Word Parts Dictionary
THIRD EDITION

Word Parts Dictionary

Standard and Reverse Listings of Prefixes, Suffixes, Roots and Combining Forms

Third Edition

MICHAEL J. SHEEHAN

To Betty Lou —

May you never be at a loss for words.

Mike Sheehan

McFarland & Company, Inc., Publishers

Jefferson, North Carolina

Library of Congress Cataloguing-in-Publication Data

Names: Sheehan, Michael J., 1939– author.
Title: Word parts dictionary : standard and reverse listings of prefixes,
suffixes, roots and combining forms / Michael J. Sheehan.
Description: Third edition. | Jefferson, North Carolina : McFarland &
Company, Inc., Publishers, 2021
Identifiers: LCCN 2020049170 | ISBN 9780786494347 (paperback : acid free paper) ∞
ISBN 9781476642109 (ebook)
Subjects: LCSH: English language—Suffixes and prefixes—Dictionaries. |
English language—Reverse indexes.
Classification: LCC PE1175 .S45 2021 | DDC 423/.1—dc23
LC record available at https://lccn.loc.gov/2020049170

British Library cataloguing data are available

ISBN (print) 978-0-7864-9434-7
ISBN (ebook) 978-1-4766-4210-9

On the cover: Background image © 2021 Shutterstock

Printed in the United States of America

McFarland & Company, Inc., Publishers
Box 611, Jefferson, North Carolina 28640
www.mcfarlandpub.com

To my son, Michael:
hic est filius dilectus meus
in quo mihi complacui

Table of Contents

Preface

The Third Edition

The *Word Parts Dictionary* is a specialized work of reference designed to make access to useful word parts swift and simple. Professional wordsmiths will find it a convenient way to jumpstart their research—to begin a process that will invariably be deeper and longer—but anyone fascinated by the quirkiness, flexibility, and power of English will find hours of interesting information to peruse.

This third edition builds on what has come before. Part I (the dictionary proper) contains 429 new entries, some of historical interest, but most of contemporary interest. Part II (the reverse dictionary) has 791 new entries. Part III (categories) has 274 new entries, and it adds two new categories, Emotional States and Mental Processes. This brings the new material to 1,494 entries not contained in the first two editions.

The Second Edition

Aside from catering to those who wish to expand their vocabulary, the purpose of this dictionary is to provide word parts in convenient form to those who may be interested in deciphering or inventing words bearing an established and embedded meaning. This includes students, academicians, inventors, advertising agencies, authors, readers, librarians, scientists, scholars, word buffs, historians, avid amateurs, cruciverbalists, and anyone else with a vested interest in words, professional or personal.

Because comprehensiveness was a goal, some of the examples included as illustrations are no longer current. Along with contemporary usages, you will occasionally find words that are obsolescent, obsolete, rare, antiquated, and archaic. You may even find a hapax legomenon or two. This provides a trip through the history of the English language, a guide to word parts that once were—and still could be—vital and expressive, and it places at your fingertips the snap-together tools to create words yet to be. It also provides a glimpse of

1

the immense inventive possibilities provided to English by Greek and Latin borrowings.

Part I, the Dictionary, benefits from many additions, the most noticeable of which will be the freshly embedded etymologies. In addition, examples have been doubled. In Part II, the Finder, well over 1,000 new terms have been added. In Part III, Categories, three entirely new categories have been added (*Eating, Experts,* and *Measurement Science*), and the others have been expanded when possible. So, while the second edition builds on the strengths of the first, it contains measurable improvements.

The First Edition

This dictionary is based on word parts—those prefixes, suffixes, combining forms and roots that show up repeatedly to form words—and is meant to be used in conjunction with a standard dictionary and a thesaurus. It can help to retrieve words only dimly remembered, or it can lead to specific new words which otherwise might never have been discovered. And since a single recurrent letter combination often unlocks the partial meaning of dozens of words, it can act as an efficient way to expand one's general vocabulary.

The *Word Parts Dictionary* is divided into three sections.

Part I, the standard Dictionary, allows a reader to find the meaning of word parts conveniently arranged in alphabetical order, together with an example. For instance, Part I would reveal that the word part **-nov-** can mean either "new" (novelty) or "nine" (novenary), so the user would then become alert to context clues. This section is particularly useful to the person who has set out to expand his or her vocabulary. It is also a convenient place to consult to find actual examples after using Section II. Generally, one example is provided for each meaning.

Part II, the Finder, allows a user to start with a meaning or concept and then find the word parts which express that meaning. It is a reverse dictionary. For instance, one would learn that the meaning "color" is carried by the word parts **chromato-, -chrome, chromo-, -chroous, -pigm-, -tinct-,** and **-ting-**. Armed with that information, a user could then consult his or her memory or turn to the appropriate pages of a standard dictionary to find a variety of words which a thesaurus would not have contained. The alternative to finding such word parts is endless paging through an unabridged dictionary.

Part III, Categories, is also a reverse dictionary, but this time with the word parts arranged in clusters of meaning. For example, Part III would enable a reader to find, in one convenient listing, word parts that express many specific colors. Each color would also appear in Part II, of course, but in an isolated, alphabetical fashion.

This dictionary focuses on four kinds of word parts.

Prefixes (*pre*): A prefix is a syllable, group of syllables, or word united with or joined to the beginning of another word to alter its meaning or create a new word. For example, **re-** is a prefix in the word "redevelop." The hyphen at the end of the prefix indicates that it usually starts a word.

Suffixes (*suf*): A suffix is a syllable, group of syllables, or word added at the end of a word or word base to change its meaning, give it grammatical form, or form a new word. For example, **-ette** is a suffix in the word "kitchenette." The hyphen at the start of the suffix indicates that it normally ends a word.

Combining forms (*comb*): A combining form is a word form that occurs only in compounds, or in compounds and derivatives, and that can combine with other such forms or with prefixes and suffixes to form a word. For example, **cryo-** is one of the combining forms in the word "cryogenic," and **-genic** is the other one. The hyphens indicate that **cryo-** usually starts the word in which it appears and that **-genic** usually ends the word in which it appears.

Bases (*base*): A base is a stem or a root, a generally short letter combination that conveys a recurrent meaning all by itself without being involved in a compound word. Prefixes and suffixes may be added to it. For example, **-dict-** is a base in the word "predictable." The two hyphens indicate that it may appear at any location in a word: front, back, or middle. Thus, we have "dictation," "contradict," and "predictable."

PART I

Dictionary

(Prefixes, bases, combining forms,
and suffixes, with examples)

A

a-¹ *see* **ad-**

a-², **ab-**, **abs-** [L. *ab-*, away from] *pre* from; off; away; down (avert, abduct, abscond)

a-³, **an-** [Gr. *a-* without] *pre* not; without (anoxia, anandrous)

-a⁴ [L. suf -*a*] **1.** *suf* singular feminine ending (Roberta); **2.** plural ending (data, phenomena)

abact- [L. *abigere/abact-*, drive away] *base* steal cattle (abaction, abactor)

abdic- [L. *abdicare*, to reject] *base* detach, reject (abdicable, abdication)

abdit- [L. *abditus*, secret, hidden] *base* hidden, abstruse (abdite, abditory)

abdomino- [L. *abdomen*, belly] *comb* abdomen (abdominocentesis, abdominoscopy)

abduct- [L. *abductus*, carried away] *base* carried away (abduction, abductor)

aberr- [L. *aberro*, to go astray] *base* wander, diverge (aberrancy, aberration)

abhor- [L. *abhorreo*, to shrink back in dread] *base* recoil, be disgusted by (abhorrence, abhorrent)

abiet- [L. *abies*, silver fir] *base* fir (abietic, abietite)

abig- [L. *abigo*, to drive away] *base* drive away (abigate, abigation)

ablat- [L. *ablatio*, a taking away] *base* removal, subtraction (ablation, ablatitious)

-able [L.–*abilis*, capable of] **1.** *suf* able to (durable); **2.** capable of being (drinkable); **3.** worthy of being; (lovable); **4.** having qualities of (comfortable); **5.** tending to (peaceable)

ableps- [Gr. *ablepsia*, blindness] *base* blindness (ablepsia, ablepsy)

ablut- [L. *ab-* + *luere*, to wash] *base* bathe; wash away (ablution, ablutionary)

-ably [L. suf -*abilem*] *suf* adverb form of **-able** (affably, unspeakably). *See* **–ible**

abol- [L. *abolere*, to destroy] *base* eradicate, make void (abolish, abolition)

abom- [L. *abominari*, to loathe] *base* disgusting, revolting (abominate, abomination)

abrad-, **abras-** [L. *abradere*, to scrape] *base* scraping, grinding (abrade, abrasive)

abrog- [L. *abrogare*, repeal] *base* abolish (abrogative, abrogator)

abul- [Gr. *aboulia*, indecisiveness] *base* indecisiveness (aboulia, abulia)

ac-¹ *see* **ad-**

-ac² [Gr.–*akos*, pertaining to] *suf* of; pertaining to (cardiac, celiac). *See* **-ic**

academ- [Gr. *academia*, Plato's school] *base* academy (academese, academic)

acantho- [Gr. *akanthos*, thorn] *comb* spiny; thorny (acanthocyte, acanthophorous)

acar-, **acari-**, **acarin-**, **acaro-** [Gr. *akari*, mite] *comb* mite; tick (acarine, acariasis, acarinosis, acarophobia)

accipit- [L. *accipiter*, bird of prey] *base* falcon; hawk (accipitral, accipitrine)

accit- [L. *accitare*, a summons or call] *base* (accite)

-acea [L. -*acea*, pl. neut.] *suf* plural for names of animal classes or orders (Cetacea, Crustacea)

-aceae [L. -*aceae*, pl. suff.] *suf* plural for names of plant families or orders (Liliaceae, Rosaceae)

-acean, **-aceous** [L.–*aceus*, nom. masc. sing.] *suf* of the nature of; like; characterized by; belonging to (crustacean, crustaceous)

aced- [Gr. *accedes*, heedless] *base* indifference (acedia, acedious)

acer-¹ [L. *acerbus*, harsh] *base* sharp; needle-like (acerose, acrid)

acer-² [L. *acer*, maple] *base* maple (acerate, aceric)

acer-³ [L. *acerosus*, full of chaff, husky] *base* mixed with chaff (acerose, acerote)

acerb- [L. *acerbus*, harsh] *base* harsh; bitter (acerbic, exacerbate)

acerv- [L. *acervare*, to heap up] *base* heap (acervate, acervose)

acesc- [L. *acescere*, turn sour] *base* turn acid or sour (acescence, acescent)

acest- [Gr. *akestos*, healed] *base* healing (acesodyne, acestoma)

acet-, aceto-, acetyl- [L. *acere*, to be sour] *comb* acetic; acetyl; vinegar (acetamid, acetometer, acetylcholine)

acetabul- [L. *acetabulum*, cup-shaped vessel] *base* saucer (acetabular fractures, acetabuliform)

acetar- [L. *acetaria*, salad plants] *base* salad (acetarious, acetary)

achat- [Gr. *axates*, an agate] *base* agate (achate)

acheron- [Gr. *akheron*, river of the Lower World] *base* hell; underworld (Acherontia, acherontical)

achlu- [Gr. *akhluo*, to grow dark] *base* darkness (achluophobia)

aci- [L. *acicula*, small needle] *base* needle (acicular, aciculate)

acid- [L. *acidus*, sharply sour] *comb* sour (acidify, acidosis)

acinaci- [L. *acinus*, berry growing in a cluster] *comb* scimitar (acinacifolious, acinaciform)

acini- [L. *acinus*, berry growing in a cluster] *comb* grape (acinarious, aciniform)

-acious [L.–*acius*, abounding in] *suf* characterized by; full of (audacious, mendacious)

acipenser- [Gr. *akkipesios*, sturgeon] *base* sturgeon (acipenserine, acipenseroid)

-acity [L. suf.–*acitas*] *suf* quality of (tenacity, vivacity)

acolyt- [Gr. *akolouthos*, follower] *base* attendant (acolyte, acolyteship)

acop- [Gr. *a-*, not + *kopos*, fatigue] *base* soothing horse salve (acopic, acopon)

acor [L. *acere*, to be sour] *base* acid taste or sourness (acor, acoric)

acosm- [Gr. *a-*, not + *kosmos*, ordered universe] *base* nonexistence (acosmic, acosmism)

acou-, acoust- [Gr. *akouein*, to hear] *comb* hearing; sound (acouesthesia, acoustical)

acras- [Gr. *akrasia*, bad mixture] *base* intemperance (acrasia, acrasial)

acrid- [L. *acridium*, grasshopper] *base* grasshopper (acridian, acridid)

acrim- [L. *acris*, bitter, sharp] *base* bitterness (acrimonious, acrimony)

acro- [Gr. *akhros*, furthest, highest, pointed] **1.** *comb* pointed (acrocephaly); **2.** highest (acrospire); **3.** extremity (acroataxia)

acroa- [Gr. *akroama*, something heard] *base* oral (acroamatic, acroasis)

acromio- [Gr. *akromion*, point of the shoulder blade] *comb* upper arm; shoulder (acromion, acromioclavicular)

actino- [Gr. *aktis*, ray] **1.** *comb* [zoology] possession of tentacles (actinomorphic); **2.** [physics/chemistry] presence of actinic rays (actinometry); **3.** light ray (actinotherapy)

acu-, acul- [L. *aculeatus*, prickly] *comb* sharp (acumen, aculeate)

aculei- [L. *aculeatus*, prickly] *base* spine (aculeiform, aculeolate)

acuti- [L. *acutus*, sharp] *comb* sharp-pointed (acutifoliate, acutilobate)

-acy [L.–*acia*, state of] *suf* quality; position; condition (democracy, primacy)

acyro- [Gr. *a-*, lacking + *kuros*, authority] *comb* incorrect use of words (acyrological, acyrology)

ad-[1] [L. *ad-*, toward] **1.** *pre* motion toward (advance); **2.** addition to (admit); **3.** nearness to (adjoin) NOTE: ad- can change to: **a-** (ascribe); **ab-** (abbreviate); **ac-** (acclaim); **af-** (affirm); **ag-** (aggrade); **al-** (allege); **an-** (announce); **ap-** (approve); **ar-** (arrive); **as-** (assent); **at-** (attrition)

-ad[2] [Gr. n. suffix] *suf* of or relating to; used to form names of **1.** collective numerals (monad); **2.** some poems (Iliad); **3.** some plants (cycad)

-ad[3] [L. *ad-*, toward] *suf* [anatomy] toward; in the direction of (dextrad, dorsad)

adag- [L. *adagium*, proverb] *base* proverb (adage, adagial)

adamant- [Gr. *adamantinos*, rock-hard] *base* unyielding, immovable

-ade [L. suf.–*atus*] **1.** *suf* the act of

(blockade); **2.** product of (pomade); **3.** participant (brigade); **4.** drink made from (lemonade)

adelph- [Gr. *adelphos*, brother] *base* brother (adelphous, Philadelphia)

adempt- [L. *ademptio*, removal] *base* removal (adempt, ademption)

aden-, adeni-, adeno- [Gr. *aden*, gland] *comb* gland or glands (adenalgia, adeniform, adenography)

adephag- [Gr. *adephagia*, gluttony] *base* voracious appetite (Adephaga, adephagia)

ader- [L. *adaeratio*, evaluation] *base* evaluation (adaeration, aderation)

adip-, adipo- [L. *adeps*, fat] *comb* fat (adipose, adipocellular)

adjut-, adjuv- [L. *adjutare*, assist] *base* help (adjutant, adjuvant)

adnat- [L. *adnatus*, added] *base* added (adnate, adnation)

ador- [L. *ador*, spelt] *base* spelt (ador)

adren-, adreno- [L. *ad-*, to + *renes*, kidney] *comb* adrenal gland (adrenalitis, adrenotoxin)

adrog- [L. *adrogare*, adopt] *base* adopt (adrogate, adrogation)

adscitit- [L. *adsciticius*, additional] *base* additional (adscititious, adscititiously)

adul- [L. *adulari*, to fawn upon] *base* flattery (adulation, adulatory)

adular- [NL. *Adula*, a mountain group in the Grison Alps] *base* blue (adularia, adularescent)

adunc- [L. *aduncus*, hooked] *base* hooked; bent inward (aduncate, aduncous)

adust- [L. *adustus*, sunburned, scorched] *base* burned, scorched (adust, adustible)

adven- [L. *advenire*, coming from outside, foreigner] *base* foreign (advenient, adventitious)

adyt- [Gr. *aduton*, not to be entered] *base* innermost part of a temple (adyt, adytum)

-ae [L. nom. pl. *-ae*] *suf* plural ending (antennae, minutiae)

aed- [Gr. *aedes*, unpleasant] *base* yellow fever mosquito (Aedes)

-aede- [Gr. *aidoia*, private parts] *base* genitals (aedeagus). *Also* **aedoe-** (aedoeomania)

aedi- [L. *aedes*, edifice] *base* temple; shrine; habitat (aedicule, aedile). *See* **edi-**

aegag- [Gr. *aigagros*, wild goat] *base* wild goat (aegagropila, aegogrus) *Also* **egag-**

aegr- [L. *aegrotare*, to be sick] *base* illness (aegritude, aegrotat)

aei- [Gr. *aei*, ever] *base* always; ever; continued (aeipathy)

aeluro- *see* **ailuro-**

-aemia [Gr. *aima*, blood] *comb* blood condition (acetonaemia, hyperaemia). *See* **-emia**

-aen(io)- [L. *aeneus*, brazen] *base* brass (aeneous, aeniolithic)

aeon- [Gr. *aion*, immeasurable period of time] *base* eternity (aeonial, aeonic) *Also* eon-

aequor- [L. *aequor*, level, as a calm, smooth sea] *base* sea; ocean (Aequoria, aequorial)

aer-, aeri-, aero- [Gr. *aer*, air] *comb* air; gas (aerate, aeriferous, aerobatics)

aerug- [L. *aerugo*, rust of copper] *base* green-blue; verdegris (aeruginous, aerugo)

aerumn- [L. *aerumna*, toil] *base* toil; trouble (aerumnous)

aescul- [L. *aesculus*, Italian oak] *base* horse chestnut (aesculetin, aesculin). *Also*, **escul-**

aestiv- [L. *aestivus*, of summer] *base* summer (aestival, aestivate) *Also*, **estiv-**

aestu- [L. *aestuare*, to boil] *base* boil up (aestuation, exaestuating). *Also* **estu-** (estuosity)

aet- [Gr. *aetos*, eagle] *base* eagle (Aëtian, aetites)

aetheo- [Gr. *a-*, not + *ethos*, custom] *base* unusual (aetheogam, aetheogamous)

aetio- [Gr. *aitia*, cause] *base* cause (aetiologue, aetiology). *See* **etio-**

aev- [L. *aevum*, age] *base* time; age (aeviternal, mediaeval)

af- *see* **ad-**

afflat- [L. *af-*, to + *flare*, blow] *base*

breathe on; inspiration (afflate, afflatus)

Afro- [L. *Afer*, African] *comb* African (Afro-American, Afroasiatic)

ag- *see* **ad-**

agalma- [Gr. *agalma*, work of art] *base* image; statue (agalmatolite, stylagalmatic)

agam- [Gr. *agamos*, unmarried] *base* nonsexual (agamic, agamist)

agap- [Gr. *agape*, love] *base* love (agape, agapetae)

agar- [Gr. *Agaria*, town in Sarmatia] *base* mushroom (agariciform, agaricoid)

agath- [Gr. *agathos*, good] *base* good (agathism, agathopoietic)

agati- [Gr. *akhates*, agate < River Achates in Sicily] *comb* agate (agatiferous, agatiform)

-age [L. suff.*–aticum*] **1.** *suf* act; condition; result of (marriage); **2.** amount; number of (acreage); **3.** cost of (postage); **4.** place of (steerage); **5.** collection of (peerage); **6.** home of (hermitage); **7.** to act (forage)

agelast- [Gr. *agelastos* not laughing] *base* humorless (agelast, agelastic)

agger- [L. *agger*, materials heaped up] *base* accumulated, piled up (aggeration, aggerose)

agglut- [L. *ad-*, to + *glutinare*, to glue] *base* stick to (agglutination, agglutinogen)

agil- [L. *agilis*, easily moved, nimble] *base* swift, active, nimble (agile, agility)

agito- [L. *agitare*, < *agere*, to drive] *comb* excited; restless (agitomania, agitophasia)

agmat- [Gr. *agmat*, fragment] *base* fracture; break (agmatology, catagmatic)

agn- [L. *agnus*, lamb] *base* lamb (agnel, agnification)

agnat- [L. *agnatus*, relation on the father's side] *base* relation through the male line (agnate, agnatic)

agnit- [L. *agnitio*, perception] *base* acknowledgement (agnition, agnize)

agnoi- [Gr. *agnoia*, ignorance] *base* ignorance (agnoiologist, agnoiology)

-agnosia [Gr. *a-*, without + *gnosis*, knowledge] *comb* loss of knowledge (prosopoagnosia, simultanagnosia)

-agogue [Gr. *agein*, to drive] **1.** *comb* leading; directing (pedagogue); **2.** inciting (demagogue); *adj.* **-agogic** (hemagogic)

agon- [Gr. *agein*, to drive] *base* contest; struggle (antagonist, protagonist)

agora- [Gr. *agora*, marketplace] *comb* open space (agoranome, agoraphobic)

agra-[1] [L. *agrarius*, land] *base* cultivated land (agrarian, agrarianism)

-agra-[2] [Gr. *agra*, a seizing] *comb* sudden pain; seizure (coxagra, pellagra)

agramm- [Gr. *agrammatos*, illiterate] *base* illiterate (agrammatic, agrammatist)

agraph- [Gr. *agraphia*, unwritten] *base* writing difficulty (agraphia, agraphic)

agrest- [L. *agrestis*, rural < *ager*, field] *base* rural; field (agrestic, agrestian)

agri- [L. *ager*, field] *comb* field; earth; soil (agriculture, agribusiness)

agrio- [Gr. *agrios*, savage] *base* wild; savage (agriologist, agriology)

agro- [Gr. *agros*, field] *comb* field; earth; soil (agrobacterium, agronomy)

agrost- [Gr. *agrostis*, grass] *base* grass (agrostography, agrostology)

-agrypn- [Gr. *agrein*, hunt + *hupnos*, sleep] *base* sleeplessness (agrypnocoma, agrypnode)

-aholic [Eng. compression of *alcoholic*] *comb* person addicted to or obsessed with ___ (chocaholic, workaholic)

aichm- [Gr. *aichme*, point of a spear] *base* needle (aichmomania, aichmophobia)

aichur- [Gr. *aichme*, point of a spear] *base* pointed (aichurophobia)

ailuro- [Gr. *ailouros*, cat] *comb* cat (ailurophile, ailurophobia). *Also* **aeluro-** (aeluromania)

-aire [adaptation of Fr. *millionaire*] *suf* person characterized by or occupied with (billionaire, legionnaire)

aischro- [Gr. *aischros*, distasteful] *base* smut; obscenity (aischrolatria, aischrologia)

aisthes-/esthes- [Gr. *aisthesis*, internal senses] *base* perception (aesthesia, aesthesis) al-¹ *see* ad-

al-² [Arabic *al*, the] *comb* the (alchemy, algebra)

-al³ [L.–*alis*, adj. suf.] **1.** *suf* belonging to; like; of (theatrical); **2.** nouns from adj. (perennial); **3.** act or process of (acquittal); **4.** [chemistry] having aldehydes (chloral)

ala- [L. *ala*, wing] *base* wing (alar, alation)

alabast- [Gr. *alabastros*, alabaster] *base* alabaster (alabastrian, alabastrine)

alacr- [L. *alacer*, lively] *base* promptness (alacrify, alacrity)

alaud- [L. *alauda*, lark] *base* skylark (Alaudidae, alaudine)

alaz- [Gr. *alazon*, braggart] *base* full of arrogance (alazon, alazony)

-alb- [L. *albus*, white] *base* white (albino, album)

albug- [L. *albugo*, disease of the eye] *base* white spot on the eye the color of egg white (albugo, albuginous)

alcelaph- [Gr. *alke*, elk + *elaphos*, deer] *base* antelope (alcelaphine, Alcelaphinae)

alcid- [L. *alca*, auk] *base* auk (Alcidae, alcidine)

alea- [L. *alea*, game of chance] *base* dice; chance (aleatoric, aleatory)

alectoro-, alectryo- [Gr. *alektrion*, cock] *comb* cock; rooster (alectoromachy, alectryomancy)

alemb- [L. *alembicare*, distil] *base* refine (alembicate, alembication)

-ales [L. pl. suf.] *suf* ending for scientific Latin names of plant orders (Agavales, Liliales)

aleth- [Gr. *alethes*, truth] *base* truth (alethic, alethiology)

aletud- [L. *aletudo*, grossness] *base* fatness (aletude, aletudinous)

aleuro- [Gr. *aleuron*, meal] *base* flour (aleuromancy, aleurone)

alex-, alexi-, alexo- [Gr. *alexein*, ward off] *comb* to ward off; keep away (alexiteric, alexipyretic, alexocyte)

alg- [L. *algere*, to be cold] *base* cold (algid, algidity)

alge-, algesi-, -algia, algo-, -algy [Gr.

algos, pain] *comb* pain (algetic, algesiometer, neuralgia, algophobia, coxalgy)

algos- [L. *algosus*, abounding in seaweed] *base* covered in seaweed (algose, algous)

ali-¹ [L. *ala*, wing] *comb* wing (aliferous, aliform)

-ali-² [L. *alius*, other] *base* another; other (alien, alienation)

alibil- [L. *alibilis*, nutritious] *base* nourishing, nutritious (alibility, alible)

alica [L. *alica*, spelt] *base* hulled grain, especially spelt (alica)

-alim- [L. *alere*, to nourish] *base* nourishment; food (alimentary, alimentation)

-aliph- [Gr. *alephein*, to anoint with oil] *base* unguent; fat (aliphatic)

-alis [L. suf.–*alis*] *suf* ending for scientific Latin names (Australis, borealis)

alkal- [Arabic *al-qali*, potash] *base* alkali (alkalescence, alkaliferous)

-allac-, -allag- [Gr. *allasein*, to exchange] *base* exchange; mutually binding (synallactic, synallagmatic)

allant(o)- [Gr. *allas*, sausage] **1.** *comb* membrane: fetal (allanto-chorion); **2.** sausage-shaped (allantoid)

-allaxis- [Gr. *allaxis*, to exchange] *base* exchange (morphallaxis, trophallaxis)

allect- [L. *allectare*, to allure, entice] *base* allure, attract (allection, allective)

allegor- [Gr. *allegorikos*, allegory] *base* allegory (allegoric, allegorically)

allelo- [Gr. *allos*, other] *comb* of one another; reciprocal (allelomorph, allelopathy)

alli- [L. *alium*, garlic] *base* garlic (alliaceous, Allium)

allo- [Gr. *allos*, other] *comb* variation; reversal; departure from normal (allonym, allopathy)

allotrio- [Gr. *allotrios*, strange] *comb* abnormal, unnatural (allotriolith, allotriophagy)

allubesc- [L. *allubescere*, begin to please] *base* content (allubescent, allubescency)

-ally [ON suf.–*liga*, bind] *suf* to form certain adverbs (abdominally, terrifically)

alman- [Arabic *al-manak*, the calendar] *base* almanac (almanac, almanacking)

alog(o)- [Gr. *a-*, not + *logos*, reason] *base* unreasonable (alogism, alogotrophy)

alopec- [Gr. *alopekia*, fox mange] *base* fox (alopecoid); baldness (alopecia)

alphito- [Gr. *alphiton*, barley] *base* barley (alphitomancy, alphitomorphous)

alter- [L. *alter*, other] *comb* another; other (alter, alternate)

altercat- [L. *altercatio*, dispute, debate] *base* dispute, wrangle (altercation, altercative)

alti-, alto- [L. *altus*, high] *comb* high (altimeter, altocumulus)

altric- [L. *altrix*, female nourisher] *base* nestling (altricial)

alumino- [L. *alumen*, alum] *comb* aluminum (aluminosilicate, aluminothermic)

alut- [L. *aluta*, soft leather] *base* leather (alutaceous, alutation)

alv- [L. *alvus*, belly] *base* belly (alviducous, alvine)

alve- [L. *alveus*, basket, beehive] *base* beehive (alveary, alveated)

alveolo- [L. *alveus*, a cavity] 1. *comb* connected with alveolus (alveolodental); 2. small cavity; socket (alveolopalatal)

alyt- [Gr. *alutes*, police officer] *base* police officer (alytarch)

-am- [L. *amare*, to love] *base* love; friendship (amity, amorous)

amar- [L. *amarus*, bitter] *base* sour (amaretto, amarine)

amaranth- [Gr. *a-*, not + *marainein*, to wither] *base* purple (amaranthine, amaranthoid)

amath- [Gr. *amathos*, sand] *base* dust (amathigerous, amathophobia)

amaur- [Gr. *amaros*, dark] *base* dim; dark (amaurosis, amaurotic)

amaxo- [Gr. *amaxis*, little wagon] *base* automobile (amaxomania, amaxophobia)

ambag- [L. *ambi*, around + *agere*, to drive] *base* oblique; indirect (ambagious, ambagatory)

ambi-, ambo- [L. *ambi*, around] *comb* both; around (ambience, amboceptor). *See* **amphi-**

ambig- [L. *ambi*, around + *agere*, to drive] *base* uncertain (ambiguity, unambiguous)

amblos/t- [Gr. *amblosis*, miscarry] *base* abortive birth (amblosis, amblotic)

ambly- [L. *amblus*, dim, dulled] *comb* dullness; dimness (amblyopia, Amblystoma)

ambul- [L. *ambulare*, to walk] *comb* walk (ambulatory, somnambulate)

amebi-, amebo- [Gr. *amoibe*, change] *comb* ameba (amebicide, amebocyte)

amelo- [short form of *enamel* < Fr. *enamayller*] *comb* enamel (ameloblast, amelogenesis)

amen(it)- [L. *amoenitas*, pleasantness] *base* pleasant, agreeable (amenable, amenity)

amensi- [L. *a-*, not + *mens*, mind] *base* amnesia (amensiphobia)

ament-¹ [L. *a-*, not + *mens*, mind] *base* insanity; feeble-mindedness (amentia, amenty)

ament-² [L. *amentum*, strap] *base* catkin (amentaceous, amentiferous)

ametro- [Gr. *ametros*, irregular] *comb* irregular, imperfect (ametrometer, ametropia)

amic-¹ [L. *amicus*, friend] *base* friend (amicable, amicableness)

-amic² [ML *am(monia)*, ammonia + *-ic*] *suf* amide related (allocinnamic, lactamic acid)

amita- [L. *amita*, paternal aunt] *base* aunt (amitate, amitation)

ammino- [am(monia) + *-ine*] *comb* containing ammines (ammino-chloride)

ammo- [Gr. *ammos*, sand] *comb* sand (ammochryse, ammodromous)

ammonio-, ammono- [ML. *ammonia*, from *sal ammoniac* < Gr. *Ammon*, Egyptian deity] *comb* containing ammonia (ammonioferric, ammonotelic)

amn- [L. *amnis*, river] *base* river (amnicoline, amnicolist)

amnes- [Gr. *a-*, not + *mnesthai*, to

remember] *base* forgotten (amnesia, paramnesia)

amnio- [Gr. *amnion*, membrane around the fetus] *comb* amniotic sac; membrane: fetal (amniocentesis, amnioscopy)

amorpho- [Gr. *a-*, without + *morphe*, shape] *comb* shapeless; irregularly shaped (amorphous, amorphogranular)

-ampel- [Gr. *ampelos*, vine] *base* vine (ampelography, ampelopsis)

amphi-, ampho- [Gr. *amphi*, on both sides] *comb* on both sides; surrounding (amphibology, amphoteric). *See* **ambi-**

-ampl- [L. *amplus*, spacious] *base* large (amplification, amplifier)

ampull- [Gr. dimin. of *amphoreus*, jar with two handles] *base* bottle (ampulla, ampullaceous)

amycho- [Gr. *amussein*, lacerate] *base* scratch; irritate (amychophobia, amyctic)

amygdalo- [Gr. *amugdale*, almond] *comb* almond-shaped (amygdalotomy, amygdalophenin)

amyl-, amylo- [Gr. *amulon*, starch] *comb* of starch (amylamine, amylometer)

an-[1] [variant of Gr. *a-*, not] *pre* not; lacking (anacanthous, anarchy)

an-[2] *see* **ad-**

-an[3] [L. suf.*–anus*] **1.** *suf* belonging to; of; characteristic of (diocesan); **2.** born in; living in (American); **3.** believing in; following (Mohammedan)

ana-[1] [Gr. *ana*, up] *pre* up; upon; back; again; anew; throughout (anabolism, anaphylaxis)

-ana[2] [L. suf. *-ana*] *suf* plural: collective (Americana, Victoriana)

anabol- [Gr. *anabole*, toss up, ascend] *base* ascend (anabolic, anabolism)

anacamp- [Gr. *anakampsis*, bending back] *base* reflection (anacampsis, anacamptic)

anacard- [Gr. *ana*, resembling + *kardia*, heart] *base* cashew (anacardiaceous, anacardic)

anagog- [Gr. *anagoge*, religious ecstasy] *base* mystical (anagogic, anagogy)

anagram- [Gr. *anagrammatizein*, transpose letters] *base* anagram (anagrammatic, anagrammatist)

analect- [Gr. *analegein*, to gather up] *base* literary fragments (analect, analects)

anaps- [Gr. *an-*, upwards + *apsis*, arch] *base* turtle (anapsid, anapsida)

anat- [L. *anas*, duck] *base* duck (anatiferous, anatine)

anathem- [Gr. *anathema*, an accursed thing] *base* curse (anathema, anathematize)

anatoc-[Gr. *anatokismos*, compound interest] *base* compound interest (anatocism)

-ance [L. suf.*–antia*] **1.** *suf* the act of (utterance); **2.** quality or state of being (vigilance); **3.** a thing that ___ (conveyance); **4.** a thing that is ___ (dissonance); *n.* **-ancy** (constancy, vacancy)

anchi- [Gr. *anchi*, near] *base* connected (anchimere, anchithere)

ancip- [Gr. *anceps*, two-headed] *base* doubtful; two-edged (ancipital, ancipitous)

ancis- [Gr. *ankistron*, hook] *base* hook-shaped (ancistroid)

-ancon- [Gr. *ankon*, elbow] *base* elbow (anconad, anconitis)

ancylo- [Gr. *ankulos*, crooked] *comb* bent; crooked; stiff (ancylomele, ancylostomiasis). *Also* **ankylo-** (ankyloglossia)

ancylostom- [Gr. *ankulos*, crooked + *stoma*, mouth] *base* hookworm (Ancylostoma)

ancyr- [Gr. *ankura*, anchor] *base* anchor (Ancyrene, ancyroid)

ando- [Japanese *ando*, volcanic soil] *base* volcanic soil (andic, andosol)

andro-, -andry [Gr. *andros*, man] *comb* man; male (androgenous, polyandry)

-androus [Gr. *-androus*, having men] **1.** *comb* man; male (polyandrous); **2.** *BOT*: having stamens (diandrous)

-ane [Gr.*–ene*, fem. adj. suf.] *suf* a saturated hydrocarbon (hexane, methane)

anemo- [Gr. *anemos*, wind] *comb* wind (anemometer, anemophilous) anet- [Gr. *anetos*, relaxed] *base* soothing (anetic, anetodermia)

aneth- [Gr. *anethon*, anise or dill] *base* dill (anethated, anethene)

angar- [Gr. *angareia*, courier] *base* to force labor from (angariate, angariation)

angel- [Gr. *angelos*, messenger] *base* angel (angelic, angelification)

angin- [Gr. *ankhone*, strangling] *base* strangulation; heart attack (angina, angina pectoris)

angio- [Gr. *angos*, vessel] *comb* vessel; case; pot (angiocarp, angioma)

Anglo- [L. *Angli*, the English people] *comb* English (Anglo-Irish, Anglomania)

angui- [L. *angere*, throttle or choke] *base* snake (anguiform, anguine)

anguill- [Gr. *enchelos*, eel] *base* eel (anguilliform, anguillous)

angul- [L. *angulus*, angle] *base* angle (angularity, angulation)

angur- [Gr. *angourion*, watermelon] *base* watermelon (Anguria)

angusti- [L. *angustus*, constricted] *comb* narrow (angustation, angustifoliate)

anhel- [L. *anhelare*, to draw breath] *base* breathing, inhaling (anhelant, anhelation)

anhydro- [Gr. *an-*, without + *hudor*, water] *comb* anhydride (anhydroglucose, anhydrous)

anil- [L. *anilis*, pert. to an old woman] *base* old woman (anile, anility)

-anim- [L. *anima*, soul] *base* spirit; life (animation, animatronics)

anis- [L. *anisum*, anise] *comb* oil of anise (anisamide, anisanalyde)

aniso- [Gr. *an-*, not + *isos*, equal] *comb* unequal; dissimilar (anisogamy, anisometropia)

ankylo- [Gr. *ankulos*, crooked] *comb* bent; crooked; stiff (ankylosaur, ankylosis). *Also* ancylo-

-ann-, -enn- [L. *annus*, year] *base* year; (annual, biennial); yearly (anniversary)

annon- [L. *annona*, provisions] *base* provisions (annonary)

annul- [L. *annulus*, ring] *comb* ring (annular, annulation)

ano-[1] [Gr. *ano*, upward] *pre* upward; above (Anostoma, anotropia)

ano-[2] [L. *anus*, ring] *comb* anal; ring-shaped (anoplasty, anorectal)

anom-, anomo- [Gr. *an-*, not + *homos*, same] *comb* unusual; irregular; abnormal (anomalous, anomocarpous)

anomalo- [Gr. *an-*, not + *homalos*, even] *comb* irregular; uneven (anomalogonatous, anomalous)

anophel- [Gr. *an-*, without + *ophelos*, advantage] *base* mosquito (Anopheles, anopheline)

anosm- [Gr. *an-*, not + *osme*, smell, without smell] *base* lack of smelling (anosmia, anosmic)

ansa- [L. *ansa*, handle] *base* handle (ansated, ansation)

anser- [L. *anser*, goose] *base* goose (anserine, anserous)

-ant [L. suf.–*ant*] 1. *suf* performing an act (defiant); 2. person who performs (accountant); 3. impersonal physical agent (lubricant)

antagon- [Gr. *antaginistes*, opponent] *base* opponent (antagonal, antagonist)

ante- [L. *ante*, before] *pre* before in time, order, or position (antecedent, antedate)

antero- [L. *anterus*, preceding] *comb* anterior; front (anterolateral, anteroparietal)

-anthema [Gr. *antheein*, to blossom] *comb* rash; eruption (enanthema, exanthema)

-antherous [Gr. *anthos*, flower] *comb* flowering; having anthers (anantherous, isantherous)

antho- [Gr. *anthos*, flower] *comb* of flowers (anthocarpous, anthomania)

-anthous [Gr. *anthos*, flower] *comb* having flowers of a specified kind or number (ananthous, monanthous)

anthraco- [Gr. *anthrak*, charcoal] *comb* coal; carbuncle (anthracomancy, anthracometer)

anthropo- [Gr. *anthropos*, human

being] *comb* human (anthropology, anthropophagus)

anthyp- [Gr. *anthypo*, in turn] *base* counter [anthypophora, anthypophoretic]

anti- [Gr. *anti*, opposite] **1.** *pre* against; hostile (antilabor); **2.** operating against (antiballistic); **3.** preventing, curing, neutralizing (antitoxin); **4.** opposite; reverse (antiperistalsis); **5.** rivaling (antipope)

antio- [Gr. *anti*, opposite to] *comb* set against (antiodont, antiopelmous)

-antiq- [L. *antiquus*, old] *base* old; ancient (antiquarian, antiquated)

antl- [Gr. *antlion*, bucket] *base* bucket (antlia, antliate)

antro- [Gr. *antron*, cave] *comb* nearly closed cavity; antrum (antral, antrozous)

anu- [L. *anus*, ring] *base* circular; ring-shaped (annulus, anus)

anur-[1] [Gr. *an-*, no + *oura*, tail] *base* tailless (anura, anurous)

anur-[2] [Gr. *an-* no + *ouron*, urine] *base* absence of urine (anuresis, anuria)

-anus [L. adj. suf.*–anus*] *suf* scientific word ending (Platanus, Raphanus)

aorto- [Gr. *aeirein*, to lift] *comb* aorta (aortoclasia, aortography)

ap- *see* **ad-**

apag- [Gr. *apagein*, lead off] *base* lead away (apagoge, apagogic)

apat- [Gr. *apate*, deceit] *base* illusion, deceit (apatite, Apatornis)

apeir- [Gr. *a-*, without + *peras*, an end] *base* infinite; endless (apeirogon, Apeiron)

apeps- [Gr. *a-*, not + *peptein*, digest] *base* indigestion (apepsia, apepsy)

apert- [L. *apertus*, open] *base* open (apertometer, aperture)

aphan- [Gr. *aphanes*, unmanifest] *base* invisible, obscure (aphanite, aphanozygous)

aphe-, -aphia [Gr. *haphe*, touch] *comb* sense of touch (aphephobia, dysaphia)

aphn- [Gr. *aphneios*, wealthy] *base* rich, wealthy (aphnologist)

aphor- [Gr. *aphorismos*, a distinction]

base pithy expression (aphorism, aphorist)

aphr- [Gr. *aphros*, foam] *base* foam (aphrite, Aphrodite)

aphrodisio- [Gr. *aphrodisiakos*, venereal < Aphrodite] *base* sexual (aphrodisiac, aphrodisian)

api- [L. *apis*, bee] *comb* bee (apiary, apiculture)

-apical, apico- [L. *apex*, summit] *comb* apex; tip (periapical, apicotomy)

apio- [Gr. *apion*, pear] *base* pear (apiocrinite, apioid)

apo- [Gr. *apo*, off] *pre* off; from; away from; separation (apoblast, apocopate)

apocris- [Gr. *apokrisis*, answer] *base* to give or receive answers (apocrisiary)

apodemi- [Gr. *apodemia*, journey] *base* journey (apodemialgia)

apolaust- [Gr. *apolaustos*, enjoyable] *base* enjoyment; self-indulgence (apolaustic, apolausticism)

apor(et)- [Gr. *aporos*, doubtful] *base* doubt (aporia, aporetic)

aposem- [Gr. *apo-*, detached + *sema*, sign, repellant] *base* warning signal (aposematic, aposeme)

apostem- [Gr. *apostema*, distance, abscess] *base* abscess (apostemation, apostematous)

appell- [L. *appellare*, to address or accost] *base* call to; name (appellation, appellative)

appet- [L. *appetere*, to strive after] *base* craving (appetite, appetizer)

apr- [L. *aprum*, wild boar] *base* wild boar (apricide, aprine)

apricat- [L. *apricus*, open to the sun] *base* sunbathing (apricate, aprication)

-aps-, -apt-[1] [Gr. *hapsis*, to fasten] *base* joining (synapse, synaptic)

-apsia [Gr. *hapsis*, to fasten] *comb* touch (parapsia)

apt-[2] [L. *aptus*, fastened] *base* ability (apt, aptitude)

aqua-, aque-, aqui- [L. *aqua*, water] *comb* water; (aquatic, aqueduct, aquiculture)

aquil- [L. *aquila*, eagle] *base* eagle (aquilated, aquiline)

ar-[1] *see* **ad-**

-ar^2 [L. suf.–*aris*] **1.** *suf* pertaining to (angular); **2.** one who ___ (burglar); **3.** connected with ___ (collar)

arach- [Gr. *arakis*, leguminous plant] *base* peanut; ground nut (arachidic, Arachis)

arachn-, arachno- [Gr. *arachen*, spider] *comb* spider; cobweb (arachnephobia, arachnodactylia)

araio- [Gr. *araios*, thin] *comb* thin, light (araiocardia)

-araneo- [L. *aranea*, spider] *base* spider (araneal, araneology)

arat- [L. *aratus*, plow] *base* farming; tillage (aration, aratory)

-arbor- [L. *arbor*, tree] *base* tree (arboraceous, arboretum)

arbusc- [L. *arbuscula*, shrub] *base* shrub, tuft (arbuscle, arbuscular)

arcan- [L. *arcanus*, secret < *arca*, chest] *base* secret (arcana, arcane)

arch-^{1} [Gr. *arkos*, chief] *pre* main; chief; principal (archbishop, archrival)

-arch^2 [Gr. *archein*, to be first] *comb* ruler (matriarch, patriarch)

archaeo-, archeo- [Gr. *arkhaios*, ancient] *comb* ancient; original (archaeology, Archeozoic)

archi- [Gr. *archi*, first] *pre* [biology] primitive (archiplasm, archistome)

-archy [Gr. *archein*, to be first] *comb* rule; government (monarchy, oligarchy)

arci- [L. *arcus*, bow] *base* arch; bow (arciform; arcigerous)

arct- [Gr. *arktia*, moth] *base* moth (arctian)

arcto- [Gr. *arktos*, bear] *comb* bear (arctic, cynarctomachy)

arctoid- [Gr. *arktos*, bear] *base* raccoon; weasel (Arctoidea, arctoidean)

ard-^{1}, **ars-** [L. *ardere*, to burn] *base* burn (ardor, arson)

-ard^2, **-art** [O.F. n. suf.–*ard*] *suf* one who is or does too much (drunkard, braggart)

ard-^{3}, **ardu-** [L. *arduus*, hard or steep] *base* erect; steep; laborious (arduity, arduous,)

arde- [Gr. *erodios*, heron] *base* heron (ardeid, ardeine)

ardelio- [L. *ardelio*, meddler] *base* busybody (ardelio, ardelion)

ardu- [L. *arduus*, steep, difficult] *base* difficult (arduously, ardurous)

aren- [L. *arena*, sand] *comb* sand (arenaceous, arenicolous)

arenaceo- [L. *arena*, sand + suf. -*aceus*] *comb* sandy (arenaceo-argillaceous, arenaceocalcareous)

arene- [L. *aranea*, spider] *base* spider (areneiform)

areo-^{1} [Gr. *Ares*, planet Mars] *comb* Mars (areocentric, areology)

areo-^{2} [Gr. *araios*, thin; not dense] *base* thin; rare (areometer, areostyle)

areto- [Gr. *arete*, virtue] *comb* virtue (aretologist, aretology)

arg- [Gr. *argos*, idle] *base* idle, unused (argamblyopia)

argent-, argenti-, argento- [L. *argentum*, silver] *comb* silver (argentite, argentiferous, argento-cuprous)

argillaceo- [Gr. *argillos*, white clay] *comb* clay (arenaceo-argillaceous)

argillo- [Gr. *argillos*, white clay] *comb* clay (argillo-calcareous, argilloarenaceous)

argyro- [Gr. *argyros*, silver] *comb* silver (Argyropelecus, argyrophyllus)

-aria [L. pl. n, suf.–*aria*] *suf* [botany/zoology] used to form names of groups and names of genera (Alternaria, Planaria)

-arian [L. comp. suf.] *suf* age; sect; occupation; social belief (humanitarian, Unitarian)

arid- [L. *aridus*, dry] *base* dry (aridity, aridness)

ariet- [L. *arietare*, to butt like a ram] *base* ram (arietate, arietation)

-arious [L. adj. suf.] *suf* relating to; connected with (gregarious, vicarious)

-aris [L. suf.–*aris*] *suf* scientific word ending (Muscularis, Polaris)

arist- [Gr. *ariston*, breakfast, lunch] *base* dining (aristology, aristologist)

aristo- [Gr. *aristos*, best] *comb* best (aristocracy, aristotype)

arithm- [Gr. *arithmos*, number] *base* number (arithmancy, arithmetic)

-arium [L. neut. suf.] *suf* location; receptacle (aquarium, solarium)

arm- [Gr. *arma*, weapon] *base* weapon (armament, armory)

Armeno- [Gr. *Armenios*, Armenia] *comb* Armenia (Armenophile, Armenophobia)

arment- [L. *armentum*, herd of cattle] *base* herd (armental, armentose)

armill- [L. *armilla*, bracelet, hoop] *base* bracelet, hoop (armillary, armillary)

armo- [L. *armus*, shoulder] *base* shoulder (armomancy)

aroma- [Gr. *aroma*, sweet smell] *base* fragrance (aromatic, aromatherapy)

arrept- [L. *arripere*, snatch away] *base* carry off, carry away (arreption, arreptitious)

arrheno- [Gr. *arreno*, male] *comb* male (arrhenotokous, arrhenotoky)

arsenio-, arseno- [Old Iranian *zarna*, golden] *comb* having arsenic (arsenolite, arsenopyrite, arseniosiderite)

artemes- [L. *artemesia*, wormwood] *base* wormwood (artemesia, artemisinin)

arterio- [Gr. *arteria*, artery] *comb* artery (arteriosclerosis, arteriovenous)

arthr-, arthro- [Gr. *arthron*, joint] *comb* connected with a joint (arthrectomy, arthrodynia)

arthropod- [Gr. *arthro*, joint + *pod*, foot] *base* millipede (arthropodal, arthropodan)

arti- [L. *ars*, art + *factum*, something made] *comb* workmanship (artifact, artifice)

-articul- [L. *articulus*, small joint] *base* joint (articulated, multiarticular)

artio- [Gr. *artios*, even] *comb* even number (artiad, Artiodactyla)

artiodactyl- [Gr. *artios*, even + *daktulos*, finger or toe] *base* cloven-footed (artiodactyl, artiodactylous)

arto- [Gr. *artos*, bread] *comb* bread (artocarpous, artophagous)

artuat- [L. *artuare*, torn in pieces] *base* dismembered limbs (artuate, artuose)

arundi- [L. *harundo*, a reed] *base* reed (arundiferous, arundinaceous)

arv- [L. *arvum*, arable land] *base* plowed land (arval)

arvicol- [L. *arvum*, field + *colere*, dwell] *base* meadow mouse (arvicoline, arvicolous)

-ary [L. suf.*–arius*] **1.** *suf* relating to; like (legendary); **2.** thing/person connected to (military)

aryt- [Gr. *arytaina*, a funnel] *base* funnel (arytenoids, arytenoidal)

aryteno- [Gr. *arytaina*, funnel] *comb.* vocal cord cartilage (aryteno-epiglottic, arytenoid)

as-[1] *see* **ad-**

as-[2], **asin-** [L. *asinus*, ass] *base* jackass (asinine, asininity)

asbest- [Gr. *asbestos*, unquenchable] *base* asbestos (asbestic, asbestiform)

asbol- [Gr. *asbole*, soot] *base* soot (asbolan, asbolite)

ascari- [Gr. *askaris*, intestinal worm] *comb* intestinal worm (ascariasis, Ascaridae)

ascid- [Gr. *askidion*, little leather bag] *base* molluscs with leathery tunic (ascidian, Ascidium)

asco- [Gr. *askos*, bag] *comb* [botany] sac (ascocarp, ascophore)

-ase [suf. from *diastase* < Gr. *diastasis*, separation] *suf* names of enzymes (amylase, angiotensinase)

-asis *see* **–iasis**

-asm [Gr. suf.*–asmos*] *suf* result of an action (enthusiasm, orgasm)

asmato- [Gr. *asma*, song] *comb* song (asmatographer, asmatography)

aspala- [Gr. *aspalaks*, mole] *base* mole (aspalasoma)

asper- [L. *asper*, rough] *comb* rough (asperation, asperity)

aspido- [Gr. *aspid*, shield] *base* shield (aspidomancy, Aspidogaster)

assentat- [L. *assentari*, to agree in a servile manner] *base* to agree obsequiously (assentation, assentacious)

assid- [L. *assiduous*, sitting down to] *base* unceasing (assiduity, assiduous)

-ast [Gr. suf.*–astes*] *suf* one who is ___ (chiliast, enthusiast)

astac- [Gr. *astakos*, lobster or crawfish] *base* lobster (astacian, astacite)

aster-[1] [Gr. *aster*, star] *comb* star (asteraceous, asteria)

-aster[2] [L. suf.*–aster*] *suf* diminution; inferiority; worthlessness; slight resemblance (parasitaster, poetaster) *contemptuous diminutive*

asteroid- [Gr. *aster*, star + *eidos*, form] *base* starlike; starfish (asteroidal, asteroidean)

asthen-, astheno- [Gr. *asthenes*, without strength] *comb* weakness (asthenopia, asthenobiosis). *See* **-esthenia**

astigm- [Gr. *a-*, not + *stigma*, point] *base* structural eye defect (astigmatic, astigmatism)

astra- [Gr. *astrapaios*, of lightning] *comb* lightning (Astrapaeus, astraphobia)

astragalo- [Gr. *astragalos*, a bone] *comb* anklebone; dice; (astragalonavicular, astragalomancy)

astro- [Gr. *aster*, star] *comb* star; celestial activity (astrologer, astronomy)

asty- [Gr. *astu*, city] *base* city (astyclinic)

at- *see* **ad-**

-ata [L. suf.*–ata*] *suf* result of; plural ending (Articulata, stomata)

atax-, ataxi-, -ataxia, ataxio-, ataxo- [Gr. *a-*, without + *taktos*, order] *comb* confusion; disorder (ataxaphasia, ataxiamnesic, psychataxia, ataxiophemia, ataxophobia)

-ate[1] [L. suf.*–atus*] *v.* **1.** *suf* to become (maturate); **2.** cause to become (invalidate); **3.** form or produce (salivate); **4.** provide or treat with (refrigerate); **5.** put in the form of; form by means of (delineate); **6.** to arrange for (orchestrate); **7.** to combine; infuse; treat with (chlorinate)

-ate[2] [L. suf.*–atus*] *adj.* **1.** *suf* characteristic of (collegiate); **2.** having; filled with (passionate); **3.** [biology] having or characterized by (caudate)

-ate[3] [L. suf.*–atus*] *n.* **1.** *suf* office; function; agent; official (directorate); **2.** person or thing that is the object of an action (legate); **3.** [chemistry] a salt made from an acid ending in -ic (nitrate)

ate-[4] [Gr. *Até*, goddess of mischief] *base* ruinous; reckless impulse (atemania, atephobia)

atelia-, atelo- [Gr. *a-*, without + *telos*, completion] *comb* incomplete; undeveloped (myelatelia, atelocardia)

ather- [Gr. *atherine*, smelt] *base* smelt (atherine, atherinid)

atherm- [Gr. *athermantos*, unheated] *base* blocking heat (athermancy, athermic)

athero- [Gr. *athere*, porridge] *comb* deposit: soft materials (atherogenic, atheromatous)

athet- [Gr. *athetein*, to reject] *base* rejection (athetesis, athetize)

athlet- [Gr. *athletikos*, champion] *base* athlete (athletic, athleticism)

-athlon, -athon [extraction from Gr. village *Marathon*] *suf* event; contest (pentathlon, walkathon)

-atic [L. suf.*–aticus*] *suf* of the kind of (chromatic, dramatic)

-atile [L. suf. *-atilis*] *suf* possibility; quality (versatile, volatile)

-ation [L. suf. *-atio*] **1.** *suf* the act of (alteration); **2.** condition of being (gratification); **3.** the result of (compilation)

-ative [L. suf.*–ativus*] *suf* relating to; tending to (correlative, demonstrative)

atlanto- [Gr. god *Atlas*] *comb* [anatomy] pertaining to the atlas, top vertebra (atlantoaxial, atlanto-occipital)

atlo- [Gr. god *Atlas*] *comb* of the neck (atlo-axoid, atloid)

atmo- [Gr. *atmos*, vapor] *comb* steam; vapor; air (atmologist, atmosphere)

-ator [L. suf. *-tor*] *suf* doer; agent; actor (adjudicator, educator)

-atory [L. suf. *-orius*] *suf* of the nature of; pertaining to; produced by (accusatory, celebratory)

atrament- [L. *atramentum*, black ink < *ater*, black] *base* ink, inky (atramental, atramentarious)

atra(t)- [L. *atratus*, blackened] *base* black (atrament, atrate)

-atresia [Gr. *a-*, not + *tretos*, perforated] *comb* imperforate; lacking an opening (colpatresia, proctatresia)

atreto- [Gr. *a-*, not + *tretos*, perforated]

comb imperforate; lacking an opening (atretocyst, atretorrhinia)

atrio- [L. *atrium*, central hall] *comb* cavity, esp. a chamber of the heart (atriopore, atrioventricular)

atro- [L. *ater*, black] *comb* black (atroceruleus, atrorubent)

atroc- [L. *atrox, atroc-*, savage, cruel] *base* terrible, heinous (atrocious, atrocity)

-atrophia, atrophic [Gr. *a-*, without + *trephein*, to nourish] **1.** *comb* malnutrition (metatrophia); **2.** progressive decline (neuratrophia, myotrophic)

atto- [Old Norse *attjan*, eighteen] *pre* one-quintillionth–10^{18} (attogram, attotesla)

atychi- [Gr. *atucheo*, to fail] *base* failure (atychimania, atychiphobia)

auant- [Gr. *auantikos*, wasted] *base* wasting away (auantic)

-auchen- [Gr. *auchen*, neck] *base* neck (Auchenia, maerauchenia)

aucup- [L. *aucupari*, to catch birds] *base* hunt fowl (aucupate, aucupation)

audac- [L. *audax*, bold] *base* boldness (audacious, audacity)

audi-, audio- [L. *audire*, to hear] *comb* hearing (auditorium, audiology)

-aug- [L. *augere*, to increase] *base* grow; increase (augment, augmentation)

augur- [perh. L *augere*, to promote] *base* soothsaying; divination (augurous, augury)

aul-[1] [Gr. *aule*, hall] *base* collegiate hall (aulary, aulicism)

aul-[2] [Gr. *aulein*, to play the flute] *base* flute (aulete, auletic)

aul-[3] [Gr. *aule*, court] *base* courtly (aulic, aulicism)

auranti- [L. *aurantium*, an orange] *base* orange (aurantiaceous, Aurantieæ)

aur(i)-[1] [L. *aurus*, ear] *comb* ear (auricle, auriform)

aur(i)-[2], **auro-** [L. *aurum*, gold] *comb* gold (auriferous, aurous)

auricalc- [Gr. *aurichalkon*, yellow copper ore] *base* copper; gold-colored (auricalceous, aurichalcite)

auriculo- [L. *auricula*, outer ear] *comb* outer ear; lobe (auriculo-temporal, auriculoventricular)

aurif- [L. *aurum*, gold + *-fer*, producing] *base* producing or working gold (auriferous, aurifex)

aurig- [L. *auriga*, chariot] *base* coach or carriage (aurigal, aurigation)

-auror- [L. *aurora*, dawn] *base* dawn (auroral, aurorean)

aurora- [L. *aurora*, dawn] *comb* radiant emissions in both hemispheres (aurora australis, aurora borealis)

auster- [Gr. *austerikos*, severe] *base* harsh (austerely, austerity)

austro- [L. *auster*, south wind] **1.** *comb* wind: south (austromancy); **2.** eastern (Austro-Hungarian)

authen- [Gr. *authentikos*, original, authoritative] *base* credible, genuine (authentic, authenticate)

authi- [Gr. *authi*, on the spot] *base* in situ (authigenic, authigenesis)

auto- [Gr. *autos*, self] *comb* self; self-moving (autobiography, autoclastic)

autumn- [L. *autumnus*, autumn] *base* fall (autumnal, autumnity)

auxano-, auxeto-, auxo- [Gr. *auxesis*, increase] *comb* increase; growth (auxanogram, auxetophone, auxochrome)

auxil- [L. *auxilium*, help] *base* help; assistance (auxiliary, auxiliate)

avar- [L. *avaritia*, covetousness] *base* greed (avarice, avaricious)

aven- [L. *avena*, oats] *base* oats (avenaceous, avenage)

avern- [L. *Lake Avernus*, considered the entrance to hell] *base* hellish (avernal, Avernian)

avia-, avio- [L. *avis*, bird] **1.** *comb* bird (aviary); **2.** flight (avionics, aviator)

avid- [L. *avidus*, greedy] *base* eager (avidly, avidity)

avion- [Fr. *avion*, aviator] *base* of flying (avionic, avionics)

avit- [L. *avitus*, grandfather] *base* grandfather (avital, avitic)

avoc- [L. *avocare*, call off or away] *base* diversion, secondary pursuit (avocation, avocational)

-avunc- [L. *avunculus*, uncle] *base* uncle (avuncular, avunculate)

axen- [Gr. *a-*, not + *xenikos*, alien] *base* self-contained (axenic, axenical)

axi-, axio-¹, axo-, axono- [L. *axis*, pole of the earth] *comb* related to an axis (axial, axiomesial, axometer, Axonophora)

-axill- [L. *axilla*, armpit] *base* armpit (axillar, periaxillary)

axin- [Gr. *axine*, ax] *base* ax (axinite, axinomancy)

axio-² [Gr. *axios*, worth] *comb* values (axiology, axiopisty)

axung- [L. *axis*, axle + *ungere*, to grease] *base* lard-like, greasy (axunge, axungious)

azal- [Gr. *azaleos*, dry] *base* dry (azalea, azaleine)

azo- [Gr. *a-*, not + *ksoein*, to live] *comb* [chemistry] nitrogen (azobenzene, azotobacter)

-azur- [Persian *lajward*, lapis lazuli] *base* sky-blue (azureous, azurite)

B

baccato- [L. *bacca*, berry] *comb* bearing berries (baccate, baccato-tuberculous)

bacci- [L. *bacca*, berry] *comb* berry (bacciform, baccivorous)

bacill-, bacilli-, bacillo- [L. *bacillum*, rod or staff] *comb* rod-shaped bacillus (bacillemia, bacilliform, bacillotherapy)

back- [Dan. *bag*, back] 1. *comb* of the back (backache); 2. behind (backfield); 3. prior (backdate); 4. opposing (backlash)

bact- [Gr. *Baktrionos*, of Bactria] *base* two-humped Asian camel (bactrian)

-bacter, bacteri-, bacterio- [Gr. *bakterion*, little stick] *comb* of bacteria (aerobacter, bactericide, bacteriology)

bacul- [L. *bacul*, rod] *base* rod, stave (baculine, baculometry)

baityl- [Gr. *baitylos*, meteor stone] *base* metor stone (baetyl, baetylic)

bajulat- [L. *bajulare*, to carry] *base* to carry, as a porter (bajulate, bajulation)

bal- [L. *balare*, to bleat, talk foolishly] *base* bleat (balant, balle)

balaen- [L. *balaena*, whale] *base* whale (Balaenidae, balaenoid)

balani-, balano- [Gr. *balanos*, acorn] *comb* acorn; gland (balaniferous, balanitis)

balatro- [L. *balatro*, jester] *base* buffoon (balatronic, balatrophobia)

balaust- [Gr. *balaustion*, flower of the wild pomegranate] *base* pomegranate (balaustine, Balaustion)

balbut- [L. *balbus*, stammering] *base* stutter; stammer (balbutiate, balbutient)

ball- [L. *ballare*, to dance] *base* dance (ballo, ballade)

ballist- [Gr. *ballein*, to throw] *base* projectile (ballistic, ballistics)

balneo- [L. *balnaeum*, warm bath] *comb* baths; bathing (balneary, balneology)

Balto- [L. *Balticus*, Baltic] *comb.* Baltic + (Balto-Lithuanian, Balto-Slavic)

bambus- [L. *bambusa*, bamboo] *base* bamboo (bambusaceous, bambusicoline)

banaus- [Gr. *banausikos*, of mechanics] *base* mechanical (banausian, banausic)

bapt- [Gr. *baptein*, to dip] *base* dip (baptize, baptosaurus)

-bar [Gr. *baros*, weight] *comb* atmospheric pressure; weight (decibar, isobar)

barath- [Gr. *barathron*, abyss, deep pit] *base* pit (barathrum)

barb- [L. *barba*, beard] *comb* beard; tufted (barbate, barbellate)

barbar- [Gr. *barbaros*, foreign] *base* barbarian (barbarian, barbarocracy)

bari-, baro- [Gr. *baros*, weight] *comb* atmospheric pressure; weight (baritone, barometer)

bary- [Gr. *baros*, weight] *comb* heavy; difficult (barycentric, baryphonia)

bas- [L. *basium*, kiss] *base* kiss (basial, basiator)

basal- [Gr. *bassus*, deep] *base* deep sea region (Bassalia, Bassalian)

bascaud- [L. *bascauda*, basket] *base* basket (bascaud, bascaudal)

Basco- [Fr. *Basque*, Basque] *comb* Basque (Bascologist, Bascology)

basi-, baso- [Gr. *basis*, base] *comb* [biology] the base; at or near base (basidigitale, basocellular)

-basia [Gr. *basis*, step] *comb* [medicine] ability to walk (abasia, dysbasia)

basiat- [L. *basium*, kiss] *base* kiss (basiate, basiation)

basidio- [L. *basidium*, base] *comb* base (basidiomycetes, basidium)

basil- [Gr. *basileus*, king] *base* king; royal (basilic, basilica)

bassar- [Gr. *bassaris*, fox] *base* fox (Bassaricyon, Bassarididae)

-bat-[1] [Gr. *bainein*, go] *base* walk; go; pass (diabatic, katabatic)

bat-[2] [L. *battare*, hit, strike] *base* beat time (battue, battuta)

bat-[3] [Gr. *batos*, bramble] *base* bramble (batologist, batology)

bathmo- [Gr. *bathmos*, threshold] *comb* excitability, responsiveness (bathmotropic, bathmotropism)

batho-, bathy- [Gr. *bathos*, depth] *comb* depth; deep (bathometer, bathysphere)

bato-[1] [Gr. *batos*, passable] *comb* height (batomania, batophobia)

bato-[2] [Gr. *batos*, bramble-bush] *comb* brambles (batologist, batology)

batracho- [Gr. *batraxos*, frog] *comb* frog; toad (batrachoid, batrachophagous)

batto- [Gr. *battos*, stammerer] *comb* repetition (battologize, battology)

bdell- [Gr. *bdella*, leech] *base* leech (bdellatomy, bdellometer)

be- [L.-*bi* in *ambi*, both] **1.** *pre* around (beset); **2.** completely (besmear); **3.** away (bereave); **4.** about (bemoan); **5.** make (besot); **6.** furnish with (befriend); **7.** cover(ed) with; (becloud)

beati- [L. *beatus*, happy] *base* happy; blessed (beatific, beatitude)

becc- [L. *beccare*, to peck with a beak] *base* peck (abeche, beccafico)

bech- [Gr. *bexikos*, cough] *base* cough (bechic, bechical)

-bell-[1] [L. *bellum*, war] *base* war (bellicose, belligerence)

bell-[2] [L. *bella*, lovely] *base* beautiful (belle, belletrist)

bellat- [L. *bellator*, warrior] *base* warlike, soldier (bellatory, bellatrice)

bellu- [L. *bellua*, beast] *base* beast (belue, belluine)

-belo- [Gr. *belos*, arrow] *base* arrow (beloid, belomancy)

-belon- [Gr. *belone*, needle] *base* needle; pin; sharp object (belonite, belonoid)

bene- [L. *bene*, well] *pre* good; well (benefactor, beneficence)

benig- [L. *benignus*, kind, affable] *base* kind, gracious (benign, benignant)

benzo- [It. *benzoinzo*, frankincense] *comb* [chemistry] benzine; (benzo-phenone, benzopyrene)

beryl- [Gr. *berrulos*, beryl] *base* pale sea green (beryline, berylloid)

besti- [L. *bestia*, beast] *base* beast (bestiary, bestiocracy)

betul- [L. *betulla*, birch] *base* birch (Betula, betulaceous)

bi- [L. *bi*, two] **1.** *pre* having two (biangular); **2.** on both sides; in two ways (bilingual); **3.** every two (biweekly); **4.** using two (bilabial); **5.** involving two (bipartisan); **6.** [botany/zoology] twice; doubly; in pairs (bipinnate); **7.** [chemistry] having twice as many atoms or chemical equivalents for a definite weight of the other constituent of the compound (sodium bicarbonate); **8.** organic compounds having a combination of two radicals of the same composition (biphenyl)

bib- [L. *bibere*, to drink] *base* drink (bibulous, imbibe)

biblio- [Gr. *biblion*, book] **1.** *comb* of

books (bibliography); **2.** of the Bible (bibliomancy)

bili- [L. *bilis*, bile] *comb* gall; bile (biliary, biligenic)

-bility [L. suf.–*bilitas*] *suf* power to do or be (credibility, responsibility)

bin- [L. *bini*, two by two] *pre* two (binary, binaural)

bio- [Gr. *bios*, life] *comb* living; life (biograph, biology)

-biosis, -biotic [Gr. *bios*, life] *comb* way of living (parabiosis, symbiosis, aerobiotic)

-bis- [L. *bis*, twice] *pre* two; twice (biscroma, bisferious)

blaes- [L. *blaesus*, lisping or stammering] *base* stammering (blaesitas, blaesiloquent) *Also* **bles-**

bland- [L. *blandus*, flattering] *base* flattery (blandiloquence, blandishment)

-blast, -blastic, blasto-, -blasty [Gr. *blastos*, germ or sprout] *comb* formative; germinal; embryonic; developing (mesoblast, osteoblastic, blastoderm)

blat- [L. *blatire*, prattle, babble] *base* babble, bellow (blather, blatteration)

blatt-[1] [L. *blatta*, cockroach] *base* cockroach (Blatta, blattiform)

blatt-[2] [L. *blatta*, purple silk] *base* purple (blatta, blattean)

-ble *see* **-able**

blenn-, blenno- [Gr. *blennos*, mucus] *comb* mucus; slime (blennadenitis, blennostasis)

-blep- [Gr. *blepso*, I see] *base* sight (ablepsia, ablepsy)

blepharo- [Gr. *blepharon*, eyelid] *comb* eyelid (blepharospasm, blepharotomy)

blesi- [L. *blaesus*, lisping or stammering] *base* stammering (blesiloquent)

-bly *see* **-ably**

-bole [Gr. *ballein*, to throw] *comb* thrown down/out/in/together/beyond (amphibole, hyperbole)

bolet- [Gr. *boletes*, type of mushroom] *base* fungus; mushroom (boletic, boletus)

-bolic, bolo-[1]**, -boly** [Gr. *ballein*, to throw] *comb* thrown down/out/in/

together/beyond (catabolic, bolometer, epiboly)

bolo-[2] [Gr. *bole*, throw, glance, ray] *base* ray; radiant energy (bolometer, bolometric)

-bomb- 1. [L. *bombus*, bumblebee] *base* bee (bombilation); **2.** [L. *bombyx*, silkworm] silk; silkworm (bombic, bombycinous) **3.** [L. *bombare*, to buzz] buzzing or droning sound (bombilate, bombilation)

bon- [L. *bonus*, good] *base* good (bona fide, bonanza)

borbor-[1] [Gr. *borborugmos*, bowel rumbling] *base* intestinal rumbling (borborygmus, borborygmic)

borbor-[2] [Gr. *borboros*, filthy talk] *base* filthy talk (Borborite, borborology)

borea- [Gr. *boreas*, north wind] *base* north (boreal, borean)

boro- [Pers. *burah*, borax] *comb* [chemistry] boron (boroflouride, borosilicate)

-bosc-[1] [OHG *busc*, a thicket] *base* mass of growing trees or shrubs (boscage, bosky)

-bosc-[2] [Gr. *boskein*, to feed] *base* to feed (Boscades, hippoboscid)

-boss- [Gr. *bossen*, strike or beat] *base* protuberant part (bosselated, emboss)

bostrych- [Gr. *bostruchos*, curl or lock of hair] *base* coiled or curled (bostrychite, bostryx)

botano- [Gr. *botane*, herb or plant] *comb* plant (botanical, botanomancy)

botaur- [L. *bos*, ox + *taurus*, bull] *base* bittern (Botaurinae, botaurus)

-bothr- [Gr. *bothros*, pit or trench] *base* pitted; grooved (bothrenchyma, Bothrophera)

botry(o)- [Gr. *botrus*, grape cluster] *comb* grapes; clustered like grapes (botryose, botyroidal)

-botul- [L. *botulus*, sausage] *base* sausage (botuliform, botulism)

bou-, bu- [Gr. *bous*, ox] *comb* ox; cow (boustrophedon, bulemia)

-bound 1. [OE *bindan*, place under bond] *comb* constrained (snowbound); **2.** [ON *bua*, to get ready] going toward (homebound, westbound)

-bov- [L. gen. case *bovis*, ox] *base* cow (boviculture, bovine)

brachi-, brachio- [L. *brachium*, arm] *comb* arm; upper arm (brachialgia, brachiopod)

brachisto- [Gr. *braxis*, short] *comb* short (brachistocephaly, brachistochrone)

brachy- [Gr. *braxis*, short] *comb* short (brachycardia, brachycerous)

bract- [L. *bractea*, gold-leaf veneer] *base* thin plate; leaf (bracteate, bracteiform)

brady- [Gr. *bradys*, slow] *comb* slow; delayed (bradyarthria, bradyphasia)

-branchia, branchio- [Gr. *branchia*, gills] *comb* gills (pulmobranchia, branchiopod)

brassic- [L. *brassica*, cabbage] *base* broccoli; cabbage (Brassica, brassicacious)

bregm- [Gr. *bregma*, front of the skull] *base* fore part of the head; the sinciput (bregma, bregmatic)

brepho- [Gr. *brephos*, babe] *comb* baby (brepholatry, brephotrophic)

brevi- [L. *brevis*, short] *comb* brief; little; short (brevifoliate, breviloquence)

broch- [L. *brochatus*, having projecting teeth] *base* having tusks (Brochata, brochate)

brom-, bromo-¹ [Gr. *broma*, food] *comb* stench (bromidrosis, bromopnea)

bromato- [Gr. *broma*, food] *comb* food (bromatography, bromatology)

bromel- [L. *Bromelia*,< Swed. botanist Olaf Bromel] *base* pineapple (Bromelia, bromeliaceous)

bromo-² [Gr. *bromos*, stench] *comb* [chemistry] bromine (bromoderma, bromogelatin)

bronch-, bronchi-, bronchio-, broncho- [Gr. *bronchos*, windpipe] *comb* the windpipe (bronchadenitis, bronchiectasis, bronchiogenic, bronchoscope)

bronto- [Gr. *bronte*, thunder] **1.** *comb* thunder (brontograph); **2.** [paleontology] hugeness (brontosaurus)

-brotic [Gr. *brotikos*, inclined to eat] *comb* corrosive; inclined to eat (diabrotic, scolecobrotic)

bruch- [Gr. *brouchos*, wingless locust] *base* beetle (bruchid, Bruchidae)

brum- [L. *bruma*, winter] *base* winter; foggy (brumal, brumous)

brun- [Fr. *brun*, dimin. of brown] *base* dark brown (brunette, brunneous)

brux- [Gr. *brukein*, to gnash] *base* grind (bruxism, bruxomania)

bryo- [Gr. *bruon*, moss] *comb* moss (bryology, bryophyte)

bu- *see* bou-

bubal- [Gr. *boubalos*, antelope, buffalo] *base* antelope; buffalo (bubaline, Bubalus)

bubo- [Gr. *boubon*, groin] *base* groin (bubonic, bubonocele)

buccin- [L. *bucina*, trumpet < Gr. cow's horn] *base* trumpet (buccinal, buccinatory)

bucco- [L. *bucca*, cheek] *comb* cheek (buccal, buccolabial)

bucerat-, bucorac- [Gr. *bous*, ox + *keras*, horn] *base* hornbill (Buceratinae, Bucoracinae)

bufo- [L. *bufo*, toad] *comb* toad (bufoniform, bufotoxin)

bulbi-, bulbo- [L. *bulbus*, bulb] *comb* bulb; bulbous (bulbiform, bulbospinal)

-bulia [Gr. *boule*, will] *comb* will; (abulia, dysbulia)

bulim- [Gr. *boulimos*, ravenous hunger] *base* eating disorder (bulimia, bulimic)

bullat- [L. *bulla*, bubble] *base* bubble; blister (bullate, bullescence)

-bulum [L. –*bulum*, names of instruments] *suf* indicating an instrument (acetabulum, infundibulum)

buno- [Gr. *bonnos*, hill or mound] *base* elevated (bunodont, bunotherian)

-burg, -burgh [OE *burg*, town] *comb* city; town; village (Vicksburg, Pittsburgh)

-burger [Ger. city *Hamburg*] *comb* sandwich made on a roll or bun (cheeseburger, mooseburger)

burs-, burso- [L. *bursa*, pouch] *comb* pouch; purse; sac (bursar, bursopathy)

buteo- [L. *buteo*, buzzard-hawk] *comb* hawk; buzzard (Buteoninae, buteonine)

butyro- [L. *buturum*, butter] *comb* butter (butyraceous, butyrometer)

bux- [L. *buxeus*, box tree] *base* box-tree (buxeous, buxiferous)
by- [L.–*bi*< *ambi*, both] **1.** *pre* near; close by (bystander); **2.** side (bystreet); **3.** secondary (by-product)
-byon- [Gr. *buein*, to stuff] *base* plug; stuff (rhinobyon)

-byss-[1] [Gr. *bussos*, depth] *base* depth (hypabyssal, hyperbyssal)
-byss-[2] [Gr. *bussos*, flax-like] *base* flax (byssaceous, byssinosis)

C

caball- [Gr. *kabales*, pack horse] *base* horse (caballaria, caballine)
caca- [Gr. *kakke*, excrement] *base* excrement (cacagogue, cacatory)
-cace [Gr. *kake*, bad, flawed] *base* disease, deformity (chilocace, stomacace)
cachex- [Gr. *kachexia*, disease] *base* ill health (cachectic, cachexia)
cachin- [L. *cacinnare*, to laugh immoderately] *base* laugh (cachinnate, cachinnation)
caco- [Gr. *kakos*, bad] *comb* bad; poor; harsh (caconym, cacophony). *Also* **kako-** (kakistocracy)
cact- [Gr. *cactos*, prickly plant] *base* cactus (cactaceous, cactoid)
cacumin- [L. *cacumina*, summit] *base* tip (cacuminal, cacuminate)
cad- [L. *cadere*, to fall] *base* fall (cadence, cadenza)
cadav- [L. *cadaver*, corpse] *base* corpse (cadaveric, cadaverous)
-cade [suf. from *cavalcade*] *comb* procession; parade (aquacade, motorcade)
caduc-[1] [L. *caducus*, fleeting] *base* transitory; perishable (caducicorn, caducous)
caduc-[2] [L. *caducium*, herald's staff] *base* herald, messenger (caducean, caduceator)
cadus- [L. *cadus*, large vessel] *base* cask, barrel (cade, cade-bow)
caec- [L. *caecus*, blind] **1.** *base* blind (caecilian); **2.** intestinal pouch (caeciform)
caed- *see* **-cide**
cael- [L. *caelestis*, celestial] *base* heavens (caelestial, caelometer). Also **cel-** (celestial) *see* **celest-**

caelat- [L. *caelator*, engraver] *base* embossed, engraved (celature)
caelib- [L. *caelebs*, unmarried] *base* unmarried, celibate (celibatarian, celibate)
caeno-[1], **ceno-**, **coeno-** [Gr. *koinos*, common] *comb* in common (caenobite, cenobite, coenobium)
caeno-[2] [Gr. *kainos*, recent] *comb* new (caenogenesis, Caenozoic). *Also* **caino-** (cainophobia)
caep- [L. *caepa*, onion] *base* caper (cepaceous, cepivorous)
caerimon- [L. *caerimonia*, sacred ceremony] *base* ceremony (ceremony, unceremoniously)
caes- [L. *caesius*, bluish-gray] *base* blue; gray; green (caesiellus, caesious)
caesur- [L. *caesura*, a cutting, hewing off] *base* metrical pause (caesura, caesural)
-caine [taken from *cocaine*, coca + *-ine*] *comb* synthetic alkaloid in anesthetic drugs (lidocaine, novocaine)
cal-, cale- [L. *calere*, to be warm] *base* heat (decalescence, caleficient)
calam- [L. *calamus*, reed] *base* reed (calamarious, calamiform)
calamist- [L. *calamistratus*, curled] *base* curled, frizzled (calamistrate, calamistration)
calamit- [L. *calamitas*, damage, misfortune] *base* trouble, adversity (calamitous, calamity)
calar-, calat- [L. *calare*, to proclaim solemnly] *base* inserted (intercalary, intercalated)
calathi- [Gr. *kalathos*, basket] *comb* cup; basket (calathiform, calathus)

calcaneo- [L. *calx*, heel] *comb* heel-bone (calcaneo-fibular, calcaneum)

calcareo- [L. *calcarius*, pert. to lime] *comb* of lime (calcareosulfurous, calcariferous)

calcat- [L. *calcatorium*, a wine press] *base* treading (calcate, calcation)

-calce- [L. *calceus*, shoe] *base* shoe (discalceate, discalced)

calci- [L. *calx/calc-*, lime] *comb* calcium; lime (calcification, calcify)

calcitr- [L. *calcitrare*, to kick] *base* kick (calcitrant, recalcitrant)

-calcul- [L. *calculus*, pebble] *base* count; pebble (calculary, calcu-lator)

-cali- [Gr. *kalia*, hut] *base* nest; hut (caliological, caliology)

calic- [L. *calix/calic-*, cup] *base* like a cup (calicula, calicular) *Also* **calyc-**

calig- [L. *caligo*, gloom, mist] *base* fog; mist (caliginous, caligo)

callain- [Gr. *kallais*, turquoise] *base* turquoise (callainite)

calli- [Gr. *kalos*, beautiful] *comb* beautiful (calligraphy, callipygous)

callid- [L. *callidus*, shrewd, worldly] *base* crafty (called, callidity)

callithri- [Gr. *kalos*, beautiful + *trix*, hair] *base* marmoset (callithricid, callithrix)

callo- [Gr. *kalos*, beautiful] *comb* beautiful (callomania, callotechnics)

callos- [L. *callosus*, thick-skinned] *base* hardened (callose, callosity)

calo-, calori- [L. *calor*, heat] *comb* heat (caloreceptor, calorimeter)

calumn- [L. *calumnia*, slander] *base* slander (calumniate, calumniator)

calv- [L. *calva*, scalp without hair] *base* bald (calvarium, Calvary)

calyc- [Gr. *kaluk*, cup-shaped] *base* cup-shaped (calycanthemy, calyciferous)

calypto- [Gr. *kaluptos*, covered] *comb* hidden; covered (calyptoblastic, calyptomerous)

calyptri- [Gr. *kaluptra*, veil] *base* hood (calyptriform, calyptrimorphous)

camar- *see* **camer-**

-camb- [L. *cambire*, to exchange] *base* change; exchange (cambistry, excambition)

cambar- [L. *camarus*, sea-crab] *base* crayfish variety (cambarine, cambaroid)

cameli- [Gr. *kamelos*, camel] *base* camel (camelid, cameline)

camer- [Gr. *kamara*, vault] *base* vault (Camarasaurus, camerastoma)

camis- [L. *camisia*, nightgown] *base* tunic, shirt (camisated, camisole)

-camp-[1] [L. *campus*, field] *base* field (campaign, campestral)

-camp-[2] [Gr. *kampe*, caterpillar] *base* caterpillar (campodeiform, campophagine)

campan- [L. *campana*, bell] *base* bell (campaniform, campanology)

campho- [Arab. *kafur*, bitter aromatic] *comb* camphor (camphogen, campholide)

-campsis, campto- [Gr. *kamptos*, bent] *comb* bent (phallocampsis, camptomelia)

campylo- [Gr. *kampilos*, bent or curved] *comb* crooked; bent (campylospermous, campylotropal)

can-[1] [L. *canis*, dog] *base* dog (canid, canine)

can-[2] [L. *canus*, hoary] *base* gray (canescence, canescent)

can-[3] [Gr. *kanastron*, wicker basket] *base* small container (canister, cannister)

canal- [L. *canalis*, channel, groove] *base* groove (canaliculated, canalirostrate)

cancel- [L. *cancellarius*, chancellor] *base* chancellor (cancellarian, cancellariate)

cancell- [L. *cancellatus*, latticed] *base* barrier; latticed (cancellate, cancellous)

cancr- [L. *cancer*, crab] *base* crab (cancriform, cancrine)

cand- [L. *candidus*, bright] *base* white (candescent, candidate)

canicul- [L. *canis*, dog] *base* relating to the dog-days (canicular, canicule)

canitud- [L. *canitudo*, gray color, hoariness] *base* gray, hoary (canitude, canitudinous)

cann- [L. *canna*, reed] *base* reed (cannula, cannoid)

canon- [Gr. *kananikos*, rule] *base* authorized (canonic, canonical)

canor- [L. *canorus,* tuneful, melodious] *base* melodious (canor, canorously)

canthar- [L. *cantharus,* drinking vessel] *base* cup, laver (cantharus, canthari)

cantho- [Gr. *kanthos,* corner of the eye] *comb* eye: corner of (canthectomy, canthoplasty)

-cap- [L. *capere,* seize] *base* take; hold; receive (captivate, recapture). *Also* cep/cip (receptacle, recipient)

capel- [Gr. *kapelos,* shopkeeper] *base* shopkeeper (capelocracy, capelocratic)

capilli- [L. *capillus,* hair] *comb* hair (capillaceous, capilliform)

capist- [L. *capistrare,* to tie with a halter, to muzzle] *base* to muzzle (capistrate, capistration)

-capit- [L. *caput,* head] *base* head (capital, decapitate)

-capnia, capno- [Gr. *kapnos,* smoke] *comb* smoke; vapor; carbon dioxide (acapnia, capnomancy) *Also* kapno- (kapnography)

capri- [L. *caper/capr-,* goat] *base* goat (Capricorn, capriform)

capsuli-, capsulo- [L. *capsa,* chest] *comb* capsule (capsuliform, capsulolenticular)

carbo- [L. *carbo,* coal] *comb* [chemistry] carbon (carbohydrate, carboniferous)

carbol- [L. *carbo,* coal] *base* of phenol (carboloc, carbolize)

carbon- [L. *carbonem,* charcoal] *base* charcoal (carbonaceous, carbonify)

carcer- [L. *carcer,* prison] *base* jail (carceral, incarcerate)

carcharin- [Gr. *karxaros,* jagged] *base* shark (carcharinid, carcharoid)

carcin(o)- [Gr. *karkinos,* crab, cancer] *comb* cancer; crab (carcinogenesis, carcinophagous)

cardam- [Gr. *kardamon,* cress] *base* cress (cardamine, cardamom)

cardi-, -cardia, cardio-, -cardium [Gr. *kardia,* heart] *comb* heart (cardiagra, tachycardia, cardiology, myocardium)

cardo- [Gr. *kardos,* thistle] *comb* thistle (cardophagous)

carico- [L. *carex/caric-,* sedge] *base* sedge (caricography, caricologist)

carid- [Gr. *karis,* shrimp or prawn] *base* shrimp, prawn (caridean, caridomorphic)

-carin- [L. *carina,* keel] *base* keel; ridge (carinate, carinula)

cario- [L. *caries,* decay] *comb* tooth disease; caries (cariogenic, carious)

carni- [L. *caro,* flesh] *comb* flesh (carnality, carnivore)

carnoso- [L. *caro,* flesh] *comb* fleshy (carnoso-fibrous, carnoso-tube-rose)

carot- [Gr. *karos,* stupor] *base* stupefying; soporific (carotic, carotid)

-carp, -carpic, carpo-[1], -carpous [Gr. *karpos,* fruit] *comb* fruit; seeds (endocarp, endocarpic, carpophore, monocarpous)

carpho- [Gr. *karphos,* straw] *comb* straw; dry (carpholite, carphology)

carpo-[2] [Gr. *karpos,* wrist] *comb* wrist; (carpocerite, carpoptosis)

cartilag- [L. *cartilago,* gristle] *base* cartilage (cartilage, cartilaginous)

carto- [L. *carta,* a card] *comb* map; card; piece of paper (cartographer, cartomancy). *Also* charto- (chartometer)

caryo- [Gr. *karuon,* nut] *comb* nucleus (cartophyllus, caryopsis). *Also* karyo- (karyokinesis)

cas- [L. *casus,* fall] *base* fall (cascade, grammatical case)

case- [L. *caseus,* cheese] *base* cheese (caseation, casefied)

cassidi- [L. *cassis,* helmet] *base* helmet (cassidiform, cassidula)

cassiter- [Gr. *kassiteros,* tin] *base* tin (cassiterite, cassiterotantalite)

-cast [ON *casta,* to throw, scatter] *comb* transmit (broadcast, telecast)

castan- [L. *castanea,* chestnut] *base* brown; chestnut (castaneous, castanet)

castella- [L. *castellum,* castle] *base* fortification (castellar, incastellate)

castig- [L. *castigare,* correct] *base* chasten; reprove (castigate, castigatory)

castor- [L. *castor,* beaver] *base* beaver (castoreum, castorine)

castr- [L. *castra,* camp] *base* camp (castrametation, castrensian)

casuar- [L. *casuarius*, cassowary] *base* cassowary (Casuariidae, casuary)

cata-, cath- [Gr. *kata*, down] *pre* down; through; against; completely (catabolism, cathartic). *Also* **kata-** (katabatic)

catagelo- [Gr. *katagelos*, mockery] *base* ridicule (catagelomania, catagelophobia). *Also* **katagelo-**

cataglott- [Gr. *kataglottisma*, lascivious kiss] *base* tongue-kissing (cataglottism, cataglottistic)

catagm- [Gr. *kata*, intensive + *agnunai*, break in pieces] *base* fracture (catagmatic, catagmatical)

cataphract- [Gr. *kataphraktes*, mail-clad] *base* scaly or horny-armored (cataphracted, cataphractic)

catech- [Gr. *katechein*, to instruct] *base* oral instruction, esp. Q & A (catechetics, catechism)

caten- [L. *catena*, chain] *base* chain (catenary, concatenation)

caterv- [L. *caterva*, a crowd, troop] *base* band, troop (caterve, catervation)

cathar- [Gr. *katharos*, clean, pure] *base* clean; purge; purify (catharize, catharsis)

cathart- [Gr. *katharein*, to cleanse] *base* buzzard (Cathartes, cathartine)

-cathex- [Gr. *kathexis*, retention] *base* retention (acathexis, hypercathexis)

cathis- [Gr. *cathizein*, to sit] *base* sit; seat (cathisma, cathismata)

cathodo- [Gr. *kathodos*, a going down] *comb.* cathode + (cathodo-excitation, cathodo-luminescence)

catill- [L. *catillus*, dish, plate] *base* plate (catillate, catillation)

catoptro- [Gr. *katoptron*, mirror] *comb* mirror (catoptrics, catoptromantic)

cattall- [Gr. *katallaktikos*, having to do with exchange] *base* money exchange (catallactically, catallactics)

caudo- [L. *cauda*, tail] *comb* tail (caudo-femoral, caudotibial)

cauli-, caulo- [L. *caulis*, a stalk] *comb* stem; stalk (caulicolous, caulocarpic)

caum- [Gr. *kauma*, heat] *base* heat (caumatic, caumesthesia)

caupon- [L. *caupo*, huckster] *base* huckster; innkeeper (cauponate, cauponation)

-caust- [Gr. *kaustos*, capable of burning] *base* burn (caustic, holocaust)

caut- [L. *cautela*, caution] *base* heed; carefulness (cautelous, precautionary)

cauter- [Gr. *kauter*, branding iron] *comb* caustic; burning (cauterize, cautery)

cava-, -cave, cavi-, cavo- [L. *cavus*, hollow] *base* hollow (cavate, concave, cavernicolous, cavicorn)

caval- [L. *caballus*, horse] *base* horse (cavalier, cavalry)

-ce *suf* multiplicative suffix (thrice, twice)

cebo- [L. *cebus*, monkey] *comb* monkey (Cebidae, cebocephalic)

cecid- [Gr. *kekis*, gallnut] *base* gall: tumorous plant tissue (Cecidomyia, cecidomyian)

cec- [L. *cecus*, blind] *base* blindness (cecity, cecutiency)

ceco- [L. *cecus*, blind] *comb* intestinal pouch; cecum; (cecostomy). *Also* **caec-** (caeciform)

-ced-, -cess- [L. *cedere*, yield] *base* move; go; give way (concede, procession). *See* **-cid-**

cedr- [L. *cedrus*, cedar] *base* cedar (cedrine, cedron)

celad- [Fr. *celadon*, pale green] *base* pale green (celadon, celadonikte)

-cele [Gr. *kele*, tumor] *comb* tumor; swelling (adenocele, cystocele); hernia; (bubonocele, perineocele)

-celer- [L. *celer*, swift] *base* speed (accelerate, celerity)

celest- [L. *coelum*, heaven] *base* heavens (celestial, celestify)

celido- [Gr. *kelis*, a spot] *comb* spot; surface marking (celidography)

celio- [Gr. *koilia*, belly] *comb* abdomen; (celiomyositis, celiotomy)

celli- [L. *cella*, cell] *comb* cell (celliferous, celliform)

cello- [L. *cella*, chamber] *comb* cellulose (cellobiose, cellophane)

celluli-, cellulo- [L. *cellula*, little cell] *comb* cell; cell wall (celluliferous, cellulo-fibrous)

celo-[1] [Gr. *koilos*, hollow] **1.** *comb*

celom (celomate); **2.** hernia (celotomy); **3.** abdomen (celoscope). *Also* **coelo-** (coeloscope)

-**celo-**[2] [Gr. *kelos*, dry, burnt] *base* dry; burnt (celosia)

celsi- [L. *celsus*, lofty] *base* dignity; eminence; lofty position (celsitude, celsity)

Celto- [Gr. *keltos*, Western people] *comb* Celt; Celtic (Celto-Germanic, Celtomania)

cen- [L. *cena*, dinner] *base* meal (cenation, cenatory)

-**cene** [Gr. *kainos*, new] *comb* geological epoch (Eocene, Miocene)

ceno-[1] [Gr. *kainos*, new] *comb* new; recent (cenogenesis, Cenozoic). *Also* **caeno-, caino-, kaino-** (Caenozoic, Cainozoic, Kainozoic)

ceno-[2] [Gr. *koinos*, common] *comb* in common; common (cenobite, cenogonous). *Also* **coeno-** (coenobite)

ceno-[3] [Gr. *kenos*, empty] *comb* empty (cenotaph, cenotaphic). *Also* **keno-** (kenosis)

cenoto- [Gr. *kainos*, new] *comb* new (cenotomania, cenotophobia) *Also* **cainoto-, kainoto-** (cainotophobia, kainotophobia)

-**centered** [Gr. *kentron*, center of a circle] *comb* focused on (child-centered, market-centered).

-**centesis** [Gr. *kentesis*, pricking] *comb* puncture (amniocentesis, pericardiocentesis)

centi- [L. *centum*, hundred] **1.** *comb* hundred-fold (centipede); **2.** hundredth part (centigram)

centri-, centro- [Gr. *kentron*, center of a circle] *comb* center (centripetal, centrobaric)

-**centric** [Gr. *kentron*, center of a circle] *comb* **1.** having ___ center (polycentric) **2.** focused around ___ (etho-centric)

-**cep-**[1] [L. *capere*, take] *base* take (accept, receptor). *See* -**cap-**

-**cep-**[2] [L. *cepa*, onion] *base* onion; bulb (cepaceous, cepivorous)

cephal-, -cephalic, cephalo-, -cephalous, -cephaly [Gr. *kephale*, head]

comb head; skull (cephalitis, dolichocephalic, cephalopod, brachycephalous, dolichocephaly)

cephalopod- [Gr. *kephale*, head + *pous*, foot] *base* squid (Cephalapoda, cephalopodal)

-**ceptor** [L. *capere*, to take] *comb* taker; receiver (chemoceptor, neuroreceptor)

cera- [L. *cera*, wax] *base* wax (ceraceous, cerein)

ceramo- [Gr. *keramos*, potters' clay] *comb* ceramic (ceramean, ceramodontia)

ceras- [L. *cerasus*, cherry] *base* cherry (cerasin, cerasinous)

cerato- [Gr. *keras*, horn] *comb* horn; hornlike (ceratocele, ceratophyllous). *Also* **kerato-** (keratoglobus)

cerator- [Gr. *keras*, horn + *hris*, snout] *base* rhino (ceratorhine, Ceratorhina)

cerauno- [Gr. *keraunos*, thunderbolt] *comb* thunder (ceraunic, ceraunoscope). *Also* **kerauno-** (keraunoscope)

-**cerca, -cercal, cerco-** [Gr. *kerkos*, tail of a beast] *comb* having a ___ tail (Schistocerca, heterocercal, Cercopithecus)

cerebri-, cerebro- [L. *cerebra*, brain] *comb* brain (cerebritis, cerebrospinal)

ceri-, cero- [L. *cera*, wax] *comb* wax (ceriferous, ceromancy)

-**cern-** [L. *cernere*, perceive] *base* to sift (discern, excernent)

cerr- [L. *cerrus*, oak] *base* evergreen oak (cerrial, cerris)

cerul- [L. *caerulus*, dark blue] *base* blue (cerulean, cerulescent)

cerumini- [L. *cera*, wax] *comb* waxlike secretion (ceruminiferous, ceruminous)

cerus- [L. *cerussa*, white lead] *base* white (ceruse, cerussal)

-**cerv-** [L. *cervus*, deer] *base* deer; elk; moose (cervicide, cervine)

cervico- [L. *cervix*, neck] *comb* cervical; of the neck (cervicodorsal, cervicispinal)

cervis- [L. *cervesia*, beer] *base* beer (cervisial, cervisomania)

cespit- [L. *caespes*, turf or sod] *base* growing in dense tufts or clumps (cespitose, cespitulose) *Also* **cespi-toso-** *comb* (cespitoso-arboriform, cespitoso-ramose)

-cess-, -ced- [L. *cedere*, yield] *base* move; go; give way (procession, concede)

cessat- [L. *cessatio*, a tarrying, stopping] *base* cease (cessation, intercession)

cest- [Gr. *kestos*, girdle] *base* tapeworm (cestoid, Cestoidea)

-cet- [Gr. *ketos*, whale] *base* whale (cetaceous, cetology)

-chaem- [Gr. *khamai*, on the ground] *base* low (chaemacephalic). *Also* **-cham-**

chaeti-, chaeto-, -chaeta [L. *chaeta*, bristle] *comb* hair; bristle; seta (chaetiferous, chaetophorous, Spirochaeta)

chalast- [Gr. *khalastikos*, laxative] *base* laxative; relaxant (chalastic)

chalax- [Gr. *khalaxes*, hailstone] *base* hailstone (chalaxa, chalaxite)

chalco- [Gr. *khalkos*, copper] *comb* copper; brass (chalcocite, chalcography)

chalic- [Gr. *khalik*, gravel] *base* particles, gravel (Chalicomys, chalicosis)

chalyb- [Gr. *khalups*, steel] *base* steel (chalybean, chalybeous). *See* **iron**

chamae- [Gr. *khamai*, on the ground] *comb* low-growing; dwarflike (chamaecephaly, chamaedorea)

chao- [Gr. *khaos*, chaos] **1.** *base* abyss (chaology, chaotic); **2.** atmosphere (chaomancy)

charadr- [Gr. *kharadra*, cleft, ravine] *base* sandpiper, snipe, plover, woodcock (charadrine, charadrioid)

charis- [Gr. *xaris*, grace, favor] *base* gift of leadership (charism, charismatic)

charit- [L. *caritas*, love] *base* love (charitably, charity)

charto- [L. *charta*, paper] *comb* paper; map (chartomancy, chartometer) *Also* **carto-**

chasmo- [Gr. *khasma*, gulf, yawning hollow] *comb* fissure (chasmogamy, chasmophobia)

cheilo- [Gr. *kheilos*, lip] *base* lip (Cheilanthes, cheiloplasty). *See* **chilo-**

cheima- [Gr. *kheima*, frost, winter] *comb* cold (cheimaphilic, cheimaphobia)

cheir(o)- [Gr. *kheir*, hand] *comb* hand (Cheiranthus, macrocheiria). *See* **chiro-**

-chela, cheli- [Gr. *kele*, claw] *comb* claw (isochela, cheliferous)

chelid- [Gr. *khelidon*, swallow] *base* a swallow (chelidonian)

-chelo(n)-, chelys [Gr. *khelus*, turtle] *base* turtle (chelonian, Lepidochelys)

chemo- [L. *chimia*, alchemy] *comb* chemicals; (chemosmosis, chemotherapy)

cheno- [Gr. *khen*, goose] *base* goose (chenomorphic, chenopod)

cherm- [Gr. *xermaodion*, large stone] *base* stone missile (chermadic, chermadion)

chero-[1] [Gr. *khara*, joy, delight] *comb* happy (cheromania, cherophobia)

chero-[2] [Gr. *khoiros*, young pig] *base* hyrax (cherogril)

cherso- [Gr. *khersos*, dry land] *base* dry (chersonese, Chersydrus)

-chezia [Gr. *khezein*, to defecate] *comb* defecation condition (dyschezia, hematochezia)

chias-, chiasto- [Gr. *khiazein*, marked with crossed lines] *comb* paired; diagonal (chiasmus. chiastic, chiastolite)

chicor- [Gr. *kikhoreia*, succory, endive] *base* chicory (chicoried, chicory)

chili- [Gr. *khilioi*, thousand] *comb* one thousand (chiliasm, chiliastic)

chilo- [Gr. *kheilos*, lip] *comb* lip (chilognathous, chiloplasty)

chilopod- [Gr. *kheilos*, lip + *pous*, foot] *base* centipede (chilopodal, chilopodifirm)

chim- [Gr. *khimaira*, fabled monster] *base* unreal; fantastic (chimera, chimerical)

Chino- [Sanskrit *cinah*, Chinese people] *comb* Chinese (Chino-Japanese, Chino-Tibetan). *See* **Sino-**

-chion- [Gr. *khion*, snow] *base* snow (Chionis, chionodoxa). *See* **-chium**

chiro- [Gr. *kheir*, hand] *comb* hand (chirognomy, chiromancy). *Also* **cheiro-**

chirur- [Gr. *khirourgos*, doing by hand] *base* surgeon (chirurgery, chirurgic)

-chium [Gr. *khion*, snow] *base* snow (hedychium, sisyrinchium) *see* **-chion-**

chlamyd- [Gr. *khlamus*, mantle]

comb cloak; sheath (chlamydeous, chlamydospore)

chloro- [Gr. *khloros,* greenish-yellow] **1.** *comb* green (chlorophyll); **2.** . having chlorine; (chloroform)

choano- [Gr. *khoane,* funnel] *comb* funnel (choanocyte, choanoid)

chol-, chole-,cholo- [Gr. *khole,* bile] *comb* bile; gall; anger (cholagogue, cholecyst, chololith)

chomo- [Gr. *xoma,* heaped-up earth] *comb* debris (chomophyte, chomophytic)

chondr-, chondrio-, chondro- [Gr. *khondros,* cartilage, grain] *comb* cartilage ;(chondrify, chondriosome, chondroblast)

chord-, -chorda [Gr. *khorde,* string of a musical instrument] *comb* cord; sinew (chorditis, Protochorda). *Also* **cord-** (cordotomy)

-chorea, choreo- [Gr. *khorea,* dance] *comb* involuntary movement; spasm; dance (labiochorea, choreophrasia)

chori- [Gr. *khoris,* asunder] *comb* apart; separate (choripetalous, choryphyllus)

chorio- [Gr. *khorion,* membrane] *comb* membrane; skin (choriocapillaris, choriocele)

choristo- [Gr. *khoristos,* separate] *comb* apart; separate (choristophyllus, choristopodous)

choro- [Gr. *khoros,* place, country] *comb* region; land (chorology, chorometry)

choroid- [Gr. *khorion,* membrane + *eidos,* form] *comb* membrane; skinlike (choroideremia, choroiditis)

chrem-, chremat- [Gr. *khremata,* money, wealth] *base* wealth; money (chrematistic, chrematistics)

chreo- [Gr. *khreios,* useful] *comb* useful (chreotechnical, chreotechnics)

chresis- [Gr. *khresthai,* to use] *base* used for doing (catachresis, catachrestical)

chresmo- [Gr. *khresmo,* oracle] *comb* oracle (chresmomancy, chresmological)

chresto- [Gr. *khrestos,* worthy, useful] *base* useful (chrestomathic, chrestomathy)

chrism- [Gr. *chrisma,* anointing] *base* anointing (chrismal, chrismatory)

Christo- [Gr. *khristos,* the anointed one] *comb* Christ (Christocentric, Christomaniac)

chromato- [Gr. *khromat,* color] *comb* color; chromatin (chromatogenous, chromatopathic)

-chrome, -chromy [Gr. *khromat,* color] **1.** *comb* color (lithochromy, monochrome); **2.** chromium (ferrochrome)

chromo- [Gr. *khromat,* color] *comb* color (chromogenic, chromosome)

chrono-, -chronous [Gr. *khronos,* time] *comb* time (chronography, chronometer, isochronous)

-chroous [Gr, *khroia,* color] *comb* colored (allochroous, xanthocroous)

chrys(o)- [Gr. *khrusos,* gold] *comb* yellow; golden (chrysoberyl, chrysocarpous)

chthono- [Gr. *khthonos,* earth] *comb* earth (chthonic, chthonography)

chyl-, chyli-, chylo-, -chylia [Gr. *khulos,* juice, moisture] *comb* connected with chyle; digestive fluid; gastric juice (chylaqueous, chyliferous, chylocyst, achylia)

chymo- [Gr. *khymos,* juice] *comb* partially digested food (chymification, chymotrypsin)

-chys-, -chyt- [Gr. *khein,* to pour] *base* to pour (synchysis, synchytic)

-cib- [L. *cibus,* food] *base* food (cibarian, cibarious)

cica- [L. *cicatrix,* scar] *base* scar (cicatricose, cicatrix)

cichlo- [Gr. *cikhla,* bird like a thrush; also a sea fish] *base* thrush (cichlomorphous); fish (Cichla)

cichor- [Gr. *cikhorion,* chicory] *base* chicory (cichoraceous, Cichorium)

cicin- [Gr. *kikinos,* castor oil] *base* castor oil (cicinie)

ciconi- [L. *ciconia,* stork] *comb* stork (ciconian, ciconiiform)

cicur- [L. *cicurare,* to tame] *base* tame (cicurate, cicuration)

-cid- [L. *cadere,* to fall] *base* fall (deciduous, incident) *see* **-ced-, -cess-**

-cidal, -cide, -cidious, -cidism [L. *caedere*, to kill] *comb* killing (homicidal, patricide, parricidious, suicidism)

cilii-, cilio- [L. *cilium*, eyelid] *comb* cilia; hairlike process (ciliiferous, cilioretinal)

cimic- [L. *cimex/cimic-*, bug] *base* bug (cimicoid, Cimicifuga)

cimol- [Gr. *Kimolos*, name of an island] *base* chalk; light earth (cimolian, cimolite)

-cinc- [L. *cingere*, to gird, encircle] *base* ring; girdle (cincture, pre-cinct)

cinchon- [Sp. town *Chinchon*] *base* quinine (cinchonism, cinchotannic)

cincinn- [L. *cincinnus*, curl] *base* curl (cincinnal, Cincinnurus)

cine- [Gr. *kinein*, to move] *comb* movement; movie (cinematography, cinenchyma). *Also* **kine-** (kinescope)

ciner- [L. *cinis*, ashes] *base* ashes (cineraceous, incinerate)

-cing- [L. *cingere*, to gird] *base* ring; girdle (cingulated, circumcingle)

cinque- [Fr. *cinq*, five] *base* five (cinque, cinquefoil)

-cion [L.–*tio*, state or condition of being] *suf* variation of **-tion** (coercion, suspicion)

ciono- [Gr. *khion*, pillar, uvula] *base* uvula (cionitis, cionotomy)

-cip- [L. *capere*, to take] *base* take (anticipate, recipient). *See* **-cap-**

circin- [L. *circinare*, to make round] *base* round (circinal, circinate)

circul- [L. *circularis*, circular] *base* circle (circulate, circulatory)

circum- [L. *circum*, around, about] *suf* around; about; surrounding (circumscribe, circumstances)

cirrh- [Gr. *kirros*, tawny] *base* yellow appearance (cirrhosis, cirrhotic)

cirri-, cirro- [L. *cirrus*, curl or tuft] *comb* curl; ringlet; tendril (cirrrigerous, cirrocumulus)

cirso- [Gr. *kirsos*, enlargement of a vein] *comb* enlarged vein (cirsoid, cirsotomy)

cis-[1] [L. *cis*, on this side] *suf* on this side

of; near (cisalpine, cisatlantic). *See* **citra-**

-cis-[2], **-cise-** [L. *caedere*, to cut] *base* cut; cut off (incision, precise)

ciss- [Gr. *kissos*, ivy] *base* ivy (cissoid, cissoidal)

-cisto- [L. *cista*, box, chest] *base* chest; container (cistern, cistophorous)

-cit- [L. *citare*, to stimulate] *base* arouse (incite, recitation)

cithar- [Gr. *kithara*, type of lyre] *base* ancient stringed instrument (citharistic, citharaoedic)

citra- [L. *citer*, hither] *comb* on this side of; near (citracaucasian, citramontane). *See* **cis-**

citro- [L. *citrus*, citron tree] *comb* citric; lemon-colored (citrometer, citrine)

civ- [L. *civis*, city] *base* citizen (civic, civilization)

clado-, -cladous [Gr. *klados*, branch] *comb* branch (cladogenous, cladophyll, acanthocladous)

-claim, clam- [L. *clamare*, to call out] *comb* say; speak; tell (exclaim, exclamation)

clar- [L. *clarus*, clear] *base* clear (clarified, clarity)

-clasia, -clasis, -clastic [Gr. *klastos*, broken] *comb* break; fracture; fragment (osteoclasia, onychoclasis, aclastic)

-clasm, clasmato- [Gr. *klasma*, fragment] *comb* fragment (clasmatocyte, cataclasm)

clathr- [Gr. *klethron*, lattice] *base* lattice; bars (clathrate, clathroid)

claud- [L. *claudus*, lame] *base* lame (claudicant, claudication)

claustro- [L. *claustrum*, closed place] *comb* closed; shut (claustral, claustrophobia)

-clav- [L. *clavus*, nail] *base* nail (clavus, inclavate)

clavato- [L. *clavatus*, club-shaped] *comb* studded; club-shaped (clavato-elongate, clavato-turbinate)

clavi-[1] [L. *clavis*, key] *comb* key; collarbone (clavichord, clavicle)

clavi-[2] [L. *clava*, knotty branch or club] *base* club (clavicorn, claviform)

-cle [L. suf.–*culus*] **1.** *suf* diminutive spelling (particle); **2.** place; means (receptacle)

cleido- *see* **clido-**

-cleisis [Gr. *enkleiein*, to shut up] *comb* closure (colpocleisis, iredencleisis)

cleisto- [Gr. *kleistos*, closed] *comb* shut; closed (cleistocarp, cleistogamic)

clem-[1] [Gr. *klemat*, vine] *base* vine (clematine, clematis)

clem-[2] [L. *clemens*, mild] *base* mercy; leniency (clemency, clement)

clepto- [Gr. *kleptein*, steal] *comb* robber (clepsamnia, cleptobiosis). *See* **klepto-**

clerico- [L. *clericus*, clergyman] *comb* clerical and __ (clerico-liberal, clerico-political)

clero- [Gr. *kleros*, lot, share] *comb* chance; lot (cleromancy, cleronomy)

-clesis [Gr. *klesis,* calling, invitation] *suf* invocation (epiclesis)

clethr- [Gr. *klethra*, alder] *base* alder (clethra, Clethraceae)

clido- [Gr. *kleidos*, key] **1.** *comb* key (clidomancy); **2.** clavicle (clidomastoid). *Also* **cleido-** (cleidomancy)

climac- [Gr. *klimakter*, step of a staircase or ladder; critical period of life] *base* stairs; ladder rungs (climacophobia, climacteric)

clin- [Gr. *kline*, bed] *base* bed (clinical, clinoid)

-clinal, -clinate, -cline, -clinic, clino-, -clinous [Gr. *klinein*, to bend or slope] *comb* sloped; bent; directed toward; inclined (anticlinal, proclinate, incline, matroclinic, clinodiagonal, patroclinous)

-clisis [Gr. *klinein*, to lean] *comb* proneness; bending (enclisis, pathoclisis)

clisto- [Gr. *kleistos*, able to close] *comb* closed; closeable (clistocarp, clistogamous)

-clit- [Gr. *klinein*, to lean] *base* bend; inflect; lean (enclitic, heteroclital)

-clithr- [Gr. *kleithria*, keyhole, chink] **1.** *base* closed; shut (clithral); **2.** keyhole (clithridiate)

-cliv- [L. *clivus*, rising ground] *base* slope (acclivity, proclivity)

cloac- [L. *cloaca*, common sewer] *base* sewer; bowel cavity (cloacal, intracloacal)

-clonic, -clonus [Gr. *klonos*, confused motion or turmoil] *comb* spasm; twitching (synclonic, myoclonus)

-clud-, -clus- [L. *claudere*, to shut] *base* closed; shut (exclude, reclusive)

clupe- [L. *clupea*, small river fish] *base* herring (clupeiform, clupeoid)

clype- [L. *clypeus*, shield] *comb* like a shield (clypeate, clypeiform)

-clysis [Gr. *kluzein*, to wash out] *comb* irrigation (peritoneoclysis, venoclysis)

clysm-, clyst- [Gr. *kluzein*, to wash out] *base* enema (clysmic, clysterize)

-cnem- [Gr. *kneme*, lower part of the leg] *base* leg; tibia (cnemial, gastrocnemius)

cnes- [Gr. *knesis*, scratching] *base* scratch (acnestis)

cnido- [Gr. *knide*, nettle] *comb* nettle; stinging organ (cnidoblast, cnidophore)

co-[1] [L. pref. *com-*, with] **1.** *suf* together; with (co-operation); **2.** joint (co-owner); **3.** equally (coextensive); **4.** complement of (cosine). NOTE: **co-** can change to: **col-** (colleague); **com-** (commingle); **con-** (convulse); **cor-** (correlate)

-co[2] [abbrev. < *company*] *suf* trade names (Amoco, Pepsico)

cobalti-, cobalto- [Ger. *kobalt*, demon of the mines] *comb* cobalt (cobalti-cyanide, cobalto-cyanide)

-coccal, -coccic, cocco-, -coccoid, -coccus [Gr. *kokkos*, berry, kernel] *comb* of or like a bacterium; bacteria names; berry-like; grainlike (staphylococcal, staphylococcic, coccobacillus, staphylococcoid, staphylococcus)

cocci-, -coccus [Gr. *kokkos*, berry, kernel] *comb* berry-shaped (coccigerous, streptococcus)

coccy-, coccygo- [Gr. *kokkyx*, coccyx] *comb* coccyx (coccyalgia, coccygodynia)

cochin- [L. *coccinus*, scarlet < Gr. *kokkos*,

berry] *base* crimson dyestuff (cochineal, cochinillifera)

cochle(a)- [Gr. *kochlias*, snail] *base* snail (cochleate, cochleiform)

cochlear(i)- [L. *cochlear*, spoon] *base* spoon (cochlear, cochleariform)

cochlio- [Gr. *kochlias*, snail] *comb* spiral; twisted (cochliocarpous, cochliodontoid)

-coct- [L. *coquere*, to cook] *base* cook; boil (coctible, decoction)

codico- [L. *codex/codic-*, manuscript] *base* manuscript (codicologically, codicologist)

-codonic [Gr. *kodon*, bell] *comb* bell-shaped (adelocodonic, phanerocodonic)

-coele [Gr. *koilos*, hollow] *comb* cavity; chamber (blastocoele, hydrocoele)

coeli- [L. *coelum*, heaven] *comb* heaven; sky (celestial, coelicolist)

coelo-, -coelous [Gr. *koilos*, hollow] *comb* hollow (coelodont, procoelous)

coen-¹ [L. *cena*, principal meal] *base* meal (cenacle, coenaculous)

coen-² [L. *coenum*, dirt, mire] *base* filth, mud (coenose, coenosity)

coeno- [Gr. *koinos*, common] *comb* in common (coenobite). *Also* **ceno-** (cenobite)

cogit- [L. *cogitare*, to think] *base* know; think (cogitation)

-cogn-¹ [L. *cogitare*, to think] *base* know (recognize, cognition)

-cogn-² [L. *gnatus, natus*, born] *base* allied by blood (cognate, cognation)

coimet- [Gr. *koimeterion*, burial ground] *base* cemetery (coimetrophobia). *Also* **coemet-**

coit- [L. *coire*, come together] *base* intercourse; coming together (coition, coitus)

col-¹ *see* **co-**

col-² [L. *colum*, strainer or sieve] *base* strain; filter (colander, colation)

colaco- [Gr. *kolak*, parasite] *base* parasite (colacobiosis, colacobiotic)

colaph- [Gr. *kolaphos*, blow, buffet] *base* beat, buffet (colaphic, colaphize)

colar-, colat- [L. *colare*, to strain] *base* strain (colarin, percolated)

-cole, -colent [L. *colere*, to inhabit] *comb* [botany] inhabit; habitat (arboricole, accolent). *See* **-colous**

coleo- [Gr. *koleos*, sheath] *comb* sheath; scabbard (coleorhiza, coleophyllous)

coleopter- [L. *coleopterum*, beetle] *base* beetle (coleopteran, coleopterous)

coli-¹, colo- [Gr. *kolon*, intestine] *comb* colon (coliform, coloenteritis)

coli-² [L. *colum*, strainer or sieve] *comb* sieve (coliform)

coll-¹ [L. *collum*, neck] *base* neck; collar (decollate, colliform)

coll-² [Gr. *kolla*, glue] *base* glue (collenchyma, collencyte)

coll-³ [L. *collis*, hill] *base* hill (colliculate, colliculus)

-colleto- [Gr. *kolla*, glue] *base* one who glues or fastens (colletic, colletocystophore)

collic- [L. *colliculus*, little hill] *base* little hill (collicular, colliculate)

collodio- [Gr. *kollodes*, like glue] *comb* collodion (collodio-chloride, collodiotype)

colluct- [L. *colluctari*, to contend together] *base* strife, conflict (colluctancy, colluctation)

collut- [L. *col*, together + *colluere*, wash] *base* mouthwash (collution, collutorium)

collyb- [Greek *kollybistes*, money-changer] base money-changer (colliby, collybist)

colo- [Gr. *kolos*, docked, defective] *base* curtailed; mutilated (Colobus, colocephalous)

colob- [Gr. *kolobos*, docked, curtailed] *base* docked (colobin, colobus)

-colous [L. *colere*, to inhabit] *comb* growing in; living among (arenicolous). *See* **-cole**

colp(o)- [Gr. *kolpos*, womb] *comb* vagina (colpocele, colpoplasty)

colubri- [L. *coluber*, serpent] *comb* snake (colubriform, colubrine)

columb- [L. *columba*, dove] *base* dove; pigeon (columbaceous, columbarium)

columelli- [L. *columella*, little column]

comb small column (columellar, columelliform)

column- [L. *columna*, column] *base* pillar (columnar, columniferous)

coly- [Gr. *koluein*, to hinder] *comb* inhibitory (colyone, colytic) *Also* **koly-**

-com- [Gr. *komeo*, to attend to] *base* treatment (gerocomic, gerocomy)

-coma[1], comi-, como- [Gr. *kome*, hair] *comb* having hair or a hairlike structure (Abrocoma, comiferous, comophorous)

coma-[2] [Gr *koma*, deep sleep] *base* pert. to a coma (comatose, comatosity)

combur- [L *comburere*, burn up, consume] *base* burn (comburence, comburent)

comest- [L. *com-*, intensifier + *edere*, to eat] *base* edible (comestible, comestibles)

comico- [Gr. *komikos*, pert. to revelry] *comb* humorous (comico-cynical, comicography)

comit-[1] [L. *comis*, courteous, friendly] *base* affable; courteous (comitive, comity)

comit-[2] [L. *comitari*, to accompany] *base* companion (comitative, comitatus)

comminat- [L. *com-*, intensifier + *minari*, to threaten] *base* menace, threaten (commination, comminatory)

compag- [L. *compago*, fastening, joining] *base* framework, connected parts (compaginate, compagination)

conat- [L. *conari*, attempt, undertake] *base* attempt; desire to (conation, conative)

concavo- [L. *concavus*, hollow] *comb* concave (cancavo-concave, concavo-convex)

concess- [L. *concedere*, to grant] *base* grant; yield (concession, concessory)

conchi- [L. *concha*, shell] *comb* shell (conchiferous, conchiform)

concinn- [L. *concinnus*, fitly put together] *base* adjusted; suitable; harmonious (concinnation, inconcinnity)

-cond- [L. *condere*, put together] *base* put together (condite, incondite)

condyl- [Gr. *kondulos*, knuckle, knob]

comb knob; protuberance (condylar, condyloid)

confin- [L. *confinis*, bordering] *base* bordered, shut in (confines, confinement)

conger- [L. *congerere*, bring together] *base* pile (congeriate, congeries)

congru- [L. *congruere*, agree] *base* come together (congruency, incongruent)

coni-[1], -conia, conio- [Gr. *konis*, dust] *comb* dust; granules (coniosis, fibroconia, coniofibrosis). *Also* **konio-** (koniosis)

coni-[2], cono- [Gr. *konos*, cone] *comb* cone (coniferous, conodont)

conico- [Gr. *konos*, cone] *comb* conical (conico-cylindrical, conicoid)

conist- [Gr. *konis*, dust, ashes] *base* dust (conistery)

conjugato- [L. *con-*, together + *jugum*, yoke] *comb* coupled; paired (conjugative, conjugato-palmate)

connict- [L. *con-*, with + *nictare*, to wink] *base* blink (connictation. connictatory)

conniv- [L. *con-*, with + *nivere*, to wink] *base* blink (connivance, connive)

connochaet- [Gr. *konnos*, beard + *khaite*, mane] *base* gnu (connochaetes)

conoido- [Gr. *konoeides*, cone-shaped] *comb* nearly conical (conoidical, conoido-hemispherical)

conop- [Gr. *konops*, gnat] *base* gnat (Conopidae, Conops)

consil- [L. *con-*, together + *salire*, to leap] *base* in accord; agreeing (consilience, consilient)

cont- [Gr. *kontos*, pole] *base* pole (cont, contist)

contig- [L. *contingere*, to touch] *base* adjacent (contiguity, contiguous)

contin- [L. *continere*, hold together] *base* unceasing (continuation, continuous)

contorto- [L. *con-*, together + *torquere*, to twist] *comb* twisted (contorto-foliaceous, contortuplicate)

contra-, contro- [L. *contra*, against] *pre* against; contrary; opposite (contraband, contradiction, controversy)

contre- [Fr. *contre*, against] *pre* opposite (contrecoup, contretemps)

contum- [L. *contumax*, stubborn] *base*

insolence; stubborness (contumacious, contumely)

convexo- [L. *convexus*, arched] *comb* rounded; convex (convexo-concave, convexo-convex)

-cop- [Gr. *koptein*, to beat] *base* beat; strike (apocope, syncope)

coph- [Gr. *kophos*, deaf] *base* deaf (cophosis, Cophyla)

copi- [L. *copia*, plenty] *base* abundance (copious, copiousness)

copro- [Gr. *kopros*, dung] *comb* excrement; filth (coprolite); obscenity (coprology)

coraci-, coraco- [Gr. *korax*, raven] **1.** *comb* coracoid bone; beaklike (coraco-acromial); **2.** crow; raven (coraciiform, coracomorphic)

coralli- [Gr. *kouralion*, coral] *comb* coral (coralligenous, corallidomous)

corb- [L. *corbus*, basket] *base* basket (corbiculate, corbula)

cord- [Gr. *korde*, string of a musical instrument] *comb* cord; sinew (cordillera, cordotomy) *Also* **chord** (chorditis)

cordato- [Gr. *kardia*, heart] *comb* heart-shaped (cordate-oblong, cordato-ovate)

cordi- [Gr. *kardia*, heart] *comb* heart (cordiality, cordiform)

core-[1], **coreo-, -coria, coro-** [Gr. *kore*, the pupil] *comb* pupil of the eye (corelysis, coreoplasty, isocoria, coroplastic). *Also* **-koria** (leukokoria)

core-[2] [Gr. *koris*, bedbug] *base* bug (Coreoidea, coreopsis)

-cori- [L. *corium*, leather] *base* leather (coriacious, coriuym)

cormo- [Gr. *kormos*, tree trunk] *comb* trunk; stem (cormophyte, cormophyly)

-corn, corni- [L. *cornu*, horn] *comb* horn (unicorn, corniform)

corneo- [L. *corneus*, horny] **1.** *comb* with a horny admixture (corneo-silicious); **2.** cornea of eye (corneoiritis)

cornic- [L. *corniculum*, little horn] *base* little tentacles; antennae (cornicular, corniculate)

cornu- [L. *cornu*, horn] *base* horn (cornupete, cornucopia)

coro- [Gr. *koros*, satiety] *comb* satiety (acoria)

corolli- [L. *corolla*, little crown] *comb* crown; flower garland (corolliflorous, corolliform)

coron- [Gr. *korone*, crow] *base* crow's beak (coronoid)

coroni-, corono- [L. *corona*, crown] *comb* crown (coroniform, coronofacial)

-corp- [L. *corpus*, body] *base* body; bulk (corporal, incorporate)

corrig- [L. *corrigere*, to correct] *base* correction (corrigent, incorrigible)

corrugato- [L. *cor*, together + *rugare*, to wrinkle] *comb* wrinkled (corrugated, corrugato-striate)

cortici-, cortico- [L. *cortex/cortic-*, bark, rind] *comb* bark; cortex (corticiform, corticotropin)

corusc- [L. *coruscare*, to flash] *base* flash; gleam (coruscate, coruscation)

corv- [L. *corvus*, raven] *base* crow; magpie, raven (corviform, corvine)

corybant- [Gr. *Korybas*, priest of Cymbele in Phrygia] *base* frenzied (corybantic, corybantism)

coryd- [Gr. *korudos*, lark] *base* lark (Corydalis, Corydonix)

corymbi- [Gr. *korumbos*, head or cluster] *comb* cluster (corymbiferous, corymbulose)

coryn- [Gr. *korune*, club] *base* rod; club (coryniform, corynoid)

-coryph- [Gr. *koruphe*, highest point] *base* top; summit (corypheus, coryphodon)

corys- [Gr. *korus*, helmet] *base* helmet (corysterium, coryza)

corytho- [Gr. *koruthos*, crested] *comb* crested (Corythosaurian, Corythosaurus)

coscino- [Gr. *koskinon*, sieve] *comb* sieve (coscinomancy, Cosinoptera)

-cosm, cosmo- [Gr. *kosmos*, universe] *comb* world; universe (macrocosm, cosmotheism)

costi-, costo- [L. *costa*, a rib] *comb* rib (costiform, costotome)

coturn- [L. *coturnix*, quail] *base* quail (Coturniculus, coturnine)

cotyle-, cotyli-, cotylo- [L. *cotula*, vessel or hollow] *comb* cup-shaped; hollow; hipjoint socket (cotyledonary, cotyliform, cotylosacral)

counter- [L. *contra*, against] **1.** *comb* opposite; contrary to (counterclockwise); **2.** in retaliation (counterplot); **3.** complementary (counterpart)

coupho- [Gr. *kouphos*, tender] *comb* frail; fragile; tender (coupholite). *Also* **koupho-** (koupholite)

coxo- [L. *coxa*, hip] *comb* hip (coxodynia, coxofemoral)

-cracy [Gr. *kratos*, strength, rule] *comb* form of government (democracy, theocracy)

-craft [Swed. *kraft*, strength] *comb* work; skill; art; practice of (filmcraft, woodcraft)

cranio- [L. *cranium*, skull] *comb* skull (cranioclasm, craniofacial)

-cranter- [Gr. *kranteres*, wisdom teeth] *base* wisdom teeth (diacranteric, syncranterian)

crapul- [L. *crapula*, drunkenness] *base* excessive drinking (crapulence, crapulent)

-crasia [Gr. *krasis*, excess] **1.** *comb* mixture (spermacrasia); **2.** loss of control (coprocrasia). *Also* **-crasy** (idiocrasy)

crasp- [Gr. *kraspedon*, edge or border] *base* bordered (Craspedacusta, craspedote)

-crass- [L. *crassus*, dense, solid] *base* thickened; condensed (crassiped, incrassated)

crastin- [L. *cras*, tomorrow] *base* delay (crastination, procrastinate)

-crat [Gr. *kratos*, strength, rule] *comb* participant in government (democrat, theocrat)

-crataeg- [Gr. *krataigos*, flowering thorn] *base* hawthorn (crataegin, Crataegus)

crater- [Gr. *krater*, vessel] *base* bowl (cratera, crateriform)

crateri- [Gr. *krater*, crater of a volcano] *base* crater (crateral, crateriform)

cratic- [L. *cratis*, hurdle] *base* lattice (craticle, craticulated)

-crease [L. *crescere*, to grow] *comb* grow (increase, decrease)

crebr- [L. *creber*, frequent] *base* frequent (crebrity, crebrous)

crebri- [L. *creber*, closely placed] *comb* ridged (crebricostate, crebrisulcate)

-cred- [L. *credere*, to believe] *base* belief; trust (credulity, incredible)

-crem- [L. *cremare*, to burn] *base* burn (crematorium, incremable)

cremast- [Gr. *kremaster*, suspender] *base* suspended (cremaster, cremasteric)

cremno- [Gr. *kremnos*, overhanging cliff] *base* precipice (cremnomania, cremnophobia)

cremo- [Gr. *kreman*, to hang] *comb* hanging (cremaster, cremocarp)

cren-[1], crenato-, crenulato- [Late L. *crenatus*, notched] *comb* notched; scalloped (crenellation, crenato-serrate, crenulato-dentate)

cren-[2] [Gr. *krene*, a spring] *base* fountain; spring (apocrenic, crenic)

creo- [Gr. *kreas*, flesh] *comb* flesh (creophagous, creosote) *Also* **kreo-** (kreophagy)

-crep- [Gr. *krepis*, boot, base] *base* shoe (crepidarian, hippocrepian)

-crepit- [L. *crepare*, to crackle] *base* |crack; creak; crackle (crepitation, decrepit)

-crepus- [L. *creper*, dusky] *base* twilight (crepuscular, crepusculous)

-cresc- [L. *crescere*, increase] *base* grow; build up (crescitive, decrease)

crescenti- [L. *crescens*, increasing] *base* crescent (crescentiform, crescentoid)

cretaceo- [L. *creta*, chalk] *comb* [geology] chalk formation (cretaceo-oolitic, cretaceo-tertiary)

crev- [L. *crepare*, to crack] *base* crack; rift (crevasse, crevice)

cribri- [L. *cribrum*, sieve] *comb* sieve (cribriform, cribrose)

cricet- [It. *criceto*, hamster] *base* gerbil; hamster (cricetine, Cricetodon)

crico- [Gr. *krikos*, ring] *comb* ring; circle (crico-arytenoid, cricothyroid)

crimin[1]- [L. *crimen*, crime] *base* crime (criminal, incriminate)

crimin[2]- [Gr. *krima*, judgment] *base* distinguish, differentiate (discriminate, indiscriminate)

-crin- [Gr. *krinon*, lily] *base* cup-shaped; calyx (crinoidal, crinoidean)

crini- [L. *crinis*, hair] *comb* hair (criniferous, crinite)

crino-, -crine [Gr. *krinein*, to separate] *comb* secretion (crinogenic, endocrine)

crio- [Gr. *krios*, a ram] *comb* a ram (criocephalous, criocerate)

-crisp- [L. *crispus*, curled] *base* curl; wrinkle (crispate, incrispated)

crist- [L. *crista*, crest] *base* crested (cristate, cristiform)

crit-[1] [Gr. *krites*, a judge] *base* judge; decide (critical, criticism). *Also* krit- (kritarchy)

-crit[2] [Gr. *kritein*, to separate] *comb* separate (hematocrit, microhematocrit)

criterio- [Gr. *kriterion*, test, standard] *base* criterion (citeriology, criterion)

crith- [Gr. *krithe*, barley] *comb* barley (crithology, crithomancy)

critico- [Gr. *krites*, judge] *comb* critical and (critico-historical, critico-theological)

croce- [L. *crocus*, saffron] *base* saffron (croceal, croceous)

crocodil- [Gr. *krokodeilos*, lizard, crocodile] *base* crocodile (crocodilian, crocodility)

cromny- [Gr. *krommuon*, onion] *base* onion (cromnyomancy, cromnyophobia)

cross- [< *across*, transverse] *comb* transverse; contrary (cross-reference, crossroads)

crosso- [Gr. *krossoi*, fringe or border] *comb* fringed; tasseled (Crossopterygian, Crossorhinus)

-crot- [Gr. *krotos*, striking, clapping] *base* beat; strike (anacrotic, catacrotic)

crotal- [Gr. *krotalon*, a rattle] *base* rattlesnake (crotaliform, crotaline)

crotaph- [Gr. *krotaphos*, the temple] *base* the temple (crotaphion)

crouno- [Gr. *krounos*, spring] *comb* spring water (crounotherapy)

cruci- [L. *crux*, cross] *comb* cross (crucial, cruciferous)

-cruent- [L. *cruentus*, bloody] *base* bloody (cruentate, incruent)

cruor- [L. *cruor*, blood] *base* blood (chlorocruorin, cruorin)

-crur- [L. *crus*, the leg] *base* leg (bicrural, crural)

crus-/crust- [Gr. *kruein*, to strike] *base* rhythmic beat (anacrusis, anacrustic)

crymo-, cryo- [Gr. *krumos*, cold] *comb* cold; freezing (crymophilic, cryogenics)

cryph- [Gr. *kryphios*, hidden] *base* concealed (apocryphical, Apocrypha)

crypto- [Gr. *kruptos*, secret, hidden] *comb* secret; hidden; covered (cryptodirous, cryptogram)

crystallo- [Gr. *krustallos*, clear ice] *comb* crystal (crystallogenic, crystalloid)

cteino- [Gr. *kteinein*, to kill] *comb* destructive (cteinophyte)

cteno- [Gr. *kteis*, comb] *comb* comb (ctenobranch, ctenoid)

ctet- [Gr. *ktetos*, that may be acquired] *base* acquired characteristics (ctetology, ctetologist)

-cub- [L. *cubare*, to lie down] *base* lie; recline (cubicle, incubator)

cubi-, cubo- [Gr. *kubos*, a die or cube] *comb* cube; dice (cubicontravariant, cubo-octahedron)

cubil- [L. *cubile*, nest] *base* nest (cubilose)

-cubist [Gr *kubos*, a die] *comb* dice player (philocubist, misocubist)

cubito- [L. *cubitum*, elbow] *comb* [anatomy] ulna and ___ (cubito-carpal, cubitidigital)

cucul- [L. *cuculus*, cuckoo] *comb* cuckoo; roadrunner (cuculiform, cuculine)

cuculli- [L. *cucullus*, cap, hood] *comb* hood; cowl (cucculate, cuculliform)

cucumi- [L. *cucumis*, cucumber] *comb* cucumber (cucumiform, Cucumis)

cucurbit- [L. *curcurbita*, gourd] *base* gourd (cucurbital, cucurbitine)

-cula, -cule, [L. *culus*, dim. suf.] *suf* diminutive (Auricula, molecule)

culici- [L. *culex*, gnat or flea] *base* gnat; mosquito (culiciform, culicifuge)

culin- [L. *culina*, kitchen] *base* kitchen (culinarian, culinary)

culmi- [L. *culmus*, stalk] *comb* plant stem; straw (culmicolou, culmiferous)

culmin- [L. *culmen*, summit] *base* peak; top (culminant, culmination)

culp- [L. *culpare*, to blame] *base* fault; blame (culpable, exculpate)

cult- [L. *cultus*, worship, cultivation] *base* worship (cultish, cultism)

cultel- [L. *culter*, knife] *base* knife (cultellary, cultellation)

cultri- [L. *culter*, knife] *comb* knife (cultrirostral, cultrivorous)

-culture [L. *cultus*, attended to] *comb* tillage; raising (agriculture, viniculture)

-culum, -culus [L. *ulus*, dim. suf.] *suf* diminutive (curriculum, fasciculus)

cuma- [Gr. *kuma*, wave] *base* wave; surf (cumaceous, cumaphytism)

-cumb- [L. *cumbere*, to lie down] *base* lie; recline (incumbent, recumbent)

cumulo- [L. *cumulare*, to heap up] *comb* heaplike; cumulus and ___ (cumulonimbus, cumulostratus)

cunct- [L. *cunctari*, to delay] *base* delay; tardy action (cunctation, cunctator)

cunei-, cuneo- [L. *cuneus*, wedge] *comb* wedge (cuneiform, cuneo-scaphoid)

cunic- [L. *cuniculus*, rabbit] *base* hare; rabbit (cuniculate, cuniculous)

cunicul- [L. *cuniculum*, underground passage; warren] *base* underground (cunicular, cuniculate)

cup- [L. *cupere*, to desire] *base* desire (concupiscence, cupidity)

cupreo-, cupri-, cupro-, cuproso- [L. *cuprium*, copper] *comb* copper; (cupreo-violaceous, cupriferous, cupromagnesite, cuproso-ferric)

cupress- [Gr. *kuparissos*, cypress] *base* cypress (cupressineous, Cupressus)

cupuli- [L. *cupa*, cup] *comb* cup (cupuliferous, cupuliform)

cur- [L. *cura*, health, attention] *base* health; healing (curate, curative)

curculion- [L. *curculio*, weevil] *base* weevil (Curculio, curculionid)

curcum- [Arabic *kurkum*, turmeric] *base* turmeric (curcuma, curcumin)

-cur(r)-, -curs- [L. *currere*, to run] *base* run; go (recurrent, cursory)

curt- [L. *curtus*, docked; mutilated] *base* short; abbreviated (curtail, curtate)

curvi- [L. *curvare*, make crooked] *comb* curved; bent (curvicaudate, curvilinear)

cusp- [L. *cuspis*, point, spear] *base* point (cuspated, cuspid)

cuss- [L. *quatere*, strike forcibly] *base* strike; shake (concussion, percussion)

custod- [L. *custos*, guardian] *base* watchman (custodial, custodianship)

cutaneo- [L. *cutaneus*, of the skin] *comb* skin (cutaneo-osseous, cutaneo-skeletal)

cuti- [L. *cutis*, skin] *comb* skin (cuticle, cutisector)

-cy [L. suf.–*cia*] 1. *suf* quality; fact of being; state; condition (democracy); 2. position; rank; (captaincy)

-cyam- [Gr. *kuamos*, bean] *base* bean (cyamoid, hyoscyamine)

cyano- [Gr. *kuanois*, dark blue] 1. *comb* dark blue (cyanosis); 2. cyanide (cyanohydrin)

cyathi-, cyatho- [Gr. *kuathos*, cup] *comb* cuplike (cyathiform, cyatholith)

cyber- [Gr. *kubernan*, to steer] *comb* relating to computers (cyberphobia, cyberspace)

cyclo- [Gr. *kuklos*, circle] *comb* wheel; circle; cycle (cyclograph, cyclometer)

cyclorraph- [Gr. *kuklos*, circle + *raphe*, a seam] *base* fly (Cyclorhapha, cyclorhaphous)

cyclostom- [Gr. *kuklos*, circle + *stoma*, mouth] *base* eel (cyclostomate, cyclostomatous)

cyem- [Gr. *kuema*, embryo] *base* embryo (cyema, cyemology)

cyesi-, -cyesis [Gr. *kuesis*, conception] *comb* pregnancy (cyesiognosis, polycyesis)

cygn- [Gr. *kuknos*, swan] *base* swan (cygneous, cygnine). *Also* cycn- (cycnean)

cylico- [Gr. *kulix*, cup] *base* bowl

(cylicomancy, cylicotomy). *Also*
kylixo-
cylindro- [Gr. *kulindros*, cylinder, roller]
comb cylinder (cylindro-conical,
cylindro-ogival)
cyma-, cymato-, cymo- [Gr. *kuma*,
wave] *comb* wave; billow (cyma-
graph, cymatolite, cymoscope) *Also*
kymo- (kymograph)
cymbi-, cymbo- [Gr. *kumbe*, boat;
bowl] *comb* boat; bowl (cymbiform,
cymbocephalic)
cyn-, cyno- [Gr. *kuon*, dog] *comb* dog
(cynanthropy, cynophobia) *Also*
kyno-
cyo- [Gr. *kuos,* fetus] *comb* fetus (cyo-
genic, cyophoria)
cyper- [Late L. *cyperus*, sedge] *base* sedge
(cyperaceous, cyperologist)
cyphell- [Gr. *kuphella*, hollow of the
ear] *base* cuplike (cyphella, cyphellae-
form)
cypho- [Gr. *kuphoma*, hump] *comb*
humped; bent; crooked (cyphonism,
cyphosis). *Also* **kypho-** (kyphosis)
cypriani- [Gr. *kuprios*, pert. to Cyprus,
famous for worshipping Venus] *base*
lewd; harlot (Cyprian, cyprianite)

cyprid- [Gr. *kuprios*, pert. to
Cyprus] *base* sexual (Cypridacea,
cypridophobia)
cyprin- [Gr. *kuprinos*, carp] *base*
carp; goldfish; minnow (cyprinid,
cypriniform)
cypsel- [L. *cypselus*, a swift] *base* swift
(cypseliform, cypseline)
cyrio- [Gr. *kurios*, authorized, proper]
base regular; proper (cyriologic,
cyriological)
cyrto- [Gr. *kurtos*, curved, arched]
comb curved; arched (cyrtoceratitic,
cyrtometer)
cyst-, -cyst, cysti-, -cystis, cysto- [Gr.
kustis, bladder, bag] *comb* like a bladder; pouch; sac; cyst (cystalgia, statocyst, cystiform,macrocystis, cystocarp)
-cyte, cyto- [Gr. *kutos*, hollow, cav-
ity] *comb* cell (lymphocyte, cytology) *Also* **cytio-** (cytioderm) and
cytulo- (cytulococcus)
-cythemia [Gr. *kutos*, hollow + *aima*,
blood] *comb* blood cell condition
(macrocythemia, leukocythemia)

D

dacn- [Gr. *daknein*, bite, sting] *base*
bite; kill (dacnidine, Tridacna) *Also*
daco- (Dakosaurus)
dacry(o)- [Gr. *dakruein*, weep] *comb* a
tear (dacryocystitis, dacryops)
dactyl-, dactylo-, -dactylous, -dactyly
[Gr. *dactulos*, finger, date] *comb* finger;
toe (dactyliology, dactylology, tridactylous, brachydactyly)
dactylio- [Gr. *dactulios*, finger ring]
comb finger ring (dactylioglyphic,
dactyliomancy)
daedal- [Gr. *Daidalos*, builder of the
Crete labyrinth] *base* cunning; skillful
(daedalenchyma, logodaedaly)
daemono- *see* **demono-**

damal- [Gr. *damalis*, heifer] *base* heifer
(damalic acid, damaluric)
danist- [Gr. *danaistes*, money-lender]
base money-lending (danism, danistic)
Dano- [L. *Danicus*, Danish] *comb*
Danish and ___ (Dano-Irish,
Dano-Norwegian)
dap- [L. *dais*, food] *base* food, feast
(dapifer, dapiferous)
dapat- [L. *dapaticus*, sumptuous] *base*
sumptuous; costly (dapatical)
daphn- [Gr. *daphne*, laurel] *base* laurel
(daphniaceous, daphnomancy)
dasy- [Gr. *dasus*, think, dense, hairy]
comb hairy or wooly; thick or dense
(Dasyprocta, dasyphyllous)

dasypod- [Gr. *dasus*, hairy or rough + *pous*, foot] *base* armadillo (Dasypodid, dasypodine)

dasyproct- [Gr. *dasus*, hairy + *proctos*, buttocks] *base* agouti (Dasyprocta, dasyproctid)

dativo- [L. *dativus*, of or belonging to] *comb* dative (dativo-gerundial, dativo-locative)

de- [L. *de-*, away from, down from, out of, etc.] **1.** *pre* away from; off (detrain); **2.** down; (decline); **3.** entirely (defunct); **4.** undo; reverse (defrost)

debil- [L. *debilis*, weak] *base* weakness (debilitate, debility)

dec(a)- [Gr. *deka*, ten] *comb* ten; (decagon, decalogue) *Also* **deka-**

decalco- [Fr. *decalquer*, counter-trace] *comb* tattoo (decalcomania, decalcophobia)

decem- [L. *decem*, ten] *base* ten (decemcostate, decemfid)

deci- [L. *decimus*, tenth] *comb* one-tenth (decimate, decimeter)

decid- [L. *de-*, down + *cadere*, to fall] falling (decidual, deciduous)

-decker [M. Du. *dec*, roof, covering] *comb* having ___ decks or in layers (double-decker, three-decker)

declin- [L. *de*, down + *clinare*, bend] *base* bending, sloping (declination, declinometer)

decliv- [L. *de*, down + *clinare*, slope] *base* sloping downward (declivate, declivity)

decoct- [L. *de*, down + *coquere*, cook] *base* boiled (decoctible, decoction)

decrep- [L. *decrepitus*, very old] *base* broken down (decrepit, decrepitude)

decresc- [L. *decrescere*, decrase] *base* wane, lessen(decrescendo, decrescent)

decub- [L. *de*, down + *cubare*, to lie] *base* lying down (decubation, decubital)

decuss- [L. *decussare*, to cross] *base* divided crosswise; x-shaped (decussate, decussative)

dedit- [L. *deditio*, surrender] *base* surrender, yielding (dedition, dedititious)

defalc- [L. *defalcare*, cut off, take away]

base default one's accounts (defalcate, defalcation)

degen- [L. *degeneratus*, ignoble] *base* decline; lose quality (degenerate, degenerative)

deglut- [L. *deglutinare*, swallow down] *base* swallowing (deglutition, deglutitory)

dehisc- [L. *dehisco*, gape, split asunder] *base* burst open (dehisce, dehiscent)

dehydro- [Gr. *de-*, privative + *hudor*, water] *comb* dehydrogenated (dehydro-chlorinate, dehydrogenizer)

de(i)- [L. *deus*, a god] *base* God (deistic, deification)

deict-, -deictic [Gr. *deiktikos*. serving to show] *base, comb* demonstrating (deictically, epideictic)

deipno- [Gr, *deipnon*, dinner] *comb* dinner (deipnophobia, Deipnosophist)

deka- [Gr. *deka*, ten] *comb* ten (dekadrachm, dekaliter) *Also* **deca-**

delect- [L. *delectare*, to delight] *base* please (delectable, delectation)

delet- [L. *delere*, blot out] *base* expunge, erase (delete, deletory)

deleter- [Gr. *deleisthai*, damage, spoil] *base* noxious, injurious (deleterious, deleteriously)

delinq- [L. *delinquere*, to fail] *base* fault (delinquency, delinquent)

deliqu- [L. *deliquescere*, to melt away] *base* melt, become liquid (deliquescence, deliquescent)

delo- [Gr. *delos*, evident] *comb* well-defined, limited (delomorphic, delomorphous)

delphin- [Gr. *delphis*, dolphin] *base* porpoise; dolphin (delphine, delphinoid)

delto- [Gr. *delta*, triangular Greek letter D] *comb* triangular (deltohedron, deltoidal)

-dema [Gr. *oidema*, swelling] *base* swelling (lymphedema, scleredema)

dement- [L. *de-*, out of + *mentis*, mind] *base* insane (dementate, dementia)

demi- [L. *dimidius*, half] **1.** *pre* half (demivolt); **2.** less than usual (demigod)

-demia [Gr. *demos*, tallow] *comb* fatty

degeneration (hypertriglyceridemia, myodemia)

demo- [Gr. *demos*, the people] *comb* people (demographics, democracy)

demono- [Gr. *daimon*, god of lower rank] *comb* demon (demonocracy, demonology)

dendri-, dendro-, -dendron [Gr. *dendron*, tree] *comb* tree; treelike (dendriform, dendrology, rhododendron)

dentato- [L. *dentis*, tooth] *comb* toothed; dentate and ___ (dentato-serrate, dentate-sinuate)

denti-, dento-, -dentate [L. *dentis*, tooth] *comb* tooth (dentiform, dentosurgical, multidentate). *Also* **dont-** (pedodontics)

deoxy- [Gr. *de-*, privative + *oxus*, sharp, acid] *comb* oxygen removed (deoxygenize, deoxyhemoglobin)

depil- [L. *de-* away + *pilus*, hair] *base* deprive of hair (depilation, depilatory)

deprav- [L. *depravare*, corrupt] *base* perverted, corrupt (deprave, depravity)

deps- [Gr. *depsein*, to knead] *base* organic compound from lichens (depsides)

deris- [L. *deridere*, laugh at] *base* mockery; scorn (derision, derisory)

derm-, -derm, derma, -derma, dermato-, -dermatous, -dermis, dermo- [Gr. *derma*, skin] *comb* skin; covering (dermabrasion, endoderm, dermatherm, scleroderma, dermatology, xerodermatous, epidermis, dermoneural)

dero- [Gr. *dere*, the neck] *base* animal neck (derotrematous, derotreme)

derog- [L. *de-*, away+ *rogare*, to question] *base* disparage (derogate, derogatory)

des- [OF *des-*, away from] *pre* missing; deprived of (desoxalic, desoxydation). *See* **dis-**

desicc- [L. *de-*, intensifier + *siccus*, dry] *base* dry (desiccate, desiccation)

desid- [L. *desiderare*, to desire] *base* wish; desire (desideration, desiderative)

-desis [Gr. *desis*, binding] *comb* binding (iridodesis, syndesis)

desit- [L. *desinere*, to cease] *base* final; conclusive (desition, desitive)

desm- [Gr. *desmos*, chain] *base* unicellular algae (desmid, desmidiology)

desmo- [Gr. *desmos*, band] *comb* bond; band; ligament (desmogen, desmognathous)

desmodont- [Gr. *desmos*, band + *odont-*, tooth] *base* bat (Desmodontes, desmodontid)

despot- [Gr. *despoteia*, master of slaves] *base* despot (despotic, despotism)

detrit- [L. *detritus*, rubbing away] *base* matter produced by wearing away (detrition, detrivorous)

deuter(o)-, deuto- [Gr. *deuteros*, second] *comb* second; secondary (deuterogamy, deutoplasm)

dexio- [Gr. *dexios*, on the right hand] *comb* on the right side (dexiocardia, dexiotropic)

dextr(o)- [Gr. *dexios*, on the right hand] **1.** *comb* on the right side (dextrocardia); **2.** [chemistry] clockwise (dextrorotatory)

di-¹ [Gr. *dis*, twice] **1.** *pre* twice; double (dichroism); **2.** having two (diacid)

di-² [L. privative] *pre* away; apart (diverse, divest). *See* **dis-**

dia- [Gr. *dia*, through] **1.** *pre* through; across (diagonal); **2.** apart; between (diaphony)

-diabol- [L. *diabolus*, devil] *base* devil (diabolic, diabolism)

dialect- [Gr. *dialegesthai,* to converse] *base* speech (dialectical, dialectition)

dialyt- [Gr. *dialytos,* separated] *base* separation (dialytic, dialytically)

diaped- [Gr. *dia*, through + *pedan*, to leap] *base* migration (diapedesis, diapedetic)

diaphano- [Gr, *diaphanes*, transparent] *comb* transparent (diaphaneity, diaphanometer)

diaphor- [Gr. *diaphorein*, perspire] *base* perspiration (diaphoresis, diaphoretic)

diaphys- [Gr. *dia-*, through + *phyein*, produce] *base* growth (diaphysis, diaphysial)

diaspora- [Gr. *diaspora*, scattering] *base* dispersion (Diaspora, diaspora)

-diastasis [Gr. *dia*, apart + *stasis*, placing]

comb displacement (adenodiastasis, myelodiastasis)

diasyrm- [*diasyrmos*, mockery] *base* ridicule (diasyrm, diasyrmic)

diatrib- [Gr. *diatribe*, school, learned discussion] *base* invective (diatribe, diatribist)

dicac- [L. *dicax*, witty talk] *base* satirical (dicacious, dicacity)

dicaeo- [Gr. *dikaiologia*, plea in defense] *base* jurisdiction (dicaeologist, dicaeology)

dicho- [Gr. *dikha*, apart] *comb* in two; split; separately (dichogamy, dichotomy)

dichro- [Gr. *dikhcroos*, two-colored] *comb* two-colored (dichromatic, dichromatism)

diclid- [Gr. *diklides*, valves] *base* valves (dicliditis, diclidotomy)

-dict- [L. *dictum*, a thing said] *base* say; speak; tell (contradiction, dictation)

dictyo- [Gr. *diktuon*, net] *comb* net (Dictyocysta, dictyogen)

did- [L. *didus*, dodo] *base* dodo (Dididae, didine)

didact- [Gr. *didaktikos*, apt at teaching] *base* teach (didactic, didacticism)

didasc- [Gr. *didaskein*, teach] *base* teach (didascalic, didascalics)

didelph- [Gr. *di-*, two + *delphus*, womb] *base* opossum (didelphian, didelphine)

didym-, didymo- [Gr. *didumos*, twin] *comb* twofold; relating to the testis (didymous; didymalgia)

dif- [L. *dis-*, apart] *pre* away; apart (differ, differentiate). *See* **dis-**

digitato- [L. *digitus*, finger] *comb* having fingerlike divisions (digitato-palmate, digitato-pinnate)

digiti- [L. *digitus*, finger] *comb* finger; toe (digitigrade, digitinerved)

digito- [NL. *digitalis*, digitalis] *comb* digitalis; foxglove (digitoleic acid, digitoxin)

dihydro- [Gr. *di-*, two + *hudor*, water] *comb* having two atoms of hydrogen in combination (dihydrobromide, dihydrostreptomycin)

dike- [Gr. *dike*, justice] *comb* justice (dikemania, dikephobia)

dilat-[1] [L. *dilitare*, dilate] *base* expansion (dilitator, dilation)

dilat-[2] [L. *dilatio*, a deferring] *base* delay (dilatoriness, dilatory)

diluv- [L. *diluvio*, deluge] *base* flood (antediluvian, diluvial)

(di)mid- [L. *dimidium*, half] *base* half (dimidiation, dimidiate)

(di)min- [L. *diminuere*, break into small pieces] *base* lessen (diminish, diminution)

dinet- [Gr. *dinetos*, whirled around] *base* rotatory (dinetic, dinetical)

dino-[1] [Gr. *deinos*, terrible] *comb* terrible; mighty; huge (dinosaur, Dinotherium)

dino-[2] [Gr. *dinos*, whirling] *comb* whirling (Dinoflagellata, dinoflagellate)

dioc- [Gr. *dioikesis*, house management] *base* bishop's domain (diocese, diocesan)

diomed- [Gr. *Diomedes*, hero at the siege of Troy] *base* albatross (Diomedia, Diomedeinae)

dior- [Gr. *dia*, through + *horizein*, to draw a boundary] *base* distinction; definition (diorism, dioristic)

dioscorea- [Gr. *Dioscorides*, famous botanist] *base* yam (Dioscorea, dioscoreaceous)

diphther- [Gr. *diphtheris*, skin, hide] *base* infectious disease (diphtheria, diphtherial)

diphy- [Gr. *diphues*, of double form] *comb* double; bipartite (diphycercal, diphyodont)

diplo- [Gr. *diploos*, double] *comb* two; double; twin (diploblastic, diplocephaly)

diplopod- [Gr. *diploos*, double + *pous*, foot] *base* millipede (Diplopoda, diplopodal)

dipso- [Gr. *dipsa*, thirst] *comb* thirst (dipsomania, dipsosis)

diptero- [Gr. *dipteros*, two-winged] *comb* having two wings (dipterology, dipterous)

dirig- [L. *dirigere*, to direct] *base* able to be steered (dirigent, dirigible)

dirit- [L. *diritas*, misfortune, cruelty] *base* dreadfulness (dirity)

dis- [L. *duo*, in two] **1.** *pre* away; apart (dismiss); **2.** deprive of (disbar); **3.** cause to be the opposite of (disable); **4.** fail; refuse to (disallow); **5.** not (dishonest); **6.** lack of (disunion) NOTE: **dis-** can change to **di-** (divest) or **dif-** (differ). *See* **des-**

discip- [L. *discipulus*, learner] *base* follower; learner (disciple, discipline)

disco- [Gr. *diskos*, disk] *comb* disk-shaped (discocarp, discophile)

discophor- [Gr. *diskos*, disk + *pherein*, to bear] *base* jellyfish; leech (discophoran, discophorous)

dissep- [L. *disseptio*, partition, divider] *base* partition (dissepiment, dissepimental)

-disso- [Gr. *dissos*, double] *base* double (dissoconch, dissogony)

disto- [<*distant*, modeled on *centro-*] *comb* remote; farther away (distobuccal, distolabial)

diures- [Gr. *diourein*, urinate] *base* pert. to urine (diuresis, diuretic)

diurn- [L. *diurnus*, daily] *base* day (diurnal, diurnation)

diuturn- [L. *diuturnus*, of long duration] *base* lasting; long duration (diuturnal, diuturnity)

divergenti-, divergi- [L. *di-*, apart + *vergere*, incline] *comb* divergent (divergentiflorous, divergivenate)

diversi- [L. *diversus*, diverse] *comb* various (diversiflorous, diversiform)

doc- [L. *docere*, teach] *base* teach (docent, indoctrinate)

docim- [Gr. *dokimastes*, assayer, examiner] *base* testing, assaying (docimastic, docimology)

dodeca- [Gr. *dodeka*, twelve] *comb* twelve (dodecagon, dodecapetalous)

dogmato- [Gr. *dogmatikos*, dogma] *comb* pertaining to dogma (dogmatology, dogmatopoeic)

dolabri- [L. *dolabra*, hatchet or ax] *comb* ax; cleaver (Dolabrifera, dolabriform)

dolatil- [L. *dolatilis*, easily hewn] *base* hew, chip (circumdolate, dolation)

dolero- [Gr. *dolos*, deceit] *comb* deceptive (dolerite, dolerophanite)

dolicho- [Gr. *dolikhos*, long] *comb* long; narrow (dolichocephalic, dolichodirous)

dolio- [L. *dolium*, very large jar] *base* barrel (dolioform, Doliolum)

-dolor- [L. *dolor*, grief or pain] *base* pain; sorrow (doloriferous, dolorific)

dolos- [L. *dolosus*, deceitful] *base* deceitful (dolose, dolosity)

-dom-[1] [L. *domus*, house, household] *base* house; dwelling (domestic, domestication)

-dom-[2] [OE *dom*, position, condition] **1.** *suf* rank of; position of; domain of (kingdom); **2.** state of being (wisdom); **3.** total of all who are (officialdom)

-don- [L. *donare*, to give] *base* give (condone, donation). *Also* **-dor-** gift (Dorothy)

-dont [Gr. *odont*, tooth] *comb* tooth (orthodontist, pedodontics). *Also* **dent-** (dentifrice)

dora- [Gr. *dora*, hide or skin] *base* fur; hide (doramania, doraphobia)

-dorm- [L. *dormire*, sleep] *base* sleep (dormant, dormitive)

dorsi-, dorso- [L. *dorsum*, the back] *comb* the back (dorsibranch, dorsoventral)

dory- [Gr. *doru*, spear] *base* spear (Doryanthes, doryphore)

dosio- [Gr. *dosis*, giving] *base* dose (dosimetric, dosiology)

dot- [L. *dotare*, to endow] *base* dowry; endowment (dotal, dotation)

dotal- [L. *dotalis*, pert. to a dowry] *base* marriage dowry (dotal, extradotal)

double- [L. *duplus*, double] *comb* in combination (double-barreled, double-breasted)

dox- [Gr. *doxazein*, to opine] *base* opinion (doxastic, doxographer)

doxol- [Gr. *doxa*, glory + *logos*, speech] *base* praise utterance (doxologize, doxology)

draco-, draconi- [Gr. *drakon*, serpent, dragon] *base* dragon (dracocephalum, draconiform)

drapeto- [Gr. *drapetes*, runaway slave]

comb flee; fugitive (drapetomania, drapetophobia)

drepani- [Gr. *drepane,* sickle] *comb* sickle (drepaniform, drepanium)

-drome, dromo-, -dromous [Gr. *dromas,* running] *comb* running; moving; race course (hippodrome, dromomania, catadromous)

droso- [Gr. *drosos,* dew, juice] *comb* dew (drosometer, drosophore)

drosophyl- [Gr. *drosos,* juice + *philos,* loving] *base* fruitfly (Drosophila, Drosophylidae)

drup- [Gr. *druppa,* stone-fruit] *base* pulpy fruit enclosing a stone (drupaceous, drupe)

dryo- [Gr. *drus,* tree] *base* tree (Dryopithecus, dryopithecine)

du- [Gr. *duo,* two] *pre* two (dual, duplicate)

dub- [L. *dubius,* doubtful] *base* doubtful (dubiety, indubitably)

-duc(e), -duct- [L. *ducere,* to lead] *base* lead (induce, conductor)

ducen- [L. *ducenarius,* two hundred] *base* two hundred (ducenarious, ducenary)

ductil- [L. *ductilis,* capable of being extended] *base* capable of being led or drawn (ductile, ductilimeter)

-dulc- [L. *dulcis,* sweet] *base* sweet (dulcet, dulcify)

dulo- [Gr. *doulos,* slave] *comb* slave (dulia, dulocracy). *Also* **doulo-** (doulocracy)

duo- [Gr. *duo,* two] *comb* two; double (duodrama, duologue)

duodec-, duodecim-, duoden- [Gr. *dodeka,* twelve] *base* twelve (duodecuple, duodecimfid, duodenary)

duodeviginti- [L. *duodeviginti,* eighteen] *comb* (duodevigintiangular)

duplicato- [L. *duplicatus,* doubled] *comb* doubly (duplicato-dentate, duplicato-pinnate)

duplici- [L. *duplicatus,* doubled] *comb* duplex (duplicidentate, duplicipennate)

dur-, duro- [L. *durus,* hard, lasting] *base* hard; lasting (endurance, durometer)

dy-, dyo- [Gr. *duo,* two] *base* two (dyad, diarchy, Dyophysite)

dyna-, dynamo-, -dyne [Gr. *dunamis,* power] *comb* power; strength; energy (dynamic, dynamogeny, heterodyne)

-dynia [Gr. *odune,* pain] *comb* pain (gastrodynia, inguinodynia)

dys- [Gr. *dus,* bad, unlucky] *pre* hard; ill; bad; difficult (dysentery, dyslexia)

-dyte- [Gr. *duein,* to dive or go into] *base* to enter; dive (ammodyte, troglodyte)

E

e- *see* **ex-**

-ea [L. suf. *-ea*] *suf* noun ending (amenorrhea, cornea)

-eae [L. suf. *-eae*] *suf* plant tribes: plural ending (Fabineae, Gramineae)

-ean [L. suf. *-ean*] *suf* belonging to; like (Aeschylean, European)

eben- [Gr. *ebenos,* ebony] *base* ebony (ebeneous, ébéniste)

ebon- [Gr. *ebenos,* ebony tree] *base* black (ebonize, ebony)

ebriet- [L. *ebrietas,* drunkenness] *base* drunkenness (ebriecation, ebriety)

ebullio- [L. *ebullire,* to bubble out] *base* boiling (ebulliometer, ebullioscope)

ebur- [L. *ebur,* ivory] *base* ivory (eburnation, eburneous)

ec- *see* **ex-**

ecchym- [Gr. *ekkeuma,* a pouring out] *base* pour out (ecchymosis, ecchymotic)

ecclesiastico- [Gr. *ekklesia,* church] *comb* of the church or clergy (ecclesiastico-conservative, ecclesiastico-military)

eccrino- [Gr. *ekkrinein,* to secrete] *base* secretion (eccrinologist, eccrinology)

-echia [Gr. *ekhein,* to hold] *comb* have;

retain (anterior synechia, posterior synechia)

echidno- [Gr. *ekhidna*, adder, viper] *comb* viper (echidnine, echidnotoxin)

echin- [L. *echinus*, prickly, hedgehog] *base* hedgehog; sea urchin; bristly (echinate, echiniform)

echinato-, echino- [L. *echinatus*, prickly] *comb* prickly; spiny (echinato-dentate, echinococcus)

echinoderm- [Gr. *ekhinos*, sea-urchin + *dermos*, skin] *base* hedgehog, sea-urchin (echinoderm, echinodermatous)

echinulato-, echinuli- [Gr. *ekhinos*, sea-urchin, prickly] *comb* prickly; spiny (echinulato-striate, echinuliform)

echo- [Gr. *ekhos*, sound] *comb* repeated sound (echolalia, echometry)

eclog- [Gr. *ekloge*, selection] *base* pastoral poem (eclogue, ecloguey)

eco- [Gr. *oikos*, house] *comb* environment (ecologist, ecosystem)

-ecoia [Gr. *ekhouein*, to hear] *comb* hearing condition (dysecoia, oxyecoia)

ecphia- [Gr. *ekphuos*, appendix] *comb* appendix (ecphyadectomy, ecphyaditis)

-ectasia, -ectasis [Gr. *ektasia*, extension] *comb* dilation; expansion (colpectasia, anectasis)

ect(o)- [Gr. *ektos*, outside] *comb* outside; external (ectocardia, ectoderm)

-ectomy [Gr. *ektome*, cutting out] *comb* surgical operation; excision; cutting (appendectomy, bursectomy)

ectro- [Gr. *ektro*, to damage] *comb* congenital absence of a part (ectrodactyly, ectromelia)

ed-[1] [L. *edere*, to eat] *base* eat (edacious, edible)

-ed[2] [OE suf. *-ede*] *suf* having; provided with; characterized by (pileated, softhearted)

edacit- [L. *edacitas*, gluttony] *base* devoted to eating (edacious, edacity)

edaph- [Gr. *edaphos*, bottom] *base* floor; ground (edaphic, edaphodont)

-edema [Gr. *oidema*, swelling, tumor] *comb* swelling (myoedema, scleredema)

-edent- [L. *edentatus*, toothless] **1.** *base* lacking teeth (edentulous); **2.** order of New World mammals which includes armadillos, sloths, anteaters (edentate)

edi- [L. *aedificare*, to build] *base* building (edicule, edifice). *Also* **aedi-**

-edr- [Gr. *edra*, seat] *base* seat (edriophthalmate, edriophthalmian)

-ee [AF *-e*, p.p.] **1.** *suf* recipient (appointee); **2.** person (employee); **3.** thing (goatee)

-een [Irish dim. *-in*] *suf* diminutive (buckeen, colleen)

-eer [L. suf. *-arius*] **1.** *suf* person who does (engineer); **2.** person who writes (sonneteer)

ef- *see* **ex-**

efferit- [L. *efferitas*, wildness] *base* fierce (efferate, efferous)

efficac- [L. *efficax/efficac-*, efficacious] *base* effective; competent (efficacious, efficacy)

effig- [L. *effigies*, imitation] *base* likeness (effigial, effigy)

egagro- [Gr. *aigogros*, wild goat] *base* wild goat (egagrophobia, egagropile)

egen(t)- [L. *egens*, needy] *base* poor (egency, egene)

egest- [L. *egestas*, poverty] *base* poverty (egestuosity, egestuous)

egestiv- [L. *egestivus*, purgative] *base* pass off (egest, egestive)

ego- [L. *ego*, I] *comb* self (egomania, egotism)

egress- [L. *egressus*, a going out] *base* depart; leave (egress, egressive)

egro- [Corrupt form of *necro-*, dead] *comb* dead (egromancy, egromantic) *see* **necro-**

Egypto- [Gr. *aiguptos*, Egypt] *comb* Egyptian and ___ (Egypto-Arabic, Egypto-Syrian)

eico- [Gr. *eikosi*, twenty] *comb* twenty (eicosanoic, eicosapentaenoic) *see* **ico-**

eid-, eido- [Gr. *eidos*, form] *comb* shape; form; that which is seen (eidetic, eidoclast)

eiren- [Gr. *eirene*, peace] *base* peace (eirenarchy, eirenical). *Also* **iren-**

eiron- [Gr. *eironeia*, dissimulation] *base* pretended ignorance (eiron, ironic)

eis- [Gr. *eis*, into] *pre* into (eisegesis, eisegetical)

eisoptro- [Gr. *eis*, into + *optos*, visible] *comb* mirror (eisoptromania, eisoptrophobia)

-eity [L. suf. *-tatem*] *suf* noun of quality or condition (contemporaneity, spontaneity)

eka- [Sanskrit *eka*, one] *comb* one (eka holmium, ekaselenium)

ekist- [Gr. *oikos*, dwelling] *comb* settlement; house (ekistician, ekistics)

-el [L. suf. *-alis*] *suf* diminutive (satchel, tunnel)

elao-, elaeo- [Gr. *elaia*, olive tree] *comb* oil (elaolite, elaeometer) *see* **eleo-**

elaph- [Gr. *elaphos*, deer] *base* deer; stag (elaphine, Elaphmyces)

-elasmo- [Gr. *elasma*, metal plate] *base* metal plate (elasmognathous, elasmosaurus)

elasto- [Gr. *elastikos*, that which drives] *comb* rubber or plastic; stretchable (elastomer, elastometry)

elat-[1] [L. *elatus*, lift up] *base* joy (elated, elation)

elat-[2] [Gr. *elatos*, ductile] *base* elastic (elater, elaterite)

electro- [L. *electrum*, amber] *comb* electrical (electrobiology, electromagnetic)

eleemosyn- [Gr. *eleemosyne*, pity] *base* alms (eleemosynary, eleemosynate)

eleg- [Gr. *elegos*, song] *base* poem (elegiac, elegiast)

elench- [Gr. *elenchos*, reproach] *base* refutation (elench, elenchical)

eleo- [Gr. *elaia*, olive tree] *comb* oil (eleoma, eleoplast) *see* **oleo-**

elephant- [Gr. *elephas*, elephant, ivory] *base* elephant (elephantiasis, elephantine)

eleuthero- [Gr. *eleutheros*, free] *comb* freedom (eleutheromania, eleutheropetalous)

elix- [L. *elixus*, boiled] *base* boil (elixated, elixation)

-ella [L. dim. *-ella*] **1.** *suf* diminutive

(umbrella); **2.** bacteria genus (salmonella)

elleips- [Gr. *elleipsis*, fall short] *base* ellipse (ellipse, ellipsis)

ellychn- [Gr. *ellychnion*, lamp wick] *base* lamp wick (elychnious)

eluct- [L. *eluctatio*, a struggle] *base* struggle (eluctation, ineluctable)

elucub- [L *elucubro*, compose by lamplight] *base* study by candlelight (elucubrate, elucubration)

elusc- [L. *eluscare*, to deprive of an eye] *base* to blind in one eye (eluscate, eluscation)

elytri- [Gr. *elutron*, a cover] *comb* wing case (elytriform, elytrine)

elytr(o)- [Gr. *elutron*, sheath] *comb* [medicine] vagina (elytrocele, elytropolypus)

em- [Gr. *en*, into; intensifier] **1.** *pre* in (embed); **2.** cause to be (empower); **3.** to place (emplacement); **4.** to restrict (embrace)

embado- [Gr. *embadon*, by land] *base* land (embadometrist, embadometry)

embamm- [Gr. *embamma*, sauce] *base* sauce (embamma)

emberiz- [Gr. *ammer*, a bunting] *base* bunting (Emberiza, emberizine)

embol-, emboli-, embolo- [Gr. *embolus*, thrown in] *comb* plug; obstruction; patch; stopper (embolism, emboliform, embololalia)

embryo- [Gr. *embruos*, growing in] *comb* fetus (embryogeny, embryology)

-eme [Gr. suf. *-ema*] *suf* [linguistics] significant contrastive unit (archiphoneme, phoneme)

-emesis, -emetic, emeto- [Gr. *emesis*, vomiting] *comb* vomiting (hematemesis, antiemetic, emetophobia)

-emia [Gr. *haima*, blood] *comb* blood condition; blood disease; (anemia, leukemia). *Also* **-aemia** (hyperaemia)

emmen- [Gr. *emmenos*, monthly] *comb* monthly; menstrual (emmeniopathy, emmenology)

emmetrop- [Gr. *emmetros*, proportional, in measure] *base* eyes normal as to refraction (emmetrope, emmetropia)

emper- [MF *empirer*, to make worse] *base* impair (emperish, emperishment)

emphas- [Gr. *emphainein*, exhibit, display] *base* stress (emphasis, emphatic)

emphys- [Gr. *emphusan*, puff up] *base* abnormal presence of air in tissue (emphysema, emphysemic)

empiric- [Gr. *empirikos*, experienced] *base* through experience and observation (empirical, empiricism)

emplect- [Gr. *emplektos*, interwoven] *base* type of masonry (emplectite, emplecton)

empor- [Gr. *emperos*, merchant, traveler] *base* trade; merchant; merchandise (emporetic, emporium)

-empt- [L. *emptus*, bought] *base* buy; take (emptional, exempt)

empyr- [Gr. *empuros*, fiery] *base* belonging to the highest heaven (empyreal, empyrean)

emul- [L. *aemulus*, envious] *base* jealous; rivalrous (emulate, emulation)

emunct- [L. *emungere*, blow the nose] *base* nose blowing; excretory (emunction, emunctory)

emydo- [Gr. *emus*, tortoise] *comb* tortoise (emydian, emydosaurian)

en-[1] [Gr. *en-*, into] **1.** *pre* in; within (energy); **2.** to place (entomb); **3.** to cause to be in (enshrine); **4.** to restrict (encircle) NOTE: **en-** becomes **em-** before B and P: (embed). *See* **eis-**

-en-[2] [OE suf. *-nian*] **1.** *suf* plural form (oxen); **2.** cause to be (weaken); **3.** cause to have (strengthen); **4.** made of (wooden); **5.** female (vixen); **6.** diminutive (kitten)

enalio- [Gr. *enalios*, of the sea] *base* of the sea (enaliosaur, enaliosaurian)

enantio- [Gr. *enantios*, opposite] *comb* opposite; (enantioblastous, enantiopathic)

-enarthra- [Gr. *enarthrosis*, a kind of jointing] *base* jointed; ball-and-socket joint (enarthrodial, enarthrosis)

encarp- [Gr. *enkarpos*, containing fruit] *base* frieze decorations (encarpus, encarpa)

encaust- [Gr. *enkaustikos*, burned in] *base* fired pigment or glaze (encaustic, encaustically)

-ence [L. suf. *-entia*] *suf* action; state; quality (excellence). *See* **-ance**

encephalo- [Gr. *enkephalos*, in the head] *comb* brain (encephalalgia, encephalocele)

enchely- [Gr. *enkelus*, eel] *base* eel, conger (Enchelycephali, enchelycephalous)

enchor- [Gr. *en*, in + *khora*, country] *base* native, indigenous (enchorial, enchoristic)

-enchyma [Gr. *enkhein*, infuse] *comb* infusion; wavy (enchymatous, protenchyma; colpenchyma)

enclit- [Gr. *en*, on + *klitikos*, leaning] *base* leaning (enclitic, encliticism)

encom- [Gr. *enkhomion*, laudatory ode] *base* praise (encomiastic, encomium)

-ency [ME suf. *-ence*] *suf* act; fact; quality; degree; state; result (complacency, emergency)

encyc- [Gr. *enkuklos*, in a circle] *base* for circulation (encyclical, encyclopedia)

endeca- [Gr. *hendeka*, eleven] *comb* eleven (endecagon, endecaphyllous). *Also* **hendeca-** (hendecasyllabic)

endo- [Gr. *endou*, within] *comb* inside; within (endocardium, endogamous)

-ene [Gr. suf. *-ene*] *suf* hydrocarbons (benzene, ethylene)

enerv- [L. *enervus*, without nerves or sinews] *base* weakness (enervated, enervose)

engastri- [Gr. *engastrimythos*, speaking from the belly] *comb* ventriloquism (engastrimyth, engastrimythian)

engraul- [Gr. *engraulis*, small fish] *base* anchovy (Engraulid, Engraulis)

engus- [Gr. *engus*, near at hand] *base* near (engyscope, engysseismologist)

engys- [Gr. *engys*, near] *base*, near (engyscope)

enigmato- [Gr. *ainigma*, riddle] *comb* obscure; enigmatic (enigmatography, enigmatology)

enisso- [Gr. *enisso*, to attack] *comb* reproach; criticism (enissomania, enissophobia)

-enn- [L. *annus*, year] *base* year (biennial, centennial). *Also* -ann- (annual)

-enne [Fr. fem. ending] *suf* feminine ending (comedienne, Parisienne)

ennea- [Gr. *ennea*, nine] *comb* nine (enneahedron, enneander)

enneacent- [Gr. *ennea*, nine + L. *centum*, one hundred] *base* nine hundred (enneacentenary)

enneaconta- [Gr. *enneaconta*, ninety] *base* ninety (enneacontahedral)

enneakaideca- [Gr. *ennea*, nine + *deka*, ten] *comb* nineteen (enneakaidecagon, enneakaidecahedron)

-ennial [L. *annus*, year] *comb* years (biennial, novennial)

-enoic [Gr. suf. *-ene* + *-ic*] *suf* unsaturated acid (eicosatrienoic, polyenoic)

enoptro- [Gr. *enoptron*, a mirror] *comb* mirror (enoptromancy)

enosi- [Gr. *enosi*, quaking] *base* terror (enosiomania, enosiophobia)

ensi- [L. *ensis*, sword] *comb* sword-shaped (ensiferous, ensiform)

-ensis [L. suf. *-iensis*] *suf* scientific derivatives of place names (canariensis, carolinensis)

-ent [L. pp. suf. *-entis*] 1. *suf* having the quality of (insistent); 2. person who (superintendent); 3. material agent (emolient). *See* -ant

enter- [L. *inter*, between] *pre* between; among; mutually (enterclose, entertain). *Usually* inter-

entero- [Gr. *enteron*, intestine] *comb* intestines (enterectomy, enteropathy)

enth- [Gr. *entheos*, internal divine power] *base* divinely inspired (entheal, entheastic)

enthym- [Gr. *enthumema*, reasoning] *base* syllogism with unstated premise (enthememic, enthymeme)

ento- [Gr. *entos*, within] *comb* within; inner (entoglossal, entophyte)

entomo- [Gr. *entomon*, insect] *comb* insect (entomogenous, entomology)

entostho- [Gr. *entosthe*, from within] *comb* from within (entosthoblast)

entre- [Fr. *entre*, within] *base* in; undertaking (entrepeneur, entrepot)

eo- [Gr. *eos*, dawn] *pre* early time period; dawn (eohippus, eolithic)

eon- [Gr. *aion*, immeasurable period of time] *base* eternity (eonial, eonic) Also aeon-

eoso- [Gr. *eos*, dawn] *comb* dawn (eosomania, eosophobia)

-eous [L. suf. *-osus*] *suf* having the nature of; like (beauteous, gaseous)

epana- [Gr. *epi*, upon + *ana*, again] *comb* repetition (epanastrophe, epanodos)

epanet- [Gr. *epainein*, to praise] *base* laudatory (epaenetic, epanetic)

-epeiro- [Gr. *epeiros*, continent] *base* mainland; continent (epeirogenic, epeirogeny)

epeo- [Gr. *epeos*, word] *base* word (epeolatrist, epeolatry)

epheb- [Gr. *ephebos*, youth] *base* adolescent (ephebic, ephebolic)

ephed- [Gr. *ephedra*, sitting upon] *base* low evergreen shrub (ephedra, ephedroid)

ephel- [Gr. *ephelis*, freckle] *base* freckle (ephelis)

ephem- [Gr. *ephemeros*, lasting for a day] *base* lasting for a day (ephemeral, ephemeris)

ephipp- [Gr. *ephippios*, saddle-cloth] *base* saddle-like (Ephippiorhynchus, ephippium)

epi- [Gr. *epi*, on or upon] *pre* on; upon; up to; over; on the outside; among; beside; following (epicardium). NOTE: epi- can change to ep- (epaxial)

epiced- [L. *epicideum*, funeral song] *base* pertaining to funeral rites (epicedial, epicedian)

epige- [Gr. *epi*, on + *gea*, earth, ground] *base* living near the ground (epigene, epigeous)

epigram- [Gr. *epigramma*, an inscription] *base* inscription, pointed saying (epigram, epigrammatic)

epiphonem- [Gr. *epiphonema*, an exclamation] *base* exclamatory rhetorical sentence (epiphonema, epiphoneme)

episcop- [L. *episcopus*, bishop] *base* bishop (episcopate, episcopicide)

episio- [Gr. *episeion,* pubes] *comb* vulva (episiorrhagia, episiotomy)

epistem- [Gr. *episteme,* knowledge] *base* knowledge (epistemological, epistemology)

epod- [Gr. *epodos,* incantation] *base* lyric poem (epodal, epode)

eponym- [Gr. *eponumos,* giving one's name to] *base* eponym (eponymic, eponymous)

epul- [L. *epularis,* pert. to a banquet] *base* feast (epulary, epulation)

epulat- [Gr. *epoulotikos,* scarred] *base* scar (epulotic, epulotical)

equ- [L. *equus,* horse] *base* horse (equestrian, equine)

equi- [L. *aequus,* equal] *comb* equal; (equidistant, equidiurnal)

equiset- [L. *equus,* horse + *seta,* a bristle] *base* horsetail (equisetiform, Equisetum)

-er [L. suf. *-arius*] **1.** *suf* person who (farmer) ; **2.** person living in (New Yorker); **3.** thing or action (double-header); **4.** repeatedly (flicker); **5.** comparative degree (cooler)

eran- [Gr. *eranos,* community meal or club] *base* club (eranist)

-erel [ME diminutive *-erel*] *suf* pejorative (doggerel, pickerel)

eremo- [Gr. *eremos,* desert] **1.** *comb* alone; solitary (eremophobia); **2.** of/in a desert (eremophyte)

-erethis- [Gr. *erethein,* to excite] *base* irritate, stimulate (erethism, erethistic)

-ergasia [Gr. *ergon,* work] *comb* interfunctioning of mind and body; work; activity (exergasia, hypoergasia) *Also* **ergasio-** (ergasiophobia)

ergato- [Gr. *ergates,* worker] *comb* worker (ergotocracy, ergatotelic)

ergo-, -ergic, -ergy [Gr. *ergon,* work] *comb* work; activity; result (ergonomics, neurergic, allergy)

ergod- [Gr. *ergon,* work + *odos,* way] *base* trajectory frequency (ergodic, ergodicity)

eric- [L. *erica,* heath] *base* heath (ericaceous, ericetal)

erinac- [L. *erinaceus,* hedgehog] *base* hedgehog (erinaceid, erinaceous)

erio- [Gr. *erion,* wool] *base* wool; fiber (Eriogaster, eriometer)

eris- [Gr. *eristikos,* given to strife] *base* controversy; strife (eristic, eristical)

-ern [L. suf. *-aneus*] *suf* direction names (southern, western)

ero- [Gr. *eros,* sexual love] *base* sexual (erogenic, erogenous)

eroso- [L. *erosus,* incised] *comb* incised; indentated (erosodentate, eroso-denticulate)

erotis-, erotet- [Gr. *erotan,* ask] *base* question (erotesis, erotetic)

eroto- [Gr. *erotikos,* pert. to love] *comb* sexual desire (erotomania, erotomaniac)

err- [L. *errare,* to wander] *base* wander (errant, erratic)

eruci- [L. *eruca,* caterpillar] *base* caterpillar (eruciform, erucivorous)

eruct- [L. *eructare,* to belch] *base* belching (eructate, eructation)

-ery [ME suf. *-erie*] **1.** *suf* a place to (brewery); **2.** a place for (nunnery); **3.** practice/act of (robbery); **4.** product/goods of (pottery); **5.** collection of (crockery); **6.** condition/state of (slavery)

erysi- [Gr. *erusipelas,* red skin] *comb* red; inflamed (erysipelas, erysipeloid)

erythro- [Gr. *eruthros,* red] *comb* red; erythrocyte (erythema, erythrocarpous)

es- *see* **ex-**

-es [suf. variation of *-s*] *suf* plural ending (dishes, wishes)

esc- [L. *esca,* food] *base* food (escal, esculent)

-esce [L. suf. *-escere,* in process] *suf* incomplete action (effervesce, incandesce)

-escence [L. suf. *-escere,* in process] n. *suf* something becoming (convalescence, excrescence)

-escent [L. suf. *-escere,* in process] adj. *suf* starting to be; becoming (adolescent, obsolescent)

eschar- [Gr. *eskhara,* scar, scab] *base*

scarring; caustic (Escharipora, escharotic)

eschato- [Gr. *eskhaton*, the end] *base* last (eschatologist, eschatology)

escul- [L. *esculentus*, good to eat] *base* food (esculency, esculent)

-ese [L. suf. *-ensis*] **1.** *suf* of a country (Portuguese); **2.** of a language (Chinese); **3.** in the style of (journalese)

-esis [Gr. suf. *-esis*, nouns of process] *suf* condition; process; action (anoesis, enuresis)

-esmus [Gr. n. suf. *-ismos*] *comb* spasm; contraction (tenesmic, tenesmus). *Also* **-ismus** (vaginismus)

eso- [Gr. *eso*, within] *comb* inner; within (esoderm, esotropia)

esoc- [L. *esox/esoc-*, pike] *base* pike, the fish (esocifor, esocoid)

esophag- [Gr. *oisophagos*, gullet] *base* gullet (esophageal, esophagus). *Also* **oesophag-** (oesophagalgia)

esoter- [Gr. *esoterikos*, inner, secret] *base* of an inner circle; select (esoteric, esoterica)

-esque [L. suf. *-iscus*] **1.** *suf* in the style of (Romanesque); **2.** like (picturesque)

-ess [Gr. suf. *-issa*] *suf* female who (actress, princess)

esse- [L. *esse*, to be] *base* being; existence (essence, essential)

-est [Gr. suf. *-istos*] *suf* superlative degree (coolest, tallest)

-esthesia, esthesio- [Gr. *aesthesis*, feeling] *comb* sensation; perception (myesthesia, esthesiogenic)

estu- [L. *aestuare*, to boil] *base* **1.** boil (estuant); **2.** tide (estuary). *Also* **aestu-**

esur- [L. *esurire*, be hungry] *base* hunger; appetite (esurient, esurine)

-et [Fr. suf. *-et*] *suf* diminutive (pullet, rivulet)

-eth [OE suf. *-the*] *suf* ordinal numbers (twentieth, fiftieth)

ethico- [Gr. *ethikos*, moral] *comb* ethical and (ethico-political, ethico-religious)

ethmo- [Gr. *ethmos*, strainer] *comb* sieve; ethmoid bone (ethmomaxillary, ethmo-turbinal)

ethno- [Gr. *ethnos*, people, nation] *comb* race; people; culture; nation (ethnocentric, ethnology)

etho- [Gr. *ethon*, being accustomed] *comb* character; behavior (ethology, ethopoietic)

-etic [Gr. suf. *-etikos*] *suf* adjective ending (kinetic, pathetic)

etio- [Gr. *aitia*, cause or reason + *logia*, discourse] *comb* cause; origin (etiologist, etiology) *Also* **aetio-** (aetiology)

-ette [OF suf. *-et*] **1.** *suf* diminutive (dinette); **2.** female (suffragette); **3.** substitute (leatherette)

-etum [L. suf. *-etum*] *suf* a grove of the plant specified (arboretum, pinetum)

etym- [Gr. *etumon*, the true, literal, historical sense of a word] *base* root or primitive meaning (etymologist, etymology)

eu- [Gr. *eu-*, good] *pre* good; well (eulogy, euphony)

eulog- [Gr. *eulogia*, praise, blessing] *base* laudatory speech (eulogize, eulogy)

-eum [Gr. suf. *-aios*] *suf* scientific name ending (ileum, peritoneum)

euphu- [Gr. *eu*, well + *phuein*, to grow] *base* affectation (Euphues, euphuistic)

-eur [L. suf. *-or*] *suf* one who (hauteur, voyeur)

euro- [Gr. *Euros*, east or east-southeast wind] *comb* east (euroboreal, Eurus)

Euro- [Gr. *Europe*, Europe] *comb* European (Eurodollars, Europocentric)

Europaeo-, Europeo- [Gr. *Europe*, Europe] *comb* European (Europaeo-Siberian, Europeo-Asiatic)

eury- [Gr. *eurus*, broad] *comb* [science] broad; wide (eurycephalic, eurystomatous)

-eus [L. suf. *-eus*] *suf* scientific name ending (aculeus, nucleus)

eusuch- [Gr. *eu*, good + *soukhos*, crocodile] *base* alligator, crocodile (Eusuchia, eusuchian)

eutax- [Gr. *eutakhs*, good order] *base* good or right order (eutaxiology, eutaxy)

evangel- [Gr. *eu*, well + *angellein*, to announce] Gospel (evangelism, evangelist) even- [OE *efen*, even] *comb* smooth; consistent (even-handed, even-tempered)

ever- [OE *aefre*, ever] *comb* always (ever-abiding, everlasting)

evitab- [L. *evitabilis*, avoidable] *base* avoidable (evitable, inevitable)

ex- [L. *ex*, out of, away from] **1.** *pre* from; out (expel); **2.** beyond (excess); **3.** away from; out of (expatriate); **4.** thoroughly (exterminate); **5.** upward (exalt); **6.** not having (exanimate); **7.** former (ex-husband). NOTE: ex- can change to: **e-** (eject); **ec-** (eccentric); **ef-** (efferent); **es-** (escape)

exa- *comb* quintillion (exahertz, exameter)

exanim- [L. *exanimare*, deprive of life] *base* without life (exanimate, exanimation)

exanthem- [Gr. *exanthema*, an eruption on the skin] *base* a rash (exanthema, exanthematic)

excern- [L. *excernere*, to excrete] *base* evacuate, discharge (excernant)

excito- [L. *excitare*, excite] *comb* [anatomy] stimulating (excitomotor, excito-nutrient)

excub- [L. *excubatio*, keeping watch] *base* watchman (excubation, excubitorium)

excuss- [L. *excutere*, shake off] *base* shake off, get rid of (excusable, excussion)

exec- [L. *exsecratio*, curse, malediction] *base* a curse (execrable, execration)

exedr- [Gr. *exedra*, hall with seats] *base* portico (exedra, exedral)

-exia *see* -orexia

exig- [L. *exigere*, to exact] **1.** *base* demanding (exigency); **2.** scanty (exiguous)

exo- [Gr. *exo*, outside] *pre* without; outside; outer part (exocardia, exogamous)

exoter- [Gr. *exoterikos*, outer] *base* outside, commonplace (exoteric, exoterically)

exousia- [Gr. *exousia*, authority] *comb* authority (exousiastic)

exped- [L. *expedire*, dispatch] *base* promptness, speed (expeditious, expeditory)

explanato- [L. *explanatus*, flattened, spread out] *comb* spread out in a plane or flat surface (explanate, explanato-foliaceous)

expurg- [L. *expurgare*, purge] *base* remove, purge (expurgate, expurge)

exsibil- [L. *exsibilare*, to hiss forth] *base* hiss (exsibilate, exsibilation)

extero- [L. *externus*, external + *-ceptor*, receive] *comb* outside (exteroceptive, exteroceptor)

extra-, extro- [L. *extra-*, beyond, outside] *pre* outside; beyond; more than; besides (extraordinary, extrovert)

exuv- [L. *exuere*, cast off, molt] *base* shed, molt, cast off (exuvial, exuviate)

-ey [variant of *-y*] *suf* characterized by; inclined to (clayey, gooey)

F

-faba-, -fabi- [L. *faba*, bean] *base* bean (fabaceous, fabiform)

fabell- [L. *fabella*, brief narrative] *base* story (fabellator, fable)

-fabr- [L. *fabricari*, make, construct] *base* make; construct (fabrication, fabricator)

fabul- [L. *fabula*, fable] *base* tale (fabulist, fabulous)

-fac-, -fec-, -fic- [L. *facere*, to do] *base* make; do (factory, efficient, fictitious)

facet- [L. *facetus*, droll, witty] *base* amusing (facetious, facetiously)

-facient [L. *facere*, to do] *comb* causing to become; making; (calefacient, liquefacient)

facil- [L. *facilis*, easy] *base* easy (facile, facilitate)

facin- [L. *facinorosus*, atrocious, wicked]

base wicked; vile (facinorous, facinorously)

facio- [L. *facies*, face] *comb* face (facioplasty, facioplegia)

factic/t- [L. *facticius*, artificial] *base* artificial (factitious, factitiousness)

factios- [L. *factiosus*, segmented] *base* forming factions (factious, factiousness)

-facture [L. *factura*, making, formation] *comb* making (manufacture, metallifacture)

facund- [L. *facundus*, fluent, eloquent] *base* eloquent (facund, facundity)

faecul-/fecul- [L. *faecula*, the lees of wine, dregs] *base* sediment (feculence, feculent)

-faga- [L. *fagus*, beech] *base* beech (fagaceous, Fagus)

fagopyr- [L. *fagopyrum*, buckwheat] *base* buckwheat (fagopyrism)

-falc- [L. *falx/falc-*, sickle] *base* sickle; hooked (falcate, falciform)

falco-, falconi- [L. *falco*, falcon < its hooked, sickle-like claws] *base* falcon; kestrel; hawk (falconine, falconry)

fam- [L. *fames*, hunger] *base* hunger (famelic, famished)

famig- [L. *famigeratio*, rumor] *base* rumor (famigerate, famigeration)

famulat- [L. *famulatio*, domestics, household] *base* serve (famulate, famulative)

fan-¹ [Gr. *phanos*, torch, lantern] *base* lighthouse; beacon (fanal)

fan-² [L. *fanum*, sanctuary, temple] *base* temple (fane, profane)

farcim- [L. *farcimen*, sausage] *base* seasoned stuffing (farciment, farciminous)

farct- [L. *farcere*, to stuff] *base* to stuff; obstruct (infarct, infarction)

farin- [L. *farina*, meal, grain] *base* flour (farinaceous, farinose)

farr-, farrag- [L. *far*, spelt] *base* mixed feed grains; spelt (confarreation, farraginous)

fasciculato- [L. *fasciculus*, small bundle] *comb* arranged in a bundle (fasciculato-glomerate, fasciculato-ramose)

fascin- [L. *fascinnum*, witchcraft] *base* bewitched (fascinate, fascinous)

fascio- [L. *fascia*, bundle or band] *comb* fibrous tissue; fascia; bundle (fasciation, fasciotomy)

fastid- [L. *fastidium*, loathing] *base* disgust (fastidious, fastidiousness)

fastig- [L. *fastigatus*, sloping] *base* gabled; pointed; tapered (fastigate, fastigiated)

fati- [L. *fatum*, fate] *base* prophet (fatidic, fatiferous)

fatisc- [L. *fatiscere*, open in chinks] *base* cleft (fatiscence, fatiscent)

fatu- [L. *fatuus*, foolish] *base* foolish (fatuitous, fatuous)

fauc- [L. *faux/fauc-*, throat] *base* throat (faucal, fauces)

faust- [L. *faustus*, favored] *base* fortune; chance (faustitude, faustity)

fav- [L. *faveolus*, honeycomb-like cell] *base* honeycomb (faveolate, faviform)

favill- [L. *favilla*, embers] *base* ashes (favillous)

favon- [L. *Favonius*, west wind] *base* west wind (favonian, favonious)

favoso- [L. *favus*, honeycomb] *comb* honeycombed (favose, favoso-dehiscent)

febri- [L. *febris*, fever] *comb* fever (febrifacient, febrifuge)

-fec-¹ [L. *facere*, to do] *base* make; do (effective). *See* fac-

-fec-² [L. *feces*, dregs] *base* filth; dregs (feculence, feculent)

fedi- [L. *federe*, to league together] *base* compact; covenant (federation, fedifragous)

fel- [L. *felis*, cat] *base* cat (Felidae, feline)

felic- [L. *felix*, happy] *base* happy (felicify, felicitation)

felli- [L. *fellitus*, steeped in gall] *base* gall (fellifluous, fellic acid)

femin- [L. *femina*, woman] *base* woman (feminine, feminization)

femto- [ON *fimmtan*, fifteen] *pre* one-quadrillionth (femtometer, femtovolt)

fener- [L. *fenus/fener-*, proceeds, profit] *base* lending on interest (fenerate, feneration)

fenest- [L. *fenestra*, window] *base* window (fenestral, defenestration)

-fer [L. *ferre*, to carry] *comb* one that bears; one that produces (aquifer, conifer)

-fer- [L. *fera*, wild animal] *base* wild animal (feral, ferine)

feret- [Gr. *pheretron*, litter, bier] *base* shrine container (feretory, feretrum)

ferit- [L. *feritas*, wildness, savageness] *base* savage (feritaceous, ferity)

ferment- [L. *fermentum*, leaven, yeast] *base* yeast (fermentable, fermentareous)

feroc- [L. *ferox/feroc-*, fiece, savage] *base* bold; fierce (ferocious, ferocity)

-ferous [L. *ferre*, to carry] *comb* bearing; producing; yielding (coniferous, pestiferous)

ferri-, ferro- [L. *ferrum*, iron] *comb* containing ferric iron (ferricyanide, ferromagnetism)

ferrug- [L. *ferrum*, iron] *base* iron-rust color (ferruginous, ferrugo)

ferul- [L. *ferula*, rod, whip] *base* rod; stalk (ferulaceous, ferule)

ferv- [L. *fervere*, boil, glow] *base* boil; glow (fervency, fervidity)

fescinn- [L. *Fescennia*, city in Tuscany] *base* obscene, scurrilous (fescinnine, Fescinnines)

-fest [L. *festum*, holiday] *comb* assembly or celebration (chilifest, songfest)

festin- [L. *festinatio*, haste] *base* haste; speed (festinate, festination)

festuc- [L. *festuca*, stalk, straw] *base* stalk; straw (Festuca, festucine)

fetid- [L. *fetidus*, stinking] *base* stink (fetid, fetidness)

fibri-/fibro- [L. *fibra*, fiber] *comb* fiber (fibriform, fibrocystic)

fibrilloso- [L. *fibrilla*, fibril] *comb* fibril-shaped (fibrilloso-squamulous, fibrilloso-striate)

fibrino- [L. *fibra*, fiber] *comb* fibrin (fibrinogen, fibrinoplastic)

fibroso- [L. *fibra*, fiber] *comb* fibrous (fibroso-calcareus, fibroso-cartilaginous)

fibul- [L. *fibula*, brooch] *base* brooch (exfibulate, suffibulum)

-fic [L. *facere*, to make] *comb* making; creating (beatific, scientific). *See* **fac-**

-fication [L. suf. *-ficatio*] *comb* a making; a creating; a causing (amplification, calcification)

fici- [L. *ficus*, fig] *base* fig (ficiform, ficoid)

fict- [L. *facere*, to make] *base* made up (fiction, fictitious)

-fid-[1] [L. *fides*, trust] *base* faith; belief (confide, fidelity)

-fid-[2] [L. *findere*, to split] *comb* cleft; segment (multifid, pennatifid)

fidic- [L. *fidicinus*, pert. to lute-playing] *base* lute (fidicinal)

figul- [L. *figulus*, potter] *base* pottery (figulate, figuline)

figur- [L. *figure*, figure] *base* form; shape (disfiguration, figurative)

fil-[1]**, fili-, filo-** [L. *filum*, thread] *comb* threadlike (filament, filigrain, filoplume)

fil-[2] [L. *filius/filia*, son/daughter] *base* child (affiliation, filial)

filamento- [L. *fila*, thread] *comb* threadlike (filamento-caudal, filamento-cribrate)

filari- [NL *filaris*, thread] *base* slender worm (filarial, filariform)

filic- [L. *filix/filic-*, fern] *base* fern (filiciform, filicology)

fim-, fimi- [L. *fimus*, dung] *comb* dung (fimetic, fimicolous)

fimbr- [L. *fimbria*, fringe] *comb* fringe; border (fimbrial, fimbricate)

fimbriato- [L. *fimbriatus*, fringed] *comb* fringed with hairs (fimbriato-ciliate, fimbriato-lacinate)

fimbrilli- [L. *fimbrilla*, small fringe] *comb* small fringe (fimbrillate, fimbrilliferous)

-fin- [L. *finis*, end] *base* end; limit (finite, infinity)

Finno- [Norse Finnr, swampy region] *comb* Finnish; (Finno-Ugrian, Finno-Ugric)

fiscal- [L. *fiscalis*, pert. to the treasury] *base* revenue (fiscal, fiscality)

fissi- [L. *fissus*, cleft] *comb* [anatomy] cleft (fissicostate, fissidactyl)

fissuri- [L. *fissura*, cleft] *comb* fissure (fissuriform)

fistul- [L. *fistula*, pipe, reed] *base* reed; pipe; tube (fistuliform, fistulous)

flabelli- [L. *flabellum*, fan] *comb* fanlike (flabellifoliate, flabelliform)

flabil- [L. *flabilis*, airy] *base* to blow (flabile, flability)

flacc- [L. *flaccus*, flabby] *base* drooping; weak (flaccid, flaccidity)

-flagel- [L. *flagellare*, scourge] *base* whip; lash (flagellate, flagelliferous)

flagit- [L. *flagitare*, urge with violence] *base* vicious; wicked (flagitious, flagitiousness)

-flat- [L. *flatus*, blowing, snorting] *base* windy; gassy (flatulence, flatulent)

flavido- [L. *flavus*, yellow] *comb* yellowish (flavido-alba, flavido-cinerascent)

-flavin [L. *flavus*, yellow] *comb* natural derivatives of flavin (lactoflavin, riboflavin)

flavo- [L. *flavus*, yellow] **1.** *comb* yellow (flavopurpurin); **2.** flavin (flavoprotein)

fleb- [L. *flebilis*, tearful] *base* weeping; doleful (flebile)

-flect-, -flex-, flexi- [L. *flectere*, bend] *base* bend (inflection, flexible, flexicostate)

-flet- [L. *fletus*, tears] *base* weep; cry (fletiferous)

flexuoso- [L. *flectere*, bend] *comb* winding; bending; undulating (flexuouso-clavate, flexuoso-convex)

-flict- [L. *flictus*, collision, dashing together] *base* to strike (afflict, conflict)

-flocc- [L. *floccus*, lock of wool] *base* wool; tuft (floccose, flocculent)

flori-, -florous [L. *flos*, flower] *comb* flower; having flowers (floriferous, multiflorous)

-flu- [L. *fluere*, flow] *base* flowing (fluent, fluid)

flucti- [L. *fluctus*, wave] *comb* undulation; wave (fluctifragous, fluctisonant)

flum- [L. *flumen*, river] *base* river (flume, fluminal)

fluo-, fluor-, fluoro- [L. *fluere*, flow] *comb* fluorine; fluorescent (fluophosphate, fluorhydric, fluoroscope)

-fluv- [L. *fluere*, flow] *base* flowing (effluvia, fluviatile)

fluvio- [L. *fluvius*, river] *comb* [geology] river; stream (fluvio-marine, fluvio-terrestrial)

fluxil- [L. *fluxilis*, fluid] *base* flow (fluxile, fluxility)

focill- [L. *focillare*, to refresh, to cherish] *base* refresh (focillate, focillation)

fod- [L. *fodere*, dig up] *base* dig; burrow (exfodiation, fodient)

foet-/fet- [L. *foetere*, to stink] *base* stench (fetid, fetor)

-fold [AS multiplicative suf. *-feald*] **1.** *suf* having parts (twofold); **2.** larger; more (hundredfold)

foliato- [L. *foliatus*, leafy] *comb* leaf-like (foliato-explanate, foliato-ramose)

folii-, folio-, -folious [L. *folium*, leaf] *comb* leaf (foliiferous, foliolar, unifolious)

follic- [L. *folliculus*, small bag] *base* tube; small bag (follicle, follicular)

fomen- [L. *fomentum*, warm lotion] *base* heat up; incite (foment, fomentation)

-foot(er) [OE *fot*, foot] *comb* so many feet long (six-footer, twelve-footer)

for- [Dan. pref. *for-*] **1.** *pre* away; apart; off (forgo); **2.** very much (forlorn)

foramin- [L. *foramina*, hole] *base* hole (foramiferous, foraminate)

-forat- [L. *forare*, to pierce] *base* pierced (biforate, perforate)

forbi- [Gr. *phorbe*, fodder, forage] *base* grasshopper (forbivorous)

-forc-, -fort- [L. *fortis*, strong] *base* strength (enforcement, fortification)

fore- [AS *fore*, before] **1.** *pre* before (forecast); **2.** front part of (forehead)

-forfic- [L. *forfex/forfic-*, scissors] *base* scissors; deeply notched (forficate, forficulate)

forficul- [L. *forficula*, earwig] *base* earwig (forficulate, forficulid)

-foris- [L. *foris*, outside] *base* outside (forisfamiliate, forisfamiliation)

-form [L. *forma*, shape] **1.** *suf* shaped like (oviform); **2.** having ___ forms (uniform)

-formic- [L. *formica*, ant] *base* ant (formicary, formication)

formo- [L. *formica*, ant] *comb*

[chemistry] formic acid (formobenzoate, formo-benzoic)

formos- [L. *formosus*, beautiful, handsome] *base* beautiful (formose, formosity)

-fornic- [L. *fornix*, arch] *base* arch; vault (fornication, forniciform)

fortuit- [L. *fortuitus*, accidental] *base* happening by chance (fortuitous, fortuity)

foss- [L. *fossilis*, dug out] *base* dig (fossil, fossorial)

fov- [L. *fovea*, pit] *base* pitted; pock-marked (foveate, foveolet)

-fract- [L. *fractus*, broken] *base* break (fraction, fracture). *Also* **-frag-** *and* **-frang-**

fracto- [L. *fractus*, broken] *comb* ragged mass of cloud (fracto-nimbus, fracto-stratus)

-frag- [L. *frangere*, to break] *base* break (fragile, fragmented). *Also* **-fract-** *and* **-frang-**

fraga- [L. *fraga*, strawberry] *base* strawberry (Fragaria, fragarol)

frambes- [L. *frambesia*, raspberry] *base* raspberry-like (frambesia, frambesioma)

Franco- [L. comb. form *Franci-*, the Franks] *comb* French (Franco-American, Franco-Canadian)

-frang- [L. *frangere*, to break] *base* break (frangible, irrefrangible). *Also* **-fract-** *and* **-frag-**

frat- [L. *frater*, brother] *base* brother (fraternity, fratricide)

-frax- [L. *fraxinus*, ash tree] *base* ash tree (fraxetin, fraxin)

-frem- [L. *fremere*, roar, growl] *base* roar; murmur, thrill (fremescent, fremitus)

frend- [L. *frendere*, to gnash the teeth] *base* grind; gnash (frendent, frendently)

frenet- [OF *frenetique*, frenzied] *base* frenzied (frenetic, frenetical)

freno- [L. *fraena*, bridle] *comb* restraining (frenosecretory, frenotomy)

friabil- [L. *friabilis*, easily broken or crumbled] *base* crumbly (friability, friable)

-frig- [L. *frigor*, cold] *base* cold (frigidity, frigorific)

-fringill- [L. *fringilla*, small bird] *base* finch (fringillaceous, fringilliform)

frix- [L. *frixura*, frying pan] *base* frying pan (frixion, frixory)

from- [Fr. *fromage*, cheese] *base* cheese (fromologist, fromology)

-frond- [L. *frondere*, to put forth leaves] *base* leaf (frondent, frondivorous)

fronto- [L. *frons*, the brow] **1.** *comb* frontal bone (fronto-parietal); **2.** meteorological front (frontogenesis)

fructi-, fructo- [L. *fructus*, fruit] *comb* fruit; fructose (fructiferous, fructosuria)

frug-¹ [L. *frux*, fruit] *base* fruit; fructose (frugiferous, frugivorous)

frug-² [L. *fruges*, fruits of the earth] *base* sparing; thrifty (frugal, frugality)

-frument- [L. *frumentum*, grain, corn] *base* grain; cereal; corn (frumentaceous, frumentarious)

frust- [L. *frustum*, piece] *base* fragment; piece (frustulent, frustulose)

fruticuloso- [L. *fruticulus*, small shrub] *comb* shrub-like (fruticuloso-hylocomiosum, fruticuloso-ramose)

-fuc- [L. *fucus*, seaweed] *base* seaweed (fucoid, fucivorous)

fucos- [L. *fucosus*, painted, colored] *base* painted (fucose, fucosity)

-fuge, fugal [L. *fugere*, flee] *comb* driving out; driving away (febrifuge, vermifugal)

-ful [OE *full*, full] **1.** *suf* full of (painful); **2.** having qualities of (masterful); **3.** having ability to (forgetful); **4.** amount that fills (handful)

-fulg- [L. *fulgur*, flashing] *base* bright; flashing (fulgurant, fulguration)

fulic- [L. *fulica*, coot] *base* coot (fulicarian, fulicinae)

-fulig- [L. *fuligo*, soot] *base* black; sooty (fuliginated, fuliginous)

fuligul- [L. *fulica*, coot] *base* sea duck (Fuligulinae, fuliguline)

fullon- [L. *fullonicus*, pert. to fullers] *base* fuller (fullonical)

-fulmin- [L. *fulminare*, hurl lightning]

base lightning; thunder (fulminant, fulmination)

-fulv- [L. *fulvus,* flame-colored] *base* tawny; yellow-brown (fulvescent, fulvous)

-fum- [L. *fumus,* smoke] *base* smoke (fumid, fumigate)

-fun- [L. *funis,* rope] *base* rope (funambulation, funambulist)

-fund- [L. *fundamentum,* bottom] *base* bottom; base (fundament, fundamental)

-fundi- [L. *funda,* sling] *base* sling (fundiform, fundiform ligament)

funeb- [L. *funebris,* funeral] *base* funeral (funebral, funebrious)

funer- [L. *funereus,* pert. to a funeral] *base* funeral (funeral, funeration)

funest- [L. *funestus,* deadly] *base* fatal; deadly; disastrous (funest, funestous)

fungi- [L. *fungus,* mushroom] *comb* fungus (fungicide, fungivorous)

funi- [L. *funis,* rope or cord] *comb* cord; rope; fiber (funiculus, funiform)

fur-¹ [L. *furia,* anger] *base* angry (furious, furor)

fur-² [Gr. *phor,* thief] *base* stealing (furacious, furacity)

-furc- [L. *furca,* fork] *base* forked (bifurcation, furcular)

-furfur- [L. *furfur,* bran] *base* bran; dandruff (furfuraceous, furfural)

furt- [Gr. *phor,* thief] *base* theft; stealth (furtive, furtively)

furunc- [L. *furunculus,* a boil] *base* having boils (furuncle, furunculosis)

-fus- [L. *fundere,* to pour] *base* flow; pour; melt (infusion, transfusion)

fusco- [L. *fuscus,* dark] *comb* dark brown; dusky; gloomy (fusco-ferruginous, fusco-piceous)

fusi-, fuso- [L. *fusus,* spindle] *comb* spindle; rod (fusiform, fusobacterium)

-fustig- [L. *fustigare,* beat with a cudgel] *base* beat; cudgel (fustigate, fustigation)

futil- [L. *futilis,* untrustworthy] *base* useless (futile, futility)

-fy [L. suf. *-ficare*] **1.** *suf* make; cause to be (deify); **2.** cause to have; imbue with (dignify); **3.** become (putrefy)

G

-gaea/-gea [Gr. *Gaea,* goddess of Earth] *comb* earth (Paleogaea, Pangea)

galact(o)- [Gr. *galakt,* milk] *comb* milk; milky (galactagogue, galactocele)

-gale¹ [Gr. *gale,* weasel, ferret] *base* weasel (phascogale, potamogale)

-gale-² [Gr. *galeos,* shark] *base* shark (galeidan, galeod)

-gale-³ [Gr. *gale,* cat] *base* cat (galeanthropy, galeophobia)

-galea- [L. *galea,* helmet] *base* helmet (galeate, galeated)

galer- [L. *galerum,* hat] *base* cap (galericulate, galericulated)

galero- [Gr. *galeros,* cheerful] *comb* cheerful (galeropia, galeropsia)

-gallinac-, -gallinag- [L. *gallina,* hen] *base* poultry: chicken, grouse, partridge, pheasant, quail, turkey, woodcock (gallinaceous, gallinaginous)

Gallo- [L. *Gallus,* a Gaul] *comb* French; Gallic (Gallomania, Gallophobia)

galvano- [It.<. *Luigi Galvani*] *comb* galvanic; electricity (galvanocaustic, galvanometer)

gamb- [L. *gamba,* hoof] *base* animal leg (gamb, gambol)

gambog- [ML gambogium,< *Camboja,* Cambodia] *base* brilliant yellow (gambogian, gambogic)

gameto- [Gr. *gamein,* to marry] *comb* gamete; union (gametophore, gametophyte)

-gammar- [Gr. *kammaros,* lobster] *base* sea crab; lobster (gammarid, gammarolite)

gamo- [Gr. *gamos,* marriage] **1.** *comb*

sexually united (gamogenesis); **2.** joined (gamosepalous)

-gamous, -gamy [Gr. *gamos*, marriage] *comb* marrying; uniting sexually (polygamous, polygamy)

gang- [Gr. *gangetikos*, Ganges] *base* Ganges River (gangetic, gangic)

ganglio- [Gr. *ganglion*, tumor] *comb* nerve cells; swelling; ganglion (ganglioform, ganglioplexus)

gangr- [Gr. *gangraina*, cancerous ulcer] *base* ulcer (gangrene, gangrenescent)

gann(it)- [L. *gannitio*, barking] *base* bark (ganne, ganning)

-gano- [Gr. *ganos*, brightness] *base* bright; shiny (ganocephalus, ganoidal)

gargar- [Gr. *gargarisma*, a gargle] *base* gargle (gargarism, gargarize)

garrul- [L. *garrulus*, chattering] *base* chatter; magpie, jay (garrulous, garruline)

gaso- [word invented by Flemish chemist Van Helmont < Gr. *chaos*] *comb* gas (gasohol, gasometer)

gastero-, -gastria, gastro- [Gr. *gaster*, stomach] *comb* stomach (gasteropod, microgastria, gastroenteritis)

gastropod- [Gr. *gaster*, stomach + *pod*, foot] *base* snail (gasteropodous, gastropodal)

-gate [< Watergate scandal] *comb* [journalism] concealed scandal (Enrongate, Irangate)

gato- [ML *gattus* < L. *cattus*, cat] *comb* cat (gatomania, gatophobia)

gaud- [L. *gaudium*, gladness, joy] *base* joy (gaudiloquence, gaudy)

gavi- [L. *gavia*, sea-mew] *base* gull (Gaviae, gavialid)

gavial- [Hindi *ghariyal*, crocodile] *base* crocodile (Gavialidae, gavialoid)

-gea- [Gr. *ge*, earth] *base* earth (epigeal, Pangea)

gecco- [NL. *geccon*, gecko] *base* gecko or wall lizard (gecconoid, geccotoid)

geisso- [Gr. *geisson*, cornice] *comb* cornice (Geissorhiza, geissospermine)

geitono- [Gr. *geiton*, neighbor] *base* neighbor (geitonogamy, geitonophobia)

-gel-[1] [L. *gelum*, frost, cold] *base* ice; frost; freeze (gelidity, regelation)

-gel-[2] [Gr. *gelan*, to laugh] *base* laughter (Gelasimus, gelastic)

gelatino- [L. *gelatus*, frozen] *comb* gelatin (gelatino-albuminous, gelatino-chlorid)

gem- [L. *gemere*, groan] *base* groan (gement, gemonies)

-gemelli- [L. *gemellus*, twin] *base* twins (Gemellaria, gemelliparous)

-gemin- [L. *geminus,* born at the same time] *base* double (gemination, geminiflorous)

gemm-[1] [L. *gemma*, swelling, bud] *base* leaf buds (gemmaceous, gemmate)

gemm-[2] [L. *gemmarius*, pert. to gems] *base* jewel (gemmary, gemmiferous)

-gen [L. *genus*, produced] **1.** *comb* something that produces; origin (oxygen); **2.** something produced (endogen). *Also* **-genic** (endogenic); **-genous** (endogenous); **-geny** (endogeny)

-genesis [Gr. *genesis*, origin, source] *comb* origination; creation; formation; evolution (abiogenesis, parthenogenesis)

-geneth- [Gr. *genethle*, race, stock, family] *base* birthday (genethliacon, genethlialogy)

-genetic [Gr. *genesis*, origin, source] *comb* origin (phylogenetic)

-genia, genio-, geny-[1] [Gr. *geneion*, chin, beard] *comb* jaw; cheek; chin (microgenia, genioplasty, genyplasty)

genic-, genu- [L. *genu*, knee] *base* knee (geniculate, genuflect)

genito- [L. *genitus*, begotten] *comb* genital (genitocrural, genitourinary)

gennem- [Gr. *gennema*, product] *base* uttered speech sounds (gennemic, gennemically)

geno- [Gr. *genos*, sex, kind] *comb* race; genetic makeup (genoblast, genotype)

gentil- [L. *genticus*, belonging to a nation] *base* nation (gentile, gentilicial)

-geny[2] [Gr. *genos*, sex, kind] *comb* product of (cosmogeny, phylogeny)

geo- [Gr. *geo*, earth, land, country] *comb* earth (geocentric, geophagy)

georg- [Gr. *georgikos*, agricultural] *base* rural occupations (georgic, georgical)

gephyr- [Gr. *gephura*, bridge] *base* bridge (gephyrocercal, gephyrophobia)

ger-[1] [L. *gerere*, carry on, perform] *base* hold; manage (gerenda, gerent)

ger-[2] [Gr. *geras*, old age] *base* old age (gerontological, geriatric)

gerasco- [Gr. *geras*, old age] *comb* aging (gerascophobia)

Germano- [L. *Germanus*, German] *comb* German (Germanophile, Germanophobe)

gero-, geronto- [Gr. *geras*, old age] *comb* old; elderly (gerodontics, gerontology)

-gerous [L. *gerere*, carry, perform] *comb* producing; bearing; carrying (cerigerous, dentigerous)

gerul- [L. *gerulum*, bearer, carrier] *base* carrier; peddlar (nugigerulous)

gest- [L. *gestor*, tale-bearer, tattler] *base* tale (gest, gesting)

gestat- [L. *gestare*, to bear or carry] *base* carrying; pregnancy (circumgestation, gestation)

gestic- [L. *gestus*, gesture] *base* to make gestures (gesticulate, gesticulatory)

-geton- [Gr. *geiton*, neighbor] *base* neighbor (Potamogeton illinoensis, Potamogeton pectinatus)

geum-, geumat- [Gr. *geusis*, sense of taste] *base* taste (geumaphobia, geumatophobia)

-geusia [Gr. *geusis*, sense of taste] *comb* taste (ageusia, parageusia)

gibboso- [L. *gibberosus*, hunched] *base* rounded; humped; convex; protuberant (gobboso-glomerate, gibboso-lobate)

giga- [Gr. *gigas*, giant] *pre* billion (gigabyte, gigacycle)

giganto- [Gr. *gigas*, giant] *comb* gigantic; large (gigantology, gigantomachia)

gilv- [L. *gilvus*, pale yellow] *base* yellow (gilvous)

gingivo- [L. *gingivoe*, the gums] *comb* gums (gingivoglossitis, gingivostomatitis)

-gingly- [Gr. *ginglumos*, hinge joint] *base* hinge (ginglyform, ginglymoid)

glabello- [L. *glaber*, smooth] *comb* space between the eyebrows (glabellous, glabello-occipital)

-glabr- [L. *glaber*, smooth] *base* smooth; bald (glabrate, glabrous)

glacio- [L. *glacies*, ice] *comb* glacier; ice (glacio-aqueous, glaciologist)

gladi- [L. *gladius*, sword] *comb* sword (gladiator, gladiolus)

gland- [L. *glans*, acorn] *base* **1.** acorn (glandiferous); **2.** yellow-brown (glandaceous)

glare- [L. *glarea*, gravel] *base* gravel; sand (glareose, glareous)

glauco- [Gr. *glaukos*, bluish-green, gray] *comb* bluish-green; gray; silvery; opaque (glaucoma, glaucopyrite)

-glea [Gr. *gloia*, glue] *comb* glue; cement (mesoglea) *Also* **-gloia, -gloea**

-gleb- [L. *glebosus*, full of clods] *base* clod; lump; dirt (glebulose, glebous)

glen- [Gr. *glene*, pupil of the eye] *base* eyeball (glene, glenoid)

gleno- [Gr. *glene*, socket] *comb* shallow joint-socket (gleno-humeral, glenovertebral)

-glia, glio- [Gr. *glia*, glue] *comb* glue; gluelike (neuroglia, glioblastoma)

glico- *see* **gluco-**

-glir- [L. *glis*, dormouse] *base* dormouse (gliriform, glirine)

glisc- [L. *gliscere*, swell up] *base* increase (gliscent)

globi-, globo- [L. *globus*, ball] *comb* round; ball-shaped; spherical (globiferous, globospherite)

gloio- [Gr. *gloia*, glue] *comb* glue (gloiocarp, Gloiopeltis)

glom- [L. *glomus*, ball, round heap] *base* cluster; ball (conglomeration, glomerulus)

glosso- [Gr. *glossa*, tongue] **1.** *comb* of the tongue (glossoplegia); **2.** the tongue plus (glossopharyngeal); **3.** of words; of language (glossology). *Also* **-glossia** (macroglossia)

-glot, glotto- [Gr. *glotta*, tongue] *comb* language, communication in; languages, knowledge of (polyglot, glottogony)

gluco- [Gr. *glukus*, sweet] *comb* glycerin; glycerol; glycogen; sugar; (glucokinase)

glum- [L. *gluma*, corn husk] *base* husk, hull (glume, glumose)

glut- [L. *gluteus*, buttocks] *base* rump (gluteofemoral, gluteus maximus)

-glutin- [L. *agglutinare*, to fasten with glue] *base* glue (agglutinate, glutinize)

glutt- [L. *gluttire*, devour] *base* eat; gulp (glutton, gluttony)

glycero-, glyco- [Gr. *glukus*, sweet] *comb* glycerin; glycerol; glycogen; sugar (glycerolysis, glycogenesis)

glycyr- [Gr. *glukus*, sweet + *hrizha*, root] *base* licorice (glycyrize, Glycyrrhiza)

-glyph [Gr. *gluphein*, carve] *comb* carve; engrave; notch (diglyph, hieroglyph)

-glypha [Gr. *gluphein*, to carve] *comb* [zoology] snakes with grooved fangs (Opisthoglypha, proteroglypha)

glypto- [Gr. *gluphein*, to carve] *comb* carved; engraved (glyptodont, glyptograph)

gnar- [L. *gnarus*, skillful, expert] *base* knowledge (gnarity)

gnatho-, -gnathous [Gr. *gnathos*, jaw] *comb* [zoology] jaw (gnathodynamics, prognathous)

gnom-[1] [Gr. *gnomon*, sundial] *base* sundial pin (gnomon, gnomonic)

gnom-[2] [Gr. *gnomai*, saying] *base* maxim (gnomic, gnomologist)

gnom-[2] [L. *gnomus*, diminutive spirit] *base* dwarf (gnome, gnomish)

-gnomy, -gnosia, -gnosis, -gnostic [Gr. *gnosis*, knowledge] *comb* judging; determining; knowledge (physiognomy, dysgnosia, diagnosis, diagnostic)

gnoto- [Gr. *gnotos*, known] *comb* known (gnotobiology, gnotobiote)

goet- [Gr. *goeteia*, witchcraft] *base* witchcraft (goetic, goety)

gog-, -gogue *see* **-agogue**

-gomph- [Gr. *gomphos*, bolt, fastening] *base* bolt; socket; nail (gomphiasis, gomphosis)

-gon, -gonal [Gr. *gonia*, angle] *comb* figure with ___ angles (pentagon, polygonal)

gonado- [Gr. *gone*, generation, seed] *comb* gonad; sex gland (gonadopathy, gonaduct)

-gone, -gonium, gono-, -gony [Gr. *gone*, generation, seed] *comb* reproduction; generation; origin; formation (myelogone, sporogonium, gonothecal, cosmogony)

gonido- [Gr. *gone*, generation, seed] *comb* reproductive (gonidogenous, gonidophore)

gonio- [Gr. *gonia*, angle] *comb* angle (goniognathous, goniometry)

gorg- [*gorgos*, fierce] *base* fierce (Gorgon, gorgonesque)

gorill- [Gr. *Gorillai*, name of a tribe of hairy women] *base* large ape (gorilla, gorilloid)

grabat- [Gr. *krabatos*, low couch, pallet] *base* couch (crabat)

-gracil- [L. *gracilis*, slender] *base* slender; lean (gracilescent, gracility)

gracul- [L. *graculus*, jackdaw] *base* jackdaw, grackle (Graculinae, graculine)

grad- [L. *gradus*, step] *base* walk; move; go (gradation, gradual)

-grade [L. *gradus*, step] *comb* a specified manner of walking or moving (plantigrade, tardigrade) *see* **-gress-**

Graeco- [L. *Graecus*, Greek] *comb* Greek (Graecomania). *Also* **Greco-** (Grecophile)

-grall- [L. *grallae*, stilts] *base* wading bird (grallae, gralline)

grallator- [L. *grallator*, one who walks on stilts] *base* stork; heron (grallatorial, grallatory)

-gram [Gr. *gramma*, what is written] **1.** *comb* written or drawn (telegram); [LL. *gramma*, a small weight] **2.** grams: x number of (kilograms); **3.** gram: fraction of (centigram)

-gramen-, -gramin- [L. *gramen*, grass] *base* grass (gramenite, graminifer-ous)

grammat- [Gr. *gramatikos*, pert. to grammar] *base* grammar (grammatical, grammaticize)

grand- [L. *grandis*, having high dignity

or rank] *comb* of the generation older than or younger than (grandfather, granddaughter)

grandi- [L. *grandis*, large] *base* great; large (grandiloquent, grandiosity)

grandin- [L. *grandinus*, full of hail] *base* hail (grandination, grandinous)

grani- [L. *granum*, grain] *comb* grain; corn (graniferous, granivorous)

graniti- [It. *granito*, grained] *comb* granite; (graniticoline, granitiform)

grano- [L. *granum*, grain] **1.** *comb* granite: like/of (granolithic); **2.** granular (granophyre)

granulo- [L. *granulus*, granular] *comb* granular (granulo-adipose, granduloma)

grao- [Gr. *graus*, old woman] *comb* old woman (graocracy)

-graph [Gr. *graphein*, write] **1.** *comb* that which writes/draws/describes (telegraph); **2.** that which is written/drawn (autograph). *Also* **-grapher** (stenographer); **-graphic** (telegraphic); **grapho-** (graphology); **-graphy** (autobiography)

grapto- [Gr. *graptos*, marked, written] *comb* writing (graptolitic, graptomancy)

grat- [L. *gratus*, pleasing] *base* thankful (grateful, gratitude)

-graticul- [L. dim. of *cratis*, wickerwork] *base* gridiron (graticulation, graticule)

-grav- [L. *gravis*, heavy] *base* weight; heavy; serious (gravigrade, gravimeter)

graveol- [L. *graveolens*, offensive smell] *base* rank smell (graveolence, graveolent)

-gravid- [L. *gravidus*, pregnant] *base* pregnant (gravidity, multigravida)

Greco- [L. *Graecus*, Greek] *comb* Greek; (Greco-Roman). *Also* **Graeco-** (Graecophile)

-greg- [L. *grex/greg-*, flock] *base* herd; flock (congregation, gregarious)

grem- [It. *gremio*, lap, bosom] *base* bosom; lap (gremial, gremiale)

-gress- [L. *gressor*, walker] *base* walk; move; go (aggressive). *See* **-grad-**

griph- [Gr. *griphos*, enigma, puzzling question] *base* riddle (griph, logogriph)

-gris- [ML *griseus*, gray] *base* gray (grisaille, griseous)

grom- [L. *groma*, surveyor's measuring-rod] *base* pert. to land-surveying (gromatic, gromatical)

gross- [L. *grossus*, thick] *base* thick (engross, gross)

grossul- [NL *grossula*, gooseberry] *base* gooseberry (grossulaceous, grossular)

-grui- [NL *grus*, crane] *base* crane (gruiform, Gruiformes)

-grum- [L. *grumus*, a little heap] *base* clot (grumous, grumousness)

grunn(it)- [L. *grunnire*, to grunt like a swine] *base* grunt (grunt, grunter)

gryll- [L. *grillus*, grasshopper, cricket] *base* cricket; grasshopper (Gryllotalpa, Gryllus)

gryp- [Gr. *grypos*, hook-nosed] *base* curved (grypanian, onychogryphosis)

gubern- [L. *gubernacula*, helm, rudder] *base* ruler; guide (gubernation, gubernatorial)

gul(os)- [L. *gula*, throat] *base* gluttony; voracity (gullet, gulosity)

gurd- [L. *gurdus*, dolt, numskull] *base* fried dough cake; unit of money (gordita, gourde)

gurg- [L. *gurges*, whirlpool] *base* gush, swirl (gurgitation, gurgle)

-gust- [L. *gustare*, taste] *base* taste; eat (gustation, gustatory)

gutti- [L. *gutta*, a drop] *base* drop; gum-yielding (guttiferous, guttulate)

gutturo- [L. *guttur*, the throat] *comb* throat (gutturo-labial, gutturo-nasal)

gymno- [Gr. *gumnos*, naked] *comb* naked; stripped; bare (gymnoblastic, gymnocarpous)

gyn-, gyno- [Gr. *gune*, female] **1.** *comb* woman; female (gynarchy); **2.** ovary; pistil (gynophore). *Also* **-gynia** (polygynia), **-gynic** (androgynic), **-gynist** (philogynist), **-gynous** (polygynous), and **-gyny** (monogyny)

gynandro- [Gr. *gune*, female + *aner*, male] *comb* of uncertain sex (gynandrosporous, gynandromorphism)

gyne-, gyneco-, gyneo- [Gr. *gune,* female] *comb* woman; female (gyne-phobia, gynecocracy, gyneolatry)

gypo- [Gr. *gups,* vulture] *base* vulture (Gypogeranus, Gypohierax)

-gypso- [Gr. *gupsos,* chalk, gypsum] *base* chalk (gypsiferous, gypsophila)

gyral- [Gr. *gyraleos,* rounded] *base* circle (gyral, gyrally)

gyro- [Gr. *guros,* circle] **1.** *comb* gyrating (gyroscope); **2.** spiral (gyroidal); **3.** gyroscope (gyrocompass)

gyroso- [Gr. *guros,* circle] *comb* marked with wavy lines (gyroso-labyrin-thiform, gyroso-rugose)

H

haben- [L. *habena,* thong, strap, strip] *base* resembling a thong (habena, habennula)

habent- [L. *habentia,* possessions] *base* possessing (non-habence)

habenul- [*habenula,* strip of diseased flesh] *base* small strip (habenula, habenular)

habil- [L. *habilis,* suitable, fit] **1.** *base* ability; equipped (rehabilitate); **2.** clothing (habiliments)

habilit- [L. *habilitas,* aptitude] *base* qualified (habilitate, habilitation)

habit- [L. *habitus,* condition, state] *base* accustomed (habituate, habituation)

habitat- [L. *habitation,* dwelling] *base* dwelling (habitation, habitative)

habitud- [L. *habitudo,* condition] *base* disposition (habitude, habitudinal)

-habro- [Gr. *habros,* graceful, delicate] *base* graceful; delicate (habroneme, habroreme)

-hadro- [Gr. *hadros,* stout, bulky] *base* thick (hadrosaur, Hadrosaurus)

haema- *see* **hema-**

haeret- *see* **heret-**

hagi-, hagio- [Gr. *hagios,* holy] *comb* saintly; holy (hagiheroical, hagiology)

halcyon- [Gr. *alkon,* kingfisher] *base* kingfisher (halcyoneum, halcyonine)

-hale [L. *halare,* to breathe] *base* breath; vapor (exhale, inhalation)

-halec- [NL *halec,* herring] *base* herring (halecoid, halecomorphic)

hali- [Gr. *hals,* the sea] *base* sea (hali-chondroid, Halicore)

-halieut- [Gr. *halieuein,* to fish] *base* fishing (halieutical, halieutics)

-halit- [L. *halare,* to breathe] *base* breath; vapor (halitosis, halitous)

halluc- [ML *hallux* < *hallus,* thumb + *hallex,* big toe] *base* toe (hallucal, hallucar)

halo- [Gr. *hals,* sea] **1.** *comb* of the sea (halosaurian); **2.** of salt (halophyte); **3.** of halogen (halogenous)

-ham-/hamat- [L. *hamus,* hook] *base* hook (hamated, hamulate)

hama- [Gr. *hama,* together with] *comb* together with; at the same time; united (hamadryad, hamarchy)

-hamart- [Gr. *hamartia,* error, sin] **1.** *base* sin (hamartiology); **2.** corporal defect (hamartoma)

hand- [AS *hentan,* hand] *comb* hand: of/with/by/for (handbell, handcuff)

-hapal- [Gr. *hapalos,* soft to the touch] *base* soft (Hapalidae, hapalote)

hapax- [Gr. *hapax,* once only] *comb* single instance (hapax legomenon, hapax legomena)

haph- [Gr. *hapalos,* soft to the touch] *base* touch (haphalgesia)

haplo- [Gr. *haplous,* single] *comb* one-fold; single (haplodont, haplography)

hapt-, hapto-[1] [Gr. *haptesthai,* to touch] *comb* touch; sensation (haptics, haptotaxis)

-hapto-[2] [Gr. *haptein,* to fasten] *base* fasten; combine (haptophore, haptotropism)

harengi- [NL *harengus,* herring] *comb* herring (harrengiform)

hariol- [L. *hariolatio*, foretelling] *base* divination (hariolate, hariolation). *Also see* "Divination" in Part III

harmat- [Gr. *harma*, war chariot] *base* car; chariot (harmatian)

harmon- [Gr. *harmonia*, joining, concord] *base* congruous (harmonization, harmony)

harpact- [Gr. *harpaktikos*, rapacious] *base* crustacean (harpacticid, harpacticoid)

harpag- [Gr. *harpage*, hook, rake] *base* hook or grapple (harpagon, Harpa-gus)

harpax- [Gr. *harpactor*, robber] *base* robber (Harpactor, harpaxophobia)

harusp- [L. *haruspex*, soothsayer] *base* divination by entrails (haruspication, haruspicy)

-hastato-, hasti- [L. *hasta*, spear] *comb* spear (hastato-lanceolate; hastiform)

-haur-, -haust- [L. *haurire*, to draw water] *base* draw (forth); drain; suck (exhauriate, haustellum)

-headed [AS *heafala*, head] **1.** *comb* having a ___ head (clearheaded); **2.** having ___ heads (two-headed)

heauto- [Gr. *heautou*, of himself] *comb* of oneself (heautomorphism, heautophony)

hebdom- [Gr. *hebdomas*, week] *base* week; seven days (hebdomadal, hebdomadary)

hebe- [Gr. *hebe*, pubescent] *comb* pubescent (hebegynous, hebepetalous)

-hebet- [L. *hebes*, blunt, sluggish] *base* dull; blunt (hebetude, hebetudinous)

Hebraico- [Gr. *Hebraios*, Hebrew] *comb* Hebrew (Hebraico-Germanic, Hebraico-Hibernian)

hecato-, hecto- [Gr. *hecato*, one hundred] *comb* one hundred (hecatophyllous, hectoliter). *Also* **hekto-** (hektograph)

hecatonicosa- [Gr. *hecato*, 100 + *icosa*, 20] *comb* one hundred twenty (hecatonicosachoron)

-heder- [L. *hedera*, ivy] *base* ivy (hederaceous, hederal)

-hedon- [Gr. *hedone*, delight] *base* pleasure (anhedonia, hedonist)

-hedral, -hedron, -hedry [Gr. *hedron*, -sided] *comb* geometric figure with x number of surfaces (hexahedral, hexahedron, hemihedry)

hedro- [Gr. *hedra*, anus] *comb* anus (hedratresia, hedrocele)

-hedy- [Gr. *hedus*, sweet] *base* sweet, pleasant (hedychium, hedyphane)

hegemon- [Gr. *hegemon*, leader, guide] *base* leader; chief (hegemonic, hegemony)

-hekisto- [Gr. *hekistos*, least, worst] *base* smallest (hekistotherm, hekisthothermic)

helc- [Gr. *helktikos*, fit for drawing] *base* draw (helctic, helctical)

helco- [Gr. *helkos*, ulcer] *comb* festering wound; ulcer (helcology, helcoplasty)

helici-, helico- [Gr. *heliks*, spiral] *comb* spiral-shaped (heliciform, helicopter)

helio- [Gr. *helios*, sun] *comb* sun; bright; radiant (heliocentric, heliocomete)

helminth(o)- [Gr. *helminth*, worm] *comb* [botany] worm; (helminthiasis, helminthogogue)

helo-[1] [Gr. *helos*, a nail] *comb* nail; spike (heloderma, helodont)

helo-[2] [Gr. *helos*, a marsh] *comb* marsh, bog (helobious, Helophilous)

helu- [L. *heluo*, glutton, squanderer] *base* gluttony (heluation, heluations)

helv- [L. *helvus*, yellow] *base* yellow (helvenac, helvolous)

Helvet- [L. *Helveticus*, the Swiss] *base* Swiss (Helvetian, Helvetic)

hema-, hemato-, hemo- [Gr. *haima*, blood] *comb* blood; (hemachrome, hematogenic, hemophilia). *Also* **haem-** (haemachrome)

hemangio- [Gr. *haima*, blood + *angaio*, vessel] *comb* blood vessels (hemangioblastoma, hemangiosarcoma)

hemer- [Gr. *hemera*, day] *base* day (hemeralopia, monohemerous)

hemi- [L. *hemi*, half] *pre* half (hemicardia, hemicylindrical)

hemiol- [Gr. *hemiolos*, one and a half] *base* one and a half (hemiologamous, hemiolia)

hemispherico- [F. *hemispherique*,

hemispherical] *comb* hemispheric (hemispherico-conical, hemispherico-conoid)

hendeca- [Gr. *hendeka*, eleven] *comb* eleven (hendecagon, hendecahedron)

-heno- [Gr. *eis/ev-*, one] *base* one (henotheism, henotic)

heort- [Gr. *heorte*, feast, festival] *base* feast day; festival (heortologist, heortology)

hepar- [Gr. *hepar*, liver] *base* anticoagulant (heparin, heparinize)

hepatic-, **hepato-** [Gr. *hepatikos*, of the liver] *comb* liver (hepaticostomy, hepatogastric)

hepta- [Gr. *hepta*, seven] *comb* seven (heptagon, heptasepalous)

heptakaideca- [Gr. *hepta*, seven + *kai*, and + *deka*, ten] *comb* seventeen (heptakaidecagon, heptakaidecahedron)

-herbi- [L. *herba*, grass] *base* plant (herbiferous, herbivorous)

-herco- [Gr. *herkos*, fence, barrier] *base* wall; barrier (hercogamous, hercogamy)

heredo- [L. *hereditas*, heirship] *comb* heredity (heredofamilial, heredomacular degeneration)

heresio- [Gr. *hairesis*, sect] *base* heresy (heresiologist, heresiography)

heret- [Gr. *haeretikos*, heretical] *base* heretic (heretical, hereticate)

heri- [L. *herus*, master] *base* master (hericide, herile)

heril- [L. *herilis*, of the master or mistress] *base* master (herile, herility)

-hermen- [Gr. *hermeneutes*, interpreter] *base* interpretation (hermeneutical, hermeneutics)

hermo- [Gr. *Hermes*, of Hermes] *comb* pertaining to the god Hermes (hermodactyl, hermoglyphic)

hernio- [L. *hernia*, hernia] *comb* hernia (herniated, herniotomy)

herp- [Gr. *herpes*, shingles] *base* shingles (herpes, herpetic)

herpeti-, **herpeto-** [Gr. *herpeton*, reptile, snake] *comb* reptile (herpetiform, herpetology)

-hesper- [L. *Hesperus*, evening star]

base west, evening (hesperanopia, Hesperian)

-hesperid- [Gr. *Hesperides*, nymphs who guarded the golden apples] *base* fleshy fruit with a leathery rind—orange, lemon, etc. (hesperidin, hesperidium)

-hesson- [Gr. *hesson*, less] *base* less; inferior (hessonite)

-hestern- [L. *hesternus*, of yesterday] *base* yesterday (hestern, hesternal)

hestho- [Gr. *hesthes*. clothing] *base* clothing; dress (hesthogenous)

hesy- [Gr. *hesu*, quiet] *base* still; quiet (Hesychasm, hesychastic)

hetaero- [Gr. *hetaira*, female companion] *base* companion; courtesan (hetaerism, hetaerocrasy)

hetero- [Gr. *heteros*, other, different] *comb* other; another; different (heteradenic, heterosexual)

hetto- [Gr. *hetton*, less] *comb* slight, less (hettocyrtosis)

-heur- [Gr. *heuretikos*, inventive] *base* discover; invent (heuretic, heuristic)

hexa- [Gr. *heks*, six] *comb* six (hexad, hexameter)

hexaconta- [Gr. *heksenta*, sixty] *comb* sixty (hexacontagon, hexacontahedron)

hexacosi- [Gr. *heksacosia*, 600] *comb* six hundred (hexacosichora, hexacosichoron)

hexadeca-, **hexakaideca-** [Gr. *heks*, six + *deka*, ten] *comb* sixteen (hexadecachoron, hexakaidecahedron)

hexakis- [Gr. *heksakis*, six times] *comb* six times (hexakisoctahedron, hexakistetrahedron)

hexametro- [Gr. *heks*, six + *metron*, measure] *comb* hexameter (hexametrographer, hexametromania)

-hexi- [Gr. *hekhein*, be in a given state] *base* habit; behavior (hexiological, hexiology)

hibern- [L. *hibernus*, of winter] *base* winter (hibernal, hibernation)

Hiberno- [L. *Hibernia*, Ireland] *comb* Irish (Hiberno-Celtic, Hibernology)

-hidro- [Gr. *hidrosis*, sweat] *base* sweat; (anhidrosis, hidrotic)

hiem- [L. *hiems*, winter] *base* winter (hiemal, hiemation)

hieraco- [Gr. *hieraks*, hawk, falcon] *comb* hawk (hieracosophic, hieracosphinx)

hiero- [Gr. *hiero*, sacred] *comb* holy; consecrated; sacred (hierocracy, hierophobia)

hilar- [Gr. *hilaros*, cheerful, jovial] *base* jocular (hilarious, hilarity)

hilasm- [Gr. *hilasmos*, means of appeasing] *base* propitiatory (hilasm, hilasmic)

Himalo- [Sansk. *hima*, snow + *alaya*, abode] *comb.* Himalaya plus (Himalo-Chinese, Himalo-Tibetan)

-himant- [Gr. *himas*, thong] *base* strap; thong (Himanthalia, Himantopus)

hind- [Goth. *hinduma*, posterior] *comb* rear; following (hindbrain, hindmost)

hinn- [L. *hinnere*, to neigh] *base* neigh (hinniate, hinnible)

hippo-, -hippus [Gr. *hippos*, horse] *comb* horse (hippocrepian, eohippus)

hippocamp- [Gr. *hippokampos*, mythical sea monster with a horse's body and a fish's tail] *base* seahorse (hippocampine, hippocampus)

hippocrepi- [Gr. *hippos*, horse + *krepis*, shoe, boot] *base* horseshoe (hippocrepian, hippocrepiform)

hippogloss- [Gr. *hippos*, horse + *glossa*, tongue] *base* halibut, flounder (Hippoglossinae, hippoglossoid)

hippur- [Gr. *hippouris*, horsetail] *base* horse (hippuric acid, hippurid)

-hircin- [L. *hircus*, goat] *base* goat (hircine, hircinous)

-hirmo- [Gr. *hermos*, connection, series] *base* series; connection (hirmologion)

hirr- [L. *hirrire*, to snarl] *base* snarling; trilling (hirrient)

hirsuto- [L. *hirsutus*, shaggy] *comb* having hair of a certain color or type (hirsuto-castaneous, hirsuto-rufus)

-hirudin- [NL *hirudo*, leech] *base* leech (hirudiniculture, hirudinid)

-hirund- [L. *hirundo*, swallow] *base* swallow; martin (hirundine, Hirundo)

hisc- [L. *hiscere*, to gape, open] *base* split open (dehisce, dehiscing)

Hispano- [L. *Hispanicus*, Spanish] *comb* Spanish (Hispano-American, Hispano-Italian)

-hispid- [L. *hispidus*, rough, shaggy] *base* shaggy; hairy (hispidating, hispidulous)

histio-, histo- [Gr. *histos*, web, tissue] *comb* tissue (histiocytoma, histology)

historico- [Gr. *historikos*, of history] *comb* historical (historico-geographical, historico-tropological)

-histrion- [L. *histrio*, stage player] *base* stage-player (histrionically, histrionics)

-hodiern- [L. *hodiernus*, of this day] *base* today (hodiern, hodiernal)

hodo- [Gr. *hodos*, way] *comb* way; road (hodograph, hodometer). *See* **odo-**

-holco- [Gr. *holkos*, furrow, track] *base* furrow (holcodont, Holcus)

holo- [Gr. *holos*, entire] *comb* complete; entire; whole; (holarthritis, holograph)

hom- [L. *homo*, human] *base* humankind (homicide, hominid)

homalo-, homolo- [Gr. *homalos*, even] *comb* even; regular; level; ordinary (homalographic, homologous)

-homar- [ML. *Homarus*, lobster] *base* lobster (Homaridae, homarine)

homeo- [Gr. *homoios*, like] *comb* similar; like (homeomorphism, homeoplastic)

homichlo- [Gr. *homikhle*, fog] *base* cloud; fog; dimness (homichlomania, homichlophobia)

homil- [Gr. *homilia*, instruction, lecture] *base* sermon (homiletics, homily)

homin- [L. *homo*, human] *base* humankind (hominiform, hominivorous)

homo- [Gr. *homos*, same] *comb* same; equal (homocarpous, homochromous)

homoeo-, homoio- [Gr. *hoimoios*, like] *comb* similar; like (homoeodont, homoiothermal)

homolo- [Gr. *homologos*, agreeing] *comb* corresponding; assenting (homologous, homolographic). *See* **homalo-**

-hood [Dan. *-hed*, quality, condition] **1.** *suf* quality; character; state; condition (childhood); **2.** whole group of ___ (brotherhood)

hoplo- [Gr. *hoplon*, large shield] *comb* weapon; armor (Hoplocephalus, hoplophorous)

-horde- [L. *hordeum*, barley] *base* barley (hordeaceous, Hordeum)

horizo- [Gr. *horizon*, horizon] *comb* horizon (horizocardia)

horm- [Gr. *hormaein*, to urge on] *base* urge; impel (hormetic, hormetically)

hormo- [Gr. *hormos*, cord, chain, necklace] *base* chainlike (hormogonium, hormogonous)

horo- [L. *hora*, hour, season] *comb* hour; time; season (horology, horoscope)

horr- [L. *horrescere*, to bristle] *base* standing on end (horrent, horrescent)

-hort- [L. *hortari*, encourage] *base* urge; encourage (exhortation, hortatory)

-horti- [L. *hortus*, garden] *base* garden (horticulture, horticulturist)

hosp- [L. *hospes*, host] *base* host (hospitable, hospitality)

-hum- [L. *humus*, ground] *base* ground (exhumation, posthumous)

humano- [L. *humanus*, human] *comb* human and (humano-solar, humano-taurine)

-humect- [L. *humectus*, moist] *base* moist; wet (humectant, humectation)

humero- [L. *humerus*, shoulder] *comb* shoulder; upper arm (humero-cubital, humeroradial)

hyalo- [Gr. *hualos*, glass] *comb* [chemistry] transparent; glassy (hyaline, hyalophane)

-hybo- [Gr. *hubos*, humpbacked] *base* hump (hybodont, Hybodontes)

-hydno- [Gr. *hudnon*, truffle] *base* truffle (hydnocarpous, Hydnum)

hydraulico- [Gr. *hudraulos*, water pipe] *comb* hydraulic (hydraulico-pneumatical, hydraulicostatics)

-hydric [Gr. *hudor*, water] *comb* the presence of x number of hydroxyl radicals or replaceable hydrogen atoms (chlorohydric, monohydric)

hydro- [Gr. *hudor*, water] 1. *comb* water (hydrometer); 2. [chemistry] hydrogen (hydrocyanic)

hydroxy- [*hydro* + *oxygen*] *comb* hydroxyl group (hydroxy-benzene, hydroxyurea)

hyeto- [Gr. *huetos*, rain] *comb* rain; rainfall (hyetal, hyetograph)

hygeio-, hygien- [Gr. *hugeia*, health] *comb* health; hygiene (hygeiolatry, hygienist)

hygro- [Gr. *hugros*, wet] *comb* wet; moisture (hygrology, hygrometer)

hylac- [Gr. *hulaktein*, to bark] *base* barking (hylactic, hylactism)

hylaeo- [Gr. *hulaios*, of wood or forest] *comb* forest (hylaeosaurus)

hyle-, hylo- [Gr. *hule*, wood] 1. *comb* wood (hylephobia, hylophagous); 2. matter (hylozoism)

hylobat- [Gr. *hulobates*, one who haunts the woods] *base* gibbon (Hylobates, hylobatine)

hymeno- [Gr. *Humen*, god of marriage] *comb* membrane (hymeneal, hymenogeny)

hyo- [shape of Gr. letter *upsilon*] *comb* hyoid bone (hyoglossal, hyoideal)

hyos- [Gr. *hus*, hog] *base* hog (hyoscyamine, Hyoscyamus)

hypegia- [Gr. *hupenguos*, liable to be called to account] *base* responsibility (hypegiaphobia)

hypengy- [Gr. *hupenguos*, liable to be called to account] *base* responsibility (hypengiomania, hypengyophobia)

hyper- [Gr. *huper*, over, above] 1. *pre* over; above; excessive (hypercritical); 2. [chemistry] maximum (hyperoxide)

-hypho- [Gr. *huphe*, web, weaving] *base* web, tissue (hyphodrome, hyphomycetes)

hypno- [Gr. *hupnos*, sleep] *comb* sleep; hypnotism (hypnophobia, hypnotic)

hypo- [Gr. *hupo*, under] 1. *pre* under; below (hypodermic); 2. less than (hypotaxis); 3. [chemistry] having a lower state of oxidation (hypophosphorous)

hypocrater- [Gr. *hupo*, under + *krater*, mixing vessel] *base* tray (hypocrateriform, hypocraterimorphous)

hypsi-, hypso- [Gr. *hupsi*, on high]

comb high; height (hypsicephalic, hypsodont)

hyraci-, hyraco- [Gr. *huraks*, shrew-mouse] *comb* hyrax: rabbit-like quadruped (hyraciform, hyracodont)

hystero-[1] [Gr. *hustera*, uterus] **1.** *comb* uterus; womb (hysterodynia); **2.** hysteria (hysteroepilepsy)

hystero-[2] [Gr. *husteros*, later] *comb* later; inferior (hysteresis, hystero-genetic)

-hystric- [L. *hystrix*, porcupine] *base* porcupine, hedgehog (hystriciasis, histricine)

I

-i [L. pl. suf. *-i*] *suf* plural ending (alumni, foci)

-ia [L. nom. suf. *-ia*] **1.** *suf* country names (India); **2.** disease names (pneumonia); **3.** festival names (Lupercalia); **4.** Gk/Lat. words (militia); **5.** plurals > Gk/Lat. (genitalia); **6.** [biology] class names (Reptilia); **7.** [botany] some generic plant names (zinnia); **8.** [chemistry] alkaloid names (strychnia)

-ial [L. suf. *-ialis*] *suf* of; pertaining to (imperial, magisterial)

iamb- [Gr. *iaptein*, to assail in words] *base* metrical foot (iambic, iambist)

-ian [L. suf. *-ianus*] *suf* **1.** relating to (Bostonian) **2.** relating to, resembling (academician)

-iana *see* **-ana**

ianth- [Gr. *ianthus*, violet-colored] *base* violet (Ianthina, ianthine)

-iasis [Gr. suf. *-iasis*] **1.** *comb* process; condition; **2.** morbid condition (hypochondriasis, psoriasis)

iasp- [Gr. *iaspis*, jasper] *base* jasper (jasper, jasper-ware)

-iatrics, -iatrist, iatro-, -iatry [Gr. *iatrikos*, of physicians] *comb* medical treatment (pediatrics, podiatrist, iatrophysical, psychiatry)

Ibero- [Gr. *Iberia*, Spain] *comb* Spanish (Iberian, Ibero-French)

-ibility, -ible, -ibly [L. suf.] *suf* capable of (sensibility, sensible, visibly)

-ic [L. suf. *-icus*] **1.** *suf* having to do with; of (volcanic); **2.** like; having the nature of; characteristic of (angelic); **3.**

produced by; caused by (symphonic); **4.** made up of; containing; consisting of; (dactylic); **5.** [chemistry] higher valence than is indicated by the suffix **-ous** (nitric); **6.** nouns from adjectives; (magic)

-ical, -ically [L. suf. *-ic* + *-al*] *suf* adjective/adverb forms parallel to **-ic** (angelical, magically)

-ice[1] [< L. suf. *-itius*] *suf* condition; state; quality of; action (malice, service)

-ice[2] *suf* feminine ending (mediatrice)

-ichno [Gr. *ikhnos*, track] *comb* [paleontology] track; trace; posture; position (ichnolite, ichnology)

ichnograph- [Gr. *ichnographia*, ground plan] *base* ground plan (ichnographic, ichnography)

ichor- [Gr. *ikhor*, juice] *comb* serous fluid (ichorremia, ichorose)

ichthyo- [Gr. *ikhthus*, fish] *comb* fish; fishlike (ichthyologist, ichthyophagous)

-ician [OF suf. *-icien*] *suf* practitioner; specialist (beautician, logician)

-icity [Fr. suf. *-icite*] *suf* nouns formed from **-ic** adjectives (authenticity, publicity)

icono- [Gr. *eikon*, image] *comb* figure; likeness; image (iconograph, iconostasis)

icosa-, icosi- [Gr. *eikosi*, twenty] *comb* [mathematics/botany] twenty (icosahedron, icositetrahedron: 24)

-ics [Gr. suf. *-ikos*] **1.** *suf* art; science (mathematics); **2.** activities; practice; properties; system (statistics)

ict- [L. *ictus*, blow, strike] *base* strike (ictic, ictus)

icter-¹, ictero- [Gr. *ikteros*, jaundice] *comb* yellow; jaundice (icteric, icteroanemia)

icter-² [Gr. *ikteros*, bird that supposedly cured jaundice] *base* blackbird; bobolink; meadowlark; oriole (Icteridae, icterine)

-id¹ [NL. suf. *-ides*] **1.** *suf* belonging to; connected with (Aeneid); **2.** animal group name (arachnid); **3.** meteor names (Perseid)

-id² [L. suf. *-idus*] *suf* filled with (morbid, vivid)

-ida [L. suf. *-ida*] *suf* [zoology] order/class names (Annelida, Acarida)

-idae [Gr. suf. *-idai*] *suf* [zoology] family names (Felidae, Laniadae)

-idan [L. suf. *-id* + *-an*] *suf* [zoology] of or pertaining to (arachnidan, araneidan)

-ide [< ox*ide*] *suf* [chemistry] compound names (cyanide, chloride)

idea-, ideo- [Gr. *idea*, form, idea] *comb* idea; creation (ideation, ideology)

-ides [Gr. suf. *-ides*] *suf* [science] name endings (cantharides)

-idine [L. suf. *-id* + *-ine*] *suf* chemical compound related to another (pyridine, toluidine)

idio- [Gr. *idios*, one's own] *comb* one's own; distinct; personal (idiocrasy, idiomorphic)

-idion [Gr. dim. suf. *-idion*] *suf* diminutive (enchiridion, pyramidion)

idiot- [Gr. *idiotikos*, unskilled, ignorant] *base* ignorant (idiocy, idiotic)

-idium [< Gr. dim. suf. *-idion*] *suf* [science] diminutive (aecidium, phyllidium)

idolo- [Gr. *eidolon*, idol] *comb* idol (idoloclast, idolomancy)

idon- [L. *idoneus*, fit] *base* suitable (idoneal, idoneus)

-ie [ME dim. suf. *-ie*] *suf* diminutive (doggie, sweetie)

-ier [ME suf. *-ier*] *suf* person concerned with (courier, glazier)

-iferous *see* -ferous

-ific *see* -fic

-ification *see* -fication

-iformes [L. sci. order suf. *-iformes*] *suf* [zoology] names: having the form of (Passeriformes, Pelicaniformes)

-ify *see* -fy

ignar- [L. *ignarus*, unacquainted with, unaware] *base* ignorant (ignaro)

ignav- [L. *ignavus*, slothful] *base* sluggish (ignave, ignavy)

igneo- [L. *igneus*, of fire] *comb* fire (igneo-aqueous, igneo-metamorphic)

ignesc- [L. *ignescere*, to burn] *base* burst in flames (ignescent, ignescents)

igni- [L. *ignis*, fire] *base* fire (igniferous, ignipuncture)

il- *see* in-

-il, -ile [L. suf. *-ilis*] *suf* like; having to do with; suitable for (civil, docile)

ilast- [Gr. *ilasseai*, to appease] *base* propitiatory, conciliatory (ilastic, ilastical)

ileo-, ilio- [NL *ilium*, ilium] **1.** *comb* of the ileum (ileostomy); **2.** ileac plus (iliosacral)

-ilia [L. suf. *-ilius*] *suf* able to be ___ (juvenilia, memorabilia)

ilic- [L. *ilex/ilic-*, holm oak, holly] *base* holly (ilicate, ilicic)

-ility [L. suf. *-ilitas*] *suf* quality; condition (sensibility)

-illa [L. dim. suf. *-illus*] *suf* diminutive (banderilla, cedilla)

illaes- [L. *illaesus*, unhurt, unharmed] *base* unhurt (illaese, illaesive)

illat- [L. *illation*, a carrying or bringing in] *base* inference (illation, illative)

illeceb- [L. *illecebra*, enticement, lure] *base* alluring (illecebration, illecebrous)

-illo [L. dim. suf. *-illus*] *suf* diminutive (cigarillo, lapillo)

illyngo- [Gr. *illingos*, spinning around] *base* vertigo (illyngomania, illyngophobia)

im- *see* in-

-im [Heb. plu. suf. *-im*] *suf* Hebrew plural ending (cherubim, seraphim)

imbri- [L. *imber/imbr-*, shower] *base* rain; rain tile (imbriferous, imbricated)

imbricato- [L. *imbricatus*, covered with gutter tiles] *comb* composed of parts which overlap like tiles (imbrication, imbricato-granulous)

immer- [L. *immerens*, undeserving] *base* lacking merit (immerit, immeritorious)

immuno- [L. *immunis*, exempt from public service or charges] *comb* resistant to disease; immune (immunochemistry, immunotherapy)

immut- [L. *im-*, privative + *mutabilis*, changeable] *base* unalterable (immutability, immutable)

impari- [L. *impar*, unequal] *comb* odd-numbered; unpaired (imparipinnate, imparisyllabic)

imped- [L. *impedire*, to hinder] *base* snare; delay (impedance, impediment)

impens- [L. *impensa*, outlay, cost] *base* pay (impensible, impensively)

imper- [L. *imperare*, to command] *base* power; authority (imperative, imperial)

impet- [L. *impetus*, a rushing upon] *base* rush; assault (impetuosity, impetus)

impigrit- [L. *impigritas*, activity, indefatigableness] *base* diligence (impigrity, impigrous)

impud- [L. *impudicitia*, lewdness] *base* immodesty (impudicity, impudicous)

impuls- [L. *impulsus*, a pushing against] *base* pressure (impulse, impulsive)

in-[1] [L. *in*, into; *in*, not] **1.** *pre* within; inside; into; toward (inbreed); **2.** intensifier (instigate); **3.** not; without (insane). NOTE: **in-** can change to: **il-** (illuminate); **im-** (impossible); **ir-** (irrigate)

-in[2] [L. suf. *-inus*] *suf* [chemistry] names of neutral substances (albumin, insulin)

-ina [L. fem. suf. *-ina*] **1.** *suf* feminine ending (ballerina); **2.** characterized by (sonatina); **3.** [biology] name endings (Nemertina)

-inae [L. pl. suf. *-inae*] *suf* names of subfamilies of animals (Caninae, Felinae)

inan- [L. *inanis*, void] *base* empty; foolish (inane, inanity)

inaug- [L. *inaugurare*, to consecrate after checking omens] *base* start, install (inaugural, inaugurate)

incess- [L. *in*, privative + *cessare*, to cease] *base* unceasing (incessable, incessant)

incic- [L. *incicur*, wild] *base* wild (incicurable, incicuration)

incip- [L. *in*, on + *capere*, to take] *base* take in hand; begin (incipience, incipient)

incisi-, inciso- [L. *incisio*, a cutting into] *comb* cut into (incisiform, inciso-lobate)

inconcin- [L. *inconcinnus*, awkward] *base* clumsy (inconcinnity, inconcinnous)

increp- [L. *in*, on + *crepare*, make a noise] *base* scold; rebuke (increpation, increpatory)

incudo- [L. *incus*, anvil] *comb* small bone of the ear (incudo-malleal, incudo-stapidial)

-indag- [L. *indagare*, to search] *base* trace; search; investigate (indagation, indigative)

indi-, indo-[1] [Gr. *indikon*, indigo] *comb* indigo; metallic violet-purple (indirubin, indophenol)

indig- [L. *indigus*, in need] *base* destitute (indigence, indigent)

-indigen- [LL *indigenus*, native] *base* native (indigenous, indigenously)

Indo-[2] [Gr. *Indo*, Indian] *comb* India (Indo-Chinese, Indo-Malayan)

inducto- [L. *in*, into + *ducere*, to lead] *comb* electrical induction (inductometer, inductoscope)

-ine [L. suf. *-inus*] **1.** *suf* of; like; pertaining to; characterized by (canine); **2.** feminine ending (heroine); **3.** abstract noun ending (discipline); **4.** commercial names (Vaseline); **5.** [chemistry] names of: halogens (iodine); alkaloid/nitrogen bases (morphine); hydrides (stibine); **6.** of the nature of (crystalline)

inebr- [L. *in*, into + *ebriare*, to make drunk] *base* drunk (inebriant, inebriated)

inequi- [L. *in*, privative + *aequus*,

even] *comb* unequal (inequidistant, inequilobate)

infern- [L. *infernus*, underground] *base* underworld; hell (infernal, inferno)

infero- [L. *inferus*, low] *comb* underneath; low; below (inferolateral, inferoposterior)

infra- [L. *infra*, below] *pre* below; beneath (infrabuccal, infrastructure)

infundib- [L. *infundibulum*, funnel] *base* funnel (infundibulate, infundibuliform)

-ing [OE suf. *-ing*] **1.** *suf* belonging to; descended from (atheling); **2.** present participle (shifting sand); **3.** act of; process (talking); **4.** produced by (painting); **5.** material for (roofing)

ingen- [L. *ingenium*, natural capacity, gifted] *base* versatile; clever (ingenious, ingenuity)

ingress- [L. *ingressus*, a going into] *base* enter (ingress, ingressive)

inguino- [L. *inguinalis*, of the groin] *comb* inguinal; groin (inguino-femoral, inguino-scrotal)

-ini [NL. suf. *-ini*] *suf* [zoology] group names (Acanthurini, Salmonini)

inimic- [L. *inimicus*, enemy] *base* hostile (inimical, inimicitous)

iniq- [L. *iniquitas*, injustice] *base* bad; uneven (iniquitous, iniquity)

init- [L. *initium*, beginning] *base* begin; enter (initialize, initiate)

innato- [L. *innatus*, inborn] *comb* inborn; natural (innato-erumpent, innato-sessile)

ino- [Gr. *iz/inos*, fiber] *comb* fiber; fibrous growth (inocarpin, inolith)

inquis- *see* **-quire**

insecti-, insecto- [L. *insectum*, insect] *comb* bug (insecticide, insectology)

insul- [L. *insula*, island] *base* island (insularity, insulation)

insuls- [L.*insulsus*, tasteless] *base* insipid, stupid (insulse, insulsity)

integri-/integro- [L. *integer*, whole] *comb* whole (integripallial, integropalliate)

inter- [L. *inter*, between] **1.** *comb* between; among (interchange); **2.**

mutual; reciprocal; with each other; (interact)

interno-, intero- [L. *internus*, inner] *comb* internal; inside; within (internomedial, interoceptive)

intestini, intestino- [L. *intestinum*, intestine] *comb* intestine (intestiniform, intestino-vesical)

intra- [L. *intra*, within] *comb* within; inside (intracellular, intramural)

intrit- [L. *intrita*, a mash or paste of lime, clay, etc.] *base* paste (intrite)

intro- [L. *intro*, within] *comb* into; within; inward (introgression, introvert)

intubac- [L. *intubaceous*, pert. to endive] *base* endive (intubaceous)

intyb- [Gr. *intybos*, endive] *base* endive (intybe, intybous)

inund- [L. *inundatus*, inumdated] *base* flood; overflow (inundate, inundation)

inutil- [L. *inutilis*, useless] *base* useless (inutile, inutility)

-invid- [L. *invidia*, envy] *base* envy; resentment (invidious, invidiously)

involucr- [L. *involvere*, wrap or roll up] *base* wrapped (involucral, involucriform)

-involver- [L. *involvere*, wrap or roll up] *base* wrapping; covering (involveriform)

iodi-, iodo- [Gr. *iodes*, like a violet] *comb* iodine (iodiform, iodoform)

-ion [L. suf. *-ion-*] **1.** *suf* act; process (solution); **2.** state; condition (ambition)

iono-, ionto- [Gr. *ion*, something that goes] *comb* ion (ionophore, iontophoresis)

-ior [ME suf. *-eor*] **1.** *suf* one who ___ (warrior); **2.** comparative form (inferior)

-ious [L. suf. *-ius*] *suf* characterized by; having (ambitious, contentious)

ipse- [L. *ipse*, self] *base* self (ipseity, ipsilateral)

ir- *see* **in-**

-ira-, -irasc- [L. *ira*, anger] *base* hatred; anger (irate, irascible)

-iren- [Gr. *eirene*, peace] *base* peace (irenic, irenics)

irid-, iris- [Gr. *iris*, rainbow] *base* rainbow (iridial, iridescence, irisopsia)

iridico-, iridio- [Gr. *iris, irid-* rainbow] *comb* iridium (iridico-potassic, iridio-cyanide)

irido- [NL *iris, irid-,* iris] *comb* iris (iridectomy, iridomotor)

isch-, ischur- [Gr. *ischein*, to hold] *comb* restriction; deficiency (ischemia, ischuretic)

ischi-, ischio- [Gr. *ischiadikos*, of the hips] *comb* hip; ischium (ischialgia, ischiocapsular)

-ise [var. of *-ize* < L. *-itius*] *suf* quality; condition; function (franchise, merchandise)

-ish [OE suf. *-isc*] **1.** *suf* national connection (Irish); **2.** characteristic of; like (devilish); **3.** tending to (bookish); **4.** somewhat; rather (whitish); **5.** approximately (thirty-ish)

-isk [Gr. suf. *-iskos*] *suf* diminutive (asterisk, obelisk)

-ism [Gr. suf. *-ismos*] **1.** *suf* act; result of; practice (terrorism); **2.** condition of being (barbarism); **3.** qualities characteristic of; conduct characteristic of; (patriotism); **4.** doctrine; theory; principle of (socialism); **5.** devotion to (nationalism); **6.** instance of; example of; peculiarity of (Gallicism); **7.** abnormal condition caused by __ (alcoholism)

-ismus [L. suf. *-ismus*] *suf* spasm; contraction (strabismus, vaginismus). *See* **-esmus**

iso- [Gr. *iso*, equal] *comb* equality; identity; similarity (isochronal, isodactylous)

isoptero- [Gr. *iso*, equal + *pteron*, wing] *base* termite; white ant (Isoptera, isopterous)

-ist [Gr. suf. *-istes*] *suf* practitioner; believer; person skilled in (lobbyist, theorist)

isthm- [Gr. *isthmos*, narrow passage] *base* narrow passage; neck of land (isthmian, isthmiate)

-istic, -istical [suf. *-ist* + *-ic* + *-al*] *suf* tending towards; acting like (communistic, egotistical)

istiophor- [Gr. *istiov*, sail + *phoros*, bearing] *base* marlin; sailfish (Istiophoridae, istiophorid)

Italo- [L. *Italia*, Italy] *comb* Italy (Italo-Byzantine, Italophile)

-ite [Gr. suf. *-ites*] **1.** *suf* native; inhabitant; citizen of (Brooklynite); **2.** adherent; believer (Benthamite); **3.** manufactured product (dynamite); **4.** fossil (coprolite); **5.** bodily organ part (somite); **6.** salt or ester of an acid ending in *-ous* (nitrite); **7.** mineral or rock (anthracite)

itea- [Gr. *itea*, willow] *comb* willow tree (Itea, iteatic)

-iter- [L. *iterare*, to repeat] *base* repeat (iteration, reiterate)

ithy- [Gr. *ithus*, straight] *comb* erect; straight (ithyphallian, ithyphallic)

-itic [Gr. suf. *-ites* + *-ic*] *suf* relating to; of (dendritic, syphilitic)

-itiner- [L. *itinerari*, go on a journey] *base* journey (itinerant, itinerary)

-ition *see* **-ation**

-itious [L. suf. *-icius*] *suf* having the nature of; characterized by (ambitious, fictitious)

-itis [Gr. suf. *-itis*, now used to mean affliction] *suf* inflammation; disease (appendicitis, bronchitis)

-itive *see* **-ative**

-itol [suf. *-ite* + *ol*] *suf* Used to form the names of polyhydric alcohols other than di- or trihydric alcohols (dulcitol, mannitol)

-ity [L. suf. *-itas*] *suf* state; character; condition (nobility, stability)

-ium [L. suf. *-ium*] *suf* noun ending (delirium, opprobrium)

-ive [L. suf. *-ivus*] **1.** *suf* related to; belonging to; (negative); **2.** tending to (creative)

-ivus [L. suf. *-ivus*] *suf* [science] name endings (ampliativus, exfoliativus)

-ixo- [Gr. *iksos*, birdlime] *base* mistletoe; sticky or clammy like birdlime (ixia, ixolite)

ixobrych- [Gr. *iksos*, birdlime + *brukso*, eat greedily] *base* bittern (ixobrychus)

ixod- [Gr. *iksos*, birdlime + *eidos*, form] *base* tick (Ixodes, ixodicide)

-ization [suf. *-ize* + *-ation*] *suf* used to form noun from **-ize** verb (acclimatization, realization)

-ize [Gr. suf. *-izein*] **1.** *suf* cause to be or become; resemble; make (sterilize); **2.** become like (crystallize); **3.** subject to; treat with; combine with; (oxidize); **4.** engage in; act (theorize)

J

-jact-, -jacula-, -ject- [L. *jactare*, to throw, agitate] *base* hurl; throw (jactation, ejaculation, inject)

jactan- [L. *jactans*, bragging] *base* boasting (jactancy, jactant)

jaun- [OF *jaunisse*, yellowness] *base* yellow (jaundice, jaundiced)

jecor- [L. *jecur*, liver] *base* liver (jecorary, jecorin)

-jejuno- [L. *jejunus*, fasting, barren] *comb* of the jejunum (jejunocolostomy, jejunoduodenal)

-jent- [L. *jentaculum*, breakfast] *base* breakfast (jentacular, jenticulation)

-joco(s)-, -jocu(l)- [L. *jocare*, to jest] *base* joke; jest (jocosity, jocularity)

journ- [L. *diurnalis*, daily] *comb* day; daily (journalism, journalistic)

juba- [L. *juba*, mane] *base* mane (juba, jubate)

-jubil- [L. *jubilare*, shout for joy] *base* joy; elation (jubilation, jubilee)

jud- [L. *judicare*, to judge] *base* wisdom; law; justice (judiciously, judgment)

Judaeo-, Judeo- [Gr. *Ioudaia*, Judea] *comb* Jewish (Judaeophobia, Judeo-Christian)

Judaico- [Gr. *Ioudaia*, Judea] *comb* Judaic (Judaico-Christian, Judaico-Moslem)

jug- [L. *jugare*, to yoke] *base* yoke (abjugate, conjugate)

jug(it)- [L. *jugitas*, continuance, duration] *base* perpetual (jugial)

juglan- [L. *juglan*, walnut] *base* walnut (Juglandaceae, juglandaceous)

jugo-, jugulo- [L. *jugum*, yoke] *comb* neck; throat; yoke (jugo-maxillary, jugulocephalic)

-juli- [L. *iulus*, catkin] *base* catkin (julaceous, juliferous)

jument- [L. *jumentum*, beast of burden] *base* beast of burden; having a strong animal odor (jumentarious, jumentous)

jun- [L. *juvenis*, young] *base* young (junior, juniorship)

-junc- [L. *juncus*, a rush] *base* a rush (Junaceae, juncaceous)

junct- [L. *jungere*, to join] *comb* join (conjunction, juncture)

jur-, juris- [L. *jurare*, to swear] *comb* law (juridical, jurisprudence)

jurg(at)- [L. *jurgatorius*, quarrelsome] *base* rebuke (objurgation, objurgatory)

juscul- [L. *jusculum*, broth] *base* broth (Muraena jusculum)

-juss[1]- [L. *jubere*, to command] *base* command (fidejussionary, jussive)

juss-[2] [L. *jus*, broth, soup] *base* broth (jussel, jussulent)

-jut-, -juv- [L. *adjuvare*, to aid] *base* aid; help (adjutant, adjuvant)

juven- [L. *juvenis*, youth] *comb* young; immature (juvenescent, juvenile)

juxta- [L. *juxta*, near] *comb* near; beside; close by (juxtapose, juxtaposition)

K

kair- [Gr. *kairos*, right or proper time]
base fullness of time (kairos, kairine)

kaki-, kako- [Gr. *kakos*, bad] *comb* bad;
evil (kakistocracy, kakogenesis). *Also*
caco- (cacophony)

kakorrhaph- [Gr. *kakos*, bad
+ *rhaphe*, seam] *base* failure
(kakorrhaphiophobia)

-kal- [Gr. *kalos*, beautiful] *base* beautiful
(kaleidoscope, kallynteria)

kal(i)- [Ar. *qali*, potash] *comb* potassium
(kaligenous, kaliopenia)

kamp- [Gr. *kampe*, caterpillar] *base* wingless insect (campodean, lasiocampid)
Also camp-²

kar- [Gr. *karon*, caraway] *base* caraway
plant (caraway, caraway-comfit)

karm- [Sansk. *karma*, fate, desrtiny] *base*
fate (karma, karmic)

karyo- [Gr. *karuon*, nut] *comb* [biology]
nucleus (karyokinesis, karyolysis).
Also caryo- (caryopsis)

kata- *see* cata-

katheno- [Gr. *kata*, according to + *eis/
ein-*, one] *comb* each; every; one by one
(kathenotheism, kathenotheistic)

kathis- [Gr. *kathizein*, to seat] *base* sit;
seat (kathisophobia, kathismata)

kelo- [Gr. *kelis*, scar] *comb* scar (keloid,
kelotomy)

kelyph- [Gr. *keluphos*, sheath] *base* shell;
pod (kelyphite, kelyphitic)

keno- [Gr. *kainos*, empty] *comb* empty
(kenosis, kenotic)

kephalo- [Gr. *kephale*, head] *comb* head
(kephalometer, kephalotomy). *Also*
cephalo- (cephalopod)

kera-, kerato- [Gr. *keras*, horn] 1. *comb*
horn; hornlike; horny tissue; (keracele,
keratogenous); 2. cornea (keratotomy). *Also* cerato- (ceratosaur)

keraulo- [Gr. *keras*, a horn + *aulos*, a pipe,
flute] *comb* hornblower; organ stop
name (keraulophon)

kerauno- [Gr. *kerauno*, thun-
der] *comb* thunder

(keraunograph, keraunophobia). *Also*
cerauno- (ceraunoscope)

keri-, kero- [Gr. *keros*, wax] *base* wax
(keritherapy, kerosene)

kery- [Gr. *kerugma*, proclamation] *base*
proclamation; preaching (kerygma,
kerygmatic)

keto- [Ger. *keton* < acetone] *comb* ketone;
organic chemical compound (ketoaci-
dosis, ketogenesis)

kibdelo- [Gr. *kibdelos*, spurious] *base*
adulterated; spurious (kibdelophane,
kibdelo-sporangium)

kil-, kill- [Gael. *ceall*, church] *comb* cell;
church; burying place (Kilpatrick,
Kilkenny)

kilo- [Gr. *khilioi*, thousand] *comb* thousand (kilogram, kilometer)

-kin [Du. dim. suf. *-ken*] *suf* diminutive
(catkin, lambkin)

kinesi-, -kinesia, -kinesis, kineso- [Gr.
kinesis, movement] *comb* movement;
muscular activity (kinesiology, hyper-
kinesia, telekinesis, kinesodic)

-kinetic, kineto- [Gr. *kinein*, to move]
comb motion (hyperkinetic, kineto-
graph). *See* cine-

-kinin [Gr. *kinein*, set in motion] *suf*
hormone names (bradykinin, cyto-
kinin)

kino- [Gr. *kinein*, set in motion] *base*
movement; muscular activity (kinocil-
ium, kinoplasmic)

kio- [Gr. *kion*, column] *comb* uvula (kiot-
ome, kiotomy)

klepto- [Gr. *kleptein*, steal] *comb* steal
(kleptomania, kleptomaniac). *Also*
clepto- (cleptobiosis)

klino- [Gr. *klinein*, to slope] *comb* sloped;
bent (klinocephalic, klinometer). *Also*
clino- (clinograph)

klope- [Gr. *klope*, theft] *comb* steal
(klopemania, klopephobia)

kniss- [Gr. *knisa*, savor and steam of
burnt sacrifice] *base* incense (knissomancy, knissophobia)

koilo- [Gr. *koilos*, hollow] *comb* hollow (koilon, koilonychia)

koin- [Gr. *koinonia*, fellowship] *base* common (koine, koinonia). *See* **ceno-**[2]

koll(o)- [Gr. *kolla*, glue] *comb* glue (kolloxylin). *Also* **coll-** (colloblast, colloidal)

kolon- [Gr. *kolon*, colon] *comb* colon (colonitis, colonoscopy)

koloph- [Gr. *kolophon*, top, finishing touch] *base* summit, finishing touch (colophon, colophonize)

koloss- [Gr. *kolossos*, gigantic] *base* enormous (colossal, Colossus of Rhodes)

kolpo- [Gr. *kolpos*, womb, vagina] *comb* vagina (kolpalgia, kolpocele). *Also* **colpo-** (colpocele, colposcope)

koly- [Gr. *kolouo*, curtail, abridge] *comb* inhibit; restrain (kolypeptic, kolytic)

-kompo- [Gr. *kompos*, boast] *base* boasting (kompological, kompology)

koni(o)- [Gr. *konia*, dust] *comb* dust (konimeter). *Also* **conio-** (conidium, coniomycetes)

kopo- [Gr. *kopos*, fatigue] *base* exhaustion (kopophobia). *Also* **copo-** (copiopia, copodyskinesia)

kopro- [Gr. *kopros*, dung] *comb* filth; excrement (koprophilia). *See* **copro-**

-koria [Gr. *kore*, pupil] *comb* pupil of the eye (leukokoria). *Also* **-coria** (anisocoria)

koupho- [Gr. *kouphos*, light in weight] *base* light, fragile (koupholite). *Also* **coupho-** (coupholite)

krato- [Gr. *kratos*, strength] *comb* resistant, firm (kratogen, kratogenic)

krauro- [Gr. *krauros*, dry] *comb* dry (kraurosis)

kreo- [Gr. *kreas*, flesh] *comb* flesh (kreophagous). *Also* **creo-** (creophagists)

-krio- [Gr. *krio*, ram] *base* ram (krioboly). *Also* **crio-** (criocephalous, criophoric)

krymo-, kryo- *See* **crymo-**

kryo- [Gr. *kruos*, frost] *comb* frost; cold (kryometer). *Also* **cryo-** (cryobiologist, cryogen)

kud- [Gr *kudos*, praise or renown] *base* credit or congratulations (kudize, kudos)

kuttaro- [Gr. *kuttaros*, cavity] *comb* cavity (kuttarosome)

kyano- *see* **cyano-**

kylixo- [Gr. *kuliks*, cup, vase] *base* bowl (kylixes, kylixomancy)

kyma-, kymo- [Gr. *kuma*, wave] *comb* wave; (kymatism, kymograph). *Also* **cymo-** (cymophane)

kyno- [Gr. *kuon*, dog] *comb* dog (kynophagous). *Also* **cyno-** (cynocephalic, cynosure)

kypho- [Gr. *kuphosis*, hump] *comb* hump (kyphoscoliosis, kyphosis). *Also* **cypho-** (cyphonism)

-kyrio- [Gr. *kurios*, having authority] *base* authorized; proper (kyriolexy). *Also* **cyrio-** (cyriologic, cyriological)

kyto- [Gr. *kutos*, hollow] *comb* cell (kytometry). *Usually* **cyto-** (cytoblast, cytopathic)

L

-lab-[1] [L. *labare*, to totter] *base* totter; shake; weaken (labefaction, labefy)

lab-[2] [Gr *labreia*, boast] *base* gossip (lab, labbing)

labar- [Gr. *labaron*, standard] *base* banner; standard (labarum)

-labe [Gr., *lab*, to seize] *base* instrument (astrolabe, litholabe)

-labido- [Gr. *labis, labid-*, forceps] *base* forceps (labidometer, Labidura)

labil- [L. *labilis*, slippery] *base* fall, lapse (labile, lability)

labio- [L. *labium*, lip] *comb* lips, labia (labiodental, labipalpus)

-labor- [L. *labor*, toil] *base* work (laboratory, laboriousness)

labro- [Gr. *labros*, fierce, greedy] *base* greedy, furious (Labridae, Labrosaurus)

labrusc- [L. *labrusca*, wild vine] *base* wild vine (labrusca, labruscose) labrynthi-, labryntho- [Gr. *laburinthos*, labyrinth] *comb* labyrinth-like (labrynthiform, labrynthodont)

lac- [L. *lac*, milk] *base* milk; milky-white (lactation; lacteous)

-lacco- [Gr. *lakkos*, pit] *base* reservoir (laccolite, laccolithic)

-lacer- [L. *laceratos*, torn] *base* mangle (lacerable, laceration)

lacert- [L. *lacerta*, lizard] *base* lizard (lacertiform, lacertilian)

lach- [Gr. *lachanizo*, to be weak] *base* negligent (laches, lachousness)

-lachan- [Gr. *lachanon*, vegetable] *base* vegetable (lachanopolist, lachanopoll)

-lacin- [L. *lacinia*, a flap] *base* fringed; jagged (laciniform, laciniolate)

lacrim-, lacrimo- [L. *lacrima*, tear] *comb* tears; crying (lachrimation, lacrimonasal). *Also* lachrym- (lachrymose)

lacti-, lacto- [L. *lac*, milk] 1. *comb* milk (lactiflorous); 2.[chemistry] lactic acid (lactophosphate)

lactuc- [L. *lactuca*, lettuce] *base* lettuce (lactucarium, lactucic)

-lacun- [L. *lacuna*, ditch, pit] *base* cavity; hole (lacunary, lacunose)

-lacus- [L. *lacus*, lake] *base* lake; pool (lacustral, lacustrine)

ladron- [L. *latro*, robber] *base* steal (ladrone, ladronism)

laeo-, laevo- [Gr. *laios*, left] 1. *comb* on the left (laeotropic); 2. counterclockwise (laevorotation). *Also* levo- (levogyrate)

laes-/les- [L. *laesura*, hurting or injury] *base* damage (leased, lesion)

laet- [L. *laetans*, joyful] *base* cheer (elated, laetification)

-lagen- [Gr. *lagunos*, flask] *base* flask (lageniform, Lagenorhynchus)

-lagnia [Gr. *lagneia*, lust] *comb* desire; coition; fetish (algolagnia, kleptolagnia)

lago- [Gr. *lagos*, hare] *comb* [zoology] hare (lagopodus, lagotic)

-lalia [Gr. *lalein*, talk, chatter] *comb* speech disorder (coprolalia, echolalia)

lall- [L. *lallum*, lullaby] *base* childish utterance (lallate, lallation)

lalo- [Gr. *lalein*, talk, chatter] *comb* babbling; speech defect (lalopathy, lalophobia)

lamb- [L. *lambere*, lick] *base* lick (lambent, lambitive)

lamelli- [L. *lamella*, plate] *comb* plate; layer; scales (lamellibranch, lamelliform)

lamini-, lamino- [L. *lamina*, thin plate] 1. *comb* plate; layer (laminiferous); 2. blade of the tongue (laminoalveolar)

-lampad- [Gr. *lampadias*, torchbearer] *base* torch; lamp (lampadite, lampadomancy)

lampro- [Gr. *lampros*, bright] *comb* clear; distinct (lamprophony, lamprophyre)

lampyr- [Gr. *lampuris*, glow-worm] *base* firefly (lampyrid, lampyrine)

-lana- [Gr. *lenos*, wool] *base* wool (lanary, lanate). *See* lani-

lanci- [L. *lancea*, lance] *base* lance (lanceolated, lanciform)

-land [Goth. *land*, land, country] 1. *comb* a kind of land (highland); 2. territory or country (England); 3. place with a specified character (cloudland)

languid- [L. *languidus*, faint, weak] *base* weak (languid, languidly)

lani- [Gr. *lenos*, wool] *base* wool; (laniferous, lanigerous). *See* lana-

-lania- [L. *laniare*, tear, lacerate] *base* to tear; butcher (laniary, Lanius)

laniar- [L. *laniarium*, pert. to a butcher] *base* canine tooth (laniariform, laniarious)

lanist- [L. *lanista*, gladiator trainer] *base* trainer of gladiators (lanista)

lanug- [L. *lanugo*, down, wooly substance] *base* hair; down (lanuginous, lanugo)

laparo- [Gr. *lapara*, the flank, loins] *comb* abdominal wall; flank; loins (laparocele, laparotomy)

-lapid- [L. *lapis*, stone] *base* stone; gem (lapidary, lapidification)

lapp- [L. *lappa*, a burr] *base* burr (lappacean, lappaceous)

laps- [L. *lapsus*, falling] *base* slip away; error; fall (collapse, elapsed)

laqu- [L. *laqueus*, noose] *base* band, noose (laquear, laquearian)

lar- [Gr. *laros*, ravenous sea bird] *base* gull (Laridae, larine)

-largi- [L. *largus*, abundant] *base* abundant; copious (largifluous, largiloquent)

larix- [L. *larix*, larch] *base* larch (larix, larixinic)

larvi- [L. *larva*, ghost, mask] *comb* larva (larviform, larvigerous) ;

laryngo- [Gr. *larunks*, throat, gullet] *comb* windpipe; larynx (laryngoscope, laryngotracheal)

lasciv- [L. *lascivus*, unrestrained] *base* wanton (lascivious, lasciviousness)

lasio- [Gr. lasio, shaggy, hairy] base shaggy (lasiocampid, lasionite)

-lass- [L. *lassus*, faint, weary] *base* weary (lassate, lassitude)

lat-¹ [L. *latus*, broad, wide*]* *base* extent, scope (latitude, latudinal)

lat-² [Gr. *laas*, stone quarry] *base* stone quarry (latomy)

latax- [Gr. *lataks*, water quadruped] *base* otter (Latax)

latebr- [L. *latebra*, hiding place] *base* lurking hole (latebricole, latebrous)

laten- [L. *latens*, hidden] *base* concealed (latency, latent)

later-¹ [L. *later*, brick] *base* brick (lateritious, laterite)

-later² [Gr. *latreia*, worship] *comb* one who worships (artolater, gastrolater). *See* **-latry**

lateri-, latero- [L. *later-*, side] *comb* on the side (laterigrade, laterodeviation)

lathro- [Gr. *lathraios*, hidden] *base* hidden; beetle (lathrobiiform, Lathrobiiformes)

lati- [L. *latus*, broad] *comb* wide; broad (latidentate, latipennate)

latib- [L. *latibulus*, lurking place] *base* hiding place (latibulate, latibulize)

latici- [L. *latex/latic-*, liquid] *comb* latex (laticiferous)

latio- [L. *latio*, a bringing] base motion; bringing (legislation, lation)

latr- [Gr *latreia*, divine service] *base* worship of God (latria, latrial)

-latra- [L. *latrare*, to bark] *base* barking (latrant, latration)

latro- [L. *latrinatio*, highway robbery] *base* robber (latrocination, latronage)

latrodect- [Gr. *latris*, robber + *dexomai*, of a hunter waiting for game] *base* black widow spider (Latrodectus)

latrunc- [L. *latrunculus*, highwayman] *base* robber (latruncular, latrunculate)

-latry [Gr. *latreia*, worship] *comb* excessive devotion; worship of; (bardolotry, idolatry). *See* **-later**

-laud- [L. *laudare*, to praise] *base* praise (applaud, laudatory)

lauri-, lauro- [L. *laurus*, laurel] *base* laurel (lauriferous, laurine, lauromitrile)

laut- [L. *lautus*, washed] *base* purify (lauter, lautermash)

-lav- [L. *lavare*, to wash] *base* wash (lavage, lavatory)

-lax- [L. *laxare*, to loosen] *base* loose, open (laxative, relaxation)

lazul- [Pers. *lazhward*, blue color] *base* blue (lazuline, lazulite)

-le [OE suf. *-le*] *suf* **1.** small (icicle); **2.** person who does (beadle); **3.** something used for doing (girdle); **4.** frequent (wriggle)

leb- [Gr. *lebes*, basin] *base* basin (lebes)

lecano- [Gr. *lekos*, dish, pot] *comb* basin; pan; dish (lecanomancy, lecanorine)

lechrio- [Gr. *lechrios*, slanting] *comb* slanting (lechriodont, lechriopyla)

lecith-, lecitho- [Gr. *lekithos*, yolk] *comb* egg yolk (lecithin, lecithoprotein)

-leco- [Gr. *lekos*, dish or plate] *base* dish (lecotropal)

-lect-¹ [L. *lectio*, reading] *base* read (lectionary, lecture)

-lect-² [L. *lectus*, picked] *base* picked (elected, select)

lecti-¹, **lectu-** [L. *lectualis*, pert, to a bed] *base* bed, couch (lectisternium, lectual)

lecti-² [L. *lectica*, litter, sedan] *base* transporation for the sick (lectisternium, lectual)

lecyth- [Gr. *lekythos*, pert. to an oil-flask] *base* flask (lecyth, lecythid)

-**leg-**[1] [L. *legere*, to read] *base* read (leg-enda, legendary)

leg-[2] [L. *lex, leg-*, law] *base* law (legality, legislation)

legat-[1] [L. *legatio*, ambassador] *base* representative (delegate, legate)

legat-[2] [L. *legatum*, bequest] *base* bequest (legacy, legatary)

-**legia** [L. *legere*, to read] *comb* reading (bradylegia, tachylegia)

leio- [Gr. *leios*, smooth] *comb* smooth (leiomyoma, Leiophyllum). *Also* **lio-**

lemb- [Gr. *lembos*, sailboat] *base* vessel for distilling (alembic, alembicate)

-**lemma**[1] [Gr. *lemma*, thing taken for granted] *comb* assumption; proposition (dilemma, pentalemma)

-**lemma**[2] [Gr. *lemma*, rind or husk] *comb* rind; peel; husk (neurilemma, sarcolemma)

-**lemnisc-** [L. *lemniscus*, ribbon] *base* ribbon (lemniscate, lemniscus)

lemur- [L. *lemures*, ghost, specter] *base* tarsier (Lemuridae, lemuroid)

-**len-** [L. *lenis*, soft] *base* gentle; mild; soothing (lenient, lenity)

lenim- [L. *lenimen*, soothing remedy] *base* oily ointment (leniment, liniment)

-**lenocin-** [L. *leno*, pander] *base* allure; entice (lenocinant, lenocinium)

lent-[1] [L. *lentus*, slow] *base* slow (lentitude, lentitudinous)

lent-[2] [L. *lens/lent-*, lens] *base* lens (lenticular, lentiform)

-**lent**[3] [L. suf. *-lentus*] *suf* full of (pestilent, turbulent)

lentic- [L. *lenticula*, lentil, lens] *base* lentil-shaped (lenticel, lenticular)

lentig- [L. *lentigo*, lentil-shaped spot] *base* freckle (lentiginose, lentigo)

lentitud- [L. *lentitudo*, sluggishness] *base* sluggish (lentitude, lentitudinous)

-**leo-** [L. *leo*, lion] *base* lion (Leonides, leonine)

lepid- [L. *lepidus*, charming] *base* pleasant (lepid, lepidity)

lepido- [Gr. *lepis*, a scale] *comb* [botany/zoology] scaly; (lepidocrocite, lepidodendron)

lepidopter- [Gr. *lepis*, scale + *pteron*, wing] *base* butterfly (lepidopterist, lepidopterology)

lepo- [Gr. *lepos*, husk or scale] *comb* husk or scale (lepocyte, lepolyte)

-**lepor-** [L. *lepus/lepor-*, hare] *base* hare (leporiform, leporine)

lepra-, lepro- [Gr. *lepra*, leprosy] *comb* leprosy (lepraphobia, leprologist)

-**lepsia, -lepsis, -lepsy, lepti-, -lep-tic** [Gr. *lambanein*, to take] *comb* fit; attack; seizure (Epilepsia, catalepsis, catalepsy, epileptiform, narcoleptic)

lepti-, lepto- [Gr. *leptos*, thin, slender] *comb* narrow; thin; fine; frail (leptiform, leptocephaly)

-**less** [AS *leas*, free] *suf* without; lacking; incapable of being (lawless, thankless)

lesto- [Gr. *lestes*, robber] *comb* thief; robber (lestobiosis, Lestodon)

-**let** [Fr. dim. suf. *-let*] **1.** *suf* small (hamlet); **2.** band (anklet)

leth-[1] [Gr. *lethe*, oblivion] *base* forgetfulness; drugged state (lethargy, lethonomania)

leth-[2] [L. *lethalis*, mortal, deadly] *base* deadly (lethal, lethiferous)

leuco-, leuko- [Gr. *leukos*, white] *comb* colorless; white (leucocyte, leukemia)

-**levi-** [L. *levitas*, lightness] *base* airy; light (levitate, levity)

-**levig-** [L. *levigare*, make smooth] *base* smooth; polished (levigated, levigation)

levo- [L. *laevus*, left] **1.** *comb* on the left (levogyrate); **2.** counterclockwise (levorotatory). *Also* **laevo-** (laevorotation)

levul- [L. *laevus*, left + *-ule* + *-ose*] *base* sugar (levulinic, levulose)

-**lexia, -lexis, -lexy** [Gr. *leksis*, speaking] *comb* speech, reading (dyslexia, catalexis, kyriolexy)

lexico- [Gr. *leksikon*, lexicon] *comb* word; vocabulary (lexicographer, lexicology)

-**libano-** [Gr. *libanos*, frankincense tree] *base* incense (libanomancy, libanotophorousy)

libell- [L. *libellus*, little book] *base* dragonfly (libelluline, libelluloid)

-liber- [L. *liber*, free] *base* free (liberation, liberty)

libid- [L. *libido*, desire] *base* desirous; lustful (libidinous, libinidously)

libit- [L. *libitina*, undertaker] *base* undertaker (Libitina, libitinarian)

-libr- [L. *liber*, written material < tree bark] *base* book (librarian, library)

-libra- [L. *libra*, pound] *base* balance; scale (libration, libratory)

libri- [L. *liber*, inner bark] *base* bark; book (libriform, libricide)

licheno- [Gr. *leiken*, tree moss] *comb* lichen; skin disease (lichenologist; licheno-lupoid)

lien(o)- [L. *lien*, spleen] *comb* spleen (lieno-gastric, lienomalacia)

-liga- [L. *ligare*, to bind] *base* tie; bind (ligament, ligature)

ligamenti-, ligamento- [L. *ligamentum*, a tie or band] *comb* having ligaments (ligamentiferous, ligamento-muscular)

ligni-, ligno- [L. *lignum*, wood] *comb* wood (lignivorous, lignoceric)

liguli- [L. dim. *ligula*, little tongue] *comb* tonguelike; strap (liguliflorate, liguliform)

ligur- [L. *lingere*, to lick] *base* lick (ligurate, ligurrition)

ligyr- [Gr. *ligaino*, cry aloud] *base* noise (ligyrophobia)

-like [AS *gelic*, like] 1. *suf* characteristic of; suitable for (warlike); 2. in the manner of (bird-like)

lilaps- [Gr. *lailaps*, hurricane, tempest] *base* tornado; hurricane (lilapsomania, lilapsophobia)

lili- [L. *lilium*, lily] *base* lily (liliaceous, liliform)

-lim- [L. *limus*, mud] *base* mud (limicoline, limicolous)

-limac- [L. *limax/limac-*, snail] *base* snail; slug (limaceous, Limacina)

limat- [L. *limatus*, polished] *base* polished (limation, limature)

limbat- [L. *limbatus*, edged] *base* bordered, margined (limbate, limbation)

limen- [Gr. *limen*, harbor, haven] *base* harbor (limenarch, Limenitis)

-limin- [L. *limen*, threshold] *base* threshold (eliminate, liminal)

limno- [Gr. *limen*, pool, lake, marsh] *comb* lake; pond; marsh (limnology, limnophagous)

limo-[1] [L. *limus*, mud] *comb* clayey and (limo-cretaceous, limosity)

limo-[2] [Gr. *limos*, hunger] *comb* fasting; famine (limotherapy)

limpid- [L. *limpidus*, clear, clean] *base* clear (limpid, limpidity)

lin-, linon- [Gr. *linon*, cord, fishing line] *base* string, web (linitis, linonophobia)

linar- [L. *linum*, flax] *base* flax (Linaria, linigerous)

linct- [Gr. *liktes*, licking] *base* licking (lincture, linctus)

lineo- [L. *linea*, line] *comb* line (lineolate, lineo-polar)

-ling[1] [ME suf. *-ling*] *suf* person or thing belonging to or concerned with (underling, worldling)

-ling[2] [Goth. suf. *-liggs*] *suf* diminutive (duckling, stripling)

-ling[3] [ME suf. *-ling*] *suf* direction; extent; condition (darkling, groveling)

ling-[4] [L. *lingere*, to lick] *base* lick (lingible)

lingui-, linguli-, linguo- [L. *lingua*, tongue] *comb* language; tongue (bilingual, lingulate, linguopalatal)

lino- [Gr. *linon*, flax] *base* flax (linamarin, linigerous)

lint- [L. *linteum*, linen] *base* linen (lintearious, lint-white)

lipar- [Gr. *liparos*, oily] *base* grease; fat (Liparia, liparocele)

lipo-[1] [Gr. *lipos*, fat, lard] *comb* fatty (lipogenous, liposuction)

lipo-[2] [Gr. *lipein*, to leave] *comb* lacking; without (lipocephalous, lipostomosis)

lipp- [L. *lippus*, bleary-eyed] *base* bleary-eyed (lippitude, lippitudinous)

lipsano- [Gr. *lipares*, earnest in praying] *comb* relics (lipsanographer, lipsanotheca)

-liqu- [L. *liquare*, to melt] *base* melt; make liquid; dissolve (liquefaction, liquescent)

lir- [L. *liro*, plow] *base* deviate from the straight (delirifacient, delirious)

lirell- [dim. of *lira*, furrow] *base* narrow and furrowed (lirellate, lirelliform)

-lirio- [Gr. *leirion*, lily] *base* lily (liriodendrin, Liriodendron)

-liss(o)- [Gr. *lissos*, smooth, bare] *base* smooth (lissoflagellate, lissotrichous)

-litan- [Gr. *litaneia*, an entreating] *base* prayer; entreaty (litaneutical, litany)

-lite [Gr. *lithos*, stone] *suf* names of minerals; stone (aciculate, chrysolite)

liter- [L. *litera*, letter] *base* of words (literary, literate)

-lith [Gr. *lithos*, stone] *comb* stone (acrolith, monolith)

-lithic [Gr. *lithos*, stone] *comb* stone-using stage (Eolithic, neolithic)

litho- [Gr. *lithos*, stone] *comb* stone; rock; calculus (lithoglyph, lithosphere)

litig- [L. *litigare*, carry on a suit] *base* quarrel; lawsuit (litigation, litigious)

-littor- [L. *litus/litor-*, shore] *base* shore (littoral, Littorina)

-litu- [L. *lituus*, trumpet] *base* clarion, trumpet (lituate, lituiform)

litur- [L. *lituro*, erase] *base* erase (litura, liturate)

livid- [L. *lividus*, black and blue] *base* black and blue (lividity, lividness)

lixiv- [L. *lixivius*, lye] *base* lye; alkaline (lixivation, lixiviate)

lobi-, lobo- [Gr. *lobos*, lobe] *comb* lobe (lobigerous, lobiole)

lobulato- [dim. of Gr. *lobos*, lobe] *comb* having small lobes (lobulato-crenate, lobulato-glomerate)

locat- [L. *loco*, hire out, rent] *base* hire out (allocate, allocation)

lochio- [Gr. *lochios*, of childbirth] *comb* childbirth (lochiometritis, lochioperitonitis)

loco- [L. *locus*, place] **1.** *comb* from place to place (locomotive); **2.** a particular place (locodescriptive)

-locu- [L. *locutus*, spoken] *base* word; speech; discourse (elocution, interlocutor). *Also* **-loqu-** (eloquence)

locul- [L. *loculus*, compartment] *base* box, cell (loculament, loculicidal)

locuplet- [L. *locuples*, enrich] *base* make rich (locupletive, locuplete)

locust- [L. *locusta*, locust] *base* cricket; locust; grasshopper (locustarian)

lodic- [L. *lodex/lodic-*, coverlet] *base* blanket; rug; scale (lodicula, lodicule)

logad- [Gr. *logades*, conjunctivae] *base* conjunctivitis (logadectomy, logaditis)

-logia [Gr. *logos*, word] *comb* speech (bradylogia, paromologia)

-logic, -logical [Gr. *logike*, reasoning] *comb* of a science (geologic, biological)

-logist[1] [Gr. *logike*, reasoning] *comb* one versed in __ (biologist, philologist)

logist-[2] [Gr. *logistes*, accountant] *base* accountant (logist, logists)

logo- [Gr. *logos*, word] *comb* word; speech; discourse (logographic, logorrhea)

-logue [Gr. *logos*, word] *comb* kind of speaking or writing (dialogue, monologue)

-logy [Gr. *logos*, word] **1.** *comb* kind of speaking (eulogy); **2.** science; doctrine; theory/study of (geology, theology)

-loimo- [Gr. *loimos*, plague] *base* pestilence (loimography, loimology). *Also* **loemo-** (loemology)

loligo- [L. *loligo*, cuttlefish] *base* squid (loligopsid, Loligopsis)

lom- [Gr. *loma*, hem or fringe] *base* fringed (lomarioid, lomatine)

-lonch- [Gr. *lonkhe*, spear head] *base* spearhead (lonchidite, Lonchitis)

longi- [L. *longus*, long] *comb* long (longicorn, longipennate)

lophio-, lopho- [Gr. *lophos*, crest] *comb* [zoology/anatomy] crest; ridge (lophiodont, lophocercal)

-loqu- [L. *loquere*, to speak] *base* talk; speech (eloquence, grandiloquent). *See* **locu-**

loquel- [L. *loquela*, speech] *base* speech (loquel, loquels)

-lor- [L. *lorum*, thong or strap] *base* thong; strap (Loranthus, lorate)

lordo- [Gr. *lordosis*, bend back] *comb* hump (lordoscoliosis, lordosis)

-lorica- [L. *lorica*, corselet] *base* covering; hard shell (illoricated, loricate)

loutro- [Gr. *loutron*, bathing place] *comb* bath (loutrophobia, loutrophoros)

lox- [Gr. *loxeia*, childbirth] *base* childbirth (lochia, lochial)

loxo- [Gr. *loksos*, slanting] *comb* [medicine/zoology] slanting; oblique (loxodromics, loxotomy)

-lubric- [L. *lubricare*, make smooth] *base* smooth; slippery (lubrication, lubricity)

luc-, luci- [L. *lux/luc-*, light] *comb* light; clear; dawn (lucidity, lucifugal, antelucan)

lucern- [L. *lucerna*, lamp] *base* lamp (lucernal, Lucernaria)

-lucr(i)- [L. *lucrum*, gain] *base* profit; gain (lucriferous, lucrific)

-luct-[1] [L. *luctus*, sorrow] *base* sorrow (luctisonant, luctual)

luct-[2] [L. *luctatio*, wrestle, struggle] *base* wrestle (luctation, luctatory)

lucubr- [ML *lucubrum*, faint light] *base* work; nocturnal study (lucubration, lucubratory)

lucul- [L. *luculentus*, brilliant] *base* bright (lucule, luculent)

-lude [L. *ludus*, play, diversion] *comb* a play; to play with (interlude, prelude)

ludif- [L. *ludificare*, make sport of] *base* hoax; deception (ludification, ludificatory)

-luetic [L. *lues*, plague] *comb* syphilis (luetic, paraluetic)

lugub- [L. *lugeo*, to mourn] *base* mournful (lugubriosity, lugubrious)

-lum- [L. *lumen*, light] *base* light (illumination, luminosity). See -luc-

lumbo- [L. *lumbus*, loin] *comb* loin; lumbar (lumbodorsal, lumbosacral)

-lumbric- [L. *lumbricus*, intestinal worm] *base* worm (lumbricide, lumbriciform)

luni- [L. *luna*, moon] *comb* moon; (lunistitial, lunitidal)

lunu- [L. *lunula*, little moon] *comb* crescent; moon-shaped (lunulated, lunulet)

-lup- [L. *lupinus*, of a wolf] *base* wolf; (lupine, Lupinus)

lupan- [L. *lupanar*, brothel] *base* brothel (lupanar, lupanary)

lur- [L. *luridus*, pale yellow, wan] *base* yellow-brown (lurid, luridly)

lurc- [L. *lurco*, eat voraciously] *base* gluttonize (lurcate, lurcation)

lurido- [L. *luridus*, pale yellow, wan] *comb* yellow (lurido-cinerascent, lurido-whitish)

-lusc- [L. *luscus*, one-eyed] *base* one-eyed (eluscate, Luscinia)

lustr- [L. *lustrum*, purificatory sacrifice] *base* shining; splendor (illustrious, lustral)

lut- [L. *lutum*, mud] *base* mud (lutarious, lutulent)

luteo- [L. *luteus*, golden-yellow] *comb* yellow; (luteo-cobaltic, luteofulvous)

lutjan- [NL *lutjanus*, snapper] *base* snapper (lutjanid, Lutjanidae)

lutr- [L. *lutra*, otter] *base* otter (Lutridae, lutrine)

lux- [L. *luxo*, to dislocate] *base* dislocate (eluxate, luxation)

-ly [OE suf. *-lice*] 1. *suf* characteristic of; suitable to (earthly); 2. happening every ___ (hourly); 3. in a specified way (harshly); 4. in some direction (outwardly); 5. in some order (thirdly)

lyc-, lyco- [Gr. *lukos*, wolf] *comb* wolf (lycanthropy, lycomania)

-lych- [Gr. *lukhnos*, lamp] *base* lamp (lychnapsia, lychnic)

lyg- [Gr. *lugaios*, gloomy] *base* dark; murky (lygaeid, Lygaeus)

lygod- [Gr. *lugos*, willow twig] *base* fern (Lygodiaceae, Lygodium)

lymphaden(o)- [NL *lympha*, lymph + Gr. *aden*, gland] *comb* lymph nodes (lymphadenoma, lymphadenopathy)

lymphangio- [NL *lympha*, lymph + Gr. *angeion*, vessel] *comb* lymphatic vessels (lymphangioplasty, lymphangitis)

lymphato- [NL *lymphaticus*, of the lymph] *comb* lymphatic (lymphatolysis)

lympho- [NL *lympha*, lymph] *comb* of the lymph; (lymphocyte, lymphosarcoma)

lync- [Gr. *lunks*, lynx] *base* lynx (lyncean, Lynceus)

lyo- [Gr. *luein*, dissolve] *comb* dissolution (lyomerous, lyophilic)

lype- [Gr. *lupe*, grief, distress] *comb* sadness; grief (lypemania, Lyperanthus)

lyri- [L. *lyra*, lyre] *base* lyre (lyriferous, lyriform)

lyrico- [Gr. *lurikos*, sung with a lyre] *comb* lyric (lyrico-dramatic, lyrico-epic)

lysi-, -lysis, lyso-, -lyte, -lytic, -lyze [Gr. *lusis*, a setting free] *comb* freeing; relieving; breaking up; dissolving; destroying (lysimeter, lysogen, electrolysis, gazolyte, paralytic, paralyze)

-lysso- [Gr. *lussa*, canine madness] *base* rabies (lyssic, lyssophobia)

-lyte [Gr. *lutos*, loosed] *comb* decomposed substance; dissolved (electrolyte, hydrolyte)

lyxo- [< xylose, 1st syllable reversed, Gr. *ksulon*, wood] *base* artificial sugar (lyxoflavin, lyxose)

M

-ma [Gr. *suf. -ma*] *suf* result of action (dogma, enigma)

macar- [Gr. *makar*, blessed, happy] *base* happy; blessed (macarism, macarize)

macell- [Gr. *makellos*, market] *base* meat market (macellarious)

macer- [L. *maceratus*, softened] *base* soften, soak (macerate, maceration)

-machaero- [Gr. *makhaira*, sword] *base* sword (machaerodont, Machaeropterus) *Also* **machair-**

macho-, -machy [Gr. *makhe*, fight] *comb* struggle; contest; battle; fight (machopolyp, hieromachy)

maci- [L. *macere*, be lean] *base* thin; lean (macilence, macilent)

macrit- [L. *macritas*, leanness, poorness] *base* lean (macritude, macritudinous)

macro- [Gr. *makros*, long] *comb* long; large (macrobiotics, macrocosm)

macropod- [Gr. *makropous*, long-footed] *base* kangaroo (macropodal, macropodine)

macrur- [L. *macrurus*, long-tailed] *base* shrimp (macruran, macrural)

mact- [L. *mactare*, to sacrifice] *base* immolation; sacrifice (mactation, mactator)

-macul- [L. *macula*, spot, stain] *base* spot; stain (immaculate, maculation)

mad- [L. *madere*, to be wet] *base* wet; moist (madefacient, madefaction)

madar- [Gr. *madaros*, bold] *base* hair loss (madarosis)

maest- [It. *maestro*, composer, conductor] *base* skilled master (maestria, maestro)

magad- [Gr. *magadizein*, to sing in octaves] *base* sing in octaves (magadize, magadizing)

mageir- [Gr. *mageiros*, cook] *base* cook (mageiric, mageiricophobia). *Also* **magir-** (magiric, magirology)

magic- [Gr. *magikos*, magic] *base* magic (magical, magician)

-magist- [L. *magister*, chief, director] *base* master; head; authority (magisterial, magistrate)

magma(t)- [Gr. *magma*, unguent] *base* unguent, semi-solid material (magma, magmatic)

magneto- [Gr. *magnes*, Magnesia, Thessaly] *comb* magnetic force (magneto-electric, magnetometer)

magni- [L. *magnus*, great, large] *comb* great; large (magniloquent, magnitude)

mago- [Gr. *magos*, magical] *comb* magic (mago-chemical, magomany)

magud- [Gr. *magudarus*, the stalk] *base* stalk (magydare)

maha- [Sanskrit *maha*, great] *base* mastery; control (maharanee, mahatma)

maieusio- [Gr. *maieusis*, childbirth]

base childbirth (maieusiomania, maieusiophobia)

maieut- [Gr. *maieutikos,* of midwifery] *base* bringing forth; midwifery (maieutic, maieutical)

-maj- [L. *major,* greater] *base* great; large (majoration, majority)

mal-[1] [L. *malus,* bad] *comb* bad; wrong; ill (maladroit, malcontent)

mal-[2] [L. *mala,* cheek] *base* cheek (malar)

-malacia, malaco- [Gr. *malakos,* soft] **1.** *comb* soft (gastromalacia); **2.** mollusks (malacology)

-malax- [L. *malaxare,* soften] *base* soften, knead (malaxate, malaxation)

Malayo- [Portuguese *malayo,* Malay land] *comb* Malay (Malayo-Indonesian, Malayo-Polynesian)

male- [L. *malus,* bad] *comb* evil (malediction, malefaction)

-mali- [L. *malum,* apple] *base* apple (malicorium, maliform)

malleo- [L. *malleus,* hammer] *comb* hammer (malleo-incudal, malleoramate)

-mallo- [Gr. *mallos,* lock of wool] *base* wool (mallophagan, mallophagous)

malneiro- [L. *malus,* bad + Gr. *neiros,* dream] *comb* nightmare (malneirophobia, malneirophrenia)

mammato- [L. *mammatus,* having breasts] *comb* rounded clouds (mammato-cumulus)

mammi-, mammo- [L. *mamma,* breast] *comb* breasts (mammiferous, mammogram)

mammilli- [L. dim. of *mamma,* breast, nipple] *comb* nipple (mammilated, mammilliform)

-man [Sanskrit *manu,* man < Manu, mythical father of the human race] *comb* human; male (anchorman, woodsman)

-mancy, -mantic [Gr. *manteia,* divination] *comb* divination (necromancy, necromantic)

-mand- [L. *mandare,* to entrust] *base* command; oblige (mandate, mandatory)

mandibulo- [L. *mandibulum,*

jaw] *comb* jaw (mandibuliform, mandibulo-maxillary)

manduc- [L. *manducare,* to chew] *comb* chew; eat (manducation, manducatory)

mangan-, mangani-, mangano-, manganoso- [L. *manganium,* manganese] *comb* manganese (manganbrucite, manganicyanide, manganosiderite, manganoso-manganic)

mani-, manu- [L. *manus,* hand] *comb* hand; (manipulate, manuscript)

-mania [L. *mania,* madness] **1.** *comb* mental disorder (kleptomania); **2.** excessive craving (bibliomania)

mano- [Gr. *manos,* rare] *comb* thin; rare (manometer, manometric)

mansue- [L. *mansuetus,* tame] *base* tame; mild (mansuete, mansuetude)

mantic- [L. *mantica,* wallet, purse] *base* small bag (manticulate, manticulation)

manub- [L. *manubiae,* booty] *base* booty (manubial, manubiary)

manubr- [L. *manubrium,* handle, hilt] *base* handle (manubrial, manubriated)

manul- [L. *manulea,* tunic sleeve] *base* sleeve (manuleated, manuleation)

marasm- [Gr. *marasmos,* withering, wasting away] *base* wasting, withering (marasmic, marasmus)

-marc- [L. *marcescere,* wither, shrivel] *base* faded; withered (marcescent, marcescible)

mare- [L. *mare,* sea] *comb* sea (mareogram, mareography)

marg- [L. *margo,* border] *base* border; verge (marginal, marginate)

margarit- [Gr. *margarites,* pearl] *base* pearl (margaritaceous, margaritiferous)

-margy [Gr. *margos,* raging mad] *base* raging mad (gastrimargy, gastromargy)

mari- [L. *mare,* sea] *comb* sea (mariculture, marigraph)

marit- [L. *maritus,* of marriage] *base* spouse; marriage (marital)

-marm- [L. *marmor,* marble] *base* marble (marmoration, marmoreal)

-marsup- [L. *marsupium,* pouch] *base* pouch (marsupial, marsupiated)

martyr- [Gr. *martur*, witness] *base* martyr (martyrdom, martyrology)

-mas [mass < L. *missa*, dismissal] *comb* feast day (Christmas, Martinmas)

maschal- [Gr. *maskhale*, armpit] *base* armpit (maschaladenitis, maschaliatry)

masculo- [L. *masculus*, masculine] *comb* male (masculonuclear, masculo-nucleus)

mass- [Gr. *masson*, great, uncountable] *base* huge (massive, massivity)

masso- [Gr. *massein*, to knead] *comb* massage (massotherapist, massotherapy)

-mastia, masto- [Gr. *mastos*, breast] *comb* [medicine/zoology] breast: of or like (macromastia, mastodynia)

mastic- [L. *masticare*, chew] *base* chew (mastication, masticatory)

mastigo- [Gr. *mastiks*, whip] *comb* whiplike; scourge bearing (mastigophore, mastigopod)

masto- [Gr. *mastos*, breast] *comb* breast (mastodont, mastodynia)

mastoido- [Gr. *mastoeides*, like the breast] *comb* mastoid (mastoideum, mastoido-humeral)

-mateo- [Gr. *mataios*, vain, foolish] *base* unprofitable; useless; vain (mataeology, mateotechny)

mater-, matri-, matro- [L. *mater*, mother] *comb* mother (maternity, matriarchy, matroclinous)

matertera- [L. *matertera*, maternal aunt] *base* aunt on mother's side (materteral)

-math- [Gr. *manthanein*, to learn] *comb* learn (opsimath, polymath)

mathet- [Gr. *matheteia,* instruction] *base* learning (mathetic, mathetical)

matur- [L. *maturare*, to make ripe] *base* ripe (maturation, maturity)

-matut- [L. *matutinum*, morning] *base* morning (matutinal, matutine)

maxi- [L. *maximus*, largest] *comb* very large; very long (maxibudget, maxicoat)

maxillo- [L. *maxilla*, jaw] *comb* of the maxilla; jaw (maxilliform, maxillo-palatine)

mazo-¹ [L. *maza*, placenta] *comb* placenta (mazolysis, mazolytic)

mazo-² [Gr. *maksos*, breast] *comb* breast (mazologist, mazoplazia)

-meal [OE *mael*, appointed time] *comb* measure (heapmeal, piecemeal)

meato- [L. *meatus*, a passage] *comb* passage; channel (meatometer, meatoscopy)

mech- [L. *moechus*, adulterer] *base* adulterer (mechal, mechation)

mechanico- [Gr. *mechanikos*, pert. to machines] *comb* partly mechanical (mechanico-acoustic, mechanico-chemical)

mechano- [Gr. *mechane*, machine] *comb* machines (mechanochemical, mechanotherapy)

-meco- [Gr. *mekos*, length] *base* length (mecodont, mecometer)

-mecon- [Gr. *mekon*, poppy] *base* poppy; opium (meconic, meconidine)

-med- [Gr. *medos*, bladder] **1.** *base s.* bladder (medorrhea); **2.** *pl.* genitals (medorthophobia)

medi-, medio- [L. *medius*, middle] *comb* middle (medicommisure, mediodorsal)

mediastino- [L. *mediastinus*, medial] *comb* membranous partition (mediastino-pericardial, mediastinoscopy)

medico- [L. *medicus*, physician] *comb* medical; of healing (medicochirurgical, medico-legal)

medo- [Gr. *medos*, penis] *comb* penis (medorrhea, medorrhinum)

medull- [L. *medullosus*, full of marrow] *base* marrow, pith (medullary, medullose)

medus- [L. *medusa*, jellyfish] *base* jellyfish (Medusidae, medusiform)

mega- [Gr. *megas*, large, great] **1.** *comb* large; powerful (megaphone); **2.** a million of (megacycle)

megachiropter- [Gr. *megas*, large + *cheir*, hand + *pteron*, wing] *base* fruit- bat (megacheiropteran, megachiropterous)

megalo-, -megaly [Gr. *megas/megal-*, large] **1.** *comb* large; powerful (megalomania); **2.** abnormal enlargement (megalocardia, hepatomegaly)

meio- [Gr. *meion*, less] *comb* less (meiosis). *Also* **mio-** (miogeosyncline, Miolithic)

meizo- [Gr. *meizon*, greater] *comb* greater (meizoseismal, meizoseismic)

melan-, melano- [Gr. *melas/melan-*, black] *comb* black; very dark (melanosis, melanocomous)

-mele [Gr. *melos*, limb] *comb* limb; extremity (phocomele)

meleagr- [L. *meleagris*, turkey] *base* turkey (Meleagridinae, meleagrine)

melet- [Gr. *meletan*, to study, meditate] *base* meditation (meletetics)

-melia-[1] [Gr. *melos*, limb] *comb* limb; extremity (macromelia)

-melia-[2] [Gr. *melia*, a type of ash tree] *base* ash tree (meliaceous, melial)

melin- [L. *meles/melin-*, badger] **1.** *base* badger (meline); **2.** tawny (meline)

-melior- [L. *melior*, better] *base* make better; improve (ameliorate, meliorism)

melisso- [Gr. *melissa*, bee] *base* bee (Melissa, melissean)

melitto- [Gr. *melitta*, bee] *base* bee (melittology, melliturgy)

mell(i)- [Gr. *meli*, honey] *comb* honey; sweet (mellifluous, mellivorous)

melo-[1] [Gr. *melos/melod-*, melody] *comb* song; music (melodious, melomania)

melo-[2] [Gr. *mela*, cheeks < *melon*, apple] *comb* cheek; (meloplastic, meloplasty)

melo-[3] [Gr. *melos*, limb] *comb* limb; extremity (melorheostosis, melorheostoses)

membrani/o- [L. *membrana*, skin] *comb* membrane plus (membraniform, membranocartilaginous)

memor- [L. *memor*, mindful] *base* remembering (memorial, memory)

mendac- [L. *mendax/mendac-*, lying, false] *base* falsehood (mendacious, mendacity)

mendic- [L. *mendicare*, to beg] *base* beggar; poor (mendicant, mendication)

-menia [Gr. *men*, month] *comb* [medicine] pertaining to the menses (catamenia, paramenia)

meningo- [Gr. *menig/mening-*,

membrane] *comb* [medicine/anatomy] related to the meninges (meningocele, meningococcus)

-menisc- [Gr. *meniskos*, dim. of moon] *base* crescent-shaped (meniscoid, meniscus)

meno-[1] [Gr. *men*, month] **1.** *comb* [medicine] pertaining to the menses (menopause); **2.** month (menology)

meno-[2] [Gr. *menein*, to remain] *comb* persisting (menobranchus, menorhynchus)

mens- [L. *mensis*, month] *base* month; menses (mensual; menstrual)

-ment[1] [L. suf. *-mentum*, result of an act] **1.** *suf* result; product (pavement); **2.** instrument; means (adornment); **3.** process of doing (measurement); **4.** state of being acted on (disappointment)

ment-[2] [L. *mens/ment-*, mind] *base* mind; thought (mental, mentation)

menth- [L. *mentha*, mint] *base* mint (menthaceous, menthol)

mentig- [L. *mentigo*, eruption or scab] *base* pustular eruption (mentiginous, mentigo)

mento- [L. *mentum*, chin] *comb* chin (mentohyoid, mentoplasty)

-mentul- [L. *mentula*, penis] *base* penis (mentula, mentulate)

mephit- [L. *mephitis*, pestilential exhalation] *base* skunk (mephitic, Mephitinae)

-mer, -meran [Gr. *meros*, part] *comb* part; unit (isomer, heteromeran). *Also* **-mere** (blastomere). *See* **mero-**[1]

merac- [L. *meracus*, pure, unmixed] *base* unmixed (meracious, meracity)

-merc- [L. *mercari*, trade or buy] *base* goods (mercantile, mercantilism)

merced- [L. *merces*, salary] *base* hireling (mercedary, mercede)

-merd- [L. *merda*, dung] *base* dung (immerd, merdivorous)

-mere [Gr. *meros*, part] *comb* part; unit (blastomere). *See* **-mer** and **mero-**[1]

meretric- [L. *meretrix/meretric-*, prostitute] *base* harlot (meretricious, meretriciousness)

-merge, -merse [L. *mergere*, dive, dip]
comb plunge; dip (submerge, immerse)

merid- [L. *meridies*, midday] *base* noon
(antemeridian, postmeridian)

merinth- [Gr. *merinthos*, cord, line,
string] *base* bind (merinthophobia)

meristi- [Gr. *meristos*, divided] *comb*
divided (meristematic, meristiform)

merluc- [L. *merlucus*, haddock] *base* hake
(merlucine, merlucoid)

mero-¹, meri-, -meris, -merous, -mery
[Gr. *meros*, part] *comb* part; unit; partial; having ___ parts; (meroblast, meri-
hedric, Piptomeris, heteromerous,
gonomery)

mero-² [Gr. *meros*, thigh] *comb* thigh
(merocele, merocerite)

merul- [L. *merula*, blackbird] *base* blackbird (Merula, meruline)

mesati- [Gr. *mesatos*, midmost] *comb*
medium (mesaticephaly, mesatipelvic)

mesmer- [< *Franz Mesmer*, German phy-
sician] *base* hypnotism (mesmerism,
mesmeromania)

meso- [Gr. *mesos*, middle] 1. *comb* in the
middle (mesocarp); 2. [anatomy] a
mesentery (mesogastrium)

mess- [L. *messis*, harvest] *base* reaper
(Messidor, messor)

meta-¹ [Gr. *meta*, beside] 1. *pre* changed
(metamorphosis); 2. after (metaphysics); 3. behind; in back (metathorax);
4. beyond; higher (metapsychosis)

meta-² [Gr. *meta*, beside] [chemistry]
1. *pre* polymer of (metaldehyde); 2.
derivative of (metaprotein); 3. acid
containing less water combined with
the anhydride than other acids of the
same non-metallic element (metaphos-
phoric); 4. characterized by substitutes
in the 1,3 position in the benzene ring
(metacoumarate)

metabol- [Gr. *metabole*, change] *base* of
metabolism (metabolic, metabolism)

metacarpo- [Gr. *meta*, beyond + *karpos*,
wrist] *comb* metacarpus plus (metacar-
pophalangeal, metacarpotrapezial)

metalli-, metallo- [Gr. *metallon*,
mine] *comb* metal (metalliferous,
metallochrome)

metatarso- [Gr. *meta*, beyond + *tarsos*,
tarsus] *comb* metatarsus plus (metatar-
sodigital, metatarso-phalangeal)

metax- [Gr. *metaksa*, silk] *base* silk
(metaxin, metaxite)

-meter [Gr. *metron*, measure] 1. *comb*
device for measuring (barometer); 2.
so many meters (kilometer); 3. fraction of a meter (centimeter); 4. having
___ metrical feet (penta-meter)

metho- [Gr. *methu*, mead] *comb* methyl;
mead (methoxyl; methomania)

methoxy- [Gr. *methu*, mead + *okhus*,
sharp] *comb* methoxy group (methoxy-
caffeine, methoxychlor)

methyl- [Gr. *methu*, mead] *comb* methyl
group (methyl-benzene, methyldopa)

methys- [Gr. *methusis*, drunkenness]
base drunk; intoxicated (methysis,
methystic)

metopo- [Gr. *metopon*, forehead]
comb forehead (metoposcopical,
metoposcopy)

metr- [Gr. *metron*, poetic meter] *base*
poem (metrical, metrician)

metra-, metro-¹ [Gr. *metra*, womb] *comb*
uterus (metratonia, metrorrhagia)

-metric, -metrics, metro-², -metry [Gr.
metrikos, rel. to measurement] *comb*
measure (geometric, econometrics,
metrology, chronometry)

-metrio- [Gr. *metrios*, moderate] *base*
moderate (metriocephalic)

mezzo- [Ital. *mezzo*, middle] *comb* middle; half (mezzo-rilievo, mezzotint)

mic- [L. *mica*, crumb] *base* particle (mica,
micelle)

micro- [Gr. *mikros*, small] 1. *comb* little;
small (microbarograph); 2. abnormally
small (microcephalic); 3. enlarging
what is small; (microscope); 4. relation
to microscopes (microchemistry); 5.
one millionth part of (microgram)

microchiropter- [Gr. *mikros*, small +
kheir, hand + *pteron*, wing] *base* insectivorous bat (microchiropteran)

-mict- [L. *mingere*, urinate] *base* urine
(micturate, micturient). *See* -ming-

-mictic [Gr.*miktos*, blended] *comb* mixed
(hemictic, holomictic)

mid- [Old English *midd*, central] *comb* middle part (midbrain, midseason)

migma- [Gr. *migma*, mixture] *base* mixture of solid and molten rock (migmatic, migmatite)

-milit- [L. *militare*, serve as a soldier] *base* soldier (militancy, military)

milli- [L. *millia*, thousand] **1.** *comb* one thousandth part of (millimeter); **2.** one thousand (millifold)

milv- [L. *milvus*, the kite] *base* kite—the bird (Milvinae, milvine)

-mim- [Gr. *mimeisthai*, imitate] **1.** *base* imitate (mimetic); **2.** mockingbird (mimine)

min- [L. *minari*, threaten] *base* threat (minacious, minatory)

-ming- [L. *mingere*, to discharge urine] *base* urine (mingent, retromingent). *See* **-mict-**

mini- [L. *minimus*, least] *comb* smaller; shorter; lesser than usual (miniskirt, minimart)

miniac- [L. *miniaceus*, vermillion] *base* reddish-orange (miniaceous)

mio- [Gr. *meion*, less] *comb* less; diminished (miosis, miotaxy). *Also* **meio-** (meiosis)

-mir- [L. *mirari*, to wonder] *base* wonder (admiration, mirabilia)

mis- [Gothic *missa*, wrong, bad] *pre* wrong; bad (miscalculate, misrule)

-misc- [L. *miscere*, mix] *base* mixed (immiscible, miscellaneous)

miser- [L. *miser*, wretched, pitiable] *base* distressed (miserable, miserably)

-miserat- [L. *miserari*, bewail, pity] *base* show compassion (commiserate, uncommiserated)

miso- [Gr. *misos*, hatred] *comb* hated; hating (misogamy, misogyny)

-miss-, -mit-[1] [L. *mittere*, send] *base* send (dismiss, remit)

mit-[2]**, mito-** [Gr. *mitos*, thread] *comb* thread (mitosis, mitochondria)

miti-[1] [L. *mitis*, mild] *base* mild; soothing (mitigate, mitigatory)

miti-[2] [Dutch *mit*, woodworm] *base* mite (miticidal, miticide)

mitri- [L. *mitri*, miter, turban] *base* miter (Mitrephorus, mitriform)

mixo- [Gr. *mikso*, mixed] *comb* mixed (mixogamous, mixogamy)

mixti- [L. *mixtus*, mixed] *comb* mixed (mixtiform, mixtilineal)

-mnem-, -mnesia, -mnesis [Gr. *mnasthai*, remember] *base* memory (mnemonics, amnesia, anamnesis)

-mo [< duodeci*mo*, in twelve] *suf* printing books: a suffix to the number designating one of the equal parts into which a sheet is divided, the size of a page varying with the size of the sheet folded (12mo, twelvemo)

-mob- [L. *mobilis*, moveable] *base* move (immobility, mobile)

-mobile [< auto*mobile*] *comb* special type of vehicle (Batmobile, bookmobile)

-mochl- [Gr. *mokhlikos*, lever] *base* lever (hypomochlion, mochlic)

modic- [L. *modicitas*, moderate, insignificant] *base* small (modicity, modicum)

modul- [L. *modulari*, regulate] *base* regulate (modulate, modulatory)

mogi- [Gr. *mogis*, hardly] *comb* with difficulty (mogigraphia, mogilalia)

mol-, molin- [L. *molere*, grind] *base* grind (molar, molariform, molinologist)

-molend- [L. *molendinum*, mill-house] *base* mill (molendarious, molendinary)

molit- [L. *molitio*, an attempt] *base* undertaking (demolition, molition)

-moll- [L. *mollis*, soft] *base* soft; (emollient, mollify)

mollusc- [L. *molluscum*, mollusk] *base* mollusk (molluscan, molluscous)

molybdo- [Gr. *molubdos*, lead] *comb* lead (molybdeniferous, molybdocolic)

molys- [Gr. *molunsis*, staining] *base* dirt (molysite, molysmophobia)

momen- [L. *momen*, motion] *base* motion (momentum)

-mon- [L. *monere*, warn] *base* warn; (admonish, monitorial)

monach- [L. *monachus*, monk] *base* monk (monachal, monachism)

monet- [L. *moneta*, the mint] *base* coinage (demonetize, monetary)

-monil- [L. *monile*, necklace] *base* necklace (monilated, moniliform)

mono- [Gr. *monos*, alone, single] **1.** *comb*

single; alone; one (monoclinal); **2.** containing one atom (monochloride); **3.** one molecule thick (monolayer)

monotrem- [Gr. *monos*, single + *trema*, hole] *base* platypus (monotremal, Monotremata)

-monstr- [L. *monstrare*, to show] *base* show; (demonstrate, monstrance)

mont- [L. *montanus*, mountain] *base* mountain (montagnard, montane)

-mony [L. suf. *-monia*] *suf* resulting state (patrimony, queremony)

-mor-[1] [L. *mos/mor-*, manner, custom] *base* usage; custom (morality, mores)

-mor-[2] [L. *morum*, blackberry, mulberry] *base* mulberry (moriform, morula)

-mora- [L. *mora*, delay] *base* delay (moration, remorate)

-morb- [L. *morbus*, disease] *base* sickly; diseased (morbidity, morbiferous)

morbilli- [L. dim. of *morbus*] *base* measles (morbilliform, morbillous)

-mord- [L. *mordax/mordac-*, biting] *base* sharp; biting; acrid (mordacity, mordant)

mori- [L. *morum*, mulberry] *base* mulberry (moric acid, moriform)

-moriger- [L. *morigerari*, comply with] *base* obedient; submissive (morigeration, morigerous)

-morilli- [Fr. *morille*, morel] *base* fungus; morel (morilliform)

mormo- [Gr. *mormo*, imaginary monster] *base* imaginary monster (mormo, mormoopid)

moro- [Gr. *moros*, foolish] *base* foolish (morology, moronic)

moros- [L. *morosus*, sullen, peevish] *base* surly (morose, morosity)

-morph, -morphic, -morphism, morpho-, -morphosis, -morphous [Gr. *morphe*, shape] *comb* having a specified form (pseudomorph, anthropomorphic, monomorphism, morphology, cytomorphosis, isomorphous)

mort-, morti- [L. *mor/mort-*, death] *comb* death (immortality, mortify)

-mosch- [Gr. *moschos*, musk] *base* musk (moschiferous, moschine)

-most [Old English *mest*, most] *suf* superlatives (foremost, hindmost)

motil- [L. *motilis*, motile] *base* capable of motion (motile, motility)

-motive [Fr. *motif*, that causes motion] *comb* moving (automotive, locomotive)

moto- [L. *motor*, mover] *comb* motor (motocross, moto-sensitive)

-mouthed [Old English *muth*, mouth] *comb* having a ___ mouth; having ___ mouths (foul-mouthed, large-mouthed)

mov- [L. *movere*, move] *base* move (movable, remove)

muci-, muco- [L. *mucus*, mucus] *comb* snot; mucous membrane (muciparous, mucoprotein)

mucid- [L. *mucidus*, moldy] *base* musty (mucidness, mucidous)

mucoso- [L. *mucosus*, slimy] *comb* partly mucous (mucoso-granular, mucoso-saccharine)

-mucro- [L. *mucro*, sharp point] *base* sharp tip or point (mucroniferous, mucronulate)

-mug- [L. *mugire*, bellow] *base* bellow (mugient, remugient)

mugil- [L. *mugil*, mullet] *base* mullet (mugiliform, mugiloid)

mulc-, mult- [L. *molitura*, toll paid to a grinder] *base* toll, fine (mulctuary, multure)

mulie(b)r- [L. *mulier*, woman] *base* woman (muliebrity, mulierose)

muls- [L. *mulsus*, mixed with honey] *base* mixed with honey (mulse, mulsed)

mult(i)- [L. *multus*, many] **1.** *comb* having many (multicolored); **2.** more than two (multilateral); **3.** many times (multimillionaire)

mummi- [Hindi *mum*, embalming wax] *base* mummy (mummiform, mummify)

mun- [L. *munus*, a present] *base* gift (munificent, remunerate)

-mund-[1] [L. *mundus*, world] *base* world (mundane, mundivagant)

-mund-[2] [L. *mundare*, cleanse] *base* cleanse (mundation)

muniment- [L. *munimentum,* fortification, deed] *base* charter (muniment, muniments)

-mur-[1] [L. *mus/mur-,* mouse] *base* mouse (murine)

-mur-[2] [L. *murus,* wall] *base* wall (immured, mural)

-mur-[3] [Fr. *mure,* mulberry] *base* mulberry (muriform)

muraen- [L. *murena,* eel] *base* moray (muraenid, muraenoid)

murc- [L. *murcus,* mutilated] *base* truncated, slothful (murcid, murcous)

-muri- [L. *muria,* brine] *base* brine (muriacite, muriatic)

muriat- [L. *muria,* brine] *base* chloride (muriated , muriatic)

-muric- [L. *murex/muric-,* pointed rock, spire] *base* pointed; sharp (muricated, muricatohispid)

musa- [Arabic *muze,* banana] *base* banana (Musaceae, musaceous)

-musc-[1] [L. *musca,* fly] *base* fly (Musca, musciform)

-musc-[2] [L. *muscus,* moss] *base* moss (emuscation, muscicole)

muscar- [L. *muscarium,* fly brush] *base* brush (muscariform, muscatorium)

muscicap- [L. *musca,* fly + *capere,* take] *base* flycatching bird; thrush (Muscicapidae, muscicapine)

musculo- [L. *musculus,* muscle] *comb* muscle (musculocutaneous, musculophrenic)

musico- [Gr. *mousike,* melodic art] *comb* music (musicodramatic, musicophobia)

muso- [Gr. *mousa,* muse] *base* poem (musomania, musophobia)

muss- [L. *mussitare,* murmur] *base* mutter; murmur (mussitate, mussitation)

-mustel- [L. *mustella,* weasel] **1.** *base* weasel; badger; skunk; polecat; ermine; marten; mink; wolverine; ferret (musteline); **2.** tawny (musteline)

-mut- [L. *mutare,* change] *base* change (immutable, mutability)

-mutil- [L. *mutilare,* mutilate] *base* maim (mutilate, mutilation)

-mutu- [L. *mutuus,* interchanged] *base* reciprocal (mutual, mutuality)

-mycete, myceto- [Gr. *mukes/muket-,* fungus] *comb* fungus of a specified group (schizomycete, mycetoma)

-mycin [< *myc*(o) + *-in*] *comb* derivative of a specified substance from bacteria or fungi; antibiotic (neomycin, streptomycin)

myco- [Gr. *mukes,* fungus] *comb* mushroom; fungus (mycobiont, mycology)

mycter- [Gr. *mukter,* snout] *comb* sneer; scoff; nose (Mycteria, mycterism)

mycto- [Gr. *mukter,* nostril] *comb* lanternfish (myctophid, myctophiform)

myda- [Gr. *mudan,* to be damp] *base* putrid (mydatoxin, mydin)

-myelia, myelo- [Gr. *muelos,* marrow] *comb* spinal cord; marrow (micromyelia, myelogenic)

myia- [Gr. *muia,* fly] *base* fly (myiasis, Myodioctes)

mylo- [Gr. *mule,* millstone, molar] *base* molar (mylodont, myloglossus)

myo-[1] [Gr. *mus,* muscle] *comb* [medicine/anatomy] muscle (myocardium, myodynamia)

myo-[2] [Gr. *mus,* mouse] *base* mouse (myomancy, myomorph)

myop- [Gr. *muopia,* short-sighted] *base* short-sightedness (myopia, myopic)

myox- [Gr. *muoksos,* dormouse] *base* dormouse (myoxine, Myoxus)

myria- [Gr. *murios,* numberless] **1.** *comb* numerous; many (myriapod); **2.** ten thousand (myriameter). *Also* **myrio-** (myriophyllus)

myric- [Gr .*myrike,* low shrub] *base* aromatic shrub (myrica, myrica wax)

myringo- [L. *myringa,* membrana tympani] *base* tympanic (myringitis, myringoplasty)

myrist- [Gr. *muristikos,* fragrant (nut)] *base* nutmeg (myristic, myristicivorous)

myrmeco-, myrmic- [Gr. *murmek-,* ant] *comb* ant (myrmecology, myrmicine)

myrmecophag- [Gr. *murmek-,* ant + *phagein,* eat] *base* anteater (myrmecophagine, mymecophagous)

myrio- [Gr. *moira*, fate] *base* dirge, lament (myriologist, myriologue)

myro- [Gr. *muron*, unguent] *comb* ointment; perfume (myronic, myropolist)

-myrti- [Gr. *murtos*, myrtle] *base* myrtle (myrtaceous, myrtiform)

mysi- [Gr. *mysis*, closing] *base* a genus of crustaceans (mysid, Mysis)

myso- [Gr. *musos*, uncleanness] *comb* dirt (mysophobia, mysomania). *Also* **miso-** (misophobia)

myster- [L. *mysterium*, secret rites] *base* mystery (mysteriarch, mysteriosophy)

mystico- [Gr. *mustikos*, secret] *comb* partly mystical (mystico-allegoric, mystico-religious)

mythico- [Gr. *muthos*, myth] *comb* partly mythical (mythico-magical, mythico-romantic)

mytho- [Gr. *muthos*, myth] *comb* myth; story (mythoclast, mythological)

-mytil- [Gr. *mutilos*, sea-mussel] *base* mussel (mytilaceous, mytiliform)

-myxia, myxo- [Gr. *muksa*, nostril, mucus] *comb* slime; mucus (hypomyxia, myxomycete)

-myz- [Gr. *muzein*, suck] *base* suck (myzont, myzostoma)

N

-nacar- [Pg. *nacar*, mother-of-pearl] *base* orange-red, scarlet (nacarat, nacarine)

naev- [L. *naevus*, mole] *base* blemish, birthmark (naevoid, naevous)

nano- [L. *nanus*, dwarf] **1.** *comb* dwarfism; (nanocephalous); **2.** one-billionth (nanosecond). *Also* **nanno-** (nannofossil)

-nao- [Gr. *naos*, temple] *base* temple (naological, naology)

-napi- [L. *napus*, turnip] *base* turnip (napifolious, napiform)

narco- [Gr. *narkoun*, benumb] *comb* numbness; stupor (narcolepsy, narcomatous)

nard- [Gr. *nardinos*, nard] *base* nard (nardiferous, nardine)

-nari- [L. *naris*, nostril] *base* nostrils (naricorn, nariform)

narr- [L. *narrare*, report] *base* relate; tell (narrative, narrator)

nasc- [L. *nasci*, be born] *base* born (nascent, nascently)

nasi-, naso- [L. *nasus*, nose] *comb* nose; nasal (nasicornous, nasolabial)

-nastic, -nasty [Gr. *nastos*, pressed close] *comb* plant growth: unequal by some specified means or in a specified direction (hyponastic, hyponasty)

nasut- [L. *nasutus*, long-nosed] *base* long-nosed, sagacious (nasute, nasuteness)

-nata- [L. *natare*, swim] *base* swim; (natation, natatorium)

-natal- [L. *natalis*, pert. to birth] *base* birth (antenatal, neonatal)

-nati- [L. *nates*, buttocks] *base* buttocks (naticine, natiform)

-natremia [Gr. *natrion*, sodium] *comb* sodium; (hyponatremia, pseudohyponatremia)

natro- [L. *natrium*, sodium] *comb* containing sodium (natrolunite, natrochalcite)

-natured [L. *natura*, natural constitution] *comb* having a ___ nature or temperament (good-natured, mean-natured)

naus- [Gr. *nausia*, ship] *base* sick; seasick (nausea, nauseous)

-naut-, -nav-, navic- [Gr. *nautikos*, pert. to ships] *base* ship; sea (nautical, navigate, naviculoid)

navig- [L. *navigare*, go by sea] *base* voyage (navigable, navigation)

ne- [Gr. *ne*, not] *pre* not (nescience, nescient)

-nebul- [L. *nebula*, cloud, vapor] *base* cloud; mist; vapor (nebuliferous, nebulous)

necro- [Gr. *nekros*, dead body] *comb*

death; corpse; dead tissue (necrolatry, necrology)

-nect- [L. *necto*, join together] *base* fastened (connect, disconnected)

nectar- [Gr. *nectar*, drink of the gods] *base* sweet plant fluid (nectareal, nectarean)

necto- [Gr. *nektos*, swimming] *comb* swimming (nectosome, nectozooid)

necyo- [Gr. *nekus*, corpse] *comb* demon; damned spirit (necyomancer, necyomancy)

nefand- [L. *nefandus*, atrocious] *base* heinous (nefandous, nefandousness)

nefar- [L. *nefarius*, immoral] *base* wicked (nefarious, nefariously)

-neg- [L. *negare*, deny] *base* deny (negation, negativist)

neglig- [L. *negligens*, heedless] *base* heedless (negligent, negligible)

-negot- [L. *negotium*, business] *base* business (negotiation, renegotiate)

-nema- [Gr. *nema*, thread] *base* thread (hyalonema, nemalite)

nemato- [Gr. *nema/nemat-*, thread] *comb* thread; threadlike (nematoblast, nematocyst)

nemert- [Gr. *nemerteia*, a sea nymph] *base* marine flatworm (nemertean, nemertine)

nemesis [Gr. *nemesis*, goddess of vengeance] *base* arch enemy (nemesis, nemesistic)

nemor- [Gr. *nemos*, wooded pasture] *base* woods; forest (nemoral, nemorous)

neo- [Gr. *neos*, new, young] 1. *comb* new; recent; latest (neo-classic); 2. [geology] chronologically last part of a period (Neocene)

neosso- [Gr. *neossos*, young bird] *comb* young birds (neossology, neossoptile)

nep- [Gr. *nepos*, infant] *base* postembryonic (nepionic, nepionical)

nephal- [Gr. *nephalios*, sober] *base* sober; abstinent (nephalism, nephalist)

nephelo-, nepho- [Gr. *nephele*, cloud] *comb* cloud ;(nephelometer, nephology)

nephro- [Gr. *nephros*, kidney] *comb* kidney (nephrologist, nephrotomy)

nepi- [Gr. *nepios*, infant] *base* infant (nepiology, nepionic)

-nepo- [L. *nepos*, nephew] *base* nephew (nepotic, nepotism)

-ner- [Gr. *Nereus*, sea-god] *base* liquid (aneroid, nereocystis)

-nerter- [Gr. *nerteroi*, the dead] *base* the dead (nerterologist, nerterology)

nerv-, nervi-, nervo- [L. *nervus*, sinew, fiber, nerve] *comb* nerve (nervosity, nervifolious, nervovital)

nesc- [L. *nesciens*, ignorant] *base* ignorance (nescience, nescient)

nesid- [Gr. *nesidion*, island] *base* insulin precursor in the islets of Langerhans (nesidioblast, nesidioblastic)

neso- [Gr. *nesos*, island] *comb* island (Nesomys, Nesotragus)

-ness [AS suf. *-nes*] *suf* condition; quality of (greatness, sweetness)

neuro- [Gr. *neuron*, nerve] *comb* nervous system; nerve (neurography, neuropath)

neus(t)- [Gr. *neuston*, swimming] *base* clustered (neuston, synneusis)

neutro- [L. *neuter*, neither] *comb* neutral (neutropenia, neutrophile)

nev-, nevo- [L. *naevus*, mole] *base* birthmark; mole (nevoid, nevus)

-nex- [L. *nexus*, a bond] *base* connect; bind (annex, nexus)

nic- [Gr. *nike*, victory] *base* victory (epinician, epinicion)

-nict- [L. *nictitare*, wink] *base* wink (nictation, nictitate)

nid-, nidi- [L. *nidus*, nest] *base* nest (nidal, nidification)

nidor- [L. *nidor*, vapor, aroma] *base* smell (nidorosity, nidorous)

nigri-, nigro- [L. *niger*, black] *comb* black (nigricauline, nigrofuscous)

nihili- [L. *nihil*, nothing] *comb* nothing (nihili-parturient, nihility)

-nik *suf* one who is associated with ___ (beatnik, peacenik)

nim- [L. *nimius*, excessive] *base* superfluous (nimiety, nimious)

nimb- [L. *nimbus*, cloud] *base* cloud; rainstorm (nimbiferous, nimbification)

ning- [L. *ninguis*, snow] *base* snow (ninguid)

nipha- [Gr. *nipha*, snow] *comb* snow blindness (niphablepsia, niphotyphlosis)

nitid- [L. *nitidus*, shining, bright] *base* lustrous; bright (nitidiflorous, nitidity)

nitro- [L. *nitrum*, niter] **1.** *comb* presence of nitrogen compounds (nitro-cellulose); **2.** the presence of the NO_2 radical (nitrobenzene); **3.** niter (nitrobacteria)

-niv- [L. *nix/niv-*, snow] *base* snow (nival, niveous)

noci- [L. *nocere*, harm] *comb* hurt; pain; injury (nociceptor, nocivous)

nocti- [L. *nox/noct-*, night] *comb* night (noctiferous, noctilucent)

noctilion- [L. *noctilio*, family of bats] *base* bat (Noctilio, noctilionid)

noctui- [L. *noctua*, family of moths] *base* noctuid moth (noctuidous, noctuiform)

nocturn- [L. *nocturnus*, of the night] *base* at night (nocturnal, nocturnally)

nocu- [L. *nocuus*, harmful] *base* harmful (innocuous, nocuous)

-nod- [L. *nodus*, knot] *base* knot, knob (nodulated, nodulose)

-noe- [Gr. *noema*, thought, perception] *base* thought; intellect (noematic, noetic)

-noia [Gr. *nous*, mind] *comb* thought (metanoia, paranoia)

-nom-, -nym- [L. *nomen* name + Gr. *onoma*, name] *base* name (nomenclature, synonymous)

nomato- *see* **onomato-**

-nomia [L. *nomen*, name] *comb* name (anomia, paranomia)

nomo- [Gr. *nomos*, law] *comb* law; custom (nomotropic, nomology)

-nomy [Gr. *nomos*, arranging] *comb* systematized knowledge of (agronomy, astronomy)

non-[1] [L. *non*, not] *pre* negative; not (nonconforming, nondescript)

non-[2] , **nona-** [L. *nonus*, ninth] *base* nine, ninth (nonagon, nonan)

nonagen-, nonages- [L. *nonaginta*, ninety] *base* ninety (nonagenarian, nonagesimal)

-noo- [Gr. *noos*, mind] *base* mind (noögenism, nooscopic)

Normanno- [L. *Normannus*, Norman] *comb* Norman (Normanno-Gallican, Normanno-Saxonic)

normo- [L. *normalis*, right-angled] *comb* usual; normal (normoblastic, normotensive)

noso- [Gr. *nosos*, disease] *comb* disease (nosology, nosophobia)

nosocom- [Gr. *nosokomeion*, infirmary] *base* hospital (nosocomial, nosocomially)

nosto- [Gr. *nostos*, return] *comb* a return; nostalgia (nostology, nostomania)

nota-, noto-[1] [Gr. *notos*, the back] *comb* the back; dorsum (notancephalia, notochord)

notar- [L.*notarius*, clerk] *base* official witness (notarize, notary)

-notho- [Gr. *nothos*, spurious] *base* spurious; false (Notholaena, nothosaurus)

-noto-[2] [Gr. *notos*, the south] *comb* south (Notornis, notothere)

-nov-[1] [L. *novus*, new] *base* new (innovation, renovate)

-nov-[2] [L. *novem*, nine] *base* nine (November, novenary)

-noverc- [L. *noverca*, stepmother] *base* stepmother (novercal, novercant)

-nox- [L. *noxa*, injury] *base* harmful; (noxiousness, obnoxious)

-nub-, -nupt- [L. *nubere/nuptus*, wed] *base* marry (connubial, nuptial)

-nubi- [L. *nubes*, cloud] *base* cloud (nubiferous, nubigenous)

nuci- [L. *nux/nuci-*, nut] *comb* nut (nuciferous, nucifragous)

nuclei-, nucleo- [L. *nucleus*, kernel] *comb* nucleus: relation to; kernel (nucleiform, nucleoplasm)

nudi- [L. *nudus*, naked] *comb* naked; bare (nudibranchiate, nudiflorous)

-nuga- [L. *nugae*, trifles] *base* trifling (nugation, nugatory)

nulli- [L. *nullus*, not any] *comb* none (nullify, nulliparous)

-num- [L. *numerare*, to number] *base* count (enumerate, numerous)

-numisma- [Gr. *numisma*, money] *base* coinage (numismatics, numismatist)

nummi- [L. *nummus*, coin] *comb* coin; disk (nummiform, nummulary)

nummul- [L. *nummularius,* currency changing] *base* money changer (nummular, nummulary)

nuncup- [L. *nuncupare*, call by name] *base* declare, name (nuncupate, nuncupatory)

nundin- [L. *nundinare*, trade] *base* market; commerce (nundinal, nundination)

-nupt- [L. *nubere/nuptus*, wed] *base* wed (nuptial, prenuptial)

nur(us)- [L. *nurus*, daughter-in-law] *base* daughter-in-law (nurine)

nuta- [L. *nutare*, to nod] *base* sway; nod (nutant, nutation)

-nutr- [L. *nutrire*, nourish] *base* nourish (malnutrition, nutriment)

-nychia *see* **onycho-**

nycta-, nycti-, nycto- [Gr. *nux/nuct-*, night] *comb* night (nyctalopia, nyctitropic, nyctophobia)

-nym- *see* **-nom**

nympho- [Gr. *numphe*, bride; nymph; pupa] **1.** *comb* labia minora (nymphotomy); **2.** nymphs (nympholepsy); **3.** pupa of an insect (nymphiparous)

nystag- [Gr. *nustagmos*, drowsiness] *base* twitchy eye (nystagmoid, nystagmus)

-nyxis [Gr. *nuksis*, pricking] *base* stabbing, pricking (keratonyxis, scleronyxis)

O

-o [It. suf. *-o*] **1.** *suf* informal abbreviation (ammo); **2.** person associated with (politico)

oario- [Gr. *oarion*, little egg] *comb* ovary (oariocele, oariopathy). *See* **ovario-**

ob- [L. *ob-*, toward, upon, about, for] **1.** *pre* to; toward; before (object); **2.** opposed to; against (obnoxious); **3.** upon; over (obfuscate); **4.** completely; totally (objurgate). NOTE: **ob-** can change to: **o-** (omission); **oc-** (occur); **of-** (offer); **op-** (oppose)

obdur- [L. *obdurare*, harden] *base* stubborn, inflexible (obdurate, obdure)

obel- [L. *obelus*, critical mark shaped like an obelisk] *base* obelisk mark (obelize, obelus)

obes- [L. *obesus*, fat] *base* fat; heavy (obese, obesity)

obit- [L. *obitus*, death] *base* death (obitual, obituary)

objurg- [L. *obiurgare*, to reprimand] *base* rebuke, rail against (objurgate, objurgative)

oblit- [L. *obliterare*, to erase] *base* erase (obliterate, obliteration)

obliv- [L. *oblivium*, forgetfulness] *base* forgotten; lost to memory (oblivious, oblivescence)

oblongo- [L. *oblongus*, rather long] *comb* with oblong extension (oblongo-elliptic, oblong-ovate)

obol- [Gr. *obolos*, a silver coin] *base* ancient silver coin (obol, obolary)

obscur- [L. *obscurus*, dark, shady] *base* dark (obscurant, obscurity)

obsol- [L. *obsoletus*, worn out] *base* outmoded (obsolescence, obsolete)

obstin- [L. *obstinatus*, resolute] *base* stubborn (obstinacy, obstinately)

obstrep- [L. *obstreperus*, clamorous] *base* argumentative (obstreperous, obstreperousness)

obturat- [L. *obturatus*, closed, stopped up] *base* shut, occlude (obturation, obturator)

obtusi- [L. *obtusus*, blunted, dull] *comb* obtuse; blunted (obtusifolious, obtusi-pennate)

-occid- [L. *occidens*, setting sun] *base* west; (occident, occidental)

occipito- [L. *occiput*, back of the head]

comb occipital; skull (occipito-axial, occipito-parietal)

occlud-/occlus- [L. *occludere*, shut up or close] *base* close; obstruct (occlude, occlusion)

occult- [L. *occultus*, concealed] *base* hidden (occult, occultation)

ocelli- [L. *ocelus*, little eye] *comb* spot; eyelet (ocelliform, ocelliferous)

ochlo- [Gr. *okhlos*, crowd] *comb* crowd; mob (ochlocracy, ochlophobia)

ocho-¹ [Gr. *okhos*, carriage] *base* vehicle (ochophobia, ochomania)

ocho-² [Gr. *okhos*, anything that holds] *base* capacious; ample (ochopetalous)

ochreo- [L. *ochreus*, containing ochre] *comb* containing ochre; light brownish yellow (ochreo-ferrous, ochreo-testaceous)

ochro- [Gr. *okhros*, pale yellow] *comb* pale yellow (ochrocarpous, ochroleucous)

ociv- [Fr. *oisif*, idle] *base* sloth, laziness (ocivitous, ocivity)

-ock [Ger. suf. forming diminutives] *suf* diminutive: small (hassock, hillock)

ocno- [Gr. *oknos*, hesitation] *comb* clinging insecure personality (ocnophil, ocnophilic)

-ocracy [Gr. *kratos*, strength, authority] *comb* the rule of any class (plutocracy, tradeocracy)

octa-, octi-, octo- [Gr. *okto*, eight] *comb* eight (octagon, octipara, octobrachiate)

octakaideca- [Gr. *okto*, eight + *kai*, and + *deka*, ten] *comb* eighteen (octakaideca-hedral, octakaidecahedron)

octan- [Gr. *okto*, eight] *base* eighth (octandrous, octant)

octocent- [L. *octo*, eight + *centenarius*, consisting of a hundred] *base* eight hundred (octocentennial, octocentenary)

octogen-, octoges- [L. *octogenarius*, eighty] *base* eighty (octogenarian, octogesimal)

oculi-, oculo- [L. *ocularius*, pert. to the eye] *comb* eye (oculiform, oculomotor)

ocy- *comb* [Gr. *okus*, swift] swift (ocydrome, ocypodan)

-ode¹ [Gr. *hodos*, way] *comb* way; path (cathode, electrode)

-ode² [Gr. *odes*, of the nature of] *suf* like (geode, phyllode)

odi- [L. *odium*, hatred] *base* hatred (odious, odium)

-odic [Gr. stem -*od*, smell] *comb* smell (cacodic, euodic)

-odin [Gr. *odis*, birth] *comb* type of gamete release by a coelomate (idiodinic, porodinic)

odo- [Gr. *hodos*, way] *comb* road; journey (odometer). *See* **hodo-**

odoben- [Gr. *odous*, tooth + *baino*, walk, step] *base* walrus (odobenidae)

-odont, odonto- [Gr. stem *odont-*, tooth] *comb* tooth (macrodont, odontoblast)

odori-, odoro- [L. *odor*, smell] *comb* smell; scent (odoriferant, odoroscope)

-odus [Gr. *odous*, tooth] *comb* having teeth; names of genera (ceratodus, Machairodus)

-odynia, odyno- [Gr. *odune*, pain] *comb* pain in ___ (osteodynia, odynophagia)

oeco- [Gr. *oikos*, house] *comb* environment (œcological, œcology). *See* **eco-**

oego- [Gr. *oigein*, to open] *base* open (œgopsid). *Also* **oigo-** (oigopsid)

oeno- [Gr. *oinos*, wine] *comb* wine (œnomania, œnophile). *Also* **eno-** (enophile)

oesophago- *see* **esophag-**

off-¹ [ME *of*, separation] *comb* away from (offbrand, offcolor)

-off² [< horse racing: *they're off and running*] *suf* a competition (bakeoff, cookoff)

ogdo- [Gr. *ogdoas*, eight in number] *comb* eight (ogdoad, ogdoastich)

-oid, -oidal [Gr. *eidos*, resemblance] *suf* shape; like; resembling (spheroid, trapezoidal)

-oidea [NL. sci. suf. -*oidea*] *comb* names of zoological classes; names of entomological superfamilies; (Molluscoidea, Nautiloidea)

-oigo- [Gr. *oigein*, to open] *base* open (oigopsid, Oigopsidae)

oiko- [Gr. *oikos*, house] *comb* environment (oikofugic, oikoid). *See* **eco-**

oino- [Gr. *oinos*, wine] *comb* wine (oino-
logical, oinomania). *See* **œno-**

-ol [Abbrev. of L. *oleum*, oil] *suf* [chemis-
try] **1.** alcohol or phenol (menthol); **2.**
same as **-ole** (anethol)

-ola [L. suf. *-olus/-a/-um*, somewhat] *suf*
diminutive (aureola, variola)

-ole[1] [Abbrev. of L. *oleum*, oil] *suf* [chem-
istry] **1.** compound: closed-chain
with five members (pyrrole); **2.**
names of certain aldehydes and ethers
(anethole)

-ole[2] [L. suf. *-olus/-a/-um*, somewhat] *suf*
diminutive (foveole, variole)

olea-, -oleic, oleo- [Ge. *elaia*, olive tree]
comb oil; olein; oleic (oleaginous, pal-
mitoleic, oleomargarine)

olecran- [Gr. *olekranon*, elbow] *base*
elbow (olecranarthritis, olecranon)

-olent [L. *olere*, to smell] *base* giving out a
smell (grateolent, redolent)

oler- [L. *olus/oler-*, pot-herb] *base* vegetables; pot-herbs (oleraceous,
olericulture)

olfacto- [L. *olfacere*, to smell] *comb* smell
(olfactometer, olfactory)

oligo- [Gr. *oligos*, little] *comb* few; deficiency of (oligoglottism, oligophrenia)

olisto- [Gr. *olisthein*, to slip] *comb* glide or
slip (olistolith, olistrome)

olit- [L. *holitor*, kitchen-gardener] *base*
vegetables (olitory)

oliv-, olivaceo- [L. *oliva*, olive]
comb dusky green (olivaceous,
olivaceo-cinereous)

-ologist [Gr. *logos*, discourse] *comb* specialist (mixologist, proctologist)

-oma, -ome [Gr. suf. *-oma*, tumor] *suf*
morbid growth; tumor; neoplasm; formation (sarcoma, phyllome)

omalo- *see* **homalo-**

ombro- [Gr. *ombros*, rain shower]
comb rain; shower (ombrometer,
ombrophilous)

ommat- [Gr. *omma/ommat-*, eye] *base*
eye (ommatophore, ommatophorous)

omni- [L. *omnis*, all] *comb* all; every-
where (omniscient, omnivorous)

omo-[1] [Gr. *omos*, shoulder] *comb* shoulder (omodynia, omohyoid)

omo-[2] [Gr. *omos*, raw] *base* raw (omopha-
gia, omophagous)

omphac- [Gr. *omphaks*, unripe grape]
base green like an unripe grape
(omphacine, omphacite)

omphalo- [Gr. *omphalos*, the navel]
comb navel; umbilicus (omphalitis,
omphalophlebitis)

-on [< *ion*] *suf* [chemistry] **1.** elementary
particle (gluon); **2.** inert gas (neon)

oncho- [Gr. *onkos*, barb] *comb* barb, hook
(onchocerciasis, onchocercosis)

onco- [Gr. *onkos*, mass] *comb* tumor
(oncologist, oncotomy)

-one [Gr. fem. suf. *-one*] *suf* [chemistry] a
ketone (acetone, nitrone)

oneiro- [Gr. *oneiros*, dream] *comb* dream
(oneirocritic, oneirodynia)

-oner- [L. *onus/oner-*, burden] *base* burden (onerative, onerous)

-onic [Gr. fem. suf. *-one* + *-ic*, of the
nature of] *suf* names of acids (galac-
tonic, gluconic acid)

onio- [Gr. *onios*, for sale] *base* buy (onio-
mania, oniophobia)

-onisc- [Gr. *oniskos*, woodlouse] *base*
woodlouse (Oniscidae, onisciform)

ono- [Gr. *onos*, ass] *base* donkey; beast of
burden (onology, Onopordon)

-onocrot- [Gr. *onokrotalos*, pelican] *base*
pelican (onocrotal, onocrotalus)

onom-, onomato- [Gr. *onoma*,
name] *comb* name (onomastic,
onomatopoeia)

-onomasia [Gr. *onomasia*, name]
suf name, naming (antonomasia,
paronomasia)

onto- [Gr. *on/ont-*, being] *comb* being;
existence (ontogenesis, ontology)

onych-, -onychia, onycho- [Gr. *onuks*,
fingernail] *comb* claw; nail (onychosis,
leukonychia, onychophagy)

-onym, -onymy [Gr. *onoma*, name]
comb name (paranym, pseudonym,
synonymy)

oo- [Gr. *oon*, egg] *comb* egg; ovum
(oocystic, oogamous)

oophoro- [Gr. *oon*, egg + *pherein*, to

bear] *comb* ovary (oophorectomy, oophoritis)

op- [Gr. *ops*, eye] *comb* eye (opalgia, optics)

-opac- [L. *opacus*, shady] *base* shade; dimness (opacate, opacity)

-oper-[1] [L. *opus/oper-*, work] *base* work; labor (operate, operosity)

-oper-[2] [L. *operculare*, furnish with a lid] *base* lid; cover (inoperculate, operculum)

ophel- [Gr. *ophellimos*, beneficial] *base* advantageous, satisfying (ophelimity)

-ophidia, ophidio- [Gr. *ophis/ophid-*, serpent] *comb* [medicine] venemous snakes (Thanatophidia, ophidiophobia)

ophio- [Gr. *ophis*, serpent] *comb* snake (ophiomancy, ophiolatry)

ophry- [Gr. *ophrys*, eyebrow] *base* eyebrow (ophritis, ophryosis)

ophthalmo- [Gr. *ophthalmos*, eye] *comb* eye (ophthalmodynia, ophthalmoscope)

-opia [Gr. *ops*, eye] *comb* eye defect; vision (amblyopia, diplopia)

opim- [L *opimus*, fruitful] *base* sumptuous (opime, opimus)

opio- [Gr. *opion*, opium] *comb* poppy juice (opiomania, opiophagy)

-opiso- [Gr. *opiso*, behind, again] *base* backwards (opisometer, opisometry)

opistho- [Gr. *opisthen*, behind] *comb* behind; dorsal (opisthodont, opisthopterous)

opo- [Gr. *opos*, juice] *comb* juice (opobalsam, opopanax)

oporo- [Gr. *opora*, fruit-time] *comb* fruit (oporopolist, oporopolistic)

oppositi- [L. *oppositus*, opposite] *comb* opposite (oppositiflorous, oppositifolious)

opsi-[1] [Gr. *opse*, late] *comb* late (opsigamy, opsimathy)

opsi-[2] [Gr. *opsis*, eye] *comb* sight; eye (opsin, opsiometer)

-opsia [Gr. *opsia*, sight or vision] *comb* sight; view (dysopsia, hemianopsia)

-opsis [Gr. *opsis*, sight] **1.** *comb* see; (synopsis); **2.** likeness; resembling (coreopsis, stereopsis)

opso-[1] [Gr. *opsis*, sight] *comb* eye (opsoclonus)

opso-[2] [Gr. *opsonein*, to prepare food] cooked meat; relish; rich fare; provisions; sweets (opsomania, opsonium)

-opsy [Gr. *opsia*, sight] *comb* examination (autopsy, biopsy)

-opt-[1] [L. *optio*, choice] *base* wish; choice (optional)

-opt-[2] [L. *optimus*, best] *base* best (optimism, optimum)

optico- [Gr. *optikos*, of seeing] *comb* pertaining to sight (optico-ciliary, optico-kinetic)

opto- [Gr. *optikos*, of seeing] *comb* sight; eye (optometry, optostriate)

opul- [L *opulentia*, wealth] *base* riches (opulence, opulent)

opus- [L. *opus*, work] *base* work (opus, opuscular)

or-[1] [L. *os/or-*, mouth] *base* mouth (oral, orifice)

-or[2] [Gr. suf. *-tor*, nouns of agent] *suf* person or thing that (counselor, inventor)

-or[3] [L. n. suf. *-or*] *suf* quality; condition (horror, odor)

orag- [F. *orage*, storm] *base* storm (orage, oragious)

-orama [Gr. *orama*, that which is seen] *comb* display; spectacle (georama, panorama)

-orat- [L. *oratus*, spoken] *base* speak (orator, oratorical)

orbiculato- [L. *orbiculus*, small disk] *comb* partly rounded (orbiculato-cordate, orbiculato-elliptical)

orbito- [L. *orbita*, orbit] *comb* orbit; circle (orbitonasal, orbitorostral)

-orches- [Gr. *orkestra*, part of the stage where the chorus danced] *base* dance (orchesography, orchestic)

orchido-[1] [L. *orchis*, orchid] *comb* orchid (Orchidacae, orchidology)

orchido-[2] [Gr. *orkhis*, testicle] *comb* testicle (orchidotomy)

orchio- [Gr. *orkhis*, testicle] *comb* testicle (orchialgia, orchiocele)

ordin- [L. *ordo*, order] *base* position in a series (ordinability, ordinal)

orect-, -orexia [Gr. *orektikos*, pert. to

appetite] *comb* appetite (orectic, dysorexia)

organo- [Gr. *organon*, organ] *comb* organ; organic (organography, organoplasty)

orgi- [Gr.*orgia*, secret rites] *base* licentious behavior (orgiac, orgiastic)

-orial [L suf. *-or*, one who + *-ialis*, relating to] *suf* pertaining to an action (conspiratorial, memorial)

orient- [L. *oriens*, rising] *base* east; sunrise (orientalism, orienteering)

-orious [L suf. *-orius*] *suf* relating to; characterized by (censorious, meritorious)

orismo- [Gr. *horismos*, bounding, defining] *comb* definition; boundary (orismological, orismology)

-orium [L. *-orium*, place for] *suf* a place for ___ (auditorium, exploratorium)

orneo-, orni-, ornitho-, orno- [Gr. *orneion*, bird] *comb* bird (orneoscopic, orniscopic, ornithology, ornomancy)

oro-[1] [L. *os/or-*, mouth] *comb* mouth; (oro-anal, orolingual)

oro-[2] [Gr. *oros*, mountain] *comb* mountain (orogenic, orology). *Also* **oreo-** (oreology)

orrho- [Gr. *oros*, serum, whey] *comb* serum (orrhocyst, orrhoid)

ortho- [Gr. *orthos*, straight] **1.** *comb* straight; regular; upright (orthodontia); **2.** right angle (orthorhombic); **3.** proper; correct; standard (orthography); **4.** [chemistry] that acid of a group containing the same nonmetallic element that has the largest number of OH groups per atom of the nonmetal (orthophosphoric); **5.** [medicine] correction of; deformities (orthopedics)

-ory [L. suf. *-orium*] **1.** *suf* having the nature of (hortatory); **2.** a place for ___ (observatory)

ortyg- [Gr. *ortuks/ortug-*, quail] *base* quail (ortygan, Ortiginae)

orycto- [Gr. *oruktos*, dug out] *comb* dug up: fossil or mineral (oryctological, orictologist)

-oryzi- [Gr. *oruksa*, rice] *base* rice (oryzivorous, Orizopsis)

oscheo- [Gr. *oskheon*, scrotum] *comb* scrotum (oscheitis, oscheocele)

-oscill- [L. *oscillare*, to swing] *base* swing (oscillation, oscillatory)

oscin- [L. *oscen*, singing bird] *base* songbirds (oscine, Oscines)

-oscit- [L. *oscitare*, to gape, yawn] *base* yawn (oscitancy, oscitation)

oscul- [L. *osculari*, to kiss] *base* kiss (osculation, osculatory)

-ose[1] [Fr. suf. *-ose* < Gr. *-os*] **1.** *suf* carbohydrate (cellulose); **2.** protein hydrolysis: product of (proteose)

-ose[2] [L. suf. *-osus*] *suf* full of; containing; like (verbose). *See* **-osity**

-osis [Gr. suf. *-osis*] **1.** *suf* state; condition; action (osmosis); **2.** abnormal condition; diseased condition (neurosis, tuberculosis)

-osity [L. suf. *-ositas*] *suf* full of; containing; like (generosity, verbosity). *See* **-ose**[2]

-osmia [Gr. *osme*, odor] *comb* smell; odor (anosmia, parosmia)

osmio- [Gr. *osme*, odor] *comb* osmium (osmio-chloride, osmiophilic)

osmo-[1] [Gr. *osme*, odor] *comb* smell; odor (osmoceptor, osmodysphoria)

osmo-[2] [Gr. *osmos*, impulsion] *comb* osmosis; (osmogene, osmolarity)

osphresio- [Gr. *osphresis*, smelling] *comb* odor; sense of smell (osphresiology, osphresiophobia)

osphy-, osphyo- [Gr. *osphus*, the loin] *comb* loins (osphyalgia, osphyocele)

-ossi, osseo-, osteo- [Gr. *osteon*, bone] *comb* bone (ossification, osseomucin, osteoplasty)

ossifrag- [L. *ossifraga*, sea-eagle < *os*, bone + *frag-*, to break] *base* osprey (ossifrage, ossifragous)

osti- [L. *ostium*, gate] *base* gate; opening (ostiolate, ostiole)

-ostraca, ostraco- [Gr. *ostrakon*, a shell] *comb* shell (Leptostraca, ostracoderm)

ostre-, ostrei-, ostreo- [Gr. *ostreion*, oyster] *comb* oyster (ostreaceous, ostreiform, ostreophage)

ot-, oto- [Gr. *ous/ot-*, ear] *comb* ear (othemorrhagia, otopyosis)

-ota [Gr. suf. *-ote*] *suf* plural ending of taxonomic names (amniota, biota)

-ote [Gr. suf. *-otes*] *suf* singular ending of taxonomic names (amniote, eukaryote)

oti- [L. *otium*, leisure] *base* idleness; leisure (otiose, otiosity)

-otic [Gr. suf. *-otikos*] **1.** *suf* affected with; of (sclerotic); **2.** producing (narcotic)

oulo-[1] [Gr. *oulan*, gums] *comb* gums (oulitis, oulorrhagy)

oulo-[2] [Gr. *oulas*, wooly] *base* curly, wooly (oulopholite, oulotrichous). *Also* **ulo-**

ourano- [Gr. *ouranos*, sky] *comb* heavens (ouranography, ouranomancy). *See* **urano-**

ouro- [Gr. *ouron*, urine] *comb* urine (ouromancy, ouromelanin). *Also* **uro-**

-ous [L. suf. *-osus*, full of] **1.** *suf* characterized by; having; full of (generous); **2.** [chemistry] having a valence lower than in a compound whose name ends in -ic (sulfurous)

-ousia, -ousian [Gr. *ousia*, substance] *comb* essence; substance (homoousia, heteroousian)

out- [O.E. *ut*, out] **1.** *comb* situated at; outside (outpatient); **2.** going away; outward (outcast); **3.** better; greater; more than (outsell)

ovario- [L. *ovum*, egg] *comb* ovary (ovariocentesis, ovariotomy). *See* **oario-**

ovato- [L. *ovum*, egg] *comb* egg-shaped (ovato-deltoid, ovato-oblong)

over- [O.E. *ofer*, over] **1.** *comb* above; upper; superior; eminent (overbearing); **2.** beyond normal; excessive (overrate); **3.** passing across; passing beyond (overshoot); **4.** moving lower (overwhelm)

ovi-[1] [L. *ovum*, egg] *comb* egg; ovum (oviduct, ovigenous)

ovi-[2] [L. *ovis*, sheep] *comb* sheep (ovibovine, ovicide)

ovo- [L. *ovum*, egg] *comb* ovum; ovally (ovococcus, ovolecithin)

oxa-, oxo- [< *oxygen*] *pre* [chemistry] presence of oxygen (oxazine, oxopolysaccharide)

oxy-[1] [Gr. *oksus*, sharp] *comb* sharp; pointed; acute; acid (oxycephalic, oxyphonia)

oxy-[2] [< *oxygen*] *comb* oxygen-containing (oxyacetylene, oxygenous)

oxyur- [Gr. *oksus*, sharp + *oura*, tail] *base* worm (oxyuricide, oxyurous)

ozo- [Gr. *ozein*, smell] *comb* smell (ozocerite, ozostomia)

ozono- [Gr. *ozein*, smell] *comb* ozone (ozonolysis, ozonometry)

ozostom- [Gr. *ozostomos*, having bad breath] *base* bad breath (ozostomatic, ozostomia)

P

pabul- [L. *pabulum*, fodder] *base* fodder (pabular, pabulum)

pac- [L. *pax/pac-*, peace] *base* peace (pacific, pacifist)

paca- [L. *pacare*, to pacify] *base* appeasement (pacation, pacative)

pachno- [Gr. *pakhno*, hoarfrost, rime] *comb* frost (pachnolite)

pachy- [Gr. *pakhus*, thick] *comb* thick; large; massive (pachycardia, pachycephaly)

pachyderm- [Gr. *pakhus*, thick + *derma*, skin] *base* elephant; tapir (pachydermatous, pachydermoid)

pacif- [L. *pacification*, peace-making] *base* peace-making (pacification, pacifist)

pact- [L. *pactum*, agreement] *base* agreement (pact, paction)

paedo-[1] [Gr. *pedon*, soil] *comb* dirt; soil (paedogenic). *Usually* **pedo-** (pedocal)

paedo-[2] [Gr. *pais/paid-*, child] *comb* child; immature; doll (paedomorphic). *Usually* **pedo-** (pedophile)

-pagia [Gr. *pagos*, something fixed] *comb* conjoined twins (ectopagia, sternopagia)

pagin- [L. *pagina*, page] *base* page-related (paginal, pagination)

pago- [Gr. *pagos*, frost] *comb* cold; frost (pagophagia, Pagophila)

pagur- [Gr. *pagouros*, crab] *base* hermit crab (pagurian, paguroid)

-pagus [Gr. *pagos*, something fixed] *comb* conjoined twins (diplopagus, thoracopagus)

-paizo- [Gr. *paizo*, play with] *base* love-play (paizogonous, paizogony)

pala- [L. *pala*, shovel, spade] *base* spade-shaped (palaceous, palette-knife)

palato- [L. *palatum*, palate] *comb* palate; roof of mouth (palatoglossal, palatonasal)

palea- [L. *palea*, chaff] *base* chaff; chaff-like (paleaceous, paleaeform)

paleo- [Gr. *palaios*, ancient] **1.** *comb* ancient; prehistoric (Paleozoic); **2.** primitive (paleolithic); **3.** paleontological (paleozoology). *Also* **paeleo-** (paeleozoic)

palest- [Gr. *palaistra*, wrestling] *base* wrestling (palestral, palestric)

-pali-, palil-, -palin- [Gr. *palin*, again] *base* over; again (paliphrasia, palilogy, palingenesis)

pallia-, pallio- [L. *pallium*, cloak, mantle] *comb* pallium; mantle (palliament, palliopedal)

pallidi- [L. *pallidus*, pale] *comb* pale (pallidiflorous, pallidiventrate)

pallio- [L. *pallium*, cloak] *comb* mantle, pallium (pallio-cardiac, palliovisceral)

pallo- [Gr. *pallein*, quiver, quake] *comb* vibrations (pallometric, pallometrical)

palma-, palmi- [L. *palma*, palm tree] *base* palm tree (palmaceous, palmacite, palmicolous)

palmati-, palmato- [L. *palmatus*, marked with the palm of the hand] *comb* like the palm of the hand (palmatifid, palmatopeltate)

-palp- [L. *palpare*, to stroke] *base* touch; feel (palpable, palpiform)

palpebra- [L. *palpebra*, eyelid] *base* eyelid (palpebral, palpebrate)

paludi-, palus- [L. *palus/palud-*, swamp, marsh] *base* marsh (paludicole, palustrine)

palumb- [L. *palumbis*, pigeon or dove] *base* pigeon (palumbine, palumbus)

palyn- [Gr. *pale*, fine meal or dust] *base* pollen (palynology, palynomorph)

-pampin- [L. *pampinus*, tendril] *base* vine; tendril (pampinary, pampiniform)

pan-[1] [Gr. *pas/pan-*, all] **1.** *comb* all (pantheism); **2.** common to all/every (Pan-American); **3.** belief in a unified group (Pan-Slavism)

pan-[2] [L. *panis*, bread] *base* bread (panary, panivorous)

pancrat- [Gr. *pankration*, physically powerful] *base* highly skilled (pancratic, pancratist)

pancreato-, pancreo- [NL *pancreas*, pancreas] *comb* of the pancreas (pancreatotomy, pancreopathy)

pand- [L. *pandus*, arched, bowed, warped] *base* bending under a weight, esp. in architecture (pandation)

pandicul- [L. *pandiculari*, stretch oneself] *base* stretched out (pandiculated, pandiculation)

pandur- [L. *pandura*, musical instrument] *base* fiddle (pandurate, panduriform)

pann- [L. *pannus*, a cloth] *base* rag-like, cloth-like (Pannaria, pannose)

-pannychy [Gr. *pannukios*, lasting all night] *comb* lasting all night (psychopannychistic, psychopannychy)

pant-, panto- [Gr. *pas/pant-*, all] *comb* all; every (pantalgia, pantograph)

-papaver- [L. *papaver*, poppy] *base* poppy (Papavereae, papaverous)

papil- [L. *papilio*, butterfly] *base* butterfly (papilionaceous, papilionine)

papilli-, papillo-, papilloso- [L. *papilla*, nipple, pimple] *comb* papillary; nipple-like (papilliform, papillomatosis, papilloso-asperate)

papp- [L. *pappus*, down, fuzz] *base* plant down (pappiferous, pappose)

papulo- [L. *papula*, pustule] *comb* papule; skin elevation (papulation, papuliferous)

papyro- [L. *papyrus*, paper] *comb* papyrus (papyral, papyrology)

par-[1] [L. *pars/part-*, portion] *base* fraction; portion (partition, tripartite)

par-[2] [L. *parus*, titmouse] *base* titmouse; chickadee (Parinae, parine)

para-[1] [L. *parare*, prepare] **1.** *comb* protecting from (parapet); **2.** using a parachute (paratroop)

para-[2] [Gr. *para*, beside] **1.** *pre* beside; beyond (parallel); **2.** [chemistry] an isomer, modification, polymer, derivative of a specified substance (paradichlorobenzene); **3.** [medicine] secondary capacity; accessory capacity (paramedical); **4.** [medicine] functionally disordered; abnormal (parafunctional); **5.** [medicine] like; resembling (paracholera)

-para[3] [L. *parus*, bearing] *comb* woman who has given birth; parturient (multipara, primipara)

paral- [Gr. *paralios*, by the sea] *base* seashore (paralian, paralic)

paralip- [Gr. *paraleipein*, omit] *base* neglect; omission (paralipomena, paralipsis)

paraphil- [Gr. *para*, beyond + *philia*, sexual interest] *base* unusual sexual practices (paraphilia, paraphiliac)

parasit- [Gr. *parasitos*, one who eats at another's table] *base* parasite (parasitical, parasiticide)

parc- [L. *parcus*, sparing] *base* frugality (parciloquy, parcity)

pard- [Gr. *pardos*, pard] *base* leopard (pardalotus, pardine)

paremio- [Gr. *paroimia*, proverb, maxim] *comb* proverb (paremiographer, paremiology)

pares- [Gr. *paresis*, relaxation] *base* paralysis (paresis, pareso-analgesia)

pari- [L. *par*, equal] *comb* equal (paridigitate, paripinnate)

-paria [L. *par*, equal] *comb* genera and order of trilobytes; cheeks (Hypoparia, Opisthoparia)

parieto- [L. *paries/pariet-*, wall] *comb* forming a cavity; parietal; wall (parietofrontal, parietomastoid)

pariso- [Gr. *parisos*, almost equal] *comb* evenly balanced; almost equal (parisology, parison)

paroch- [L. *parochia*, parish] *base* limited, provincial (parochial, parochialness)

parod- [Gr. *parodia*, burlesque poem or song] *base* satirization (parodistic, parody)

paroem- [Gr. *paroimia*, proverb] *base* proverb (paroemiographer, paroemiology). *Also* **parem-** (paremiography)

-parous [L. *parus*, bearing , producing] *comb* producing; bearing; bringing forth (oviparous, viviparous)

pars- [L. *parsimonia*, frugality] *base* spare; save (parsimonious, parsimony)

partheno- [Gr. *parthenos*, virgin] *comb* virgin (parthenogenesis, parthenology)

parti- [L. *pars/part-*, part] *base* division; part (parti-colored, partition)

-partur- [L. *parturire*, bring forth] *base* giving birth (parturifacient, parturition)

parvi-, parvo- [L. *parvus*, little] *comb* small (parvifolious, parvoline)

pascu- [L. *pascuum*, pasture] *base* grazing (pascuant, pascuous)

pasi- [Gr. *pasi*, for all] *comb* all; universal; gestures to communicate (pasigraphic, pasigraphy, pasimology). *See* **pan-**

-passeri- [L. *passer*, sparrow] *base* perching bird; sparrow (passeriform, passerine)

pastin- [L. *pastinaca*, parsnip] *base* parsnip (pastinaceous, pastinacine)

pate- [L. *patere*, lie open] *base* revelation (patefaction, patefy)

-pated [poss. L. *patena*, dish] *comb* head: type of (bald-pated, muddle-pated)

patell- [L. *patella*, pan] *base* kneecap (patellar, patelliform)

-pater- [L. *pater*, father] *base* father (paternalism, paternity)

-path, -pathic, patho-, -pathy [Gr. *pathos*, suffering, misery] *comb* suffering; disease; feeling (psychopath, telepathic, pathopoeia, antipathy)

patri- [L. *pater/patr-*, father] *comb* father (patriarch, patrimony)

patroc- [L. *patrocinium*, protection] *base* support; defend (patrocinate, patrociny)

patroio- [Gr. *patrios*, hereditary] *comb* ancestor (patroiomania, patroiophobia)

patru- [L. *patruus*, father's brother] *base* uncle (patruel, patruity)

patul- [L. *patulus*, lying open] *base* open; spread out (patulent, patulous)

pauc-, pauci- [L. *paucus*, few, little] *comb* few (paucity, pauciflorous)

paulo- [Gr. *paula*, pause] *comb* pause (paulocardia, paulo-post)

paup- [L. *pauper*, poor] *base* poor (pauper, pauperize)

pauro- [Gr. *pauros*, little, small] *base* little, small (paurometabolous, pauropod)

paus- [Gr. *pausis*, cessation] *base* pause (andropause, menopause)

-pavid- [L. *pavidus*, fearful] *base* fearful (impavidity, pavid)

-pavon- [L. *pavo*, peacock] **1.** *base* peacock (pavonian); **2.** peacock blue (pavonine)

pax- [L. *pax*, peace] *comb* peace (Pax Germanica, Pax Romana)

paxill- [L. *paxillus*, stake, peg] *base* pillarlike; stalklike (paxilla, paxillose)

-pecca- [L. *peccare*, to sin] *base* fault; sin; disease (impeccable, peccant)

pect-[1] [L. *pectus/pector-*, breast bone] *base* breastbone (pectoral, pectoriloquial)

pect-[2] [Gr. *pectos*, curdled] *base* coagulated (pectic, pectin)

pectinato- [L. *pectinare*, to comb] *comb* like the teeth of a comb (pectinato-denticulate, pectinato-fimbricate)

pecu- [L. *pecus*, farm animal] *base* cattle (pecuarious, pecudiculture)

pecul- [L. *peculari*, to embezzle] *base* embezzle (peculation, peculator)

-pecun- [L. *pecunia*, wealth] *base* money (impecunious, pecuniary)

ped-[1], **-pede, pedi-, pedo-**[1] [L. *pes/ped-*,

foot] *comb* foot (pedal, centipede, pedicure, pedopathy). *Also* **pod-** (tripod)

ped-[2] [Gr. *pais/paid-*, child] *comb* child (pedagogy)

ped-[3] [Gr. *pedon*, soil] *comb* dirt, soil (pedology, pedocal)

pedati- [L. *pedatus*, having feet] *comb* pedately; like a foot (pedatifid, pedatisect)

-pedia [Gr. *paideia*, instruction] *comb* teach (encyclopedia, pharmacopedia)

pedicul- [L. *pediculus*, louse] *base* lice (pediculosis, pediculous)

pedio- [Gr. *pedion*, a plain] *base* flat surface; plain (pedion, pedionomite)

pedipalp- [L. *pes/ped-*, foot + *palpus*, feeler] *base* scorpion (pedipalpate, pedipalpous)

pedo-[2] [Gr. *paid-*, child] *comb* child (pedobaptism, pedodontia)

pedo-[3] [Gr. *pedon*, dirt] *comb* dirt; soil (pedocal, pedosphere)

pegm- [Gr. *pegmat-*, fastened together] *base* framework; fastening (pegmatite, pegmatoid)

pego- [Gr. *pege*, spring, fountain] *base* spring; fountain (pegomancy)

peino- [Gr. *peina*, hunger] *comb* hunger (peinotherapy)

peir- [Gr. *peiran*, attempt] *base* try; experiment (peirameter, peirastic)

pejor- [L. *pejor*, worse] *base* worse (pejorative, pejority)

-pel- [L. *pellere*, drive] *base* push; drive (propel, repel). *Also* **-pul-** (propulsion)

pelad- [Fr. *peler*, strip of hair] *base* bald (peladic, pelade)

pelag- [Gr. *pelagos*, the sea] *base* sea (archipelago, pelagic)

pelarg- [Gr. *pelargos*, stork] *base* stork (pelargic, pelargomorph)

pelec- [Gr. *pelekus*, ax] *base* hatchet (pelecoid, pelecypod)

pelecan- [Gr. *pelekan*, pelican] *base* pelican (pelecanid, Pelecanus)

pelico- [Gr. *pelika*, pelvis] *comb* pelvis (pelicology, pelicometer)

pelios- [Gr. *pelios*, livid] *base* livid (peliosis, peliosis hepatitis)

pell-, pelli- [Gr. *pella*, skin, hide] *base* skin; hide (pellagra, pellibranchiate)

-pelm-, -pelmous [Gr. *pelma*, sole of the foot] *base* sole of the foot (antiopelmous, pelmatogram, desmopelmous)

pelo- [Gr. *pelos*, mud, mire] *comb* mud; clay (Pelodytes, pelophilous)

pelor- [Gr. *pelor*, monster] *base* monster (pelorization, pelorize)

pelt-, pelti-, pelto- [Gr. *pelte*, small shield] *comb* shield (peltate, peltiferous, peltogaster)

peltati-, peltato- [Gr. *pelte*, small shield] *comb* shield-shaped (peltatifid, peltatodigitate)

pelvi- [L. *pelvis*, pelvis] *comb* pelvis; pelvic; basin-shaped (pelvimeter, pelvisacrum)

pemm- [Gr. *pemma*, cake of dressed food] *base* cake of dried meat + (pemmican, pemmicanize)

pemphig- [Gr. *pemphig*, blister] *base* blister (pemphigoid, pemphigus)

pemphred- [Gr. *pemphredon*, kind of wasp] *base* wasp (Pemphredon, Pemphredoninae)

-pend- [L. *pendere*, hang] **1.** *base* hang (pendant); **2.** pay; weigh (expend). *Also* **-pens-** (pension)

pendulin- [L. *pendulus*, hanging] *base* birds with hanging nests (penduline, Pendulinus)

pen(e)- [L. *pene*, almost] *comb* almost; nearly (penannular, peninsula)

-penia [Gr. *penia*, poverty, need] *comb* poverty; deficiency; tightening (kaliopenia, neutropenia)

penit- [L. *penitentia*, repentance] *base* repentance (penitent, plenitude)

pennati- [L. *pennatus*, furnished with wings] *comb* feather (pennatifid, pennatilobate)

penni- [L. *penna*, feather] *comb* feather; featherlike (penniferous, penniform)

-penny [OE *penig*] *comb* monetary unit (catch-penny, halfpenny)

peno- [Gr. *poine*, penalty] *base* punishment (penologist, penology)

penta- [Gr. *pente*, five] *comb* five (pentacapsular, pentamerous)

pentakaideca- [Gr. *pente*, five + *kai*, and + *deka*, ten] *comb* fifteen (pentakaidecahedral, pentakaidecahedron)

pentaconta- [Gr. *pentekonte*, fifty] *comb* fifty (pentacontadrachn, pentecontaglossal)

pentecost- [Gr. *pentekonta*, fifty] *base* fifty (Pentecost, pentecostal)

penth- [Gr. *penthos*, grief, sorrow] *base* grief (nepenthe, nepenthean)

penther- [Gr. *penthera*, mother-in-law] *base* mother-in-law (pentheraphobia)

penur- [L. *penuria*, scarcity] *base* poverty; lack (penurious, penury)

-peo- [Gr. *peos*, penis] *base* penis (peotillomania, peotomy)

pepo- [Gr. *pepon*, large ripe melon] *base* gourd, melon, pumpkin (peponida, peponium)

peps-, -pepsia, pept-, pepto- [Gr. *pepsis*, digestion] *comb* digest (pepsinogen, dyspepsia, peptic, peptogenic)

per- [L. *per*, through] **1.** *pre* through; away (percolate); **2.** completely; very (persuade); **3.** [chemistry] containing a specified element or radical in its maximum or a relatively high valence (perchlorate)

percepto- [L. *percipere*, to perceive] *comb* perceived (percepto-diagnostic, percepto-motor)

perces- [L. *perca*, perch] *base* barracuda, mullet (Percesoses, Percesocine)

percesoc-, -perci-, -perco- [L. *perca*, perch] *base* barracuda; perch (percesocine, perciform, percomorph)

perd- [L. *perdere*, to lose] *base* destroy; lose (perdifoil, perdition)

-perdic- [L. *perdrix*, partridge, quail] *base* partridge (Perdicinae, perdicine)

perdri- [L. *perdrix*, partridge, quail] *base* partridge (perdricide, perdrigon)

peregrin- [L. *per*, through + *ager*, field] *base* travel; wander (peregrinate, peregrine)

perempt- [L. *perimere*, to destroy] *base* destructive; decisive (perempt, peremptory)

perenn- [L. *per*, through + *annus*, year] *base* lasting (perennial, perennibranch) perfid- [L. *perfidus*, treachery] *base* deceitful (perfidious, perfidy)

-pergamen- [L. *pergamina*, parchment] *base* parchment (pergameneous, pergamentaceous)

peri- [Gr. *peri*, around, about] **1.** *pre* around; surrounding (periscope, periadenitis); **2.** near (periblepsis, perigee)

pericardiaco-, pericardio- [Gr. *peri*, around + *kardia*, heart] *comb* relating to the sac surrounding the heart; pericardial (pericardiaco-phrenic, pericardiostomy)

pericul- [L. *periculum*, danger] *base* danger (periculant, periculous)

perineo- [Gr. *perineon*, perineum] *comb* perineum (perineocele, perineoplasty)

periosteo- [Gr. *peri*, around + *osteon*, bone] *comb* periosteum; bone membrane (periosteophyte, periosteotome)

perisso- [Gr. *perissos*, irregular, superfluous] *comb* uneven; strange; redundant (perissodactyl, perissology)

perister- [Gr. *peristera*, pigeon] *base* pigeon (peristeronic, peristeropod)

peritoneo- [Gr. *peri*, around + *teinein*, to stretch] *comb* peritonium; abdominal sac (peritoneoclysis, peritoneoscopy)

perm- [L. *permeare*, to pass through] *base* capable of being passed through (permeate, permeable)

perman- [L. *per*, through + *manere*, to remain] *base* lasting; remaining (permanency, permanent)

pernic- [L. *perniciosus*, deadly] *base* harmful (pernicious, perniciousness)

pero- [Gr. *peros*, maimed] *comb* maimed; malformed (perocephalus, perodactyly)

peroneo- [Gr. *perone*, brooch, pin, fibula] *comb* peroneal; fibula (peroneo-calcaneal, peroneotibial)

peroxy- [Gr. *per*, through + *oxy*, oxygen] *comb* peroxy group (peroxynitrate, peroxyborate)

perpet- [L. *perpetuus*, constant] *base* unceasing (perpetual, perpetuate)

pers- [L. *persea*, fruit-bearing tree] *base* avocado (Persea)

persic- [L. *persicum*, peach] *base* peach (persicaria, persicot)

-person [L. *persona*, actor's mask] *comb* person in a specialized activity (chairperson, spokesperson)

perturb- [L. *perturbare*, to trouble] *base* disturb (perturbation, perturbatory)

pertuss- [L. *per*, intensifier + *tussis*, cough] *base* pert. to a cough (pertussal, pertussis)

perul- [L. *perula*, wallet or pocket] *base* bud scaly cover (perula, perulate)

-pervic- [L. *pervicax*, obstinate] *base* stubborn (pervicacious, pervicacity)

pesso- [Gr. *pessis*, oval gaming stone] *comb* pebble (pessomancy)

-pessul- [L. *pessulus*, bolt of a door] *base* bolt (pessular, pessulus)

pesti- [L. *pestis*, plague] *comb* injurious plant or animal; pest; plague (pestiferous, pestilence)

-pet- [L. *petere*, to seek] *base* seek; ask; require (compete, petition)

peta- [Gr. *pente*, five] *comb* quadrillion (petabyte, petameter)

-petal [L. *petere*, to seek] *comb* moving toward; seeking (acropetal, centripetal)

petalo- [Gr. *petalon*, leaf] *base* leaf (petalocerous, petalomania)

petas- [Gr. *petasmos*, something spread out] *base* appendage in male crustacean (petasma, petasmata)

petill- [Fr. *pétiller*, to sparkle] *base* effervesce (petillant, petillateō)

petri-, petro- [Gr. *petra*, rock] *comb* rock; stone (petrifaction, petroglyph)

petro- [Gr. *petra*, rock + *elaion*, oil] *comb* petroleum (petrodollars, petropolitics)

petrosel- [L. *petroselinum*, parsley] *base* parsley (petroseline, petroselinum)

-peuce- [Gr. *peuke*, pine] *base* pine (Peucaea, peucedaneous)

-pexy [Gr. *peksis*, putting together] *comb* fixation: surgical (nephropexy, orchidopexy)

-phacell- [Gr. *phakellos*, bundle] *base* bundle (phacellate, phacellus)

phaco- [Gr. *phakos*, lentil; lens of the

eye] *comb* lens; lentil-shaped (phacitis, phacolytic). *Also* **phako-** (phakocyst, phakoscope) *See* **-phakia**

-phaein, phaeo- [Gr. *phaios*, dusky] *comb* dusky; gray; muddy brown (haemophaein, phaeophyl). *Also* **pheo-** (pheochrome)

-phaeno- [Gr. *phainein*, to show] *base* showing (phaenocarpous, phaenogamous). *Also* **pheno-** (phenocryst, phenomenon)

-phage, phago-, -phagous, -phagy [Gr. *phagein*, to eat] **1.** *comb* eating; destroying; **2.** phagocyte (xylophage, phagocytosis, xylophagous, anthropophagy)

-phagia [Gr. *phagos*, eating] *comb* eating, ingesting (odynophagia, polyphagia)

-phakia [Gr. *phakos*, lentil] *comb* lens (aphakia, microphakia). *See* **phaco-**

-phalacr- [Gr. *phalakros*, bald] *base* bald (phalacrocorax, phalacrophobia)

phalacrocorac- [L. *phalacrocorax*, cormorant] *base* cormorant (phalacrocoracidae, phalacrocoracine)

-phalaen- [Gr. *phalaina*, moth] *base* moth (phalaenoid, Phalaenopsis)

-phalang- [Gr. *phalanks*, bone of finger or toe] *base* **1.** finger or toe bone (phalangeal, phalanx) **2.** marsupial mammal (phalanger, Phalangeridae) **3.** tracheate spider (Phalangidea, phalangidean) **4.** a soldier belonging to a phalanx (phalangite)

phaler- [Gr. *phaleris*, coot] *base* coot (phaleridine, Phaleris)

phall(o)- [Gr. *phallus*, penis] *comb* penis (phallalgia, phallocampsis)

-phane, -phanic, -phany [Gr. *phanein*, to show] *comb* appearance; resemblance (allophane, urophanic, epiphany)

phanero- [Gr. *phaneros*, visible, evident] *comb* visible; manifest (phanerocodonic, phanerogam)

phantas- [Gr. *phantasma*, appearance, apparition] *base* illusion (phantasmagoria, phantasmal)

-phar- [Gr. *pharos*, lighthouse] *base* lighthouse (pharology, pharos)

pharmaco- [Gr. *pharmakon*, drug,

medicine] *comb* drugs (pharmacomaniacal, pharmacotherapy)

pharyngo- [Gr. *pharanks*, throat] *comb* the pharynx (pharyngalgia, pharyngology)

phasc- [Gr. *phaskos*, tree moss] *base* moss (Phascaceae, Phascum)

phascolo- [Gr. *phaskolos*, leather bag] *comb* wombat (phascolome, Phascolomyidae)

-phaseol- [Gr. *phaselos*, kind of bean] *base* kidney bean (phaseolite, phaseologist)

-phasia, -phasic, -phasis, -phasy [Gr. *phasis*, speech or utterance] *comb* speech disorder (aphasia, dysphasic, emphasis, aphasy)

-phasian- [Gr. *phasianos*, pheasant] *base* pheasant (phasianine, phasianoid)

phasm- [Gr. *phasma*, apparition] *base* apparition; walking-stick insect (Phasmidae, phasmophobia)

phat-[1] [Gr. *phatos*, spoken] *base* speak (emphatic, phatic)

phat-[2] [Gr. *phatein*, tooth socket] *base* tooth socket (phatnoma, phatnorrhea)

phaulo- [Gr. *phaulos*, bad, worthless] *comb* worthless (ethnophaulism, phaulographic)

pheg- [Gr. *phegos*, oak] *base* beech (Phegopteris)

-phein- [Gr. *phaos*, gray, dusky] *base* dusky (hemophein, phyllophein). *See* **phaeo-**

phello- [Gr. *phellos*, cork] *comb* cork (phellogen, phelloplastic)

-phemia, -phemy [Gr. *pheme*, voice, speech] *comb* speech disorder (paraphemia, heterophemy)

phenac-, phenakist- [Gr. *phenaks*, imposter] *base* imposter (phenacite, phenakistoscope)

phenanthro- [Gr. *phaineo*, bring to light + *anthrak*, coal] *comb* [chemistry] (phenanthrene , phenanthroline)

pheng(o)- [Gr. *phengos*, light] *base* light; luster (phengite, phengophobia)

phenic- [Gr. *phoiniks*, purplish-red] *base* purple (phenicine, phenicopter)

pheno- [Gr. *phainein*, show] **1.** *comb*

appearance; (phenomenon); **2.** phenyl group (phenomenology, phenoxide)

pheo- [Gr. *phaios*, dusky] *comb* dusky; gray (pheochrome, pheochromocytoma). *Also* **phæo-** (phæophile)

-pher [Gr. *phoros*, carrying] *comb* bearing; carrying (Christopher, chronopher)

phial- [Gr. *phiale*, shallow dish] *base* vessel (phial, phialine)

philatel- [Gr. *philos*, love + *ateles*, prepaid, free of tax] *base* postage stamp (philatelic, philately)

-phile, -philic, -philism, philo-, -philous [Gr. *philos*, love] *comb* favorably disposed to; loving; liking (Anglophile, Francophilic, bibliophilism, philology, photophilous)

-philia, -philiac [Gr. *philia*, attraction] **1.** *comb* tendency toward (hemophilia, hemophiliac); **2.** abnormal attraction to (coprophilia, logophilia)

philomel- [Gr. *philomela*, nightingale] *base* nightingale (philomel, philomelian)

philosophico- [Gr. *philosophia*, love of knowledge and wisdom] *comb* philosophical and ... (philosophico-historic, philisophico-religious)

-phim- [Gr. *phimosis*, a muzzling] *base* narrow (phimosis, phimotic)

phlebo- [Gr. *phleps*, vein] *comb* vein (phlebography, phlebotomy)

phlegm- [Gr. *phlegma*, fire, phlegm] *base* phlegm (phlegmagogic, phlegmatic)

-phloem- [Gr. *phloios*, bark] *base* tree bark (epiphloem, metaphloem)

phlog-, phlogo- [Gr. *phlox*, a flame] *comb* inflammation (phlogistic, phlogogenous)

phloro- [Gr. *phloios*, bark] *comb* crystalline compound (phlorectin, phlorizin)

phlyct- [Gr. *phluktaina*, blister, pustule] *base* blister (phlyctenoid, phlyctenous)

-phobe, -phobia, -phobic, phobo- [Gr. *phobos*, fear] *comb* fear; hatred; dread (Francophobe, claustrophobia, ailurophobic, phobophobia)

phoco- [Gr. *phoke*, seal] *comb* seal: sea mammal (phocine, phocomelia)

phoecaen- [Gr. *phokaina*, porpoise] *base* porpoise (phocaenine, Phoecaenoides)

phœnicopt- [Gr. *phoiniks*, purple-red + *kerkos*, tail] *base* flamingo (phoenicopterid, phœnicopterous)

pholc- [Gr. *pholkos*, squint-eyed] *base* type of spider (Pholcidae, Pholcus)

pholid-, -pholis [Gr. *pholiz*, scale] *base* scales (pholidosis, pholidote, Conopholis)

-phone, phono-, -phony [Gr. *phone*, sound] *comb* sound; tone; speech; voice (megaphone, phonology, cacophony)

phonetico- [Gr. *phonetos*, to be spoken] *comb* phonetic and (phonetico-etymological, phonetico-grammatical)

-phor, -phora, -phore, -phorous [Gr, *pherein*, to bear] *comb* bearer; producer (phosphor, Cladophora, carpophore, gonophorous)

-phoresis [Gr. *phoresis*, being carried] *comb* transmission (cataphoresis, diaphoresis)

phoro- [*phorein*, to bear] *comb* bearing (phoroplast, phorozoon)

phos- [Gr. *phos*, light] *base* light (phosphene, phosphor)

phospho-, phosphoro- [Gr. *phos*, light + *pherein*, to bear] *comb* phosphorus (phosphoprotein, phosphoroscope)

photo- [Gr. *phos*, light] **1.** *comb* of light (photocampsis, photodynamics); **2.** of photography (photographic, photomontage)

-phragma, phragmo- [Gr. *phragma*, fence, partition] *comb* barrier; wall; fence (diaphragma, phragmophorous)

phraseo- [Gr. *phrasis*, speech] *comb* phrase; verbal expression (phraseogram, phraseology)

-phrasia [Gr. *phrasis*, speech] *comb* speech defect (bradyphrasia, paraphrasia)

-phrastic [Gr. *phraksein*, to declare] *comb* word choice (holophrastic, periphrastic)

-phrat- [Gr. *phrater*, brother, clansman] *base* clan (phratric, phratry)

phreato- [Gr. *phrear*, artificial well] *base* well (phreatic, phreatophyte)

phreni-, phreno- [Gr. *phren*, diaphragm, mind, will] *comb* **1.** mind (phrenology); **2.** diaphragm (phrenic)

-phrenia [Gr. *phren*, diaphragm, mind, will] *comb* mental disorder (hebephrenia, schizophrenia)

-phrenic, phrenico-, phreno- [Gr. *phren*, diaphragm, mind, will] **1.** *comb* diaphragm; midriff (gastrophrenic); **2.** mental condition; mind (schizophrenic, phrenicotomy, phrenogastric)

phricto- [Gr. *phriktos*, producing a shudder] *comb* shudder (phrictopathic)

phron- [Gr. *phronesis*, wisdom, prudence] *base* sound judgment (phronesis, phronetal)

phrontis- [Gr. *phrontis*, thought, meditation] *base* thought, consideration (phrontisterion, phrontistery)

phryno- [Gr. *phrunos*, toad] *comb* toad (phrynoderma, Phrynosoma)

phthart- [Gr. *phthartos*, corruptible] *base* destructive; deadly (phthartic, Phthartolatrae)

phthino- [Gr. *phthinein*, waste away] *comb* wasting away; decay (phthinode, phthinoplasm)

-phthir- [Gr. *phtheir*, louse] *base* louse (phthiriasis, phthirophagous). *Also* **phthyr-**

phthisi-, phthisio-, -phthisis, -phthysis [Gr. *phthinein*, waste away] *comb* wasting away; decay; tuber-culo-sis (phthisiology, phthisio-genesis, myelophthisis, panmyelophthysis)

-phthong [Gr. *phthongos*, voice, sound] *comb* voice; sound (aphthong, diphthong)

-phthor- [Gr. *phthora*, destruction] *base* corruption (blastophthoria, thelyphthoric)

-phyceae, -phyceous, phyco- [Gr. *phukos*, seaweed] *comb* seaweed (Rhodophyceae, Rhodophyceous, phycology)

-phygo- [Gr. *phugein*, shun, avoid] *base* shun; flee (apophyge, phygogalactic)

-phylactic, phylacto-, -phylax, -phylaxis [Gr. *phulakter*, guard] *comb* protection; defense; guard (prophylactic, phylactocarp, chartophylax, tachyphylaxis)

-phyletic [Gr. *phule*, tribe] *comb* origin (monophyletic, polyphyletic)

-phyll, phyllo-, -phyllous [Gr. *phullon*, leaf] *comb* leaf (sporophyll, phyllophagous, monophyllous)

phylo- [Gr. *phule*, tribe] *comb* tribe; race; phylum (phyloanalysis, phylogenesis)

phym-, -phyma [Gr. *phuma*, tumor] *comb* tumor; swelling; outgrowth; (phymatosis, osteophyma)

-phyr-, -phyre, -phyric [Gr. *phurein*, mix, mingle] *comb* **1.** mix; mingle (haunophyr) **2.** porphyritic rock (granophyre, orthophyric)

physa- [Gr. *phusa*, bellows, wind] *base* flatulence (physagogal, physagogue)

physali- [Gr. *phusa*, bellows, wind] *comb* bladder; bubble (physaliphore, physalite)

physc- [Gr. *phuske*, blister, sausage] *base* swelling; potbelly (physconic, physcony)

physeter- [Gr. *phuseter*, blowpipe, type of whale] *base* sperm whale (Physeteridae, physeterine)

physi-, physico-, physio- [Gr. *phusis*, nature] *comb* nature; natural; physical; bodily (physitheism, physicochemical, physiography)

-physis [Gr. *phusis*, natural growth] *comb* growth (apophysis, prophysis)

physo- [Gr. *phusa*, breath, air bubble] **1.** *comb* tendency to swell (physocele); **2.** relating to air or gas (physometra); **3.** bladder (physogastric)

-phyta, -phyte, phyti-, -phytic, phyto- [Gr. *phuton*, plant] *comb* plant; flora; vegetation (Bryophyta, microphyte, phytiform, holophytic, phytogenesis)

piac- [L. *piare*, to appease] *base* expiatory; wicked (piacular, piacularity)

-piceo- [L. *piceus*, pitch-black] *comb* black-tinged (piceo-ferruginous, piceo-testaceous)

-pici- [L. *picus*, woodpecker] *base* woodpecker (picarian, piciform)

pico- [Sp. *pico*, small quantity] *comb* one-trillionth (picoampere, picogram) picro- [Gr. *pikros*, bitter] *comb* bitter (picroerythrin, picrtoxin)

-pict- [L. *pictura*, painting] *base* paint (depiction, pictorial)

-piesis [Gr. *piesis*, pressure] *comb* pressure (anisopiesis, hyperpiesis)

piezo- [Gr. *piezein*, press] *comb* pressure; strain (piezo-electricity, piezometer)

pigm- [L. *pigmentum*, paint] *base* paint; color (pigment, pigmentation)

-pign- [L. *pignus*, pledge] *base* pledge; pawn; mortgage (impignorate, pignoration)

-pigr- [L. *piger*, slow, sluggish] *base* slow; sluggish; slothful (impigrity, pigritude)

pil-, pili-, pilo- [L. *pilus*, hair] *comb* hair; (depilatory, piliform, piloerection)

-pile- [L. *pileus*, cap] *base* cap (pileated, pileolus)

piloso- [L. *pilosus*, hairy] *comb* hairy (piloso-fimbriate, piloso-hispid)

pilul- [L. *pilula*, pill, pellet] *base* pill (pilular, pilulous)

pimel-, pimelo- [Gr. *pimele*, fat] *comb* fat; fatty (pimelitis, pimelosis)

pin- [L. *pinus*, pine] *base* pine (pinaceous, pinaster)

-pinac- [Gr. *pinaks*, tablet] *base* tablet; slab (pinacocyte, pinacoid). *Also* -pinak- (pinakoid)

-pingu- [L. *pinguis*, fat] *base* fat (pinguescence, pinguid)

pinnati-, pinnato- [L. *pinnatus*, pinnate] *comb* like a feather; pinnately (pinnatifid, pinnato-pectinate)

pinni- [L. *pinna*, fin, flipper] *comb* fin; flipper (pinnigrade, pinniped)

pino- [Gr. *pinein*, to drink] *comb* drink (pinocytic, pinocytosis)

pio- [Gr. *pion*, fat] *comb* fat (Piophila, pioscope)

-piper- [L. *piper*, pepper] *base* pepper (piperaceous, piperic)

-piq- [Fr. *piquer*, prick, sting] *base* stinging; sharp (piquant, pique)

pirat- [Gr. *peirates*, to attack] *base* plunderer (pirate, piratical)

piri-, piro- [L. *pirum*, pear] *comb* pear (piriform, piroplasmosis). *See* pyri-

pisci- [L. *piscis*, fish] *comb* fish (piscicolous, piscivorous)

pisi- [L. *pisum*, pea] *comb* pea (pisidiid, pisiform)

piss- [Gr. *pissa*, pitch] *base* pitch, tar (pissasphalt, pissoceros)

pist-, pisti- [Gr. *pistis*, faith] *base* faith (pistology, pistiology)

pistac- [L. *pistake*, pistachio] *base* pistachio (pistachio-nut, pistacite)

pistill- [L. *pistillium*, pistil] *base* pistil (pistillar, pistillode)

pistor- [L. *pistor*, baker, grinder] *base* baking (pistorial, pistorian)

pithec-, -pithecus [Gr. *pithekos*, ape] *comb* primate; apelike (pithecoid, Australopithecus)

pithi- [Gr. *peithein*, to persuade] *comb* persuasion (pithiatism, pithiatric)

pitta- [Gr. *pitta*, pitch] *base* like pitch (pittacal, pittizite)

pituit- [L. *pituita*, mucus, phlegm] *base* phlegm (pituital, pituitous)

-pityr- [Gr. *pituron*, bran] *base* bran (pityriasis, pityroid)

-plac- [L. *placare*, to appease] *base* please; appease (implacable, placidity)

placenti- [L. *placenta*, cake] *comb* placenta (placentiferous, placentiform)

placo- [Gr. *plaks*, tablet, plate] *comb* flat plate (placodermal, placoid)

plag- [L. *plagiarius*, kidnapper > *plaga*, trap] *base* kidnap; seize (plagiarist, plagiarize)

plagio- [Gr. *plagios*, oblique] *comb* slanting; oblique (plagioclastic, plagiotropic)

-plakia [Gr. *plaks*, flat surface] *comb* [medicine] patch (erythroplakia, leukoplakia)

planari- [L. *planus*, flat] *comb* in one plane; flat (planariform, planarioid)

-plang- [L. *plangere*, to strike noisily] *base* strike; beat (plangency, plangent)

plani-, plano-[1] [L. *planus*, flat] *comb* level; plane; flat (planimeter, plano-concave)

-plania, plano-[2] [Gr. *planos*, wandering] *comb* wandering; moving (uroplania, planogamete)

-plant- [L. *planta*, sole of the foot] *base* sole of the foot (plantar, plantigrade)

-plasia, -plasis [Gr. *plasis*, molding, configuration] *comb* development; growth; change (hypoplasia, cataplasis)

-plasm, plasmato-, plasmo- [Gr. *plasma*, formed, imaged] *comb* fluid cell substances of an animal or vegetable (endoplasm, plasmatoparous, plasmolysis)

-plast, -plastic, plasto- [Gr. *plastos*, formed, molded] *comb* molded; formed (protoplast, protoplastic, plastotype)

-plasty [Gr. *plastos*, formed, molded] **1.** *comb* forming: act or means (genioplasty); **2.** plastic surgery: specific part of the body (thoracoplasty); **3.** plastic surgery: tissue from specified source (autoplasty); **4.** plastic surgery: for a specific purpose (kineplasty)

plat-¹ [Gr. *platis*, flat, wide] *base* flat (platen, platform)

plat-² [L. *plata*, silver, precious metal] *base* silver (plateresque, platinum)

platini-, platino- [L. *platinum*, platinum, silvery-white element] *comb* platinum (plantiniferous, platinocyanide)

platy- [Gr. *platis*, flat, wide] *comb* broad; flat (platycephaly, platypus)

-plaud-, -plaus- [L. *plaudere*, to clap, strike] *base* clap (plaudits, plausible)

plaustr- [L. *plaustrum*, wagon, cart] *base* cart; wagon (plaustral, plaustrary)

-pleb- [L. *plebs*, common people] *base* common people (plebiscite, plebeian)

pleco-, plecto- [Gr. *plekein*, twist, twine] *comb* twist; twine; plait (plecopteran, plectognath)

pleg- [Gr. *plege,* a strike] *base* hammering (plegnic, plegometer)

-plegia, -plegy [Gr. *plege*, stroke] *comb* paralysis (hemiplegy, paraplegia)

pleio- [Gr. *pleion*, more] *comb* more (pleiochasial, pleiomastia)

-pleisto- [Gr. *pleistos*, most] *comb* most (Pleistocene, pleistodox)

plemyr- [Gr. *plemura*, flood tide] *base* flood-tide (plemyrameter). *Also* **plemmir-** (plemmirrulate)

-plen-, -pler(o)-, -plet- [L. *plenus*, full] *base* fill; full (replenish, pleroma, complete)

pleo-, pleon-, plio- [Gr. *pleion*, more] *comb* more; increased (pleomorphic, pleonasm, Pliosaurus). *Also* **pleio-** (pleiomorphy)

pleonec-, pleonex- [Gr. *pleonektikos*, greedy] *base* greed; avarice (pleonectic, pleonexia)

plero- [Gr. *pleres*, full, satisfied] *comb.* full (pleroma, plerophory)

plesio- [Gr. *plesios*, near] *comb* near (plesiomorphous, plesiosaurus)

pless(i)- [Gr. *plessein*, to strike] *comb* striking; percussion (plessimeter, plessor)

pleth- [Gr. *plethein*, full] *base* excessive (plethora, plethoric)

plethys- [Gr. *plethus*, fullness] *comb* increase; large number (plethysmograph, plethysmometry)

pleuro- [Gr. *pleura*, the side] **1.** *comb* side: on or near (pleurodont); **2.** pleura: of or near (pleurotomy); **3.** pleural (pleuropneumonia)

-plex [L. *plex*, fold] *comb* network; folds; layers (contraplex, decemplex)

-plexia [Gr. *plessein*, to strike] *comb* stroke (apoplexia, parapoplexia)

plicato-, plici- [L. *plicare*, to fold] *comb* folded (plicato-lobate, pliciform)

plinthi- [Gr. *plinthos*, brick, tile] *comb* brick; squared stone (plinthiform, plinthlike)

plio- *See* **pleo-**

plisio- [Gr. *plusios*, rich] *comb* wealthy (plusiocrasy, plusiophobia)

ploc- [Gr. *plokos*, woven, plaited] *base* weaver bird (Ploceidae, ploceiform)

-ploid [Gr. *eidos*, form] *comb* chromosones: of a specified multiple of (diploid, haploid)

plor- [L. *plorare*, to weep, lament] *base* cry (implore, ploration)

plum-, plumi- [L. *pluma*, feather] *comb* feather (plumage, plumiform)

plumb-, plumbo- [L. *plumbum*, lead] *comb* lead (plumbism, plumbocalcite)

pluri- [L. *plus/plur-*, more] *comb* several; many (pluriflorous, pluriparous)

pluto- [Gr. *ploutos*, wealthy] *comb* wealth (plutocracy, plutology)

pluvial- [L. *pluvia*, rain] *base* plover (pluvialiform, pluvialine)

pluvio- [L. *pluvia*, rain] *comb* rain (pluviograph, pluvious)

-pnea, pneo- [Gr. *pnein*, to breathe] *comb* breath; respiration (dyspnea, pneograph)

pneum-, pneumato- [Gr. *pneuma*, wind, breath, spirit] **1.** *comb* air vapor (pneumatophore); **2.** breathing (pneumatometer); **3.** spirits (pneumatology)

pneumo-, pneumono- [Gr. *pneuma*, wind, breath, spirit] *comb* lungs; air; gas (pneumobacillus, pneumonophorous)

pneusio-, -pneustic [Gr. *pneusis*, breathing] *comb* breathing (metapneustic, pneusiobiognosis)

-pnig- [Gr. *pnigein*, to choke] *base* choke; suffocate (pnigalion, pnigophobia)

-pocul- [L. *poculum*, goblet, cup] *base* drink; cup (poculent, poculiform)

-pod, -poda, -pode, podo-, -podous [Gr. *pous/pod-*, foot] **1.** *comb* foot (pleopod, Cephalopoda, pseudopode, podomere, cephalopodous); **2.** having ___ feet (tripod)

podag- [Gr. *podagra*, gout] *base* gout (podagra, podagrical)

podic- [L. *podex/podic-*, rump] *base* **1.** rump (podical) **2.** grebe (Podicipedidae)

-podium [L. *podium*, raised platform] *comb* supporting part; footstalk; (mesopodium, monopodium)

poe- [Gr. *poa*, grass] *base* grass (poephagous, Poephila)

poecilo- [Gr. *poikilos*, various, many-colored] *comb* irregular; many-colored (poecilomere, poecilonymy). *Also* **poicilo-** (poicilothermous)

pogon-, pogono- [Gr. *pogon*, beard] *comb* beard (pogoniasis, pogonotrophy)

-poiesis, -poietic [Gr. *poiein*, to make] *comb* making; forming; producing (leukopoiesis, onomatopoietic)

poikilo- [Gr. *poikilos*, various, many-colored] *comb* irregular; varied (poikiloblast, poikiloderma)

poimen- [Gr. *poimen*, shepherd] *base* pastoral (poimenic, poimenics)

poine- [Gr. *poinao*, to avenge, punish] *base* punishment (poinemania, poinephobia)

polari- [L. *polaris*, polar] *comb* polar (polari-guttulate, polarimetry)

-pole [Gr. *poles*, seller, dealer] *comb* dealer (bibliopole, pharmacopole)

-polem- [Gr. *polemos*, war] *base* war (polemicist, polemics)

polio- [Gr. *polios*, gray] *comb* gray; gray matter (poliomyelitis, polioviral)

-polis, polit- [Gr. *polis/polit-*, city] *comb* city (metropolis, politician)

politico- [Gr. *polis/polit-*, city] *comb* political (politico-commercial, politico-religious)

pollaki- [Gr. *pollakis*, many times] *comb* many times (pollakiuria, pollakanthous)

pollic- [L. *pollex/pollic-*, thumb, great toe] *base* thumb (pollicar, pollicate)

pollin(i)- [L. *polis/pollin-*, fine dust, flour] *comb* pollen (pollination, pollinosis)

pollinct- [L. *pollingere*, wash a corpse before a funeral] *base* corpse-washing (pollinctor, pollincture)

pollut- [L. *polluere*, to dirty, violate] *base* taint (pollutant, pollution)

poly- [Gr. *pollos/pollu-*, many] **1.** *comb* more than one (polychromatic); **2.** more than usual; excessive (polyphagia); **3.** many kinds or parts (polymorphous)

polymorpho- [Gr. *pollos*, many + *morphe*, form] *comb* multiform (polymorphocellular, polymorphonucleated)

polyped- [Gr. *poly*, much + *pedein*, to jump] *base* tree toad (Polypedates, polypedatid)

pomar- [L. *pomarium*, fruit garden] *base* orchard (pomarious, pomary)

pomerid- [L. *pomeridianus*, post meridian] *base* afternoon (pomeridian)

pomi-, pomo- [L. *pomum*, fruit,

apple] *comb* fruit; apple (pomiform, pomology)

-pomp- [Gr. *pompe*, a sending, procession] **1.** *base* release; sending away (hypnopompic); **2.** conductor; guide (psychopomp)

pomph- [Gr. *pomphos*, bubble, blister] *base* blister (pomphologous, pompholyx)

-pon-, -pos- [L. *ponere*, to place] *base* to place (opponent, opposition)

-pond- [L. *pondus*, weight] *base* weight; (ponderous, preponderant)

ponero- [Gr. *poneros*, injurious] *comb* evil; wicked; useless (ponerine, ponerology)

pong- [Fr. *pongo*, orangutan] *base* gorilla; orangutan (pongid, pongo)

-ponic [Gr. *penesthai*, to labor] *base* cultivation (geoponic, hydroponic)

pono- [Gr. *ponos*, toil, distress, suffering] *comb* hard work; pain; fatigue (ponograph, ponophobia)

pont-[1] [L. *pons/pont-*, bridge] *base* bridge (pontal, pontiff)

pont-[2] [Gr. *pontos*, sea] *base* Black Sea region (Hellespont, Pontic)

pontic- [Gr. *pontikos*, sour, astringent] *base* sour, tart (Pontic, ponticity)

popin- [L. *popina*, eating-house] *base* excessive eating and drinking (popinal, popination)

poplit- [L. *poples/poplit-*, back of the knee] *base* back of knee (popliteal, popliteus)

-popul- [L. *populus*, the people] *base* people (depopulate, population)

porc-, porcin- [L. *porcus*, hog] *base* pork (porcelain, porcine)

pori-, poro- [L. *porus*, pore] *comb* pore; channel (poriferous, porencephalia)

porno- [Gr. *porne*, prostitute] *comb* harlot (pornocracy, pornography)

poroso- [L. *porosus*, full of pores] *comb* filled with pores (poroso-punctate)

porphyro- [Gr. *porphura*, purple] *comb* purple (porphyritic, porphyrogenite)

porr(ac)- [L. *porrum*, leek] *base* leek; green (porraceous, porre)

porrect- [L. *porrigere*, stretch, extend] *base* extend (porrect, porrection)

-porrig- [L. *porrigo*, dandruff] *base* dandruff (porriginous, porrigo)

-port- [L. *portare*, to carry] *base* carry (import, portable)

portent- [L. *portentum*, sign] *base* indicator (portention, portentive)

portic- [L. *porticus*, colonnade] *base* colonnade (portico, porticoed)

porto- [L. *porta*, city gate, door] *comb* portal; entrance (portobilioarterial, portosystemic)

portulac- [L. *portulaca*, purslane] *base* purslane (portulaca, portulaceous)

-pos- *see* **-pon-**

posio- [Gr. *posis*, drinking] *base* drinking (aposia, posiomania)

poso- [Gr. *posos*, how much] *comb* dose (posological, posology)

post- [L. *post*, behind] **1.** *pre* after in time; following; later (postgraduate); **2.** after in space; behind (postaxial, postprandial)

postero- [L. *posterus*, later, next] *comb* posterior; behind (postero-lateral, postero-mesial)

postul- [L. *postulare*, demand, claim] *base* request, claim (postulant, postulate)

pot-, poto- [L. *potare*, to drink] *comb* drink (potable, potomania)

potamo- [Gr. *potamos*, river] *comb* river (potamography, potamolo-gist)

-poten- [L. *potentia*, power] *base* power; ability (impotency, potential)

poticho- [Fr. *potiche*, kind of pot] *comb* porcelain (potichomania, potichomanist)

pov- [OF *poverte*, destitution] *base* poor (impoverished, poverty)

practic- [Gr. *praktike*, efficacious] *base* practical (practice, practicable)

-pragia [Gr. *prassein*, to achieve] *comb* a quality of action (bradypragia)

pragmat- [Gr. *pragmatikos*, factual, business-like] *base* practical (pragmatic, pragmatics)

-prand- [L. *prandium*, late breakfast, luncheon] *base* dinner (postprandial, preprandial)

-pras- [Gr. *prasaios*, leek-green] *base* leek-green (prase, prasine)

praso- [Gr. *prasaios*, leek-green] *comb* leek (prasolite, prasophagous)

-prat- [L. *pratum*, meadow] *base* meadow (pratal, Praticola)

-prav- [L. *pravus*, wicked, bad] *base* crooked; wrong; bad (depravity, impravable)

-praxia, -praxis [Gr. *praksis*, action] *comb* movement; action (hyperpraxia, parapraxis)

pre- [L. *prae*, before] **1.** *pre* before in time; earlier; prior to; (presuppose); **2.** before in place; anterior; in front of (preaxial); **3.** before in rank; superior; surpassing (preeminent); **4.** in preparation for (preschool). *Also* **prae-** (praenomen)

-preca- [L. *precari*, to pray] *base* entreat; pray (imprecation, precarious)

precip- [L. *praeceps/praecipit*, headlong] *base* steep; headlong (precipice, precipitant)

precis- [L. *praecise*, shortened] *base* curtailed, exact (précis, precision)

pred- [L. *praedare*, to plunder] *base* robbery (predation, predatory)

-prehend, -prehens- [L. *prendere*, to grasp, seize] *base* hold; seize (apprehend, apprehensive)

presby- [Gr. *presbus*, old] *comb* old age (presbyacusis, presbyopia)

presbyter- [Gr. *presbuteros*, elder] *comb* elder; priest (presbyteral, presbytery)

prester- [Gr. *prester*, whirlwind, waterspout] *base* whirlwind, engorged vein (prester, presternal)

preter- [L. *praeter*, beyond, over] *pre* past; beyond; outside the bounds (preternatural, preternuptial)

pri-, prion- [Gr. *prion*, a saw] *base* a saw (priodont, prionodont)

priap- [L. *Priapus*, god of procreation] *base* lascivious (priapic. priapism)

prid- [L. *pridianus*, day before] *base* yesterday (pridian)

prim-, primi-, primo- [L. *primus*, first] *comb* first; original; early (primacy, primigravida, primogenitor)

primaver- [Sp. *primavera*, springtime] *base* spring (pasta primavera, primaveral)

princip- [L. *principalis*, chief, first] *base* chief; first; main (principal, principiate)

prion- [Gr. *prion*, a saw] *base* a saw (prionodont, Prionurus)

prior- [L. *prior*, earlier, previous] *base* superior; better (prioress, priority)

prisc- [L. *priscus*, primitive] *base* ancient; primitive (priscal, priscan)

pristin- [L. *pristinus*, former] *base* unspoiled (pristine, pristinate)

-priv-[1] [L. *privatus*, individual, private] *base* private (privacy, privilege)

-priv-[2] [L. *privare*, rob, strip] *base* divest (deprivation, privation)

privign- [L. *privignus*, born of one only of a married pair] *base* stepchild (Amanita privigna, privignal)

pro-[1] [L. *pro*, forward, onward] **1.** *pre* moving forward; moving ahead of (proclivity); **2.** forth (produce); **3.** substituting for; acting for (pronoun); **4.** defending; supporting (prolabor)

pro-[2] [Gr. *pro*, before] *pre* before in place or time; (proestrus, prologue)

prob- [L. *probare*, to test] *base* good; upright (probe, probity)

probat- [L. *probatus*, tested, proven] *base* examine (probation, probative)

probl- [Gr. *problema*, issue to be solved] *base* difficulty (problem, problematic)

probol- [Gr. *probole*, emanation] *base* emanation (probole, probolistic)

-probosc- [Gr. *pro*, before + *boskein*, to feed] *base* long flexible snout (proboscidiform, proboscis)

-probr- [L. *probrum*, shameful deed] *base* reproach (exprobration, opprobrious)

procac- [L. *procax/procac-*, forward, bold] *base* bully; insolent (procacious, procacity)

procata- [Gr. *prokata*, beforehand] *comb* anticipation (procatalepsis, procatalectic)

procell- [L. *procella*, storm, hurricane] *base* storm (Procellaria, procellous)

procer- [L. *procerus*, high, tall, long] *base* tall; long (proceritic, procerity)

procto- [Gr. *proktos*, anus] *comb* rectum (proctalgia, proctology)

procyon- [Gr. *prokuon*, the constellation known as *Canis Minor*] *base* raccoon (procyoniform, procyonine)

-prodit- [L. *proditio*, betrayal] *base* traitor (proditomania, proditorious)

profan- [L. *profanare*, to desecrate] *base* unholy, violated (profanation, profanity)

proflig- [L. *profligatus*, depraved] *base* debauched, wasteful (profligate, profligation)

-profund- [L. *profundus*, deep] *base* deep (profundiplantar, profundity)

prognos- [Gr. *progignoskein*, to know beforehand] *base* foreknowledge; forecast (prognosis, prognostication)

prohib- [L. *prohibere*, to hold off, stop] *base* hold back; forbid (prohibit, prohibitory)

proli- [L. *proles*, offspring] *comb* productive, fruitful (prolicide, proliferation)

promulg- [L. *promulgare*, make known formally] *base* disseminate (promulgate, promulgation)

prono- [L. *pronus*, bent downward] *comb* bent downward (pronograde, pronometer)

-proof [L. *probare*, to prove] 1. *suf* impervious to (waterproof); 2. protected against (weatherproof); 3. as strong as (armorproof); 4. resistive to; unaffected by (womanproof)

prophor- [Gr. *prophora*, utterance] *base* 2nd person of the Holy Trinity (prophoric)

propinq- [L. *propinquitas*, nearness] *base* closeness (propinquitous, propinquity)

propit- [L. *propitiare*, appease] *base* render favorable (propitiate, propitiation)

proprio- [L. *proprius*, one's one] *comb* one's own (proprioceptive, proprioceptor)

pror- [Gr. *prora*, ship's prow] *base* prow-shaped (prora, proral)

pros- [Gr. *pros*, to, toward] *comb* to; toward (prosenchyma, prosody)

proselyt- [Gr. *proselyth*, newcomer] *base* convert (proselyte, proselytize)

proso- [Gr. *proso*, forward] *comb* forward; anterior (prosopulmonate, prosopyle)

prosop(o)- [Gr. *prosopon*, a face] *comb* face (prosopagnosia, prosopalgia)

prostato- [Gr. *prostates*, one who stands before] *comb* of the prostate (prostatectomy, prostatocystitis)

proteo- [Gr. *proteios*, primary] *comb* protein (proteoclastic, proteolysis)

protero- [Gr. *proteros*, fore] *comb* earlier; before; former; anterior (proteroglyph, proterogyny)

proterv- [L. *protervitas*, boldness] *base* stubborn; insolent (protervity, protervous)

proto- [Gr. *protos*, first] 1. *comb* first in time; original (protocol); 2. first in importance; principal; chief (protagonist); 3. primitive (proto-Arabic); 4. [chemistry] being that member of a series of compounds having the lowest proportion of the specified element or radical; being the parent form of a specified substance (protoactinium)

protother- [Gr. *proto*, first + *ther*, wild beast] *base* platypus (Prototheria, prototherian)

prox-, proximo- [L. *proximus*, nearest] *comb* near (proxemics, proximocephalic)

prozym- [Gr. *pro*, for + *zume*, leaven] *base* yeast (prozymite, prozymogen)

-pruin- [L. *pruina*, hoarfrost] *base* frost (pruinate, pruinose)

-prur- [L. *prurire*, to itch] *base* itch (prurient, pruritic)

-psalid- [Gr. *psalis*, shears] *base* shears; scissors (psalidodect, psaloid)

psall- [Gr. *psallein*, to play on a stringed instrument] *base* lyre (psallenda, psalloid)

psamm(o)- [Gr. *psammos*, sand] *comb* sand (psammitic, psammophilous)

-psar- [Gr. *psar*, starling] 1. *base* speckled (Psaronius); 2. starling (psarolite)

psath- [Gr. *psathuros*, crumbling] *base*
friable (osteopsathyrosis)

pselapho- [Gr. *pselaphon*, feel about]
comb type of millipede (pselaphog-
nath, pselaphotheca)

psell- [Gr. *psellos*, stammering] *base* stuttering (psellism, psellismologist)

pseph(o)- [Gr. *psephos*, pebble] *comb*
pebble; counter (psephology,
psephomancy)

psett- [Gr. *psetta*, flatfish] *base* turbot
(psettaceous, psettine)

pseudo- [Gr. *pseudes*, false] **1.** *comb* fictitious; sham (pseudonym); **2.** counterfeit; spurious (pseudepigrapha);
3. closely similar or deceptively similar; (pseudomorph);**4.** illusory (pseu-
dacusis); **5.** [chemistry] an isomer or
related form (pseudocholinesterase)

psil-, psilo- [Gr. *psilos*, naked, blank]
comb bare; smooth; mere (psilan-
thropy, psilodermatous)

-psithur- [Gr. *psithurizein*, to whisper]
base whisper (psithurism)

-psittac- [L. *psittacus*, parrot] *base* parrot; macaw; parakeet (psittacine,
psittacoid)

psoa- [Gr. *psoa*, loin muscle] *base* loin
muscle (psoa, psoatic)

psoma- [Gr. *psomos*, morsel] *comb* mor-
sel (psomophagia, psomophagy)

psopho- [Gr. *psophos*, noise] *comb* noise
(psophometer, psophometric)

psor- [Gr. *psora*, itch] *comb* itch (psoriasis, psoroid)

psycho- [Gr. *psuke*, spirit, mind] *comb*
mind; mental processes (psychodectic,
psychology)

psychro- [Gr. *psuchros*, cold, chill] *comb*
cold (psychrometer, psychrophobia)

psydroc- [Gr. *psudrakion*, pimple, pus-
tule] *base* pustule (psydracious,
psydracium)

psyll-¹ [Gr. *psulla*, flea] *base* flea (Psylla,
psylly)

psyll-² [Gr. *Psulloi*, African people famed
as snake charmers] *base* snake charmer
(psyllic)

ptarm- [Gr. *ptarmos*, sneezing] *base*
sneeze (ptarmic, Ptarmica)

pteno- [Gr. *ptenos*, having feath-
ers] *comb* feathered (ptenoglossate,
Ptenopleura)

-pter, ptero-, -pterous [Gr. *pteron*, wing,
plumage] *comb* wing; wing-shaped;
feather; fin (hymenopter, pterodactyl,
homopterous)

pterido- [Gr. *pteris/pterid-*, fern] *comb*
fern (pteridology, pteromania)

ptern- [Gr. *pterna*, heel] *base* heel bone
(pterna, pternalgia)

pterocl- [L. *pterocles* < Gr. *pteron*,
wing] *base* sand grouse (pteroclid,
pteroclomorphic)

pterono- [Gr. *pteron*, wing] *comb*
wing; feather; fin (pteronomania,
pteronophobia)

pterop- [Gr. *pteropous*, wing-footed] *base*
fruit bat (pteropine, pteropodial)

pterophyll- [Gr. *ptero*, wing + *phullon*,
leaf] *base* angelfish (pterophyllous,
Pterophyllum scalare)

pterygo- [Gr. *pterugion*, little wing, fin]
comb wing; wing-shaped; feather; fin
(pterygoblast, pterygoid)

-pteryl- [Gr. *pteron*, wing, plumage] *base*
feather (pterylography, pterylosis)

ptilo-, -ptile [Gr. *ptilon*, feather]
comb wing; feathery (ptilogenesis,
protoptile)

ptis- [Gr. *ptisane*, peeled barley] *base* barley, barley-water (ptisan, ptisanery)

ptocho- [Gr. *ptokhos*, beggar] *comb* poor;
beggar (ptochocracy, ptochology)

-ptosia, -ptosis [Gr. *ptosis*, falling] *comb*
falling; drooping (phrenoptosia,
nephroptosis)

ptyal-, ptyalo- [Gr. *ptuein*, to spit] *comb*
saliva (ptyalagogue, ptyalogenic)

-ptych- [Gr. *ptukhe*, a fold] *base* folded
(ptychodont, Ptychzoön)

ptyg- [Gr. *ptygma*, anything folded] *base*
layered or folded (ptygma, ptygmatic)

-ptysis [Gr. *ptuein*, to spit] *base* spitting
(hemoptysis, ptysmagogue)

pubio-, pubo- [L. *pubis*, pubic bone]
comb pubic (pubiotomy, pubofemoral)

-puden- [L. *pudens/pudent-*, bashful,
modest] *base* shame; modesty (impudent, pudency)

pudic- [L. *pudicus*, chaste] *base* chaste (pudical, pudicity)

-puer- [L. *puer*, child] *base like a* child (puerile, puerility)

puerper- [L. *puer*, child + *parere*, bring forth] *base* childbirth (puerperal, puerperous)

pugil- [L. *pugil*, boxer] *base* attack; fight; fist (pugilism, pugilistic)

pugio- [L. *pugio*, dagger] *base* dagger (pugioniform, pugioniphobia)

-pugn- [L. *pugnare*, to fight] *base* fight; oppose (impugn, oppugn)

-pul- [L. *pellere*, to drive] *base* push; drive (appulsion, propulsion). *Also* **-pel-** (repel)

pulchr- [L. *pulchritudo*, beauty] *base* beautiful (pulchritude, pulchritudinous)

-puli- [L. *pulex/pulic-*, flea] *base* flea (pulicose, pulicosity)

pull- [L. *pullus*, chicken] *base* chicken (pullet, pullulate)

pullastr- [L. *pullastra*, young hen] *base* pigeon (pullastriform, pullastrine)

pulmo-, pulmoni-, pulmono- [L. *pulmo*, lung] **1.** *comb* lung (pulmonate); **2.** pulmonary (pulmocutaneous, pulmonigrade, pulmonogastropod)

-puls- [L. *pulsus*, a push or blow] *base* beating; knocking (pulsation, pulse)

pulver- [L. *pulvis*, dust, powder] *base* dust; ash (pulverious, pulverize)

-pulvin- [L. *pulvinus*, bolster, pillow] *base* cushion (pulvilliform, pulvinate)

pum- [L. *pumex/pumic-*, pumice] base pumice (pumicate, pumiceous)

-pun-[1] [L. *punire*, to punish] *base* punish (impunity, punishable)

-pun-[2] [L. *puniceus*, red, purple] *base* purple (puniceous, punicin)

-punct-, pung- [L. *punctum*, dot] *base* point; sharp (punctiform, pungent)

punctato- [L. *punctatus*, pointed] *comb* with points or dots (punctato-striate, punctato-sulcate)

pupa- [L. *pupa*, girl, doll] *base* **1.** pupa (puparial, pupation) **2.** puppet (pupaphobia)

pupillo- [L. *pupilla*, pupil] *comb* pupil of the eye (pupillography, pupillometer)

-pur- [L. *pus/pur-*, pus] *base* pus (purulent, suppuration)

-purg- [L. *purgare*, to cleanse] *base* cleanse (purgation, purgative)

purpureo- [Gr. *porfureos*, purple] *comb* [chemistry] purple compounds (purpureo-cobalt, purpureo-cobaltic)

purulo- [L. *purulentus*, pus-filled] *comb* pus (purulo-fibrinous, purulo-gangrenous)

pusill- [L. *pusillus*, very little] *base* petty; very small (pusillanimity, pusillanimous)

pustulo- [L. *pustula*, blister] *comb* pimple (pustuliform, pustulocrustaceous)

-put- [L. *putare*, think, suppose] *base* think (putative, reputed)

putamin- [L. *putamen*, waste, husk] *base* husk (putamen, putaminous)

putea- [L. *puteus*, a well] *base* a well (puteal, puteanic)

putre-, putri- [L. *putris*, rotten] *comb* rotten (putrefaction, putriform)

py-, pyo- [Gr. *puon*, pus] *base* pus (pyedema, pyemic, pyolymph)

pycn(i)o- [Gr. *puknos*, thick, dense] *comb* thick; compact; dense (pycnidiospore, pycnometer). *Also* **pykn(o)-** (pyknemia, pyknic)

pyelo- [Gr. *puelos*, pelvis] *comb* pelvis; kidney (pyelocystitis, pyelonephritis)

-pygia, pygo- [Gr. *puge*, rump] *comb* rump; buttocks (pygopod, steatopygia)

pygm- [L. *pugnus*, fist] *base* fist (pygmachy, pygmy)

-pyle [Gr. *pule*, gate] *comb* gate; aperture (astropyle, micropyle)

-pyle-, pylo- [Gr. *pule*, gate] *base* gate; aperture (pylemphraxis, pylephlebitis, pylon, pylorus)

pyloro- [Gr. *pule*, gate + *ora*, keeper] *comb* pylorus: stomach opening (pylorodiosis, pylorospasm)

pyo- [Gr. *puon*, pus] **1.** *comb* pus (pyogenic, pyonephrotic); **2.** suppurative (pyococcus, pyosis)

pyram- [Gr. *pyramis,* pyramid] *base* pyramid (pyramid, pyramidical)

pyren- [Gr. *puren,* fruit stone] *base* nucleated; drupaceous (pyrenemia, pyrenocarp)

pyreto-, -pyrexia [Gr. *purektikos,* feverish < *pur,* fire] *comb* fever (pyretogenesis, pyretology, eupyrexia, hyperpyrexia)

-pyrgo- [Gr. *purgos,* tower] *base* tower (pyrgocephalic, pyrgoidal)

-pyri- [L. *pirum,* pear] *base* pear (pyridion, pyriform). *Also* **piro-** (piroplasm)

pyrito- [Gr. *purites,* flint] *comb* pyrites (pyritohedral, pyritohedron)

pyro- [Gr. *pur,* fire] **1.** *comb* fire; heat (pyromania); **2.** [chemistry] a substance derived from the specified

substance by or as if by the action of heat (pyrogallol); **3.** [geology] formed by heat (pyroxenite)

pyrrho- [Gr. *purros,* reddish] *comb* reddish (pyrrhoarsenite, pyrrhocorax)

pyrrhul- [Gr. *purros,* reddish] *base* bullfinch; bunting (pyrrhula, pyrrhuline)

pyrrhulox- [Gr. *purros,* reddish] *base* cardinal (Pyrrhuloxia, pyrrhuloxine)

pysm- [Gr. *pysma,* question] base interrogatory (pysmatic)

pytho- [Gr. *puthein,* to rot] *comb* corrupt; decomposed (pythogenic, pythogenesis)

pyx- [Gr. *puksis,* box] *comb* box (pyxidate, pyxis)

Q

quadr- [L. *quadra,* square] *base* four; fourfold; square (quadrable, quadrangle)

quadragen- [L. *quadraginta,* forty] *base* forty (quadragenarian, quadragene)

quadrages- [L. *quadragesima,* Lent, 40 days] *base* forty (Quadragesima, quadragesimal)

quadrati-, quadrato- [L. *quadratus,* square] *comb* four; fourfold (quadratiformis, quadratocubic)

quadri- [L. *quattuor,* four] *base* four; fourfold (quadriceps, quadrilateral)

quadricent- [L. *quattuor,* four + *centennis,* 100 years] *base* four hundred (quadricentennial)

quadru- [L. *quattuor,* four] *base* four; fourfold (quadrumanous, quadruped)

quaest- [L. *quarere,* seek, obtain] *base* gain; money-making (quaesta, quaestuary)

quali- [L. *qualis,* of what kind?] *base* characteristics; competence (qualitative, quality)

qualm- [Ger. *qualm,* nausea] *base* nausea, sickness (qualminess, qualmish)

quanti- [L. *quantus,* how much]

comb amount; extent (quantity, quantitative)

quart-, quarter-, quarti- [L. *quartus,* fourth] *base* one-fourth (quartile, quartering, quartisect)

quasi- [L. *quasi,* about, nearly] *comb* seemingly; as if; resembling (quasi-judicial, quasi-periodic)

quass- [L. *quassare,* to shake] *base* shake; beat (conquassate, quassative)

quat-, quater-, quatr- [L. *quattuor,* four] *comb* four (quatrain, quaternion, quatrefoil)

quattuordec- [L. *quattuor,* four + *decem,* ten] *base* fourteen (quatuordecangle, quatuordecillion)

-quer-[1], querul- [L. *queri,* to complain] *base* complain (querimonious, querulous)

-quer-[2] [L. *quaere,* to ask] *base* question (query, querying)

querc-, querci- [L. *quercus,* oak] *comb* oak (quercine, quercivorous)

-quest- [L. *inquirire,* to inquire] *base* inquiry (inquest, request)

quid- [L. *quid,* what] *base* nature; essence (quiddative, quiddity)

quiesc- [L. *quiescere*, keep quiet, rest] *base* quiet (acquiesce, quiescent)

quin-¹ [L. *quinque*, five] *base* five; multiple of five (quinary, quinate)

quin-² [SA *kina*, Peruvian bark] *base* quinine (quinidamine, quinology)

quincent- [L. *quinque*, five + *centenarius*, having 100] *base* five hundred (quincentenary, quincentennial)

quindec(em)- [L. *quinque*, five + *decem*, ten] *base* fifteen (quindecemvirate, quindecima)

quinquagen- [L. *quinquaginta*, fifty] *base* fifty (quinquagenarian, quinquagenary)

quinquages- [L. *quinquaginta*, fifty] *base* fifty (Quinquagesima Sunday, quinquagesimal)

quinque- [L. *quinque*, five] *comb* five (quinquefoliant, quinquennial)

quint-¹, quinti- [L. *quinque*, five] *comb* five; multiple of five (quintuplets, quintilateral)

quint-² [L. *quintus*, fifth] *comb* one-fifth (quintan, quintile)

-quire, -quiry [L. *quaerere*, to seek] *comb* seek; search for (require, inquiry)

-quis- [L. *quaerere*, to seek] *base* seek; search for (inquisition, requisition)

quisquil- [L. *quisquiliae*, rubbish] *base* worthless (quisquilian, quisquilious)

quot- [L. *quoties*, how many] *base* how many (quota, quotient)

quotid- [L. *quot*, as many as + *dies*, day] *base* daily (quotidian, quotidianly)

R

rabid- [L. *rabidus*, frenzied] *base* raging (rabidly, rabidness)

-racem- [L. *racemus*, cluster of grapes] *base* cluster (racemation, racemiform)

rachi-, rachio- [Gr. *rakhis*, spine] *comb* relating to the spine (rachicentesis, rachiometer). *See* -**rrhachia**

-rad- [L. *radius*, ray] *base* ray; rod; spoke (irradiate, radial)

-rade [L. *radere*, scrape away] *base* wear off (abrade, corrade)

radiati-, radiato- [L. *radiatus*, radiate] *comb* ray-like (radiatiform, radiato-striate)

radici- [L. *radix/radic-*, root] *comb* root (radiciform, radicicolous)

radiculo- [L. *radiculus*, rootlet] *comb* radicle; rootlike part (radiculoganglionitis, radiculose)

radio- [L. *radius*, ray] **1.** *comb* ray; ray-like (radiolarian); **2.** by radio (radiotelegram); **3.** [anatomy] radius and (radiobicipital); **4.** [medicine] by radiant energy (radiotherapy); **5.** [physics] radioactive (radiothorium)

raduli- [L. *radula*, scraper, rasp] *base* sharp-pointed; rasp-like (raduliferous, raduliform)

rall- [L. *Rallus*, the rail—a bird] *base* the rail (ralliform, ralline)

rament- [L. *ramentum*, shavings] *base* scaly (ramentaceous, ramentiferous)

rami- [L. *ramus*, branch] *comb* branch (ramification, ramiflorous)

ramoso- [L. *ramosus*, full of branches] *comb* branchy (ramoso-palmate, ramoso-subpinnate)

ramul- [L. *ramulus*, little branch] *base* twig (ramuliferous, ramulose)

rancid- [L. *rancidus*, putrid] *base* rotten (rancidification, rancidness)

rang(if)- [L. *rangifer*, reindeer] *base* reindeer, caribou (rangerine, rangiferine)

rani- [L. *rana*, frog] *comb* frog (raniform, raniverous)

rap- [L. *rapere*, to seize] *base* snatch; seize (rapacious, rapture)

-raphan- [Gr. *raphanis*, radish] *base* radish (raphania, raphanus)

raphi(d)- [Gr. *raphis/raphid-* needle] *base* needle (raphidiferous, raphigraph)

raptor- [L. *raptor*, robber] *base* falcon (Raptores, raptorial)

rasor- [L. *radere/rasus*, to scrape] *base* scratching, shaving (Rasores, rasorial)

rat- [L. *ratis*, raft] *base* emu; ostrich (Ratitae, ratite)

-rater [L. *reri/ratus*, to think, judge] *comb* specified rate or class (first-rater, second-rater)

-ratio- [L. *ratio*, reasoning] *base* reasoning; thought (irrational, rationalize)

rauc- [L. *raucus*, hoarse] *base* hoarse; boisterous (raucity, raucously)

re- [L. *re-*, back, again] **1.** *pre* back (restore); **2.** again; anew (retell)

recidiv- [L. *recidivare*, relapse] *base* relapse (recidivism, recidivist)

recti- [L. *rectus*, straight] *comb* straight; right (rectirostral, rectitude)

recto- [L. *rectum*, rectum] *comb* rectal (rectogenital, rectoscope)

recurvi-, **recurvo-** [L. *recurvus*, bent back] *comb* bent back (recurvirostral, recurvo-ternate)

-red [OE *raeden*, condition] *suf* condition; state (hatred, kindred)

regi- [L. *rex/reg-*, king] *base* of a king (regible, regicide)

regin- [L. *regina*, queen] *base* queen (reginal, reginist)

regm- [Gr. *regmunai*, to break] *base* separation, splitting (regma, regmacarp)

-regn- [L. *regnum*, kingdom] *base* royal; ruling (interregnum, regnant)

rego- [Gr. *rhegos*, blanket, rug] *comb* covering (regolith, regolithic)

regul- [L. *regula*, rule] *base* standard pattern (irregular, regulations)

-rel [OF -*erel*, diminutive suffix] *suf* diminutive (kestrel, wastrel)

religio- [L. *religiosus*, religious] *comb* religion (religio-educational, religio-mystical)

relinq- [L. *relinquere*, to leave] *base* leave; jilt; abandon (relinquish, unrelinquished)

reliq- [L. *reliquiae*, relics] *base* remains; relic (reliquarian, reliquary)

-reme, **-remi-** [L. *remus*, oar] *base* oar (trireme, remiform)

remig- [L. *remigare*, of rowing] *base* rowing (remigration, remigatory)

reni-, **reno-** [L. *renes*, kidneys] *comb* kidney (reniform, renovascular)

rep- [L. *rapere*, to snatch] *base* snatch; seize (subreption, surreptitious)

repando- [L. *repandus*, bent back] *comb* bent back (repando-dentate, repando-lobate)

repert- [L. *reperire*, invent, discover] *base* inventory (repertoire, reportorial)

-rept [L. *repere*, to creep] *base* creep; crawl (reptation, reptatorial)

reptil- [LL. *reptilis*, reptile] *base* reptile (reptilian, reptilivorous)

repud- [L. *repudium*, rejection] *base* jilt; reject (repudiate, repudiatory)

resino- [L. *resina*, resin] *comb* resin (resino-extractive, resino-vitreous)

respirato- [L. *respirare*, to breathe out] *comb* respiratory (respirato-prehensory, respirato-pulmonary)

-resti- [L. *restis*, cord, rope] *base* cord; cordlike (restibrachial, restiform)

reti- [L. *rete*, net] *base* net (reticular, retiform)

reticulato-, **reticulo-** *comb* net; network (reticulato-venose, reticulo-ramose)

retino- [NL *retina*, retina] *comb* of the retina (retinogen, retinoschisis)

retro- [L. *retro*, back, behind, formerly] *comb* backward; back; behind (retroactive, retroflex)

retuso- [L. *retusus*, blunt, weakened] *comb.* weakened (retuso-umbilicate, retuso-conical)

rhabdo- [Gr. *rhabdos*, rod] *comb* rod; wand (rhabdocoele, rhabdomancer)

-rhachia *see* **rachia-** *and* **-rrhachia**

rhachio-, **rhacio-** [Gr. *rhachis*, spine] *comb* spine (rhachiomyelitis, rhaciotomy)

-rhag-[1] [Gr. *rhagodes*, like grapes] *base* grape (rhagon, rhagose)

rhag-[2] [Gr. *rhagas*, fissure] *base* scars, skin cracks (rhagades)

-rhage *see* **-rrhage**

-rhamn [Gr. *rhamnos*, buckthorn] *base* buckthorn (rhamneous, rhamnose)

rhampho- [Gr. *rhamphos*, curved beak] *comb* beak (rhamphoid, rhamphotheca)

rhap- [Gr. *rhapis*, rod] *base* tapered, wand-like (Rhapidophyllum, Rhapis)

rhaphio- [Gr. *rhaphion*, needle] *comb* needle-like (Rhaphiodopsis, Rhaphiosaurus)

-rhaphy *see* **-rrhaphy**

-rhaps- [Gr. *rhaptein/rhaps-*, stitch or fasten together] *base* stitched; strung together (rhapsodomancy, rhapsody)

-rhea *see* **-rrhea**

rhed- [L. *rheda*, carriage] *base* carriage (rhedarious, rhedarium)

rhegma- [Gr. *rhegma*, a break] *comb* fracture; break (rhegma, rhegmatogenous)

rhema- [Gr. *rhematikos*, belonging to a verb] *base* word; verb (epirrhema, rhematic)

rheo- [Gr. *rhein*, to flow] *comb* flow; current (rheoscope, rheostat)

rhesto- [Gr. *rhaio*, to destroy] *comb* broken down (rhestocythemia). *Also* **rhaesto-**

rhet- [Gr. *rhetor*, a speaker] *base* say; speak (rhetorical, rhetorician)

-rheum- [Gr. *rheuma*, a flow] *base* flow; stream (rheumatic, rheumatoid)

-rhexis *see* **-rrhexis**

rhigo- [Gr. *rhigos*, cold] *comb* cold; frost (rhigolene, rhigosis)

rhino- [Gr. *rhis/rhin-*, nose] *comb* nose (rhinencephalon, rhinology)

rhipi-, rhipido- [Gr. *rhipis/rhipid-*, fan] *comb* fan (rhipidate, rhipidoglossate)

rhizo- [Gr. *rhiza*, root] *comb* root (rhizomorph, rhizophagous). *See* **-(r)rhiza**

rhodo- [Gr. *rhodon*, rose] *comb* rose; rose-red (rhodochrome, rhodolite)

-rhoeica *see* **-rrhoeica**

rhombi-, rhombo- [Gr. *rhombos*, rhomb, lozenge] *comb* rhombus (rhombiform, rhombohedral)

-rhonch- [Gr. *rhonkhos*, snoring, snorting] *base* snoring (rhonchal, rhonchisonant)

-rhopal- [Gr. *rhopalikos*, like a club] *base* club; cudgel (rhopalocerous, Rhopalodon)

rhopheo- [Gr. *rhophein*, gulp down] *comb* aspirate (rhopheocytosis)

-rhopo- [Gr. *rhopos*, petty wares] *base* petty; restricted (rhopographer, rhopography)

rhyaco- [Gr. *rhuaks*, a stream] *comb* torrent, stream (rhyacolite, Rhyacophilus)

rhyncho- [Gr. *rhunkhos*, snout] *comb* snout; beak (rhynchophore, rhyncosaurian). *See* **-rrhyncha**

rhyparo-, rhypo- [Gr. *rhuparos*, foul, dirty] *comb* dirt; filth (rhyparographer, rhypophagy). *Also* **rypo-** (rypophagy)

rhyss- [Gr. *rhusos*, drawn up, wrinkled] *base* wrinkled (Rhyssa, Rhyssodidae)

rhythm- [L. *rhythmus*, harmony] *base* rhythm (rhythmic, rhymical)

rhyti- [Gr. *rhutis*, a wrinkle] *comb* wrinkle (rhytidectomy, rhytidoma)

ribes- [Pers. *ribaj*, gooseberry] *base* gooseberry (ribes, Ribesieae)

-ric [OE *rice*, realm, province] *comb* jurisdiction; realm (abbotric, bishopric)

ricinol- [L. *ricinus*, error for *cicinus*, castor oil] *comb* castor oil (ricinolamide, ricinolein)

rict- [L. *rictus*, open-mouthed] *base* gaping (rictal, ricture)

-ridden [past participle of *ride*] *comb* obsessed or burdened with (guilt-ridden, priest-ridden)

-rig- [L. *rigare*, to water] *base* wet (irrigate, rigation)

rigesc- [L. *rigescere*, grow stiff or numb] *base* stiff; rigid (rigescence, rigescent)

-rim- [L. *rima*, crack, opening] *base* opening; crack (rimiform, rimose)

ringi- [L. *ringi*, to gape] *base* open-mouthed (ringent, Ringiculidae)

-rip- [L. *ripa*, river bank] *base* river; water (riparian, ripicolous)

-ris- [L. *ridere/ris-*, to laugh] *base* laugh (risibility, risible)

riv- [L. *rivus*, a stream, channel] *base* grooved; pert. to a stream (rivose; rivulose)

-rix- [L. *rixari*, to brawl] *base* quarrel (rixation, rixatrix)

rizi-, ryzi- [Gr. *oruksa*, rice] *base* rice (oryzivorous, riziform)

-robor-[1] [L. *roborare*, to strengthen] *base* strength (roborant, roboration)

-robor-[2] [L. *robur*, oak, hard wood] *base* oak (roborean, roboreous)

rod- [L. *rodere*, to gnaw] *base* eat away (corrode, erode)

roentgeno- [<Wilhelm Konrad Roentgen] *comb* X-rays (roentgenology, roentgenotherapy)

-rog- [L. *rogare*, to ask] *base* ask; question (interrogate, rogatory)

Romano- [L. *Romanus*, Roman] *comb* Roman and (Romano-Byzantine, Romano-Lombardic)

romantico- [Fr. *romant*, romance, novel] *comb* romantic (romantico-heroic, romantico-historical)

rond- [ME *ronde*, round] *base* circular (rondache, rondure)

-ror- [L. *ros/ror-*, dew] *base* dew (roriferous, rorifluent)

roscid- [L. *roscidus*, dewy] *base* dewy (roscid, roscidating)

roseo- [L. *roseus*, rosy] *comb* [chemistry] reddish salts (roseo-cobaltic, roseochrome)

-rostell- [L. *rostellum*, little beak] *base* snout; radicle (rostellate, rostelliform)

rostrato-, rostri-, rostro- [L. *rostratus*, having a beak or hook] *comb* beak; (rostrato-nariform, rostriform, rostrocarinate)

rot-, roti-, roto- [L. *rota*, wheel] *comb* turn; wheel (rotation, rotiform, rotograph)

rotundi-, rotundo- [L. *rotundus*, round] *comb* round (rotundifoliate, rotundo-tetragonal)

-rrhachia [Gr. *rakhis*, spine] *comb* spine (glycorrhachia). *See* **rachio-**

-rrhage, -rrhagia [Gr. *regnunai*, burst forth] *comb* abnormal discharge; excessive flow (hemorrhage, menorrhagia)

-rrhaphy [Gr. *rhaptein*, to sew] *comb* suture (arteriorrhaphy, cystorrhaphy)

-rrhea [Gr. *rroia*, flux, flow] *comb* flow; discharge (diarrhea, logorrhea). *Also* **-rrhœa** (diarrhœa). *See* **rheo-**

-rrhexis [Gr. *rheksis*, a breaking] *comb* rupture; bursting (karyorrhexis, myorrhexis). *See* **rhegma-**

-rrhiza [Gr. *rhiza*, root] *comb* root (mycorrhiza, pseudomycorrhiza). *See* **rhizo-**

-rrhoeic, -rrhoeica [Gr. *rroia*, flux, flow] *comb* flow (seborhoeic, seborrhoeica)

-rryncha [Gr. *rhunkhos*, snout] *comb* snout; beak (auchenorrhyncha, oxyrryncha). *See* **rhyncho-**

-rub- [L. *rubedo*, redness] *base* red; (rubedity, rubescent)

rubig- [L. *rubiginosus*, rusty] *base* rust (rubiginose, rubiginous)

-ruct- [L. *ructare*, to belch] *base* belch; emit (eructation, eruction)

-rud- [L. *rudis*, imperfect] *base* rough; elementary (rudimentary, rudiments)

ruder- [L. *ruderare*, cover with rubbish] *base* stone fragments; rubble; rubbish (ruderal, ruderation)

rufi-, rufo- [L. *rufus*, red] *comb* red (ruficaudate, rufo-fulvous)

-rug- [L. *ruga*, wrinkle] *base* wrinkle; (erugate, rugose)

rumen- [L. *rumen*, throat, gullet] *base* ruminant stomach (rumenitis, rumenotomy)

rumin- [L. *ruminans*, cud-chewing] *base* cud-chewing; ponder (ruminant, ruminate)

runc- [L. *runcare*, to weed] *base* weed (aberuncate, runcation)

runcin- [L. *runcina*, plane] *base* sawtoothed (runcinate, Runcinidae)

runo- [L. *runa*, rune] *comb* rune (runographic, runology)

rupes-, rupic- [L. *rupes/rupic-*, rock] *base* rock (rupestrine, rupicolous)

rupicap- [L. *rupes*, rock + *capra*, goat] *base* chamois (Rupicapra, rupicaprine)

rupo-[1] [Gr. *rhuparos*, foul, dirty] *base* filth (rupophobia). *See* **rhypo-**

rupo-[2] [Gr. *rhupos*, sealing wax] *base* impressing a coin or medal on sealing wax (rupography, rupographical)

-rupt- [L. *ruptura*, a breaking] *base* burst; break (disruption, eruption)

rur- [L. *rus/rur-*, the country] *base* the country (rural, rurigenous)

Russo- [L. *Russus*, Russia] **1.** *comb* Russia (Russophobe); **2.** Russian and (Russo-Japanese)

rustic- [L. *rusticus*, rural] *base* rural (rustical, rusticality)

rut- [L. *rutaceus*, of or belonging to rue] *base* rue (Rutaceae, rutaceous)

-rutil- [L. *rutilus*, red, yellowish-red] *base* shining; reddish (rutilant, rutilate)

-ry *See* -ery

rypo- [Gr. *rhuparos*, foul, dirty] *base* filth (rypophagy). *Also* rupo-

S

-s [OE -*es*, pl. suf.] *suf* plural ending (dogs, zebras)

sabell-, sabul- [L. *sabulum*, sand, gravel] *base* sand; grit (sabellan, sabulosity)

saburr- [L. *saburra*, sand] *base* sand (saburral, saburration)

-sacc- [L. *saccus*, bag] *base* pouch; bag; cyst (saccate, sacculation)

saccharo- [Gr. *sakkhraron*, sugar] **1.** *comb* sugar (saccharometer); **2.** saccharin and (saccharo-mucilaginous)

saccomy- [Gr. *Saccomys*, pocket-mouse] *base* rodent with cheek pouches (saccomyian, saccomyoid)

sacerdot- [L. *sacerdos/sacerdot-*, priest] *base* priest (sacerdotal, sacerdotalize)

saco- [Gr. *sakos*, shield] *base* shield-like; type of beetle (Sacodes, Sacoglossa)

-sacr- [L. *sacrare*, dedicate, consecrate] *base* holy; set apart (sacrament, sacrificial)

sacro- [L. *sacrum*, the sacrum] *comb* sacral and (sacrospinal, sacrovertebral)

saen- [Gr. *sainein*, wag the tail] *base* annelids (Saenuridomorpha, Saenuris)

safran- [Fr. *safran*, saffron] *base* yellow; saffron (saffranin, saffranophile)

sagac- [L. *sagax/sagac-*, acute, perceptive] *base* intellectually discerning (sagacious, sagacity)

sagen- [Gr. *sagene*, large fishing net] *base* like a fishing net (Sagenaria, sagene)

sagin- [L. *sagina*, fattening] *base* fattening (saginate, sagination)

-sagitt- [L. *sagitta*, arrow, bolt] *base* like an arrow (sagittal, sagittate)

sagma- [Gr. *sagma*, pack-saddle] *base* like a saddle (Sagmarius, sagmatorhine)

salac- [L. *salax/salac-*, lustful] *base* lecherous (salacious, salacity)

salar- [L. *salarium*, military allotment for salt] *base* pay, earnings (salariat, salaried)

-salebr- [L. *salebrosus*, rugged] *base* rough; uneven (salebrosity, salebrous)

-sali- [L. *sal*, salt] *base* salt (desalination, salinity)

-salic- [L. *salix/salic-*, a willow] *base* willow (salicaceous, salicetum)

salino- [L. *salinus*, of salt] *comb* salt and (salinometry, salinosulphureous)

saliv- [L. *saliva*, spittle] *base* spit (salivary, salivation)

salmoni- [L. *salmo*, salmon] *base* salmon (salmonic, salmoniform)

salpingo- [Gr. *salpinks*, trumpet] **1.** *comb* of a fallopian tube (salpingocyesis, salpingotomy); **2.** of a eustachian tube (salpingitis, salpingonasal)

sals- [L. *salsus*, salted] *base* salted (salsamentarious, salsuginous)

-salta- [L. *saltare*, dance, leap] *base* leap; dance (saltation, saltatory)

saltu- [L. *saltuosus*, wooded] *base* of woods (saltuary)

-salub- [L. *salubris*, healthful] *base* healthy (salubrious, salubrity)

saluti- [L. *salutifer*, health-bringing] *comb* remedial; medicinal (salutiferous, salutigerous)

-salv- [L. *salvare*, save] *base* save (salvage, salvation)

sambuc-¹ [L. *sambucus*, elder tree] *base* elder tree (sambuca, sambucene)

sambuc-² [Gr. *sambyke*, stringed

instrument] *base* small, shrill harp (Sambuca)

-san- [L. *sanare*, heal] *base* health; healing (sanatorium, unsanitary)

sanct-, sancti- [L. *sanctus*, holy] *comb* holy (sanctuary, sancticolist)

sandal- [Gr. *sandalon*, sandal] *base* sandal (sandalled, sandaliform)

sangui-, sanguineo-, sanguino- [L. *sanguis*, blood] *comb* blood (sanguicolous, sanguineo-vascular, sanguino-purulent)

sanguisug- [L. *sanguisuga*, bloodsucker] *base* leech (sanguisugent, sanguisugous)

sanid- [Gr. *sanidion*, small board or plank] *base* glassy feldspar (sanidine, sanidinic)

sapid- [L. *sapidus*, savory] *base* savory (sapidity, sapidness)

-sapien- [L. *sapientia*, wisdom] *base* wise (sapience, sapiently)

sapon-, saponi- [L. *sapo*, soap] *comb* soap (saponaceous, saponification)

sapor-, savor- [L. *sapor*, taste, flavor] *base* of taste (saporific, saporous, unsavory)

sapphir- [L. *sapphirus*, sapphire] *base* sapphire (sapphiric, sapphirine)

sapro- [Gr. *sapros*, rotten] *comb* [biology] dead; putrefying; decaying (saprogenic, saprophagous)

-sarc-, sarco- [Gr. *sarks/sark-*, flesh] *comb* flesh; tissue (ectosarc, sarcology)

sarcin- [L. *sarcina*, a bundle] *base* bundle (sarcina, sarcinic)

sarcul- [L. *sarculare*, to hoe] *base* hoe (sarculate, sarculation)

sardon- [Gr. *sardanios*, scornful laughter] *base* scornful mockery (sardonic, sardonicism)

sariss- [Gr. *sarissa*, long Macedonian lance] *base* long Macedonian lance (sarissa, sarissae)

-sarmass- [Gr. *sarks*, flesh + *masso*, knead] *base* erotic caressing, loveplay (sarmassation, sarmassophile)

sarment- [L. *sarmentum*, twigs, brushwood] *base* stem; runner (sarmentaceous, sarmentose)

saro- [Gr. *saron*, broom] *base* hairlike, brushlike (Sarothamnus, sarothrum)

sartor- [L. *sartor*, tailor] *base* tailor (sartorial, sartorius)

sat- [L. *satis*, sufficient] *base* full; replete (insatiable, satiety)

satellit- [L. *satellite*, attendant] *base* satellite (satellitic, satellitious)

satir- [L. *satira*, ridiculing literary work] *base* mockery (satirical, saritist)

sativ- [L. *sativus*, sown or planted] *base* sown; planted (sative, sativous)

sator- [L. *sator*, sower] *base* sow (satorious)

satur- [L. *satur*, full] *base* full (saturate, saturation)

satyr- [Gr. *satyros*, lusty woodland demon] *base* satyr (satyresque, satyriasis)

sauciat- [L. *sauciare*, to wound] *base* wound (sauciate, sauciation)

-saur, sauro-, -saurus [Gr. *sauros*, lizard] *comb* lizard (dinosaur, saurophagous, icthyosaurus)

sax-, saxi- [L. *saxus*, rock] *comb* rock; stone (saxatile, saxicoline)

scabi- [L. *scabere*, to scratch] *base* itch (scabiophobia, scabiosity)

scaev- [L. *scaevus*, left-handed] *base* left-sided; unlucky (scaevity, Scaevola)

-scal- [L. *scala*, ladder, flight of stairs] *base* climb; ladder (escalation, scalariform)

scaleno- [Gr. *skalenos*, uneven] *comb* scalene; unequal (scalenohedral, scalenohedron)

scalpelli- [L. *scalpellum*, surgical knife] *comb* scalpel (scalpelliform)

-scalpri- [L. *scalprum*, chisel] *base* chisel (scalpriform)

-scan- [L. *scandere*, to climb] *base* climb; scan (scansion, scansorial)

scandal- [Gr. *skandale*, snare, trap] *base* scandal (scandalist, scandalize)

-scape [Du, *landschap*, lay of the land] *comb* view; scenery (cityscape, seascape)

scapho- [Gr. *skaphe*, tub, skiff] *comb* boat-shaped (scaphocephalic, scaphoid) scapi- [L. *scapus*, stem or stalk] *comb* stalk; shaft (scapiform, scapigerous)

scapo- [Gr. *skapos*, rod] *comb* rodlike (scapolite, scapolitization)

scapuli-, scapulo- [L. *scapula*, shoulder] *comb* scapula and; shoulder blade (scapulimancy, scapuloclavicular)

scarab- [L. *scarabaeus*, beetle] *base* beetle (scarabaeid, scaraboid)

scato- [Gr. *skor/skat-*, dung] *comb* excrement; feces (scatology, scatophagous)

scatur- [L. *scatere*, to bubble up, gush] *base* spring of water (scaturient, scaturiginous)

-scel- [Gr. *skelos*, leg] *base* leg (isosceles, scelidosaur)

sceler- [L. *scelus/sceler-*, crime] *base* wicked (scelerous, scelestic)

-scelia [Gr. *skelos*, leg] *comb* [medicine] condition of the legs (macroscelia, microscelia)

sceno- [Gr. *skene*, stage, scene] *comb* scene (scenographer, scenography)

scept- [Gr. *skeptron*, staff, symbol of power] *base* scepter (sceptered, sceptral)

sceuo- [Gr. *skeuos*, a vessel] *base* vessel; utensil (sceuophorion, sceuophylax)

-schem- [Gr. *schema*, shape, figure] *base* appearance; form (schematic, schematism)

schismato-, schismo- [Gr. *schisma*, cleft, split] *comb* split (Schismatobranchia, schismopnea)

schisto- [Gr. *schistos*, easily cleft] *comb* split; cleft (schistocephalus, schistoprosopia)

schizo- [Gr. *schizein*, to cleave, split] *comb* split; cleavage; division (schizocarp, schizogenesis)

-schœno- [Gr. *schoinos*, rush] *base* rope (schœnobatic, schœnocaulon)

schol- [L. *schola*, school] *base* school (scholar, scholastic)

-sci- [L. *scire*, to know] *base* know (omniscient, scientific)

-scia- [Gr. *skia*, shade, shadow] *base* shadow (macroscian, sciamachy). *Also* scio- (sciomancy). *See* skia-

scilli-, scillo- [Gr. *skilla*, squill, sea-onion] *comb* squill-shaped; pointed (scillitoxin, scillocephalous, scillocephalus)

scinci-, scinco- [L. *scincus*, skink] *comb* skink; lizard (scinciform, scincoid)

-scind- [L. *scindere*, to cut off] *base* detach (abscond, rescindable)

-scintill- [L. *scintilla*, spark] *base* spark (scintilla, scintillation)

-scio-[1] [Gr. *skia*, shade] *base* shadow (sciomancy, sciomantic). *Also* -scia- (macroscian)

scio-[2] [L. *sciolus*, one who knows little] *comb* shallow knowledge (sciolism, sciolus)

scirrho- [Gr. *skirros*, hard] *comb* hard cancer (scirrhoma, scirrhosarca)

sciss- [L. *scindere*, cut or divide] *base* cut; divide (scissible, scission)

-sciur- [Gr. *skiouros*, squirrel < shade-tailed] *base* squirrel; marmot (sciurine, sciuromorphic)

sclero- [Gr. *skleros*, hard or harsh] 1. *comb* hard (sclerometer); 2. of the sclera (sclerotomy)

-scob- [L. *scobis*, sawdust, filings] *base* sawdust (scobiform, scobina)

scoleci-, scoleco- [Gr. *skoleks*, worm] *comb* worm (scoleciform, scolecobrotic)

scoli(o)- [Gr. *skolios*, bent, curved] *comb* bent; crooked (scoliosis, scoliotic)

scolo- [Gr. *skolops*, stake, thorn] *comb* pointed like a spike (scolophore, scolopsite)

scolopac- [L. *scolopax*, snipe] *base* snipe; woodcock (scolopaceous, scolopacine)

scolopendri- [L. *scolopendra*, milliped] *base* centipede (scolopendriform, scolopendrine)

scolyt- [Gr. *skoluptein*, crop, strip, peel] *base* bark-beetle (scolytoid, Scolytus)

scombr- [Gr. *skombros*, mackerel] *base* mackerel (scombrid, scombroid)

scomm- [Gr. *skomma*, jest, taunt, jeer] *base* mocking (scomm, scommatic)

scopa- [L. *scopa*, brush, broom] *base* twigs; broom; brush (scoparious, scopate). *Also* scopi-

-scope, -scopic, scopo-, -scopy [Gr.

skopein, to see] *comb* sight; observation; examination (telescope, microscopic, scopophilia, bioscopy)

scopeli- [Gr. *skopelos*, high rock] *base* bony fish; Scopelidae (scopeliform, scopeloid)

scophthalm- [Gr. *skopein*, to look, watch + *ophthalmos*, eye] *base* turbot (scophthalmus)

scopi- [L. *scopa*, twigs, shoots, broom] *base* twig; broom (scopiferous, scopiform)

scopul- [Gr. *skopelos*, cliff, promontory] *base* crag; cliff (scopulosity, scopulous)

scopuli- [L. *scopulae*, little broom] *comb* brush-like (scopuliform, scopulipede)

scor- [Gr. *skor*, dung] *base* fecal matter (scoracratia, scoretemia)

-scorb- [ML. *scorbutus*, scurvy] *base* scurvy (scorbutic, scorbutigenic)

-scoria- [Gr. *skoria*, refuse, dross] *base* slag (scoriaceous, scoriform)

-scoro- [Gr. *skordon*, garlic] *base* garlic (scorodite, scoro-doprasum)

scorp- [Gr. *skorpios*, scorpion] *base* scorpion (scorpioid, scorpioidal)

-scort- [L. *scortator*, fornicator] *base* fornication; harlot (scortation, scortatory)

Scoto- [Gr. *Skotoi*, people in the northern part of Britain] *comb* Scottish and (Scoto-Irish, Scoto-Welsh)

scoto- [Gr. *skotos*, gloom] *base* darkness; dimness (scotoma, scotophobia)

-scrib-, -script- [L. *scribere*, write] *base* write (scribacious, manuscript)

scrin- [L. *scrinium*, box, shrine] *base* chest; shrine (scrine, scrinium)

-scrobic- [L. *scrobis*, ditch, dike, trench] *base* furrowed; pitted (scrobiculate, scrobiculus)

-scrot- [L. *scrotum*, scrotum] *base* scrotum; testicular sac (scrotiform, scrotocele)

scrup- [L. *scrupulus*, little pebble] *base* conscience-troubling (scrupulosity, scrupulous)

-scrut- [L. *scrutari*, search or examine] *base* examine; search (inscrutable, scrutinize)

-sculpt- [L. *sculpere*, carve or chisel] *base* sculpt (resculpt, sculptor)

scurril- [L. *scurra*, buffoon] *base* coarse, indecent (scurrile, scurrilous)

-scut- [L. *scutum*, shield] *base* shield; scale (scutate, scutiform)

scutel- [L. *scutella*, salver, tray] *base* dish (scutelliform, scutelligerous)

scyllio- [Gr. *skulion*, dogfish] *comb* a type of shark (scylliodont, Scylliorhinus)

scyphi-, scypho- [Gr. *skuphos*, drinking cup] *comb* cup; [botany] cup-shaped part (scyphiform, scyphomancy)

Scytho- [Gr. *Skuthes*, a Scythian] *comb* Scythian and (Scytho-Aryan, Scytho-Greek)

scyto- [Gr. *skutos*, hide, skin] *comb* leathery skin (scytodepsic, scytodermatous)

se- [L. *se*, without, apart, away] *pre* away from (seclude, secret)

-seb-, sebo- [L. *sebum*, tallow, fat] *base* tallow; grease (sebaceous, seborrhea)

sebasto- [Gr. *sebastos*, reverend] *comb* of religion (sebastomania, sebastophobia)

-sec-, -sect- [L. *secare*, cut] *base* cut (secant, intersection)

-secul- [L. *saecularis*, of an age or period] *base* worldly; temporal (secularism, secularize)

secundi-, secundo- [L. *secundus*, following] *comb* second (secundipara, secundogeniture)

securi- [L. *securi*, ax or hatchet] *comb* ax; hatchet (securiferous, securiform)

-secut- [L. *sequor/secut-*, to seek] *base* follow (consecutive, persecute). *See* -seq-

-sed- [L. *sedere*, to sit] *base* sit (sedent, sedentary)

sedat- [L. *sedatus*, composed] *base* allay; calm (sedate, sedation)

sedecim- [L. *sedecim*, sixteen] *base* sixteen (sedecimal, sedecimarticulate)

sedul- [L. *sedulous*, careful] *base* diligent (sedulity, sedulously)

segn- [L. *segnitia*, slowness] *base* sloth; sluggishness (segnitude, segnity)

seiro- [Gr. *seiron*, garment] *comb* type of algae (Seirospora, seirospore)

-seism, -seismal [Gr.*seisma*, shaking] *comb* earthquake wave (bradyseism, coseismal)

seismo- [Gr. *seismos*, earthquake] *comb* earthquake (seismograph, seismology)

sela- [Gr. *selas*, brightness] *comb* flash; lightning (selaphobia, Selaphorus)

selach- [Gr. *selachos*, sea-fish, shark] *base* shark (selachoid, selachology)

seleno- [Gr. *selene*, moon] *comb* moon (selenography, selenological)

self- [AS. *seolf*, self] *comb* oneself (self-denial, self-closing)

selli- [L. *sella*, saddle] *comb* saddle (selliform)

sema-, -seme, semeio-, semio- [Gr. *sema*, sign] *comb* sign; signal; symbol; token; symptom (semaphore, microseme, semeiology, semiotics)

semel- [L. *semel*, once] *comb* once (semelparity, semelparous)

semi- [L. *semi*, half] **1.** *pre* half (semidiameter); **2.** partly; imperfectly (semicivilized); **3.** twice per ___ (semiannual)

semin- [L. *seminalis*, relating to seed] *base* seedbed; germinal (seminal, seminality)

semit- [L. *semita*, narrow way, path] *base* fasciole (semita, semital)

semno- [Gr. *semnos*, revered, sacred] *comb* honored; sacred (semnopithece, Semnopithecus)

semper- [L. *semper*, always] *base* always (sempervirent, sempervivum)

-sen- [L. *senilis*, of old age] *base* old (senility, seniority)

sena- [L. *seni*, six] *base* six (senarius, senary)

-sens-, -sent- [L. *sensus*, perception] *base* feel (sensitive, sentimental)

sensori- [L. *sensorium*, organ of sensation] *comb* pertaining to the senses or to sensations (sensoridigestive, sensorimotor)

sep- [Gr. *sepsis*, decay] *base* putrid (sepedogenesis, sepsometer)

-sepalous [Gr. *skepe*, covering] *comb* having a specific kind or number of sepals (antisepalous, trisepalous)

sepi-¹ [Gr. *sepios*, cuttlefish] *base* cuttlefish (sepia, sepiacean)

sepi-² [L. *saepes/sepes*, hedge or fence] *base* hedge, fence, separation (sepicolous, sepiment)

sept- [L. *septem*, seven] *base* seven (septan, September)

septem- [L. *septem*, seven] *comb* seven (septempartite, septemvirate)

septen- [L. *septentrio*, north] *base* north (septentrion, septentrionate)

septendecim- [Latin *septem*, seven + *decem*, ten] *base* seventeen (septendecimal)

septi-¹ [L. *septem*, seven] *comb* seven (septifolious, septilateral)

septi-², septico- [Gr. *septos*, made rotten + *aima*, blood] *comb* decomposed; vitiated (septicemia, septico-pyaemia)

septim- [L. *septimus*, seventh] *base* seventh (septimal, septimole)

septingenti- [L. *septingenti*, seven hundred] *base* seven hundred (septingentenary)

septo-¹ [Gr. *septos*, made rotten] *comb* decomposed; vitiated (septogenic, septometer)

septo-² [L. *septum*, fence] *comb* dividing wall (septocephalic, septonasal)

septuagen- [L. *septuagenarius*, seventy] *base* seventy (septuagenarian, septuagenary)

septuages- [L. *septuagesima*, seventieth] *base* seventy (Septuagesima Sunday, septuagesimal)

septuagint- [L. *septuaginta*, seventy] *base* seventy (Septuagint, septuagintal)

sepul- [L. *sepulcrum*, burial place] *base* grave; tomb; burial (sepulcher, sepulchral)

-seq- [L. *sequor*, to follow] *base* follow (consequence, sequential). *See* -secut-

-ser- [L. *serare*, to join] *base* bar; bolt (reseration, seraglio)

serang- [Gr. *seranks*, cavern] *base* cave (serangitis)

Serbo- [Fr. *Serbe*, a Serbian] *comb* Serbia (Serbo-Croatian, Serbo-Italian)

seri-, sericeo-, serico- [Gr. *Ser*, the Seres,

northern China] *comb* silk (serigraph, sericeo-tomentose, sericostoma)

serio- [L. *serius*, grave, earnest] *comb* partly serious (serio-comedic, serio-comic)

serm- [L. *sermo*, discourse] *base* sermon (sermonize, sermonology)

sero- [L. *serum*, serum] *comb* serum; (serology, seropurulent)

serot- [L. *serotinus*, late, backward] *base* late in occurrence or development (serotine, serotinous)

serpen- [L. *serpens/serpent-*, snake] *base* snake (serpentiform, serpentine)

serrati-, serrato- [L. *serra*, a saw] *comb* saw-toothed (serratirostral, serrato-crennate)

serri- [L. *serra*, a saw] *comb* [entomology/zoology] a saw (serricorn, serrirostrate)

serv- [L. *servire*, to serve] *base* attendant; slave (servant, servitude)

-serve [L. *servare*, to keep or protect] *comb* keep; attend to (preserve, reservation)

sesam- [Gr. *sesame*, sesame] *base* sesame (sesamine, seasminoid)

sesqui- [L. *sesqui-*, more by one half] *comb* one and one half (sesquibasic, sesquicentennial)

sesquipedal- [L. *sesqui-*, one half more + *pes/ped*, foot] *base* long words < Horace: "words a foot and a half long" (sesquipedalian, sesquipedalophobia)

-sess- [L. *sedere/sess-*, to sit] *base* sit; perch (insessorial, sessile)

setaceo- [L. *seta*, bristle] *comb* bristles and (setaceo-rostrate)

seti- [L. *seta*, bristle] *base* bristle (setiferous, setiparous)

setul- [L. *setula*, little bristle] *base* little bristle (setuliform, setulose)

sexagen- [L. *sexageni*, sixty each] *base* sixty (sexagenary, sexagenarian)

sexages- [L. *sexagesimus*, sixtieth] *base* sixty (Sexagesima Sunday, sexagesimal)

sexcent- [L. *sex*, six + *centenarius*, of one hundred] *base* six hundred (sexcentenary)

sexi- [L. *sex*, six] *comb* six (sexipolar, sexisyllabic)

sext- [L. *sextanus*, sixth] *comb* sixth (sextan, sextant)

sexti- [L. *sextanus*, sixth] *comb* six (sextipartite, sextisection)

she- [OE *sio*, she] *comb* female (she-bear, she-wolf)

-ship [AS *scapan*, shape] **1.** *suf* quality; condition; state of (friendship); **2.** rank; office; status (kingship); **3.** ability; skill (leadership); **4.** collective: all individuals of a specified class (readership)

-siagon- [Gr. *siagon*, jawbone] *base* jawbone (siagon, siagonology)

sial-[1] [Gr. *sialon*, spittle] *base* saliva (sialogogic, sialorrhea)

sial-[2] [Gr. *sialis*, kind of bird] *base* **1.** bluebird (Sialia) **2.** neuropterous insect (Sialidae)

-sibil- [L. *sibilare*, to hiss, whistle] *base* hiss; whistle (sibilant, sibilation)

sica- [L. *sica*, dagger] *base* knife; dagger (sicarian, sicarius)

-sicc- [L. *siccare*, to dry] *base* dry (desiccate, siccate)

Siculo- [Gr. *Sikeloi*, Sicilians] *comb* Sicilian (Siculo-Arabian, Siculo-Punic)

-sid- [L. *sidere*, to sit] *base* inhere; sit in (insident, reside)

-sider(e) [L. *sidus/sider-*, star] *comb* star (hagiosidere, sidereal)

sidero-[1] [Gr. *sideros*, iron] *comb* iron (siderazote, siderolite)

sidero-[2] [L. *sidus/sider-*, star] *comb* star (siderostat, siderostatic)

siderodromo- [Gr. *sideros*, iron + *dromos*, running] *comb* railroad— invented word (siderodromomania, siderodromophobia)

-sigil- [L. *sigillum*, little mark or token] *base* seal; signet (sigillary, sigillation)

sigma- [Gr. *sigma*, the letter s] *comb* S-shaped (sigmaspiral, sigmation)

siliceo-, silici-, silico- [L. *silex/silic-*, flint] *comb* [chemistry] silica: containing or relating to (siliceo-calcareous, siliciferous, silico-alkaline)

silicul- [L. *silicula*, little husk or pod] *base* seed-vessel, pod (silicular, siliculose)

silig- [L. *siligo*, fine wheat] *base* winter wheat (siliginose, siliginous)

siliqu- [L. *siliqua*, husk or pod] *base* pod (siliquiferous, siliquiform)

sillo- [Gr. *silos*, satire] *comb* of satire (sillograph, sillographist)

silph- [Gr. *silphe*, beetle] *base* carrion-beetle; larva (silphid, silphology)

-silur- [Gr. *silouros*, river-fish] *base* catfish (silurid, siluroid)

Siluro- [Gr. *Silures*, the Silures, a people of ancient Britain] *comb* Silurian (Siluro-Cambrian, Siluro-Devonian)

silvi- [L. *silva*, forest] *comb* tree; forest (silvicolous, silviculture). *Also* **sylvi-**

sim- [L. *simia*, ape, monkey] *base* ape; chimp (simian, Simiidae)

-simil- [L. *similis*, like or akin] *base* like; resembling (dissimilarity, similitude). *Also* **simul-** (simulation, simulatory)

-simo- [Gr. *simos*, snub-nosed] *base* snub-nosed (Simenchelys, simosaurus)

-simul- [L. *simul*, together] *base* at the same time (simultaneity, simultaneous)

sinap- [Gr. *sinapi*, mustard] *base* mustard (Sinapis, sinapism)

sindon- [Gr. *sindon*, muslin] *base* shroud (sindonologist, sindonology)

singult- [L. *singultus*, hiccup, throat rattle] *base* hiccup; sob (singultous, singultient)

sinistro- [L. *sinister*, left] *comb* left: of, at, using (sinistro-cerebral, sinistrogyric)

sino- [L. *sinus*, curve, bend, bay] *comb* sinus (sino-auricular, sinorespiratory)

Sino- [Gr. *Sinai*, the Chinese] *comb* Chinese: people/language (sinology, Sino-Soviet)

-sinu- [L. *sinus*, a bend or fold] *base* bending; winding (insinuate, sinuous)

sinuato-, sinuoso- [L. *sinus*, a bend or fold] *comb* wavy; uneven (sinuato-dentate, simuoso-lobate)

-sion *see* **-ion**

siphoni-, siphono- [Gr. *siphon*, tube, pipe] *comb* tube; pipe; siphon (siphoniform, siphonostele)

sipuncul- [L. *sipunculus*, little tube or siphon] *base* spoonworm (sipunculacean, sipunculiform)

-sis [Gr. *-sis*, a suf. in nouns of action] *suf* action; condition (analysis, stasis)

-siti- [L. *sitire*, to thirst] *base* thirst (insitiency, sitient)

-sitia, sitio-, sito- [Gr. *sitos*, food] *comb* food; eating; appetite (asitia, sitiophobia, sitology)

sitt- [Gr. *sitte*, a kind of woodpecker] *base* nuthatch (Sittinae, sittine)

situ- [L. *situare*, to place] *base* located; inherent (situate, situation)

-size, -sized [L. *assidere*, to sit down while assessing a tax] *comb* having a specified size (life-size, small-sized)

skeleto- [Gr. *skeleton*, skeleton] *comb* skeleton (skeletology, skeleto-trophic)

-skeps/-skept [Gr. *skepsis*, inquiry] *base* self-absorbed, doubtful (omphaloskepsis, skeptic)

skeuo- [Gr. *skeuos*, vessel, implement] *base* decorated vessel; utensil (skeuomorph, skeuomorphic)

skia- [Gr. *skia*, shadow] *comb* shadow (skiagraphy, skiascopy). *See* **scia-**

Slavo- [Gr. *Sklabos*, a Slav] *comb* Slav; (Slavo-Lithuanian, Slavophile)

smaragd- [Gr. *smaragdos*, light-green precious stone] *base* emerald (smaragdine, smaragdochalcite)

smegma- [Gr. *smegma*, soap] *base* sebaceous secretion (smegma, smegmatic)

sobol- [L. *soboles*, sprout or shoot < *sub*, under + *olere*, to grow] *base* shoot or creeping underground stem (soboles, soboliferous)

socer- [L. *socer*, father-in-law] *base* father-in-law (soceraphobia)

socio- [L. *sociare*, to join or accompany] *comb* society; social (sociobiological, sociogeny)

sodal- [L. *sodalitas*, fellowship] *base* association (sodalitious, sodality)

sodio- [NL. *soda*, alkaline substance] *comb* sodium (sodio-hydric, sodio-platinic)

-soever [OE *swa*, so + *ever*, a generalized, indefinite appendage] *comb* any

___ of those possible; (whatsoever, whosoever)

sol-[1] [L. *sol*, sun] *comb* sun (solar energy, solarium)

sol-[2] [L. *solum*, ground, floor, bottom] *base* of the ground (solary)

solen-, soleno- [Gr. *solen*, channel or pipe] *comb* [zoology] channel; pipe (solenoid, solenoglypha)

soli- [L. *solus*, alone] *comb* alone (solitary, solitude)

-solu-, -solv- [L. *solvere*, to dissolve] *base* melt; dissolve (soluble, solvant)

-soma [Gr. *soma*, body] *comb* [zoology] names of genera (Schistosoma, Trypanosoma)

somato-, -somatous [Gr. *soma/somat-*, of the body] *comb* body (somatogenic, somatology, macrosomatous)

-some[1] [Gr. *soma*, body] *comb* body; (acrosome, chromosome)

-some[2] [OE *-sum*, tending to be] *suf* like; tending to be (loathsome, tiresome)

-some[3] [OE *-sum*, numerical suffix] *suf* number: in a specified (threesome, foursome)

somn(i)- [L. *somnus*, sleep] *comb* sleep (somnambulant, somniferous)

son-, soni-, sono-, sonoro- [L. *sonus*, sound] *comb* sound (sonancy, soniferous, sonogram, sonoro-sibilant)

sophron- [Gr. *sophron*, self-control] *base* self-control (sophronist, sophronize)

-sophy [Gr. *sophos*, wise] *comb* knowledge; thought (misosophy, philosophy)

-sopor- [L. *sopor*, sleep] *base* sleep (soporific, soporous)

-sor- [Gr. *soros*, a heap] *base* heap (sorosis, sorotrochous)

-sorb-[1] [Gr. *sorbere*, suck in, swallow up] *base* soak up (absorbent, sorbefacient)

-sorb-[2] [L. *sorbus*, service-tree] *base* mountain ash (sorbic, sorbite)

-sord- [L. *sordes*, filth, dregs] *base* dirt; filth (insordescent, sordid)

soredi- [Gr. *soros*, a heap] *comb* reproductive unit of lichens (sorediferous, sorediform)

soric- [L. *sorex/soric-*, shrew] *base* shrew (soricident, soricine)

soro- [Gr. *soros*, heap] *base* accumulation (sorites, sorotrochous)

-soror- [L. *soror*, sister] *base* sister (sororicide, sorority)

-sote [Gr. *sozein*, to save] *comb* preserver (creosote)

-soter- [Gr. *soter*, savior] *base* salvation (autosoteric, soteriology)

spad- [Gr. *spadiks*, nut-brown, palm-colored] *base* brown (spadiceous)

spadici- [NL *spadix/spadic-*, palm-like] *comb* succulent spike (spadicifloral, spadiciform)

spalac- [Gr. *spalaks/spalac-*, mole] *base* mole-rat (Spalacidae, spalacine)

spano- [Gr. *spanos*, scarce or rare] *comb* scarce (spanemia, spanopnea)

sparasso-, sparax- [Gr. *sparassein*, to tear] *comb* laceration; tearing (sparassodont, sparaxis)

sparg- [L. *spargere*, to sprinkle, strew] *base* sprinkle; scatter (spargefication, sparger)

spars- [L. *sparsus*, scattered, sprinkled] *base* thinly scattered (sparsile, sparsity)

spasmato-, spasmo- [Gr. *spasmos*, a spasm] *comb* spasm; contraction (spasmatomancy, spasmology, spasmolysis)

spathi- [Gr. *spathe*, a broad flat blade] *base* spatula; broad blade (spathiform, spathiopyrite, spatuliform)

spatilo- [Gr. *spatile*, excrement] *comb* excrement (spatilomancy)

spatul-, spatuli- [L. *spatula*, broad blade] *base* shoulder; spatula-shaped (spatulamancy, spatuliform)

-spec(t)-, -spic- [L. *spectare*, see, behold] *base* look; see (spectator, conspicuous)

-specific [L. *species*, kind + *ficus*, made] *comb* applied or limited to the particular item named (age-specific, culture-specific)

specio- [L. *species*, species] *comb* specific (speciographic, speciology)

spectr- [L. *spectrum*, apparition] *base* ghost (spectral, spectrality)

spectro- [NL *spectrum*, spectrum] **1.** *comb* radiant energy as exhibited in a spectrum (spectrogram); **2.** of/by a spectroscope (spectro-heliogram); **3.** mirror (spectrophobia)

specul- [L. *specula*, watchtower] *base* reflective thought (speculation, speculative)

speleo-, spelunc- [Gr. *spelaion*, cave] *base* cave (speleologist, speluncar)

sper- [L. *sperare*, hope] *base* hope (sperable, sperate)

-sperg-, -spers- [L. *spargere*, to sprinkle] *base* sprinkle (insperge, inspersion)

-sperm, sperma-, -spermal, spermatio-, spermato, spermi-,-spermic, spermo-,
-spermous [Gr. *sperma*, seed] *comb* seed; germ; beginning (gymnosperm, spermaphore, gymnospermal, spermatiogenous, spermatocyte, spermiducal, endospermic, spermogonium, monospermous)

speus- [Gr. *speusis*, haste] *base* made in haste (speustic)

sphacel- [Gr. *sphakelos*, gangrene] *base* gangrene (sphacelate, sphaceloderma)

sphag- [Gr. *sphage*, throat] *base* throat (sphagitis, sphagiasmus)

-sphagn- [Gr. *sphagnos*, kind of moss] *base* moss (sphagnicolous, sphagnologist)

-sphair- [Gr. *sphaira*, ball] *base* tennis (sphaeristerium, sphairistic)

-sphal- [Gr. *sphaleros*, slippery, uncertain] *base* error (sphalerite, sphalma)

-sphec- [Gr. *spheks/sphek-*, wasp] *base* wasp; hornet (Sphecidae, sphecoid)

sphenisc- [Gr. *spheniskos*, little wedge] *base* penguin (spheniscan, speniscomorph)

spheno- [Gr. *sphen*, wedge] **1.** *comb* wedge-shaped (sphenogram); **2.** sphenoid bone (sphenoccipital)

-sphere, spherico-, sphero- [Gr. *sphaira*, ball, sphere] *comb* sphere (stratosphere, spherico-cylindrical, spherocyte). *Also* **sphaero-** (sphaeroblast)

-sphingo- [Gr, *sphingein*, to shut tight or close] *base* bound tightly (sphingometer, sphingomyelin)

-sphrag- [Gr. *sphragis*, signet or seal] *base* seal; signet (sphragistes, sphragistic)

sphygmo- [Gr. *sphugmos*, pulse] *comb* pulse (sphygmograph, sphygmology)

sphyr- [Gr. *sphura*, hammer, mallet] *base* hammer (sphyrelaton)

sphyraen- [Gr. *sphura*, hammer, mallet] *base* barracuda; hammer-fish (Sphyraena, sphyraenoid)

sphyrn- [Gr. *sphura*, hammer] *base* hammer-head shark (Sphyrna, sphyrnine)

spici- [L. *spica*, point or spike] *base* spiked (spiciferous, spiciform)

spicul-, spiculi-, spiculo- [L. *spiculum*, little point or spike] *comb* spiky; pointed (spicular, spiculiferous, spiculofibrous)

-spil- [Gr. *spilos*, spot] *base* spotted basalt; speck (spilite, spilosite)

spini-, spino-, spinoso-, spinuloso- [L. *spina*, thorn, backbone] *comb* spine (spini-acute, spinocerebellar, spinoso-dentate, spinuloso-serrate)

-spinthar- [Gr. *spinther*, spark] *base* spark (spinthariscope, spinthere)

spiri- [L. *spira*, coil or spire < Gr. *speira*] *comb* coil; spiral (spiriferous, spiriform)

spiro-[1] [L. *spirare*, to breathe] *comb* respiration; breath (spirograph, spirometer)

spiro-[2] [Gr. *speira*, coil or spire] *comb* spiral; coil (spirochete, Spyrogyra)

-spiss- [L. *spissus*, thick, compact] *base* thick; dense (inspissation, spissitude)

-splachn- [Gr. *splanchnon*, moss] *base* moss (splachnoid, Splachnum)

splanchno- [Gr. *splanchna*, viscera] *comb* viscera (splanchnic, splanchnology)

splenico-, splen(o)- [Gr. *splen*, spleen] *comb* spleen (splenico-phrenic, splenocele)

spodo- [Gr. *spodos*, ashes] *base* ashes (spodogenous, spodomancy)

spol- [L. *spoliare*, spoil, pillage] *base* spoil, deprive (spoliate, spoliative)

spondylo- [Gr. *spondulos*, vertebra, joint] *comb* vertebra (spondylalgia, spondylitis)

spongi-, spongio-, spongo- [Gr. *spongos*, sponge] *comb* sponge-like

(spongiculture, spongiocyte, spongolith)

spor- [Gr. *sperein*, to sow or scatter] *base* scatter (sporadic, sporadically)

-spore, spori-, sporo-, -sporous [Gr. *sporos*, seed] **1.** *comb* spore; seed (teliospore, sporiferous, sporocarp); **2.** specific number/kind of spores (monosporous)

-spum- [L. *spuma*, foam] *base* foam; froth (spumescence, spumiferous)

spur- [L. *spurius*, false] *base* false (spurious, spuriousness)

-spurc- [L. *spurcus*, foul, impure] *base* dirty; foul (conspurcation, spurcitious)

-squal- [L. *squalus*, shark] *base* shark (squaliform, squaloid)

squamato-, squamo-, squamoso-, squaroso- [L. *squama*, scale] *comb* squama; scalelike (squamato-granulous, squamo-cellular, squamoso-dentated, squaroso-laciniate)

stabil- [L. *stabilire*, to make firm] *base* lasting; fixed (destabilize, stability)

-stact- [Gr. *staktos*, dropping, oozing out] *base* drop (stacte, stactometer)

-stagm- [Gr. *stagma*, a drop] *base* drop (stagma, stagmoid)

-stagn- [L. *stagnare*, to form a pool of standing water] *base* pool (stagnant, stagnicolous)

-stal- [Gr. *stalsis*, checking of a flow] *base* motion; contraction (antiperistalsis, peristalsis)

-stalac(ti)-, -stalag- [Gr. *stalaktos*, dropping] *base* dropping; dripping (stalactite, stalagmite)

stamini- [L *stamen*, thread, fiber] *comb* stamen (staminiferous, staminigerous)

-stann- [L. *stannum*, tin] *base* tin (stannic, stanniferous)

-stap- [L. *stapes*, stirrup] *base* stirrup; stapes (stapedectomy, stapediferous)

staphylo- [Gr. *staphule*, bunch of grapes] **1.** *comb* uvula; grapelike (staphylorrhaphy); **2.** staphylococcus (staphylodermatitis)

stasi-, -stasis, -stasia [Gr. *stasis*, a stoppage] *comb* standing still; balance; arrest; halt (stasimetry, phlebostasis, menostasia)

stasio- [Gr. *stasis*, party, faction] *comb* political party (stasiologist, stasiology)

-stat [Gr. *statos*, standing, fixed] *comb* scientific instrument (aerostat, thermostat)

stathmo- [Gr. *stathmos*, day's journey] *base* stage of development (stathmograph, stathmokinesis)

stato- [Gr. *statos*, standing, fixed] *comb* stationary; stabilized (statoblast, statocyst)

stauro- [Gr. *stauros*, a cross] *comb* cross (stauraxonia, staurophobia)

-stead [OE *stede*, place] *comb* place (bedstead, homestead)

stearo-, steato- [Gr. *stear/steat-*, fat, tallow, suet] *comb* fatty substance (stearoglucose, steatopygia)

-stegano- [Gr. *steganos*, covered] *base* covered (steganography, steganopodous)

stegno- [Gr. *stegnos*, watertight, tightly covered] *comb* constricting; styptic (stegnotic, thecostegnosis)

stego- [Gr. *stegein*, to cover] *comb* covered; closed (stegocephalous, stegosaur)

stel- [Gr. *stele*, block or slab] *base* monument, pillar (stellar, stele)

-stell- [L. *stella*, star] *base* star (interstellar, stellate)

stellio- [L. *stellio*, newt] *base* lizard; newt (stellion, Stellionidae)

-stema- [Gr. *stema*, filament] *base* filament (stemapod, stemonozone)

stemma- [Gr. *stemma*, wreath, garland] *base* circular (stemma, stemmatous)

sten(o)- [Gr. *stenos*, narrow] *comb* small; thin; narrow; abbreviated (stenocardia, stenographer)

stentor- [Gr. *Stentor*, A Greek herald in the Trojan war with a trumpet-like voice—*Homer*] *base* having a powerful voice (stentorian, stentorophonic)

step- [OE *steop*, affinity arising from remarriage] *comb* relationship not by blood (stepchild, stepfather)

stephan- [Gr. *stephane*, crown, wreath]

base intersection of coronal suture and temporal ridge (stephanial, stephanion)

-ster [AS *-estre*, suf. designating occupation] **1.** *suf* person who is/does/creates ___ (spinster); **2.** person associated with ___ (gangster)

sterco- [L. *stercus*, dung] *comb* dung; feces (stercoraceous, stercoricolous)

stereo- [Gr. *stereos*, solid, hard, stiff] *comb* three-dimensional; solid (stereoscope, stereometry)

-sterigm- [Gr. *sterigma*, prop, support] *base* prop; support (sterigma, sterigmatic)

stern- [NL *sterna*, tern] *base* tern (Sterninae, sternine)

sterni-, **sterno-** [NL *sternum*, breastbone] *comb* sternum and; breastbone (sterniform, sternoclavicular)

-sternut- [L. *sternutatio*, a sneeze] *base* sneeze (sternutation, sternutatory)

-sterquil- [L. *sterquilinium*, dunghill] *base* dunghill (sterquilinian, sterquilinious)

sterr- [Gr. *sterros*, stiff, solid] *base* solid fibrous connections, strong alloy (sterraster, sterro-metal)

-stert- [L. *stertere*, to snore] *base* snore (stertor, stertorous)

stetho- [Gr. *stethos*, breast] *comb* chest; breast (stethoscope, stethoscopy)

-sthenia, **sthen(o)-** [Gr. *sthene*, strength] *comb* strength; force; power (hypersthenia, hyposthenuria)

stibio- [Gr. *stibi*, a sulphuret of antimony] *comb* [chemistry] black antimony (stibiconite, stibiotrimethyl)

stibo- [Gr. *stibos*, footstep] *comb* footprint (stibogram)

-stich, **-stichia**, **sticho-**, **-stichous** [Gr. *stikhos*, row, line] *comb* row; line; verse (heptastich, tristichia, stichometry, tristichous)

-stict- [Gr. *stiktos*, spotted, dappled] *base* spotted (laparostict, stictiform)

-stig- [Gr. *stizein*, to prick] *base* to punctuate; to goad; stimulate (instigate, instigation)

-stigm- [Gr. *stigma*, a mark] *base*

mark; point; dot; puncture; tattoo (pterostigma, stigmatized)

stigno- [Gr. *stizo*, mark with a pointed instrument] *comb* writing (stignomancy)

stilb- [Gr. *stilbein*, to glitter, shine] *base* lustrous (Stilbacae, stilbite)

-still- [L. *stilla*, a drop] *base* drop (stillatitious, stilliform)

stilo- [L. *stilus*, pointed instrument] *comb* pointed (stilogonidium). *See* **stylo-**

-stilpno- [Gr. *stilbein*, to glitter, shine] *base* glittering (stilpnomelane, stilpnosiderite)

stimul- [L. *stimulus*, goad] *base* activity-quickening (stimulation, stimulatory)

-stip-[1] [L. *stipes*, a post] *base* stalk; support (stipel, stipitate)

-stip-[2] [L. *stipare*, to crowd, press together] *base* press together; pack (constipation, stipate)

stipul- [L. *stipulari*, make firm] *base* condition for (stipulation, stipulative)

-stiri- [L. *stiria*, icicle] *base* icicle (stiriated, stirious)

-stirp- [L. *stirps*, stock, stem, race] *base* stem; stock (exstirpate, stirpiculture)

stoa- [Gr. *stoa*, colonnade] *base* portico, colonnade (stoa)

-stoch- [Gr. *stokhos*, aim, shot, guess] *base* guess (stochastic, stochasticity)

-stoicheio- [Gr. *stokhazesthai*, to aim at] *base* estimating elements (stoicheiological, stoicheiometry)

stol- [L. *stolo/stolon-*, shoot, branch, sucker] *base* branch (stolonate, stoloniferous)

stomati-, **stomato-**, **-stome**, **-stomous** [Gr. *stoma*, mouth, entrance] *comb* [medicine/botany] mouth (stomatiferous, stomatalgia, cyclostome, megastomous)

-stomy [Gr. *stoma*, opening, entrance] *comb* surgical opening into ___ (colostomy, ileosigmoidostomy)

stone- [OE *stan*, stone] *comb* very; completely (stone-broke, stone-deaf)

stop- [L. *stoppa*, tow fiber] *base* tow (stope, stopine)

-storgy [Gr. *storge*, natural love or affection] *base* affection (astorgy, philostorgy)

-stori- [aphetic form of *history*] *base* tales; legends (storiologist, storiology)

-strab-, strabism- [Gr. *strabismos*, squinting] *base* squinting (strabotomy, strabismometer)

-stragul- [L. *stragulum*, a cover] *base* covering; pallium (stragular, stragulum)

-strain [L. *stringere*, to draw tight] *comb* restrict; bind (constrain, restrain)

-stram(in)- [L. *stramen*, straw] *base* straw (stramage, stramineous)

strangul- [Gr. *strangale*, halter] *base* choke (strangulate, strangulation)

-strat- [Gr. *strategos*, a general] *base* army tactics; direction (strategic, strategy)

strati-, strato- [L. *stratum*, layer] *comb* layer; stratum (stratification, stratosphere)

-stren- [L. *strenuus*, quick, active] *base* strong; with effort (strenuous, strenuously)

strep-, strepi- [L. *strepere*, to make a noise] *base* noisy (obstreperous, strepitous)

strepho-, strepsi-, strepto- [Gr. *strepho*, twist, turn] *comb* turned; twisted (strephosymbolia, strepsipterous, streptococcal)

-stress *see* -ess

stria-, striato-, strio- [L. *stria*, furrow, channel] *comb* furrow; groove (striaform, striatocrenulate, striomuscular)

-strict [L. *stringere*, to draw tight] *comb* tightly drawn; limited (restriction)

-strid-, stridul- [L. *stridere*, give a harsh or shrill sound] *base* creak; harsh noise (strident, stridulation)

-strig- [L. *striga*, furrow] *base* furrow; channel (striga, strigated)

strigi- [Gr. *striks/strig-*, screech-owl] *base* owl (strigiform, strigine)

strigil- [L. *strigilis*, a scraper] *base* scraping instrument; curry comb-like (strigil, strigilate)

-string- [L. *stringere*, to draw tight] *base* constricted (astringent, stringent)

-strob- [Gr. *strobos*, twisting, turning] *base* twisting; spinning (strobic, strobilation)

strobil- [LL. *strobilus*, pine-cone] *base* pine cone (strobiliform, strobilite)

-strom- [L. *stroma*, covering] *base* connected structure (stroma, stromatiform)

-stromb- [Gr. *strombos*, something twisted or whorled] *base* spiral; twisted (strombiform, strombite)

strombuli- [NL. *strombulus*, little top] *base* twisted like a top (strombuliferous, strombuliform)

strongyl- [Gr. *strongulos*, round, spherical] *base* round (strongylate, strongyloid)

-stroph- [Gr. *strophe*, a turning round] *base* turn; twist (strophiolate, strophiole)

struct- [L. *struere*, pile up, build] *comb* arrange; put together (constructive, deconstruction)

strum-, -struma-, strumi- [L. *struma*, scrofulous tumor] *base* goiter; swelling; tumor (strumectomy, strumatic, strumiferous)

-struthio- [Gr. *struthion*, ostrich] *base* ostrich (struthioid, struthious)

-stult- [L. *stultus*, foolish, silly] *base* foolish (stultify, stultiloquy)

-stup- [L. *stupere*, be struck senseless] *base* senseless (stupefaction, stupor)

stupr- [L. *stuprare*, to ravish] *base* fornicate; rape (stuprate, stupration)

sturion- [ML *sturio*, sturgeon] *base* sturgeon (sturionic, sturionian)

-sturn- [L. *sturnus*, starling] *base* starling; swallow (strurniform, sturnoid)

styg- [Gr. *Stux/Stug-*, river of the lower world] *base* hellish (Stygia, Stygian)

styl- [L. *stylus*, pointed instrument for writing] *base* pen (styliform, stylography)

stylo-¹ [L. *stilus*, stake, point] **1.** *comb* pointed; sharp (stylate); **2.** styloid: bony process (stylohyoid)

-style, stylo-² [Gr. *stulos*, pillar] *comb* column; pillar (pyrgostyle, stylolite, stylospore)

styph- [Gr. *styphos*, astringent] *base* astringent (styphnate, styphnic)

-stypt- [Gr. *stuptikos*, astringent] *base* astringent (styptic pencil, stypticity)

-suad-, -suas- [L. *suasio*, counseling, exhortation] *base* urge (dissuade, persuasion)

suav- [L. *suavis*, sweet, agreeable] *base* sweet (suaveolent, suavity)

sub- [L. *sub-*, under] **1.** *pre* under; below (submarine); **2.** lower in rank; inferior to (subaltern); **3.** to a lesser degree; slightly (subtropical); **4.** division (sublet); **5.** [chemistry] less than the normal amount of ___ ; basic (subchloride); **6.** [mathematics] ratio inverse to a given ratio (subduplicate). NOTE: **sub-** can change to: **su-** (suspect); **suc-** (succeed); **suf-**(suffocate); **sug-**(suggest); **sum-** (summon); **sup-** (support); **sur-** (surrogate); **sus-** (suspend)

subagit- [L. *subagitare*, to move back and forth down below] *base* sexual intercourse (subagitation, subagitatory)

-suber- [L. *suber*, cork] *base* cork (subereous, suberose)

subero- [L. *suber*, cork] *comb* suberic acid (suberiferous, subero-pyroxylic)

subig- [L. *subigere*, to pound or knead] *base* knead (subigate, subigation)

subit- [L. *subitus*, sudden, unexpected] *base* sudden; hasty (subitaneous, subitary)

subsesqui- [L. *sub-*, under + *sesqui*, one half more] *pre* [chemistry] elements combined in the proportion of 2 to 3 (subsesquiacetate, subsesquialterate)

subter- [L. *subter-*, below, secret] *pre* below; under; less than; secretly (subterfluous, subterfuge)

-subul- [L. *subula*, awl] *base* awl (subulicorn, subuliform)

suc- [L. *succus*, juice] *base* juice (succivorous, succulent)

-succino- [L. *succinus*, of amber] *comb* amber (succinic, succino-sulphuric)

sucho- [Gr. *soukhos*, crocodile] *base* crocodile (suchospondylian, suchospondylous)

sucr- [Fr. *sucre*, sugar] *base* sugar (sucro-acid, sucrose)

sud-, sudori- [L. *sudare*, to sweat] *comb* sweat; perspiration (sudatory, sudorific)

-suet- [L. *suetus*, customary, familiar] *base* custom (assuetude, consuetude)

suffrag- [L. *suffragium*, voting tablet, judgment] *base* voting (suffrage, suffragette)

-suge [L. *sugere*, to suck] *base* suck (potisuge, sugent)

sugill- [L. *sugillare*, beat black and blue] *base* bruise (sugillate, sugillation)

sui-[1] [L. *sui*, of oneself] *base* oneself (suicide, suicism)

sui-[2]**, suid-** [L. *sus/sui-*, swine] *base* pig; boar (suilline, suidian)

sulc- [L. *sulcus*, a furrow] *base* groove (sulcation, sulcus)

sulcato- [L. *sulatcus*, furrowed] *comb* furrowed; grooved; cleft (sulcato-areolate, sulcato-rimose)

sulfato- [L. *sulpur*, brimstone, sulpher] *comb* sulfate (sulfatidates). *Also* **sulphato-** (sulphato-acetic, sulphato-carbonate)

sulfo- [L. *sulpur*, brimstone, sulpher] *comb* sulfur; sulfonate sulfonic acid (sulfocyanogen). *Also* **sulpho-** (sulpho-indigotic)

sulfureo [L. *sulpur*, brimstone, sulpher] *comb* sulfureous (sulfureo-nitrous, sulphureo-virescent)

sumpt- [L. *sumptus*, expense] *base* costly (sumptuosity, sumptuous)

super- [L. *super*, above] **1.** *pre* over; above; on top (superstructure); **2.** higher in rank/position; superior to (superintendent); **3.** greater in quality/amount/degree; surpassing; (superabundance); **4.** greater or better (supermarket); **5.** greater than normal (supersaturate); **6.** extra; additional (supertax); **7.** to a secondary degree (superparasite); **8.** [chemistry] large amount of ___ (superphosphate)

supero- [L. *superus*, above, upper] *comb* [anatomy] on the upper side (supero-dorsal, supero-posterior)

supin- [L. *supinare*, bend or lay backward] *base* lying down (supination, supine)

supra- [L. *supra*, on the upper side] *pre* above; over; beyond (supra-acromial, supraliminal)

sur- [Fr. *sur*, above] *pre* over; upon; above; beyond (surface, surpass)

sura- [L. *sura*, calf of the leg] *base* calf of the leg (sural, sural artery)

surcul- [L. *surculare*, to prune] *base* grafting; twig (surculigerous, surculose)

-surd- [L. *surdus*, deaf] *base* deaf (absurd, surdity)

-surg- [L. *surgere*, to lift up, raise] *base* rise (insurgent, resurgent)

sursum- [L. *sursum*, upward] *comb* upward (sursumduction, sursumversion)

suspir- [L. *suspirium*, sigh, difficult breathing] *base* sigh (suspiration, suspirious)

-susurr- [L. *sussurare*, to whisper] *base* whisper; murmur (insusurration, sussurus)

-sutil- [L. *sutilis*, sewn together] *base* stitch; sew (consutile, inconsutile)

sutor- [L. *sutor*, cobbler] *base* cobbler (sutorial, sutorious)

-syc- [Gr. *sukon*, fig] *base* fig (sycoma, sycosis)

-sychno- [Gr. *sukhnos*, many, frequent] *base* many (sychnocarpous)

syllab- [Gr. *syllabanein*, place together] *base* syllable (syllabic, syllable)

sylleps- [Gr. *sullepsis*, conception] *base* pregnancy (syllepsiology, syllepsis)

sylv-/sylvi- [L. *silva*, forest] *base* of trees (sylvan, sylviculture). *Also* **silv-**

symm- [Gr. *symmakos*, fighting together] *base* alliance (symmachy)

symmetr- [Gr. *summetria*, proportion] *base* symmetry (asymmertrical, symmetry)

symphyo- [Gr. *sumphues*, growing together] *comb* growing together (symphyantherous, symphyogenesis)

sympos- [Gr.*symposion*, drinking party] *base* conference (symposiarch, symposium)

syn- [Gr. *sun*, with, together] *pre* with; together; at the same time; by means of; (synagogue, synallagmatic). NOTE: **syn-** can change to: **sy-** (syzygy); **syl-** (syllogism); **sym-** (symbiosis); **sys-** (system)

synax- [Gr. *synaxis*, meeting for worship] *base* gathering together (synaxarion, synaxis)

synchro- [Gr. *sunkhronos*, contemporaneous] *comb* synchronized (synchromesh, synchronism)

syndesmo- [Gr. *sundesmos*, ligament] *comb* ligament; binding together (syndesmodontoid, syndesmoplasty)

synec-/-synœc- [Gr. *sunekheia*, connection, continuity] *base* community (synectic, synœcology)

syngam- [Gr. *syngameo*, unite] *base* interbreeding, fusion (syngamic, syngamy)

synod- [Gr. *synodos*, assembly] *base* assembly (synodal, synodic)

syntagm- [Gr. *syntagma*, arranged in order] *base* sequential relationship (syntagma, syntagmatic)

syphili-, syphilo- [NL *Syphilis*, a character in a poem by Hieronymus Frascatorius] *comb* syphilis (syphilitic, syphilophobia)

-syr- [Gr. *surinks/suring-*, tube, pipe] *base* **1.** reed; pipe; tube (syringe, siringium); **2.** Eustachian tube (syringeal, syrinx)

syrigma- [Gr. *surigmos*, whistle] *comb* whistle, ringing sound (syrigmophonia, syrigmus)

syringo- [Gr. *surinks/suring-*, tube, pipe] *comb* tube-shaped cavity (syringocarcinoma, syringomyelitis)

syrm- [Gr. *syrein*, to drag] *base* mockery (diasyrm, syrmatic)

Syro- [Gr. *Suros*, Syrian] *comb* Syrian and (Syro-Arabian, Syro-Phoenician)

-syrt- [L. *syrtis*, sand-bank] *base* quicksand (syrtic, syrtis)

systol- [Gr. *systole*, contraction] *base* contraction (systole, systolic)

T

-tab- [L. *tabere*, melt, waste away] *base* emaciated; wasted away (tabefy, tabescent)

taban- [L *tabanus*, horse-fly] *base* horse-fly (tabanid, Tabanus)

tabell- [L. *tabella*, tablet, ballot] *base* tablet; ballot (tabella, tabellary)

tabern- [L. *taberna*, hut, tent] *base* sacred receptacle (tabernacle, tabernacular)

tacho- [Gr. *takhus*, swift] *comb* speed (tachograph, tachometer)

tachy- [Gr. *takhus*, swift] *comb* rapid; swift; fast (tachycardia, tachygraphy)

tacit- [L. *tacitus*, silent, done without words] *base* quiet (tacit, taciturn)

-tact- [L. *tangere/tact-*, to touch] *base* touch (contact, tactile)

-tactic, -tactous [Gr. *taktos*, arranged or arrayed] *comb* order; arrangement (heterotactous, syntactic)

taeni-, taenio- [L. *tainia*, ribbon, tape] *comb* ribbon; or band; tapeworm (taeniafuge, taeniosomous). *Also* teni- (teniacide)

tagm- [Gr. *tagma*, something arranged] *base* distinct unit or segment (tagmatics, tagmeme)

-tain [L. *tenere*, to hold] *comb* hold (maintain, retain). *See* -ten-

-tainment [L. *tenere*, to hold] *comb.* genre combining entertainment with information (edutainment, infotainment)

tal- [L. *talis*, such, like, similar] *base* retaliation (taliation, talion)

tala-, tali-, talo- [L. *talus*, ankle] *comb* ankle (taligrade, talocalcaneal)

talip- [L. *talipes*, club foot] *base* club foot (talipedic, talipes)

talpi- [L. *talpa*, mole] *base* mole (talpicide, talpine)

tamieut- [Gr. *tamieuein*, to save] *base* sparing (isotamieutic)

-tang- [L. *tangere*, to touch] *base* touch (intangible, tangent)

tanno- [Fr. *tanin*, tannin] *base* tannin (tannometer, tannogallate)

tantal- [Gr. *Tantalos*, son of Zeus punished for revealing godly secrets] *base* tease (tantalize, tantalizingly)

tany- [Gr. *tanyein*, to stretch] *base* a type of fly (tanystome, tanystomous)

tapes- [Gr. *tapetion*, carpet] *base* layer (tapesium, tapestry)

tapet- [Gr. *tapes/tapet-*, carpet, rug] *base* like a carpet (tapesium, tapetum)

-taph, tapho-, taphro- [Gr. *taphos*, grave, tomb] *comb* tomb; pit (cenotaph, taphophobia, taphrenchyma)

-tapino- [Gr. *tapeinos*, low, base] *comb* low, dejected (tapinocephalic, tapinosis)

tarand- [Gr. *tarandos*, reindeer] *base* reindeer (tarandre, tarandus)

tarass- [Gr. *taraksis*, confused] *base* confused (tarassis)

-tard- [L. *tardare*, to go slow] *base* slow; delay (retardation, tardigrade)

tarso- [L. *tarsus*, broad, flat surface] 1. *comb* instep (tarso-metatarsus); 2. eyelid cartilage (tarsoplasty)

tartr(o)- [Fr. *tartre*, tartar] *comb* tartar; tartaric acid (tartromethylates, tartrovinic acid)

-taseo-, -tasi- [Gr. *tasis*, stretching, tension] *base* tension (taseometer, tasimetric)

tatus- [Fr. *tatusie*, armadillo] *base* armadillo (tatusia, Tatusiidae)

tauri-, tauro- [Gr. *tauros*, bull] 1. *comb* of/like a bull (tauricide, tauromachy); 2. [chemistry] taurine (taurocholate)

taurotrag- [Gr. *tauros*, bull + *tragos*, goat] *base* eland (taurotragus)

tauto- [Gr. *tauton*, the same] *comb* the same; identical (tautochronous, tautology)

tax- [NL. *taxus*, yew] *base* yew (Taxaceae, taxaceous)

taxi-, -taxia, -taxis, taxo-, -taxy [Gr. *taksis*, order, arrangement] *comb* arrangement; order (taxidermy, heterotaxia, parataxis, taxonomy, homotaxy)

techno-, -techny [Gr. *tekhne*, art, handicraft] **1.** *comb* art; science; skill (technocracy); **2.** technical; technological (technochemistry, pyrotechny)

tecno- [Gr. *teknon*, child] *comb* child (tecnology, tecnonymy)

-tect- [L. *tectus*, covered] *base* roof; cover (protection, tectiform)

tecton- [Gr. *tektonikos*, of construction] *base* earth's structural crust; building (Tectonarchinae, tectonics)

-teen [AS *tene*, ten] *suf* ten and; numbers: cardinal (nineteen, sixteen)

teg-, tegu- [L. *tegmen*, cover] *base* cover (tegmental, tegument)

tegul- [L. *tegula*, tile] *base* tile; scale (tegular, tegulated)

-teicho- [Gr. *teikhos*, wall] *base* wall (teichopsia, teichoscopy)

teino- [Gr. *tenein*, to stretch, extend] *base* adjustable (teinoscope)

tek- [Gr. *teknon*, child] *base* child (ateknia, teknonymous)

tel-[1] [L. *tela*, web] *base* web; something spun (telarian, telary)

tel-[2] [L. *telum*, dart] *base* dart (Telifera, teliferous)

tele- [Gr. *tele*, afar] **1.** *comb* at a distance; far (telegraph); **2.** television (telecast)

teleio-, teleo-, telo- [Gr. *telos*, end, completion] *comb* end; purpose; final stage (teleiosis, teleology, telophase)

telesi- [Gr. *telos*, end, accomplishment] *comb* effectual (telesiurgic, tesleiurgics)

telesm- [Gr. *telesma*, religious rite, consecration] *base* talisman (telesmatical, telesmatically)

teleuto- [Gr. *teleute*, completion] *comb* final stage (teleutofrom, teleutospore)

tellin- [Gr. *telline*, kind of shell-fish] *base* bivalve mollusk (Tellina, tellinite)

tellur- [L. *tellus/tellur-*, earth] *base* earth (intratelluric, tellurian)

-telmat- [Gr. *telma/telmat-*, marsh] *base* a bog (Telmatodytes, telamatology)

telson- [Gr. *telson*, boundary, limit] *base* final segment (telson, telsonic)

temen- [Gr. *temenos*, sacred enclosure] *base* of land dedicated to a god (temenos, Temenuchus)

temer- [L. *temere*, by chance, rashly] *base* reckless (temerity, temerous)

-temerat- [L. *temerare*, to violate] *base* violate (intemerate, temeration)

temno- [Gr. *temnein*, to cut] *comb* cut (apotemnophilia, temnospondylous)

-temp- [L. *temperare*, to proportion] *base* regulate; mix (temper, temperament)

tempest- [L. *tempestivus*, timely, seasonal] *base* timely (tempestive, tempestivity)

-tempor- [L. *tempus/tempor-*, season, time] *base* time (contemporary, temporal)

temporo- [L. *tempora*, the temples] *comb* temple of the head (temporo-auricular, temporo-maxillary)

-temul- [L. *temulentia*, intoxicated] *base* drunkenness (temulency, temulent)

-ten- [L. *tenere*, to hold, keep] *base* hold (tenable, tenacious). *See* **-tain**

tend- [L. *tendere*, to stretch] *base* stretch (contend, distend, tendon)

-tene [Gr. *tainia*, band] *comb* [biology] ribbon-shaped (diplotene, pachytene)

-tenebr- [L. *tenebrae*, darkness] *base* darkness (tenebrific, tenebrosity)

tener- [L. *tener*, tender] *base* tenderness (tenerity, tenerous)

tenes- [Gr. *tenesmos*, straining] *base* straining (tenesmus, tenesmic)

-teni- [Gr. *tainia*, band, ribbon] *base* tapeworm; ribbon-like (teniacide, teniafuge). *Also* **taeni(i)-** (taeniiphobia)

teno-, tenonto- [Gr. *tenon*, tendon] *comb* tendon (tenotomy, tenontodynia)

tensio- [L. *tensio*, stretching] *comb* stretch; strain (tensiometer, tensiometric)

tentaculi- [NL *tentaculum*, feeler] *comb* tentacle (tentaculiferous, tentaculiform)

tentig- [L. *tentigo*, tension, lust] *base* lascivious (tentigo, tentiginous)

tentor- [L. *tentorium*, tent] *base* canopy (tentorial, tentorium)

tenui- [L. *tenuis*, thin] *comb* slender; thin; narrow (tenuifolious, tenuirostral) tepe- [L. *tepere*, to be lukewarm] *base* lukewarm (tepefaction, tepefy)

tephro- [Gr. *tephra*, ashes] **1.** *comb* ashes (tephromancy); **2.** gray (tephroite, tephromalacia)

ter- [L. *ter*, thrice] *comb* thrice (tercentenary, tercentennial)

tera- [Gr. *teras*, monster] *comb* one trillion (terabit, terahertz)

terato- [Gr. *teras/terat-*, monster] *comb* prodigy; monstrosity (teratogenic, teratology)

terebinth- [Gr. *terebinthos*, the turpentine-tree] *base* turpentine (terebinthinate, terebinthine)

terebr- [L. *terebra*, a borer] *base* bore; penetrate (terebration, terebratuline)

tered- [Gr. *teredon*, ship-worm] *base* worm (teredines, teredo)

tereti-, tereto- [L. *teres/teret-*, round, smooth] *comb* rounded (tereticaudate, teretosetaceous)

tergi-, tergo- [L. *tergum*, back] *comb* the back (tergiversation, tergolateral)

-termin- [L. *terminus*, boundary] *base* end; limit (interminable, termination)

termit- [NL *termes/termit-*, white ant] *base* termite (termitarium, termitophagous)

-tern-, ternati- [L. *terni*, by threes] *base* three; triple (ternate, ternati-pennate)

terps- [Gr. *terpein*, to delight] *base* enjoy dancing (Terpsichore, terpsichorean)

-terr- [L. *terra*, earth, land] *base* earth (subterranean, territorial)

-tert- [L. *tertius*, third] *base* third (tertial, tertiary)

tessel- [L. *tesselare*, form with small blocks] *base* mosaic (tessellate, tessellation)

tessera- [Gr. *tessares*, four] *comb* four (tesserace, tesseraglot)

tesseradeca- [Gr. *tessares*, four + *dekas*, ten] *comb* fourteen (tessaradecad, tesseradecasyllabon)

testaceo- [L. *testaceus*, covered with a shell] *comb* **1.** shell (testaceography, testaceology); **2.** [*botany/zoology*] reddish-brown; dull brick color (testaceo-fuscous, testaceo-piceous)

testud- [L. *testudo*, tortoise] *base* turtle (testudinal, testudineous)

tetano- [L. *tetanus*, tetanus] *comb* tetanus; stiff (tetanigenous, tetanospasmin)

tetarto- [Gr. *tetartos*, fourth] *comb* one fourth (tetartohedral, tetartopyramid)

tetra- [Gr. *tetra*, four] *comb* four (tetrablastic, tetragamy)

tetracyclo- [Gr. *tetra*, four + *kuklikos*, in a circle] *comb* with four circles; with four atomic rings (tetracyclic, tetracycline)

tetradeca- [Gr. *tetra*, four + *deka*, ten] *comb* fourteen (tetradecapod, tetradecapodous). *Also* tetrakaideca- (tetrakaidecahedron)

tetrakis- [Gr. *tetrakis*, four times] *comb* four times (tetrakisdodecahedron, tetrakishexahedron)

tetrao- [Gr. *tetraon*, pheasant, grouse] *base* grouse; ptarmigan (tetraonid, tetraonine)

tetrazo- [Gr. *tetra*, four + *azo*, nitrogen] [*chemistry*] **1.** *comb* compound with 4 atoms of nitrogen (tetrazone); **2.** presence of four azo groups (tetrazolyl)

teuth- [Gr. *teuthis*, cuttlefish] *base* cuttlefish; squid (teuthologist, teuthology)

teuto- [L. *Teutoni*, German tribe] *comb* German (Teutonicism, teutophobia)

tex- [L. *texere*, to weave] *base* weave (textile, texture)

text- [L. *textum*, tissue] *base* tissue (textoblastic, textoma)

-th-[1] [AS suf. *-th* for abstract nouns] **1.** *suf* act of (stealth); **2.** state of being/having; quality of being/having (wealth)

-th-[2] [AS suf. *-tha* used to form ordinal numerals] *suf* numbers: ordinal (fifth, sixteenth)

thalamo- [Gr. *thalamos*, inner chamber, bedroom] *comb* thalamus (thalamocortical, thalamocrural)

thalasso-, thalatto- [Gr. *thalassa*, sea] *comb* sea; marine (thalassocracy, thalattology)

thalero- [Gr. *thaleia*, blooming] *comb* blooming; fresh (thalerophagous)

thall-, thallo- [Gr. *thallos*, a green shoot] *base* **1.** green plant (thallus, thallophyte) **2.** thallium (thallious oxide)

thamn- [Gr. *thamnos*, bush, shrub] *base* bush; shrike (thamnium; thamnophile)

thanato- [Gr. *thanatos*, death] *comb* death (thanatology, thanatopsis)

thaumato- [Gr. *thauma/thaumat-*, a wonder] *comb* wonder; miracle (thaumatology, thaumaturgic)

theatro- [Gr. *theatron*, place to view shows] *comb* theater (theatromania, theatrophobia)

-theca, theci-, theco- [Gr. *theke*, case, box] *comb* sheath; container; case; cover (sarcotheca, theciform, thecostegnosis)

-thei- [NL *thea*, tea] *base* tea (theic, theiform)

thelo- [Gr. *thele*, teat] *comb* nipple (perithelium, Thelotrema)

thely- [Gr. *thelukos*, feminine] *comb* female (Thelygonum, thelytoky)

then- [Gr. *thenar*, palm or sole] *base* palm, sole (thenad, thenar)

theo- [Gr. *theos*, god] *comb* god (theocentric, theology)

-thera [Gr. *theran*, to hunt] *base* catcher; trap (oenothera)

theraphos- [Gr. *theraphion*, little wild beast] *base* tarantula (theraphose, theraphosid)

-there, therio-, thero- [Gr. *ther*, wild beast] **1.** *comb* extinct mammalian form (megathere); **2.** beast (theriomorphic, theropod)

-therm, thermo-, -thermy [Gr. *thermos*, warm] *comb* heat; hot (isotherm, thermodynamics, diathermy)

-thesis, -thetic [Gr. *thesis*, putting, placing] *comb* set; put; place (hypothesis, antithetic)

-thesmo- [Gr. *thesmos*, law] *base* law (thesmophilist, thesmothete)

thesp- [Gr. *Thespis*, father of stage tragedy] *base* actor (thespian, thespianism)

thia-, thio- [Gr. *theion*, sulfur] *comb* sulfur (thiabendazole, thioaldehyde)

thigmo- [Gr. *thigma*, touch] *comb* touch (thigmokinesis, thigmotropism)

thino- [Gr. *this/thin-*, the shore] *base* beach; seashore (Thinocorus, thinolite)

-thlips- [Gr. *thlibein*, to press, distress] *base* pressure (thlipsencephalus, thlipsis)

thneto- [Gr. *thnetos*, mortal] *comb* mortal (thnetopsychism, Thnetopsychitae)

thoraci-, thoracico-, thoraco- [Gr. *thoraks*, a breastplate] **1.** *comb* thorax and (thoracispinal, thoracico-abdominal); **2.** thorax; chest (thoracoplasty)

thras- [Gr. *Thraso*, bragging soldier in Terence's *Eunuchus*] *base* brag; boast (thrasonical, thrasonically)

thremm- [Gr. *thremma/thremmat-*, nursling] *base* breed; propagate (thremmatology)

thren- [Gr. *threnos*, wailing, lamentation] *base* lamentation (threnetic, threnody)

threp/s/t- [Gr. *threphein*, to nourish] *base* nourish; nurse (threpsology, threpterophilia)

thripto- [Gr. *threpteon*, who must be fed to live] *base* mortal (triptophobia)

-thrix- [Gr. *thriks*, hair] *base* hair (streptothricial, streptothrix)

-throated [OE *throte*, throat] *comb* throat: specific kind (large-throated, ruby-throated)

thrombo- [Gr. *thrombos*, clot of blood] *comb* blood clot (thrombo-arteritis, thrombo-phlebitis)

thumo- [Gr. *thumos*, soul] *comb* soul (thumomancy)

-thur- [L. *thus/thur-*, incense] *base* incense (thurible, thurifer)

-thy- [Gr. *thuma*, sacrifice] *base* offering; sacrifice (idolothyus, thymiaterion)

-thylac- [Gr. *thulaks*, pouch] *base* pouch (thylacine, thylacothere)

-thymia[1] [Gr. *thumos*, soul] *comb* mental disorder (alexithymic, dysthymia)

-thymia[2] [Gr. *thumion*, burn as incense] *base* perfume; incense (thymiama, thymiatechny)

thymo- [Gr. *thumos*, thymus; soul] **1.** *comb* thymus (thymokinetic); **2.** mind; soul; mood; emotions (thymogenic, thymopathy)

-thyrea, thyreo-, thyro- [*thureos*, large oblong shield] *comb* thyroid (hypothyrea, thyreotomy, thyromegaly)

thyrsi-, thyrso- [Gr. *thursos*, stalk, stem] *comb* stalk; stem; inflorescence (thyrsiflorous, thyrsocephalic)

-thysan- [Gr. *thusanos*, a tassel] *base* fringe; tassel (thysanopter, thysanurous)

tibicin- [L. *tibicinare*, play the flute] *base* flute (tibicinate, tibicinist)

tibio- [L. *tibia*, shinbone, pipe] *comb* tibia and (tibioperoneal, tibiotarsal)

-tic *see* -ic

ticho- [Gr. *teikhos*, wall] *base* wall (Tichodroma, tichorhine)

-tight [ON *thehtr*, tight] *comb* impervious to (airtight, watertight)

tigr- [Gr. *tigris*, tiger] *base* tiger (Tigridia, tigrine)

tilia- [L. *tilia*, linden-tree] *comb* lime; linden (Tiliaceae, tiliaceous)

-till- [Gr. *tillein*, to pluck, tear] *base* to pluck (peotillomania, trichotillomania)

-tim-[1], timor- [L. *timor*, fear] *base* fear; dread (timidity, timorous)

tim-[2] [Gr. *time*, honor] *base* honor (timarchy, tomocracy)

timbro- [Fr. *timbre*, postage-stamp] *comb* postage stamp (timbrology, timbrophilic)

-timo- [Gr. *time*, honor, worth] *base* honor (timocracy, timocratic)

-tinct-, -ting- [L. *tingere/tinct-*, to dye] *base* stain; color (intinction, tingible)

tinea- [L. *tinea*, gnawing worm] *base* moth; ringworm (tineid, Tineidae)

tinn-, tintinn- [L. *tinnire*, to ring] *base* jingling; ringing; bell (tinnitus, tintinnabular)

-tion, -tious [OF -*cion*, state of being what the p.p. imports] **1.** *suf* act of (correction); **2.** state of being (elation, ambitious); **3.** thing that is (creation)

tiro- [L. *tiro*, young soldier] *base* beginner (tiro, tirocinium) *Also* tyro

titano-[1] [Gr. *Titan*, mythological deity] *comb* titan; superhuman (titanosaur, titanotherioid)

titano-[2] [NL *titanium*, titanium] *comb* titanium (titaniferous, titano-cyanide)

tithym- [Gr. *tithymallos*, spurge] *base* spurge (tithymal)

titillo- [L. *titillare*, to tickle] *base* scratch; tickle (titillation, titillatory)

-titub- [L. *titubare*, to stagger] *base* stagger (titubate, titubation)

-tmesis [Gr. *tmesis*, a cutting] *comb* cutting (neurotmesis, tmesis)

-tocia, toco- [Gr. *tokos*, birth] *comb* childbirth; labor (dystocia, tocolytic). *Also* toko- (tokogony)

-toky [Gr. *tokos*, birth] *comb* childbearing (arrenotoky, thelytoky)

toler- [L. *tolerare*, to endure] *base* bearable (tolerable, tolerance)

-tolypeut- [ML *Tolypeutes*, armadillo < Gr. *tolupe*, ball] *base* armadillo (Tolypeutes, tolypeutine)

-tome, -tomous [Gr. *tomos*, cutting] *comb* [medicine] cutting instrument (bronchotome, osteotome, orthotomous)

toment- [L. *tomentum*, stuffing of hair, feathers, wool] *base* covered with fine hairs (tomentose, tomentous)

tomo-, -tomous, -tomy [Gr. *temnein*, to cut] *comb* cutting; dividing; surgery (tomography, dichotomous, appendectomy)

-ton [AS *tun*, town] *comb* town (Hampton, Washington)

-tonia [Gr. *tonos*, tone] **1.** *comb* tone; muscle tension (isotonia); **2.** personality disorder (catatonia)

-tonic [Gr. *tonos*, tone] **1.** *comb* notes in a musical scale (pentatonic); **2.** musical intervals (diatonic); **3.** phonetic units of stress (pretonic); **4.** muscle contraction (myatonic); **5.** pathological spasms (vagatonic); **6.** restorative substance (hematonic); **7.** solution (isotonic)

-tonitru- [L. *tonitrus*, thunder] *base* thunder (tonitrous, tonitrual)

tono- [Gr. *tonos*, tone] *comb* tension; pressure (tonometer, tonotechnic)

tonsillo- [L. *tonsilla*, tonsil] *comb* tonsil (tonsillitis, tonsillotomy) tonsor- [L. *tonsor*, barber, clipper] *base* shave; barber (tonsorial, tonsorious)

-toothed [AS *toth*, tooth] *comb* specific number/kind of teeth (big-toothed, gap-toothed)

toph- [L. *tophus*, loose, porous stone] *base* stone-like deposit (tophaceous, tophus)

topiar- [L. *topiarius*, ornamental gardening] *base* landscape gardening (topiarian, topiary)

topo-, -topy [Gr. *topos*, a place] *comb* place; topical (topology, somatotopy)

toreut- [Gr. *toreuma/toreumat-*, work in relief] *base* embossing metal or ivory (toreumatography, toreutics)

tormin- [L. *tormina*, bowel pain] *base* bowel pain (tormina, torminal)

tormo- [Gr. *tormos*, hole, socket] *comb* socketed (tormodont)

torn-[1] [L. *tornare*, to turn] *base* twisted; spiral (tornadic, Tornatellidae)

torn-[2] [Gr. *tornos*, rounding tool] *base* insect wing angle (tornal, tornus)

torp- [L. *torpere*, be numb or stiff] *base* 1. numbness (torbid, torporific); 2. electric ray fish (Torpedinoidea, torpedinous)

torq- [L. *torquree*, twist] *base* twisting force (torque, torqued)

torr- [L. *torrere*, parch] *base* parched, dry (torrefy, torrid)

-tors-, -tort- [L *torquere/tort-*, to twist] *base* twisted (torsion, distorted)

torul- [L. *torus*, swelling, protuberance] *base* elevated; beadlike (toruliform, torulis)

torv- [L. *torvus*, grim] *base* fierce-looking (torvid, torvidity)

-tory *see* -ory

toti- [L. *totus*, all] *comb* whole; entire (totipalmate, totipresent)

tox-, toxi-, toxico-, toxo-[1] [Gr. *toksikon*, poison] *comb* poison; infection (toxemia,toxituberculide, toxicogenic, toxoplasma)

toxo-[2] [Gr. *tokson*, a bow] *comb* archery (toxophilitic, toxophily)

-trab- [L. *trabs*, a timber] *base* beam (trabeation, trabeculate)

trachelo- [Gr. *trakhelos*, neck] *comb* neck; (trachelodynia, trachelokyphosis)

tracheo- [Gr. *trakheia*, windpipe] 1. *comb* windpipe (tracheotomy); 2. trachea and (tracheobronchial)

trachy- [Gr. *trakhus*, rough] *comb* rough (trachycarpous, trachyglossate)

-tract- [L. *trahere*, to pull, draw] *base* draw; pull (detract, retraction)

tragelaph- [Gr. *tragos*, goat + *elaphos*, deer] *base* antelope (tragelaphine, tragelaphus)

trago- [Gr. *tragos*, goat] *comb* goat (tragopan, tragopogon)

traject- [L. *trajicere*, to throw across] *base* crossing, path (trajection, trajectory)

trans- [L. *trans*, across, on the other side] 1. *pre* across; over; on the other side; to the other side (transatlantic); 2. change thoroughly (transliterate); 3. transcending; above and beyond (trans-sonic)

transverso- [L. *trans*, across + *vertere*, to turn] *comb* transverse; crosswise (transversocubital, transversomedial)

trapezi- [Gr. *trapezion*, four-sided table] *base* trapezoid (trapeziform, trapezoid)

traul- [Gr. *traulos*, stuttering] *base* stammering (traulism)

traumato- [Gr. *trauma*, wound] *comb* wound; injury (traumatologist, traumatopnea)

trecent- [L. *tres*, three + *centum*, hundred] *comb* three hundred (trecentene, trecentist)

tredecim- [L. *tres*, three + *decem*, ten] *base* thirteen (tredecile, tredecimal)

trega- [*trillion* + *mega*, trillion] *comb* trillion (tregadyne, trega-hertz)

tremo- [L. *tremere*, to tremble] *base* shaking; tremble (tremogram, tremorless)

trench- [L. *truncare*, cut off, lop] *base* cutting; keen (trenchant, trenchantly)

-trepid- [L. *trepidus*, agitated] *base* scared; agitated (intrepid, trepidation)

trepo- [Gr. *trepo*, to turn] *base* syphilis (treponemiasis, treponemicidal)

-tresia [Gr. *tresis*, perforation] *comb* perforation (atresia, proctotresia)

-tress [Gr. *-issa*, fem. suf.] *suf* feminine ending (actress, procuress)

tri- [L. *tri-*, three < *tres*] **1.** *comb* three; three parts (triplane); **2.** three times; into three (trisect); **3.** every three; every third (triannual); **4.** [chemistry] having three atoms; having three equivalents of; having three groups (tribasic)

triaconta- [Gr. *triakontas*, thirty] *comb* thirty (triacontahedral, triacontarchy)

triakis- [Gr. *triakis*, thrice] *comb* three (triakisoctahedron, triakistetrahedron)

triangulato- [L. *triangulatus*, having three angles] *comb* triangulate (triangulato-subovate, trianguloid)

tribo- [Gr. *tribos*, rubbing] *comb* friction (tribadism, tribology)

-trice [L. *-trix*, fem. suf.] *suf* feminine ending (advocatrice, genetrice). NOTE: **-trix** is now preferred

triceni- [L. *triceni*, thirty] *base* thirty (tricenary, tricennial)

tricent- [L. *trecenti*, three hundred] base three hundred (tricentenary, tricentennial)

-trich, -tricha, -trichia, -trichous, -trichy [Gr. *triks*, hair] *comb* [zoology] creature with hairlike structures (hypotrich, Gastrotricha, oligotrichia, peritrichous, lissotrichy)

trichec- [NL *trichechus*, walrus] *base* manatee; walrus (trichechine, Trichechoidea)

tricho- [Gr. *triks*, hair] *comb* hair (trichocarpous, trichology)

trient- [L. *trientalis*, one-third] *base* third (triental, Trientalis)

triethyl- [L. *tri-*, three + Gr. *aither*, ether] *comb* [chemistry] three ethyl groups (triethylamine, triethylcarbinol)

triges- [L. *trigesmus*, thirtieth] *base* thirty (trigesimal)

trigint- [L. *triginta*, thirty] *base* thirty (trigintal, trigintennial)

trigono- [Gr. *trigonos*, three-cornered] *comb* three-cornered; triangular (trigonocephalic, trigonodont)

tring- [Gr. *trungos*, a bird] *base* sandpiper (tringine, tringoid)

trinitro- [Gr. *tri*, three + *nitro*, natron] *comb* [chemistry] three atoms of nitrogen; (trinitrocresol, trinitroglycerin)

trioxy- [Gr. *tri*, three + *oksus*, sharp] *comb* having 3 atoms of oxygen (tryoxymethylene, trioxynaphthalene)

triphth- [Gr. *triphthos*, waste matter] *base* waste (triphthemia)

triplicato- [L. *triplicare*, to triple] *comb* triplicate (triplicato-pinnate, triplicato-ternate)

-triplo- [Gr. *triplios*, threefold] *base* threefold; triple (triploblastic, triplopia)

-tripsy [Gr. *tribein*, to rub] *comb* crushing; friction (lithotripsy, neurotripsy)

tripud- [L. *tripudium*, leaping, dancing] *base* dance; exult (tripudiate, tripudiation)

triquadr- [L. *tri-*, three + *quad-*, four] *base* three-fourths; three units divided four ways (triquadrantal, triquadrifid)

tris- [Gr. *treis*, three] *base* tripled (trisoctahedron, tristetrahedron)

triskaideka- [Gr. *treiskaideka*, thirteen] *comb* thirteen (triskaidekaphobia)

trism- [Gr. *trismos*, spasm] *base* lockjaw (trismus, trismic)

trist- [L. *tristis*, sad] *base* grief; sadness (tristimania, tristful)

trit- [L. *terere*, grind, thresh] *base* friction; threshing (triturate, triturature)

-tritic- [L. *triticum*, wheat] *base* wheat (triticeous, Triticum)

trito- [Gr. *tritos*, third] *comb* third (tritocere, tritomesal)

triv- [L. *trivialis*, of the three crossroads] *base* commonplace (trivial, trivialize)

-trix [L. *-trix*, fem. suf.] *suf* female agent (consolatrix, executrix)

troch-, trochi-, trocho- [Gr. *trokhos*, a wheel] *comb* wheel; pulley; rounded (trochlear, actinotrocha, trochiferous, trochocardia)

-trocha [Gr. *trokhos*, wheel] *comb* [zoology] having a band (cephalotrocha, mesotrocha)

trochalo- [Gr. *trokhalos*, round] *comb* rolling; rotary (trochalopod, Trochalopteron)

trochil- [NL. *trochilus*, humming-bird] *base* hummingbird (trochilidist, trochiline)

trochlea- [L. *trochlea*, pulley] *base* pulley-like (trochlear, trochleate)

-trocto- [Gr. *troktes*, kind of fish] *base* trout (troctolite)

-trog- [Gr. *trogon*, having been gnawed] *base* to gnaw (trogonine, Trogosita)

-troglo- [Gr. *trogle*, hole, cave] *base* hole; cave (troglodyte, troglodytic)

troglodyt- [NL. *Troglodytes*, cave dwellers] *base* wren (Troglodytes, troglodytine)

-tromo- [Gr. *tromos*, trembling] *base* earth tremor (tromometer, tromometry)

-tron, -tronic [< *(elec)tronic*] *comb* names of devices used in electronic or subatomic experiments (animatronic, cyclotron)

-trope, -tropic, -tropism, tropo-, -tropous, -tropy [Gr. *trope*, turning] *comb* responding to a specific stimulus; turning; changing (heliotrope, phototropic, thermotropism, tropophilous, phototropous, entropy)

-troph, -trophic, tropho-, -trophy [Gr. *trophe*, nourishment] *comb* nutrition; food; nourishment (heterotroph, autotrophic, trophoplasm, atrophy)

tropido- [Gr. *tropis/tropid-*, keel] *base* keel-shaped (Tropidogaster, tropidosternal)

tropo- [L. *tropus*, figure in rhetoric] *comb* figurative, metaphorical (tropological, tropology)

trucid- [L. *trucidare*, to kill] *base* kill; slaughter (contrucidate, trucidation)

trucul- [L. *truculentia*, savageness] *base* savage, harsh (truculence, truculent)

-trude, -trus- [L. *trudere*, to thrust] *base* push; thrust (protrude, intrusion)

trunc- [L. *truncare*, to cut off, reduce] *base* cut, reduced in size (truncate, truncation)

-trutt- [ML. *trutta*, a trout] *base* trout (trutta, truttaceous)

trygon- [Gr. *trugon*, sting-ray] *base* sting-ray (Trigon, Trygonidae)

trypano- [Gr. *trupanon*, a borer] **1.** *comb* parasite; borer (trypanolytic, trypanosome); **2.** injection (trypanophobia)

trypet- [Gr. *trupetes*, a borer] *base* fruitfly (Trypeta, Trypetidae)

trypo- [Gr. *trypa*, hole] *base* perforation (trypograph, trypophobia)

tsio- [Chinese *ch'a*, tea] *base* tea (tsiology, tsiologis)

tuberculo- [L. *tuberculum*, small tuberosity] **1.** *comb* tuberculous (tubercular); **2.** tubercle bacillus (tuberculoid); **3.** tuberculosis (tuberculocidin)

tubi-, tubo- [L. *tubus*, tube] *comb* tube (tubiflorous, tubotorsion)

tubuli-, tubulo- [L. *tubulus*, small tube] *comb* tubule; small tube (tubulidentate, tubulocyst)

-tude [L. *-tudo*, suf. for abstract nouns] *suf* state of being; quality of being (plenitude, solitude)

-tum- [L. *tumere*, to swell] *base* swelling (detumescence, tumescent)

tupai- [Malay *tupaya*, squirrel-shrew] *base* squirrel-shrew (Tupaia, tupaiid)

-turb- [L. *turbare*, to agitate] *base* confuse; disturb (perturbation, turbulent)

-turbar- [L. *turba*, turf] *base* peat bog (turbarian, turbary)

turbinato- [L. *turbinatus*, shaped like a cone] *comb* top-shaped (turbinato-cylindrical, turbinate-lentiform)

turbo- [L. *turbo*, a top] *comb* consisting of; or driven by a turbine; (turbogenerator, turbotrain)

turd- [L. *turdus*, a thrush] *base* thrush; robin; bluebird (turdine, turdoid)

-turg- [L. *turgere*, to swell out] *base* swelling (turgescent, turgid)

Turko- [ML *Turcus*, Turk] *comb* Turkey; (Turko-Russian). *Also* **Turco-** (Turcophobe)

-turp- [L. *turpis*, foul, base] *base* pollute; disgrace (turpify, turpitude)

-turri- [L. *turris*, tower] *base* tower (turriculated, turriferous)

turtur- [L. *turtur*, a turtle] *base* turtle-dove (Turtur, turturring)

tus- [L. *tundere/tus-*, to thump, strike] *base* strike; bruise (contusion, obtuse)

-tuss- [L. *tussis*, cough] *base* cough (antitussive, tussicular)

tutel- [L. *tutela*, guardianship] *base* protecting (tutelage, tutelary)

twi- [AS. *twi-*, two] *comb* double (twiarched, twilight)

-ty[1] [L. *-itas*, suf. for abstract nouns] *suf* quality of; condition of (humanity, novelty)

-ty[2] [AS. *-tig*, ten] *suf* times ten; tens (thirty, sixty)

-tych-, tycho- [Gr. *tukhe*, fortune] *comb* chance; occasional accident (tychastics, tychopotamic). *Also* **tich-** (dystichiphobia)

-tyl-, tylo- [Gr. *tulos*, knot, lump] *comb* knot; knob; callus; cushion (tylosis, tylopod)

tympani-, tympano- [Gr. *tumpanon*, a drum] *comb* drum; tympanum (tympaniform, tympanoplasty)

-type [Gr. *tupos*, figure or type] **1.** *comb* type; representative form; example (prototype); **2.** stamp; printing type; print; (monotype)

typhlo- [Gr. *tuphlos*, blind] **1.** *comb* cecum; intestinal pouch (typhlostomy); **2.** blindness (typhlosis)

typho- [Gr. *tuphos*, stupor] *comb* typhus; typhoid (typhogenic, typhoidal)

typo- [Gr. *tupos*, type] *comb* type (typography, typology)

tyro- [Gr. *turos*, cheese] *base* cheese (tyroleucin, tyrotoxicon)

tyto- [Gr. *tuto*, night owl] *base* barn owl (tytonid, Tytonidae)

U

uber- [L. *uber*, plentiful] *base* abundant (uberant, uberate)

-ubi- [L. *ubi*, where] *base* place; position; location ;(ubiety, ubiquitous)

udo- [L. *udus*, moist or damp] *comb* wet; damp (udometer, udometric)

Ugro- [Russ. *Ugri*, tribe dwelling east of the Ural Mountains] *comb* Ugrian (Ugro-Finnish, Ugro-Slavonic)

-ula [L. *-ula*, dim. suf.] *suf* diminutive (auricula, fibula)

-ular [L. suf. *-ula*, dim., + *-aris*, of the kind of] *suf* having the form or character of (circular, globular)

ulcer- [L. *ulcus*, open sore] *base* ulcer (ulcerated, ulcerative)

-ule [L. *-ulus*, dim. suf.] *suf* diminutive (nodule, pustule)

-ulent [L. suf. *-ulentus*, abounding in] *suf* full of (fraudulent, virulent)

-ulig- [L. *uligo*, moisture] *base* full of moisture (uliginose, uliginous)

ulm- [L. *ulmus*, elm] *base* elm (ulmaceous, ulmous)

ulno- [L. *ulna*, elbow] *comb* ulna and (ulnocarpal, ulnoradial)

ulo-[1] [Gr. *oule*, a scar] *comb* scar (uletomy, ulodermatitis)

ulo-[2] [Gr. *oulon*, gum] *comb* gums (uloglossitis, uloncus)

ulo-[3] [Gr. *oulos*, wooly] *comb* curly; crisp (Ulophocinae, ulotrichous)

-ulose [L. adj. suf *-ulosus*, marked by] *suf* characterized by; marked by (granulose, ramulose)

-ulous [L. suf. *-ulus*, full of] *suf* characterized by; full of; tending to (populous, sedulous)

ultim-, ultimo- [L. *ultimus*, last, final] *base* final; last (ultimatum, ultimogeniture)

ultra- [L. *ultra*, beyond, more] **1.** *pre* on the further side of; beyond (ultraviolet); **2.** to an extreme degree; excessive (ultramodern); **3.** beyond the range of (ultramicroscopic)

ultro- [L. *ultro*, spontaneously] *comb* voluntary; spontaneous (ultromotivity, ultroneous)

ulul-[1] [L. *ululare*, to howl] *base* wail; howl (ululate, ululation)

ulul-[2] [L. *ulula*, screech-owl] *base* owl (Ulula, ululant)

-ulum [L. neut. suf. *-ulum*, small] *suf* diminutive (cingulum, speculum)

-ulus [L. masc. suf. *-ulus*, small] *suf* diminutive (cuniculus, homunculus)

umbell-, umbelli- [L. *umbella*, sunshade] *base* sunshade; parasol (umbellated, umbellifer)

umbilici- [L. *umbilicus*, navel] *base* navel (umbiliferous, umbiliciform)

umbo- [L. *umbo*, knob, boss] *base* knob; nipple (umbonate, umbonulate)

-umbr- [L. *umbra*, shadow] *base* shadow (umbrage, umbriphilous)

umbraculi- [L. *umbraculum*, umbrella] *comb* sunshade (umbraculiferous, umbraculiform)

umbrelli- [It. *umbrella*, an umbrella] *base* umbrella (umbrelliferous, umbrelliform)

Umbro- [L. *Umbri*, ancient people of central Italy] *comb* Umbrian (Umbro-Etruscan, Umbro-Sabellian)

un- [AS. *un-*, not] **1.** *pre* not; opposite of; lack of ;(unhappy); **2.** back; reversal (unlock)

unci- [L. *uncus*, hook, barb] *comb* hook (unciferous, unciform)

-unct- [L. *unctio*, anointing] *base* ointment; oil (unctuosity, unctuous)

-unda- [L. *unda*, wave] *base* wave (exundant, inundation)

undec- [L. *undecim*, eleven] *comb* eleven (undecagon, undecennary)

under- [AS. *under*, under] **1.** *pre* lower place: in/on/to; beneath; below (undershirt); **2.** inferior rank/position; subordinate (undergraduate); **3.** amount below standard; inadequate (underdeveloped)

undeviginti- [L. *undeviginti*, nineteen] *comb* nineteen (undevigintiangular)

-undul- [L. *undulare*, to undulate] *base* wave (undulant, undulations)

ungu- [L. *unguentum*, ointment] *base* ointment; grease (unguent, unguentary)

-ungui, -ungul- [L. *unguis*, nail, claw] *base* claw; nail (unguiform, exungulate)

uni- [L. *unus*, one] *comb* having one only (unicameral, unicellular,)

-uous [L. suf. *-osus*, full of] *suf* of the nature of; consisting of (assiduous, strenuous)

-ura- [Gr. *oura*, tail] *base* tail (condylura, gastruran)

uranisco- [Gr. *ouraniskos*, roof of the mouth] *comb* hard palate (uranisconitis, uraniscoplasty)

urano- [Gr. *ouranos*, the heavens, the roof of the mouth] **1.** *comb* hard palate (uranoschisis); **2.** the heavens (uranography)

uranoso- [NL. < planet Uranus] *comb* [chemistry] containing uranium (uranosopotassic, uranothorite)

-urb- [L. *urbs*, city] *base* city (suburban, urbane)

urcei-, urceo- [L. *urceolus*, little pitcher] *base* urn; pitcher (urceiform, urceolate)

-ure [L *-ura*, suf. denoting action or process] **1.** *suf* act/result of being (exposure); **2.** agent of; instrument of; scope of (legislature); **3.** state of being (composure)

urea-, ureo- [Gr. *ouron*, urine] *comb* urine; urea (ureapoiesis, ureometer)

uredo- [L. *uredo*, a blight] *base* blight; fungus (uredinous, uredospore)

uretero- [Gr. *oureter*, urethra] *comb* urethra and (ureterolith, ureterostomy)

urethro- [Gr. *ourethra*, passage for urine] *comb* ureter and (urethrophraxis, urethroscopy)

-uretic [Gr. *ourein*, to urinate] *comb* urine (diuretic, enuretic)

-urgy [Gr. *ergon*, work] *comb* working of; fabricating (thaumaturgy, zymurgy)

uri-, urico- [Gr. *ouron*, urine] *base* uric acid; (uridrosis, uricometer)

-uria [Gr. *ouron*, urine] *comb* diseased condition of urine (acetonuria, glycosuria)

-urient [L. stem *-urien-*, desiring] *suf* desiring (esurient, parturient)

urini-, urino- [L. *urina*, urine] *comb* urinary tract; urine (uriniparous, urinometer)

uro-¹ [Gr. *oura*, tail] *comb* tail (urodele, uropod)

uro-² [Gr. *ouron*, urine] *comb* urine (urocyst, urolith)

-urs- [L. *ursus*, a bear] *base* bear (ursiform, ursine)

-urtic- [L. *urtica*, nettle] *base* nettle (urticaceous, urtical)

-ury- [Gr. *ouron*, urine] *base* urination (dysury, strangury)

-ust- [L. *ustio*, a burning] *base* burn (ustorious, ustulation)

usur- [L *usura*, usury] *base* usury (usurer, usuriously)

usurp- [L. *usurpare*, to seize for use] *base* seize (usurpation, usurpative)

utero- [L. *uterus*, the womb] *comb* uterus and (uterocopulatory, uterovaginal)

-util- [L. *utilis*, useful] *base* useful (inutile, utilitarian)

utrei-, utri-¹ [L. *utriculus*, little leather bag or bottle] *comb* leather bottle (utreiform, utriform)

utri-², **utric-** [L. *utriculus*, little leather bag or bottle] *base* sac; baglike part (utricle, utricular)

-uvi-, -uvu- [L. *uva*, grape] *base* grape (uviform, uvula)

uvulo- [L. *uvula*, cluster of grapes] *comb* uvula; (uvulatome, uvulectomy)

uxori- [L. *uxor*, wife] *base* wife (uxoricide, uxorious)

V

-vac-, -vacu- [L. *vacans*, empty] *base* empty; free (vacancy, vacuity)

vacci- [L. *vacca*, cow] *comb* cow (vaccimulgence, vaccinia)

vaccin- [L. *vaccinium*, whortleberry] *base* blueberry (Vacciniaceae, vaccinium)

vaccino- [L. *vaccinus*, of a cow] *comb* vaccine (vaccinophobia, vaccinosyphilis)

-vacil- [L. *vacillare*, to sway] *base* sway (vacillation, vacillatory)

-vad-, -vas- [L. *vadere*, to go] *base* rush; go (invade, invasion)

-vag-, -vagr- [L. *vagari*, to wander] *base* wander (vagary, vagrant)

vagini-, vagino- [L. *vagina*, sheath] *comb* sheath; vagina and (vaginipennous, vaginotomy)

vago- [L. *vagus*, wandering] *comb* vagus nerve (vagotomy, vagotropic)

vagu- [L. *vagus*, wandring, uncertain] *base* uncertain (vaguely, vagueness)

vale- [L. *vale*, farewell] *base* farewell (valediction, valedictorian)

-valent [L. *valentia*, capacity] **1.** *comb* having a specified valence (monovalent); **2.** specified number of valences (univalent); **3.** having antibodies (multivalent)

valetud- [L. *valetudo*, infirmity] *base* ill (valetudinarian, valetudinary)

valg- [L. *valgus*, bandy-legged] *base* bandy-legged (valgous, valgus)

vall- [L. *vallum*, rampart, wall] *base* wall (vallar, vallation)

valvi- [L. *valva*, leaf of a door] *comb* valve; opening (valviferous, valviform)

valvulo- [L. *valvula*, dim. leaf of a door] *comb* valve, esp. of the heart (valvulitis, valvulotomy)

vapid- [L. *vapidus*, insipid] *base* insipid (vapid, vapidity)

vapo-, vapori- [L. *vapor*, exhalation, steam] *comb* emanation; vapor (vapography, vaporimeter)

-vapul- [L. *vapulare*, to be flogged] *base* beat; flog (vapulation, vapulatory)

varan- [L. *varanus*, monitor lizard] *base* monitor lizard (varanian, varanus)

vari- [L. *variare*, to change] *comb* changed; diverse (invariable, variant)

varic-, varici-, varico- [L. *varix/varic-*, dilated vein] *base* enlarged vein (varication, variciform, varicocele)

-variol- [L. *varius*, spotted] *base* spotted; speckled (variolite, varioloid)

vasculo- [L. *vasculum*, small vessel] *comb* blood vessel (vasculitis, vasculomotor)

vasi- [L. *vas*, vessel] *comb* vessel; tube (vasifactive, vasiform)

vaso- [L. *vas*, vessel] **1.** *comb* blood vessels (vasoconstrictor); **2.** vas deferens (vasectomy); **3.** vasomotor (vasoinhibitor)

-vast- [L. *vastare*, to lay waste] *base* destroy (devastation, vastity)

vastit- [L. *vastitas*, void, vast] *base* void, vast (vastitude, vastity)

vati- [L. *vates*, seer, prophet] *comb* prophet (vaticide, vaticination)

-vect- [L. *vehere/vect-*, to convey] *base* carry (provect, vector)

vectit- [L. *vectare*, convey] *base* carry, convey (vectitation, vectitory)

vegeti-, vegeto- [L. *vegetare*, to animate] *comb* vegetable; plant (vegetivorous, vegeto-alkaline)

vel-, veli- [L. *velare*, to cover] *comb* cover; veil; sail (velated, veliferous)

-velar [L. *velare*, to cover] *comb* soft palate (labiovelar, velar)

velit- [L. *velitatio*, bickering] *base* skirmish; dispute (veltary, velitation)

vell- [L. *velle*, wish, will] *base* wish; desire (velleity)

-vellic- [L. *vellicare*, to pluck, twitch] *base* pluck; twitch; nip (vellication, vellicative)

veloci- [L. *velox/veloc-*, swift] *base* speed (velocimeter, velocipede)

-velut- [ML *velutum*, velvet] *base* velvet (velutine, velutinous)

-ven- [L. *venire*, to come] *base* come (convention, invent)

venal- [L. *venalitas*, mercenary] *base* mercenary (venality, venalization)

-venat- [L. *venatus*, hunting] *base* hunt (venatic, venatorial)

vend- [L. *vendere*, to sell] *base* sell (vendible, vendor)

vene- [L. *vena*, vein] *comb* vein (venesect, venesection)

-venefic- [L. *veneficus*, poisonous, witchcraft] *base* sorcery; witchcraft (veneficial, veneficious)

veneni-, veneno- [L. *venenum*, poison] *comb* poison (venenifluous, veneno-salivary)

-vener-[1] [L. *Venerius*, of Venus] *base* sexual desire; Venus (venereal, venery)

-vener-[2], **-venerat-** [L. *venerari*, to revere] *base* worship (venerable, veneration)

-vener-[3] [L. *venari*, to hunt or chase] *base* hunting (venatic, venation)

veni-, veno-, venoso-, -venous [L. *vena*, vein] *comb* veins (venipuncture, venostomy, venoso-reticulated, intravenous)

-vent- [L. *ventus*, wind] *base* wind; air (ventilation, ventosity)

ventri-, ventro- [L. *venter*, stomach] **1.** *comb* abdomen; belly (ventricumbent); **2.** ventral and (ventrodorsal)

ventricoso- [L. *ventricosus*, of the belly] *comb* distended abdomen (ventricoso-globose)

ventriculo- [L. *ventriculus*, ventricle] *comb* ventricle (ventriculoatrial, ventriculobulbous)

venust- [L. *venus*, like Venus] *base* beautiful (venustity, venustation)

vepri- [L. *vepris*, bramble bush] *base* bramble bush (veprecose, vepricosous)

-ver- [L. *verus*, true] *base* truth (verification, verity)

-verber- [L. *verberare*, to beat] *base* beat (reverberate, verberative)

verbi-, verbo- [L. *verbum*, a word] *comb* word; talk (verbification, verbotomy)

verbiger- [L. *verbigerare*, to talk] *base* talk (verbigerate, verbigeration)

-verd- [L. *viridis*, green] *base* green (verdant, verdure)

verecund- [L. *verecundus*, modest] *base* shame; modesty (verecund, verecundity)

veretill- [L. dim. of *veretrum*, the penis] *base* rod-like (veretilleous, veretilliform)

-verge [L. *vergere*, to bend or turn] *comb* turn; bend (converge, diverge). *See* **-vers-**

vergi- [L. *virga*, rod, twig] *comb* rod-like (vergiform). *See* **-virgul-**

verit- [L. *veritas*, truth] *base* truth (veritable, verity)

vermi- [L. *vermis*, a worm] *comb* worm; (vermicide, vermeologist)

vermin- [L. *vermineus*, of noxious

insects] *comb* vermin (vermination, verminous)

vermivor- [L. *vermis*, worm + *vorare*, to devour] *base* warbler (Vermivora); worm-eating (vermivorous)

-vern- [L. *ver*, spring] *base* spring (vernal, vernate)

vernil- [L. *vernilis*, servile] *base* slavish (vernile, vernility)

verruci- [L. *verruca*, wart] *comb* wart; growth (verruciform, verruculose)

vers-, -verse, vert- [L. *versare*, to turn] *comb* turn; direct (reversal, transverse, revert). *See* -**verge**

versif- [L. *versificare*, to versify] *base* versify (versification, versificatory)

versut- [L. *versutus*, crafty] *base* cunning (versute, versutious)

vertebro- [L. *vertebra*, a joint] *comb* vertebra (vertbrocostal, vertebroiliac)

verticill- [L. *verticcilus*, the whirl of a spindle] *base* whorled (verticillaster, verticillate-pillose)

vertig- [L. *vertiginare*, to whirl around] *base* dizziness (vertiginate, vertiginous)

-verv- [L. *vervex*, wether] *base* sheep (vervecean, vervecine)

vesan- [L. *vesanus*, madness] *base* madness (vesania, vesanic)

vesica- [L. *vesica*, the bladder, a blister] *comb* blister (vesicant, vesicatory)

vesico- [L. *vesica*, the bladder] **1.** *comb* bladder (vesicotomy); **2.** bladder and (vesicoprostatic)

vesiculi-, vesiculo- [L. *vesicula*, a vesicle] *comb* vesicle; bladder-like vessel (vesiculigerous, vesiculo-pustular)

-vesper- [L. *vesper*, evening] *base* evening (vespers, vespertine)

-vespertil- [L. *vespertinus*, of the evening] *base* bat; vampire (Vespertilio, vespertilionine)

vespi- [L. *vespa*, a wasp] *comb* wasp; hornet (vespiary, vespiform)

vest- [L. *vestis*, a garment] *comb* clothing (divest, investiture)

vestibulo- [L. *vestibulum*, a forecourt] *comb* vestibule; small cavity (vestibulo-auditory, vestibulocochlear)

vestig- [L. *vistigium*, footstep, track] *base* trace (vestige, vestigial)

-vet- [L. *veter*, old, aged] *base* old; experienced (inveterate, veteran)

vex- [L. *vexare*, to shake, jolt] *base* bother; irritate (vexation, vexatious)

vexill- [L. *vexillum*, a standard] *comb* flag; banner (vexillator, vexillology)

vi-, via- [L. *via*, way, road, journey] *comb* journey; way (multivious, viaduct)

vibro- [L. *vibrare*, to vibrate] *comb* vibration; shaking (vibrograph, vibromotor)

vicar- [L. *vicarius*, substitute] *base* substitute (vicarial, vicarious)

vice- [L. *vice*, in the place of] *comb* deputy; assistant (vice-chancellor, vice-president)

vicenn- [L. *vicies*, twenty, + *annus*, year] *base* twenty (vicennial, vicennium)

-vicesim- [L. *vicesimus*, twentieth] *base* twentieth (vicesim, vicesimal)

vicin- [L. *vicinus*, neighboring] *base* neighborhood; proximity (vicinage, vicinity)

viciss- [L.*vicis*, change] *base* mutability (vicissitude, vicissitudinous)

-vid-, -vis- [L. *videre/vis-*, to see] *base* see (video, invisible)

video- [L. *videre*, to see] *comb* televised (videoconference, videogenic)

vidu- [L. *vidua*, a widow] *base* widowed; destitute (viduage, viduation)

-viges- [L. *vigesimus*, twentieth] *base* twenty (vigesimal, vigesimation)

vigil- [L. *vigil*, awake] *base* watchful (vigil, vigilant)

viginti- [L. *viginti*, twenty] *comb* twenty (vigintiangular, vigintivirate)

-vili- [L. *vilis*, vile] *base* worthless; base (viliorate, vility)

vill- [L. *villosus*, shaggy] *base* shaggy (villiform, villose)

-ville [OF *ville*, farm, village] *comb* village (Baskerville, Smallville)

villic- [L. *villicatio*, resource management] *base* husbandry (villicated, villication)

villoso- [L. *villosus*, hairy] *comb* covered with hairlike material (villositis, villoso-scabrous). *See* **piloso-**

vimin- [L. *vimen*, twig] *base* wicker (viminal, vimineous)

-vinc- [L. *vincere*, to conquer] *base* conquer; bind (invincible, vincibility)

vindem- [L. *vindemia*, grape-gathering] *base* grape-gathering (vindemial, vindemiate)

vindic- [L. *vindicare*, justified] *base* justified (vindicable, vindicated)

vini-, vino- [L. *vinum*, wine] *comb* wine; grapes (viniculture, vinolent). *See* **viti-**

viol- [L. *violaceus*, of a violet color] *base* violet (Violaceae, violaceous)

viper- [L. *vipera*, viper, serpent] *base* snake (viperiform, viperous)

vir- [L. *virere*, to be green] *base* green (virent, virescence)

viresc- [L. *virescere*, become green] *base* becoming green (virescence, virescent)

virgin- [L. *virgo*, maiden] *base* maiden (virginal, virginity)

virgul- [L. *virgula*, a little rod] *base* rod; twig (virgulate, virgule)

-virid- [L. *viridis*, green] *base* green (viridescent, viridity)

-viridae [L. *virus*, venom + *-idae*, family suf.] *comb* virus family (Orthomyxoviridae, Picornaviridae)

-viril- [L. *virilis*, virile] *base* masculine (virilescent, virility)

-virinae [L. *virus*, venom + *-inae*, subfamily suf.] *comb* virus subfamily (Oncovirinae, Spumavirinae)

virul- [L. *virulentus*, poisonous] *base* poisonous (virulent, viruliferous)

-virus [L. *virus*, venom] *comb* virus genus (Flavivirus, retrovirus)

-vis-, -vid- [L. *videre/vis-*, to see] *base* look; see (invisible, video)

-visaged [L. *videre/vis-*, to look] *comb* having a specific kind of face (grim-visaged, round-visaged)

visc-, visco- [L. *viscum*, birdlime] *base* sticky; thick (viscous, viscometer)

viscero- [L. *viscera*, viscera] *comb* viscera (visceralgia, visceroptosis)

visib- [L. *visibilis*, seen] *base* visible (invisible, visibility)

visuo- [L. *visus*, sight] *comb* sight (visuo-auditory, visuomotor)

-vit- [L. *vita*, life] *base* alive (vital, vitality). *See* **vivi-**

vitelli-, vitello- [L. *vitellus*, yolk] *comb* yolk; germinative contents (vitelligerous, vitellogenous)

viti- [L. *vitis*, vine] *comb* vine (viticolous, viticulture)

vitia- [L. *vitium*, fault] *base* corrupt (vitiate, vitiated)

vitilig- [L. *vitiligare*, wrangle] *base* wrangle (vitiligate, vitiligation)

vitreo-, vitri-, vitro- [L. *vitreus*, of glass] *comb* glass; glassy (vitreodentin, vitriform, vitrotype)

vitric- [L. *vitricus*, stepfather] *base* stepfather (vitricophobia)

vitriolico- [ML *vitriolum*, vitriol] *comb* vitriol (vitriolicomuriated, vitriolico-neutral)

-vitul- [L. *vitulus*, veal] *base* calf (vitular, vituline)

vituper- [L. *vituperare*, to blame, censure] *base* blame; revile (vituperative, vituperator)

viverr- [L. *vivera*, a ferret] *base* civet; ferret; mongoose (Viverridae, viverrine)

vivi- [L. *vivus*, alive] *comb* living; alive (vivify, viviparous)

voc-, voci-, -voke [L. *vocare*, to call out] *comb* say; speak (invocation, vociferous, revoke)

vocif- [L. *vociferari*, cry out] *base* shout (vociferate, vociferous)

-vol- [L. *velle*, to will] *base* wish; will (volunteer, involuntary)

volit- [*volitare*, to fly] *base* flying (volitant, volitation)

volta- [<*Alessandro Volta*, scientist] *comb* [electricity] voltaic (volta-electric, volta-electrometer)

volub- [L. *volubilis*, whirling, fluent] *base* fluent; easily set in motion (volubilate, volubility)

volucr- [L. *volucer/volucr-*, fitted for flight] *base* bird (volucrary, volucrine)

volupt- [L. *voluptas/voluptat-*, pleasure] *base* pleasure (voluptuary, voluptuous)

-volut-, -volv- [L. *volvere/volut-*, to roll] *base* turn (revolution, revolve)

vomero- [L. *vomer*, ploughshare] *comb*

bone dividing the nostrils (vomero-nasal, vomero-palatine)

vomic- [L. *vomicus*, ulcerous] *base* abscess (vomica, vomicose)

-vora, -vore, -vorous [L. *vorare*, to devour] *comb* feeding on; eating (Carnivora, herbivore, omnivorous)

-vorag- [L. *vorago*, chasm, abyss] *base* chasm; whirlpool (vorageous, voraginous)

vortici- [L. *vortex/vortic-*, whirling] *comb* whirling motion; vortex (vorticiform, vorticose)

votiv- [L. *votum*, vow] *base* vow (votive, votively)

vulcan- [L. *Volcanus*, Vulcan, god of fire] *comb* volcanoes (Vulcanic, vulcanology)

-vulg- [L. *vulgus*, multitude, mass of people] *base* common; the public (divulge, vulgar)

-vuln- [L. *vulnus*, wound] *base* wound (invulnerable, vulnerose)

vulpi- [L. *vulpes*, fox] *base* fox (vulpicide, vulpine)

-vuls- [L. *vellere*, pull or pluck] *base* tear away (convulse, revulsion)

vult- [L. *vultus*, countenance] *base* likeness; visage (invultuation, vultuous)

vultur- [L. *vultur*, a vulture] *base* vulture (vulturian, vulturine)

vulvi-, vulvo- [L. *vulva*, vulva] **1.** *comb* vulva (vulviform); **2.** vulva and (vulvovaginal)

W

-ward [AS. *-weard*, in the direction of] *suf* having a specified direction (homeward, westward)

-ways [OE *weg*, to move, journey] *suf* in a specified direction, manner, or position (breadthways, sideways)

-wheeler [OE *wheol*, circle] *comb* having a specified kind or number of wheels (eighteen-wheeler, two-wheeler)

-wide [AS. *wid*, broad] *comb* throughout a given space (storewide, worldwide)

-wife [AS. *wif*, woman] *comb* traditional female role (housewife, midwife)

-wise [ME *wyse*, way, manner] **1.** *suf* in a specified; direction, manner, or position (sidewise); **2.** characteristic manner (clockwise); **3.** with regard to; in connection with (weatherwise)

with- [AS. *with-*, against] **1.** *comb* away; back (withdraw); **2.** against; from (withhold)

-witted [OE *i-wit*, faculty] *comb* having a specified kind of intelligence (dim-witted, quick-witted)

-woman [OE *wifmon*, woman human being] *comb* female (congresswoman, horsewoman)

-worthy [OE *wurthe*, worthy] *comb* deserving of; fit for (blameworthy, newsworthy)

X

xantho- [Gr. *ksanthos*, yellow] *comb* yellow (xanthein, xanthoderma)

-xen- [Gr. *ksenos*, a guest] *base* host (cacoxenite, metoxeny)

xenarth- [Gr. *ksenos*, strange + *arthron*, a joint] *base* sloth (xenarthral)

xeno-, -xenous, -xeny [Gr. *ksenos*, strange] *comb* stranger; foreigner (xenogamy, xenophobia, lipoxenous, lipoxeny)

xenodoch- [Gr. *ksenodokhia*, reception of strangers] *base* guest house (xenodochial, xenodochy) xeri-, xero- [Gr. *kseros*, dry] *comb* dry (xeriscape, xerotic)

xest- [Gr. *ksestos*, polished] *base* polish (Xestia, xesturgy)

xilin- [Gr. *ksulon*, cotton-tree] *base* cotton (glyoxalin, xilinous)

xiph(i)-, xipho- [Gr. *ksiphias*, a swordfish] *comb* swordlike; xiphoid process; swordfish (xiphioid, xyphophyllous)

xoan- [Gr. *ksoanon*, rough image] *base* idol (xoanon, xoanonic)

xylo-, -xylous [Gr. *ksulon*, wood] *comb* wood; (xylograph, epixylous)

xyr- [Gr. *ksuron*, razor] *base* sharp-edged; razorlike (xyrospasm, xyridaceous)

xyst-[1] [Gr. *ksuein*, to scrape, smooth, polish] *base* scraping (xyster, xystos)

xyst-[2] [Gr. *xystos*, portico] *base* exercise portico (xystarch, xystus)

Y

-y[1] [AS *-ig*, full of] **1.** *suf* characterized by; full of (healthy); **2.** somewhat; rather (chilly); **3.** tending to; inclined (drowsy); **4.** suggestive of; somewhat like (wavy)

-y[2] [L. *-ia*, noun suf.] **1.** *suf* condition of; quality (jealousy); **2.** action of (inquiry)

-y[3] [ME dim. suf. *-ie*] *suf* diminutives; terms of endearment; nicknames (Billy, kitty)

-yer [ME *-ier*, agent suf.] *suf* person concerned with (buyer, lawyer)

yester- [AS *geostran-*, of the day before] *comb* previous time (yesterday, yesteryear)

-yl [Gr. *hule*, wood, matter] *suf* [chemistry] names of radicals (butyl, methyl)

ylo- *see* hylo-

yocto- [L. *octo*, eight, > 8th power of a thousandth] *comb* septillionth (yoctogram, yoctosecond)

yotta- [L. *octo*, eight, > the 8th power of a thousand] *comb* one septillion (yottahertz, yottameter)

ypsili- [Gr. letter *upsilon*] *comb* Y-shaped (ypsiliform)

-ysis [Gr. *lusis*, a loosening] *suf* action; process (acetolysis, electrolysis). *See* -lysis

yttro- [NL > *Ytterby, Sweden*] *comb* yttrium (yttrocerite, yttrotitanite)

Z

za- [Gr. *za-*, intensive pref.] *pre* intensifier (zalambdodont, zamelodia)

zamia-, zamio- [L. *zamia*, fir-cone] *base* coniferous plant (Zamia, Zamiostrobus)

zanclo- [Gr. *zanclon*, a sickle] *comb* like a sickle (Zanclodon, Zanclognatha)

zebr- [Fr. *zebre*, zebra] *base* zebra (zebraic, zebrine)

zelo- [Gr. *zelos*, zeal] *base* zeal; emulation (zelotic, zelotypia)

zemni- [Russ. *zemnoi*, earthy] *base* mole rat (zemniphobia, zemni-rat)

zeo- [Gr. *zeein*, to boil, foam] *comb* altered; converted (zeolite, zeo-scope)

-zephyr- [Gr. *zephuros*, the west wind] *base* west wind (zephyranth, zephyrean)

zepto- [L. *septem*, seven > the 7th power of a thousandth] *comb* one-sextillionth (zeptosecond, zeptovolt)

zesto- [Gr. *zestos*, boiling hot] *comb* hot (zestocausis, zestocautery)

zetet- [Gr. *zetein*, to seek or inquire] *base* inquiring, seeking (zetetic, zetetics)

zetta- [L. *septem*, seven > 7th power of a thousand] *comb* one sextillion (zettabyte)

-zeug-, -zeux- [Gr. *zeugle*, the strap of a yoke] *base* yoked (zeuglodont, zeuxite)

zibel- [It. *zibellino*, sable] *base* sable (zibeline)

zinco- [NL *zincum*, zinc] *comb* zinc as an element in specific double compounds (zincography, zincolysis)

-zingiber- [Gr. *zingiberis*, ginger] *base* ginger (Zingiber, zingiberaceous)

ziph- [Gr. *ksiphios*, swordfish] *base* swordfish (ziphiiform, ziphioid). *Also* **xiph-**

zirconio- [Arab *zarkun*, zircon] *comb* zirconium (zirconioflouride)

zizan- [Gr. zizonion, weed] *base* weed, grass (zizania, zizany)

-zo- [Gr. *zoon*, animal] *base* animal (zoanthropy, zodiophilous)

-zoa, -zoon [Gr. *zoon*, animal] *comb* [zoology] name of group (protozoa, protozoon)

-zoic [Gr. *zoe*, life + -ic] **1.** *suf* relating to animal life (celozoic); **2.** relating to geologic ages (Cenozoic, Mesozoic)

zomb- [W. Afr. *Nzambi*, god, *zumbi*, fetish] *base* zombie (zombification, zombify)

zon-, zoni- [Gr. *zone*, a girdle, belt] *comb* girdle; band; encircling structure (zonesthesia, zonifugal)

zono- [Gr. *zone*, a girdle, belt] *comb* zoned, banded (zonochlorite, zonociliate)

zoo- [Gr. *zoon*, animal] **1.** *comb* animal; animal body (zoology); **2.** zoology and (zoochemical)

-zooid [Gr. *zoon*, living being] *comb* distinct animal (allozooid, Antherozooid)

-zoon [Gr. *zoon*, living being] *comb* animal, living thing (cryptozoon, spermatozoon)

zopher- [Gr. *zopheros*, dusky] *base* dusky (Zopherus)

zorill- [NL *zorilla*, a zoril] *base* African skunk (Zorillinae, zorilline)

zoster- [Gr. *zoster*, girdle] *base* band; shingles (zosteriform, zosterops)

zyga-, zygo-, -zygous [Gr. *zugon*, a yoke] *comb* yoke; pair; articulation (zygapophysis, zygodactyl, heterozygous)

zygomatico-, zygomato- [NL *zygomaticus*, zygoma and] *comb* [anatomy] related to the zygoma (zygomatico-auricular, zygomato-temporal)

zym-, zymo- [Gr. *zume*, leaven] *comb* fermentation; enzymes; yeast (zymurgy, zymophoric)

zyth- [Gr. *zuthos*, beer] *base* brewery; beer (zythepsary, zythum)

PART II

Finder

(Reverse Dictionary)

A

aardvark *base* -edent-
abandon *base* relinq-
abbreviated *comb* brachisto-, brachy-, brevi-, micro-, mini-, parvi-, parvo-, steno-; *base* -cort-, -curt-; *suf* -cle, -cula, -cule, -culum, -culus, -een, -el, -ella, -en, -et, -ette, -idion, -idium, -ie, -illa, -illo, -isk, -le, -let, -ling, -ock, -ola, -ole, -rel, -ula, -ule, -ulum, -ulus, -y
abdomen *comb* abdomino-, celio-, celo-[1], coelo-, laparo-, ventri-, ventro-; *distended~:* ventricoso-
abdominal sac *comb* peritoneo-
abet *base* auxil-, jut-, juv-
abhorrence *comb* miso-, -phobe, -phobia, -phobic; *base* -invid-, -ira(sc)-, odi-
ability *base* -apt-[2], -habil-, -poten-, -qual-; *suf* -bility, -ful, -ship
able to *comb* -potent; *suf* -able, -ible, -ile; *in an ~ way:* -bly; **able to be ___ :** *suf* -ilia
abnormal *comb* allo-, allotrio-, anom(o)-, poecilo-, poikilo-; *~ air in tissue base* emphys-;*~ attraction: comb* -lagnia, -philia, -philiac; *~ condition: pre* para-; *suf* -ism, -osis, -otic; *~ discharge: comb* -(r)rhage, -(r)rhagy, -(r)rhagia; *~ enlargement: comb* megalo-, -megaly; *~ smallness: comb* micro-
abode *comb* -cole, -colent, -colous, eco-, oiko-; *base* aed-, dom-, edi-
abolish *base* abrog-, fin-, perd-, termin-, vast-; *suf* -ate-[4]
about *pre* be-, circum-, peri-; *comb* amphi-; *base* -zon-, -cing-, -cinct-
above *pre* ano-[1], epi-, hyper-, ob-, super-, supra-, sur-, ultra-; *comb* over-, poly-
abscess *base* apostem-, vomic-
abscond *base* drapeto-, phygo-
absence *pre* a-, an-, dis-, ex-, il-, im-, in-, ir-, un-; *comb* lipo-; *base* -priv-; *suf* -less; *~ of an opening: comb* -atresia, atreto-; *~ of a part: comb* ectro-; *~ of urine: base* anur-[2]
absorb *comb* -sorb; *base* bib-
abstinent *base* nephal

abstruse *base* abdit-
absurd *base* fatu-, inan-, moro-, stult-, uber-
abundance *base* ampl-, copi-, larg-
abusive *comb* noci-, pesti-; *base* -nox-, pericul-
abyss *comb* barath-, batho-, bathy-; *base* -byss-, chao-
academy *base* academ-
accept *base* -cap-, -cep-, -cip-, -dyte-
accessory *pre* co-, para-[2], syn; *comb* inter-
accidents *base* -tich-, -tych(o)-
accord *pre* co-; *base* concinn-, congru-, consil-, unanim-
accountant *base* logist-[2]
accumulation *comb* cumulo-; *base* acerv-, agger-, soro-
accurate *comb* ortho-, recti-
accustomed *base* habit-
acetic *comb* acet-
acetyl *comb* aceto-, acetyl-
acid *comb* ortho-, oxy-[1]; -*base* -acerb-, acesc-, acor-, -oxal-; **formic ~:** *comb* formo-; **suberic ~:** *comb* subero-; **unsaturated ~:** *suf* -enoic
acknowledgment *base* agnit-
acorn *comb* balani-, balano-; *base* -gland-
acquire *base* -cap-, -cep-, -cip-, -dyte-; *acquired: base* ctet-
acrid *comb* picro-; *base* -acerb-, -mord-
acrimonious *base* acerb-, mord-
across *pre* dia-, per-, trans-; *comb* transverso-
act (to) *base* -fac-, -fec-, -fic-; *suf* -age, -ate, -ize
act of *comb* -craft; *suf* -ade, -age, -al, -ance, -ancy, -asis, -asm, -ation, -cy, -ence, -ency, -ery, -esis, -iasis, -ice[1], -ics, -ing, -ion, -ism, -ment, -osis, -otic, -sion, -sis, -th, -tion, -tious, -ture, -ure, -y[2], -ysis
actinic rays *comb* actino-
activity *base* stimul-; *comb* -ergasia, ergasio-, -ergic, ergo-, -ergy, -orial, -pragia, -praxia, -praxis; *suf* -esce, -escence, -escent, -esis; **muscular ~:**

comb kinesi-, -kinesia, -kinesis, kineso-, kino-; *quality of ~: comb* -pragia

actor *base* histrion-, thesp-

actual *base* ver-

acute *comb* oxy-[1]; *base* acer-, -grav-, vehem-

adamant *base* contum-, obstin-, pervic-, proterv-

added *base* adnat-

adder *base* colub-

addicted to *comb* -aholic

addition *pre* a-, ac-, ad-, af-, ag-, al-, an-, ap-, ar-, as-, at-, extra-, super-; *base* adscitit- *See* **more**

adherent *suf* -ist, ite

adjacent *base* contig-, -tang-, vicin-. *See* **near**

adjusted *base* concinn-, teino-

admirable *pre* bene-, eu-; *base* agath-, bon-, prob-

adolescent *base* epheb-

adopt *base* adrog-

adrenal gland *comb* adren(o)-

adroit *base* agil-, facil-, ingen-

adulterated *base* kibdelo-

adulterer *base* mech-

advance *pre* pro-; *base* ced-, cess-

advantageous *base* ophel-

adversarial *base* hostil-, inimic-

adversity *base* calamit-

affable *base* comit-

affectation *base* euphu-

affected with *suf* -otic

affecting *comb* -tropic

affection *base* -storgy

affinity *comb* -trope. *See* **attracted**

affluence *comb* chryso-, pluto-; *base* chrem-, -opul, pecun-

afraid *base* pavid-, tim-, trepid-. *See* **fear**

African *comb* Afro-

after *pre* meta-, post-; *comb* hystero-, opistho-, postero-, retro-

aftereffect *suf* -age, -asm, -ata, -ation, -ency, -ism, -ma, -ment, -mony, -sion, -ure

afternoon *base* pomerid-

again *pre* ana-, re-; *base* -pali(n)-

against *pre* anti-, cata-, cath-, contra-, contre-, ob-, with-; *comb* antio-, contro-, counter-, enantio-

agate *base* achat-, agati-

age *pre* eo-; *comb* chrono-; *base* aev-, -temp-; *suf* -arian. *See* **old**

agent *suf* -ant, -ate[3], -ator, -ent, -ure

agitate *base* agit-, mov-, trepid-, turb-

agouti *base* dasyproct-

agreeable *base* amen(it)-

agree(ment) *pre* co-; *base* concinn-, congru-, consil-, pact-, unanim-

agricultural *base* georg-

aid *base* -auxil-, -jut-, -juv-

ailment *pre* dys-, mal-; *comb* noso-, path, -pathic, patho-, -pathy; *base* aegr-, cachex-, -morb-, -pecca-, valetud-

air *comb* aer-, aeri-, aero-, anemo-, atmo-, physo-, -pnea, pneo-, pneumato-, pneumo-, pneumono-; *base* -flat-, -vent-

alabaster *base* alabast-

albatross *base* diomed-, -procellar-

alcohol *suf* -ol

aldehydes *suf* -al, -ole

alder *base* clethr-

algae (type of) *comb* seiro-

alike *pre* co-; *comb* equi-, homo-, iso-, pari-, tauto-

alive *comb* bio-, -biosis, quick-, vivi-, -zoic, zoo-, -zooid; *base* -anim-, vita-

alkaline *base* alkal-, lixiv-

alkaloid names *suf* -ia; *~ synthetic: comb* -caine; *~ with nitrogen bases:* -ine

all *pre* be-, cata-, cath-, de-, kata-, ob-, per-; *comb* holo-, omni-, pan-[1], panto-, pasi-, toti-

allay *base* sedat-

allegory *base* allegor-

alliance *base* symm-

allied *~ by blood base* cogn-[2]; *~ by friendship comb* socio-; *base* -am-, amic-[1], comit-

alligator *base* -eusuch-

allow *base* conced-, concess-

alloy *base* sterr-

allure *base* allect-, illeceb-, lenocin-

almanac *base* alman-

almond *comb* amygdal(o)-

almost *comb* pene-

alms *base* eleemosyn-

alone *pre* mono-; *comb* eremo-, soli-, uni-

alteration *pre* meta-, trans-; *comb* -plasia,

-plasis, -tropic, zeo-; *base* -mut-, -vari-, -vert-. *See* **change**
aluminum *comb* alumino-
alveolus *comb* alveolo-
always *comb* ever-; *base* aei-, etern-, semper-
amber *comb* succino-
ambiguous *base* ambig, ancip-, dub-, pariso-
ameba *comb* amebi-, amebo-
amend *pre* be-, em-, en-, meta-, trans-; *comb* aetio-, -blast, -blastic, blasto-, -craft, ergo-, etio-, -facient, -fic, -fication, -gen, -genesis, -genic, -genous, -geny, -parous, -plasia, -plasis, plasmo-, -plast, -plastic, plasto-, -plasty, -poiesis, -poietic, -trope, -tropic, -tropism, tropo-, -tropous, -tropy, -urgy; *base* camb-, -fabr-, -fec-, -mut-, -vari-, -vert-; *suf* -ate, en, -fy, -ize, -otic
amide *comb* -amic²; ~ *radical:* amido-
ammines *comb* ammino-
ammonia *comb* ammonio-, am-mono-
amnesia *base* amensi-, amnesi-
amniotic sac *comb* amnio-
among *pre* dia-, epi-; *comb* enter-, inter-
amount *comb* quanti-; *suf* -age, -ful, ling
ample *base* ocho-2
amplify *pre* ad-, extra-, hyper-, super-; *comb* auxano-, auxo-, multi-, myria-, myrio-, out-, over-, -plasia, pleni-, pleo-, pleio-, pleon-, plethys-, plio-, pluri-, pollaki-, poly-; *base* ampl-, -aug-, -cresc-, dilat-, -fold-, pler-, -plet-
amusing *base* facet-
anagram *base* anagram-
anal *comb* ano-², hedro-, podic-
ancestors *comb* patroio-
anchor- *base* ancyr-
anchovy *base* -engraul-
ancient *comb* archaeo-, archeo-, palaeo-, paleo-, proto-; *base* -antiq-, prisc-, -vet-; ~ **silver coin** *base* obol-
anesthetic *comb* -caine
anew *pre* ana-, re-; *base* -palin-
angel *base* angel-
angelfish *base* pterophyll-
anger *base* chol-, fur-¹, -invid-, -ira-, -margy
angle *comb* -angle, -gon, -gonal, gonio-; *base* -angul-

anguish *comb* lype-; *base* dolor-, fleb-, flet-, luct-, trist-
anhydride *comb* anhydro-
animal *comb* therio-, thero-, zoo-, -zooid; *base* -fer-, zo-; ~ *classes: suf* -acea; *early* ~ *form: comb* larvi-; ~ *group name: suf* -id¹, -ida, -idae, -iformes, -zoa, -zoic, -zoon; ~ **leg** *base* gamb-; *wild* ~: fer-. *Also see* "Animals" *in Part III*
animation *comb* bio-, -biosis, vita-, vivi-, zoo-, -zoic, -zooid; *base* -anim-
anise *base* anis-
ankle (bone) *comb* astragalo-, tala-, tali-, talo-
annelids *base* saen-
annoy *base* vex-
anointing *base* chrism-
another *comb* allelo-, allo-, alter-, hetero-; *base* -ali-²
answer *base* apocris-. *See* **say**
ant *comb* myrmec-, myrmeco-, myrmic-; *base* -formic-; *white* ~: *base* isoptero-
anteater *base* myrmecophag-
antelope *base* -alcelaph-, -bubal-, tragelaph-
antenna *base* cornic-
anterior *pre* fore-; *comb* antero-, proso-
anther *comb* -antherous
antibiotic *comb* -mycin
antibodies, having *comb* -valent
anticipation *base* procata-
anticoagulant *base* hepar-
antimony *comb* stibio-
antrum *comb* antro-
anus *comb* ano-², hedro-, podic-
any ___ of those possible *comb* -soever
aorta *comb* aorto-
apart *pre* de-, des-, di-², dia-, dis-, for-, se-; *comb* chori-, choristo-, dialy-
ape *comb* pithec-, -pithecus; *base* -sim-
aperture *base* -pylo-. *See* **hole**
apex *comb* -apical, apico-
apparel *comb* hestho-
apparent *comb* lampro, luc-, luci-; *base* -clar-
apparition *base* phantas-, phasm-
appearance *comb* -phane, phanero-, -phanic, -phany, pheno-; *base* -schem-, -spec-, -spic-
appease *base* paca-, -plac-

appendage in male crustacean *base* petas-

appendix *comb* ecphia-

appetite *comb* orect-, -orexia, -sitia, sitio-, sito-; *base* esur-

apple *base* mali-, pomi-

applied to *comb* -specific

approximately *suf* -ish

arched *comb* arci-, cyrto-; *base* -fornic-

arch enemy *base* nemesis-

archery *comb* toxo-[2]

ardor *base* ard-, alacr-, -ferv-, zelo-

arduous *pre* dys-; *comb* -bar, bary-, mogi-; *base* ardu-, stren-

argument *comb* -machy; *base* altercat-, litig-, obstrep-, pugil-, -pugn-, -rix-, vitilig-

arid *comb* carpho-, xero-; *base* arid-, -celo-, -sicc-

arm *limb:* *comb* acromio-, brachio-; *upper* ~: *comb* humero

armadillo *base* dasypod-, tatus-, -tolypeut-

Armenia + *base* Armeno-

armor *comb* hoplo-

armpit *base* -axill-, maschal-

aroma *comb* brom(o)-, odori-, odoro-, olfacto-,-osmia, osmo-, osphresio-, ozo-, ozono-

aromatic shrub *base* myric-

around *pre* be-, circum-, peri-; *comb* ambi-, ambo-, amphi-; *base* -cing-, -cinct-, -zon-

arouse *comb* agito-; *base* -cit-

arrange(ment) *comb* -tactic, -tactous, -taxis, taxo-, -taxy; *base* -pos-, -struct-; *suf* -ate

arrest *stop:* *comb* stasi-, -stasis, -stat, stato-

arrogant *base* alaz-

arrow *base* belo-, -sagitt-

arsenic *comb* arseno-

art *comb* craft-, -ship, techno-, -techny; *suf* -ics

artery *comb* arterio-, -venous

articulation *comb* zyga-, zygo-

artificial *base* factic-, factit-

asbestos *base* asbest-

ascend *base* anabol-

ashes *comb* ciner-, pulver-, spodo-, tephro-; *base* favill-

ash tree *base* -frax(in)-, -melia-[2]; *mountain* ~: sorb-[2]

as if *comb* pseudo-, quasi-

ask *base* -pet-, -quir-, -quis-, -rog-

aspirate *comb* rhopheo-

ass *base* as-, ono-

assault *base* impet-

assaying *base* docim-

assemblage *base* synod-; *suf* -ad, -age, -ery, -hood, -ship

assemble *base* -fabr-, -fac-, -fec-, -fic-, -struct-

assenting *comb* homolo

assign *base* -locat-

assist *base* -auxil-, -jut-, -juv-

assistance *base* -(ad)jut-, -(ad)juv-, auxil-

assistant *comb* vice-

association *base* sodal-

assumption *comb* -lemma[1]

astragalus *comb* astragalo-, talo-

astringent *base* styph-, stypt-

at *pre* ad-, juxta-; ~ *the same time:* *pre* co-, syn-; *comb* -simul-

athlete *base* athlet-

atlas *map:* *comb* carto-; *vertebra:* *comb* atlanto-, atlo-

atmosphere *comb* -bar, baro-; *base* chao-

atrophy *base* -tabe-

attack *fight:* *base* -pugil-, -pugn-; *seizure:* *comb* -agra, -lepsia, -lepsis, -lepsy, -leptic

attempt *base* conat-, peir-

attend to *comb* -serve; *attendant:* *base* -acolyt-, serv-

attracted to *comb* -phile, -philia, -philiac, -philic, -philism, philo-, -philous, -trope, -tropic, -tropism, -tropous, -tropy; *base* allect-, -urient

augmented *pre* ad-, extra-, hyper-, super-; *comb* auxano-, auxo-, multi-, myria-, myrio-, out-, over-, -plasia, pleni-, pleo-, pleio-, pleon-, plethys-, plio-, pluri-, pollaki-, poly-; *base* ampl-, -aug-, -cresc-, dilat-, -fold-, pler-, -plet-

auk *base* alcid-

aunt *base* -amita-, -matertera-

auricle *comb* atrio-

austere *base* auster-

authority *comb* exousia-; *base* imper-, magist-

authorized *base* canon-; *comb* cyrio-,
  kyrio-
automobile *comb* amaxo-, -mobile; *base*
  harmat-, -ocho-
avarice *base* avar-, avid-, cup(id)-, edac-,
  gulos-, pleonec-, pleonex-
avocado *base* pers-
avoid *base* avers-, drapeto-, evitab-, fug-,
  phygo-

away (from) *pre* ab-, abs-, apo-, be-, de-,
  des-, di-², dia-, dif-, dis-, e-, ec-, ef-, ex-,
  for-, off-¹, se, with-; *comb* ectro-
awl *base* subul-
ax *base* axin-, dolabri-, securi-, pelec-
axis *comb* axi-, axio-¹, axo-

B

babble *base* blat-
baby *comb* brepho-, nepi-
bacillus *comb* bacill-, bacilli-, bacillo-
back *pre* ana-, re-, un-, with-; *comb* retro-;
  the ~: *comb* back-, dorsi-, dorso-, nota-,
  noto-, tergi-, tergo-; **~ of the knee:** *base*
  poplit-
backbone *comb* rachi-, rachio-, rhach-,
  rhachio-
backward *comb* opiso-, retro-
bacteria *comb* bacter-, bacteri-, bacterio-,
  coccal, -coccic, cocco-, coccoid, -coc-
  cus, mycin; *base* -ella
badger *base* -melin-, -mustel-
bad(ly) *pre* dys-, mis-; *comb* caco-,
  -iniq-, kaki-, kako-, mal-¹, male-, perv-,
  ponero-, -prav-, -turp-, vitia-
bag(like) *comb* angio-, asco-, bursi-,
  burso-, ceco-, chlamyd-, chrysali-,
  coleo-, cyst-, -cyst, cysti-, cysto-, follic-,
  pericardiaco-, pericardio-, peritoneo-,
  phasco- physa-, physali-, physo-, -theca,
  theco-, typhlo-, utri-², utric-, vesico-;
  base -sacc-, -thylac-
baking *base* pistor-
balance *comb* counter-, libra-, pariso-,
  stasi-, -stasis, -stat, stato-
bald *base* alopec-, -calv-, glabr-, madar-,
  -pelad-, -phalacr-
ballot *base* tabell-, suffrag-
ball-shaped *comb* globi-, globo-, -sphere,
  sphero-; *base* -glom-. See **circle**
Baltic + *base* Balto-
bamboo *base* bambus-
ban *pre* anti-; *base* imped-, prohib-
banana *base* musa-

band *comb* desmo-, syndesmo-, taeni-,
  teni-, -trocha , zon-, zoni-, zoster-; *base*
  laqu-, -lemnisc-, liga-, zoster-; *suf* –let;
  ~ of people: *base* caterv-
bandy-legged *base* valg-
bang *comb* plessi-, -cuss-; *base* -cop-,
  -crot-, plang-, -puls-, -tus-, -vapul-,
  -verber-
banner *comb* labar-, vexill-
bar *base* clathr-, -ser-
barbarian *base* barbar-
barbed *base* hamat-
barber *base* tonsor-
bare *comb* gymno-, nudi-, psilo-. See
  bald
bark *dog:* *base* gann(it)-, hylac-, latr-;
  tree: *base* cortici-, libri-, phloem-
barley *comb* alphito-; *base* crith-, horde-,
  ptis-
barracuda *base* -perces-, sphyraen-
barrel *base* cadus-, dolio-
barrier *comb* herco-, septo-, parieto-,
  -phragma, phragmo-; *base* cancell-,
  claustr-, -mur-
base *foundation:* *comb* basi-, basidio-,
  basio-, baso-, fund-; *base* -radic-;
  evil: *pre* dys-, mis-; *comb* caco-, iniq-,
  kak(o)-, mal(e)-, ponero-; *base* -prav-,
  sceler-, turp-, vili-
basic *base* prim-, -rud-; *chemistry:* *pre*
  sub-
basin (shaped) *base* leb-; *comb* cylico-,
  kylixo-, lecano-, pelvi-
basket *base* bascaud-, calath-, -corb-
Basque *comb* Basco-
bat *base* desmodont-, megacheiropter-,

microcheiropter, noctilion-, -pterop-, -vespertil-
bath(ing) *comb* balneo-; *base* -ablut-, -lav-, loutro-
battle *comb* macho-, -machy; *base* -bell-, -pugil-, -pugn-
beach *base* littor-, thino-; *See* **sand**
beacon *base* fan-
beadlike *base* torul-
beak *comb* coraci-, coraco-, rhampho-, rhyncho-, rostrato-, rostri-, rostro-, -rrhyncha; *base* -aquil-, coron-. *See* **nose**
beam *base* trab-
bean *base* cyam-, fab-, phaseol-
bear ~ *animal:* *comb* arcto-; *base* -urs-; ~*carry:* *comb* -fer, -ferous, -gerous, -parous, -pher, -phore, -phorous; *base* -port-, -vect-
bearable *base* toler-
beard *comb* pogon(o)-; *base* -barb(a)-
bearing *comb* -fer, -ferous, -gerous, -parous, -pher, phor-, -phore, -phorous; *base* -port-
beast *comb* -there, therio-, thero-; *base* bellu-, besti-, fer-
beat *comb* -cuss-, plessi-, rhabdo-; *base* colaph-, -cop-, -crot-, fustig-, plang-, puls-, quass-, vapul-, -verber-; ~ *time* *base* bat-[2]
beautiful *comb* calli-, callo-; *base* bell-[2], formos-, kal-, pulchr-, venust-
beaver *base* -castor-
become *suf* -ate[1], -en, -fy; ~*like:* -ize; ~*liquid:* *base* deliqu-
becoming *comb* -facient; *suf* -esce, -escence, -escent
bed *base* clin-, lecti-[1], lectu-
bee *comb* api(o)-, melisso-, melitto-; *base* -bomb-; ~ *hive:* -alve-
beech *base* faga-, pheg-
beer *base* cervis-, zuth-
beetle *base* bruch-, coleopter-, lathro-, saco-, scarab-; *bark-beetle:* *base* scolyt-; *carrion-beetle:* *base* silph-
before *pre* ante-, fore-, ob-, pre-, pro-[2]; *comb* antero-, protero-, proto-, retro-; *base* prior-
beggar *comb* ptocho-; *base* mendic-
begin(ning) *comb* -phyletic, spermato-,

-spemous; *base* incip-, -init-; *suf* -esce, -escence, -escent. *See* **origin**
beginner *base* tiro-, tyro-
behavior *comb* etho-; *base* hexi-
behind *pre* meta-, post-; *comb* after-, back-, hind-, opistho, postero, retro-; *base* terg-
being *comb* onto-; *base* -esse-
belch *base* eruct-, -ruct-
belief *comb* -ousia; *base* -cred-, -fid-[1]; *suf* -ism
believer *suf* -ist, -ite
believing in *suf* -an
bell *base* campan-, -tintinn-; ~ *shaped:* *comb* -codonic
belligerence *base* chol-, -invid-, -ira-, -margy
bellow *base* blat-, -mug-
belly *comb* abdomino-, celio-, celo-, coelo-, laparo-, ventri-, ventro-; *base* -alv-. *See* **stomach**
belonging to *suf* -acean, -aceous, -ad,-al[3], -an[3], -ar, -arious, -ary, -atic, -ative, -atory, -eae, -ean, -eous, -ery, -etic, -ial, -ian, -ic, -id[1], -il, -ile, -ina, -inae, -ine, -ing, -ious, -istic, -ite, -itic, -itious, -itive, -ive, -oidea, -ory, -otic, -tious, -tive, -ular. *See* **characteristic of**
below *pre* hypo-, infra-, sub-, subter-; *comb* infero-, under-
belt *comb* desmo-, syndesmo-, taeni-, teni-, -trocha , zon-, zoni-; *base* -lemnisc-, liga-, zoster-; *suf* -let
bend, bent *comb* ancylo-, ankylo-, -campsis, campto-, campylo-, -clinal, -clinate, -cline, -clinic, clino-, -clinous, -clisis, curvi-, cyrto-, -flect, flex-, flexuouso-, klino-, lechrio-, loxo-, recurvi-, recurvo-, repando-, scolio-, -tort-, -verge; *base* -clit-, cliv-, declin-, pand-, -sinu-; ~ *inward:* *base* adunc-
beneficial *base* ophel-
benefit *base* -auxil-, -jut-, -juv-
benzine *pre* meta-; *comb* benzo-, phen-
benzoyl group *base* benzoxy-
benzyl group *base* benzyloxy-
bequest *base* legat-[2]
bereavement *comb* lype-; *base* dolor-, fleb-, flet-, luct-, trist-

berry *comb* baccato-, bacci-, cocci-; *base*
-acin-
beside *pre* a-, ac-, ad-, af-, ag-, al-, an-, ap-,
ar-, as-, at-, by-, epi-, para-², peri-; *comb*
juxta-, citra-, pene-, proximo-
besides *pre* extra-
best *comb* aristo-; *base* -opt-²
bestow *base* -don-
better *comb* melior-, out-; *base* prior-
between *pre* dia-, epi-; *comb* enter-, inter-
bewitched *base* fascin-
beyond *pre* ex-, extra-, meta-, para-²,
preter-, super-, supra-, sur-, ultra-; *comb*
over-
Bible *comb* biblio-
big *base* grand-, magn-. *See* large
bile *comb* bili-, chole-, cholo-, gall-
billion *comb* giga-. *Also see* "Numbers" in
Part III
billionth *comb* nanno-, nano-
billow *comb* cyma-, cymato-, cymo-
bind *comb* sphingo-, -strain, -strict,
syndesmo-; *base* liga-, -merinth-,
nex-, -string-, -vinc-; ~ *tightly:* base
sphingo-; *binding:* comb -desis
bipartite *comb* diphy-. *See* two
birch *base* betul-
bird *comb* orneo-, orni-, ornitho-, orno-;
base -avi-, grall-, muscicap-, oscin-,
passer-, pendulin-, volucr-; ~ *lime:* base
ixo-; *weaver ~:* base ploc-
birth *comb* -genic, -natal, -para, -tocia,
-toky; *base* geneth-, -nasc-, -partur-; ~
day: geneth-
birthmark *comb* nevi-, nevo-; *base* naev-
bishop *base* episcop-; ~ *domain:* base
dioc-
biting *comb* aceto-, keto-, oxal-, oxy-; *base*
-acid-, -mord-
bitter *comb* picro-; *base* -acerb-, asper-,
botaur-, -mord-;
bittern *base* botaur-, ixobrych-
bitterness *base* acrim-
black *comb* atro-, melano-, nigri-, nigro-,
piceo-; *base* atra(t)-, -ebon-, fulig-. *Also*
see "Colors" in Part III
blackbird *base* -icter-, merul-
Black Sea region *base* pont-²
black widow *base* latrodect-
blade (broad) *comb* spathi-

bladder *comb* asco-, burs-, bursi-, burso-,
ceco-, cyst-, -cyst, cysti-, cysto-, follic-,
physa-, physali-, physo-, typhlo-, utri-,
utric-, vesico-, vesiculi-, vesiculo-; *base*
med-, -sacc-, -thylac-
blame *base* culp-, reprehen-, -vituper-
blanket *base* -lodic-
bleary-eyed *base* lipp-
bleat *base* bal-
blemish *comb* nevi-, nevo-; *base* naev-
blend *pre* co-; *comb* conjugato-, -ergasia,
gameto-, gamo-, hapto-, junct-; *base*
aps-, apt-, -greg-, -soc-; *suf* -ate, -ize
blessed *base* macar-
blight *comb* fungi-, -mycete, myceto-,
-mycin, myco-, uredo-
blind *comb* caeco-, ceco-, typhlo-; *base*
ableps-, -lusc-; *to ~ in one eye:* base
elusc-
blink *base* -conniv-, -nict-
blister *comb* phlyc-, vesica-, vesico-, vesi-
culo-; *base* bullat-, pemphig-, pomph-,
pustul-
blood *comb* haema-, haemo-, hema-,
hemato-, hemo-, sangui-, sanguineo-,
sanguino-; *base* cruent-, cruor-; ~ *clot:*
thrombo-; ~ *condition or disease:*
-aemia, -cythemia, -emia; ~ *fluid:* lym-
pho-; ~ *vessels:* hemangio-, vasculo-,
vaso-
blooming *comb* thalero-; *base* flor-, vig-
blow *wind:* base anemo-, flabil-, flat-,
vent-; *punch:* comb plessi-; *base* cop-,
-crot-, -cuss-, -plang-, puls-, -tus-,
vapul-, -verber-
blue *comb* cyano-, glauco-; *base* adular-,
aerug-, -azur-, -caes-, -cerul-, -lazul-,
-livid-, -pavon-; *bluish-green:* comb
glauco-. *Also see* "Colors" in Part III
blueberry *base* vaccin-
bluebird *base* sial-², -turd-
blunder *base* culp-, delinq-, laps-, pecc-,
sphal-
blunt *comb* obtusi-; *base* hebet-
boar *base* apr-, suid-
boasting *base* kompo-, thras-
boat (-shaped) *comb* navi-, scapho-, sca-
pulo-; *base* -cymb-
bobolink *base* -icter-
body *comb* physico-, physi-, physio-,

somato-, -some[1]; *base* -corp-; *dead ~:
comb* necro-; *base* -cadav-; *~ defect:
base* -hamart-; *~ odor:* brom-, ozos-
tom-; *~ organ part: suf* -ite
bog *base* helo-, telmat-; *peat ~: base*
turbar-
boil (up) *base* aestu-, -coct-, decoct-,
ebullio-, elix-, ferv-
boils *base* furunc-
bold *base* audac-, feroc-
bolt *base* gomph-, pessul-, -ser-
bond *comb* desmo-, ligamenti-, liga-
mento-, syndesmo-; *base* -caten-,
-vinc-; *double ~: suf* -ylene
bone *comb* ossi-, osseo-, osteo-; *forearm
~:* ulno-; *~ joining hipbones:* sacro-; *~
membrane:* periosteo-; *finger or toe ~:*
phalang-; *frontal~: base* fronto-; *bony
process: comb* stylo-; *small bone of the
ear: comb* incudo-
book *comb* biblio-; *base* -libr-; *~ size: suf*
-mo; *~ worm:* tinea-
booty *base* manub-
border *base* fimbr-, -marg-, propinq-,
prox-, termin-. *~ bordered: base*
confin-, crasp-, limbat- *See* **near** or
surrounding
bore *base* terebr-; *borer: comb* trypano-
born *comb* -genic, -natal, -para, -tocia,
-toky; *base* geneth-, -nasc-, partur-; *~
in: suf* -an
boron *comb* boro-
bosom *base* grem-
both *comb* ambi-, ambo-; *~ sides:* amphi-,
ampho-, bi-
bother *base* vex-
bottle *base* ampull-, lagen-; *leather ~:*
utrei-, utri-
bottom *pre* sub-; *comb* basi-, fund-; *base*
-radic-
boundary *comb* orismo-; *base* fin-,
termin-
bow *base* arci-
bowel cavity *base* cloac-; *~ pain: base*
tormin- *See* **intestines**
bowl *comb* cymbi-, cymbo-, crater-, cyl-
ico-, kylixo-
box *comb* pyx-; *~ tree: base* bux-, locul-
boy *base* puer-
bracelet *base* armill-

braggart *base* alaz-, iactan-
bragging *base* kompo-, thras-
brain *comb* cephal-, cerebri-, cerebro-,
encephalo-
brambles *base* bat-[3], vepri-; *comb* bato-[2]
bran *base* furfur-, pityr-
branch *comb* clado-, rami-; *base* stol-;
branchy: comb ramoso-
brass *comb* chalco-; *base* -aenio-
brave *base* audac-, feroc-
brazen *base* contum-, impud-, procac-
bread *base* arto-, pan-[2]
breakfast *base* -jent-
break(ing) *comb* -clasia, -clasis, -clas-
tic, -rhegma, -(r)rhexis; *base* agmat-,
-fract-, -frag-, -frang-, -rupt-; *broken
down: base* decrep-
breast *comb* mammi-, mammo-, mastia-,
-masto-, mazo-[2], stetho-; *base* pect-; *~
bone:* sterni-, sterno-. *See* **nipple**
breath *comb* -hale, -pnea, pneo-, pneu-
mato-, pneumo-, pneumono-, pne-
usio-, pulmo-, spiro-[1]; *base* afflat-,
anhel-; *bad ~:* -halit-, ozostom-
breed *base* thremm-
brewery *base* zuth-
brick *base* -later-, plinthi-; *~ color: comb*
testaceo-
bridge *base* gephyr-, pont-
brief *comb* brachio-, brachisto-, brachy-,
brevi-, chamae-, hekisto-, micro-,
mini-, parvi-, parvo-, steno-, tapino-;
base -cort-, -curt-, exig-; *suf* -cle, -cula,
-cule, -een, -el, -ella, -en, -et, -ette,
-idion, -idium, -ie,-illa, -illo, -isk, -kin,
-le, -let, -ling, -ock, -ola, -ole, -rel, -ula,
-ule, -ulum, -ulus, -y
bright *comb* helio-; *base* -clar-, -fulg-,
-gano-, -luc-, lucul-, -lumin-, nitid-
brine *base* muri-
bring *base* -duc-, -fer-, -latio-, -port- . *See*
carry
bring forth *comb* maieusi-, -parous; *base*
partur-
brisk *comb* ocy-, tacho-, tachy-; *base*
alacr-, celer-, festin-, veloc-
bristle *comb* chaeta-, chaeti-, chaeto-,
seti-; *bristly: base* echin-; *little ~: base*
setul-
broad *comb* eury-, lati-, platy-

broccoli *base* brassic-
broken down *comb* rhesto-
bromine *comb* bromo-
brooch *base* fibul-
broom *comb* scopa-, scopi-
broth *base* juss-²
brothel *base* lupan-
brother *comb* frater-, fratri-; *base* -adelph-
brown *comb* fusco-, -phaein, phaeo-; *base*
 aen-, brun-, castan-, -fulv-, -gland-, lur-,
 mustel-, -spad-, -testac-. *Also see* "Colors" in Part III
bruise *base* livid-, sugill-, -tus-
brush *comb* scopa-, scopi-; *base* muscar-;
 brushlike: comb scopuli-; *base* saro-
bubble *comb* pego-, physali-; *base* bullat-
bucket *base* antl-
buckthorn *base* -rhamn-
buckwheat *base* fagopyr-
bud *base* gemm-¹; *scaly cover of ~: base*
 perul-
buffalo *base* bubal-
buffet *base* colaph-
buffoon *comb* balatro-
bug *comb* cimic-, core-², entomo-,
 insecti-, insecto-
build *base* -fabr-, -fac-, -fec-, -fic-, -struct-
building *base* aedi-, edi-, tecton-
bulb(ous) *comb* bulbo-; *base* cep-²
bulge *comb* -cele, -edema, ganglio-,
 phlogo-, phym-, -phyma, physa-,
 physo-, strum(i)-; *base* aug-, cresc-,
 physc-, strum-, -tum-, -turg-; *suf* -itis
bulk *base* corp-
bull *comb* tauri-, tauro-

bullfinch *base* pyrrhul-
bull-headed *base* contum-, obstin-, per-
 vic-, proterv-
bully *base* -procac-
bundle *comb* fasciculato-, fascio-; *base*
 phacell-, -sarcin-
bunting *base* emberiz-, pyrrhul-
burden(ed) *comb* hypegia-, hypengy-,
 -ridden; *base* -oner-, paralip-
burdensome *pre* dys-; *comb* -bar, bary-,
 mogi-; *base* ardu-, stren-
burial *base* sepul-
burning *comb* causto-, igni- pyro-; *base*
 adust-, ard-¹, ars-, cauter-, celo-², com-
 bur-, combust-, crem-, ignesc-, phlog-,
 -ust-
burr *base* lapp-
burrow *base* fod-
bursting *base* dehisce-, -rrhexis-, -rupt-.
 See **breaking**
bury *base* -hum-
burying place *comb* kil(l)-. *See* **tomb**
bush *base* thamn-
business *base* -negot-, nundin-
busybody *base* ardelio-
butcher *base* lania-
butter *comb* butyro-
butterfly *base* lepidopter-, papil-
buttocks *comb* -pygia, pygo-; *base* nati-,
 podic-
buzzard *comb* buteo-; *base* cathart-
buy *comb* onio-; *base* -empt-, -merc-,
 nundin-
by *pre* ad-, by-, epi-, peri-; *comb* juxta-;
 base -prox-; *~ means of: pre* syn-

C

cabbage *base* brassic-
cactus *base* cact-
cake of dried meat *base* pemm-
calcium *comb* calc-, calci-
calf *base* **animal:** vitul-; **leg:** sura-
call *base* appell-, -claim, -clam-, -dict-,
 -nom-, -voc-; *~ upon: base* -prec-
callus *comb* tylo-
calm *base* placid-, sedat-, tranquil-
calyx *comb* calath-, calyc-, cotyle-, cotyli-,

 cotylo-, cupuli-, cyathi-, cyatho-,
 scyphi-, scypho-; *base* calic-, crin-,
 cyphell-, pocul-
camel *comb* cameli-; *base* bact-
camp *base* castr-
camphor *comb* campho-
cancel *base* oblit-
cancer *comb* scirrho-; *base* carcin(o)-
canine *comb* cyno-, kyno; *base* -can-¹; *~
 tooth: base* laniar-

canopy *base* tentor-
cap *base* galer-, -pile-
capable of being *suf* -able, -ibility, -ible,
 -ibly, -ile
capacious *base* ocho-[2]
caper (onion) *base* caep-
capsule *comb* capsuli-, capsulo-
car *comb* amaxo-; *base* harmat-
caraway plant *base* kar-
carbohydrate *suf* -ose[1]
carbon *comb* carbo-
carbon dioxide *comb* -capnia, capno-
carbuncle *comb* anthraco-
card *comb* carto-, charto-
cardinal *bird:* *base* pyrrhul-
careful *base* attent-, caut-, diligen-
caries *comb* cario-
carp *base* cyprin-
carpet *base* tapet-
caressing *base* -sarmass-
carriage *base* aurig-, rhed-
carry(ing) *comb* -fer, -ferous, -gerous,
 -parous, -pher, -phore, -phorous; *base*
 bajulat-, gestat-, -port-, -vect-, vectit-
cart *base* plaustr-
cartilage *comb* chondr-, chondrio-, chon-
 dro-, xiphi-; *base* cartilag-; *eyelid* ~:
 tarso-
carve *comb* -glyph, glypto-
case *comb* angio-, chlamyd-, coleo-,
 meningo-, -theca, theci-, theco-; *wing*
 ~: *comb* elytri-
cash *comb* -penny ; *base* chremat-,
 -numm-, -pecun-, quaest-
cashew *base* anacard-
cask *base* cadus-
cassowary *base* casuar-
cast off *base* exuv-
castor oil *base* cicin-, ricinol-
cat *comb* aeluro-, ailuro-, gato-; *base* -fel-,
 gale-[3]
catch *comb* -tain; *base* -cap(t)-, -cathex-,
 -ger-, -hapt-, -prehend, prehens-, rap-,
 rep-, -ten-; *catcher:* *base* -thera
caterpillar *base* bruch-, -camp-[2], eruc-,
 kamp-
catfish *base* silur-
cathode + *comb* cathodo-
catkin *base* ament-[2], -juli-
cattle *base* bou-, bov-, bu, pecu—

cauliflower *base* brassic-
cause, causing *pre* be-, em-, en-[2], meta-,
 trans-; *comb* aetio-, -blast, -blastic,
 blasto-, -craft, ergo-, etio-, -facient,
 -fic, -fication, -gen, -genesis, -genic,
 -genous, -geny, -parous, -plasia, -plasis,
 plasmo-, -plast, -plastic, plasto-, -plasty,
 -poiesis, -poietic, -trope, -tropic, -tro-
 pism, tropo-, -tropous, -tropy, -urgy;
 base -fabr-, -fec-, -mut-, -vert-; *suf* -ate,
 -en, -fy, -ize, -otic
caused by *suf* -atory, -ic, -ing
caustic *comb* cauter-; *base* eschar-; **acri-**
 monious: *base* acerb-, mord-
cave *comb* speleo-, troglo-; *base* serang-,
 spelunc-
cavity *comb* alveolo-, antro-, atrio-,
 -coele, coelo-, kuttaro-, parieto-, sino-,
 sinu-, syringo-, ventriculo-, vesiculo-,
 vestibulo-; *base* lacun-. *See* **hollow**
cease *comb* stasi-, -stasis, -stat; *base* ces-
 sat-, fin-, termin-
cecum *comb* ceco-, typhlo-
cedar *base* cedr-
celebration *comb* -fest, -mas; *suf* -ia
celestial activity *comb* astro-
celibate *base* caelib-
cell *comb* alveolo-, celli-, celluli-, cellulo-,
 -cyte, -cythemia, cyto-, -gonium, kyto-,
 -plasm, plasmato-, plasmo-
cellulose *comb* cello-
celom *comb* celo-[1]
Celt *comb* Celto-
cement *comb* glea-
cemetery *base* coemet-, coimet-
center *comb* centr-, centri-, -centric,
 centro-
centipede *base* chilopod-, scolopendri-
ceramic *comb* ceramo-
cereal *base* frument-, gramin-
ceremony *base* caerimon-
cervical *comb* cervico-
chaff *base* acer-[3], plea-
chain *base* caten-, vinc-; ~ *like:* *base*
 hormo-
chair *base* cathedr-, sedil-
chalk *base* cimol-, -cret-, gypso-; [geol-
 ogy] *comb* cretaceo-
chamber *comb* alveolo-, atrio-, antro-,
 -coele, coelo-, parieto-, sino-, sinu-,

sinuso-, syringo-, ventriculo-, vesiculo-, vestibulo-. *See* **hollow**

chamois *base* rupicap-

chance *comb* clero-, faust-, tycho-; *base* alea-, fortuit-

chancellor *base* cancel-

change *pre* be-, em-, en-, meta-, trans-; *comb* aetio-, -blast, -blastic, blasto-, -craft, ergo-, etio-, -facient, -fic, -fication, -gen, -genesis, -genic, -genous, -geny, -parous, -plasia, -plasis, plasmo-, -plast, -plastic, plasto-, -plasty, -poiesis, -poietic, -trope, -tropic, -tropism, tropo-, -tropous, -tropy, -urgy; *base* camb-, -fabr-, -fec-, -mut-, -vari-, -vert-, viciss-; *suf* -ate, en, -fy, -ize, -otic

channel *comb* aulo-, follic-, meato-, poro-, salpingo-, siphono-, soleno-, stria-, striato-, strio-, syringo-, tubi-, tubo-, tubulo-, vasi-; *base* solen-, strig-

character *comb* etho-, -hood, quali-; *suf* -ity

characteristic of *suf* -an^3, -ar, -ary, -ate^2, -ean, -en, -esque, -ian, -ic, -ical, -il, -ile, -ine, -ish, -istic, -like, -ly, -ous, -ular, -ulent, -ulose, -y. *See* **belonging to**

characterized by *suf* -acean, -aceous, -acious, -aire, -al, -ate, -ed^2, -eous, -ey, -ful, -gerous, -ial, -ine, -ious, -itious, -oid, -orious, -ory, -ose, -osity, -ous, -some, -ular, -ulent, -ulose, -ulous, -wise, -y^1

charcoal *base* carbon

chariot *base* harmat-

charter *base* muniment-

chasm *base* vorag-

chaste *base* pudic-

chastisement *comb* mastigo-, rhabdo-; *base* castig-, peno-, poine-, -pun-

chatter *base* garrul-. *See* **talk**

cheat *base* apat-, dolero-, ludif-

checked *comb* brady-; *base* -cunct-, imped-, -mora-, -tard-. *See* **inhibit**

cheek *comb* bucco-, -genia, genio-, geny-, mal-^{2}, mel(o)-^{2}, -paria, zygomatico-, zygomato-

cheerful *comb* chero-, galero-; *base* beati-, felic-, jubil-, macar-

cheese *comb* tyro-; *base* from-; *suf* case-

chemicals *comb* chemo-; ***chemical compound:*** -idine

cherry *base* -ceras-

chest *anatomy:* *comb* sterno-, stetho-, thoracico-, thoraco-; *base* pector-; ***container:*** *comb* cisto-, scrin-

chestnut *base* aescul-, -castan-

chew *base* manduc-, -mastic-, trog-

chickadee *base* par-^{2}

chicken *base* gallin-, pull-. *See* **cock**

chicory *base* cichor-

chief *comb* arch-^{1}, archi-, proto-; *base* hegemon-, -prim-, -princip-

child *comb* paedo-^{2}, pedi-, pedo-^{2}, proli-, tecno-; *base* -fil-^{2}, -puer-, tek-

childbirth *comb* lochio-, maieusi-, -para, -parous, -tocia, toco-, toko-, -toky; *base* lox-, -partur-, puerper-

childish utterance *base* lall-

chimpanzee *base* sim-

chin *comb* -genia, genio-, geny-, mento-

Chinese *comb* Chino-, Sino-

chip *base* dolatil-

chisel *comb* scalpri-

chloride *base* muriat-

chlorine *comb* chloro-, perchloro-

choice *base* -opt-^{1}, -vol-

choke *base* -pnig-, strangul-

chore *comb* arti-, -craft, -ergasia, ergasio-, -ergics, ergo-, -ergy, organo-, -urgy; *base* -labor-, lucubr-, oper-^{1}, -opus-, pono-^{2}

chosen *base* -lect-^{2}

chromatin *comb* chromato-

chromium *comb* -chrome

chromosones: of a specified multiple of ___ *comb* -ploid

church *comb* ecclesiastico-, kil(l)-

chyle *comb* chyl-, chyli-, chylo-

cilia *comb* cilii-, cilio-

circle, circular *comb* ano-, annul-, crico-, cyclo-, disco-, globi-, globo-, glom-, gyro-, orbito-, -sphere, sphero-, stilli-, zon-, zoni-, zono-; *base* -anu-, -cing-, -cinct-, -circin-, -circul-, -coron-, -glomer-, gyral-, -numm-, -orb-, rond-, -rot-, stemma-, -troch-

circulating *base* encyc-

citizen (of) *base* -civ-; *suf* -an, -ian, -ite

citric *base* citro-

city *comb* -burg(h), -polis, -ton, -ville;
   base asty-, -civ-, -urb-
civet *base* viverr-
clamor *base* crepit-, frem-, ligyr-,
   strep(i)-, strid-, stridul-. *See* **sound**
clan *base* -phrat-
clap *base* -plaud-, -plaus-
clarion *base* -litu-
class names *suf* -ia; *specified class: comb*
   -rater
clatter *base* -strepit-
clavicle *comb* cleido-, clido-
claw *comb* -chela, cheli-, helo-, onycho-,
   -onychia; *base* -ungui-, ungul-
clay *comb* argillaceo-, argillo-, limo-[1],
   pelo-
cleanse *comb* balneo-; *base* ablut-, cathar-,
   -lav-, -mund-[2], -purg-
clear *comb* lampro-, limpid-, luc-, luci-;
   base -clar-
cleaver *base* -dolabr-
cleft *comb* dicho-, -fid[2], fissi-, schisto-,
   schizo-, sulcato-, -tomy; *base* fatisc-,
   -par-, rim-. *See* **groove**
clergy *comb* clerico-, ecclesiastico-
clever *base* ingen-
cliff *base* cremno-, scopul-
climb *base* -ascend-, ascens-, -scal-,
   -scand-, -scans-
cloak *base* chlamyd-
clockwise *comb* dextr(o)-
clod *base* gleb-
close by *pre* a-, ac-, ad-, af-, ag-, al-, an-,
   ap-, ar-, as-, at-, by-, cis-, epi-, para-,
   peri-; *comb* citra-, juxta-, pene-, prox-
   imo-; *base* engys-, propinq-
closed, closure *comb* -atresia, atreto-,
   claustro-, cleido-, -cleisis, cleisto-,
   clisto-, stego-; *base* -clithr-, -clud-,
   -clus-, occlud-, occlus-
clot *comb* thrombo-; *base* grum-
clothing *base* habil-, hesto-, -vest-
cloth-like *base* pann-
cloud *comb* fracto-, nephelo-, nepho-,
   nimbo-; *base* homichlo-, -nebul-,
   -nubi-; *rounded~:* mammato-
cloven-footed *base* artiodactyl-
club (cudgel) *base* clavi-, coryn-, rhopal-;
   ~ foot: talip-; *~ shaped: comb* clavi-[2]
club (group) *base* eran-

clumps *comb* cespitoso-; *base* -glob-. *See*
   tufts
clumsy *base* inconcin-
cluster *base* corymbi-, glom-, neus(t)-,
   racem-
clutch *comb* -tain; *base* -cap(t)-, -cathex-,
   -ger-, -hapt-, -prehend, prehens-, rap-,
   rep-, -ten-
coach *base* aurig-
coagulated *base* pect-[2]
coal *comb* anthraco-; *base* -carb-
coarse *base* scurril-
coast *shore: base* littor-, maritim-
cobalt *comb* cobalti-, cobalto-
cobbler *base* sutor-
cobweb *base* arachn-
coccus *comb* -coccal
coccyx *comb* coccy-, coccygo-
cock *base* alector-, alectry-
cockroach *base* blatt-[1]
coercion *comb* dyna-, dynamo-, mega-,
   megalo-, -megaly, -sthenia, stheno-;
   base -forc-, -fort-, -poten-, robor-
coil *comb* cirri-, cochlio-, gyro-, helico-,
   spiri-, spiro-[2], strepto-; *base* bostrych-,
   stromb-. *See* **curl**
coin *base* monet-, numisma-, -numm-
coincide *base* concinn-, congru-, unanim-
coition *comb* -lagnia; *base* -coit-
cold *comb* cheima-, crymo-, cryo-, frigo-,
   gelo-, kryo-, pago-, psychro-, rhigo-;
   base alg-, glac-
collar *base* coll-[1]
collarbone *base* clavi-[1]
collection of *suf* -ad, -age, -ery, -hood,
   -ship
collegiate hall *base* aul-[1]
collodion *comb* collodio-
colon *comb* coli-[1], colo-, kolon-
colonnade *base* exedr-, portic-, stoa-
color *comb* chromato-, -chrome,
   chromo-; *base* -pigm-, -tinct-, -ting-;
   colored: comb -chroous; *many-colored: comb* poecilo-; *two-colored:*
   comb dichro-. *Also see* "Colors" in Part
   III
colorless *comb* leuco-, leuko-
column *comb* kio-; *base* stylo-[2]; *small ~:*
   columelli-
coma *base* coma-[2]

comb *base* cteno-, strigil-; ~ *teeth:* pectinato-

combat *comb* macho-, -machy, pugn-; *base* -bell-, pugil-

combine *pre* co-; *comb* conjugato-, -ergasia, gameto-, gamo-, hapto-[2], junct-; *base* aps-, apt-, -greg-, -soc-; *suf* -ate, -ize; **combination** *comb* double-; **combined in the proportion of 2 to 3:** *comb* subsesqui-; **combined with entertainment:** -tainment

combustible *comb* ard-, ars-

come *comb* -vene; *base* -ven(t)-; ~ *together: base* congru-

comestibles *comb* bromato-, -brotic, manduc-, opso-, -phage, phago-, -phagous, -phagy, -sitia, sitio-, sito-, -troph, -trophic, tropho-, -trophy, -vora, -vore, -vorous; *base* -alim-, -cib-, escul-, -gust-, -nutr-; **partially digested ~:** chymo-

command *base* -imper-, juss-, -mand-

commence *base* inaug-, incip-, init-

commerce *base* negot-, nundin-

commercial names *suf* -co, -ine

common *comb* caeno-[1], ceno-[2], coeno-, pan-[1]; *base* -commun-, koin-, -vulg-; **commonplace:** *base* triv-; ~ *people: comb* demo-; *base* -pleb-, -popul-

commotion *base* -agit-, -tumult-, -turb-

community *base* synœc-

compact *dense: comb* dasy-, pycno-, pykno-; *base* -crass-, -press-, -spiss-; *small: comb* brachio-, brachisto-, brachy-, brevi-, chamae-, hekisto-, micro-, mini-, nano-, parvi-, parvo-, -steno-; *base* cort-, curt-; *suf* -cle, -cula, -cule, -culum, -culus, -een, -el, -ella, -en, -et, -ette, -idion, -idium, -ie, -illa, -illo, -isk, -kin, -le, -let, -ling, -ock, -ola, -ole, -rel, -ula, -ule, -ulum, -ulus, -y

companion *base* comit-[2], hetaero-

comparable *pre* para-, quasi-; *comb* homeo-, omœo-, homoio-, homolo-, iso-, -phane, -phanic; *base* simil-; *suf* -acean, -aceous, -al, -an, -ar, -ary, -ean, -en, -eous, -esque, -ful, -ic, -il, -ile, -ine, -ing, -ish, -itious, -ize, -like, -ode, -oid, -ose, -osity, -some, -tious, -ular, -y

compartment *base* locul-

compel *base* horm-, -hort-, -suade, -suas-

competence *base* quali-

competitive event *comb* -athlon, -athon, -off[2]

complain *base* -quer-, -querul-

complement of *pre* co-

complementary *comb* counter-

complete(ly) *pre* be-, cata-, cath-, de-, kata-, ob-, per-; *comb* holo-, omni-, pan-, panto-, stone-, toti-

compound interest *base* anatoc-

compound names *comb* tetrazo-; *suf* -ide, -ole[1]

comprehension *comb* -gnomy, -gnosia, -gnosis, -gnostic, gnoto-, ideo-, -noia, -nomy, -phrenic, phrenico-, phreno-, psycho-, -sophy; *base* -cogit-, -cogn-, epistem-, ment(a)-, -noe-, -put-, ratio-, -sci-

computer *comb* cyber-

concave *comb* concavo-

concealed *pre* sub-; *comb* calypto-, crypto-; *base* abdit-, cryph-, laten-, occult-

concept *comb* -gnomy, -gnosia, -gnosis, -gnostic, gnoto-, ideo-, -noia, -nomy, phreno-, psycho-, -sophy; *base* -cogit-, -cogn-, epistem-, -noe-, -put-, ratio-, -sci-

concise *comb* brachio-, brachisto-, brachy-, brevi-, chamae-, hekisto-, micro-, mini-, parvi-, parvo-, steno-, tapino-; *base* -cort-, -curt-, exig-; *suf* -cle, -cula, -cule, -culum, -culus, -een, -el, -ella, -en, -et, -ette, -idion, -idium, -ie, -illa, -illo, -isk, -kin, -le, -let, -ling, -ock, ola, -ole, -rel, -ula, -ule, ulum, -ulus, -y

conciliatory *base* ilast-

conclude *base* -fin-, termin-

conclusive *base* desit-

condensed *comb* brachio-, brachisto-, brachy-, brevi-, chamae-, hekisto-, micro-, mini-, parvi-, parvo-, steno-, tapino-; *base* -cort-, -curt-, exig-; *suf* -cle, -cula, -cule, culum, -culus, -een, -el, -ella, -en, -et, -ette, -idion, -idium, -ie, -illa, -illo, -isk, -le, -let, -ling, -ock, -ola, -ole, -rel, -ula, -ule, -ulum, -ulus, -y; ~ *thickened: base* -crass-

condition *suf* -able, -acity, -acy, -age, -ance, -ancy, -ant, -asis, -asm, -ate, -atile, -ation, -cy, -dom, -eity, -ence, -ency, -ent, -ery, -esis, -ful, -hood, -iasis, -ice[1], -ility, -ion, -ise, -ism, -ity, -ling[3], -ma, -ment, -ness, -or[3], -osis, -otic, -red, -ship, -sion, -sis, -th, -tion, -tude, -ture, -ty[1], -ure, -y[2]; *condition for:* base stipul-

conduct *behavior:* comb etho-; base hexi-; **lead:** comb –arch, -duce, -duct-, magist-; basenhegemon-, -reg-

conductor *base* -pomp-

cone *comb* coni-[2], conico-, cono-, conoido-; *pine ~:* strobil-

confer *base* -don-

conference *base* sympos-

configuration *comb* topo-

confine *comb* sphingo-, -strain, -strict, syndesmo-; *base* -liga-, -merinth-, -string-, -vinc-

conflict *comb* macho-, -machy; *base* -bell-, -pugil-, -pugn-; *base* collect-

confusion *comb* atax-, ataxi-, -ataxia, ataxio-, ataxo-; *base* misc-, tarass-, -turb-

conger *base* enchely-

congratulations *base* kud-

congruous *base* harmon-

connected (with) *base* anchi-, hirmo-, nex-; *suf* -ar[2], -arious, -ary, -id[1], -wise; *~ twins:* comb -pagia, -pagus; *connected structure:* base strom-

conquer *base* vict-, -vinc-

conscience-troubled *base* scrup-

consecrated *comb* hagio-, hiero-; *base* -sacr-, -sanct-

consequence *comb* ergo-, -ergic, -ergy; *suf* -age, -asm, -ata, -ation, -ency, -ism, -ma, -ment, -mony, -sion, -ure

consideration *base* phrontis-

consistent *comb* even-

constitution *comb* -ousia, -ousian; *base* quid-

constrained *comb* -bound

constriction *comb* lepto-, stegno-, steno-; *base* -stal-, sphingo-, -strict-, string-. *See* tightening

construction *comb* -craft, ergo-, -fic, -urgy; *base* -fabr-, -fac-, -fic-. *See* **make**

contagious *base* -tapin-

container *comb* angio-, asco-, bursi-, burso-, ceco-, chlamyd-, chrysali-, cisto-, coleo-, -cyst, cysti-, cysto-, follic-, meningo-, pericardiaco-, pericardio-, peritoneo-, phasco-, physa-, physali-, physo-, -theca, theci-, theco-, typhlo-, utri-, utric, vesico-; *base* -sacc-, -thylac-

containing *comb* -filled, pleni-, pleo-, pluri-; *base* -pler-, -plet-; *suf* -acious, -ate, -ic, -ful, -lent, -ose[2], -osity, -ous, -ulent, -y

contempt *base* fastid-

contentment *comb* chero-; *base* allubesc-, beati-, felic-, jubil-, macar-

contents (germinative) *comb* vitelli-, vitello-

contest *comb* -athlon, -athon, macho-, -machy, -off; *base* agon-

continent *base* -epeiro-

continual *base* aei-, assid-, contin-, incess-, perpet-

contorted *comb* contorto-, gyro-, helico-, pleco-, plecto-, spiro-, strepho-, strepsi-, strepto-; *base* -strob-, -stromb-, -stroph-, -tors-, -tort-

contraction *comb* -chorea , choreo-, -clonic, -clonus, -esmus, -ismus, spasmato-, spasmo-; *base* -stal-, systole-, vellic-

contrary *pre* anti-, cata-, contra-, contre-, contro-, cross-, dis-, hetero-, ob-, un-, with-; *comb* counter-, enantio-, oppositi-

control *base* magist-, maha-; *loss of ~:* comb -crasia

controversy *base* eris-

converge *comb* -ergasia, gameto-, gamo-, hapto-, junct-; *base* -aps-, -apt-, -greg-, -soc-; *suf* -ate, -ize

conversation *comb* -claim, logo-, -logue, -lalia, -lexia, lexico-, -lexis, -lexy, -logy, -phone, phono-, -phony, verbi-, verbo-, voc-, voci-, -voke; *base* -clam-, -dict-, -loc(u)-, -loqu-, -orat-, rhet-

convert *base* proselyt-

convex *comb* convexo-, gibboso-

cook *base* -coct-, mageir-, magir-; *cooked meat:* base opso-[2]

coot *base* fulic-, phalar-
copious *base* ampl-, copi-, largi-
copper *comb* chalco-, cupreo-, cupri-, cupro-, cuproso-; *base* auricalc-. *Also see* "Colors" *in Part III*
copy *base* -mim-
coracoid bone *comb* coraci-, coraco-
coral *comb* coralli-
cord *comb* -chorda, chord-, cordo-, funi-, tendo-; *base* cord-, resti-
core *comb* caryo-, karyo-, nucleo-
cork *comb* phello-; *base* suber-
cormorant *base* phalacrocorac-
corn *base* frument-, grani-; *ear of ~:* spici-
cornea *comb* corneo-, kerato-
cornice *comb* geisso-
corpse *comb* necro-; *base* -cadav-; *~ washing:* *base* pollinct-
corpulent *base* obes-, pingu-
correct(ion) *comb* ortho-; *base* castig-, corrig-, emend-
corresponding *comb* homolo-
corrosive *comb* -brotic
corruption *comb* lysi-, -lysis, lyso-, -lyte, -lytic, -lyze, phthino-, phthisio-, -phthisis, phthysio-, -phthysis, putri-, pyo-, pytho-, sapro-, septi-, septo-, septico-; *base* phthor-, vitia-; *moral ~:* *base* deprav-
cortex *comb* cortico-, pallio-
costly *base* dapat-, sumpt-
cost of *suf* -age
cotton *base* xilin-
couch *base* grabat-, klin-, lecti-[1], lectu-
cough *base* bech-, -tuss-
count *base* calcul-, -comput-, -num-; *counter:* *comb* pseph(o)-
counter *base* anthyp-
counterclockwise *comb* laevo-, levo-
counterfeit *comb* pseudo-
countless *comb* myrio-; *base* innum-
country *base* -rur-, -rustic-; *of a ~: suf* -ese, -ian; *~ names: comb* -land; *suf* -ia
coupled *comb* conjugato-
courtesan *comb* cypriano-, hetaero-, porno-; *base* -meretric-, scort-; *brothel:* lupan-
courtesy *base* -comit-
courtly *base* aul-[3]
cousin *base* -sobrin-

covenant *base* fedi-
cover(ed) with *pre* be-; *comb* calypto-, stegano-, stego-; *~ fine hairs: base* toment-; *~ with hairlike material: comb* villoso-
covering *comb* lamelli-, lepido-, squamo-, tecti-, tegu-, -theca, theco-, theci-, veli-; *base* involver-, lorica-, oper-[2], -scut-, strag-. *See* skin
covert *pre* sub-; *comb* crypto-; *base* clandest-, furt-
covetousness *base* avar-, cup(id)-, pleonec-, pleonex-
cow *base* bou-, bov-, bu-, -vacc-
cowardly *base* pav-, timid-, trep-
cowl *base* cuculli-
crab *comb* carcino- *base* cancr-, harpact-; *hermit ~:* pagur-; *sea ~:* gammar-
crack *comb* dicho-, -fid, fissi-, schisto-, schizo-, sulcato-, -tomy; *base* crev-, fatisc-, -par-, rim-
crackle *base* -crep-, -crepit-, strid-, stridul-
craft *base* techn-. *See* make
crafty *base* callid-
crane *comb* alector-, grallator-, grui-
crater *base* crateri-
craving *comb* eroto-, -lagnia, -mania, -orexia; *base* -appet-, conat-, -cup-, -libid-, -opt-, vell-; *suf* -urient
crawl *base* -rept-
crayfish *base* cambar-
crazy *comb* lysso-, -mania; *base* ament-, dement-
creak *base* -crep-, -crepit-, strid-, stridul-
creased *base* -rug-
create/creation *pre* be-, em-, en-, meta-, trans-; *comb* aetio-, -blast , -blastic, blasto-, -craft, ergo-, etio-, -facient, -fic, -fication, -gen, -genesis, -genic, -genous, -geny, ideo-, -parous, -plasia, -plasis, plasmo-, -plast, plastic, plasto-, -plasty, -poiesis, -poietic, -trope, -tropic, -tropism, tropo-, -tropous, -tropy, -urgy; *base* -fabr-, -fec-, -mut-, -vert-; *suf* -ate, -en, -fy, -ize, -otic
creep *base* -rept-
crescent *base* crescenti-, lunul-, menisc-
cress *base* cardam-
crest *comb* lophio-, lopho-; *base* coryth-, crist-

cricket *base* gryll-, locust-
crime *pre* dys-, mis-; *comb* caco-, enisso-,
enosio-, kak-, kako-, mal-, male-,
ponero-; *base* crimin-[1], culp-, delict-,
facin-, flagit-, hamart-, iniq-, nefar-,
pecca-, perdit-, -prav-, sceler-, scelest-,
turp-
crimson *base* cochin-
crisp *comb* ulo-[3]
criterion *base* criterio-
critical *comb* critico-, enisso-
crocodile *base* crocodil-, eusuch-,
-gavial-, sucho-
crooked *comb* ancylo-, ankylo-, -camp-
sis, campto-, campylo-, -clinal, -clinate,
-cline, -clinic, clino-, -clinous, -cli-
sis, curvi-, cypho-, cyrto-, -flect , flex-,
flexuoso-, lechrio-, loxo-, recurvo-,
repando-, scolio-, -tort, -verge; *base*
-clit-, -cliv-, sinu-
cross *comb* cruci-, stauro-
crosswise *comb* transverso-; *base* decuss-
crow *comb* coraci-, coraco-; *base* corvin-;
~'s **beak:** *base* coron-
crowd *comb* ochlo-
crown *base* corolli-, -coron-
cruel *base* agrio-, atroc-
crumbly *base* friabil-, psath-
crushing *comb* stip-[2], tribo-, -tripsy
crustacean genus *base* mysi
crust of the earth *base* tecton-
cry *tears:* *comb* dacryo-, fleb-, flet-,
lachrim(o)-, lachrym(o)-, -plor-; *call
out:* *comb* -claim; *base* -clam-, -plor-
crystal *comb* crystallo-; *crystalline compound:* phloro-
cube *comb* cubi-, cubo-; *base* tesser-
cuckoo *base* cucul-
cucumber *base* cucumi-
cudgel *base* fustig-, rhopal-
culpability *base* culp-, delinq-, laps-,
-pecca-, sphal-
cultivation *comb* –ponic; *base* agra-[1]
culture *comb* ethno-
cumulus *comb* cumulo-
cunning *base* daedal-, versut-

cup (-shaped) *comb* calath-, calyc-, cot-
yle-, cotyli-, cotylo-, cupuli-, cyathi-,
cyatho-, scyphi-, scypho-; *base* calic-,
canthar-, crin-, cyphell-, pocul-
curing *comb* -iatrics, -iatr(o)-, -iatry, med-
ico-; *base* cur-, san-
curl, curly *comb* cirrhi-, cirrho-, cirri-,
cirro-, ulo-[3]; *base* bostrych-, calamist-,
cincinn-, -crisp-. *See* **coil**
current *electrical:* *comb* rheo-; *water:*
comb fluvio-; *base* -potam-, rheum-,
-rip-; *contemporary:* *comb* co-, hama-;
base -simul-
curse *base* anathem-, exsec-
curtailed *comb* brachisto-, brachy-,
brevi-, chamae-, colo-, hekisto-, micro-,
mini-, parvi-, parvo-, steno-, tapino-;
base -curt-, exig-; *suf* -cle, -cula, -cule,
-een, -el, -ella, -en, -et, -ette, -idion,
-idium, -ie, -illa, -illo, -isk, kin, -le, -let,
-ling, -ock, -ola, -ole, -rel, -ula, -ule,
-ulum, -ulus, -y
curved *comb* ancylo-, ankylo-, -camp-
sis, campto-, campylo-, -clinal, -clinate,
-cline, -clinic, clino-, -clinous, -clisis,
curvi-, cyrto-, -flect, flex-, flexuoso-,
lechrio-, loxo-, recurvo-, repando-,
scolio-, -tort, -verge; *base* -clit-, -cliv-,
gryp-, sinu-
cushion *base* pulvin-, tylo-; *cushion stuffing:* *base* toment-
custom *base* mor-[1], nomo-, -suet-
customer *base* empt-
cut *comb* -cide, cis-[2], -cise, -ectomy,
incisi-, inciso-, -sect, temno-, -tme-
sis, -tome, tomo-, -tomous, -tomy; *base*
sec-, –scind, sciss-, trunc-
cutting *surgical:* *comb* -ectomy, -tome,
-tomy; *argument:* *base* trench-
cuttlefish *base* -teuth-, sepi(a)-
cyanogen *comb* cyano-
cycle *comb* cyclo-; *base* circul-, orb-
cylinder *comb* cylindro-
cypress *base* cupress-
cyst *base* sacc-

D

dagger *base* pugio-, sica-
daily *base* diurn-, ephem-, hemer-,
   hodiern-, journ-, quotid-
damaging *comb* noci-, pesti-; *base* laes-,
   les-, -nox-
damp *comb* hydro-, hygro-, udo-; *base*
   humect-, myda-, ulig-
dance *comb* choreo-; *base* ball-, orches-,
   orchest-, -salta-, terps-, tripud-
dandruff *base* furfur-, porrig-
danger *base* pericul-
Danish *comb* Dano-
dark(ness) *comb* ambly-, melan(o)-,
   nycto-, scoto-; *base* -achlu-, amaur-,
   fusc-, lyg-, obscur-, tenebr-
dart *base* tel-
dative *comb* dativo-
daughter *comb* fili-
daughter-in-law *base* -nur(us)-
dawn *base* -auror-, eos(o)-, luc-
day *base* diurn-, ephem-, hemer-,
   hodiern-, journ-, quotid-
daylight *base* -pheng-
deaf *base* coph-, -surd-
dealer *base* –pole
death *comb* mort(i)-, necro-, sapro-,
   thanato-; *base* exanim-, nerter-, obit-;
   deadly: funest-, leth-², phthart-
debauched *base* proflig-
debility *comb* astheno-, -atrophia, lepto-,
   -plegia, -plegy; *base* -debil-, dimin-,
   enerv-, flacc-, labe-
debris *base* chomo-
decaying *comb* cario-, lysi-, -lysis, lyso-,
   -lyte, phthino-, phthisio-, -phthi-
   sis, putre-, putri-, pytho-, sapro-,
   septi-, septico-, septo-; *base* marcesc-,
   phthor-, tabe-; *suf* -ase
deceptive *base* apat-, dolero-, dolos-, ,
   ludif-, perfid-
decide *base* crit-¹
decisive *base* perempt-
decks *comb* -decker
decline *comb* -atrophia; *base* degen-, dimin-
decomposed *comb* septi-², septico-,
   septo-¹; ~ *substance: comb* -lyte

decomposing enzyme *suf* -ase
decrease *base* decresc-, dimin-
decree *base* -imper-, juss-, -mand-
deep *comb* batho-, bathy-; *base* profund-;
   ~ *sea region* : *base* basal-
deer *base* cervi-, elaph-
default *base* defalc-
defeat *base* vict-, -vinc-
defecation *comb* -chezia, copro-, fim-,
   fimi-, kopro-, scato-, spatilo-, sterco-;
   base -fec(u)-
defect, bodily *comb* pero-; *base* -hamart-,
   -mutil-
defending *pre* pro-; *base* patroc-
defense *comb* -phylactic, phylacto-, -phy-
   lax, -phylaxis; ~ *feature: base* aposem-
deficiency *comb* isch-, oligo-, -penia
definition *comb* orismo-; *base* dior-;
   well-defined: comb delo-
deformed *comb* -cace, pero-; *base* -mutil-
degree *suf* -ency
dehydrogenated *comb* dehydro-
deity *comb* theo-; *base* dei-
dejected *comb* lype-, tapino-; *base* dolor-,
   fleb-, flet-, luct-, trist-
delayed *comb* brady-; *base* crastin-,
   -cunct-, dilat-², imped-, -mora-, -tard-.
   See **late**
delete *base* oblit-
deleterious *comb* noci-, pesti-; *base* -nox-,
   pericul-
delicate *comb* habro-, lepto-, subtil-,
   tenu-
delight *comb* chero-; *base* beati-, elat-,
   felic-, gaud-, jubil-, macar-
demanding *base* exig-
dementia *comb* lysso-, -mania; *base*
   ament-, dement-
demon *comb* daemono-, demono-; *base*
   diabol-, necyo-, satan-
demonstrating *comb* -deictic; *base*
   -monstr-
dense *comb* dasy-, pycno-, pykno-,
   -spiss-; *base* -crass-; ~ *tufts:* cespitoso-
dentate *comb* dentato-
deny *base* -neg-

deoxygenated *comb* deoxy-

depart *base* relinq-

deposit of soft materials *comb* athero-

depraved *pre* dys-, mis-; *comb* caco-, enisso-, enosio-, kak-, kako-, mal-, male-, ponero-; *base* culp-, facin-, flagit-, hamart-, iniq-, nefar-, pecca-, perdit-, -prav-, sceler-, scelest-, turp-

deprive of *pre* ab-, apo-, be-, de-, des-[1], di-, dia-, dif-, dis-, e-, ec-, ef-, ex-, for-, off-, se-, with-; *comb* ectro-; *base* -spol-

depth *comb* batho-, bathy-; *base* -byss-

deputy *comb* vice-

derivative of *pre* meta-, para-

descended from *comb* -gone, -gonium, gono-, -gony, proli-; *suf* -ing

description *comb* -graphy

desert *comb* eremo-

deserving of *comb* -worthy

designate *base* nuncup-

desire *comb* eroto-, -lagnia, -mania, -orexia; *base* -appet-, conat-, -cup-, desid-, -libid-, -opt-, vell-, vener-[1]; *suf* -urient

despot *base* despot-

destination *comb* teleo-, telo-, ultim(o)-; *base* -fin-, -termin-

destitute *comb* ptocho-, vidu-; *base* egent-, indig-, mendic-, -paup-, -pov-

destroying *comb* lysi-, lyso-, -lysis, -lytic, -lyze, -phage, phago-, -phagous, -phagy; *base* abol-, -ate-[4], perd-, perempt-, phthart-, -vast-

detach *base* abdic-, -scind-

determine *comb* -gnomy, -gnosia, -gnosis, -gnostic, gnoto-

detestation *comb* miso-, -phobe, -phobia, -phobic; *base* -invid-, -ira(sc)-, odi-

detrimental *comb* noci-, pesti-; *base* -nox-, pericul-

development *comb* -blast, -blastic, blasto-, -geny, -plasia, -plasis, -plast , -plastic, plasto-, -plasty, -trope, -tropism, tropo-, -tropous, -tropy; *base* -mut-, -vari-, -vert-; *late* ~: serot-; *stage of* ~: *base* stathmo-

deviate from the straight *base* lir-

device *electronic* ~: *comb* -tron, -tronic; *measuring* ~ *comb* -meter

devil *comb* demono-, necyo-, satan-; *base* -diabol-

devoid *comb* ceno-, keno-; *base* -erem-, (ex)haur-, inan-, -vac(u)-

devotion to, excessive *comb* -latry; *suf* -ism

devour *comb* bromato-, -brotic, manduc-, -phage, phago-, -phagous, -phagy, -sitia, sitio-, sito-, -troph, -trophic, tropho-, -trophy, -vora, -vore, -vorous; *base* -alim-, -cib-, comest-, -ed-, escul-, glutt-, -gust-

dew *comb* droso-, -ror-; *base* roscid-

diagonal *base* chias-

diaphragm *comb* phreni-, -phrenic, phrenico-, phreno-

dice *base* alea-, astragal-, clero-, cubo-; ~ **player:** *comb* -cubist

die *see* **death**

different *comb* hetero-

differentiate *base* crimin-[2]

difficult *pre* dys-; *comb* -bar, bary-, mogi-; *base* ardu-, probl-, stren-

dig *comb* orycto-; *base* fod-, -foss-

digest *comb* peps-, pept-, pepto-; *partially* ~: *comb* chymo-

digestive fluid *comb* chyli-, chylo-, chymo-

digitalis *comb* digito-

dignity *base* celsi-

dilation *comb* -ectasia, -ectasis

diligence *base* imprigrit-, sedul-

dill *base* aneth-

dimension *comb* -footer, -sized; ~ *of a sheet:* *suf* -mo; *having 3 dimensions:* *comb* stereo-. *Also see* "Dimension" in Part III

diminished *pre* demi-, hypo-, mis-, sub-, subter-; *comb* meio-, mini-, mio-, oligo-; *base* decresc-, dimin-, hesson-, -pauc-

diminution *suf* -aster[2]

diminutive ending *suf* -cle, -cula, -cule, -culum, -culus, -een, -el, -ella, -en, -et, -ette, -idion, -idium, -ie, -illa, -illo, -isk, kin, -le, -let, -ling[2], -ock, -ola, -ole[2], -rel, -ula, -ule -ulum, -ulus, -y[3]

dimness *comb* ambly-, melan(o)-, nycto-, scoto-; *base* -achlu-, amaur-, fusc-, homichlo-, lyg-, obscur-, opac-, tenebr-

dinner *comb* deipno-, prand-; *dining: base* arist-

dip *comb* -merge, -merse; *base* bapt-

directing *comb* -agogic, -agogue; *base* -vers-, -vert-

direction *comb*—ward, -ways, -wise; *suf* -ern, -ling[3]; ~ *east:* euro-, -orient-; ~ *north:* -borea, septen-; ~ *south:* -austr-, noto-; ~ *west:* hesper-, occid-, -zephyr-; *strategic ~: base* strat-. *Also see* "Direction" *in Part III*

dirge *base* myrio-

dirt *comb* blenno-, -chezia, copro-, edaph-, fim(i)-, kopro-, miso-[2], myso-, -myxia, myxo-, paedo-[1], pedo-[3], scato-, spatilo-, spurc-, stegno-, sterco-; *base* -fecu-, gleb-, hum-, macul-, molys-, rhypar-, rhypo-, rypo-, sord-

disastrous *base* funest-

discerning *comb* -gnomy, -gnosia, -gnosis, -gnostic; *base* -crit-, -judic-, sagac-, -soph-

discharge *flow: comb* rheo-, rheum-, -(r)rhage, -(r)rhagia, -(r)rhea, -(r)rhoea, -(r)rhoeica; *base* excern-, -flu(v)-, -fus-; *release: base* -miss-, -mit-, -pomp-

discipline *comb* mastigo-, rhabdo-; *base* castig-, peno-, poine-, -pun-

discontinue *comb* stasi-, -stasis, -stat; *base* fin-, termin-

discourse *comb* -claim, logo-, -logue, -lalia, -lexia, lexico-, -lexis, -lexy, -logy, -phone, phono-, -phony, verbi-, verbo-, voc-, voci-, -voke; *base* -clam-, -dict-, -loc(u)-, -loqu-, -orat-, rhet-; *defective~: comb* -lalia, lalo-, -phasia, -phasic, -phasis, -phasy, -phemia, -phemy; *base* psell-

discover *base* heur-

disease *pre* dys-, mal-; *comb* -cace, loemo-, loimo-, noso-, -path, -pathic, patho-,-pathy; *base* aegr-, -morb-, -pecca-; ~ *names: comb* -aemia, -emia; *suf* -asis, -ia, -itis, -oma, -osis; *skin ~:* derm-, licheno-; ~ *treatment: comb* -iatrics, iatro-, -iatry. *See* **disorder**

disfigured *comb* pero-; *base* -mutil-

disgorge *comb* -emesis, -emetic, emeto-

disgrace *base* sord-, turp-

disgust *base* abom-, fastid-

dish *comb* lecano-; *base* -leco-, scutel-

disk-shaped *comb* disco-; *base* -numm-

dislocate *base* –lux-

dismembered *base* artuat-

disorder *comb* atax-, ataxi-, -ataxia, ataxio-, ataxo-, -thymia, -phrenia, -phrenic; *base* -turb-; *of personality ~: comb* -tonia; *speech ~: comb* -lalia

disparage *base* derog-

dispersion *base* diaspora

display *comb* -orama, phaeno-, pheno-; *base* -monstr-

disposed *comb* -phile, -philic, -philism, philo-, -philous

disposition *base* habitud-

dispute *base* altercat-, velit-

disrespectful *base* derog-

disseminate *base* promulg-

dissimilar *comb* aniso-, anomalo-, anomo-, perisso-, poikilo-

dissolve *comb* lyo-, lysi-, -lysis, lyso-, -lyte, -lytic, -lyze; *base* -liqu-, -solu-, -solv-

distant *comb* disto-, tele-

distension *comb* -cele, -edema, ganglio-, phlogo-, phym-, -phyma, physa-, physo-, strum(i)-; *base* aug-, cresc-, physc-, strum-, -tum-, -turg-; *suf* -itis

distinct *separate: pre* dia-, dis-, for-, se-; *comb* -crit, dialy-, ideo-, proprio-, self-; ~ *unit: base* tagm-; ~ *animals: comb* -zooid. *See* **divided.** *clear: comb* lampro-, luc-, luci-; *base* -clar-

distinction *base* crimin-[2], dior-

distress *base* aerumn-, miser-, perturb-, vex-

disturb *base* perturb-, -turb-

divalent sulfur *comb* sulfo-

divergent *comb* divergenti-, divergi-, vari-; *base* aberr-, avoc-

divest *base* -priv-[2]

divide(d) *pre* sub-; *comb* dicho-, -fid, fissi-, parti-, schisto-, schizo-, tomo-, -tomous, -tomy; *base* sciss-; ~ *crosswise:* decuss-

dividing wall *comb* sept(o)-[2]

divination *comb* -mancy, -mantic; *base* augur-, hariol-, harusp-, vatic-. *Also see* "Divination" *in Part III*

divinely inspired *base* enth-
dizziness *comb* dino-[2]; *base* vertig-
do *pre* em-, en-; *comb* -craft, ergo-,
 -facient, -fic, -fication, -gen, -genesis,
 -genic, -genous, -geny, ideo-, -plast,
 -plastic, plasto-, -plasty, poiesis, -poi-
 etic,-urgy; *base* -fabr-, -fac-, -fec-[1]; *suf*
 -ate, -en, -fy, -ize
docile *base* moriger-
docked tail *base* colob-
doctor *comb* iatro-; *base* -med-
doctrine *suf* -ism, -logy
dodo *base* did-
doer *suf* -an, -ant, -ard, -arian, -art, -ary,
 -ast, -ator, -ee, eer, -en, -ent, -er, -ette,
 -ier, -ist, -le, -man, -nik, -o, -or, -person,
 -people, -ster, -woman
dog *comb* cyno-, kyno; *base* -can-[1]
dogma *comb* dogmato-
dog-star *base* canicul-
doleful *comb* lype-; *base* dolor-, fleb-,
 flet-, luct-, trist-
doll *comb* paedo-[2]
dolphin *base* delphin-
domain of *suf* -dom[2]
donkey *base* as-, ono-
door *comb* osti-, porto-; *base* valv-
dormouse *base* glir-, myox-
dorsum *comb* dorsi-, dorso-, nota-, noto-,
 opistho-; *base* -terg-
dose *comb* dosio-, poso-
dotted *comb* punctato-; *base* -stigm-
double *pre* bi-, bin-, bis-, di-[1], dy-, twi-;
 comb ambi-, ambo-, amphi-, ampho-,
 deutero-, deuto-, dicho-, diphy-, diplo-,
 disso-, double-, dui-, duo-, duplicato-,
 duplici-, dyo-, gemin-, zygo-. *Also see*
 "Numbers" in Part III
doubtful *base* ambig-, ancip-, apor-, dub-,
 –skeps, -skept , vagu-
dove *base* columb-; *turtle-dove:* base turtur-
down (from) *pre* a-, ab-, abs-, cata-, cath-,
 de-, kata-; *base* decliv-; *soft hair:* base
 lanug-; *plant down:* base papp-
downcast *comb* lype-; *base* dolor-, fleb-,
 flet, luct-, -trist-
dowry *base* dot-, dotal-
dozen *comb* dodeca-, duodec-, duo-
 decim-, duoden-
dragon *base* draco-, draconi-

dragonfly *base* libell(ul)-
drain *base* haur-, haust
draw *art:* comb -gram, graph(o)-, -pict-;
 pull: *base* -duct, ductil-, helc-, -tract-; ~
 forth: *base* -haur-, -haust-
dread *comb* -phobe, -phobia, -phobic,
 phobo-; *base* abhor-, pavid-, tim(or)-,
 trem-, trep-. *Also see* "Fear" in Part III
dreadfulness *base* dirit-
dream *comb* oneiro-
dregs *base* faecul-, fec-[2], fecul-
dress *base* hestho-
drink *comb* pino-, posi-, poto-; *base* -bib-,
 pocul-; ~ ***made from ___ :*** *suf* -ade
dripping *base* driri, stalac(ti)-, stalag-
drive *base* azal-, -pel-, -pul-
driving away, out *comb* –fuge; *base* abig-
drooping *comb* -ptosia, -ptosis; *base*
 -flacc-. *See* **bent**
drop *liquid:* comb gutti-, stilli-; *base*
 stact-, stagm-; *fall:* comb -ptosia, -pto-
 sis; *base* -cad-, -cas-, -cid-
dropping *base* stalac-, stalag-
drugs *comb* pharmaco-; *base* medic-
drum *comb* tympano-
drunk *base* crapul-, ebriet-, inebr-,
 methys-, temul-
dry *comb* carpho-, krauro-, xero-; *base*
 arid-, celo-[2], cherso-, desicc-, -sicc-, torr-
dry out *base* marces-, marcid-
duck *base* anat-, fuligul-
ductile *base* elat-[2]
dull *base* hebet-, obtus-, -tard-; ~ ***vision:***
 comb ambly-
dung *comb* -chezia, copro-, fimi-, kopro-,
 scato-, spatilo-, sterc(o)-; *base* -fec(u)-,
 -merd-, scor-; ~ ***hill:*** sterquil-
duplex *comb* duplici-
during *pre* con-, in-, inter-, per-
dusk *base* -crepus-, lyg-
dusky *comb* fusc-, fusco-, -phaein, phaeo-,
 phein-, pheo-; *base* zopher-
dust *comb* coni-[1], -conia, conio-, konio-;
 base amath-, pulver-; *dusty place:*
 conist-
duty *comb* hypegia, hypengy-; *base*
 paralip-
dwarf *comb* chamae-, nan(n)o-, *base* gnom-[3]
dwelling *comb* ekist-; *base* -aed-, -cali-,
 -dom-, -edi-; *base* habitat-; *suf* –age

E

each *comb* katheno-
eager *base* avid-, cupid-
eagle *base* aet-, aquil-
ear *comb* auri-[1], auriculo-, oto-. *See* **sound**
early *pre* ante-, pre-; *comb* prim-, primi-,
  primo-, proto-; ~ *period: pre* eo-; *comb*
  paleo-, protero-; *earlier: comb* protero-
earnings *base* salar-
earth *comb* agri-, agro-, -gaea, -gea, geo-,
  hum-; *base* -cthon-, secul-, tellur-, -terr-
earthquake *comb* -seism, -seismal,
  seismo-, tromo-
earwig *base* forficul-
east *base* euro-, -orient-
easy *base* -facil-
eating *comb* bromato-, -brotic, man-
  duc-, -phage, -phagia, phago-, -pha-
  gous, -phagy, -sitia, sitio-, sito-, -troph,
  -trophic, tropho-, -trophy, -vora, -vore,
  -vorous; *base* -alim-, -cib-, comest-,
  -ed-[1], escul-, glutt-, -gust-. ~ *disorder:*
  bulim-; ~ *oriented:* edacit- *See* "Eating
  Habits" in Section III
ebony *base* eben-
eccentric *comb* aetheo-, anom(o)-, anom-
  alo-. *See* **irregular**
educate *comb* -pedia; *base* -didact-, doc-,
  -paed-
eel *base* anguill-, -cyclostom-, enchely-,
  -muraen-
effect *comb* -ergy
effectual *base* telesi-
effervesce *base* petill-
efficient *base* efficac-, habil-, quali-
effort *base* conat-, peir-, stren-
egg *comb* oo-, ovario-, ovi-[1], ovo-; ~ *yolk:*
  lecith-, lecitho-, vitell-; ~ *shaped:*
  ovato-
Egyptian *comb* Egypto-
eight *comb* octa-, octo-, ogdo-; ~ *hundred:* octocent-. *Also see* "Numbers" in
  Part III
eighteen *comb* duodeviginti-,
  octakaideca-
eighth *base* octan-
eighty *base* octogen-, octoges-

eland *base* taurotrag-
elastic *base* elat-[2]
elation *base* jubil-
elbow *base* -ancon-, olecran-
elderly *comb* gerasco-, gero-, geronto-,
  grand-, presby-, presbyter-; *base*
  -antiqu-, -sen-, -vet-; ~ *woman:* grao-
elder tree *base* sambuc-[1]
electric(al) *comb* electro-, galvano-; ~
  induction: comb inducto-
electric ray-fish *base* torp-
elementary *base* prim-, -rud-; ~ *particle:*
  comb stoichio-; *suf* -on
elephant *base* elephant-, pachyderm-
elevation *comb* acro-, alti-, alto-, bato-,
  hypsi-, hypso-; *base* buno-, procer-;
  elevated swelling: base torul-
eleven *comb* endeca-, hendeca-, undeca-,
  undecim-. *Also see* "Numbers" in Part
  III
elk *base* cerv-
ellipse *base* elleips-
elm *base* ulm-
eloquent *base* fecund-
emaciated *base* tab-. *See* **wasting away**
emanation *comb* atmo-, -capnia, capno-,
  vapo-, vapori-; *base* nebul-, probol-
embarrassment *base* pud-, verecund-
embezzle *base* pecul-
emboss(ed) *base* caelat-, toreut-
embryo(nic) *comb* -blast, -blastic,
  blasto-, -blasty; *base* cyem-, embry-
emendation *comb* ortho-; *base* castig-,
  emend-
emerald *base* smaragd-
eminent *comb* celsi-, over-
emit *base* -ruct-
emotions *comb* thymo-; *disordered* ~:
  -thymia. *Also see* "Emotional States" in
  Part III.
empty *comb* ceno-[3], keno-; *base* -erem-,
  (ex)haur-, inan-, -vac(u)-
emu- *base* rat-
emulation *base* zelo-
enamel *comb* amelo-
encircling *comb* zoni-, zono-

encounter *base* congress-, congru-
encourage *base* -hort-
end *comb* teleo-, telo-, ultim-, ultimo-; *base* -fin-, -termin-; **endless:** apeiro-
endive *base* intubac-, intib-
endowment *base* dot-
enduring *base* diuturn-, dur(o)-, perenn-, perm-, stabil-
enema *comb* -clysis; *base* chalast-, clysm-; clyst-
enemy *base* advers-, hostil-, inimic-
energy *comb* dyna(mo)-
engage in *suf* -ize
English *comb* Anglo-
engrave *comb* -glyph, glypto-; *base* caelat-
enigmatic *comb* enigmatico-
enjoyment *base* apolaust-
enlarged *pre* ad-, extra-, hyper-, super-; *comb* auxano-, auxo-, multi-, myria-, myrio-, out-, over-, -plasia, pleni-, pleo-, pleio-, pleon-, plethys-, plio-, pluri-, pollaki-, poly-; *base* ampl-, -aug-, -cresc-, dilat-, -fold-, pler-, -plet-; *abnormally* ~: *comb* megalo-, -megaly; ~ *vein:* *comb* cirso-
enormous *comb* bronto-, dino-, giganto-, mega-, megalo-, -megaly; *base* koloss-, mass-, vastit-
enter *comb* -dyte-, intro-; *base* ingress-, init-
enthusiasm *base* ard-, alacr-, -ferv-, zelo-
entice *base* lenocin-
entire(ly) *pre* be-, cata-, de-, kata-, ob-, per-; *comb* holo-, omni-, pan-, panto-, stone-, toti-
entrance *comb* porto-
entreaty *base* litan-, -preca-
enveloped *pre* be-; *comb* calypto-, stegano-, stego-
environment *comb* -cole, -colent, -colous, eco-, oeco-, oiko-; *base* -aed-, -dom-, -edi-
envy *base* -invid-
enzymes *comb* zym-, zymo-; *suf* -ase
epidemic *base* luet-, morb-, pestil-
epoch *comb* -cene
eponym *base* eponym-
equal(ly) *pre* co-; *comb* equi-, homalo-, homo-, homolo-, iso-, pari-, tauto-; *almost* ~: *comb* pariso-

equipped *base* habil-
equivalent *pre* para-, quasi-; *comb* homeo-, omœo, homoio-, homolo-, iso-, -phane, -phanic; *base* simil-; *suf* -acean, -aceous, -al, -an, -ar, -ary, -ean, -en, -eous, -esque, -ful, -ic, -il, -ile, -ine, -ing, -ish, -itious, -ize, -like, -ode, -oid, -ose, -osity, -some, -tious, -ular, -y
eradicate *base* abol-
erase *base* litur-, oblit-
erect *comb* ithy-, ortho-, recti-; *base* ard-[3]
ermine *base* mustel-
error *base* culp-, delinq-, laps-, pecc-, sphal-
eruption *comb* -anthema
erythrocyte *comb* erythro-
essence *base* -ousia, -ousian, quid-
estimate *base* stoicheio-
eternal *comb* ever-; *base* aeon-, eon-, etern-, perpet-, semper-
ethers *suf* -ole
ethical *comb* ethico-
ethmoid bone *comb* ethmo-
European *comb* Euro-, Europaeo-, Europeo-
eustachian tube *comb* salpingo-
evaluation *base* ader-
even *level:* *comb* homalo-, homolo-, plani-, plano-, plate-, platy-; *number:* artio-. *See* **equal**
evening *comb* -noct(i)-, nyct(o)-; *base* crepus-, -vesper-
event *comb* -athlon, -athon, -machy, -off. *See* **festival**
evergreen shrub *base* ephed-
everlasting *base* aei-, assid-, contin-, incess-, perpet-
every *comb* katheno-, omni-, pan-, pant(o)-
evil *pre* dys-, mis-; *comb* caco-, iniq-, kaki-, kako-, -mal(e)-, ponero-; *base* -prav-, sceler-, turp-
evolution *comb* -genesis. *See* **creation**
exact *base* precis-
examination *comb* -opsy, -scope, -scopic, scopo-, -scopy; *base* -(in)quir-, -(in)quis-, probat-, -scrut-
example of *comb* -type; *suf* -ism
excessive *pre* hyper-, super-, ultra-; *base* nim-, pleth-; *comb* over-, poly-; ~

craving: comb -lagnia, -mania; *~ devotion: comb* -latry; *suf* -ism; *~ drinking and eating: base* crapul-, popin-; *~ flow: comb* -(r)rhagia, -(r)rhage, -(r)rhagy

exchange *base* -allac-, -allag-, -allaxis-, camb-

excision *comb* -(ec)tomy

excite *comb* agito-; *base* -cit-; *excitability: comb* bathmo-

exclaim *base* clam-, epiphonem-, vocif-

exclude *pre* ab-, apo-, be-, de-, des-, di-, dia-, dif-, dis-, e-, ec-, ef-, ex-, for-, off-, se-, with-; *comb* ectro-; *base* -spol-

excrement *comb* -chezia, copro-, fimi-, kopro-, scato-, spatilo-, sterco-; *base* caca-, -fec(u)-, -merd-

exertion *comb* –ergasia, ergasio-, -ergoc, ergo-, -ergy, -orial, -pragia, -praxia, -praxis; *suf* –esce, -escence, -escent, -esis; *quality of ~: comb* -pragia

exhaustion *comb* pono-; *base* -fatig-, -kopo-, -lass-

exhibit *comb* phaeno-, pheno-; *base* -monstr-

existence *comb* onto-; *base* -esse-

exit *base* egress-, relinq-

expansion *comb* -ectasia, -ectasis; *base* -dilat-

expensive *base* sumpt-

experienced *base* empiric-, -vet-

experiment *base* peir-

expert *comb* -logist. *Also see* "Experts" in Part III

expiatory *base* piac-

expunge *base* delet-

extended *comb* dolicho-, -footer, longi-, macro-, maxi-; *base* porrect-, procer-; *~ words:* sesquipedal-

extent *comb* quant(i)-; *base* lat-[1]; *suf* -age, -ful, -ling[3]

external *comb* ect(o)-, exo-, extra-

extinct mammal form *comb* -there, therio-, thero-

extol *base* laud-

extra *pre* hyper-, super-. *See* **increased**

extremity *comb* acro-, aorto-, -mele, -melia[1], melo-[3]

exultation *comb* chero-; *base* beati-, felic-, jubil-, macar-, tripud-

eye *comb* eid(o)-, oculi-, oculo-, op-, ophthalmo-, -opia, opsi-, -opsia, -opsis, opso-[2], -opsy, optico-, opto-, -scope, -scopic, -scopy; *base* blep-, ommat-, -spec-, -spic-, -vid-, -vis-; *cornea of ~: comb* corneo-, kerato-; *corner of ~:* canth(o)-; *~ covering:* sclero-; *~ defect: base* albug-, astigm-; *eyeball:* glen; *iris of~:* irido-; *~lash:* cili-; *~ lid:* blepharo-, palpebra-, tarso-; *one-eyed:* lusc-; *pupil of ~:* core(o)-, -coria, coro-, -koria, pupillo-; *~ retina:* retino- *See* "Body" in Part III

eyebrows *base* ophry-; *space between ~:* glabello-

eyelet *comb* ocelli-

F

fabricate/fabrication *pre* be-; *comb* -craft, ergo-, -facient, fic-, -fication, -plastic, -plast, plasto-, -plasty, -poiesis, -poietic, -urgy; *base* aedi-, edi-, -fabr-, -fac-, -fec-; *suf* -ate, -fy, -ize

face *comb* facio-, prosop(o)-, -visaged; *base* vult-

faceted *comb* -hedral, -hedron

faction *base* factios-

fact of being *suf* -cy, -ency

faded *base* -marc-

fail(ure) *pre* dis-; *base* atychi-, kakorrhaph-

fainting *base* asthen-

faith *comb* -ousia; *base* -cred-, -fid-[1], -pist-; *suf* -ism

fake *See* **false**

falcon *base* accipit-, falconi-, raptor-

fall *base* -autumn-

falling *comb* -ptosia, -ptosis; *base* -cad-, -cas-, -cid-, decid-, laps-

fallopian tube *comb* salpingo-

false *comb* mytho-, pseudo-; *base* fict-, kibdelo-, -mendac-, notho-, spur-
fame/famous *base* celebr-, laud-, -lustr-
family *base* cogn-, famil-, stirp-
family names [zoology] *suf* -idae
famine *comb* limo-²
fan *base* rhipi-; ~ *like:* flabelli-, rhipido-
fantastic *base* chim-
far *comb* disto-, tele-
farewell *base* vale-
farming *base* agricol-, agricult-, arat-
fascia *comb* fascio-
fasciole *base* semit-
fast *comb* ocy-, tacho-, tachy-; *base* alacr-, -celer-, veloc-
fasten *base* -hapto-², -nect-, pegm-; ~ *one who:* comb colleto-. *See* **bind**
fasting *comb* limo-²
fat *comb* adip(o)-, lipo-¹, pimel(o)-, pio-, stearo-, steato-; *base* aletud-, -aliph-, lipar-, -obes-, -pingu-, sebo-; ~ *degeneration:* comb -demia
fatal *base* funest-, phthart-
fate *base* karm-
father *comb* pater-, patri-
father-in-law *base* socer-
fatigue *comb* pono-; *base* -fatig-, -kopo-, lass-
fattening *base* sagin-
fault *base* culp-, delinq-, laps-, -pecca-, sphal-
fear *comb* -phobe, -phobia, -phobic, phobo-; *base* pavid-, tim(or)-, -trem-, -trep-. *Also see* "Fear" in Part III
feast *base* dap-, epul-
feast day *base* heort-; *suf* -fest, -ia, -mas
feather(like) *comb* penni-, pennati-, pinnati-, pinnato-, pinni-, plum(i)-, pteno-, pter, ptero-, pterono-, -pterous, pterygo-, -pteryl, ptilo-; *wing ~; comb* pterono-. *See* **wing**
feces *comb* -chezia, copro-, fim(i)-, kopro-, scato-, spatilo-, sterco-; *base* -fec(u)-, -merd-, scor-
feeble *comb* astheno-, -atrophia, lepto-, -plegia, -plegy; *base* -debil-, dimin-, enerv-, flacc-, labe-
feeding on *comb* bromato-, -brotic, manduc-, -phage, phago-, -phagous, -phagy, -sitia, sitio-, sito-, -troph, -trophic,

tropho-, -trophy, -vora, -vore, -vorous; *base* -alim-, -bosc-, -cib-, -gust-
feel *comb* -aphia, -apsia, hapt(o)-, -path, -pathic, patho-, -pathy, sensi-, senso-, sensori-, thigmo-; *base* -palp-, -sens-, -sent-, -tact-, -tang-
feet long *comb* -foot(er)
feign *comb* pseudo-; *base* -simula-
felicity *comb* chero-; *base* beati-, felic-, jubil-, macar-
female *comb* gyn(e)-, gyneco-, gyneo-, gyno-, -gynous, -gyny, -para, she-, thely-, -wife, -woman; *base* femin-, muliebr-, mulier-; *suf* -a⁴, -en, enne, -ess, -ette, -ice², -ine, -stress, -trice, -trix; *elderly ~:* grao-
fence *comb* -phragma, phragmo-; *base* sepi-²
ferment *social: base* -agit-, -tumult-, -turb-
fermentation *comb* zym(o)-
fern *comb* pterido-; *base* filic-, lygod-
ferret *base* mustel-, viverr-
ferric iron *comb* ferri-
fervor *base* ard-, alacr-, -ferv-, zelo-
festival (names) *comb* -athon, -fest , -mas; *base* -heort-; *suf* -ia
fetish *comb* -lagnia
fetus *comb* brepho-, cyo-, embryo-, kyo-; ~ *membrane: comb* allanto-, amnio-
fever *comb* febri-, pyreto-, -pyrexia
few *comb* oligo-; *base* pauc(i)-
fiber *base* erio-, fibri-, funi-, ino-
fibril-shaped *comb* fibrilloso-
fibrin *comb* fibrino-
fibrous matter *comb* fibro-, fibroso-, funi-, strom-; ~ *growth:* ino-; ~ *tissue:* fascio-
fibula *base* peroneo-
fictitious *comb* mytho-, pseudo-; *base* fict-, kibdelo-, -mendac-, notho-
fiddle *base* pandur-
field *comb* agri-, agro-; *base* agrest-, camp-¹
fierce *base* efferit-, ferit-, feroc-, gorg-, labro-, torv-
fifteen *base* pentakaideca-, quindec-. *Also see* "Numbers" in Part III
fifth *comb* quint-²
fifty *base* pentaconta-, pentacosta-, quinquagen-, quinquages-

fig *base* -fici-, -syc-
fight *comb* macho-, -machy, pugn-; *base* -bell-, pugil-
figurative *comb* tropo-
figure *comb* icono-, -form; *base* schem-; ~ *with (x) angles:* -gon; ~ *with (x) surfaces:* -hedral, -hedron
filament *comb* fili-, filio-, filamento-, filo-, mito-, nemato-; *base* stema-
filled with *comb* -filled, plen(i)-; *base* -pler-, -plet-; *suf* -acious, -ate, -ic, -id², -ful, -ose, -osity, -ous, -ulent, -y
filter *base* col-²
filth *comb* blenno-, -chezia, copro-, fim(i)-, kopro-, miso-, myso-, -myxia, myxo-, paedo-, pedo-, rhyparo-, rhypo-, scato-, spatilo-, spurc-, stegno-, sterco-; *base* coen-², -fec-², molys-, rhypar-, rupo-, rypo-, sord-; *filthy talk:* borbor-²
fin *comb* pinni-, pterygo-
final stage *comb* eschato-, teleio-, teleo-, telo-, ultim(o)-; *base* desit-, -fin-, -termin-
finch *base* fringill-
find *base* heur-
fine *delicate:* *comb* habro-, lepti-, lepto-, subtil-, tenu-; *monetary:* *base* mulc-, mult-
finger *comb* -dactyl, dactylo-, -dactylous, -dactyly, digiti-; ~ *like:* *comb* digitato-; ~ *ring:* *comb* dactylio-
fingernail *comb* -onychia, onycho-
finishing touch *base* koloph-
Finnish *comb* Finno-
fir *base* abiet-
fire *comb* igneo-, igni-, pyr(o)-; *base* ard-, ars-, flagr-, flamm-, incend-, phlog-
fired pigment or glaze *base* encaust-
firefly *base* lampyr-
firm *comb* duro-, sclero-; *base* krato-
first *comb* arch-, fore-, pre-, primi-, primo-, pro-, proso-, protero-, proto-; *base* -princip-
fish(like) *comb* icthyo-, pisci-; *bony~:* scopeli; *electric ray-fish:* *base* torp-; *hammer ~:* *base* sphyraen-; *sea ~:* *base* cichlo-
fishing *base* halieut-, riv-; ~ *net:* *base* sagen-

fissure *comb* chasmo-, fissuri-, rim-
fist *base* pug-, pygm-
fit *seizure:* *comb* -agra, -lepsia, -lepsis, -lepsy, -leptic; *capable:* *comb* -worthy; *suf* -able, -ibility, -ible, -ile
five *comb* cinque-, penta-, quin-, quinque-, quint(i)-; ~ *hundred:* quincent-. *Also see* "Numbers" in Part III
fixation *comb* -lagnia, -philia; *surgical ~:* -pexy
fixed *comb* stasi-, -stasis, -stat, stato-; *base* stabil-
flag *comb* vexillo-
flamingo *base* phoenicopter-
flammable *comb* ard-, ars-
flank *comb* laparo-
flash *comb* sela-; *base* corrusc-, -fulg-, stilpno-
flask *base* ampul-, lagen-, lecyth-
flat *comb* plain-, plani-, plano-¹, plat-¹, platy-; ~ *plain:* pedion-
flattery *base* adul-, bland-
flatulence *comb* physa-
flavin *comb* -flavin, flavo-
flaw *base* culp-, delinq-, laps-, pecc-, sphal-
flax *comb* byssi-, linar-; *base* lino-
flea *base* psyll-², puli-
flee *base* avers-, drapeto-, fug-, -phygo-
flesh *comb* carni-, carnoso-, creo-, kreo-, -sarc, sarco-. *See* **skin**
flexible *base* agil-, facil-, ingen-
flight *comb* avi; *base* -fug-. *See* **flying**
fling *comb* -bole, -bolic, bolo-, -boly; *base* ballist-, -jact-, -jacula-, -ject-
flipper *comb* pinni-, pterygo-
flock *base* -greg-
flog *comb* -cuss-, plessi-, rhabdo-; *base* -cop-, -crot, fustig-, plang-, puls-, quass-, vapul-, -verber-
flood *base* -antlo-, diluv-, inund-; ~ *tide:* plemyr-
floor *soilbed:* *base* edaph-
flora *comb* botano-, herbi-, -phyte, phyto-; *base* veget-; *suf* -aceae, -ad, -ales, -eae, -ia
flounder *fish:* *base* hippogloss
flour *comb* aleuro-; *base* farin-
flower *comb* -antherous, antho-, -anthous, flori-, -florous; ~ *garland:* *base* corolli-

flow(ing) *comb* rheo-, rheum-, -(r)rhage, -(r)rhagia, -(r)rhea, -(r)rhoea, -(r)rhoeica; *base* -flu(v)-, fluxil-, -fus-
fluent *base* volub-
fluid *comb* -plasm, plasmo-; *base* -liqu-, -ner-
fluorescence *comb* fluo(ro)-
fluorine *comb* fluo-, fluor(o)-
flute *comb* aulo-; *base* aul-², tibicin-
fly *insect: base* cyclorraph-, musc-¹, myia-, tany-
flying *comb* aero-, avia-, avio-, aviono-; *base* volit-. *See* **wing**
foam *base* aphro-, -spum-
focused on *comb* -centered, -centric
fodder *base* pabul-
foe *base* advers-, hostil-, inimic-
fog *comb* fracto-, nephelo-, nepho-; *base* brum-², calig-, homichlo-, nebul-, -nub-
fold *comb* -plex, plicato-, plici-, -ptych; *base* ptyg-
follow(ing) *pre* epi-, meta-, post-; *comb* after-, hind-, postero-; *base* -secut-, -sequ-; *suf* -an; *follower base* discip-
folly *see* **foolish**
food *comb* bromato-, -brotic, manduc-, opso-, -phage, phago-, -phagous, -phagy, psomo-, -sitia, sitio-, sito-, -troph, -trophic, tropho-, -trophy, -vora, -vore, -vorous; *base* -alim-, -cib-, dap-, escul-, -gust-, -nutr-; *partially digested* ~: chymo-. *Also see* "Food" and "Eating Habits" in Part III.
foolish *base* fatu-, inan-, moro-, stult-
foot *comb* ped-¹, pedati-, -pede, pedi-, pedo-¹, -poda, -pode,-podium, -pod, podo-, -podous, -pus *base* -plant-; ~ *sole:* -pelm-, plant-
footprint *comb* ichno-, stibo-
for *pre* pro-
forbid *base* prohib-
force *comb* dyna-, dynamo-, mega-, megalo-, -megaly, -sthenia, stheno-; *base* angar-, -forc-, -fort-, -poten-, robor-
forceps *base* labido-
forearm *comb* ulno-
forecast *base* prognos-
forehead *comb* metopo-
foreign(er) *comb* perisso-, xeno-; *base* adven-, -ali-

foreknowledge *base* prognos-
foremost *comb* arch-, archi-, proto-; *base* -prim-, -princip-
forest *comb* dendri-, dendro-, -dendron, hylaeo-, saltu-, silvi-, xylo-; *base* arbor-, nemo(r), -sylv-
forever *comb* ever-; *base* etern-, perpet-, semper-
forget *base* amnes-, leth-; *forgotten: base* obliv-
forked *base* -furc-
form, a *comb* eid(o)-, -form, -morph, -morphic, -morphism, morpho-, -morphous; *base* -figur-, -schem-
form, to *pre* be-; *comb* aetio-, etio-; *base* -fabr-, fac-, fec-, fic-; *formed like: suf* -ular
formation *pre* em-, en-, meta-, trans-; *comb* -blast, -blastic, blasto-, -craft, ergo-, etio-, -facient, -fic, -fication, -gen, -genesis, -genic, -genous, -geny, -gone, -gonium, gono-, -gony, -parous, -plasia, -plasis, plasmo-, -plast, -plastic, plasto-, -plasty, -poiesis, -poietic, -trope, -tropic, -tropism, tropo-, -tropous, -tropy, -urgy; *base* -fec-, -mut-, -vert-; *suf* -ate, -en, -fy, -ize, -otic
former *comb* ex-, protero-
fornicate *base* copul-, scort-, stupr-
fortification *base* castella-
fortune *luck: comb* tycho-; *base* faust-; *wealth: comb* pluto-; *base* opul-
forty *base* quadragen-, quadrages-
forward *pre* fore-, pre-, pro-¹; *comb* antero-, proso-
fossil *base* oryct-; *suf* -ite
foul *dirt: comb* blenno-, -chezia, copro-, edaph-, fim(i)-, kopro-, miso-, myso-, -myxia, myxo-, paedo-, pedo-, scato-, spatilo-, spurc-, stegno-, sterco-; *base* -fecu-, gleb-, hum-, macul-, molys-, rhypar-, rhypo-, rypo-, sord-; *evil: pre* dys-, mis-; *comb* caco-, iniq-, kak(o)-, mal(e)-, ponero-, -prav-, turp-
foundation *comb* base-, basi-, baso-
fountain *base* cren-², pego-
four(th) *comb* quadr-, quadrato-, quadri-, quadru-, quart-, quarter-, quarti-, quat-, quater-, tetarto-, tetra-, tessera-; ~ *cycles:* tetra-, cyclo-; ~ *hundred:*

quadricent-; ~ *times:* tetrakis-. *Also see* "Numbers" *in Part III*

fourteen *base* quattuordec-, tessaradeca-, tetradeca-, tetrakaideca-

fowl *base* gallin-; *hunting ~: base* aucup-

fox *base* alopec-, bassar-, vulpi-

foxglove *comb* digito-

fraction *base* -par-[1], parti-; *~ of a meter: comb* -meter

fracture *comb* -clasia, -clasis, -clastic, rhegma-, -(r)raghia, -(r)rhexis; *base* agmat-, -fract-, frag-, -frang-, -rupt-; *bone ~:* catagm-

fragile *See* **frail**

fragment *comb* -clasm, clasmato-, -fid; *base* frust-, -par-; *stone ~: base* ruder-

fragrance *base* aroma-

frail *comb* lepti-, lepto-; *base* -asthen-, coupho-, -debil-, koupho-

framework *base* compag-, pegm-

fraudulent *base* apat-, dolero-, ludif-

freckle *base* ephel-, lentig-

free *comb* eleuthero-; *base* -liber-, vac(u)-

freeing *comb* lyo-, lysi-, -lysis, lyso-, -lyte, -lytic, -lyze; *base* -liqu-, -solu-, -solv-

freezing *comb* cheima-, crymo-, cryo-, frigo-, gelo-, kryo-, pago-, psychro-, rhigo-; *base* alg-, gel-[1], glac-

French *comb* Franco-, Gallo-

frenzied *base* corybant-, frenet-

frequent *comb* pluri-, pollaki-, poly-; *base* crebr-; *suf* -le. *See* **repeatedly**

fresh *comb* thalero-; *base* -nov-

friable *base* psath-

friction *comb* tribo-, -tripsy; *base* trit-

fried dough cake *base* gurd-

friendship *comb* socio-; *base* -am-, amic-[1], comit-

frieze decorations *base* encarp-

fright *see* **fear**

frigid *see* **freezing**

fringe *comb* crosso-; *base* -fimbr-, lacin-, lom-, thysan-; *small ~:* fimbrilli-; *~ with hairs:* fimbriato-

frizzled *base* calamist-

frog *comb* batracho-, bufo-, phryno-, rani-; *base* polyped-

from *pre* a-[2], ab-, abs-, apo-, e-, ex-, with-

front *pre* ante-, pre-, pro-; *comb* antero-, fore-, proso-; *~ of the head: base* bregm-

frontal bone *comb* fronto-

frost *base* cryo-, gel-[1], kryo-, pachno-, pago-, pruin-, rhigo-

froth *base* -spum-

fructose *comb* fructi-, fructo-

frugality *base* parc-

fruit *comb* -carp, -carpic, carpo-[1], -carpous, pomi-, pomo-; *base* -frug-[1], oporo-; *~ sugar:* fructi-, fructo-; *~ with leathery rind: base* hesperid-; *~ surrounding a stone: base* drup-

fruitfly *base* drosophyl-, trypet-

fruitful *comb* proli-

frying pan *base* frix-

fugitive *base* drapeto-

full (of) *comb* -filled, pleni-, pleo-, plero-, pluri-; *base* -pler-, plero-, plet-, sat-, satur-; *suf* -acious, -ate, -ic, -ful, -ilent, -ose[2], -osity, -ous, -ulent, -y

fuller *cloth: base* fullon-

fullness of time *base* kair-

fun *comb* chero-

function *suf* -ate[3], -ise

functionally disordered *pre* para-

funeral rites *base* epicid-, funeb-, funer-, thren-

fungus *comb* fungi-, morilli-, -mycete, mycet(o)-, -mycin, myco-, uredo-; *base* bolet-

funnel *comb* choano-, infundibuli-; *base* aryt-

fur *base* dora-

furious *base* chol-, -invid-, -ira-, labro-, -margy

furnish with *pre* be-; *suf* -ate

furrow *comb* holco-, stria-, striato-, strio-, sulcato-; *base* -scrobic-, strig-; *furrowed: base* lirell-

fusion *pre* co-; *comb* conjugato-, -ergasia, gameto-, gamo-, hapto-, junct-; *base* aps-, apt-, -greg-, -soc-, syngam-; *suf* -ate, -ize

futile *base* futil-, inutil-, mataeo-

G

gable *base* fastig-
gain *base* lucr-, quaest-
gall *bile: comb* bili-, chol(e)-, gall-; *base*
  felli-; *tumorous plant tissue:* cecid-
galvanic *comb* galvano-
gambling *base* alea-
gamete *comb* gameto-; *type of: base* -odia
Ganges *base* gang-
ganglion *comb* ganglio-
gangrene *base* sphacel-
gap *base* -apert-, -cav-, fenest-, foram-,
  œgo-, oigo-, osti-, patul-, pylo-, rim,
  valv-
gaping *base* rict-
garb *base* habil-, hesto-, -vest-
garden *comb* horti-
gargle *base* gargar-
garland *comb* corolli-
garlic *base* alli-, scoro-
gas *comb* aeri-, aero-, gaso-, pneumo-;
  inert ~: suf -on; *stomach ~:* flat-,
  physa-, physo-
gash *comb* -cide, cis-, -cise, -ectomy,
  inciso-, -sect, temno-, -tmesis, -tome,
  tomo-, -tomous, -tomy; *base* sec-
gastric *comb* chyli-, chylo-, chyma-
gate *comb* porto-; *base* osti-, -pyl-
gathered together *comb* cumulo-; *base*
  acerv-, -sor-, synax-
gecko *base* gecco-
gelatin *comb* gelatino-
gem *base* lapid-
generate *comb* aetio-, etio-, -gen, geno-,
  -genesis, -genic, -genous, -geny, -gone,
  -gonium, gono-, -gony, -phyletic. *See*
  cause
genital(s) *comb* genito-; *base* -aede-,
  med-; *female ~: comb* colp(o)-, ely-
  tr(o)-, kolpo-, vagini-, vagino-; *male*
  ~: comb peo-, phall(o)-; *base* med-,
  mentul-
gentle *base* -len-, mansue-, miti-, moll-
genuine *base* authen-
geological epoch *comb* -cene, -zoic
geometric figure *comb* -gon, -hedral,
  -hedron

gerbil *base* cricet-
German *comb* Germano-, Teutano-,
  Teuto-
germinal *comb* -blast, blasto-, -blasty,
  -carp, -carpic, carpo-, -carpous,
  sperma-, -spermal, spermatio-, sper-
  mato-, spermi-, -spermic, spermo-,
  -spermous, sporo-; *base* semin-
germs *comb* bacilli-, bacillo-, -bacter, bac-
  teri-, bacterio-
gesture *base* gestic-, pasi-
get *base* -cap-, -cep-, -cip-, -dyte-
ghost *base* phantas-, phasm-, spectr-
gibbon *base* hylobat-
gift *base* don-, dor-, mun-
gigantic *comb* bronto-, dino-, giganto-,
  mega-, megalo-, -megaly, super-. *See*
  large
gills *comb* -branchia, branchio-
ginger *base* zingiber-
giraffe *base* artiodactyl-
girdle *comb* zoni-, zono-; *base* -cing-, zos-
  ter-. *See* band
give *base* -don-; *~ birth: base* -partur-; *~*
  way: base -ced-, -cess-
glacier *comb* glacio-
gland *comb* adeni-, adeno-, balani-, bal-
  ano-; *swollen ~: base* strum(i)-
glans *comb* balano-
glass(y) *comb* crystallo-, hyalo-, vitreo-,
  vitri-, vitro-; *glassy feldspar:*
  base sanid-. *See* mirror
gleam *comb* sela-; *base* corrusc-, -fulg-,
  gano-, lustr-, rutil-, stilpno-
glide *base* olisto-
glittering *base* stilpno-
globe *comb* ano-, annul-, crico-, cyclo-,
  disco-, globi-, globo-, glom-, gyro-,
  orbito-, -sphere, sphero-, stilli-,
  zon-, zoni-; *base* -anu-, -cing-,
  -cinct-, -circin-, -circul-, -coron-,
  -glomer-, -numm-, -orb-, -rot-,
  -troch-
gloomy *base* fusc-, obscur-, tenebr-
glowworm *base* lampyr-
glue (like) *comb* colleto-, -glea, -glia,

glio-, gloio-, glutin-, kollo-; *base* coll-²; *one who glues: base* colleto-

glum *comb* lype-; *base* dolor-, fleb-, flet, luct-, -trist-

glutted *comb* -filled, pleni-, pleo-, plero-, pluri-; *base* -pler-, -plet-; *suf* -acious, -ate, -ic, -ful, -ilent, -ose, -osity, -ous, -ulent, -y

gluttony *base* adephag-, gul(os)-, helu-, lurc

glycerin, glycerol, glycogen *comb* glico-, gluco-

gnash *base* brux-, frend-, mol-

gnat *base* conop-, culici-

gnaw *base* -trog-. *See* **chew**

gnu *base* connochaet-

go *comb* -grade, -motive, -plania , plano-; *base* -bat-, -ced-, -cess-, -cur(s), -grad-, -gress-, -mob-, -vad-, -vas-; *~ away:* out-; *~ into:* -dyte-; *~ forward:* pro-; *~ toward:* -bound, -petal

goad *base* horm-, -hort, -suade, -suas-, -stig-

goal *comb* teleo-, telo-, ultim(o)-; *base* -fin-, -termin-

goat *comb* capri-, egagro-, trago-; *base* aegag-, egag-, hircin-

goblet *base* pocul-

God *comb* theo-; *base* dei-

goiter *base* strum(i)-

gold(en) *comb* auri-², auro-, chrys(o)-; *gold-working: base* aurif- *Also see* "Colors" in Part III

goldfish *base* cyprin-

gonad *comb* gonado-

good *pre* bene-, eu-; *base* agath-, bon-, prob-; *~ order: base* eutax-

goodbye *base* vale-

goods *base* empor-, -merc-

goose *base* anser-, cheno-

gooseberry *base* grossul-, ribes-

gorgeous *comb* calli-, callo-; *base* kal-, pulchr-

gorilla *base* gorill-, -pong-

gospel *base* evangel-

gossip *base* lab-²

gourd *base* cucurbit-, pepo-

gout *base* podag-

government *comb* -archy, -cracy, -crat(ic); *base* gubern-

grab *base* rap-, rep-. *See* **grasp**

graceful *comb* habro-

gracious *base* benig-

grackle *base* gracul-

grafting *base* surcul-

grain *comb* grani-; *base* farr-, farrag-, -frument-

gram *comb* -gram

grammar *base* grammat-

grandfather *base* avit-, av(us)-

grandmother *base* av(ia)-

granite *comb* graniti-; *like, of ~:* grano-

grant *base* concess-, don-

granular *comb* coni-, -conia, conio-, granulo-

grape (like) *comb* acini-, botry-, staphylo-, vini-, vino-, viti-; *base* racem-, -rhag-, -uvi-, -uvu-; *gathering ~: base* vindem-

grapple *base* harpag-

grasp *comb* -tain; *base* -cap(t)-, -cathex-, -ger-, -hapt-, -prehend, prehens-, -ten-

grass *base* agrost-, gramin-, poe-

grasshopper *base* acrid-, forb-, gryll-, locust-

grave *comb* -taph, tapho-; *base* sepul-

gravel *base* chalic-, glare-

gray *comb* glauco-, -phaein, phaeo-, pheo-, polio-; *base* caesi-, -can-², cani-tud-, -gris-, -tephr-. *Also see* "Colors" in Part III

grazing *base* pascu-

grease *base* axung-, lipar-, sebo-, unct-, ungu-

great *size: comb* macro-, magni-, maxi-, plethys-; *base* -ampl-, grandi-, -maj-; *suf* -fold. *See* **gigantic**

greater *pre* super-; *comb* meizo-, out-

grebe *base* podic-

greed(y) *base* avar-, avid-, cup(id)-, edac-, gulos-, labro-, pleonec-, pleonex-

Greek *comb* Graeco-, Greco-; *base* Hellen-

green *comb* chloro-, glauco-, olivaceo-; *base* aerug-, -beryl-, caes-, oliv-, por-rac-, pras-, smaragd-, thall-, thal-las-, verd-, -vir-, virid-; *like an unripe grape: base* omphac-; *turning ~:* viresc- *Also see* "Colors" in Part III

gridiron *base* graticul-

grief *comb* lype-; *base* dolor-, fleb-, flet-, luct-, penth-, trist-

grind *base* -brux-, frend-, mol-
grit *comb* ammo-, aren-, arenaceo-, glare-,
psammo-, sabell-, sabul-
groan *base* gem-
groin *comb* bubo-, inguino-
groove *comb* bothr-, canali-, -glyph,
glypto-, stria-, striato-, strio-, sulcato-;
base canal-, sulc-; *grooved: base* riv-.
See cleft
grope *base* pselaph-
ground *base* edaph-, geo-, -hum-, sol-^{2},
-terr-; ~ *plan: base* ichnography-; *living near the* ~: *base* epige-; *under* ~:
base cunicul-
group (of) *suf* -age, -ery, -hood, -ship
group names [zoology] *comb* -zoa,
-zoon; *suf* -ini
grouse *base* gallinac-, tetrao-; *sand* ~:
base pterocl-
grove *suf* -etum
grow, growth *comb* auxano-, auxeto-,
auxo-, -blast, -blastic, blasto-, -blasty,

-colous, -crease, -culture, -nastic,
-nasty, onco-, -physis, -plasia, -plasis, -plast, -plastic, plasto-, plethys-,
verruci-; *base* -aug, -cresc, diaphys-,
glisc-; *suf* -oma, -ome; ~*in:* -cole,
-colent, -colous; *fibrous growth: comb*
ino-; ~ *together:* symphyo-
grunt *base* grunn(it)-
guard *comb* -phylactic, phylacto-, -phylax, -phylaxis
guess *base* -stoch-
guide *base* gubern-, -pomp-
guilt *base* -culp-
gull *base* gavi-, lar-
gullet *comb* esophago-, œsophago-
gulp *base* glutt-
gums *comb* gingivo-, oulo-, ulo-^{2}
gum-yielding *comb* gutti-
gush *base* gurg-
gyrating *comb* gyro-
gyroscope *comb* gyro-

H

habit *base* -hexi-
habitat *comb* -cole, -colent, -colous, eco-,
oiko-; *base* -aed-, -dom-, -edi-
hailstone *base* grandin-, chalax-
hair/hairlike *comb* capilli-, -chaeta, chaeto-, cilii-, cilio-, -coma, comi-, como-,
crin(i)-, dasy-, fimbr-, fimbrilli-, pili-,
pilo-, piloso-, -trich, -tricha, tricho-,
villoso-; *base* hirsut-, hispid-, lanug-,
saro-, -thrix, vill-; *covered with fine*
hair: base toment-
hair removal *base* depil-
hake *base* merluc-
half *pre* demi-, hemi-, semi-; *comb* dicho-,
mezzo-; *base* dimid-
halibut *base* hippogloss-
halogen *comb* halo-; *suf* -ine
halt *comb* stasi-, -stasis, -stat, stato-; *base*
fin-, termin-
hammer *comb* malleo-; *base* mall-, pleg-,
sphyr-; ~ *fish: base* sphyraen-
hampered *comb* brady-; *base* -cunct-,
imped-, -mora-, -tard-

hamster *base* cricet-
hand *comb* cheiro-, chiro-, hand-, mani-,
manu-
handle *base* ansa-, manubr-
hang *comb* cremo-; *base* -pend-, -pens-
happening every ___ *suf* -ly
happiness *comb* chero-^{1}; *base* beati-,
felic-, jubil-, macar-
harbor *base* limen-
hard *comb* duro-, sclero-; *base* callos-;
~ *palate: comb* uranisco-, urano-; ~
shell: base lorica-; ~ *work: comb* pono-.
See difficult
hare *base* cunic-, lago-, lepor-
harlot *comb* cypriano-, hetaero-, porno-;
base meretric-, scort-
harmful *comb* noci-, pesti-; *base* nocu-,
-nox-, pericul-, pernic-
harmony *pre* co-; *base* concinn-, congru-,
-eiren-, -iren-, -pac-, -pax, unanim-
harp *small: base* sambuc-^{2}
harsh *comb* caco-; *base* acerb-, asper-, auster-, trucul-

haste *base* alacr-, celer-, festin-, speus-, subit-; *comb* ocy-, tacho-, tachy-

hatchet *base* dolabr-, pelec-, securi-

hate(d) *comb* miso-, -phobe, -phobia, -phobic; *base* -invid-, -ira(sc)-, odi-

haul(ing) *comb* -fer, -ferous, -gerous, -parous, -pher, -phore, -phorous; *base* -port-, -vect-

having *comb* -echia; *suf* -acean, -aceous, -al, -ate², -ed², -ful, -gerous, -ial, -ine, -ious, -itious, -ory, -ous, -some, -ulent, -ulous, -wise, -y; *base* -ten-; ~ *parts: comb* -fold; ~ *qualites of: comb* -able

hawk *base* accipit-, buteo-, falco-, hieraco-

hawthorn *base* -crataeg-

hazard *base* pericul-

head *comb* capit-, cephal-, -cephalic, cephalo-, -cephalous, -cephaly, cranio-, kephalo-; *having a __ head:* -headed; *type of ~:* -pated

headlong *base* precip-

headstrong *base* contum-, obstin-, pervic-, proterv-

healing *comb* -iatrics, -iatr(o)-, -iatry, medico-; *base* acest-, cur-, san-

health *comb* hygeio-, hygien-; *base* salub-, san-. See **sickness**

heap(ing) *comb* cumulo-; *base* acerv-, agger-, soro-

hearing *comb* acou-, acoust-, audi(o)-, auri-, echo-, -ecoia, oto-, -phone, phono-, -phony, -phthong, soni-, sono-, sonoro-; *base* acroa-. *Also see* "Senses" in Part III

heart *comb* cardi-, -cardia, cardio-, -cardium, cordato-, cordi-, pericardiaco-, pericardio-; ~ *attack: base* angin-; ~ *cavity: comb* atrio-; ~ *shaped: comb* cordato-

heartbreak *comb* lype-; *base* dolor-, fleb-, flet-, luct-, trist-

heat *comb* cal(e)-, calo-, calor(i)-, pyr(o)-, -therm, thermo-, -thermy; *base* aest-, caum-, ferv-; *heat up: base* fomen-; *heat-blocking: base* atherm-

heath *base* eric-

heave *comb* -bole, -bolic, bolo-, -boly; *base* -ballist-, -jact-, -jacula-, -ject-

heavens *comb* coeli-, ourano-, urano-; *base* cael-, cel-, celest-

heavy *comb* -bar, bari-, baro-, grav(i)-; *base* -obes-, -pond-

Hebrew *comb* Hebraico-; ~ *plural ending: suf* -im

hedge *base* sepi-²

hedgehog *comb* echinoderm-; *base* echin-, erinac-

heed *comb* -serve; *base* caut-

heedless *base* neglig-

heel-bone *comb* calcaneo-, ptern-

heifer *base* damal-

height *comb* acro-, alti-, alto-, bato-¹, hypsi-, hypso-; *base* procer-

heinous *base* atroc-, nefand

hell *base* acheron-, avern-, infern-, -styg-

helmet *base* cassidi-, corys-, -gale-

help *base* -(ad)jut-, -(ad)juv-, -auxil-

helpful *comb* chreo-, chresto-; *base* -util-

hemispheric *comb* hemispherico-

hen *base* gallin-

heptillion *comb* yotta-; ~ *th:* yocto-. *Also see* "Numbers" in Part III

herald *base* caduc-²

herd *base* arment-, -greg-

heredity *comb* heredo-

heresy *base* heresio-; *base* heret-

Hermes *comb* hermo-

hermit *base* eremit-; ~ *crab:* pagur-

hernia *comb* -cele, celo-¹, hernio-

heron *base* arde-, grallator-

herring *comb* harengi-; *base* clupe-, halec-

hesitate *base* cunct-

hew *base* dolatil-

hexameter *comb* hexametro-

hexillion *comb* zetta-; ~ *th:* zepto-. *Also see* "Numbers" in Part III

hiccup *base* singult-

hidden *pre* sub-; *comb* calypto-, crypto-; *base* abdit-, -cryph, occult-, laten-, lathro-; *hiding place:* latebr-, latib-. See **covered**

hide *animal: comb* dora-, pelli-; *conceal: See* **hidden**

high(er) *pre* meta-, super-; *comb* acro-, alti-, alto-, hypsi-, hypso-

higher valence *pre* per-; *suf* -ic

highest *comb* acro-; ~ *heaven: base* empyr-

highway *comb* hodo, -ode, odo-; *base* -iter-, -via-

hill *base* coll-[3]
Himalaya + *comb* himalo-
hinge *base* gingly-
hip *comb* cotyle-, cotyli-, cotylo-, coxo-, ischi(o)-
hireling *base* merced-
hire out *base* -locat-
hiss *base* exsibil-, -sibil-
historical *comb* historico-
hit *comb* plessi-; *base* cop-, -crot-, -cuss-, -plang-, puls-, -tus-, vapul-, -verber-
hoard *comb* cumulo-; *base* acerv-, -sor-
hoarse *base* rauc-
hoary *base* canitud-
hoax *base* ludif-
hoe *base* sarcul-
hog *base* hyos-
hold *comb* -tain; *base* -cap(t)-, -cathex-, -ger-[1], -hapt-, -prehend, prehens-, -ten-; ~ *back:* prohib-
holder *comb* angio-, asco-, bursi-, burso-, ceco-, chlamyd-, chrysali-, cisto-, coleo-, -cyst, cysti-, cysto-, follic-, meningo-, pericardiaco-, pericardio-, peritoneo-, phasco-, physa-, physali-, physo-, -theca, theci-, theco-, typhlo-, utri-, utric, vesico-; *base* -sacc-, -thylac-
hole *base* cav-, foramin-, lacun-, troglo-. *See* **opening**
holler *base* clam-, vocif-
hollow *comb* cava-, -cave, cavi-, cavo-, -coele, coelo-, cotyle-, cotyli-, cotylo-, koilo. *See* **cavity**
holly *base* ilic-
holy *comb* hagio-, hiero-, sanct(i)-; *base* -sacr-
home (of) *comb* eco-, ekist-, nosto-, oeco-, oiko-; *base* aed-, -dom-, edi-; *suf* -age
honest *base* prob-
honey *comb* mell(i)-; ~ *mix:* base muls-
honeycomb *comb* favoso-; *base* fav-
honor *base* tim-[2], timo-; *honored: comb* semno-
honorable *pre* bene-, eu-; *base* agath-, bon-, prob-
hood *base* calyptri-, cuculli-
hook *base* hamat-, harpag-, -unci-; *hooked: base* adunc-, falc-; ~ *shaped: base* ancis-

hookworm *base* ancylostom-
hoop *base* armill-
hope *base* -sper-
horizon *comb* horizo-
hormone names *comb* -kinin
horn, hornlike *comb* cerat(o)-, -corn, corneo-, corni-, cornu-, kera-, kerato-
hornbill *base* bucerot-, bucorac-
hornblower *comb* keraulo-
hornet *comb* vespi-; *base* -sphec-
horse *comb* equ(i)-, hippo-, -hippus; *base* caball-, caval-, hippur-
horsefly *base* taban-
horseshoe *base* hippocrepi-
horsetail *base* equiset-
hospital *base* nosocom-
host *base* -hosp-, -xen-
hostile *pre* anti-; *base* inimic-
hot *comb* cal(e)-, calo-, calor(i)-, pyr(o)-, thermo-, -thermy; *base* aestu-, caum-, ferv-
hour *comb* horo-
house *comb* eco-, ekist-, oeco-, oiko-; *base* aed-, -dom-1, edi-; *suf* -age
howl *base* ulul-[1]
how many *base* quot-
hub *comb* centr-, centri-, -centric, centro-
huckster *base* caupon-
huge *comb* bronto-, dino-, giganto-, mega-, megalo-, -megaly; *base* coloss-, mass-, vastit-
hull *ship: base* naut-; *husk: base* follic-, -lemma[2], putamin-
human *comb* anthrop(o)-, humano-, -man; *base* hom-, homin-. *See* **people**
humid *comb* hydro-, hygro-, udo-; *base* humect-, madefac-, -rig-
hummingbird *base* trochil-
humorless *base* agelast-
humorous *comb* comico-
hump *comb* cypho-, gibboso-, hybo-, lordo-, scoli-; *base* -kyph-
hundred *comb* cent(i)-, hecato-, hecto-, hekto-; ~ *twenty:* hecatonicosa-. *Also see* "Numbers" in Part III
hunger *base* esur-; ~ *for: comb* eroto-, -lagnia, -mania, -orexia, peino-; *base* -appet-, conat-, -cup-, esur-, fam-, -libid-, -opt-, vell-; *suf* -urient
hunt *base* venat-

hurl *comb* -bole, -bolic, bolo-, -boly; *base* ballist-, -jact-, -jacula-, -ject-
hurricane *base* lilaps-
hurry *base* accel-, celer-, festin-. See **rush**
hurt *comb* noci-; *base* -nox-, vuln-. *See* **pain**
husband *base* conjug-, marit-
husbandry *base* villic-
hushed *comb* hesy-; *base* -plac-, quiesc-, -tacit-
husk *comb* follic-, -lemma², putamin-; *base* acer-³, glum-, lepo-
hut *base* -cali-
hydraulic *comb* hydraulico-

hydrides *suf* -ine
hydrocarbon *suf* -ene; ~ *radical:* *suf* -ylene; ~ *paraffin series: suf* -ane; ~ *plus nitrogen: comb* diazo-, phenanthro-
hydrogen *comb* -hydric
hydroxyl *radicals: comb* -hydric; ~ *group: comb* hydroxy-
hygiene *comb* hygeio-, hygien-; *base* salub-, san-
hyoid bone *comb* hyo-
hypnotism *comb* hypno-; *base* mesmer-
hyrax- *comb* chero-², hyraci-, hyraco-
hysteria *comb* hyster(o)-

I

ice *comb* glacio-, pago-; *base* gel-¹
icicle *base* stiri-
icon *comb* icono-
idea *comb* -gnomy, -gnosia, -gnosis, -gnostic, gnoto-, ideo-, -noia, -nomy, phreno-, psycho-, -sophy *base* -cogit-, -cogn-, epistem-, -noe-, -put-, ratio-, -sci-
identical *pre* co-; *comb* equi-, homo-, iso-, pari-, tauto-
idiot *base* fatu-, inan-, moro-, stult-
idle *base* arg-, oti-, pigrit-
idol *comb* idolo-; *base* xoan-
ignorant *base* agnoi-, hebet-, idiot-, ignar-, nesc-, ningat-, obtus-, -tard-
ileac plus, ileum *comb* ileo-, ilio-
ill(ness) *pre* dys-, mal-; *comb* noso-, -path, -pathic, patho-, -pathy; *base* aegr-, -morb-, -pecca-, valetud-; ~ *health: base* cachex-; ~ *names: comb* -aemia, -emia; *suf* -asis, -ia, -itis, -oma, -osis; ~ *treatment: comb* -iatrics, iatro-, -iatry. *See* **disorder**
illiterate *base* agramm-
illumination *comb* actino-, luci-, phengo-, phos-, photo-; *base* clar-, -luc-, -lum-
illusory *comb* pseudo-; *base* apat-, -phantas-, phasm-, spur-
image *comb* icono-; *base* agalma-
imaginary monster *base* mormo-

imbibe *comb* pino-, poto-; *base* -bib-, pocul-
imitate *base* emul-, -mim-
immature *comb* paedo-², pedo-; *base* juven-. *See* **undeveloped**
immense *comb* bronto-, dino-, giganto-, mega-, megalo-, -megaly
immobility *comb* -plegia, -plegy
immodesty *base* impud-
immolation *base* mact-, -thy-
immorality *pre* dys-, mis-; *comb* caco-, enisso-, enosio-, kak-, kako-, mal-, male-, ponero-; *base* culp-, facin-, flagit-, hamart-, iniq-, nefar-, pecca-, perdit-, -prav-, sceler-, scelest-, turp-
immortal *comb* ever-; *base* etern-, perpet-, semper-
immovable *comb* stasi-, -stasis, -stat, stato-; *base* stabil-
immune *comb* immuno-
impaired *base* emper-, vitia-
impartial *comb* equi-
impede *comb* isch-, koly-, -penia, rhopo-, -strain, -strict; *base* angust-, -string-; *suf* -en
impel *base* horm-
imperfection *base* culp-, delinq-, laps-, -pecca-, sphal-
imperfect(ly) *pre* demi-, hemi-, semi-; *comb* ametro-, -atelia, atelo-

imperforate *comb* -atresia, atreto-
impervious to *comb* -proof, -tight
impetus *base* horm-
important *base* grav-
imposter *base* phenac-, phenak-
impoverished *comb* ptocho-, vidu-; *base* -mendic-, -paup-, penur-, -pov-
improved *comb* melior-, out-
impulse *base* ate-⁴
in *pre* eis-, em-, en-¹, il -, im-, in-, ir-; *comb* endo-, ento-, entre-, eso-, inter(o)-, intra-, intro-; ~ *a specified way:* *suf* -ly, -ways, -wise; ~ *back:* *pre* meta-; *comb* post-, postero-; ~ *common:* *comb* caeno-, ceno-; ~ *front of:* *pre* ante-, fore-, ob-, prae-, pre-, pro-; ~ *some order:* *suf* -ly; ~ *the direction of:* *suf* -ad, -ly, -ward, -ways, -wise; ~ *the manner of:* *suf* -like, -ways; ~ *the style of:* *suf* -ese, -esque
inaccuracy *base* culp-, delict-, laps-, pecc-, sphal-
inadequacy *comb* isch-, oligo-, -penia
inaudible *comb* hesy-; *base* -plac-, quiesc-, -tacit-
inborn *comb* innato-
incapable of being *suf* -less. *See* **not**
incense *comb* -thymia²; *base* kniss-, liban-, thur-
incessant *base* assid-, contin-, incess-, perpet-
incipient *base* incip-, -init-; *suf* -esce, -escence, -escent.
incised *comb* eroso-. *See* **groove**
inciting *comb* -agogic, -agogue; *base* fomen-
incline *comb* -clinal, -clinate, -cline, -clinic, clino-, -clinous, -clisis, lechrio-, loxo-, plagio-; *base* -cliv-
incomplete *pre* demi-, hemi-, semi-; *comb* -atelia, atelo-; *suf* -esce, -escence, -escent
incorrect *base* dys-, mis-; ~ *use of words:* *comb* acyro-
increased *pre* ad-, extra-, hyper-, super-; *comb* auxano-, auxo-, multi-, myria-, myrio-, out-, over-, -plasia, pleni-, pleo-, pleio-, pleon-, plethys-, plio-, pluri-, pollaki-, poly-; *base* -aug-, -cresc-, diaphys-, -fold-, glisc-,-pler-, -plet-. *See* **grow**

indecent *base* scurril-
indecisiveness *base* abul-
indefinite *base* ambig, dub-, ancip-
index *comb* sema-, -seme, semeio-, semio-
India *comb* Indo-²
indicate *comb* phaeno-, pheno-; *base* -monstr-
indifference *base* aced-
indigence *comb* -penia, ptocho-, vidu-; *base* -mendic-, -paup-, penur-, -pov-
indigenous *base* enchor-
indigestion *base* apeps-
indigo *comb* indi-, indo-¹
indirect *comb* loxo-, plagio-; *base* ambag-
indisposed *pre* dys-, mal-; *comb* noso-, path, -pathic, patho-, -pathy; *base* aegr-, cachex-, -morb-, -pecca-, valetud-
individual *suf* -aholic, -aire, -an, -ant, -ard, -arian, -art, -ary, -ast, -ate, -ator, -ee, -eer, -en, -ent, -er, -ette, -eur, -fer, -ician, -ier, -ior, -ist, -le, -ling, -man, -nik, -o, -or, -person,-people, -ster, -woman, -yer
indolent *base* pigr-
inebriated *base* inebr-, methys-, temul-
ineffectual *base* futil-, inutil-, mataeo-
inert gas *suf* -on
inexpensive *base* vili-
infection *comb* lysi-, lyso-, -lysis, -lyte, -lytic, -lyze, phthisio-, -phthisis, phthysio-, -phthysis, putre-, putri-, pyo-, pytho-, sapro-, septi-, septico-, septo-, toxi-, toxico-, toxo-; *base* diphther-, phthor-, vitia-
inference *base* illat-
inferiority *pre* hypo-, sub-, under-; *comb* hystero-²; *base* hesson-; *suf* -aster²
infinity *base* apeiro-. *See* **forever**
infirm *pre* dys-, mal-; *comb* noso-, path, -pathic, patho-, -pathy; *base* aegr-, cachex-, -morb-, -pecca-, valetud-
inflammation *comb* erysi-, phlog(o)-; *suf* -itis. *See* **swelling**
inflect *base* -clit-
inflexible *stubborn:* *base* contum-, obdur-, obstin-, pervic-, proterv-; *stiff:* *comb* ancylo-, ankylo-, tetano-
inflorescence *comb* thyrsi-, thyrso-
infuse *comb* -enchyma²; *suf* -ate
ingest *comb* bromato-, -brotic, manduc-,

-phage, phago-, -phagous, -phagy,
-sitia, sitio-, sito-, -troph, -trophic, tro-
pho-, -trophy, -vora, -vore, -vorous;
base -alim-, -cib-, comest-, -ed-, escul-,
glutt-, -gust-

inguinal *comb* inguino-

inhabit(ant) *comb* -cole, -colent, -colous;
suf -an, -ite

inhale *comb* -hale, -pnea, pneo-, pneu-
mato-, pneumo-, pneumono-, pne-
usio-, pulmo-, spiro-; *base* afflat-,
anhel-

inhere *base* -sid-, situ-

inhibit *comb* coly-, freno-, isch-, koly-,
-penia, -strain, -strict; *base* -string-; *suf*
-en. *See* **checked**

iniquity *pre* dys-, mis-; *comb* caco-, iniq-,
kak(o)-, mal(e)-, ponero-; *base* -prav-,
sceler-, turp-

initial *comb* arch-, fore-, pre-, primi-,
primo-, pro-, proso-, protero-, proto-;
base -princip-

initiate *base* inaug-, incip-, init-

injection *base* trypan-

injudicious *base* fatu-, inan-, moro-, stult-

injurious *comb* noci-, pesti-; *base* del-
eter-, -nox-, pericul-

injury *comb* noci-, traumato-; *base* -nox-

ink *base* atrament-

inner circle *base* esoter-

inner sanctum *base* adyt-

innkeeper *base* caupon-

inquiry *base* erot-, -quest-, -quir-, -rog-

insanity *comb* lysso-, -mania; *base* ament-
[1], dement-

insatiable *base* avid-, edac-, gulos-

inscribe *comb* -gram, -graph, -grapher,
-graphic, grapho-, -graphy, grapto-,
-logue; *base* epigram-, -scrib-, -script-,
typo-

insect *comb* cimic-, core-[2], entomo-,
insecti-, insecto-; ***neuropterous* ~:** base
sial-[2]; ***walking stick* ~:** *base* phasm- ~
wing angle: *base* torn-[2]. *See* **mite**

insecure *base* ocno-

insert *base* calar-, calat-, pon-, pos-

inside *pre* eis-, em-, en-[1], il -, im-, in-[1],
ir-; *comb* endo-, ento-, entre-, eso-,
inter(o)-,interno-, intra-, intro-; *from
the* ~: entostho-

insipid- *base* insuls-, vapid-

in situ *base* authi-

insolent *base* contum-, impud-, procac-,
proterv-

inspection *comb* -opsy, -scope, -scopic,
scopo-, -scopy; *base* -(in)quir-, -(in)
quis-, -scrut-

inspiration *base* afflat-

install *base* inaug-

instance of *suf* -ism

instantly *base* subit-

instep *comb* tarso-

instruct *comb* -pedia; *base* catech-,
-didact, didasc-, doc-, -paed-

instrument (of) *suf* –bulum, -ment[1],
-ure; ~ *for scraping:* base strigil-; **medical** ~: -tome; *scientific* ~: -stat

insufficient *pre* demi-, hemi-, semi-; *comb*
-atelia, atelo-

insulin precursor *base* nesid-

insult *base* contum-

intact *pre* be-, cata-, de-, kata-, ob-, per-;
comb holo-, omni-, pan-, panto-, stone-,
toti-; *base* integr-

intellect *comb* -gnomy, -gnosia, -gnosis,
-gnostic, -gnoto, ideo-, -noia, -nomy,
phren(o)-, psycho-, -sophy, thymo-,
-witted; *base* -cogit-, -cogn-, ment(a)-,
-noe-, -put-,ratio-, -sci-

intelligent *base* sapien-

intelligible *generally:* base exoter-; ~
only to a few: base esoter-

intemperance *base* acras-

intensifier *pre* em-, en-, in-, za-

interbreeding *base* syngam-

intercourse *comb* -lagnia; *base* -coit-,
copul-, subagit-

interfunctioning *comb* -ergasia, ergasio-

intermix *pre* co-; *comb* conjugato-,
-ergasia, gameto-, gamo-, hapto-, junct-;
base aps-, apt-, -greg-, -soc-; *suf* -ate, -ize

internal *pre* eis-, em-, en-[1], il -, im-, in-[1],
ir-; *comb* endo-, ento-, entre-, eso-,
inter(o)-, interno-, intra-, intro-; *from
the* ~: entostho-

interpretation *base* -hermen-

interrogate *base* -pet-, -quir-, -quis-,
-rog-, pysm-

intestinal pouch *comb* caeco-, ceco-,
typhlo-

intestines *comb* entero-, ileo-, ilio-, intestino-, jejuno-; *base* viscer-; ***rumbling of*** *~ base* borbor-¹; *~ **worm:*** ascari-
intimidated *base* -pavid-, -tim-, trepid-. See **fear**
intoxicated *base* crapul-, -inebr-, -methys-, temul-
intractable *base* contum-, obstin-, pervic-, proterv-
invective *base* diatrib-
invent *base* -heur-
inventory *base* repert-
inverse *pre* anti-, contra-, contre-, dis-, hetero-, ob-, un-; *comb* back-, counter-, enantio-, oppositi-
investigate *base* indag-
invisible *pre* sub-; *comb* calypto-, crypto-; *base* aphan-, occult-
invocation *suff* –clesis
involucre *base* involucr-
involuntary movement *comb* -chorea-, choreo-, -clonic, -clonus, spasmo-; *base* -stal-; *suf* -esmus, -ismus

iodine *comb* iodi-, iodo-
ion *comb* iono-, ionto-
irate *base* chol-, -invid-, -ira-, -margy
iridium *comb* iridico-, iridio-
iris *comb* irido-
Irish *comb* Hiberno-
iron *comb* ferri-, ferro-, sidero-¹
irregular *comb* allo-, ametro-, anomalo-, anomo-, poecilo-, poikilo-; *~ **shape:*** *comb* amorpho-
irridium *comb* iridico-, iridio-
irrigation *comb* -clysis; *base* chalast-, clysm-, clyst-
irritate *base* amycho-, erethis-, vex-
ischium *comb* ischi(o)-
island *base* insul-, neso-
isomer *comb* pseudo-
isthmus *base* isthm-
Italy *comb* Italo-
itch *comb* acari-, scabi-; *base* -prur-, psor-
ivory *base* ebur-
ivy *base* ciss-, -heder-

J

jackass *base* as-², asin-
jackdaw *base* gracul-
jagged *comb* serrato-; *base* cren-¹, lacin-
jail *base* -carcer-
jam *comb* emboli-, embolo-; *base* -byon-, -farct-
jasper *base* iasp-
jaundice *comb* icter(o)-
jaw *comb* genia-, genio-, geny-¹, gnatho-, -gnathous, mandibulo, maxillo-; *~ **bone:*** *base* -siagon-
jay *base* garrul-
jealous *base* -emul-
jeer *comb* catagelo-, katagelo-
jejunum *comb* jejuno-
jellyfish *base* discophor-, medus-
jeopardy *base* pericul-
jerk *comb* -chorea, choreo-, -clonic, -clonus, -esmus, -ismus, spasmo-, -tonic; *base* -stal-, -vellic-
jest *base* joco(s)-, jocu(l)-
jewel *base* -gemm-²

Jewish *comb* Judaico-, Judaeo-, Judeo-
jilt *base* relinq-, repud-
jingling *base* tinn-
job *comb* arti-, -craft, -ergasia, ergasio-, -ergic, ergo-, -ergy, organo-, -urgy; *base* -opus-, pono-; *suf* -arian
jocular *base* hilar-
join *comb* -ergasia, gameto-, gamo-, hapto-, junct-; *base* -aps-, -apt-¹, -greg-, -soc-; *suf* -ate, -ize; *~ **together:*** *pre* co-; *comb* conjugato; *base* zeug-, zeux-
joint ***body*** *~: comb* arthr(o)-, articul-; *~ **socket:*** gleno-; ***jointed:*** *base* -enarthra-
joke *base* joco(s)-, jocu(l)-
journey *comb* hodo-, -ode, odo-, via-; *base* apodemi-, -itin-, peregrin-
joy *comb* chero-; *base* beati-, elat-, felic-, gaud-, jubil-, laet-, macar-
judging *comb* -gnomy, -gnosia, -gnosis, -gnostic; *base* -crit-¹, -judic, krit-, -soph-
jug *base* urcei-

juice *comb* opo-; *base* -suc-
jump *base* -salta-
junction *pre* co-; *comb* conjugato-, -ergasia, gameto-, gamo-, hapto-, junct-; *base* aps-, apt-, -greg-, -soc-; *suf* -ate, -ize

jurisdiction *suf* -dom, -ric
justice *comb* dike-; *base* jud-
justified *base* vindic-
juvenile *comb* paedo-, pedi-, pedo-, proli-, tecno-; *base* -fil-, -puer-, tek-

K

kangaroo *base* macropod-
keel *base* -carin-; ***keel-shaped:*** *comb* tropido-
keen *base* -acer(b)-, trench-
keep *comb* -serve, -tain; *base* custod-, -ten-; *~ away:* *comb* alex-, alexi-, alexo-
keg *comb* dolio-
kernel *comb* caryo-, karyo-; *base* -nucl-
kestrel *base* falco-
ketone *comb* keto-; *suf* -one
key *comb* clavi-[1], cleido-, clido-; *~ hole:* *base* clithr-
kick *base* -calcitr-
kidnap *base* plag-, rap-, rep-
kidney *comb* nephro-, pyelo-, reni-, reno-
kidney-bean *base* phaseol-
killing *comb* -cidal, -cide, -cidious, -cidism, cteino-; *base* -dacn-, trucid-
kind *category:* *comb* -type; *suf* -atic; ***gentle:*** *base* benig-, -len-, mansue-, miti-, moll-
kindle *comb* causto-, igni- pyro-; *base* ard-[2], ars-, cauter-, celo-, combust-, crem-, phlog-, -ust-
kinetic *comb* cine-, -drome, dromo-, -dromous, excito-, kine-, -kinesi(a), -kinesis, -kinetic, kineso-, kineto-, kino-, -motive, -pragia, -praxia, -praxis, tremo-; *base* -stal-
kinfolk *base* cogn-, famil-, stirp-
king *base* basil-, reg(n)-

kingfisher *base* halcyon-
kinked *comb* cirri-, cochlio-, gyro-, helico-, spiro-, strepto-; *base* stromb-. *See* **curl**
kiss *base* bas-, basiat-, oscul-; ***tongue ~:*** cataglott-
kitchen *base* culin-
kite *bird:* *base* milv-
knack *base* -apt-, -habil-, -poten-, -qual-; *suf* -bility, -ful, -ship
knavish *pre* dys-, mis-; *comb* caco-, kak-, kako-, mal-, male-, ponero-; *base* facin-, flagit-, iniq-, nefar-, perdit-, -prav-, sceler-, scelest-, turp-
knead *base* subig-
knee *base* gen(u)-; ***back of ~:*** *base* poplit-; ***~cap:*** patell-
knife *comb* cultell-, cultri-, sica-
knit together *base* -hapto-, pegm-
knob *comb* clavato-, tylo-; *base* condyl-, nod-, umbo-
knock *base* -puls-
knot *base* -nod-, -tylo-
knowledge *comb* -gnomy, -gnosia, -gnosis, -gnostic, gnoto-, ideo-, -noia, -nomy, -phrenic, phrenico-, phreno-, psycho-, scio-[2], -sophy; *base* -cogit-, -cogn-, epistem-, gnar-, ment(a)-, -noe-, -put-, ratio-, -sci-; *~ of language:* *comb* -glot, glotto-
kudu *base* tragelaph-

L

labia minora *comb* nympho-
labor *childbirth:* *comb* lochio-, -para, -parous, -tocia, toco-, toko-, -toky;

work: *comb* -craft, ergic, -ergy, ergo-, -urgy; *base* ardu-, oper-[1], pono-

laborious *pre* dys-; *comb* -bar, bary-, mogi-; *base* ard³-, stren-
labyrinth-like *comb* labrynthi-, labryntho-
laceration *comb* sparasso-; *base* -sparax-
lacking *pre* a-, an-¹, dis-, ex-, il-, im-, in-, un-; *comb* lipo-²; *base* penur-, -priv-; *suf* -less; ~ *a part:* *comb* ectro-; ~ *an opening:* *comb* -atresia, atreto-; ~ *merit:* *base* immer-; ~ *teeth:* *base* edent-
lactic *comb* lacto-
ladder *base* scala-; ~ *rung:* climac-
lady *comb* gyn(e)-, gyneco-, gyneo-, gyno-, -gynous, -gyny, -para, thely-, -wife; *base* -femin-, muliebr-, mulier-; *suf* -en, -enne, -ess, -ette, -ice, -ine, -stress, -trice, -trix
lake *comb* limno-; *base* lacus-
lamb *base* -agn-
lame *base* claud-, debil-
lamentation *base* myrio-, thren-
lamp *base* lampad-, lucern-, lychn-; ~ *wick:* *base* ellychn-
lamprey *base* cyclostom-
lance *base* lanci-
land *comb* agri-, agro-, choro-, geo-; *base* embado-, tellur-, -terr-; ~ *dedicated to a god:* *base* temen-; *strip of ~:* isthm-
landscaping *base* topiar-
language *comb* -glossia, gloss(o)-, -glot, glotto-, lingui-, linguo-; *suf* -ese. See **word**
lap *base* grem-
lapse *base* labil-
larch *base* larix-
lard-like *base* axung-
large(r) *pre* super-; *comb* -fold, macro-, magni-, maxi-, pachy-, plethys-; *base* -ampl-, grandi-, -maj-. See **gigantic**
lark *base* coryd-
larva *comb* larvi-; *base* silph-
larynx *comb* guttur-, laryngo-
lascivious *base* orgi-, priap-, salac-, tentig-
lash *base* flagell-
lassitude *comb* pono-; *base* -fatig-, -kopo-, lass-
last *base* eschato-, -fin-, termin-, -ultim-
lasting *base* diuturn-, dur(o)-, perenn-, perm-, stabil-; ~ *all night:* *comb* -pannychy

late *comb* opsi-¹, serot-. See **tardy**
later *pre* meta-, post-; *comb* hystero-²
latest *comb* neo-
latex *comb* latici-
lattice *base* cancell-, clathr-, cratic-
laudatory *base* epanet-, eulog-
laugh *comb* gel-²; *base* cachinn-, -ris-
laurel *base* daphn-, lauri-
law *comb* juris-, nomo-, thesmo-; *base* jud-, jur-, leg-², regul-
lawless *comb* anomo-
lawsuit *base* litig-
laxative comb -clysis; *base* chalast-, clysm-, clyst-
layer(ed) *comb* -decker, lamelli-, lamini-, lamino-, -plex, strati-, strato-, tapes-
lazy *base* murc-, ociv-, oti-, pigrit-
lead *conduct:* *comb* -arch, -duce, duc(t)-, magist-; *base* hegemon-, -reg-; *metal:* *comb* molybdo-, plumbo-
leadership gift *base* charis-
leading *comb* -agogic, -agogue; *being led:* *base* ductil-; ~ *away:* *base* apag-
leaf *comb* folii-, folio-, -folious, petalo-, -phyll, phyllo-, -phyllous; *base* bract-, clad-, frondi-; ~ *buds:* *base* gemm-¹; ~ *like:* *comb* foliato-
lean *comb* angusti-, dolicho-, lepto-, mano-, stegno-, steno-, tenu-; *base* areo-, gracil-, isthm-, maci-, macrit-, stal-, strict-
leaning *base* enclit-
leap *base* salta-
learn *comb* disc-, -math, mathet-, soph-
leather(y) *comb* scyto-; *base* alut-, cori-, pelli-, utri-¹; ~ *bottle:* utrei-, utric-
leave *base* relinq-
lecherous *base* orgi-, priap-, salac-, tentig-
leech *base* bdell-, discophor-, hirud-, sanguisug-
leek *base* porr-, praso-
left *comb* laeo-, laevo-, levo-, sinistro-; ~ *handed:* scaev-
leg *base* -cnem-, -crur-, -scel-; *condition of ~:* *comb* -scelia; ~ *of an animal:* *base* gamb-
legend *comb* mytho-, stori-; *base* fabul-, -narr-
legumes *comb* legumini-
leisure *base* oti-

lemon *base* hesperid; ***lemon-colored***: *comb* citro-
lending *base* fener-
length *base* meco-. *See* **long**
leniency *base* clem-[2]
lens *comb* phaco-, phako-, -phakia; *base* lent-[2]
lentil-shaped *comb* phaco-; *base* lentic-
leopard *base* pard-
leper *comb* lepra-, lepro-
less(en) *pre* demi-, hypo-, mis-, sub-, subter-; *comb* hetto-, meio-, mini-, mio-, oligo-; *base* decresc-, dimin-, hesson-, -pauc-
lettuce *base* lactuc-
level *comb* homalo-, homolo-, plain-, plani-, plano-[1], platy-; *base* plat-
lever *base* -mochl-
lewd *base* cypriani-
liability *comb* hypegia-, hypengy-; *base* paralip-
lice *comb* pedicul-, phthiro-
licentious *base* orgi-, priap-, salac-, tentig-
lichen *comb* licheni-, licheno-; ***lichen compound:*** deps- (depside); ***reproductive unit:*** *comb* soredi-
lick *base* lamb-, ligur(r)-, linct-, ling-[4]
licorice *base* glycyr-
lid *base* oper-[2]
lie ***untruth:*** *base* mendac-; ***recline:*** *base* -cub-, -cumb-, decub-
life *comb* bio-, -biosis, vita-, vivi-, zoo-, -zoic, -zooid; *base* -anim-; ~ ***less:*** *base* exanim-
ligament *comb* desmo-, ligamenti-, ligamento-, syndesmo-
light ***not dark:*** *comb* actino-, luci-, phengo-, phos-, photo-; *base* clar-, -luc-, -lum-; ***not heavy:*** *base* koupho-, levi(t)-
lighthouse *base* fan-, phar-
lightning *comb* astra-, sela-; *base* astraph-, fulgur-, fulmin-
like *pre* para-, quasi-; *comb* homeo-, omœo-, homoio-, homolo-, iso-, -phane, -phanic; *base* simil-; *suf* -acean, -aceous, -al[3], -an, -ar, -ary, -ean, -en, -eous, -esque, -ful, -ic, -il, -ile, -ine, -ing, -ish, -itious, -ize, -like, -ode[2], -oid, -ose[2], -osity, -some[2], -tious, -ular, -y

likeness *comb* icono-, -opsis, -vult-; *base* effigy-
liking *comb* -phile, -philia, -philiac, -philic, -philism, philo-, -philous
lily *base* lili-, -lirio-
limb *comb* -mele, -melia[1], melo-[3]
lime *CaO:* *comb* calcareo-; *base* calc-; ***fruit:*** tilia-
limit *comb* isch-, koly-, -penia, -strain, -strict ; *base* -fin-, -string-, termin-; *suf* -en; ~ ***limited to:*** *comb* -specific, specio-; ***having well-defined limits:*** *comb* delo-
linden *base* tilia- (tiliaceous)
line *comb* lineo-, -stichia, sticho-, -stichous; ***wavy ~:*** *comb* gyroso-
linen *base* lint-
link *pre* co-; *comb* conjugato-, -ergasia, gameto-, gamo-, hapto-, junct-; *base* aps-, apt-, -greg-, -soc-; *suf* -ate, -ize
lion *base* leo(n)-
lips *comb* cheilo-, chilo-, labio-; *base* labi-
liquid *base* flu-, -ner-; ***make ~:*** *base* liqu-. *See* **water**
literary fragments *base* analect-
little *comb* brachisto-, brachy-, brevi-, chamae-, micro-, mini-, nano-, parvi-, parvo-, pauci-, steno-; *base* -curt-, exig-, modic-, pauro-; *suf* -cle, -cula, -cule, -culum-, -culus, -een, -el, -ella, -en, -et, -ette, -idion, -idium, -ie, -illa, -illo, -isk, -kin, -le, -let, -ling, -ock, -ola, -ole, -rel, -ula, -ule, -ulum, -ulus, -y; ~ ***hill:*** *base* colic-
liver *comb* hepatico-, hepato-; *base* jecor-
livid *base* pelios-
living *comb* bio-, vivi-, -zoic, -zooid; *base* -anim-, -vit-; ~ ***among:*** *comb* -colous; ~ ***in:*** *suf* -an
lizard *comb* -saur, sauro-, -saurus, scinci-, scinco-; *base* gecco-, lacert-, stellio-
load *base* oner-
loaded *comb* -filled, pleni-, pleo-, plero-, pluri-; *base* -pler-, -plet-; *suf* -acious, -ate, -ic, -ful, -ilent, -ose, -osity, -ous, -ulent, -y
lobe *comb* lobulato-; ***ear:*** *comb* auriculo-
lobster *base* astac-, -gammar-, homar-
location *comb* -land, loc(o)-, situ-, -stead, topo-, -topy; *base* ubi-; *suf* -age, -arium,

-ary, -ensis, -ery, -orium, -ory. *Also see* "Location" in Part III
lock *comb* clido-; *base* cleid-; *lockjaw:* trism-
locust *base* locust-
lofty *base* celsi-
loins *comb* laparo-, lumbo-, osphy(o)-; ~ *muscle*: *base* psoa-
long *comb* dolicho-, -footer, longi-, macro-, maxi-; *base* procer-; ~ *duration*: *base* diuturn-; ~ *words*: sesquipedal-
look *comb* eid(o)-, oculo-, ommat-, -opia, opsi-, -opsia, -opsis, opso-, -opsy, ophthalmo-, optico-, opto-, -scope, -scopic, scopo-, -scopy, visuo-; *base* -blep-, -scrut-, -spec-, -spic-, -vid-
loosen *comb* lyo-, lysi-, -lysis, lyso-, -lyte, -lytic, -lyze; *base* -lax-, -liqu-, -solu-, -solv-
loss *base* perd-
loss of control *comb* -crasia, -crasy
loss of knowledge *comb* -agnosia
loss of quality *base* degen-
lot *comb* clero-
lotus *comb* loto-
loudness *base* crepit-, frem-, ligyr-, strep(i)-, strid-, stridul-. *See* **sound**
louse *base* pedicul-, phthir-, phthyr-
love *comb* -phile, -philia, -philiac, -philic, -philism, philo-, -philous; *base* -agap-, -am-, charit-
loveplay *comb* paizo-, paraphil-, sarmass-
low(er) *pre* hypo-, infero-, infra-, sub-, subter-, under-; *comb* chamae-, infero-, tapino-; *base* hystat-; ~ *growing*: *comb* chamae-
luck *base* faust-, tych-
ludicrous *base* fatu-, inan-, moro-, stult-
lukewarm *base* tepe-
lumbar *comb* lumbo-
lump *base* gleb-, glom-
lunch *base* prand-
lung(s) *comb* -pnea, pneo-, pneumato-, pneumo-, pneumono-, pulmo-, pulmoni-, pulmono-, spiro-
lurking-hole *base* latebr-
lust *comb* eroto-, -lagnia, -mania; *base* appet-, -cup-, -libid-, tentig-
luster *comb* sela-; *base* -fulg-, gano-, lustr-, nitid-, pheng-, rutil-, stilb-, stilpno-
lute *base* fidic-
lye *base* lixiv-
lying down *base* -cub-, -cumb-, supin-
lymph(atic) *comb* lymphato-, lympho-; ~ *nodes*: *comb* lymphadeno-; ~ *vessels*: *comb* lymphangio-
lynx *base* lync-
lyre *base* lyri-, psall-
lyric *comb* lyrico-; ~ *poem*: *base* epod-

M

macaw *base* psittac-
Macedonian lance *base* saris-
machine(s) *comb* mechano-
mackerel *base* scombr-
mad *comb* -margy; *base* frenet-, -fur-, -ira-
made of *suf* -en, -ic
madness *comb* lysso-, -mania; *base* ament-, dement-; *base* vesan-
magic *base* magic-, mago-
magnetic force *comb* magneto-
magnify *base* ampl-, aug-. *See* **increased**
magpie *base* corv-, garull-
maiden *base* virgin-
maim(ed) *comb* pero-; *base* -mutil-
main *comb* arch(i)-[1], proto-; *base* -prim-, -princip-; ~ *land*: *comb* epeiro-
make, making *pre* em-, en-; *comb* -craft, ergo-, -facient, -fer, -fic, -fication, -gen, -genesis, -genic, -genous, -geny, -gerous, ideo-, -parous, -phor, -phorous, -plast, -plastic, plasto-, -plasty, poiesis, -poietic, -urgy; *base* -fabr-, -fac-, –facture , -fec-1; *suf* -ate, -atory, -en, -ic, -ing, -fy, -ize, -otic; ~ *rich*: *base* locuplet-
Malay *comb* Malayo-
male *comb* andr(o)-, -androus, -andry, arrheno-, -man, masculo-; *base* viril-

malevolent *pre* dys-, mis-; *comb* caco-,
iniq-, kak(o)-, mal(e)-, ponero-; *base*
-prav-, sceler-, turp-
malformed *comb* pero-; *base* -mutil-
malfunction *pre* dys-
malnutrition *comb* -atrophia, -atrophic
manage *base* ger-¹
manatee *base* trichec-
mane *base* jubat-
manganese *comb* mangani-, mangano-
mangle *comb* sparasso-; *base* lacer-, lania-,
sparax-. *See* **maim**
manifest *comb* luci-, phanero-, pheno-;
base -clar-
mankind *comb* anthropo-
manner *comb* -wise
mantle *comb* pallio-
manufactured product *suf* -ite
manuscript *base* codico-
many *comb* multi-, myria-, myrio-, pluri-,
poly-, sychno-; ~ *colored: comb* poe-
cilo-; ~ *times: comb* pollaki-. *See*
increased
map *comb* carto-, charto-
maple *base* acer-²
marble *base* -marm-
margined *base* limbat-
marine *comb* halo-, mari-, thalasso-,
thalatto-; *base* naut-, nav-, pelag-; ~
flatworm: base nemert-
mark *comb* celido-; *base* stigm-
market *base* negot-, nundin-
marlin *base* istiophor-
marmoset *comb* callithri-
marmot *base* sciur-
marriage *comb* gameto-, gamo-, -gamous,
-gamy; *base* conjug-, marit-, -nub-,
-nupt-
marrow *comb* -myelia, myelo-; *base*
medull-
Mars *comb* areo-¹
marsh *comb* helo-², palud-, palus-, ulig-
marsupial mammal *base* phalang-
marten *base* mustel-
martin *base* hirund-
martyr *base* martyr-
masculine *comb* andro, -androus, -andry,
arrheno-, masculo-; *base* viril-
masonry type *base* emplect-
massage *comb* masso-

massive *comb* bronto-, dino-, giganto-,
mega-, megalo-, -megaly, pachy-
master *comb* magist-, maha-; *base* heri-,
heril-, maest-
mastoid *comb* mastoido-
matching *pre* para-, quasi-; *comb* homeo-,
omœo, homoio-, homolo-, iso-,
-phane, -phanic; *base* simil-; *suf* -acean,
-aceous, -al, -an, -ar, -ary, -ean, -en,
-eous, -esque, -ful, -ic, -il, -ile, -ine, -ing,
-ish, -itious, -ize, -like, -ode, -oid, -ose,
-osity, -some, -tious, -ular, -y
material for *suf* -ing
matter *comb* hylo-
maxilla *comb* maxillo-
maxim *base* gnom-²
maximum *pre* hyper-
meadow *base* prat-; ~ lark: icter-
meager *comb* oligo-, -penia, ptocho-,
vidu-; *base* -mendic-, -paup-, penur-,
-pov-
meal *comb* deipno-; *base* cen-, coen-,
prand-. *See* **food**. *Also see* "Food" in
Part III
meaning *base* etym-
means *suf* -cle, -ment¹
measles *base* morbilli-
measure *comb* -meal, -meter, -metric(s),
metro-, -metry. *See* "Measurement Science" in Part III
meat *comb* -burger, carni-, carnoso-, creo-,
kreo-, -sarc, sarco-; ~ market: macell-
mechanical *comb* mechanico-; *base*
banaus-
meddler *base* ardelio-
medical *comb* medico-; *base* -san-; ~
treatment: *comb* -iatrics, iatro-, -iatry
medicine *base* pharma(co)-; *medicinal:*
comb saluti-
mediocre *pre* hypo-, sub-, under-; *comb*
hystero-; *base* hesson-; *suf* -aster
meditate *base* melet-
medium *comb* mesati-, metrio-. *See*
middle
meeting *base* congress-, congru-
melodious *base* canor-
melon *base* pepo-
melt *comb* lyo-, lysi-, -lysis, lyso-, -lyte,
-lytic, -lyze; *base* deliqu-, fus-, -liqu-,
-solu-, -solv-

membrane *comb* chorio-, choroid-, hymeno-, membrano-; *eyeball ~:* sclero-; *fetal ~:* allant(o)-, amnio-; *~ partition:* comb mediastino-; *mucous ~:* comb muci-, muco-, mucoso-; *~ sheath:* comb meningo-
memory *comb* -mnesia, -mnesis; *base* -mem-, -mnem-
menace *base* comminat-, min-
meninges *comb* meningo-
menstrual *comb* emmen-, -menia, men(o)-
mental *comb* -gnomy, -gnosis, -gnostic, -gnoto, ideo-, -noia, -nomy, phren(o)-, psycho-, -sophy, thymo-; *base* -cogit-, -cogn-, -noe-, -put-, -ratio-, -sci-; *~ disorder:* comb -mania, -phrenia, -phrenic, phrenico-, phreno-, -thymia[1]
mercenary *base* venal-
merchandise *base* empor-, empt-
mercy *base* clem-[2], mansue-
mere *comb* psilo-
mesentery *comb* meso-
messenger *base* caduc-[2]
metabolism *base* metabol-
metacarpus *comb* metacarpo-
metal *comb* metalli-, metallo-; *~ plate:* base -elasmo-
metaphorical *comb* tropo-
metatarsus *comb* metatarso-
meteor names *suf* -id[1]; *~ stone:* base baetyl-
meteorological front *comb* fronto-
method *comb* -craft; *suf* -ade, -age, -al, -ance, -ancy, -asis, -asm, -ation, -cy, -ence, -ency, -ery, -esis, -iasis, -ice, -ics, -ing, -ion, -ism, -ment, -osis, -otic, -sion, -sis, -th, -tion, -tious, -ture, -ure, -y, -ysis
methoxy group *comb* methoxy-
methyl *comb* metho-
metrical *foot: base* iamb-; *~ pause: base* caesur-
middle *comb* centri-, -centric, centro-, medi(o)-, mesati-, mesio-, meso-, mezzo-, mid-
midriff *comb* -phrenic, phrenico-, phreno-
midwifery *base* maieut-
mighty *comb* dino-. *See* powerful

migration *base* diaped-, peregrin-
mild *base* -len-, mansue-, miti-[1], moll-
milk(y) *comb* galact(o)-, lacti-, lacto-
mill *base* molend-
million *comb* mega-
millionth *comb* micro-
millipede *base* arthropod-, diplopod
mind *comb* -gnomy, -gnosis, -gnostic, -gnoto, ideo-, -noia, -nomy, phreni-, phreno-, psycho-, -sophy, thymo-, -witted; *base* -cogit-, -cogn-, ment-[2], -noe-, noo-, -put-, -ratio-, -sci-; *~ disorder:* comb -mania, -phrenia, -phrenic, -thymia
mine *base* bothro-
mineral *suf* -ite, -lite
mingle *comb* -phyr, -phyre, -phyric
mink *base* mustel-
minnow *base* cyprin-
minor *insignificant: base* -nuga-. *See small child:* comb paedo-, pedi-, pedo-, proli-, tecno-; *base* -fil-, -puer-, tek-
mint *base* menth-
miracle *comb* thaumato-
mirror *comb* catoptro-, eisoptro-, enoptro-, spectro-
miscarriage *base* amblos-, amblot-
misery *base* aerumn-
missile *base* ballist-
missing *pre* a-, an-, des-[1], dis-, ex-, il-, im-, in-, ir-, un-; *comb* lipo-; *base* paralip-, -priv-; *suf* -less; *~ a part:* comb ectro-; *~ an opening:* comb -atresia, atreto-
mist *comb* fracto-, nepho-, nephelo-; *base* calig-, -nebul-, -nub-
mistake *base* culp-, delict-, laps-, pecc-, sphal-
mistletoe *comb* ixo-
mite *comb* acari-, acarin-, acaro-, miti-[2]. *See* termite
miter *base* mitri-
mixed, mixture *comb* -crasia, mixo-, mixti-, -phyr, -phyre, -phyric; *base* farrag-, –mictic , -misc-, -temp-; *~ with honey: base* muls-; *mixture of solid and molten rock: base* magma
mob *comb* ochlo-
mobility *comb* cine-, -drome, dromo-, -dromous, excito-, kine-, -kinesi(a)-, -kinesis, -kinetic, kineso-, kineto-,

kino-, -motive, -pragia, -praxia, -praxis, tremo-; *base* -stal-

mockery *base* deris-, satir-, scomm-, sytm-

mockingbird *base* -mim-

moderate *base* metrio-. *See* **medium**

modern *comb* neo-. *See* **new**

modesty *base* -pud-, verecund-

modification *comb* allo-, anomalo-, anomo-, poikilo-; *base* -mut-. *See* **change**

moisture *comb* hydro-, hygro-; *base* humect-, mad-, ulig-

molded *comb* -plast, -plastic, plasto-, -plasty

mole *blemish:* *base* nev(o)-; *animal:* *base* aspala-, talp-

mole rat *base* spalac-, zemni-

mollusks *comb* malaco-; *base* mollusc-; *bivalve ~:* *base* tellin-; *~with leathery tunics:* *base* ascid-

molt *base* exuv-

money *comb* -penny ; *base* chremat-, monet-, -numm-, -pecun-, quaest-; *~ exchange:* *base* cattall-; *~ changer:* *base* collyb-, nummul-; *~ lender:* *base* danist-

mongoose *base* viverr-

monitor lizard *base* varan-

monk *base* monach-

monkey *base* cebo-, pithec-

monster *comb* terato-; *base* pelor-

month *base* mens-

monthly *base* emmen-

monument *base* ste-

mood *comb* thymo-

moon *comb* luni-, lunu-, seleno-

moose *base* cervi-

moral *pre* bene-, eu-; *base* agath-, bon-, prob-

moray *base* muraen-

morbid condition *comb* -iasis; *suf* -oma

morel *base* morilli-, psomo-

more *pre* ad-, extra-, super-; *comb* aux-ano-, auxeto-, auxo-, multi-, myria-, myrio-, out-, over-, -plasia, pleni-, pleo-, pleio-, pleon-, plethys-, plio-, pluri-, pollaki-, poly-; *base* -aug-, -cresc-, -fold-, -pler-, -plet-. *See* **addition**

morning *base* -matut-

mortal *base* thneto-, thripto-

mortgage *base* -pign-

mosaic *base* tessel-

mosquito *comb* anophel-, culici-; *base* aed-

moss *comb* bryo-; *base* phasc-, musc-[2], sphagn-, splachn-

most *comb* pleisto-

moth *base* arct-, lepidopter-, noctui-, pha-laen-, tinea-

mother *comb* mater-, matri-, metr-, -para; *birth ~:* *comb* -para[3]

mother-in-law *base* socrus-, penther-

motion *comb* cine-, -drome, dromo-, -dromous, excito-, kine-, -kinesi(a), -kinesis, -kinetic, kineso-, kineto-, kino-, -motive, phoro-, -pragia, -praxia, -praxis, tremo-; *base* momen-, -stal-; *capable of ~:* *base* motil-; *easily set in ~:* *base* volub-

motivating *base* stimul-

motor *comb* moto-

mountain *comb* oreo-, oro-[2]; *base* -mont-; *~ash:* sorb-[2]

mourning *comb* lype-; *base* dolor-, -fleb-, -flet-, -luct-, lugub-, trist-

mouse *base* mur-[1], myo-[2] ; *meadow mouse:* *base* arvicol-

mouth *comb* -mouthed, or-[1], oro-, sto-mato-, -stome, -stomous; *open ~:* *base* ringi-; *roof of ~:* *comb* palato-, ura-nisco-, urano-; *~ wash:* collut-

move *comb* -grade, -motive, -plania, plano-[2]; *base* -bat-, -ced-, -cess-, -cur(s)-, -grad-, -gress-, -mob-, -mot-, mov-, -vad-, -vas-; *~ away:* *comb* allelo-, out-; *~ forward:* *comb* pro-; *~ toward:* *comb* -petal; *movement:* *comb* kinesi-, -kine-sia, -kinesis, kineso-, -praxia, -praxis

movies *base* cine-

muck *comb* blenno-, -chezia, copro-, lim-, muci-, muco-, myco-, myso-, -myxia, myxo-, p(a)edo-, scato-, stegno-, sterco-; *base* -fecu-, -fim-, molys-, rhypar-

mucus *comb* blenno-, muci-, muco-, mucoso-, -myxia, myxo-

mud *comb* pelo-; *base* -lim-, lut-

mulberry *base* -mor-[2], -mur-[3]

mulish *base* contum-, obstin-, pervic-, proterv-
mullet *base* mugil-, perces-
multiform *comb* polymorpho-
multiple *suf* -ce
multitude *comb* ochlo-
mummy *base* mummi-
murder *comb* -cidal, -cide, -cidious, -cidism; *base* dacn-, trucid-
murky *comb* ambly-, melano-, nycto-, scoto-; *base* achlu-, amaur-, fusc-, lyg-, obscur-, opac-, tenebr-
murmur *base* frem-, mussit-, susurr-
muscle *comb* musculo-, myo-[1], -tonic; ~ *tension:* -tonia
mushroom *comb* agar-, fungi-, myco-; *base* bolet- *see* **fungus**
music *comb* melo-[1], musico-, -tonic
musk *base* -mosch-
muskrat *base* cricet-
mussel *base* mytil-
mustard *base* sinap-
musty *base* mucid-

mutable *pre* be-, em-, en-, meta-, trans-; *comb* aetio-, -blast, -blastic, blasto-, -craft, ergo-, etio-, -facient, -fic, -fication, -gen, -genesis, -genic, -genous, -geny, -parous, -plasia, -plasis, plasmo-, -plast, -plastic, plasto-, -plasty, -poiesis, -poietic, -trope, -tropic, -tropism, tropo-, -tropous, -tropy, -urgy; *base* camb-, -fabr-, -fec-, -mut-, -vari-, -vert-, viciss-; *suf* -ate, en, -fy, -ize, -otic
mutilated *base* colo-
mutter *see* **murmur**
mutual *pre* co-, enter-, inter-, syl-, sym-, syn-, sys-; *comb* allelo-, hama-, symphyo-, synchro-; *base* -allac-, -allag-, -allaxis-, -mutu-
muzzle *base* capist-
myrtle *base* myrti-
mystery *base* myster-
mystical *comb* mystico-
myth *comb* mythico-, mytho-; *base* anagog-

N

nail *comb* helo-[1], onych-,-onychia, onycho-, scolo-; *base* clav-, ungui-, ungul-
naked *comb* gymno-, nudi- psilo-
name *comb* nomato-, -nomia, onomato-, -onym; *base* appell-, -nom-, -nym-, -onomasia; *to name: base* nuncup-
names of ~ *acids: suf* -onic; ~ *alcohols: suf* -itol; ~ *animals: suf* -id, -ida, -idae, -iformes, -zooic; ~ *bacteria: suf* -ella; ~ *classes: suf* -acea, -aceae, -ia, -oidea; ~ *companies: suf* -co, -ine; ~ *compounds: suf* -ide, -idine; ~ *country: comb* -land; *suf* -ia; ~ *directions: suf* -ern; ~ *diseases: comb* -aemia, -emia; *suf* -asis, -ia, -itis, -osis; ~ *electronic devices: comb* -tron; ~ *enzymes: suf* -ase; ~ *families: suf* -idae; ~ *festivals: comb* -fest, -mas; *suf* -ia; ~ *genera: suf* -aria, -odus, -soma; ~ *groups: comb* -zoa, -zoon; *suf* -aria, -id, -ini; ~ *hormones: suf* -kinin; ~ *meteors: suf* -id; ~ *minerals: suf* -lite; ~ *neutral substances: suf* -in ; ~

numerals, collective: suf -ad; ~*orders: suf* -acea; ~ *plants: suf* -ad, -ales, -ia; ~ *radicals: suf* -yl; ~ *super-families: suf* -oidea; *taxonomic* ~: *suf* -ota, -ote
narcotics *comb* leth-, mecon-, narco-
nard *base* nard-
narrow *comb* angusti-, areo-, dolicho-, isthm-, lepti-, lepto-, stegno-, steno-; *base* lirell-, -phim-, -stal-, -strict-, -tenu-; ~ *outlook: base* paroch-
nasal *comb* nasi-, naso-, rhino-
nation *base* gentil-
nationality *suf* -an, -ean, -ian, -ish, -ite, -n
native *base* enchor-, indigen-; *suf* -ite
natural *comb* innato-, physico-, physi-, physio-
nature *comb* -ousia, -ousian; *base* quid-; *having the* ~ *of: comb* -natured; *suf* -eous
nausea *base* qualm-
navel *comb* omphalo-, umbilici-
near *pre* a-, ac-, ad-, af-, ag-, al-, an-, ap-,

ar-, as-, at-, by-, cis-[1], epi-, para-, peri-; *comb* juxta-, citra-, pene-, plesio-, prox-imo-; *base* engus-, engys-, propinq-. *See* **adjacent**

nebulous *base* ambig, dub-, ancip-

neck *comb* atlo-, cervico-, coll-[1], jugo-, jugulo-, trachelo-; *base* -auchen-; *animal ~: comb* dero-; *~ of land: base* isthm-

necklace *base* monil-

nectar *comb* nectari-

needle *comb* aci-, acicul-; *base* acer-[1], -aichm-, -belon-, raphid-; *needle-like: comb* rhaphio-

negatives *pre* a-, ab-, an-, anti-, apo-, cata-, de-, dis-, dys-, ex-, il-, im-, in-, ir-, mal-, mis-, ne-, non-[1], ob-, un-; *comb* anti-, -atresia, atreto-, contra-, counter-, ectro-, lipo-, mal-, neutro-, nihil-, no-, nulli-, with-; *base* -priv-; *suf* -less

neglect *base* paralip-

negligent *base* lach-

neigh *base* hinn-

neighbor *base* geiton(o)-, -geton; *neigh-borhood: base* vicin-

nematodes *comb* nemato-

neoplasm *suf* -oma

nephew *base* nepo-

nerve *comb* ganglio-, nervi-, nervo-, neuro-

nest *base* -cali-, cubil-, nid(i)-

nestling *base* altric-

net/network *comb* dictyo-, -plex, reti-, reticulato-, reticulo-; *fishing net: base* sagen-

nettle *comb* cnido-; *base* -urtic-

neutral(izing) *pre* anti-; *comb* neutro-

neutral substances *suf* -in

new *comb* caeno-[2], caino-, cainoto-, -cene, ceno-[1], cenoto-, kaino-, kainoto-, neo-, thalero-; *base* -nov-[1]

newt *base* stellio-

NH *comb ~ acid radicals:* -imido; *~ non-acid radicals:* imino-

nicknames *suf* -y[3]

night *comb* nocti-, nycta-, nycti-, nycto-; *base* -crepus-, nocturn-, -vesper-; *all ~: comb* -pannychy

nightingale *base* philomel-

nightmare *base* malneiro-

nimbleness *comb* ocy-, tacho-, tachy-; *base* alacr-, celer-, festin-, veloc-

nine *comb* ennea-, nona-; *base* -nov-[2]; *~ hundred:* enneacent-. *Also see* "Numbers" in Part III

nineteen *base* enneakaideca-, undeviginti-

ninety *base* enneaconta-, nonagen-, nonages-

ninth *base* non-[2]

nip *base* vellic-

nipple *comb* mamilli-, papilli-, papillo-, papilloso-, thelo-, umbo-. *See also* **breast**

niter *comb* nitro-

nitrogen *comb* azo-, nitro-, nitroso-; *~ plus hydrocarbon:* diazo-; *~ NO radical comb* nitro(so)-

nod *base* nut(a)-

noise *base* crepit-, frem-, ligyr-, psopho-, strep(i)-, strid-, stridul-. *See* **sound**

noiseless *comb* hesy-; *base* -plac-, quiesc-, -tacit-

nonacid radical *comb* -amine, amino-

none *comb* nulli-. *See* **negatives**

nonexistence *base* acosm-

nonsense *base* fatu-, inan-, moro-, stult-

nonsexual *base* agam-

noon *base* merid-

noose *base* laqu-

normal *comb* normo-

Norman *comb* Normano-

north *base* borea-, septen-

northern lights *comb* aurora-

nose *comb* nasi-, naso-, rhino-, rhyncho-, -rrhyncha. *See* **beak**. *~ bleed:* epistax-; *~ blowing:* emunct-; *snub ~:* simo-; *sneer:* mycter-

nostalgia *comb* nosto-

nostrils *base* nari-

not *pre* a-[3], ab-, an-[1], apo-, cata-, de-, dis-, ex-, il-, im-, in-, ir-, mis-, ne-, non-[1], ob-, un-; *comb* anti-, contra-, counter-, mal-, neutro-, no-, nulli-, with-; *suf* -less

notch *comb* crenato-, crenulato-, -glyph; *base* forfic-. *See* **jagged**

notes *musical scale: comb* -tonic; *written: comb* -gram, -graph, -grapher, -graphic, grapho-, -graphy, grapto-, -logue, stigno-; *base* -scrib-, -script-, typo-

not having *pre* a-, an-, des-, dis-, ex-, il-, im-, in-, ir-, un-; *comb* -atresia, atreto-, ectro-, lipo-; *base* -priv-; *suf* -less

nothing *base* nihili-

notion *comb* -gnomy, -gnosia, -gnosis, -gnostic, gnoto-, ideo-, -noia, -nomy, phreno-, psycho-, -sophy *base* -cogit-, -cogn-, epistem-, -noe-, -put-, ratio-, -sci-

nourishment *comb* bromato-, -brotic, manduc-, opso-, -phage, -phago, -phagous, -phagy, -sitia, sitio-, sito-, -trophia, -trophic, tropho-, -trophy, -vora, -vore, -vorous; *base* -alim-, -cib-, -gust-, -nutr-, thrept-

noxious *comb* noci-, pesti-; *base* deleter-, -nox-, pericul-

nucleus *comb* caryo-, karyo-, nuclei-, nucleo-

number *base* arithm-, -numer-; *even ~:* *comb* artio-; *uneven ~: comb* impari-, perisso-; *a number of: suf* -age, -some[3]. *Also see* "Numbers" in Part III

numbness *comb* narco-; *base* torp-

numerals *base* arithm-; *cardinal ~: suf* -teen; *collective ~: suf* -ad; *ordinal ~: suf* -eth, -th. *Also* see "Numbers" in Part III

numerous *comb* multi-, myria-, myrio-, pluri-, poly-, sychno-

nurse *comb* threptero-; *base* threps-, thrept-

nut, nut-shaped *comb* caryo-, karyo-, nuci-, nucleo-

nuthatch *base* sitt-

nutmeg *base* myrist-

nutrition *comb* bromato-, -brotic, manduc-, opso-, -phage, -phago, -phagous, -phagy, -sitia, sitio-, sito-, -trophia, -trophic, tropho-, -trophy, -vora, -vore, -vorous; *base* alibil-, -alim-, -cib-, -gust-, -nutr-, thrept-

nymphs *comb* nympho-

O

oak *base* querc(i)-, robor-[2]; *evergreen ~:* cerr-

oar *comb* -reme, remi-

oats *base* aven(i)-

obedient *base* moriger-

obelisk *base* obel-

obese *comb* adip(o)-, lipo-, pimel(o)-, pio-, stearo-, steato-; *base* -aliph-, lipar-, -obes-, -pingu-, sebo-

object of an action *suf* -ate

objective *comb* teleo-, telo-, ultim(o)-; *base* -fin-, -termin-

oblige *base* -mand-

oblique *comb* loxo-, plagio-; *base* ambag-

oblong *comb* oblongo-

obscenity *base* aischro-, borbor-, copro-, fescinn-

obscure *comb* enigmato-; *base* ambig, aphan-, dub-, ancip-

obsequious agreement *base* assentat-

observe *comb* eid(o)-, oculo-, ommat-, -opia, opsi-, -opsia, -opsis, opso-, -opsy, ophthalmo-, optico-, opto-, -scope,

-scopic, scopo-, -scopy, visuo-; *base* -blep-, -scrut-, -spec-, -spic-, -vid-

obsessed with *comb* -aholic, -lagnia, -philia, -ridden

obstinate *base* contum-, obstin-, pervic-, proterv-

obstructed *comb* brady-; *base* -cunct-, imped-, -mora-, obturat-, occlud-, occlus-, -tard-

obstruction *comb* emboli-, embolo-; *base* -byon-, -farct-

obtain *base* -cap-, -cep-, -cip-, -dyte-

obtuse *comb* obtusi-

obvious *comb* lampro-, luc-, luci-; *base* -clar-

occipital *comb* occipito-

occlude *base* obturat-, occlud-, occlus-

occupation *comb* arti-, -craft, -ergasia, ergasio-, -ergic, ergo-, -ergy, organo-, -urgy; *base* -opus-, pono-; *suf* -arian

ocean *comb* halo-, mari-, thalasso-, thalatto-; *base* aequor-, naut-, nav-, pelag-

ochre *comb* ochreo-

odd-numbered *comb* impari-
odor *comb* brom(o)-, -odic, odori-,
odoro-, -olent, olfacto-, -osmia, osmo-
¹, osphresio-, ozo-, ozono-; *base* fet-,
nidor-. *See also* "The Senses" in Section III
of *suf* -acean, -aceous, -ac², -ad², -al, -an,
-ar, -arious, -ary, -atic, -ative, -atory,
-eae, -ean, -eous, -ery, -etic, -ial, -ian,
-ic, -id, -il, -ile, -ina, -inae, -ine, -ing,
-ious, -istic, -ite, -itic, -itious, -itive,
-ive, -oidea, -ory, -otic, -tious, -tive,
-ular; ~ *one another:* *comb* allelo-
off *pre* ab-, apo-, de-, ex-, for-
offering *base* -don-, -thy-
office *suf* -acy, -ate³, -cy, -dom, -ship
offspring *comb* proli-
often *comb* pluri-, pollaki-, poly-; *base*
crebr-; *suf* -le
oil *comb* elaeo-, elaio-, eleo-, olea-, -oleic,
oleo-; *oily ointment:* *base* lenim-
ointment *comb* myro-; *base* -unct-, ungu-
old *comb* archaeo-, archeo-, eo-, gerasco-,
gero-, geronto-, grand-, paleo-, presbyo-; *base* -antiq-, -sen-, -vet-; ~ *age:*
ger-²; ~*woman:* anil-, grao-
omission *pre* a-, an-, dis-, ex-, il-, im-, in-,
ir-, un-; *comb* lipo-; *base* paralip-, -priv-;
suf -less; ~ *of an opening:* *comb* -atresia, atreto-;~ *of a part:* *comb* ectro-
on *pre* ana-, epi-, ob-, sur-; ~ *both sides:*
comb amph(i)-; ~ *the left side:* *comb*
laeo-, laevo-, levo-, sinistro-; ~ *the*
other side: *pre* trans-; ~ *the outside:* *pre*
epi-; ~ *the right side:* *comb* dexio-, dextro-; ~ *the side:* *pre* by-; *comb* lateri-,
latero-; ~ *this side of:* *pre* cis-; *comb*
citra-; ~ *top:* *pre* super-
once *comb* semel-
one *comb* eka-, haplo-, heno-, mono-,
uni-; ~ *and one-half:* *base* hemiol-;
comb sesqui-; ~ *billion:* *comb* giga-; ~
billionth: *comb* nan(n)o-; ~ *by one:*
katheno-; ~*fifth:* quint-; ~*fourth:*
comb tetarto-; ~ *half:* *comb* demi-,
dicho-, dimid-, hemi-, mezzo-, semi-; ~
heptillion: *comb* yotta-; ~ *heptillionth:*
comb yocto-;~ *hexillion:* *comb* zetta-; ~
hexillionth: *comb* zepto-; ~ *hundred:*
comb centi-, hecato-, hecto-, hekto-;

~ *hundredth:* *comb* centi-; ~ *million:*
comb mega-; ~ *millionth:* *comb* micro;
~ *quadrillion:* *comb* femto-; ~ *quadrillionth:* *comb* peta-;~ *quintillion:*
comb atto-; ~ *quintillionth:* *comb* exa-;
~ *thousand:* *comb* chili-, kilo-; ~ *thousandth:* *comb* milli-; ~ *trillion:* *comb*
pico-; ~ *trillionth:* *comb* tera-. *See also*
"Numbers" in Part III
one another *comb* allelo-
one-eyed *base* lusc-
oneself *comb* auto-, self-; *base* sui-
one's own *comb* heauto-, idio-, pro-,
prio-, self-, sui-
one who ___ *suf* -aholic, -aire, -an, -ant,
-ar², -ard², -arian, -art, -ary, -ast, -ate,
-ator, -ee, -eer, -en, -ent, -er, -ette, -eur,
-fer, -ician, -ier, -ior, -ist, -le, -man, -nik,
-o, -or, -person, -people, -ster, -woman,
-yer; ~ *is well versed in* ___: -logist; ~
worships: *comb* -later
onion *base* cep-², cromny-
ooze *base* ulig-
opaque *comb* glauco-
opening *base* -apert-, -cav-, fenest-,
foram-, œgo-, oigo-, osti-, patul-, pylo-,
rim, valv-; *lack of ~:* *comb* -atresia,
atreto-; *surgical ~:* -stomy
open-mouthed *base* ringi-
open space *comb* agora-, ceno-, keno-
operation *comb* -ectomy
opinion *base* dox-, gnom-
opium *base* -mecon-
opossum *base* didelph-
opponent *base* antagon-
oppose *comb* macho-, -machy; *base* bell-,
pugil-, -pugn-
opposite *pre* anti-, contra-, contre-, dis-,
hetero-, ob-, un-; *comb* back-, counter-,
enantio-, oppositi-
option *base* -opt-, -vol-
opulence *comb* chryso-, pluto-; *base*
chrem-, -opul-, pecun-
oracle *comb* chresmo-
oral *base* acroa-
orange *fruit:* *base* -hesperid-; *color:* *base*
auranti-. *Also see* "Colors" in Part III
orangutan *base* -pong-
orb *comb* ano-, annul-, crico-, cyclo-,
disco-, globi-, globo-, glom-, gyro-,

orbito-, -sphere, sphero-, stilli-, zon-,
zoni-; *base* -anu-, -cing-, -cinct-, -cir-
cin-, -circul-, -coron-, -glomer-,
-numm-, -orb-, -rot-, -troch-
orbit *comb* orbito-
orchard *base* pomar-
orchid *comb* orchido-[1]
order *placement:* *comb* -tactic, -tactous,
taxi-, -taxia,-taxis, taxo-, -taxy; *base*
-pon-, -pos-; *right ~: base* eutax-; *command: base* imper-, -jus-, -mand-
ordinary *comb* homalo-, homolo; *~ people: comb* demo-; *base* -pleb-, -popul-
organ *comb* organo-; *suf* -ite; *having
female ~: comb* -gynous; *having male
~: comb* -androus
organic *comb* organo-
origin *comb* aetio-, -blast, blasto-, -blasty,
-carp, -carpic, carpo-, -carpous,
etio-, -gen, -genic, -genesis, -genetic,
-genous, -geny, -gone, -gonium, gono-,
-gony, -phyletic, sperma-, spermal,
spermatio-, spermato-, spermi-, -sper-
mic, spermo-, -spermous, sporo-; *base*
-init-; *suf* -esce, -escence, -escent
original *comb* archaeo-, primi-, primo-,
proto-
originate *base* inaug-, incip-, init-
oriole *base* -icter-
osmium *comb* osmio-
osmosis *comb* osmo-[2]
osprey *base* ossifrag-
ostrich *base* -rat-, struthi-
other *comb* allo-, alter-, hetero-; *base* -ali-[2]
otter *base* latax-, -lutr-
outcome *comb* ergo-, -ergic, -ergy; *suf*

-age, -asm, -ata, -ation, -ency, -ism, -ma,
-ment, -mony, -sion, -ure
outgrowth *comb* cele-, -edema, ganglio-,
-phym(a); *base* -tum-
outmoded *base* obsol-
out of *pre* e-, ec-, ef-, ex-. *See* **outside**
outside *pre* epi-, exo-, extra-, extro-, para-,
preter-; *comb* ecto-, extero-, foris-, out-
.; *base* exoter-. *See* **out of**
outskirts *base* limin-, marg-
ovalyl *comb* oxal-, oxalo-
ovary *comb* gyn(o)-, -gynous, -gyny,
oario-, oophoro-, ovario-
over *above: pre* ano-, meta-, ob-, preter-,
super-, supra-, sur-, sursum-; *comb*
over-; *again: pre* ana-, re-; *base* -palin-;
excessive: pre hyper-, super-, ultra-;
comb over-, poly-
overflow *base* antlo-, diluv-, inund-
overlapping *comb* imbricato-
oversight *base* culp-, delict-, laps-, pecc-,
sphal-
overt *comb* lampro-, luc-, luci-, -phane,
phanero-, -phanic, -phany, pheno-;
base -clar-, -schem-, -spec-, -spic-
overthrow *base* vict-, -vinc-
overweight *base* obes-, pingu-
ovum *comb* oo-, ovario-, ovi-[1], ovo-
owl *base* strigi-, tyto-, ulul-[2]
ox *comb* bou-, bov-, bu-
oxygen *comb* oxa-, oxy-[2]; *deprived of ~:
comb* deoxy-; *having two atoms of ~:
comb* dioxy-
oyster *comb* ostrei-, ostreo-; *base* -ostrac-
ozone *comb* ozono-

P

pack together *base* stip-[2]
pad *comb* tylo-
page-related *base* pagin-
page size *suf* -mo
pain *comb* alge-, algesi-, -algia, algo-, -algy,
-dynia, noci-, -odynia, odyno-, pono-
[1]; *base* dolor-, -nox-; *sudden ~: comb*
-agra. *See* **suffering**

paint *base* fucos-,-pict-, pigm-
pairs *pre* bi- *comb* conjugato-, didymo-,
diplo-, zyga-, zygo- ; *paired: base* chias-
palate *comb* palato-, uranisco-, urano-,
velar-
pale *comb* pallidi-; *~ green base* celad-
paleontological *comb* paleo-
palliative *base* anet-, -len-, miti-[1]

pallium *comb* pallio-; *base* stragul-
palm *hand:* *comb* palmati-, palmato-; *base*
    then-; *tree: base* palmac-
pan *comb* lecano-
pancreas *comb* pancreato-, pancreo-
pander *comb* leno-
panic *comb* -phobe, -phobia, -phobic,
    phobo-; *base* pavid-, tim(or)-, -trem-,
    -trep-. *Also see* "Fear" *in Part III*
paper *comb* carto-, charto-, papyro-
papillary *comb* papilli-, papillo-,
    papilloso-
papule *comb* papulo-
papyrus *comb* papyro-
parachute (using) *comb* para-
parade *comb* -cade
paraffin series: hydrocarbon *suf* -ane
parakeet *base* psittac-
paralysis *comb* -plegia, -plegy; *base* pares-
paramount *comb* arch-, archi-, proto-;
    base -prim-, -princip-
parasite *base* colaco-, parasit-, pothiri-,
    trypano-, vermin-
parasol *base* umbell(i)-, umbrell(i)-
parched *comb* carpho-, xero-; *base* arid-,
    celo-, cherso-, -sicc-, torr-
parchment *base* pergamen-
parent form *comb* proto-
parietal *comb* parieto-
parrot *base* galli-, psittac-
parsley *base* petrosel-
parsnip *base* pastin-
part(s) *comb* -fold, -meran, -mer(e),
    mer(o)-[1], -merous, par-, parti-
participant *suf* -ade; *~ in govt: comb* -crat
particles *base* chalic-; *base* mic-; *elemen-
    tary ~: suf* -on
particular *comb* -specific
partition *comb* parieto-, -phragma,
    phragmo-, septo-; *base* dialyt-,
    dissep-,-mur-
partly *comb* demi-, hemi-, semi-; *~ seri-
    ous:* serio-
partridge *base* gallinac-, -perdic-, -perdri-
parturient *comb* -para
pass *base* -bat-; *~ off: base* egestiv-
passable *base* perm-
passage *comb* isthm-, meato-, over-,
    poro-, soleno-; *base* -bat-
past *comb* preter-

paste *base* glutin-, intrit-. *See* **glue**
pastoral *care: base* poimen-; *~ poem:
    base* eclog-
patch *comb* emboli-, embolo-, -plakia
path *comb* -ode[1], odo-; *base* -itin-, -via-
pathetic *base* fleb-, trist-
pattern *base* regul-
pause *base* paus-
pawn *base* pign-
pay *base* impens-, -pend-, -pens-, salar-
pea *comb* pisi-
peace *base* -eiren-, -iren-, -pac-, -pax-; *~
    making: base* pacif-
peach *base* persic-
peacock *base* pavon-
peak *comb* coryph-; *base* culmin-
peanut *base* arach-
pear *comb* apio-, piri-, piro-, pyri-
pearl *base* margarit-
peat bog *base* turbar-
pebble *comb* pesso-, psepho-; *base* cal-
    cul-. *See* **stone**
peck *bird: base* becc-
peculiar *comb* aetheo-, anom(o)-, anom-
    alo-. *See* **irregular**
peculiarity of *suf* -ism
pedately *comb* pedati-
peel *comb* -lemma[2]
pejorative *suf* -aster, -erel
pelican *base* onocrot-, pelecan-
pelvis *comb* pelvi-, perineo-, pyelo-
pen *base* styl-
penetrate *base* terebr-
penguin *base* sphenisc-
peninsula *base* chersones-
penis *comb* medo-, peo-, phall(o)-; *base*
    med-, mentul-
pennant *base* vexill-
penniless *comb* -penia, ptocho-, vidu-;
    base -mendic-, -paup-, penur-, -pov-
people *comb* dem(o)-, ethno-; *base*
    anthrop-, hom-, homin-, -pleb-,
    -popul-, -vulg-
pepper *base* piper-
perception *comb* -esthesia, -esthesio, per-
    cepto-; *base* aisthes-
perch *fish: base* perc- *sit: base* -sess-
percussion *comb* pless(i)-; *base* -crot-,
    -cuss-, -puls-, -tus-, vapul-, verber-
perforation *comb* –tresia, trypo-. *See* **tear**

perfume *comb* myro-, -thymia[2]
pericardial *comb* pericardiaco-,
  pericardio-
peril *base* pericul-
perineum *comb* perineo-
period *time: comb* back-, chrono-, eo-,
  horo-, paleo, protero-, yester-; **menstrual:** *comb* emmen-, -menia, meno-
periosteum *comb* periosteo-
perishable *base* caduc-, fragil-
peritoneum *comb* meso-, peritoneo-
permanent *base* diuturn-, dur(o)-,
  perenn-, perm-, stabil-
pernicious *comb* noci-, pesti-; *base* -nox-,
  pericul-
peroneal *comb* peroneo-
perpetual *base* assid-, contin-, incess-,
  jug(it)-, perpet-
person *suf* -aholic, -aire, -an, -ant, -ard,
  -arian, -art, -ary, -ast, -ate, -ator, -ee, -eer,
  -en, -ent, -er, -ette, -eur, -fer, -ician, -ier,
  -ior, -ist, -le, -ling[1], -man, -nik, -o, -or[2],
  -person, -people, -ster, -woman, -yer
personal *comb* idio-, proprio-, self-
perspiration *comb* diaphor-, sudori-; *base*
  -hidr-, -suda-
persuade *base* -duc-
pertaining to *suf* -ac[2], -acean, -aceous,
  -ad, -al, -an, -ar[2], -arious, -ary, -atic,
  -ative, -atory, -eae, -ean, -eous, -ery,
  -etic, -ial, -ian, -ic, -id, -idan, -il, -ile,
  -ina, -inae, -ine, -ing, -ious, -istic, -ite,
  -itic, -itious, -itive, -ive, -oidea, -ory,
  -otic, -tious, -tive, -ular
perverted *base* deprav-
pest *comb* pesti-, vermin-
pestilence *comb* loemo-, loimo-. *See*
  disease
petal *comb* petuli-, -sepalous
petroleum *comb* petro-
petty *base* pusill-, rhopo-
pharynx *comb* pharyngo-
pheasant *base* alector-, gallinac-, phasian-
phenanthrene *comb* phenanthro-
phenol *base* carbol-; *suf* -ol
phenyl *comb* pheno-
philosophical *comb* philosophico-
phlegm *base* phlegm-, pituit-
phonetic *comb* phonetico-; ~ **stress:**
  comb -tonic

phony *comb* kibdelo-, mytho-, pseudo-;
  base fict-, mendac-, -notho-
phosphorous *comb* phospho-,
  phosphoro-
photography *comb* photo-
phrase *comb* phraseo-
phylum *comb* phylo-
physical *comb* physi-, physico-, physio-; ~
  love: eroto-
picked *base* -lect-[2]
piece *comb* clasmato-, -fid; *base* frag-,
  frust-, -par-
pierced *base* –forat
pig *base* porcin-, sui-
pigeon *base* columb-, palumb-, perister-,
  pullastr-
pig-headed *base* contum-, obstin-, per-
  vic-, proterv-
pike *base* esoc-
pile *base* -acerv-, conger-, -cumul-
pillar *comb* column-, stylo-[2]; *base* stel-; ~
  like: paxill-; **small ~:** columelli-
pillow *base* pulvin-
pimp *base* leno-
pimple *comb* pustulo-
pin *base* acu-, belon-
pinch *base* -rrhexo-
pine *base* -peuce-, pin-; ~ *cone:* strobil-
pineapple *base* bromel- (bromeliaceous)
pinnately *comb* pinnati-, pinnato-
pipe *comb* aulo-, follic-, salpingo-,
  siphoni-, siphono-, solen(o)-, syringo-,
  tubi-, tubo-, tubuli-, vasi-; *base* calam-,
  fistul-, -syr-
pistachio *base* pistac-
pistil *comb* gyn(o)-, -gynous, -gyny; *base*
  pistil-
pit *base* barath-, -taph(o)-, taphro-
pitcher *comb* urcei-, urceo-
pitchlike *base* piss-, pitta
pith *base* medull-
pitted *base* bothr-, fov-, scrobic-
place, a *comb* -land, loco-, situ-, -stead,
  topo-,-topy, ubi-; *suf* -ensis; ~ *of: suf*
  -age; ~ *for: suf* -arium, -ary, -cle, -ery,
  -orium, ory. *Also see* "Location" *in Part*
  III
place, to *comb* -thesis, -thetic; *base* -pon-,
  -pos-; *suf* -en
placenta *base* mazo-[1], placenti-

plague *comb* pesti-
plait *comb* pleco, plecto-
plane *surface:* *comb* explanato-, plani-, plano-[1]
plankton *comb* plankti-
planted *base* sativ-
plant growth: unequal *comb* -nastic, -nasty
plant(s) *comb* botano-, herbi-, -phyte, phyto-, vegeti-, vegeto-; *suf* -ad, -aceae, -ales, -eae, -ia; *coniferous ~:* *base* zamia-, zamio-; *green ~:* *base* thall-; *~ juices:* *base* muci-; *~ sap:* *base* succi-; *~ lice:* aphido-; *tumorous ~ tissue:* *base* cecid-
plastic surgery *comb* -plasty
plate *comb* lamelli-, lamini-, lamino-, placo-; *base* bract-, catill-, -tect-; *metal ~:* *comb* elasmo-
platinum *comb* platini-, platino-
platypus *base* monotrem-, protother-
play *comb* -lude
pleasant *base* amen(it)-, lipid-
please *base* allubesc-, delect-, -plac-, volupt-
pleasure *base* -hedon-, volupt-
pledge *base* -pign-
pleura *comb* pleuro-
plover *base* charadr-, pluvial-
plowed land *base* arv-
pluck *base* -tillo-, -vellic-
plug *comb* emboli-, embolo-; *base* -byon-, -farct-
plunderer *base* pirat-
plunge *comb* -merge, -merse
plural *suf* -a, -acea, -aceae, -ae, -des[2], -eae, -en[2], -es, -i, -ia, -ata, -ota, -s; *collective ~:* *suf* -ana
pod *base* kelyph-, silicul-, siliqu-
poems *comb* rhapso-; *base* eleg-, -metr-, muso-, versif-; *suf* -ad
pointed *comb* acantho-, aceto-, acetyl-, acid-, acro-, acu-, acuti-, cusp-, mucro-, oxy-[1], scillo-, scolo-, spiculi-, spiculo-, stilo-, stylo-[1]; *base* -acerb-, aci-, -aichm-, -aichur-, -belon-, fastig-, muric-, -punct-, -piq-, -pung-, stigm-; *sharp-pointed:* *comb* raduli-
points, having *comb* punctato-
poison *comb* tox(i), toxico-, -toxin, toxo-[1], veneni-, veneno-; *base* virul-

polar *comb* polari-
pole *base* cont-
polecat *base* mustel-
police officer *base* alyt-
polished *base* levig-, limat-, xest-
political *comb* politico-
pollen *comb* palyn-, pollini-
pollute *base* -turp-
polymer of *pre* meta-
pomegranate *base* balaust-
pond, pool *comb* limno-; *base* lacus-, stagn-
ponder *base* rumin-
poor *deficient:* *comb* -isch-, oligo-, -penia; *penniless:* *comb* ptocho-, vidu-; *base* egent-, indig -, -mendic-, -paup-, penur-, -pov-; *quality:* *comb* caco-, kako-
poppy *comb* opio-, papaver-; *base* -mecon-
porcelain *base* poticho-
porcupine *base* hystric-
pore *comb* pori-, poro-, poroso-
pork *base* porcin-
porphyritic rock *comb* -phyre
porpoise *base* delphin-, phoecaen-
portal *comb* porto-
portico *base* exedr-, portic-, stoa-, xyst-[2]
portion *base* par-[1]
position *office:* *suf* -acy, -ate, -cy, -dom, -ship; *position in a series:* *base* ordin-. *See* **place**
possessing *comb* -echia; *suf* -acean, -aceous, -al, -ate, -ed, -ful, -gerous, -ial, -ine, -ious, -itious, -ory, -ous, -some, -ulent, -ulous, -wise, -y; *base* habent-, -ten-; *~ parts:* *comb* -fold
possibility *suf* -atile
postage stamp *base* philatel-, timbro-
post-embryonic *base* nep-
posterior *comb* postero-
posture *comb* ichno-
potassium *comb* kal(i)-
potbelly *base* physc-
potency *comb* dyna-, dynamo-, mega-, megalo-, -megaly, -sthenia, stheno-; *base* -forc-, -fort-, -poten-, robor-; *~ to do or be:* *suf* -bility
pottery *base* figul-
pouch *comb* angio-, asco-, burs(o)-,

-ceco, chlamyd-, chrysali-, coleo-, -cyst, cysti-, cysto-, follic-, meningo-, peri- cardiaco-, pericardio-, peritoneo-, physa-, physali-, physo-, theca-, theco-, typhlo-, utric-, vesico-; *base* marsup-, -sacc-, scrot-, -thylac-

poultry *base* gallin-

pound *comb* -cuss-, plessi-, rhabdo-; *base* -cop-, -crot-, fustig-, plang-, puls-, quass-, vapul-, -verber-

pour *base* -chys-, -chyt-, ecchym-, -flu-, -fus-

poverty *comb* -penia, ptocho-, vidu-; *base* egest-, -mendic-, -paup-, penur-, -pov-

power(ful) *comb* -crat, crato-, dyna-, dynamo-, mega-, megalo-, -megaly, stheno-; *base* -forc-, -fort-, imper-, -poten-; ~ *to do or be: suf* -bility; *powerful voice: base* stentor-

practical *base* practic-, pragmat-

practice of *comb* -craft; *suf* -ade, -age, -al, -ance, -ancy, -asis, -asm, -ation, -cy, -ence, -ency, -ery, -esis, -iasis, -ice, -ics, -ing, -ion, -ism, -ment, -osis, -otic, -sion, -sis, -th, -tion, -tious, -ture, -ure, -y, -ysis

practitioner *suf* -ician, -ist

praise *base* encom-, eulog-, -laud-

prawn *base* carid-

pray *base* litan-, orat-, -prec-, -rog-; *prayer of praise*: doxol-

preaching *base* kery-

precipice *base* -cremno-

predilection for *comb* philo-

pregnancy *comb* -cyesis, toco-; *base* ges- tat-, -gravid-, -maieusi-, sylleps-

prehistoric *comb* eo-, paleo-, proto-

preparation *pre* pre-

present *base* -don-

preserver *suf* -sote

press together *base* stip-²

pressure *comb* -bar, bar(o)-, -pie- sis, piezo-, -tonia, -tonic, tono-; *base* impuls-, thlips-

pretend *comb* pseudo-; *base* fict-, -simul-; *pretended ignorance: base* eiron-

preventing *pre* anti-; *base* imped-, prohib-

previous *pre* pre-; *comb* back-, yester-

prickly *comb* echinato-, echino-, echinu- lato-, echinuli-; *base* -urtic-

priest *base* presbyter-, sacerdot-

primary *comb* archi-, proto-; *base* -prim-, -princip-

primate *comb* -pithecus

primitive *comb* archi-, paleo-, prisc-, proto-

principal *comb* arch(i)-¹, prim-, proto-

principle of *suf* -ism

print *comb* -type

prior to *pre* pre-; *comb* back-, yester-

private *base* -priv-. See **secret**

proceed *comb* -grade, -motive, -plania, plano-; *base* -bat-, -ced-, -cess-, -cur(s), -grad-, -gress-, -mob-, -vad-, -vas-; ~ *away:* out-; ~ *into:* -dyte-; ~ *forward:* pro-; ~ *toward:* -bound, -petal

process of *comb* -craft; *suf* -ade, -age, -al³, -ance, -ancy, -asis, -asm, -ation, -cy, -ence, -ency, -ery, -esis, -iasis, -ice, -ics, -ing, -ion, -ism, -ment1, -osis, -otic, -sion, -sis, -th, -tion, -tious, -ture, -ure, -y, -ysis

procession *comb* -cade

proclamation *base* kery-

procure *base* -cap-, -cep-, -cip-, -dyte-

produce/producing *comb* -facient, -fer- ous, -fic, -fication, -gen, -genesis, -genic, -genous, -geny, -gerous, ideo-, -parous, -phor, -phorous, -plast, -plas- tic, plasto-, -plasty, poiesis, -poietic, -urgy; *suf* -ate, -atory, -ic, -fer, -ing, -otic; *productive: comb* proli-

product of *comb* -geny², -gony; *suf* -ade, -ery, -ment¹

proficiency *base* -apt-, -habil-, -poten-, -qual-; *suf* -bility, -ful, -ship

profit *base* lucri-, quaest-

profusion *base* ampl-, copi-, larg-

projectile *base* -ballist-

promoting *base* -gog-

promptness *base* alacr-, exped-

proneness *comb* -clisis

prop *base* sterigm-

propagate *base* thremm-

propel *comb* -bole, -bolic, bolo-, -boly; *base* ballist-, -jact-, -jacula-, -ject-

proper *comb* cyrio-, kyrio-, ortho-

properties *suf* -ics

prophetic *comb* fati-, vati-

propitiatory *base* hilasm-, ilast-

proportion of 2 to 3 *comb* subsesqui-
proposition *comb* -lemma[1]
prosperity *comb* chryso-, pluto-; *base*
   chrem-, -opul-, pecun-
prostate *comb* prostato-
prostitute *comb* cypriano-, hetaero-,
   porno-; *base* -meretric-, scort-;
   brothel: lupan-
protected against *comb* -proof
protecting from *comb* para-[1]; *base* tutel-
protection *comb* -phylactic, phylacto-,
   -phylax, -phylaxis
protein *comb* proteo-
protein hydrolysis *suf* -ose
protest *base* -quer-, -querul-
protoplasm *comb* -plasmo-, -plast
protuberance *comb* condyl(o)-, gib-
   boso-, hybo-, papillo-, ramoso-, thelo-,
   umbo-; *base* boss-
proverb *base* adag-, parem-, paroem-
provide *pre* be-; *base* -don-; *suf* -ate
provided with *comb* -echia; *suf* -able, -ate,
   -ed-[2], -ious, -ous
provincial *base* paroch-
proving *comb* -deictic
provisions *base* annon-, opso-[2]
prow-shaped *base* pror-
proximity *pre* a-, ac-, ad-, af-, ag-, al-, an-,
   ap-, ar-, as-, at-, by-, cis-, epi-, para-,
   peri-; *comb* juxta-, citra-, pene-, prox-
   imo-; *base* vicin-
proxy *comb* allelo-, allo-, alter-, hetero-;
   base -ali-
psychosis *comb* lysso-, -mania; *base*
   ament-, dement-
ptarmigan *base* tetraon-
pubescent *base* hebe-
pubic *comb* pubio-, pubo-
public *comb* demo-; *base* -pleb-, -vulg-
puke *comb* -emesis, -emetic, emeto-
pull *base* -tillo-, -tract-, vell-

pulley *comb* trochi-, trocho-; *pulley-like:*
   base trochlea
pulmonary *comb* pulmo-
pulse *comb* sphygmo-; *base* -crot-
pumpkin *base* pepo-
puncture *comb* -centesis; *base* stigm-
punishment *comb* mastigo-, rhabdo-;
   base castig-, peno-, poine-, -pun-[1]
pupa *comb* nympho-; *base* pupa-
pupil *eye: comb* core-[1], coreo-, -coria,
   coro-, -koria, pupillo-; *student: base*
   -discip-
puppet *base* pupa
purchase *comb* onio-; *base* -empt-,
   -merc-, nundin-
purge *base* expurg-; *enema: comb* -clysis;
   base chalast-, clysm-; clyst-
purify *base* cathar-, **purify** *base* laut-. *See*
   cleanse
purple *comb* purpureo-; *base* amaranth-,
   blatt-[2], indi-, indo-, phenic-, porphyr-,
   -pun-[2]. *Also see* "Colors" *in Part III*
purpose *comb* teleo-, telo-; *base* teleio-
purse *comb* burs(o)-, marsup-, phasco-
purslane *base* portulac-
pursue *base* secut-, sequ-
pus *comb* purulo-, pyo-. *See* **infection**
push *comb* -trude; *base* -pel-, -pul-, trus-
pustular eruption *base* mentig-, psydrac-
put *base* -pon-, -pos-; *suf* -en; ~ *in the*
   form of: suf -ate; ~ *together: comb* -the-
   sis, -thetic; *base* cond-, -fabr-, -fac-,
   -fec-, -fic-,-struct-
putrefying *comb* cario-, lysi-, lyso-, -lysis,
   -lyte, -lytic, phthino-, phthisio-, -phthi-
   sis, putre-, putri-, pytho-, sapro-, septi-,
   septico-, septo-; *base* marcesc-, myda-,
   phthor-, tabe-; *suf* -ase
pylorus *comb* pyloro-
pyramid *base* pyram-
pyrites *comb* pyrito-

Q

quadrillion(th) *comb* femto-, peta-
quaff *comb* pino-, poto-; *base* -bib-, pocul-
quail *base* coturn-, gallinac-, ortyg-
quake *base* -pav-, -trem-

qualified *comb* -potent; *suf* -able, -ible,
   -ile; *base* habilit-; *in a* ~ *way:* -bly
quality of *suf* -able, -acity, -acy, -age,
   -ance, -ancy, -ant, -asis, -asm, -ate,

-atile, -ation, -cy, -dom, -eity, -ence,
-ency, -ent, -ery, -esis, -ful, -hood,
-iasis, -ice[1], -ility, -ion, -ise, -ism, -ity,
-ling, -ma, -ment, -ness, -or[3], -osis,
-otic, -red, -ship, -sion, -th, -tion, -tude,
-ture, -ty[1], -ure, -y[2]

qualm *comb* -phobe, -phobia, -phobic,
phobo-; *base* pavid-, tim(or)-, -trem-,
-trep-. *Also see* "Fear" *in Part III*

quantity *base* -quant-; *suf* -age, -ful

quarrel *comb* -machy; *base* litig-, pugil-,
-pugn-, -rix-

quarry *base* lat-[2]

quarter *base* quadr-

quash *comb* lysi-, lyso-, -lysis, -lytic, -lyze,
-phage, phago-, -phagous, -phagy; *base*
-ate-[4], perd-, phthart-, -vast-

quaver *comb* tremo-; *base* pav-, trep-

queen *base* regin-

quell *comb* stasi-, -stasis, -stat, stato-; *base*
fin-, termin-

quest *comb* -petal, -quire, -quiry; *base*
indag-, -rog-, -scrut-

question *base* erot-, quer-[2], -quir-, -rog-;
questioning: *base* pysm-

quickness *comb* ocy-, tacho-, tachy-; *base*
alacr-, celer-, festin-, veloc-

quicksand *base* syrt-

quiet *comb* hesy-; *base* -plac-, quiesc-,
-tacit-

quinine *base* cinchon-, quin-[2]

quintillion(th) *comb* atto-, exa-

quirky *comb* aetheo-, anom(o)-, anom-
alo-. *See* **irregular**

quisling *base* prodit-

quit *base* relinq-

quite *pre* be-, cata-, cath-, de-, kata-, ob-,
per-; *comb* holo-, omni-, pan-, panto-,
stone-, toti-

quivering *comb* -chorea, choreo-, -clonic,
-clonus, -esmus, -ismus, spasmo-; *base*
-stal-, -vellic-

R

---

rabbit *base* cunic-, lago-, lepor-; ~ ***rabbit-like quadruped*:** comb hyraci-,
hyraco-

rabies *base* lyss-

raccoon *base* arctoid-, procyon-

race *group*: *comb* -ethno, geno-, phylo-

race *course comb* -drome, dromo-,
dromous

radiant *comb* helio-; *base* fulg-, nitid-; ~
***emission*:** *comb* aurora; ~ ***energy*:** *comb*
bolo-[2], radio-, spectro-

radicals *suf* -yl, -ylene; *two* ~: *comb* bi-

radicle *comb* radiculo-, rostell-

radioactive *comb* radio-

radish *base* raphan-

rag *base* pann-

raging *base* rabid-

rail *bird*: *base* rall-

railroad *base* siderodromo-

rain *comb* hyeto-, pluvio-; *base* imbri-,
nimb-, ombr-

rainbow *base* irid-

raise *cultivate*: *comb* -culture; *base*
-ponic; *lift*: levat-

ram *comb* crio-, krio-; *base* -ariet-

rank *position*: *comb* -rater; *suf* -cy, -dom[2],
-ship; *rank smell*: *base* graveol-

rap *comb* plessi-; *base* cop-, -crot-, -cuss-,
-plang-, puls-, -tus-, vapul-, -verber-

rape *base* rap-, rep-, stupr-

rapid *comb* ocy-, tacho-, tachy-; *base*
alacr-, celer-, festin-, veloc-

rare *comb* mano-, spano-; *base* -areo-[2]

rash *comb* –anthema; *base* exanthem-

rasp *base* radul-

raspberry *base* frambes-

rat *base* mur-; *mole-rat*: *base* spalac-,
zemni-

rate *comb* -rater

ratio, inverse *pre* sub-

rattlesnake *base* crotal-

raven *comb* coraci-, coraco-; *base* corvin-

ravenous *base* avid-, edac-, gulos-

raw *base* omo-[2]

ray *comb* radio-, radiato-; *base* bolo-[2], -rad-

razor *base* xyr-

reading *comb* -legia, -lexia, -lexis, -lexy;
base lect-, -leg-[1]

real *base* ver-
realm *suf* -dom, -ric
reaper *base* mess-
rear *comb* hind-. *See* **behind**
reasoning *comb* -gnomy, -gnosia, -gnosis,
　　-gnostic, -gnoto, ideo-, -noia, -nomy,
　　-phrenic, phrenico-, phreno-, psycho-,
　　-sophy, thymo-, -witted; *base* -cogit-,
　　-cogn-, ment(a)-, -noe-, -put-, -ratio-,
　　-sci-
rebuke *base* -jurg(at), increp-, objurg-
receiver *comb* -ceptor; *base* -cap-, -cip-;
　　suf -ee
recent *comb* -cene, ceno-¹, neo-, nov-
receptacle *comb* angio-, asco-, bursi-,
　　burso-, ceco-, chlamyd-, chrysali-,
　　cisto-, coleo-, -cyst, cysti-, cysto-, fol-
　　lic-, meningo-, pericardiaco-, peri-
　　cardio-, peritoneo-, phasco-, physa-,
　　physali-, physo-, -theca, theci-, theco-,
　　typhlo-, utri-, utric, vesico-; *base* -sacc-,
　　-thylac-; *suf* -arium
recipient *suf* -ee
reciprocal *pre* co-, inter-, syl-, sym-, syn-,
　　sys; *comb* allelo-, hama-, symphyo, syn-
　　chro-; *base* -allac-, -allag-, -allaxis-,
　　-mutu-
reckless *base* temer-
recline *base* -cub-, -cumb-
recognition *comb* -gnosis, -gnostic
recoil *base* abhor-
reconstructive surgery *comb* -plasty
rectification *comb* ortho-; *base* castig-,
　　emend-
rectum *comb* procto-, recto-
red *comb* carmino-, erysi-, erythro-,
　　phoeni-, pyhrro-, rhodo-, roseo-, rufi-,
　　rufo-, testaceo-; *base* coccin-, coquel-,
　　cruent-, -ereuth-, ferrug-, fuc-, grenat-,
　　-later-, minia-, murex-, nacar-, -rub-,
　　-rud-, -rut-, rutil-; ***reddish-orange:*** *base*
　　miniac-. *Also see* "Colors" in Part III
reduced *base* trunc-
redundant *comb* perisso-
reed *comb* aulo-, follic-, salpingo-,
　　siphoni-, siphono-, solen(o)-, syringo-,
　　tubi-, tubo-, tubuli-, vasi-; *base* arundi-,
　　calam-, cann-, fistul-, -syr-
refine *base* alemb-
reflection *base* anacamp-

reflective thought *base* specul-
refresh *base* focill-
refuse to *pre* dis-
refutation *base* elench-
region *comb* choro-
regular *comb* cyrio-, kyrio-, homalo-,
　　homolo-, ortho-
regulate *base* modul-, -temp-
regurgitate *comb* -emesis, -emetic, emeto-
reindeer *base* rang(if)-, tarand-
reject *base* abdic-, athet-, relinq-
rejoicing *base* laet-
relapse *base* recidiv-
relate *base* narr-
relating to *suf* -acean, -aceous, -ad²,
　　-al, -an, -ar, -arious, -ary, -atic, -ative,
　　-atory, -eae, -ean, -eous, -ery, -etic, -ial,
　　-ian, -ic, -id, -il, -ile, -ina, -inae, -ine,
　　-ing, -ious, -istic, -ite, -itic, -itious,
　　-itive, -ive, -oidea, -orious, -ory, -otic,
　　-tious, -tive, -ular
relatives *base* cogn-, famil-, stirp-; ~ ***not***
　　by blood: *comb* step-
relaxant *comb* -clysis; *base* chalax-,
　　clysm-, clyst-
release *base* -miss-, -mit-, -pomp-
relieving *comb* lyo-, lysi-, -lysis, lyso-,
　　-lyte, -lytic, -lyze; *base* -liqu-, -solu-,
　　-solv-
relics *comb* lipsano-, reliq-
religion *comb* religio-, theo-
relish *base* opso-²
remaining *base* perman-
remains *base* reliq-
remedial *comb* saluti-
remember *comb* -mnesia, -mnesis; *base*
　　-mem-, memor-, -mnem-
remote *comb* disto-, tele-
remove *pre* ab-, abs-, apo-, be-, de-, des-,
　　di-, dia-, dif-, dis-, e-, ec-, ef-, ex-, for-,
　　off-, se, with-; *comb* ectro-; *base* ablat-,
　　adempt-, expurg-
render favorable *base* propit-
repair *comb* ortho-; *base* castig-, emend-
repeatedly *comb* batto-, pollaki-;
　　base epana-, -iter-, palin-; *suf* -er; ~
　　sounded: *comb* echo-. *See* **frequent**
repentance *base* penit-
replacement *comb* allelo-, allo-, alter-,
　　hetero-; *base* -ali-

replete *comb* -filled, pleni-, pleo-, plero-, pluri-; *base* -pler-, -plet-; *suf* -acious, -ate, -ic, -ful, -ilent, -ose, -osity, -ous, sat-, satur-, -ulent, -y

reply *base* apocris-. *See* **say**

representative *base* legat-[1]

repress *comb* stasi-, -stasis, -stat, stato-; *base* fin-, termin-

reproach *comb* enisso-, enosi-; *base* castig-

reproduce *comb* aetio-, -blast, blasto-, -blasty, -carp, -carpic, carpo-, -carpous, etio-, -gen, -genic, -genesis, -genous, -geny, -gone, -gonium, gono-, -gony, -phyletic, sperma-, -spermal, spermato-, spermi-, -spermic, spermo-, sporo-; *base* -init-; *suf* -esce, -escence, -escent

reptile *comb* echidno-, -glypha, herpeto-, -ophidia, ophidio-, ophio-, -saur, sauro-, -saurus; *base* angui-, batrach-, colubr-, reptil-, -serp-, viper-

repulsion *base* fastid-

request *base* -pet-, - postul-, quir-, -quis-, -rog-

require *base* exig-, -pet-

rescued *comb* eleuthero-; *base* -liber-, vac(u)-

resembling *pre* para-, quasi-; *comb* homeo-, homoio-, homolo-, iso-, -opsis, -phane, -phanic, -phany, pheno-; *base* simil-; *suf* -acean, -aceous, -al, -an, -ar, -ary, -ean, -en, -eous, -esque, -ful, -ian, -ic, -il, -ile-, -ine, -ing, -ish, -istic, -istical, -itious, -ize, -like, -ode, -oid, -oidal, -ose, -osity, -some, -tious, -ular, -y

resentment *base* -invid-

reservoir *base* lacco-

resin *comb* resino-

resistant to *comb* -proof, -tight; *base* krato-; ~ *disease: comb* immuno-

resourceful *base* agil-, facil-, ingen-

respiration *comb* -pnea, pneo-, pneumato-, pneumo-, pneumono-, pneusio-, pulmo-, respirato-, spiro-[1]; *base* -hal-

responsibility *comb* hypegia-, hypengy-; *base* paralip-

responsive to *comb* bathmo-, -trope,

-tropic, -tropism, tropo-, -tropous, -tropy

rest *base* oti-

restless *comb* agito- *base* -turb-

restrained *comb* brady-, freno-; *base* -cunct-, imped-, -mora-, -tard-

restriction *comb* isch-, koly-, -penia, rhopo-, -strain, -strict; *base* angust-, -string-; *suf* -en. *See* **tie**

result (of) *comb* ergo-, -ergic, -ergy; *suf* -age, -asm, -ata, -ation, -ency, -ism, -ma, -ment[1], -mony, -sion, -ure

retaliation *comb* counter-; *base* tal-

retention *comb* -echia, -tain; *base* -cathex-, -ten-

reticular *comb* reticulo-

retina *comb* retino-

return *pre* re-; *comb* nosto-

reveal *comb* phaeno-, pheno-; *base* -monstr-

revenue *base* fiscal-

reversal *comb* allo-; *base* -vers-, -vert-

reverse *pre* anti-, de-

revile *base* vituper-

revulsion *comb* miso-, -phobe, -phobia, -phobic; *base* -invid-, -ira(sc)-, odi-; *base* abom-

rhinoceros *base* ceratorh-

rhombus *comb* rhombo-

rhythm *base* rhythm-; ***rhythmic beat:*** *base* -crus-, -crust-

rib *comb* costi-, costo-

ribbon *comb* taeni-, taenio-, -tene, teni-; *base* lemnisc-

rice *comb* oryzi-, rizi-, ryzi-

riches *comb* chryso-, pluto-; *base* chrem-, -opul-, pecun-

riddle *base* griph-

ridge *comb* crebri-, lophio-, lopho-; *base* -carin-

ridicule *comb* catagelo-, katagelo-; *base* diasyrm-

ridiculous *base* fatu-, inan-, moro-, stult-

rift *comb* dicho-, -fid, fissi-, schisto-, schizo-, sulcato-, -tomy; *base* crev-, fatisc-, -par-, rim-

right *comb* recti-; ~ *angle: comb* ortho-; ~ *side: comb* dexio-, dextro-; ***correct:*** *comb* ortho-; *base* emend-

righteous *pre* bene-, eu-; *base* agath-, bon-, prob-

rigid *comb* ancylo-, ankylo-, tetano-; *base* rigesc-

rind *comb* -lemma[2]

ring *comb* annul-, ano-[2], crico-, cyclo-, disco-, globo-, gyro-, -sphere, sphero-, stilli-; *base* -anu-, -cinct-, -cing-, -circin-, -circul-, -coron-, -glomer-, -numm-, -orb-, -rot-, -troch-, -zon-; *finger* ~: dactylio-; ~ *shaped:* ano-[2]

ringing *base* tinn-, tintinn-

ringlet *comb* cirr(h)i-, cirr(h)o-

ripe *base* -matur-

rise *base* -cresc-, -surg-

risky *base* pericul-

rival *pre* anti-

rivalrous *base* emul-

river *comb* fluvio-, potamo-; *base* amn-, flum-, -rip-

roach *base* blatt-

road *comb* hodo-, -ode, odo-; *base* -iter-, -via-

roadrunner *base* cucul-

roar *base* -frem-

robber *comb* clepto-, klepto-, lesto-; *base* -furt-, harpax-, latro-, latrunc-, pred-

robin *base* -turd-

robust *comb* -proof, dur(o)-; *base* -forc-, -fort-

rock *comb* -lithic, litho-, pesso-, petri-, petro-, sax(i)-; *base* -lapid-, -rupes-, rupic-; *suf* -ite

rod (shaped) *comb* bacilli-, bacillo-, bacul-, fusi-, fuso-, rhabdo-, vergi-; *base* coryn-, ferul-, -rad-, virgul-; *rodlike:* *comb* scapo-; *base* veretill-

rodent *base* arvic-, gliri-, mur-, myo-; ~ *with cheek pouches:* *base* saccomy-

rolling *comb* trochalo-

Roman *comb* Romano-

romantic *comb* romantico-

roof *comb* stego-, tecti-, tegu-; ~ *of mouth:* *comb* palato-, uranisco-

rookie *base* tiro-, tyro-

rooster *comb* alector-, alectry-

root *comb* radiculo-, rhizo-, -rrhiza; *base* -radic-, -stirp-; ~ *meaning:* *base* etym-

rope *comb* funi-, resti-, schoeno-

rose *comb* rhodo-, roseo-

rotary *comb* cyclo-, roti-, troch-, trochalo-, trochi-, trocho-; *base* dinet-

rotten *comb* lysi-, lyso-, -lysis, -lyte, phthysio-, -phthysis, putre-, putri-, pytho-, sapro-, septi-, septo-; *base* -putr-, rancid-.

rough *comb* asper-. trachy-; *base* -rud-, salebr-

round *comb* ano-, annul-, convexo-, crico-, cyclo-, disco-, gibboso-, globi-, globo-, glom-, gyro-, orbito-, rotundi-, rotundo-, -sphere, sphero-, stilli-, tereti-, tereto-, trochi-, trocho-, zon-, zoni-; *base* -anu-, -cing-, -cinct-, -circin-, -circul-, -coron-, -glomer-, -numm-, -orb-, -rot-, strongyl-; *partly* ~: *comb* orbiculato-

route *comb* -ode, odo-; *base* -itin-, -via-

routine *comb* -craft; *suf* -ade, -age, -al, -ance, -ancy, -asis, -asm, -ation, -cy, -ence, -ency, -ery, -esis, -iasis, -ice, -ics, -ing, -ion, -ism, -ment, -osis, -otic, -sion, -sis, -th, -tion, -tious, -ture, -ure, -y, -ysis

rowing *base* remig-

rows *comb* -stichia, sticho-, -stichous

royal *base* basil-, reg-, regn-

rubbing *comb* tribo-, -tripsy; *base* trit-

rubble *base* ruder-

rude *base* contum-, impud-, procac-

rue *base* rut-

rug *base* lodic-

ruination *comb* lysi-, lyso-, -lysis, -lytic, -lyze, -phage, phago-, -phagous, -phagy; *base* -ate-[4], perd-, phthart-, -vast-

rule *base* leg-[2], regul-

ruler *comb* -arch-[2], gubern-; *base* -reg-

ruling *comb* -archy, -ocracy; *base* -regn-

rumbling *base* borbor-

rumor *base* famig-

rump *comb* podic-, pygia, pygo-; *base* nati-

run *comb* -drom(e), dromo-, -dromous; *base* curr-, -cur(s)-

rune *comb* runo-

runner (plant) *base* sarment-

rupture *comb* -clasia, -clasis, clastic, frag-, -rhegma, -(r)rhexis; *base* -fract-, -frang-, -rupt-

rural *base* agrest-, rustic-
rush *hurry:* *base* curr-, impet-, -vad-,
-vas-; *plant:* -junc-

Russia(n) *comb* Russo-
rust *base* ferrug-, rubig-

S

sable *base* zibel-
sac *comb* angio-, asco-, bursi-, burso-,
ceco-, chlamyd-, chrysali, coleo-, -cyst,
cysti-, cysto-, follic-, meningo-, peri-
cardiaco-, pericardio-, peritoneo-,
physa-, physali-, physo-, -theca, theco-,
typhlo-, utri-², utric-, vesico-; *base* mar-
sup-, -sacc-, -thylac-
saccharin *comb* saccharo-
sacred *comb* hagio-, hiero-, semno-; *base-*
sacr-, -sanct-; *~ receptacle:* *base* tabern-
sacrifice *base* mact-, -thy-
sacrum *comb* sacro-
saddle *base* ephipp-, sagma-, selli-
sadness *comb* lype-, tapino-; *base* dolor-,
fleb-, flet, luct-, -trist-
safe from *comb* -proof, -tight
saffron *base* -croce-, safran-
sagacious *base* nasut-
sail *action:* *base* navig-; *object:* *comb* vel-,
veli
sailfish *base* istiophor-
saint *comb* hagio-; *base* sanct-
salad *base* acetar-
saliva *comb* ptyal(o)-, sial¹-
salmon *comb* salmoni-
salt *comb* alo-, halo-, sali-, salino-; *base*
sals-; *suf* -ate, -ite; *reddish salts:* *comb*
roseo-
salvation *base* soter-
salve *base* acop-
same *pre* co-; *comb* equi-, homo-, iso-,
pari-, tauto-; *~ time:* *comb* hama-; *base*
-simul-
sand *comb* ammo-, arenacio-, psammo-;
base aren-, glare-, sabell-, sabul-,
saburr-
sandal *base* sandal-
sand grouse *base* pterocl-
sandpiper *base* charadr-, -tring-
sandwich *comb* -burger
sapphire *base* sapphir-

sarcastic *base* acerb-, mord-
sated *comb* -filled, pleni-, pleo-, plero-,
pluri-; *base* -pler-, -plet-; *suf* -acious,
-ate, -ic, -ful, -ilent, -ose, -osity, -ous,
-ulent, -y
satellite *base* satellit-
satirical *comb* sillo-; *base* dicac-, parod-
satyr *base* satyr-
sauce *base* embamm-
saucer *base* acetabul-
sausage(-shaped) *base* allant(o)-, botul-
savage *base* agrio-, efferit-, ferit-, trucul-
save *base* pars-, salv-, serrato-
savory *base* sapid-
saw *tool:* *comb* pri-, prion-, runcin-, ser-
rato-, serri-
sawdust *base* scobi-
say *comb* -claim, logo-, -logue, -lalia,
-lexia, lexico-, -lexis, -lexy, -logy,
-phone, phono-, -phony, rhet-, verbi-,
verbo-, voc-, voci-, -voke; *base* -clam-,
-dict-, -loc(u)-, -loqu-, narr-, -orat-,
-phat-, -phem- scabbard *comb* coleo-
scale *base* -libra-; *musical ~:* *comb* -tonic
scalene *comb* scaleno-
scales *comb* lamelli-, lepido-, squamato-,
squamo-, squamoso-, squaroso-; *base*
cataphract-, lepo-, lodic-, -pholid-, -
rament-, scut-, tegul-
scalloped *comb* cren-, crenato-,
crenulato-
scalpel *comb* scalpelli-
scan *base* -scan-, -scand-
scandal *comb* –gate; *base* scandal-
scant *base* exig-
scapula *comb* scapuli-, scapulo-
scar *comb* kelo-, ulo-¹; *base* -cica-, epu-
lat-, rhag-²
scarce *comb* mano-, spano-; *base* -areo-
scared *base* -pavid-, -tim-, trepid-. *See*
fear
scarlet *base* nacar-

scatter(ed) *comb* -sperse; *base* -sparg-,
   -spars-, -spor-
scene *comb* sceno-
scenery *comb* -scape
scent *comb* brom(o)-, odori-, odoro-,
   olfacto-,-osmia, osmo-, osphresio-,
   ozo-, ozono-
scepter *base* scept-
school *base* schol-; ~ *-centered:* academ-
science *comb* -graphy, -logic, -logical,
   -logy, techno-, -techny; *suf* -ics
scimitar *comb* acinaci-
scintillation *comb* sela-; *base* -fulg-,
   stilpno-
scissors *base* forfic-, -psalid-
sclera *comb* sclero-
scoff *base* mycter-
scold *base* increp-
scope of *base* lat-¹; *suf* -ure
scorched *base* adust-
scorn *base* deris-; *scornful mockery:* base
   sardon-
scorpion *base* pedipalp-, scorp-
Scottish *comb* Scoto-
scourge *comb* cnido-, mastigo-; *base*
   flagell-, -piq-, -urtic-
scrap *comb* clasmato-, -fid; *base* frag-,
   frust-, -par-
scraping *base* abrad-, abras-, xyst-
scratch *comb* amycho-, scab-, titillo-; *base*
   cnes-, rasor-
scrotum *comb* didym(o)-, orchido-,
   orchio-, oscheo-; *base* -scrot-
scrub *comb* balneo-; *base* ablut-, cathar-,
   -lav-, -mund-, -purg-
sculpt *comb* glyph-, glypt-; *base* -sculpt-
scurrilous *base* fescinn-
scurvy *base* -scorb-
Scythian *comb* Scytho-
sea *comb* enalio-, halo-, mare-, mari-, tha-
   lasso-, thalatto-; *base* aequor-, naut-,
   nav-, navic-, pelag-; ~ *shore:* paral-,
   thino-
sea crab *base* gammar-
sea duck *base* fuligul-
seagull *base* -lar-
sea horse *base* hippocamp-
seal *animal: comb* phoc(o)-; *stamp: base*
   -sigil-, sphrag-
sealing wax *base* rupo-

search(ing) *comb* -petal, -quire, -quiry;
   base indag-, -rog-, -scrut-. *See* **turn**
   towards
seasick *base* naus-
seasoned stuffing *base* farcin-
seasons *comb* horo-; *fall: base* -autumn-;
   spring: base -vern-; *summer: base* -aes-
   tiv-; *winter: base* brum-¹, -hibern-,
   -hiem-
seat *base* cathedr-, cathis-, -edr-, kathis-,
   sedil-
sea urchin *comb* echinoderm-; *base*
   echin-
seaweed *comb* phyceae-, -phyceous,
   phyco-; *base* -fuc-; ~ *-covered: base*
   algos-
sebaceous secretion *base* smegma-
sebum *comb* sebo-
second/secondary *pre* bi-, para-², super-;
   comb deuter(o)-, deuto-, secundi-,
   secundo-. *See* **two**
second-rate *pre* hypo-, sub-, under-;
   comb hystero-; *base* hesson-; *suf* -aster
secret *pre* subter-; *comb* calypto-, crypto-;
   base arcan-, occult-
secretion *comb* crino-, -crine, eccrino-;
   waxlike ~: comb cerumini-
sect *suf* -arian
secure *comb* -proof, -tight
sedge *base* carico-, cyper-
sediment *base* faecul-, fecul-
see *comb* eid(o)-, oculo-, ommat-, -opia,
   opsi-, -opsia, -opsis, opso-, -opsy,
   ophthalmo-, optico-, opto-, -scope,
   -scopic, scopo-, -scopy, visuo-; *base*
   -blep-, -scrut-, -spec-, -spic-, -vid-. *Also*
   see "The Senses" in Part III
seeds *comb* -carp, -carpic, carpo-, -car-
   pous, -sperm, -spermal, spermatio-,
   spermato-, spermi-, -spermic, spermo-,
   -spermous, -spore, spori-, sporo-, -spo-
   rous; *base* semin-; *seed-vessel: base*
   silicul-
seek(ing) *comb* -petal, -quire, -quiry,
   zetet-; *base* -rog-, -scrut-. *See* **turn**
   towards
seemingly *pre* quasi-
segment *comb* clasmato-, dicho-, -fid²,
   fissi-, schisto-, schizo-, -tomy; *base*
   -par-, telson-

seize *comb* -tain; *base* -cap(t)-,-cathex-, -ger-, -hapt-, plag-, -prehend, prehens-, rap-, rep-, -ten-, usurp-

seizure *comb* -agra, -lepsia, -lepsis, -lepsy, -leptic

selection *base* -opt-, -vol-

self *comb* auto-, ego-, idio-, ipse-, proprio-, self-, tauto-; *base* -ille-; ~ *-contained: base* axen-; ~ *-control: base* sophron-; ~ *indulgence:* apolaust-

selfishness *base* avar-, avid-, cup(id)-, edac-, gulos-, pleonec-, pleonex-

self-moving *comb* auto-

sell *base* empor-, -merc-, vend-

semi-solid material *base* magma(t)

send *base* -miss-, -mit-[1], -pomp-

sensation *comb* -esthesia, esthesio-, hapto1-, sensi-, senso-, sensori-. *Also see* "The Senses" in Part III

senseless *base* -stup-

sensory *comb* sensori-

sepals *comb* -sepalous

separate *pre* apo-, dia-, dis-, for-, se-; *comb* chori-, choristo-, crit-[2], dicho-, dialy-; *base* regm-; *separation: comb* sepi-[2]; *base* dialyt-, dissep-

septillion *comb* yotta; **septillionth** *comb* yocto-

sequel *following: pre* epi-, meta-, post-; *comb* after-, hind-, postero-; *base* -secut-, -sequ-; *suf* -an; *outcome: comb* ergo-, -ergic, -ergy; *suf* -age, -asm, -ata, -ation, -ency, -ism, -ma, -ment, -mony, -sion, -ure

sequential relationship *base* syntagm-

Serbia *comb* Serbo-

serenity *base* -eiren-, -iren-, -pac-, -pax-

series *base* -hirmo-

serious *base* grav-; *partly* ~: *comb* serio-

sermon *base* -homil-, kery-, serm-

serous fluid *base* ichor-

serrated *comb* serrato-; *base* cren-[1], lacin-. *See* **notched**

serum *comb* oro-, orrho-, sero-

serve *base* famulat-

serviceable *comb* chreo-, chresto-; *base* -util-

sesame *base* sesam-

set *comb* -thesis, -thetic; *base* -pon-, -pos-; *suf* -en; ~ *against: pre* anti-, cata-,

cath-, contra-, contre-, ob-, with-; *comb* antio-, contro-, counter-, enantio-; ~ *apart: pre* se-; *base* sacr-

seta *comb* chaeta-, chaeto-

settlement *comb* ekist-; *base* -dom-; *suf* -age

seven *comb* hebdo-, hepta-, septem-, sept(i)-[1]; ~ *hundred:* septinginti-. *Also see* "Numbers" in Part III

seventeen *base* heptakaideca-, septendecim-

seventh *base* septim-

seventy *base* septuagen-, septuages-, septuagint-

sever *comb* -cide, cis-, -cise, -ectomy, inciso-, -sect, temno-, -tmesis, -tome, tomo-, -tomous, -tomy; *base* sec-

several *comb* multi-, pluri-, pollaki-, poly-

sew *base* -sutil-

sewer *base* cloac-

sex organs *comb* genito-; *base* -aede-; *female* ~: colpo-; *male* ~: phallo-

sexual *comb* aphrodisio-, eroto-, gameto-, gamo-, -gamous, -gamy, geno-, gonado-, -gone, -gonium, gono-, -gony, nympho-; *base* -coit-, -cyprid-, ero-, -vener-[1]; ~ *intercourse:* subagit-; ~ *uncertainty:* gynandro-; *unusual* ~ *practices: base* paraphil-

shabby *base* sord-, turp-

shadow *comb* scia-, scio-[1], skia-; *base* -opac-, -umbr-

shaft *comb* calam-, cauli-, caulo-, cormo-, culm-, ferul-, paxill-, scapi-, thyrsi-, thyrso-; *base* festuc-, stip-

shaggy *base* -hispid-, lasio-, vill-

shake off *base* excuss-

shaking *base* agit-, -cuss-, lab-, pav-, quass-, tremo-, trep-, vibro-

shallow *base* lev-, parv-

shame *base* pud-, verecund-

shape, a *comb* eid(o)-, -form, -morph, -morphic, -morphism, morpho-, -morphous; *base* -figur-, -schem-

shaped like *comb* -form, -oid, -oidal; *shaped like an -S: comb* sigma-; *shaped like a -Y: comb* ypsili-. *Also see* "Shapes" in Part III

shapeless *comb* amorpho-

shark *comb* scyllio-; *base* carcharin-, gale-², selach-, sphyrn-, squal-

sharp *comb* acantho-, aceto-, acetyl-, acid-, acro-, acu-, acuti-, cusp-, echino-, mord-, oxal-, oxy-¹, spiculi-, spiculo-, stylo-¹; *base* acer-¹, -acerb-, -acul-, aichm-, -aichur-, asper-, -belon-, muric-, -punct-, -piq-, pung-, xyr-; *~ pointed:* *comb* raduli-; *~ tip:* *base* mucro-; *~ words:* *base* acrim-

shatter *comb* -clasia, -clasis, -clastic, -rhegma, -(r)rhexis; *base* agmat-, -fract-, -frag-, -frang-, -rupt-

shave *base* rasor-, tonsor

shears *base* forfic-, psalid-

sheath *comb* angio-, chlamyd-, coleo-, meningo-, -theca, theci-, theco-, vagini-, vagino-. *See* **container**

shed *comb* lyo-, lysi-, -lysis, lyso-, -lyte, -lytic, -lyze; *base* exuv-, -liqu-, -solu-, -solv-

sheep *base* ovi-², verv-. *See* **lamb**

sheet *bed ~:* lodic-; *layer:* lamin-; *winding ~:* sindon-

shell *comb* conchi-, kelyph-, lorica-, -ostraca, ostraco-, testaceo-

shield *comb* aspido-, peltati-, peltato-, pelti-, pelto- *base* clype-, saco-, scut-

shift *base* camb-, -fabr-, -fec-, -mut-, -vari-, -vert-. *See* **change**

shingles *base* herp-, zoster-

shiny *base* fulg-, gano-, lustr-, pheng-, rutil-, sela-, stilpno-

ship *base* nau-, naut-, nav-, navic-

shirt *base* camis-

shoe *base* -calce-, -crep-; *shoemaker base* sutor-

shoot *base weapon:* -ballist-, -jacul-; *plant:* *base* sobol-, surcul-

shopkeeper *base* capel-

shore *base* littor-

shortage *comb* isch-, oligo-, -penia

shorter *comb* brachisto-, brachy-, brevi-, chamae-, hekisto-, micro-, mini-, parvi-, parvo-, steno-, tapino-; *base* -curt-, exig-; *suf* -cle, -cula, -cule, -een, -el, -ella, -en, -et, -ette, -idion, -idium, -ie, -illa, -illo, -isk, kin, -le, -let, -ling, -ock, -ola, -ole, -rel, -ula, -ule, -ulum, -ulus, -y

short-sighted *base* myop-

shoulder *comb* acromio-, humero-, omo-¹; *~ blade:* *comb* scapuli-, scapulo-; *base* armo-, spatul-

shout *base* clam-, vocif-

show *comb* phaeno-, pheno-; *base* -monstr-; *~ compassion:* *base* miserat-

showers *comb* hyeto-, pluvio-; *base* imbri-, ombr-

shrew *base* soric-, tupai-; *squirrel-shrew:* *base* tupai-

shrike *base* thamn-

shrimp *base* carid-, macrur-

shrine *comb* aedi-; *base* scrin-; *~ container:* *base* feret-

shrink *base* dimin-

shrivel *base* marces-, marcid-

shroud *base* sindon-

shrub *base* arbusc-, -bosc-¹, thamn- (thamnium); *shrublike:* *comb* fruticuloso-

shudder *comb* phricto-

shun *base* phygo-

shut *comb* -atresia, atreto-, claustro-, cleido-, -cleisis, cleisto-, stego-; *base* clithr-, -clud-, -clus-, confin-, obturat-, occlud-, occlus-

shyness *base* tim-, verecund-

Sicilian *comb* Siculo-

sickle(-shaped) *comb* drepani-, falci-, zanclo-

sickness *pre* dys-, mal-; *comb* noso-, path, -pathic, patho-, -pathy; *base* aegr-, cachex-, -morb-, naus-, -pecca-, valetud-

side *pre* by-; *on or near ~:* *comb* lateri-, latero-, pleuro-

sieve *comb* coli-², coscino-, cribri-, ethmo-

sift *base* -cern-

sigh *base* suspir-

sight *comb* eid(o)-, oculo-, ommat-, -opia, opsi-², -opsia, -opsis, opso-, -opsy, ophthalmo-, optico-, opto-, -scope, -scopic, scopo-, -scopy, visuo-; *base* -blep-, -scrut-, -spec-, -spic-, -vid-, vis-

sign(al) *comb* sema-, -seme, semeio-, semio-; *indicator:* *base* portent-

signet *base* -sigil-, sphrag-

silent *comb* hesy-; *base* -tacit-

silica/silicon *comb* siliceo-, silici-, silico-
silk *comb* metax-, seri-, sericeo-, serico-
silkworm *base* -bombyc-
silly *base* fatu-, inan-, moro-, stult-
Silurian *comb* Siluro-
silver(y) *comb* argenti-, argento-, argyro-,
    glauco-, plat-[2]. *Also see* "Colors" in Part
    III
similar *pre* para-, quasi-; *comb* -esque,
    homeo-, homoeo-, homoio-, homolo-,
    iso-, -phane, -phanic; *base* simil-; *suf*
    -acean, -aceous, -al, -an, -ar, -ary, -ean,
    -en, -eous, -esque, -ful, -ic, -il, -ile-, -ine,
    -ing, -ish, -itious, -ize, -like, -ode, -oid,
    -ose, -osity, -some, -tious, -ular, -y
simple *base* facil-. *See* single
sin *comb* enisso-, enosio-; *base* -culp-,
    hamart-, -pecca-
sincere *base* prob-, ver-
sinew *comb* chord-, -chorda, cord-
sing in octaves *base* magad-
single *comb* eka-, hapax-, haplo-, heno-,
    mono-, uni-
sink *decline: comb* -atrophia; *base* dimin-;
    decrease: base decresc-, dimin-
sinuous *comb* -enchyma[1]
siphon *comb* siphoni-, siphono-
sister *base* -soror-
sit *base* -cathis-, -kathis-, -sed-, -sess-; ~
    in: -sid-
situated *comb* out-
six *comb* hexa-, sena-, seni-, sexi-, sexti-,
    sise-; ~ *hundred:* hexacosi-, sexcent-;
    ~ *times:* hexakis-. *Also see* "Numbers"
    in Part III
sixteen *base* hexadeca-, hexakaideca,
    sedecim-
sixth *base* sext-
sixty *base* hexaconta-, sexagen-, sexages-
size *comb* -footer, -sized; ~ *of a sheet:*
    suf -mo. *Also see* "Dimension" in Part
    III
skeleton *comb* skeleto-
skill *comb* -craft, -ship, techno-; *skillful:*
    base daedal-, pancrat-
skin *comb* chorio-, cut(i)-, cutaneo-,
    -derm, -derma, dermato-, -dermatous,
    -dermis, dermo-, dora-; *base* -pell-; ~
    disease: licheno-; ~ *elevation: comb*
    papulo-; ~ *itch: comb* acar-, scabi(o)-;

base -prur-, -psor-; ~ *like: comb* cho-
    roid-. *See* flesh
skirmish *base* velit-. *See* battle
skull *comb* -cephalic, cephalo-, -ceph-
    alous, -cephaly, cranio-, occipito-,
    orbito-
skunk *base* mephit-, mustel-; *African ~:*
    base zorill-
sky *base* coeli-
skylark *base* alaud-
slab *base* -pinac-, -pinak-
slag *base* scoria-
slander *base* calumn-
slanting *comb* -clinal, -clinate, -cline,
    -clinic, clino-, -clisis, lechrio-, loxo-,
    plagio-; *base* -cliv-. *See* bent
slaughter *base* trucid-
Slav *comb* Slavo-
slave *comb* dulo-; *base* -serv-, vernil-
sleep *comb* hypno-, somni-; *base* carot-,
    -dorm-, -sopor-
sleeplessness *base* agrypn-
sleeve *base* manul-
slender *comb* lepto-, steno-, -tenu-; *base*
    -areo-, gracil-
slide *base* laps-
slightly *pre* sub; *comb* hetto-; *suf* –aster[2]
slime *comb* blenno-, -chezia, copro-, lim-,
    muci-, muco-, myco-, myso-, -myxia,
    myxo-, p(a)edo-, scato-, stegno-,
    sterco-; *base* -fecu-, -fim-, molys-,
    rhypar-
sling *base* fundi-
slip *base* olisto-
slippery *base* -lubric-
slope *comb* -clinal, -clinate, -cline, -clinic,
    clino-, -clisis, klino-, lechrio-, loxo-,
    plagio-; *base* -clit-, -cliv-, declin-
sloth *animal: base* xenarthr-; *indolence:*
    base murc-, ociv-,pigr-, segn-
slow *comb* brady-; *base* -cunct-, lent-[1],
    -pigr-, -tard-
slug *base* limac-
sluggish *base* ignav-, lenitud-, -pigr-
sly *base* daedal-
small(er) *comb* brachisto-, brachy-, hek-
    isto-, micro-, mini-, nano-, parvi-,
    parvo-, steno-; *base* -curt-, exig-,
    modic-, pauro, pusill-; *suf* -cle, -cula,
    -cule, -culum, -culus, -een, -el, -ella,

-en, -et, -ette, -idion, -idium, -ie, -illa, -illo, -isk, kin, -le, -let, -ling, -ock, -ola, -ole, -rel, -ula, -ule, -ulum, -ulus, -y; ~ *bag*: base mantic-; ~ *container*: base can-[3]; ~ *hill*: base colic-

smart base sapien-

smell *comb* brom(o)-, -odic, odori-, odoro-, -olent, olfacto-, -osmia, osmo-[1], osphresio-, ozo-, ozono-; *base* fet-, nidor-; ~ *deprivation*: base anosm-. *See also* "The Senses" in Part III

smelt base -ather-

smile base ris-

smoke *comb* -capnia, capno-; *base* -fum-

smooth *comb* even-, leio-, lisso-; *base* -glabr-, -levig-, -lubr-, psilo-

smother base -pnig(er)-

smut base aischro-

snail base cochlea-, gastropod-, limac-

snake *comb* -glypha, herpeto-, echidno-, -ophidia, ophio-; *base* angui-, colubr-, reptil-, serpen-, viper-; ~ *charmer*: psyll-

snapper base lutjan-

snare base imped-

snarling base hirr-

snatch base arrept-, -rap-, -rep-

sneer base mycter-

sneeze base ptarm-, sternut-

snipe base charadr-, scolopac-

snore base rhonch-, stertor-

snout *comb* rhyncho-, -rrhyncha; *base* mycter-, probosc-, rostell-, -rostr-. *See* **beak**

snow base -chion-, -chium-, ning-, nipha-, niv-

soak base macer-; *soak up*: *comb* -sorb[1]; *base* bib-

soap base sapon(i)-

sob base dacryo-, fleb-, flet-, lachrim-, lachrym-, plor-, singult-

sober base *abstinent*: nephal-; *serious*: grav-

social belief *suf* -arian

society *comb* anthropo-, socio-

socket *comb* alveolo-, tormo-; *base* -gomph-

sodium *comb* -natremia, natro-, sodio-

soft *comb* -malacia, malaco-; *base* hapal-, -len-, macer-, malax-, -moll-; ~ *deposit*: *comb* athero-; ~ *palate*: velar-

soil *comb* agri-, agro-, paedo-[1], pedo-[3]; *base* edaph-, -hum-, -terr-

soldier *comb* -milit-; ~ *belonging to a phalanx*: *base* phalang-

sole of the foot base pelm-, -plant-, then-

solid *comb* stereo-; ~ *connection*: *base* sterr-

solitary *comb* auto-, eremo-, mono-, soli-, uni-. *See* **one**

somewhat *pre* demi-, hemi-, semi-; *comb* -atelia, atelo-; *suf* -esce, -escence, -escent, -y[1]

son base fili-

son-in-law base -gener-

song *comb* asmato-, lyrico-, melo-[1], musico-; ~ *birds*: oscin-

soot base asbol-, fulig-

soothing base anet-, -len-, miti-[1]

soothsaying base augur-

soporific *comb* hypno-, somni-; *base* carot-, -dorm-, -sopor-

sorcery base -venefic-

sordid base sord-, turp-

soreness *comb* alge-, algesi-, -algia, algo-, -algy, -dynia, noci-, -odynia, odyno-, pono-; *base* dolor-, -nox-

sorrow *comb* lype-; *base* dolor-, -fleb-, -flet-, -luct-[1], penth-, trist-

soul *comb* pneumato-, thumo-, -thymia, thymo-; *base* -anim-, -spirit-

sound *comb* acou-, acoust-, audi(o)-, auri-, echo-, oto-, -ecoia, -phone, phono-, -phony, -phthong, soni-, sono-, sonoro-. *See* **noise**

soundness base salub-, san-; ~ *of judgment*: *base* phron-

sour base acer-, acesc-, acid-, acor-, amar-, -pontic

source *comb* aetio-, -blast, blasto-, -blasty, -carp, -carpic, carpo-, -carpous, etio-, -gen, -genic, -genesis, -genous, -geny, -gone, -gonium, gono-, -gony, -phyletic, sperma-, -spermal, spermato-, spermi-, -spermic, spermo-, sporo-; *base* -init-; *suf* -esce, -escence, -escent

south *comb* austro-, noto-

sow base sativ-, sator-, sparg-

spade-shaped base pala-

Spanish *comb* Hispano-, Ibero-

sparing base frug-[2]

spark *base* -scintill-, spinthar-
sparrow *base* passer-
sparse *comb* oligo-; *base* pars-, pauc(i)-
spasm *comb* -chorea, choreo-, -clonic, -clonus, -esmus, -ismus, spasmato-, spasmo-, -tonic; *base* -stal-, -vellic-
spatula *comb* spathi-, spatuli-
speak, speech *comb* -claim, -logia, logo-, -logue, -lalia, -lexia, lexico-, -lexis, -lexy, -logy, -phone, phono-, -phony, verbi-, verbo-, voc-, voci-, -voke; *base* -clam-, dialect-, -dict-, garrul-, -loc(u)-, -loqu-, - loquel, orat-, phat-, -phem-, rhet-; *defective~:* *comb* -lalia, lalo-, -phasia, -phasic, -phasis, -phasy, -phemia, -phemy, -phrasia; *base* psell-; **laudatory** *~:* *base* eulog-; *~ sounds:* *base* gennem-
spear *comb* hastato-, hasti-; *base* dory-; *~ head:* lonch-
specialist *suf* -ician, -ist, -ologist. *Also see* "Experts" *in Part III*
specific *comb* specio-
speckled *base* -psar-, -spil-, variol-. *See* **spotted**
spectacle *comb* -orama
specter *base* phantas-, phasm-, spectr-
spectroscope *comb* spectro-
speed *comb* tacho-, tachy-, veloci-; *base* -celer-, exped-, festin-
spelt *base* ador-, alica-
sphenoid bone *comb* spheno-
spherical *comb* ano-^{2}, annul-, crico-^{2}, cyclo-, disco-, globi-, globo-, glom-, gyro-, orbito-, sphaero-, -sphere, spherico-, sphero-, stilli-, zon-, zoni-; *base* anu-, -cing-, -cinct-, -circin-, -circul-, -coron-, -glomer-, -numm-, -orb-, -rot-, -troch-
spider *comb* arachn(o)-, araneo-; *base* arene-, phalang-, pholc-; *black widow ~:* *base* latrodect-; *tracheate ~:* *base* phalang-
spike *comb* helo-^{1}, scolo-, spiculi-, spiculo-; *~ of corn:* spici-; *succulent ~:* *comb* spadici-
spill *base* -chys-, -chyt-, -flu-, -fus-
spin *comb* gyro-^{1}; *base* -strob-
spinal cord *comb* -myelia, myelo-
spindle *comb* atractendyma-, fusi-, fuso-, fusu-

spine *comb* aculei-, rachi(o)-, rhach(i)-, -rrhachia, spini-, spino-, spinoso-, spinuloso-, spondylo-, vertebro-
spiny *comb* acantho-, aceto-, acetyl-, acid-, acro-, acu-, acuti-, cusp-, echinato-, echino-, echinulato-, echinuli-, oxal-, oxy-, spiculi-, spiculo-, stylo-; *base* -acerb-, -aichm-, -aichur-, -belon-, muric-, -punct-, -piq-, -punct-
spiral *comb* cirri-, cochlio-, gyro-, helici-, helico-, spiri-, spiro-^{2}, strepto-, stromb-, torn-
spirit *comb* pneumato-; *base* -anim-
spirits *base* phantas-, phasm-, spectr-; *damned ~:* *comb* necyo-
spitting *comb* –ptysis; *base* saliv-. *See* **saliva**
spleen *comb* lieno-, splenico-, spleno-
splendid *base* lustr-
split *comb* dicho-, -fid-, -fissi-, schismato-, schismo-, schisto-, schizo-, -tomy; *base* -crev-, *base* saliv-, -par-, regm-
spoil *comb* lysi-, lyso-, -lysis, -lytic, -lyze, -phage, phago-, -phagous, -phagy; *base* -ate-^{4}, perd-, phthart-, spol--vast-, vitia-
spoke *a brace:* *base* -rad-; *talked:* *See* **speak**
sponge-like *comb* spongio-, spongo
spontaneous *comb* ultro-
spoon *base* cochlea-
spoonworm *base* sipuncul-
spore *comb* -spore, spori-, sporo-, -sporous
spot *comb* celido-; *stain:* *base* -macul-, spil-, -tinct-, -ting-
spotted *comb* ocelli-; *base* -macul-, psar-, -spil-, -stict-, -variol-
spouse *base* conjug-, marit-, uxor-
spread *expand:* *comb* -ectasia, -ectasis; *base* -dilat-; *scatter:* *base* sparg-; *~ out:* *base* patul-
spring *leap:* salta-; *season:* primaver-, -vern-; *water:* *comb* crouno-; *base* cren-^{2}, pego-, scatur-
sprinkle *base* sparg-, -sperg-, -spers-
spun *base* tel-^{1}
spurge *base* tithym-
spurious *comb* kibdelo-, mytho-, pseudo-; *base* fict-, mendac-, -notho-

squama *comb* squamato-, squamo-, squa-
moso-, squaroso-
square *base* quadr-
squid *base* cephalopod-, loligo-, teutho-
squill-shaped *comb* scillo-
squinting *base* -strab-, -strabism-
squirrel *base* sciur-
stable *comb* stato-; *base* diuturn-, dur(o)-,
perenn-, perm-, stabil-
stag *base* cerv-, elaph-
stage *development: base* stathmo-; *final*
~: *comb* teleuto-
stage player *base* -histrion-
stagger *base* titub-
stain *base* -macul-, spil-, -tinct-, -ting-
stairs *base* -climac-
stalactite *comb* stalacti-
stalk *shaft: comb* calam-, cauli-, caulo-,
cormo-, culm-, ferul-, paxill-, scapi-,
thyrsi-, thyrso-; *base* festuc-, magyd-,
stip-¹; *hunt: base* -venat-
stamens *comb* -androus, stamini-
stammering *base* blaes-, traul-
stamp *comb* -type, sigil-; *postage* ~: *base*
philatel-, timbro-
standard *normal comb* ortho-; *base*
-regul-; *banner base* labar-
standing *on end: base* horr-; ~ *still: comb*
stasi-, -stasis, -stat, stato-
stapes *base* -stap-
staphylococcus *comb* staphylo-
star *comb* aster-¹, astro-, -sidere, sidero-²,
stelli-
starch *comb* amyl(o)-
starfish *base* asteroid-, echinoderm-
starling *base* psar-², sturn-
start *base* inaug-, incip-, init-
starting to be *suf* -esce, -escence, -escent
state of *suf* -able, -acity, -acy, -age, -ance,
-ancy, -ant, -asis, -asm, -ate, -atile,
-ation, -cy, -dom, -ence, -ency, -ent,
-ery, -esis, -ful, -hood, -iasis, -ice1,
-ility, -ion, -ism, -ity, -ling, -ma, -ment,
-mony, -ness, -or, -osis, -otic, -red,
-ship, -sion, -th, -tion, -tude, -ture, -ty,
-ure, -y
stationary *comb* stasi-, -stasis, -stat,
stato-; *base* stabil-
statue *base* agalma-
status *suf* -ship

stay *remain: base* contin-, dur-, per-
pet-; *delay: comb* brady-; *base* -cunct-,
imped-, -mora-, -tard-
steady *base* perm-, stabil-
steal *comb* clepto-, klepto-, lesto-; *base*
-furt-, harpax-, klope-, ladron-, latro-,
-rept-
steam *comb* atmo-
steel *base* chalyb-
steep *base* ard-³, precip-
steering *comb* -agogic, -agogue; *base*
-vers-, -vert-; *able to be steered: base*
dirig-, tract-
stem *comb* cauli-, caulo-, cormo-, scapi-;
base calam-, culmi-, sarment-, sobol-,
stirp-
stench *comb* brom(o)-, odori-, odoro-,
olfacto-, -osmia, osmo-, osphresio-,
ozo-, ozono-; *base* fet-, foet-, -mephit-,
nidor-, putr-
step *comb* -basia, bato-, -grade; *base*
-ambul-, -gress-
stepdaughter *base* privign-
stepfather *base* vitric-
stepmother *base* noverc-
stepson *base* privign-
sternum *comb* sterni-, sterno-
stick *comb* scop(i)-; *base* carph-, ramul-,
-sarment-, surcul-, virgul-
sticky *base* agglut-, ixo-, visc(o)-. See glue
stiff *comb* ancylo-, ankylo-, tetano-; *base*
rigesc-
still *base* eremo-, hesy-
stimulating *comb* excito-; *base* erethis-,
stig-
sting *comb* cnido-, mastigo-; *base* -piq-,
-urtic-; *stingray: base* trygon-
stink *comb* brom(o)-, odori-, odoro-,
olfacto-, -osmia, osmo-, osphre-
sio-, ozo-, ozono-; *base* fet-, -mephit-,
nidor-, putr-
stirrup *base* stap-
stitch *base* rhaps-, sutil-
stock *base* stirp-
stomach *comb* gastero-, -gastria, gastro-;
~ *opening: comb* pyloro-. See belly
stone *comb* -lith(o), pesso-, petri-, petro-,
plinthi-, psepho-, sax(i)-; *base* -lapid-,
-rup-; *suf* -lite; ~ *fragments: base*
ruder-; ~ *-like deposit: base* toph-; ~

missile: *base* cherm-; ~ *quarry*: *base* lat-²; ~ *using stage*: *comb* -lithic
stooping *comb* kypho-, scolio
stop *comb* stasi-, -stasis, -stat; *base* fin-, termin-
stopper *comb* emboli-, embolo-
stork *base* ciconi-, grallator-, pellarg-
storm *base* orag-, procell-
story *comb* mytho-; *base* fabell-, gest-
straight *comb* ithy-, ortho-, recti-
strain *comb* -piesis, piezo-, tensio-; *base* col-², colar-, colat-, tenes-, -tens-
strange(r) *comb* allotrio-, perisso-, xeno-; *base* -ali-, peregrin-
strap *base* himant-, -ligul-, lora-
stratum *comb* strati-, strato-. *See* **layer**
straw *comb* carpho-, culmi-, festuc-, stramin-
strawberry *base* fragar-
stream *comb* fluvio-, rhyaco-; *base* -potam-, rheum-, -rip-, riv-
strength *comb* dyna-, dynamo-, mega-, megalo-, -megaly, -sthenia, stheno-; *base* -forc-, -fort-, -poten-, robor-; ~ *to do or be*: *suf* -bility
strenuous *pre* dys-; *comb* -bar, bary-, mogi-; *base* ardu-, stren-
stress *importance*: *base* emphas-. For pressure, see strain.
stretch *comb* -tend, teno-, tensio-, tono-; *base* porrect-; *stretchable*: elasto-; *stretched out*: *base* pandicul-
strict *base* auster-
stricture *comb* isch-, koly-, -penia, rhopo-, -strain, -strict; *base* angust-, -string-; *suf* -en.
strife *base* colluct-, eris-
strike *comb* plessi-, -cuss-; *base* colaph-, -cop-, -crot-, flict, ict-, plang-, -puls-, -tus-, -vapul-, -verber-
string *base* linon-
stringed instrument *base* cithar-
strip *base* habenul-
stripped *comb* gymno-, nudi-, psilo-
stroke *comb* -plexia
strong *comb* -proof, dur(o)-; *base* -forc-, -fort-, stren-. *See* **strength**
structure *base* -strom-
struggle *comb* macho-, -machy; *base* agon-, eluct-

strung together *base* -rhaps-
stubborn *base* adamant-, contum-, obdur-, obstin-, pervic-, proterv-
studded *comb* clavato-
study *base* disc-, -math, soph-; *nocturnal* ~: *base* elucub-, lucubr-
stuff up *base* -byon-, farct-
stupid *base* hebet-, inan-, obtus-, -tard-
stupor *comb* carot-, narco-
sturgeon *base* acipenser-, sturi(m)-, sturion-
stutter *base* balbut-, blesi-, -psell-
styloid *comb* stylo-
styptic *comb* stegno-
suberic acid *comb* subero-
subfamilies (animals) *suf* -inae
subject to *suf* -ize
submissive *base* moriger-
subordinate *pre* sub-, under-
subsequent to *pre* cis-. *See* **following**
substance *comb* -ousia, -ousian
substitute *pre* pro-¹; *base* vicar-; *suf* -ette
subtraction *base* ablat-
succeed *base* -cap-, -cep-, -cip-
succinct *base* brev-. *See* **short**
suck *comb* -suge; *base* -haur-, -haust-, -myz-
sudden *base* subit-. *See* **quickness**
suffering *comb* -path, -pathic, patho-, -pathy. *See* **pain**
suffocate *base* -pnig-
sugar *comb* gluco-, glycero-, glyco-, levul-, saccharo-, sucr-
suggestive of *pre* para-, quasi-; *comb* homeo-, homoio-, homolo-, iso-, -phane, -phanic; *base* simil-; *suf* -acean, -aceous, -al, -an, -ar, -ary, -ean, -en, -eous, -esque, -ful, -ic, -il, -ile-, -ine, -ing, -ish, -itious, -ize, -like, -ode, -oid, -ose, -osity, -some, -tious, -ular, -y¹
suitable for *base* concinn-, idon-; *suf* -il, -ile, -like, -ly
sulfate *comb* sulfato-
sulfur *comb* sulfo-, sulfureo-, sulpho-, thia-, thio-
summer *base* aestiv-
summit *base* coryph-
summon *base* accit-, appell-, -claim, -clam-, -dict-, -nom-, -voc-; ~ *upon*: *base* -prec-

sumptuous *base* dapat-, opim-
sun *comb* helio-, sol-; ~ *bathing:* apri-
  cat-; ~ *rise: base* orient-; ~ *shade: comb*
  umbelli-, umbello-, umbraculi-
sundial pin *base* gnom-[1]
superfluous *base* nim-
superhuman *comb* titano-
superior *pre* pre-, super-; *comb* over-;
  base prior-
superlatives *suf* -est, -most
supplement *pre* a-, ac-, ad-, af-, ag-, al-,
  an-, ap-, ar-, as-, at-, co-, extra-, para-,
  super-, syn; *comb* inter-. *See* **more**
supporting *pre* pro-; *comb* -pher; *base*
  patroc-; ~ *part: comb* -podium, scapi-;
  base paxill-, sterigm-, -stip-[1]. *See*
  carrying
suppress *base* fin-, termin-
suppurative *comb* pyo-. *See* **putrefying**
supreme *comb* arch-, archi-, proto-; *base*
  -prim-, -princip-
surf *comb* cuma-
surfaces *comb* -hedral, -hedron, topo-,
  -topy; *flat ~: base* pedion-
surfeit *base* ampl-, copi-, larg-
surgeon *base* chirur-, medic-
surgical operation *comb* -ectomy, -pexy,
  -stomy, tomo-, -tomous, -tomy
surly *base* acerb-, moros-
surpassing *pre* ex-, extra-, meta-, over-,
  para-, pre-, preter-, super-, supra-, sur-,
  ultra-
surplus *base* ampl-, copi-, larg-
surrender *base* dedit-
surrounding *pre* be-, circum-, peri-; *comb*
  amphi-, ampho-; *base* -zon-, -cing-,
  -cinct-

suspended *base* cremast-
suture *comb* -(r)rhaphy
swallow *bird: base* chelid-, hirund-,
  -sturn-; *ingest: comb* -phage, phago-,
  -phagous, -phagy; *base* deglut-, -glut-
swamp *base* palud-, palus-
swan *base* cycn-, cygn-
sway *base* nuta-, -vacil-
sweat *comb* sudori-; *base* -hidr-, -suda-
sweet *comb* mell(i)-; *base* -dulc-, -hedy-,
  suav-; ~ *plant fluid: base* nectar-
swelling *comb* -cele, -edema, ganglio-,
  phlogo-, phym-, -phyma, physa-,
  physo-, strum(i)-; *base* aug-, cresc-,
  physc-, strum-, -tum-, -turg-; *suf* -itis
swift *bird: base* cypsel-; *fast: comb* ocy-,
  tacho-, tachy-; *base* -celer-, veloc-
swim *comb* necto-; *base* -nata-
swine *base* porcin-, sui-
swing *base* oscill-
swirl *base* gurg-
Swiss *base* Helvet-
sword(like) *comb* ensi-, gladi-, mach-
  aero-, xiphi-, xipho-
swordfish *comb* xiphi-, ziphi-
syllable *base* syllab-
syllogism with unstated premise *base*
  enthym-
symbol *comb* sema-, -seme, semeio-,
  semio-
symmetry *comb* pari-; *base* concinn-,
  congru-, symmetr-
synchronized *comb* synchro-
syphilis *comb* -luetic, syphilo-
Syrian *comb* Syro-
system *suf* –ics

T

---

tablet *base* pinac-, tabell-
tacit *comb* hesy-; *base* -tacit-
tactics *base* -strat-
tail *comb* caudo-, -cerca, -cercal, cerco-,
  uro-[1] ; *base* -ura-; ~ *less: base* anur-[1]
tailor *base* sartor-
taint *base* pollut-
take *base* -cap(t)-, -cep[1]-, -empt-

take hold of *comb* -tain; *base* -capt-,
  -cathex-, -cip-, -ger-, -hapt-, incip-,
  -prehend, prehens-, rap-, rep-, -ten-
taker *comb* -ceptor
tale *base* fabell-, -fabul-, gest-, mytho-,
  -narr-, stori-
talented *base* ingen-
talisman *base* telesm-

talk(ing) *comb* -claim, glosso-, -lalia,
  lalo-, -lexia, lexico-, -lexis, -lexy, logo-,
  -logue, -logy, -phone, phono-, -phony,
  verbi-, verbo-, voc-, voci-, -voke; *base*
  -clam-, -dict-, garrul-, -loc(u)-, -loqu-,
  -orat-, -phem-, rhet-; *disordered* ~ :
  base verbiger-; *filthy* ~: borbor-. *Also*
  see **speak/speech;** *foolish* ~ : bal-
tallness *comb* acro-, alti-, alto-, bato-,
  hypsi-, hypso-, longi-; *base* procer-
tallow *comb* seb(o)-
talon *base* ungui-, ungul-
tame *base* cicur-, mansue-
tan *base* fulv-. *Also see* "Colors" in Part III
tapered *base* fastig-, rhap-
tapeworm *comb* taeni-, teni; *base* cest-
tapir *base* pachyderm-
tar *base* piss-
tarantula *base* theraphos-
tardy *comb* brady-; *base* -cunct-, -tard-.
  See **late**
tarsier *base* lemur-
tartar *comb* tartro-
tasseled *base* crosso-, -thysan-
taste *comb* -geusia; *base* -geum-, -geumat-,
  -gust-, -sapor-. *Also see* "The Senses" in
  Part III
tattoo *comb* decalco-; *base* stigm-
taurine *comb* tauro-
tavern *base* caupon-
tawny *base* fulv-, melin-, mustel-
tea *base* -thei-, tsio-
teach *comb* -pedia; *base* -didact-, didasc-,
  doc-, -paed-
tear *rip:* *comb* sparasso-, sparax-; *base*
  lacer-, -lania-, sparax-, –vuls-; *cry:* *comb*
  dacry(o)-, lachrim-, lachrym-, lac-
  rimo-; *base* fleb-, flet-, -plor-
tease *comb* tantalo-; *base* vex-
technical *comb* techno-
technique *comb* -craft; *suf* -ade, -age, -al,
  -ance, -ancy, -asis, -asm, -ation, -cy,
  -ence, -ency, -ery, -esis, -iasis, -ice, -ics,
  -ing, -ion, -ism, -ment, -osis, -otic,
  -sion, -sis, -th, -tion, -tious, -ture, -ure,
  -y, -ysis
teeth *see* **tooth**
television *comb* tele-, video-
tell *comb* -claim, logo-, -logue, -lalia,
  -lexia, lexico-, -lexis, -lexy, -logy,

-phone, phono-, -phony, rhet-, verbi-,
  verbo-, voc-, voci-, -voke; *base* -clam-,
  -dict-, -loc(u)-, -loqu-, narr-, -orat-,
  -phat-, -phem-
temperament *comb* -natured
temple *head:* *comb* temporo-; *base*
  crotaph-; *church:* *comb* aedi-; *base*
  fan-², -nao-
temporal *base* -secul-
ten *comb* dec(a)-, decem-, deka-; *one*
  tenth: *comb* deci-; *ten and* __ : *suf*
  -teen; ~ *thousand:* myria-; *x times*
  ten: *suf* -ty². *Also see* "Numbers" in Part
  III
tender *comb* coupho-; *base* tener-
tending to *pre* pro-; *comb* -phile, -philia,
  -philiac, -trope, -tropic; *suf* -able, -ative,
  -ish, -istic, -istical, -ive, -like, -some²,
  -orial, -ulous, -y¹
tendon *comb* tendo-, teno-, tenonto-
tendril *comb* cirr(h)i-, cirr(h)o-, pampin-
tennis *base* sphair-
tension *comb* tasi-, taso-, -tonia, -tonic,
  tono-
tentacles *comb* actino-, tentaculi-; *base*
  brach-, cornic-, flagell-
tentative *base* ambig-, ancip-, apor-, dub-,
  vagu-
ten thousand *comb* myria-, myrio-
terminate *comb* stasi-, -stasis, -stat; *base*
  fin-, termin-
termite *base* isoptero-, termit-
tern *base* stern-
terrified *base* -pavid-, -tim-, trepid-. *See*
  fear
terrifying *comb* dino-¹
territory *suf* -land
testicle *comb* didym(o)-, orchido-²,
  orchio-, oscheo-; *base* -scrot-
testing *comb* -opsy, -scope, -scopic,
  scopo-, -scopy; *base* docim-, -(in)quir-,
  -(in)quis-, -scrut-
testy *base* acerb-, mord-
tetanus *comb* tetano-
thalamus *comb* thalamo-
thallium *comb* thallo-
thankful *base* grat-
the *pre* al-²
theater *comb* theatro-
theft *comb* clepto-, klepto-, lesto-; *base*

-furt-, harpax-, klope-, ladron-, latro-, -rept-

theory *suf* -ism, -logy

thermoelectric *comb* thermo-

thick *comb* cespitoso-, dasy-, hadro-, pachy-, pycno-, pykno-, visc(o)-; *base* -crass-, gross-, -spiss-; **thick-skinned** *base* callos-

thief *comb* clepto-, klepto-, lesto-; *base* -furt-, harpax-, ladron-, latr(o)

thigh *comb* mero-²

thin *comb* angusti-, araio-, dolicho-, lepti-, lepto-, maci-, mano-, stegno-, steno-, tenu-; *base* -areo-², gracil-, -isthm-, stal-, -strict-

thing that is ___ *suf* -ance, -ee, -er, -tion, -tious

think *see* thought

third *base* -tert-, trient-, trito-

thirst *comb* dipso-; *base* siti-. See **dry**

thirteen *base* tredecim-, triskaideka-

thirty *base* triaconta-, triceni-, triges-, trigint-

this side of *comb* citra-; *suf* cis-¹

thistles *base* cardo-

thong *base* haben-, himant-, lor-. See **strap**

thorax *comb* thoracico-, thoraco-

thorny *comb* acantho-, echino-, rhamn-, spiculi-, spiculo-, spini-; *base* -muric-, -urtic-

thought *comb* -gnomy, -gnosia, -gnosis, -gnostic, gnoto-, ideo-, -noia, -nomy, phreno-, psycho-, -sophy; *base* -cogit-, -cogn-, epistem-, -heur-, ment²-, -noe-, phrontis-, -put-, ratio-, -sci-; *insane* ~: *comb* lysso-, -mania; *base* ament-, dement-. *Also see* "Thought Processes" in Part III.

thousand *comb* chili-, kilo-; ~ **th:** milli-

thread(like) *comb* filamento-, fili-, filio-, filo-, mit²-, nemato-; *base* -nema-, stema-

threat *base* comminat-, min-

three *comb* ter-, tri-, triakis-, triplo-, trito-; *base* -tern-, -tert-; ~ **cornered:** *comb* trigono-; ~ **dimensional:** *comb* stereo-; ~ **fourths:** triquadr-; ~ **hundred:** trecent-. *Also see* "Numbers" in Part III

threshing *base* trit-

threshold *base* -limin-, marg-, propinq-, prox-

thrice *comb* ter-

thrift *base* frug-², pars-

throat *comb* gutturo-, jugo-, jugulo-, laryngo-, pharyngo-, -throated, tracheo-; *base* fauc-, jug-, sphag-

through *pre* cata-, cath-, dia-, per-, trans-

throughout *pre* ana-; *comb* -wide

throw *comb* -bole, -bolic, bolo-¹, -boly; *base* -ballist-, -jact-, -jacula-, -ject-

thrush *base* -musicap-, -turd-, cichlo-

thrust *base* -pel-, -pul-, -trude-, -trus-

thumb *base* pollic-

thunder *comb* bronte-, bronto-, cerauno-, kerauno-; *base* fulmin-, tonitr-

thymus *comb* thymo-

thyroid *comb* -thyrea, thyreo-; ~ **gland:** *comb* thyro-

tibia *comb* tibio-; *base* -cnem-

tick *base* acar-, ixod-

tickle *comb* titillo-

tide *base* aestu-, estu-

tie *comb* sphingo-, -strain, -strict, syndesmo-; *base* -liga-, -merinth-, -string-, -vinc-. See **restriction**

tiger *base* tigr-

tightening *comb* isch-, koly-, -penia, -strain, -strict; *base* -string-; *suf* -en; **tightly bound:** *base* sphingo- See **constriction**

tile *base* imbricato-, tegul-

tillage *comb* -culture; *base* arat-

tilting *comb* -clinal, -clinate, -cline, -clinic, clino-, -clisis, lechrio-, loxo-, plagio-; *base* -cliv-

time *comb* back-, chrono-, horo-, yester-; *base* -tempor-; ~ **period:** *pre* eo-; *comb* aev-, -cene, paleo-, protero-; **timely:** *base* tempest-. *Also see* "Time" in Part III

timid *base* pav-, trep-, verecund-

tin *base* cassiter-, stann-

tiny *comb* brachisto-, brachy-, brevi-, chamae-, micro-, mini-, nano-, parvi-, parvo-, pauci-, steno-; *base* -curt-, exig-; *suf* -cle, -cule, -een, -el, -ella, -en, -et, -ette, -idion, -idium, -ie, -illa, -illo, -isk, -kin, -le, -let, -ling, -ock, -ola, -ole, -rel, -ula, ule, -ulum, -ulus, -y

tip *comb* -apical, apico-; *base* cacumen-
tired *comb* pono-; *base* -fatig-, kopo-, -lass-
tissue *comb* fascio-, histio-, histo-, hypho-, -sarc, sarco-; *base* text-; **dead** ~: necro-; **horny** ~: *comb* kera-, kerato-
titan *comb* titano-[1]
titanium *comb* titano-[2]
titmouse *base* par-[2]
to *pre* a-, ac-[1], ad-[1], af-, ag-, al-[1], an-[2], ap-, ar-[1], as-[1], at-, il-, im-, in-, ir-, ob-; *comb* -bound; *base* pros-; *suf* -ad, -ly, -ward, -ways, -wise; ~ **the other side:** *pre* trans-
toad *comb* batracho-, bufo-, phryno-; **tree** ~: *base* polyped-
today *base* hodiern-
toe *comb* dactyl(o)-, -dactylous, -dactyly, digiti-; *base* halluc-
together *pre* co-[1], inter-, syl-, sym-, syn-, sys-; *comb* allelo-, hama-, symphyo-, synchro-; *base* -mutu-, -simul-
toil *base* aerumn-. *See* difficult *and* work
token *comb* sema-, -seme, semeio-, semio-
toll *base* mulc-, mult-
tomb *comb* -taph, tapho-; *base* sepulc-
tomorrow *base* crastin-
tone *comb* tonia-, -phone, phono-, -phony; *base* son-
tongue *comb* -glossia, glosso-, -glot, lamino-, lingu(o)-; *base* -ligul-; ~ **kissing:** cataglott-
tonsil *comb* tonsillo-
tooth *comb* dentato-, denti-, dento-, dont-, -odont(o)-, -odus, -toothed; **canine** ~: laniar-; ~ **disease:** *comb* cario-; **lacking** ~: *base* edent-, coryph-; **saw-toothed:** *comb* serrati-, serrato-; *base* runcin-; ~ **socket:** *base* phat-[2]; **wisdom** ~: *base* cranter-
top crest: *comb* cory-, coryph-, stromboli-; *base* cacum-, culm-; ~ **shaped:** *comb* turbinato-
topical *comb* topo-, -topy
torch *base* lampad-, lychn-
tornado *base* -lilaps-
torrent *comb* rhyaco-
tortoise *base* -chelon-, emydo-, testud-. *See* **turtle**

totally *pre* be-, cata-, cath-, de-, kata-, ob-, per-; *comb* holo-, omni-, pan-, panto-, stone-, toti-
totter *base* -lab-
touch *comb* aphe-, -aphia, -apsia, hapto-[1], sensori-, thigmo-; *base* haph-, -palp-, -sent-, -tact-, -tang-. *Also see* "The Senses" in Part III
toughness *comb* dyna-, dynamo-, mega-, megalo-, -megaly, -sthenia, stheno-; *base* -forc-, -fort-, -poten-, robor-
tour *comb* hodo-, -ode, odo-, via-; *base* -itin-, peregrin-
tow fiber: *base* stop-; **pull:** *base* -tillo-, -tract-, vell-
toward *pre* a-, ac-[1], ad-[1], af-, ag-, al-[1], an-[2], ap-, ar-[1], as-[1], at-, il-, im-, in-, ir-, ob-; *comb* -bound, -petal; *base* pros-; *suf* -ad[3], -ly, -ward, -ways, -wise
tower *base* pyrgo-, turri-
town *comb* -burg(h), -ton, -ville; *base* urb-
toxic *comb* tox(i), toxico-, -toxin, toxo-, veneno-
trace *comb* ichno-; *base* indag-, vestig-
trachea *comb* tracheo-
track *comb* ichno-
trade *base* empor-, merc-, nundin-; ~ **names:** co-[2], -ine
train transportation: *comb* siderodromo-
trainer of gladiators *base* lanist-
trait *suf* -able, -acity, -acy, -age, -ance, -ancy, -ant, -asis, -asm, -ate, -atile, -ation, -cy, -dom, -eity, -ence, -ency, -ent, -ery, -esis, -ful, -hood, -iasis, -ice, -ility, -ion, -ise, -ism, -ity, -ling, -ma, -ment, -ness, -or, -osis, -otic, -red, -ship, -sion, -th, -tion, -tude, -ture, -ty, -ure, -y
traitor *base* prodit-
trajectory frequency *base* ergod-
tranquility *base* -eiren-, -iren-, -pac-, -pax-
transcending *pre* trans-
transfer carry: *comb* -fer, -ferous, -gerous, -parous, -pher, -phore, -phorous; *base* -port-, -vect-; **change:** *base* camb-, -fabr-, -fec-, -mut-, -vari-, -vert-; *suf* -ate, en, -fy, -ize, -otic
transgression *comb* enisso-, enosio-; *base* -culp-, hamart-, -pecca-
transitory *base* caduc-

transmission *broadcast: comb* -cast; **passing through:** *comb* -phoresis
transparent *comb* diaphano-, hyalo-, -phane
transplant *base* chim-
transport *comb* -fer, -ferous, -gerous, -parous, -pher, -phore, -phorous; *base* -port-, -vect-
transverse *comb* cross-, transverso-
trap *comb* -thera
trapezoid *comb* trapezi-
travel *comb* hodo-, dromo-, odo-; *base* -itiner-, -peregrin-, -via-. *See* **wander**
tray *base* hypocrater-
treading *base* calcat-**treat with** *suf* -ate, -ize
treatment *comb* -iatrics, iatro-, -iatry; *base* -com-
tree(like) *comb* dendri-, dendro-, -dendron, silvi-, xylo-; *base* -arbor-, dryo-. *See* **woods**
tremble *comb* tremo-; *base* pav-, trep-; *earth* ~: *comb* tromo-
trepidation *comb* -phobe, -phobia, -phobic, phobo-; *base* pavid-, tim(or)-, -trem-, -trep-. *Also see* "Fear" *in Part III*
triangular *comb* delta-, triangulato-, trigono-
tribe *comb* phylo-
trifling *base* -nuga-
trillion *comb* tera-, trega-, ; -*th:* pico-
trilobytes *comb* -paria
trip *comb* hodo-, -ode, odo-; *base* -itiner-, -peregrin-, -via-
triple *comb* triplicato-, triplo-; *base* -ter(n)-
troop *base* caterv-
trouble *base* aerumn-, calamit-, perturb-. *See* **grief**
trout *base* -trocto-, trutt-
truffle *comb* hydno-
trumpet *base* buccin-, litu-
trunk *comb* cormo-. *See* **stem**
trust *base* -cred-. *See* **belief**
truth *base* aleth-, -ver-, verit-
try *base* conat-, peir-
tube *comb* aulo-, follic-, salpingo-, siphoni-, siphono-, soleno-, tubi-, tubo-, tubuli-, tubulo-, vasi-; *base* fistul-, -syr-; ~ *shaped: comb* syringo-

tuberculosis *comb* tuberculo-; *base* phthisi-, phthisio-, -phthisis
tufts *comb* cespitoso-; *base* arbusc-, barb-, carph-, crin-, crist-, flocc-
tumor *comb* -cele, onco-, phym-, -phyma, struma-; *suf* -oma
tumult *base* -agit-, -tumult-, -turb-
tunic *base* camis-
tunnel *base* cunicul-
turbine *comb* turbo-
turbot *base* psett-, scophthalm-
turkey *base* gallinac-, meleagr-
Turkey *comb* Turco-, Turko-
turmeric *base* curcum-
turn *comb* gyro-, helico-, roti-, strepho-, strepsi-, strepto-, stroph(i)-, trepo-, -verge, vortici-; *base* -vers-, -vert-, -volut-, -volv-; ~ *towards or away: comb* -trope, -tropic, -tropism, tropo-, -tropous, -tropy
turnabout *comb* allo-; *base* -vers-, -vert-
turnip *base* napi-
turpentine *base* terebinth-
turquoise *base* callain-
turtle *comb* chelo(n)-; *base* -anaps-, chelys-, -testud-, -turtura-. *See* **tortoise**
tusk *base* broch-
twelve *comb* dodeca-, duodec-, duodecim-, duoden-
twenty *comb* eico-, icosa-, icosi-, viginti-; *base* vicenn-, vicesim-, viges-; ~ *four:* icositetra-
twice *pre* bi-, di-[1]; ~ *per time period: pre* semi-
twigs *comb* scopa-, scopi-; *base* carph-, ramul-, -sarment-, surcul-, virgul-
twilight *base* -crepus-, -lyg-
twin(s) *comb* diplo-, zygo-; *base* -didym-, gemelli-, gemin-; *conjoined* ~: *comb* -pagia, -pagus. *See* **two**
twisted *comb* cochlio-, contorto-, gyro-, helico-, pleco-, plecto-, spiro-, strepho-, strepsi-, strepto-; *base* -strob-, -stromb-, -stroph-, torn-, torq-, -tors-, -tort-; ~ *like a top: comb* strombuli-
twitching *comb* -chorea, choreo-, -clonic, -clonus, -esmus, -ismus, spasmo-; *base* -stal-, -vellic-; ~ *eye base* nystag-
two *pre* bi-, bin-, bis-, di-[1], du-; *comb* ambi-, ambo-, amphi-, ampho-,

deutero-, deuto-, dicho-, diphy-, diplo-, disso-, double-, duo-, duplicato-, duplici-, dyo-, gemelli-, twi-, zygo-; *base* -didym-, gemin-; ~ **colored:** *comb* dichro-; ~ **edged:** *base* ancip-; ~ **hundred:** *base* ducen-; ~ **wings:** *comb* diptero-. *Also see* "Numbers" in Part III

tympanic *comb* myringo-, tympani-, tympano-
type *comb* -type, typo-
typhoid *comb* typho-

U

ulcer *comb* helco-; *base* gangr-, ulcer-
ulna *comb* cubito-, ulno-
umbilicus *comb* omphalo-
umbrella *comb* umbell(i)-, umbraculi-, umbrelli-
unaffected by *suf* -proof
unalterable *base* immut-
unceasing *base* assid-, contin-, incess-, perpet-
uncertain *base* ambig-, ancip-, apor-, dub-, vagu-; *of* ~ **sex:** *comb* gynandro-
uncle *base* -avunc-, patru-
unclean *comb* blenno-, -chezia, copro-, fim(i)-, kopro-, myso-, -myxia, myxo-, paedo-, pedo-, scato-, spatilo-, spurc-, stegno-, sterco-; *base* -fecu-, molys-, rhypar-, rhypo-
unconscious *base* -stup-
under *pre* hypo-, infra-, sub-, subter-; *comb* infero-, under-; *base* cunicul-; ~ **world:** acheron-, infern-
understanding *comb* -gnomy, -gnosia, -gnosis, -gnostic; *base* -crit-, -judic-, sagac-, -soph-
undertaker *base* libit-
undertaking *pre* entre-; *base* molit-
underworld *base* acheron, infern-
undeveloped *comb* -atelia, atelo-. *See* **immature**
undiscerning *base* hebet-, obtus-, -tard-
undivided *base* integ-, tot-
undo *pre* de-
undulation *comb* flexuoso-, flucti-; *base* -sinu-. *See* **wave**
uneasy *base* agit-, mov-, trepid-, turb-
unequal *comb* aniso-, inequi-, impari-, perisso-, scaleno-; ~ **growth:** *comb* -nastic, -nasty

uneven *comb* anomalo-, anomo-, perisso-, poikilo-, sinuato-, sinuoso-; *base* salebr-
unfinished *pre* demi-, hemi-, semi-; *base* -atelia, atelo-; *suf* -esce, -escence, -escent
unguent *base* -aliph-, magma(t), unct-
unhappy *comb* lype-; *base* dolor-, fleb-, flet, luct-, -trist-
unholy *base* profan-
unhurt *base* illaes **unimportant** *base* -nuga-
unicellular algae *base* desm-
union *comb* -ergasia, gameto-, gamo-, -gamous,-gamy; *base* -greg-, -junct-, -soc-
unit *comb* -mer(e), mero-; *significant linguistic* ~: *suf* -eme
unite(d) *pre* co-; *comb* conjugato-, -ergasia, gameto-, gamo-, hama-, hapto-, junct-; *base* aps-, apt-, -greg-, -soc-; *suf* -ate, -ize
universe *comb* -cosm, cosmo-; *universal:* *comb* pasi-
unlike *pre* anti-, contra-, contre-, dis-, hetero-, ob-, un-; *comb* back-, counter-, enantio-, oppositi-
unlit *comb* ambly-, melan(o)-, nycto-, scoto-; *base* -achlu-, amaur-, fusc-, lyg-, obscur-, tenebr-
unlucky *base* scaev-
unmarried *base* caelib-
unmixed *base* merac-
unpaired *comb* impari-
unprofitable *base* mataeo-
unquenchable *base* avid-, edac-, gulos-
unreal *base* chim-
unreasonable *base* alogo-

unripe grape *base* omphac-
unsatisfactory *pre* hypo-, sub-, under-;
   comb hystero-; *base* hesson-; *suf* -aster
unsaturated acid *comb* -enoic
unspecified *base* ambig, dub-, ancip-
unspoiled *base* pristin-
unstable *base* labil
untrustworthy *base* apat-, dolero-, ludif-
unusual *comb* aetheo-, allotrio-,
   anom(o)-, anomalo-; **~ sexual prac-**
   tices: *base* paraphil-. *See* **irregular**
unwell *pre* dys-, mal-; *comb* noso-, -path,
   -pathic, patho-, -pathy; *base* aegr-,
   -morb-, -pecca-, valetud-
unyielding *base* adamant-
up *pre* ana-, ano-; *comb* super-, supra-; **~**
   to: *pre* epi-
upheaval *base* -agit-, -tumult-, -turb-
upon *pre* ana-, epi-, ob-, super-, sur-
upper side *comb* supero-
upright *comb* ortho-, prob-, recti-
uproar *base* crepit-, frem-, ligyr-,
   strep(i)-, strid-, stridul-. *See* **sound**
upward *pre* ano-[1], ex-; *comb* sursum-
uranium *comb* uranoso-
urea *comb* ure(a)-

ureter *comb* uretero-, urethro-
urge *base* horm-, -hort-, -suade, -suas-
uric acid *comb* uri-, urico-
urine/urinary tract *comb* ouro-, ure(a)-,
   ureo-, uretero-, -uretic, urini-, urino-,
   uro-[2], -ury; *base* diures-, -mict-, -ming-;
   ~ absence of: *base* anur[2]; **diseased con-**
   dition of ~: *comb* -uria
urn *comb* urcei-, urceo-
usage *base* mor-[1]
used for doing *comb* -chresis; *suf* -le
useful *comb* chreo-, chresto-; *base* -util-
useless *comb* ponero-; *base* futil-, inutil-,
   mataeo-
usual *comb* normo-
usury *base* usur-
utensil *base* sceuo-, skeuo-
uterus *comb* hyster(o)-[1], metra-, metro-,
   utero-
utter *comb* -claim, logo-, -logue, -lalia,
   -lexia, lexico-, -lexis, -lexy, -logy,
   -phone, phono-, -phony, rhet-, verbi-,
   verbo-, voc-, voci-, -voke; *base* -clam-,
   -dict-, -loc(u)-, -loqu-, narr-, -orat-,
   -phat-, -phem-
uvula *comb* staphylo-, uvulo-; *base* ciono-

V

vacant *comb* ceno-, keno-; *base* -erem-,
   (ex)haur-, inan-, -vac(u)-
vaccine *comb* vaccino-
vagina *comb* colp(o)-, elytr(o)-, kolpo-,
   vagini-, vagino-. *See* **vulva**
vague *base* ambig, dub-, ancip-
vagus nerve *comb* vago-
vain *comb* mataeo-
valence *comb* -valent; **lower ~:** *suf* -ous
validating *comb* -deictic
values *comb* axio-[2]
valve *comb* valvi-, valvulo-; *base* diclid-
vampire *base* vespertil-
vanishing *base* marc-
vanquish *base* vict-, -vinc-
vapor *comb* atmo-, -capnia, capno-, -hale,
   vapo-, vapori-; *base* halit-, -nebul-
variation *comb* allo-, anomalo-, anomo-,
   poikilo-; *base* -mut-. *See* **change**

various *comb* diversi-, hetero-, vari-
vas deferens *comb* vaso-
vase *comb* urcei-
vast *comb* bronto-, dino-, giganto-, mega-,
   megalo-, -megaly
vault *base* camer-, fornic-
veal *base* vitul-
vegetable *comb* thalero-, vegeti-, vegeto-;
   base lachan-, oler-, olit-
vegetation *comb* botano-, herbi-, -phyte,
   phyto-; *base* veget-; *suf* -aceae, -ad,
   -ales, -eae, -ia
vehicle *comb* amaxo-, -mobile; *base*
   -ocho-[1]
veiled *pre* sub-; *comb* calypto-, crypto-,
   veli-; *base* occult-
vein *comb* cirso-, phlebo-, vene-, veni-,
   veno-, venoso-, -venous; **enlarged ~:**
   comb varici-, varico-

velvet *base* velut-
ventral *comb* abdomino-, celio-, laparo-, ventro-
ventricle *comb* ventriculo-
ventriloquism *base* engastri-
veracity *base* aleth-, -ver-
verb *base* rhema-
verdegris *base* aerug-
verge *base* marg-, propinq-, prox-
vermin *base* pesti-, vermin-
versatile *base* agil-, facil-, ingen-
verse *comb* rhapso-, -stichia, sticho-, -stichous
vertebra *comb* spondylo-, vertebro-; *top* ~: *comb* atlanto-, atlo-
vertigo *base* illyngo-
verve *base* ard-, alacr-, -ferv-, zelo-
very *pre* per-; *comb* stone-
vesicle *comb* vesiculi-, vesiculo-
vessel *blood:* *comb* angio-, vasculo-, vasi-, vaso-; *serving* ~: *base* -lemb-, phial , sceuo-, skeuo-
vestibule *comb* vestibulo-
viands *comb* bromato-, -brotic, manduc-, opso-, -phage, phago-, -phagous, -phagy, -sitia, sitio-, sito-, -troph, -trophic, tropho-, -trophy, -vora, -vore, -vorous; *base* -alim-,-cib-, escul-, -gust-, -nutr-; *partially digested* ~: chymo-
vibration *comb* pallo-, tremo-, vibro-
vice *comb* enisso-, enosio-; *base* -culp-, hamart-, -pecca-
vicious *base* flagit-, iniq-, perdit-, -prav-, turp-
victory *base* nic-
view, a *comb* -scape
view, to *comb* eid(o)-, oculo-, ommat-, -opia, opsi-, -opsia, -opsis, opso-, -opsy, ophthalmo-, optico-, opto-, -scope, -scopic, scopo-, -scopy, visuo-; *base* -blep-, -scrut-, -spec-,-spic-, -vid-
village *comb* -burg(h), -ton ,-ville
villainous *pre* dys-, mis-; *comb* caco-, enisso-, enosio-, kak-, kako-, mal-, male-, ponero-; *base* culp-, facin-, flagit-, hamart-, iniq-, nefar-, pecca-, perdit-, -prav-, sceler-, scelest-, turp-
vine *comb* clem-[1], viti-; *base* -ampel-, pampin-

vinegar *comb* acet(o)-, acetyl-, acid-, keto-; *See* **sharp**
violate(d) *base* profan-, temerat-
violet *comb* indo-[1]; *base* ianth-, -viol-. *Also see* "Colors" in Part III
viper *comb* echidno-
virgin *comb* partheno-
virtuous *pre* bene-, eu-; *comb* areto-; *base* agath-, bon-, prob-
virus *comb* **genus:** -virus; **family:** -viridae; **subfamily:** -virinae
viscera *comb* splanchno-, viscero-
visage *comb* facio-, prosop(o)-, -visaged; *base* vult-
visible *comb* lampro-, luc-, luci-, -phane, phanero-, -phanic, -phany, pheno-; *base* -clar-, -schem-, -spec-, -spic-, visib-
vision *comb* eid(o)-, oculo-, ommat-, -opia, opsi-, -opsia, -opsis, opso-, -opsy, ophthalmo-, optico-, opto-, -scope, -scopic, scopo-, -scopy, visuo-; *base* -blep-, -scrut-, -spec-, -spic-, -vid-
vitality *comb* bio-, -biosis, vita-, vivi-, zoo-, -zoic, -zooid; *base* -anim-
vitiated *comb* lysi-, lyso-, -lysis, -lyte, phthysio-, -phthysis, putre-, putri-, pytho-, sapro-, septi-[2], septico-, septo-[1]; *base* -marces-, -putr-, tabe-; *suf* -ase
vitriol *comb* vitriolico-
vocabulary *comb* glosso-, -glot, -lexia, lexico-, -lexis, -lexy, logo-, -logue, -logy, verbo-; *base* -lingu-, -locu-, -loqu-, rhema-
vocal cord cartilage *base* aryteno-
voice *comb* -claim, logo-, -logue, -lalia, -lexia, lexico-, -lexis, -lexy, -logy, -phone, phono-, -phony, -phthong, rhet-, verbi-, verbo-, voc-, voci-, -voke; *base* -clam-, -dict-, -loc(u)-, -loqu-, -orat-, -phat-, -phem-; *powerful* ~: *base* stentor-
void *comb* ceno-, keno-; *base* -erem-, (ex) haur-, inan-, -vac(u)-
volcano *comb* vulcan-; *volcanic soil:* *base* ando-
voltaic *comb* volta-
voluminous *base* ampl-, copi-, magn-
voluntary *comb* ultro-. *See* **free**
vomit *comb* -emesis, -emetic, emeto-

voracious *base* adephag-, avid-, edac-,
    edacit-, gulos-
vortex *comb* vortici-
vote *base* suffrag-
vow *base* votiv
voyage *base* -curs-, itiner-, -navig-, pere-
    grin-, via-

vulgar *obscene:* *base* aischro-, bor-
    bor-, copro-, fescinn-; *ordinary:* *comb*
    demo-; *base* -pleb-, -popul-
vulture *base* gypo-, -vultur-
vulva *comb* episio-, vulvi-, vulvo-. *See*
    vagina

W

wading bird *base* grallator-
wagon *base* plaustr-
wail *base* plang-, -plor-, -ulul-[1]
wait *comb* brady-; *base* -cunct-, imped-,
    -mora-, -tard-
walk *comb* -basia, bato-, -grade; *base*
    -ambul-, -bat-, -gress-
wall *comb* parieto-, -phragma, septo-; *base*
    herco-, -mur-[2], teicho-, ticho-, vall-
walnut *base* juglan-
walrus *base* oben-, odoben-, trichec-
wand *comb* rhabdo-; *base* rhap-
wander *comb* -plania, plano-[2]; *base* aberr-,
    err-, -peregrin-, -vag(r)-. *See* **travel**
wane *base* decresc-, dimin-, hesson-,
    -pauc-
wanting *pre* hypo-, sub-, under-; *comb*
    hystero-; *base* hesson-; *suf* -aster
wanton *base* lasciv-, meretric-, scort-
war *base* arm-, -bell-, bellat-, milit-,
    polem-
warbler *base* vermivor-
ward off *base* alexi-, alexo-
warmth *comb* cal(e)-, calo-, calor(i)-,
    pyro-, -therm, thermo-, thermy; *base*
    aest-, caum-, ferv-
warn *base* -mon-l *warning signal:* *base*
    aposem-
wart *base* verruci-
wash *comb* balneo-; *base* ablut-, cathar-,
    -lav-, -mund-[2], -purg-
wasp *comb* vespi-; *base* pemphred-,
    sphec-, sphek-
waste matter *base* triphth-
wasting away *comb* phthino-, phthisio-,
    -phthisis; *base* auant-, marasm-, tab-
watchman *base* excub-, custod-, vigil-
water *comb* aqua-, aque-, aqui-, hydro-,

hyeto-, hygro-; *base* -rip-; *spring of ~:*
    base scatur-
waterless *comb* carpho-, xero-; *base* arid-,
    celo-, cherso-, -sicc-
watermelon *base* angur-
wave *comb* cuma-, cyma-, cymato-,
    cymo-, -enchyma, flexuoso-, gyroso-,
    kymo-, sinuato-, sinuoso-; *base* -fluct-,
    -unda-, -undul-
wax *comb* ceri-, cero-, cerumini-, kero-;
    base cera-
way *comb* hodo-, -ode[1], odo-, via-; *base*
    -itin-; ~ *of living:* -biosis, -style
weakness *physical:* *comb* astheno-,
    -atrophia, lepto-, -plegia, -plegy; *base*
    -debil-, dimin-, enerv-, flacc-, labe-, lan-
    guid-, retuso-; *spiritual:* *base* culp-,
    delinq-, laps-, -pecca-, sphal-
wealth *comb* chryso-, pluto-; *base* aphn-,
    chrem-, -opul-, pecun-, plisio-
weapon *comb* hoplo-; *base* arm-
wear off *base* –rade
weary *comb* pono-; *base* -fatig-, kopo-,
    lass-
weasel *base* arctoid-, gale-[1], -mustel-
weave *base* tex-
web *comb* hypho-; *base* tel-[1]
wed *comb* gameto, gamo-, -gamous,
    -gamy; *base* conjug-, marit-, -nub-,
    -nupt-
wedge-shaped *comb* spheno-; *base* cuneo-
weed *base* runc-, zizan-
week *base* -hebdom-
weep *base* dacryo-, fleb-, flet-, lachrim-,
    lachrym-, plor-, singult-
weevil *base* curculion-
weight *comb* -bar, baro-, bary-, gravi-;
    base obes-, -pond-; *weigh:* *base* -pend

well *condition:* pre bene-, eu-; *base* -san-,-salub-; *water:* comb phreato-, putea-
west *base* hesper-, -occid-, zephyr-; ~ *wind:* base favon-. See **direction**
wet comb hydro-, hygro-, udo-; *base* humect-, madefac-, -rig-. See **water**
whale *base* -balaen-, cet(o)-; *sperm* ~: *base* physeter-
wheat *base* silig-, tritic-
wheedle *base* leno-
wheel comb cyclo-, roti-, trochalo-, trochi-, trocho-, -wheeler. See **circle**
where *base* -ubi-. See **location**
whip(like) comb flagello-, mastigo-; *base* lora-
whirl comb dino-², vortici-
whirlpool *base* vorag-
whirlwind *base* prester-
whisper *base* psithur-, susurr-
whistle *base* sibil-, syrigm-
white comb leuco-, leuko-; *base* -alb-, alut-, -cand-, ceruss-, ebur-, -lac-, -niv-. *Also see* "Colors" in Part III
whole pre be-, cata-, de-, kata-, ob-, per-; *comb* holo-, integri-, integro-, omni-, pan-, panto-, stone-, toti-; *base* integr-
whore comb cypriano-, hetaero-, porno-; *base* -meretric-, scort-; *brothel:* lupan-
whorled *base* verticil-
wicked(ness) pre dys-, mis-; *comb* caco-, enisso-, enosio-, kak-, kako-, mal-, male-, ponero-; *base* culp-, facin-, flagit-, hamart-, iniq-, nefar-, pecca-, perdit-, piac-, -prav-, sceler-, scelest-, turp-
wicker *base* vimin-
wide comb eury-, lati-, platy-; *base* ampl-
widow *base* -vidu-
wife comb uxori-; *base* conjug-, marit-
wild *base* agrio-, incic-; ~ *animal:* comb -there, therio-, thero-; *base* -fer-; ~ *vine:* base labrusc-
will comb -bulia, ultro-; *base* -vol-
willow *base* itea-, salic-
win *base* vict-, -vinc-
wind comb anemo-; *base* -flat-, -vent-; *north* ~: base -borea-; *south* ~: comb austro-; *west* ~: comb zephyro-; *base* favon-
winding comb flexuoso-; *base* -sinu-

window *base* -fenestr-
windpipe comb bronch(i)-, bronchio-, broncho-, laryngo-, tracheo-
wine comb oeno-, oino-, vini-, vino-, viti-; ~ **pressing** *base* calcat-
wing comb ala-, ali-¹, pteno-, -pter, pterido-, pterigo-, ptero-, pterono-, -pterous, pterygo-, pteryl-, ptilo-; *having two~:* comb diptero-; *~case:* elytri-
wink *base* conniv-, nict-
winter *base* brum-¹, cheima-, hibern-, hiema-
wipe out comb lysi-, lyso-, -lysis, -lytic, -lyze, -phage, phago-, -phagous, -phagy; *base* -ate-⁴, perd-, phthart-, -vast-
wisdom *base* -jud-, sapient-, -soph-
wish *base* desid-, -opt-¹, -vell-, -vol-
witchcraft *base* goet-, -venefic-
with pre co-, inter-, para-, syl-, sym-, syn-, sys-; *comb* allelo-, hama-, symphyo-, synchro-; *base* -mutu-
withdraw *leave:* base relinq-; *remove:* pre ab-, abs-, apo-, be-, de-, des-, di-, dia-, dif-, dis-, e-, ec-, ef-, ex-, for-, off-, se, with-; *comb* ectro-
wither *base* marasm-, marces-, marcid-
within pre eis-, em-, en-¹, il-, im-, in-¹, ir-; *comb* endo-, ento-, eso-, intero-, intra-, intro-; *from ~:* comb entostho-
without *missing:* pre a-, an-, dis-, ex-, in-; *comb* lipo-; *base* priv-; *suf* -less; *outside:* pre epi, exo-, extra-, para-, preter; *comb* ecto-, extero-, out-
witness *base* notar-
woe comb lype-; *base* dolor-, fleb-, flet-, luct-, trist-
wolf comb lyco-; *base* -lup-
wolverine *base* -mustel-
woman comb gyn(e)-, gyneco-, gyneo-, gyno-, -gynous, -gyny, -para³, thely-, -wife; *base* -femin-, muliebr-; *suf* -en, -enne, -ess, -ette, -ice, -ine, -stress, -trice, -trix; *old ~:* grao-; ~ *who has given birth:* comb -para³
womb comb hyster(o)-¹, metra-, metro-, utero-
wombat comb phascolo-
wonder comb thaumato-; *base* -mir-

wood *comb* erio-, hyle-, hylo-, ligni-, ligno-, xylo-, -xylous, ylo-
woodcock *base* -charadr-, gallinag-, scolopac-
woodlouse *base* -onisc-
woodpecker *base* -pici-
woods *base* nemo(r)-, saltu-, silv-. *See* **forest**
wool *comb* lani-; *base* -flocc-, -lana-, mallo-, -ulo-[3]; *wooly:* *comb* dasy-; *base* oulo-[2]
words *comb* -glossia, glosso-, -glot, -lexia, -lexis, lexico-, -lexy, lingu(o)-, logo-, -logue, -logy, phraseo-, -phrastic, verbi-, verbo-; *base* epeo-, -lex-, liter-, -locu-, -loqu-, rhema-, vocab-; *suf* -ese; *long ~: base* sesquipedal-; *~ unit: suf* -eme
work *comb* arti-, -craft, -ergasia, ergasio-, -ergics, ergo-, -ergy, organo-, -urgy; *base* -labor-, lucubr-, oper-[1], -opus-, pono-[2] ; *worker: comb* ergato-
workable *comb* chreo-, chresto-; *base* -util-
world *comb* -cosm, cosmo-, -gaea; *base* mund-[1], secul-, -tellur-, -terr-
worm *comb* ascari-, filari-, helminth(o)-, nemato-, scoleci-, scoleco-, taeni-,

vermi-; *base* lumbric-, oxyur-, tered-, tinea-
wormwood *base* artemes-
worry *base* vex-
worse *pre* sub-; *base* degen-, pejor-
worship *comb* -latry; *base* cult-, vener-[2], -venerat-; *one who ~: comb* -later
worthlessness *comb* phaulo-; *base* futil-, inutil-, mataeo-, -nuga-, quisquil-.-vili-; *suf* -aster[2]
worthy of being *suf* -able, axio-; *base* -dign-
wound *comb* helco-, traumato-; *base* sauciat-, -vuln-
wrangle *base* altercat-, obstrep-, vitilig-
wrapping *base* involucr-, involver-
wren *base* troglodyt-
wrestling *base* luct-[2], palest-
wrinkle(d) *comb* corrugato-, rhyti-; *base* -crisp-, rhyss-, -rug-
wrist *comb* carpo-[2]
write *comb* -gram, -graph, -grapher, -graphic, grapho-, -graphy, grapto-, -logue, stigno-; *base* -scrib-, -script-, typo-; **writing difficulty:** *base* agraph-
wrong *pre* dys-, mal-, mis-; *base* prav-. *See* **wicked**

X

xiphoid process *comb* xiphi-, xipho-
X-rays *comb* radio-, roentgeno-

X-shaped *base* decuss-

Y

yam *base* dioscorea-
yarn *story: base* fabul-, mytho-, narr-, stori-; *thread(like): comb* filamento-, fili-, filio-, filo-, mit[2]-, nemato-; *base* -nema-, stema-
yawl *base* nav-, scaph-
yawn *base* oscit-
year *base* -ann-, -enn-; *comb* -ennial; *period of two ~:* bienn-; *period of*

three ~: trienn-; *period of four ~:* quadrenn-; *period of five ~:* quinquenn-; *period of six ~:* sexenn-; *period of seven ~:* septenn-; *period of eight~:* octenn-; *period of nine ~:* novenn-; *period of ten ~:* decenn-. *See* "Numbers" in Part III
yearly *base* annivers-
yearn for *comb* eroto-, -lagnia, -mania,

-orexia; *base* -appet-, conat-, -cup-, -libid-, -opt-, vell-; *suf* -urient
yeast *base* ferment-, prozym-, zym(o)-
yell *base* -clam-, vocif-
yellow *comb* chrys(o)-, flavido-, flavo-, -icter-, lurido-, luteo-, ochreo-, ochro-, xantho-; *base* aen-, croce-, -fulv-, gambog-, gilv-, -helv-, jaun-, lur-, lut-, -melin-, safran-, vitell-; **~** ***appearance:*** *base* cirrh-; ***yellow-brown:*** *base* gland-. *Also see* "Colors" in Part III

yesterday *base* hestern-, prid-
yew *base* tax-
yield *base* ced-, -cess, dedit-
yoke *comb* jugo-, jugulo-, zyga-, zygo-; *base* zeug-, zeux-
yolk *comb* lecith(o)-, vitelli-, vitello-
young *base* jun-, -juven-, nov-. *See* **child**
Y-shaped *comb* ypsili-
yttrium *comb* yttro-

Z

zany *base* fatu-, inan-, moro-, stult-
zeal *base* ard-, alacr-, -ferv-, zelo-
zebra *base* -zebr-
zenith *comb* -apical, apico-
zero *comb* nihil-, nulli-. *See also* "Negatives" in Part III
zest *comb* agito-; *base* alacr-, ard-, avid-, cupid-, ferv-, hedon-, volupt-, zelo-

zinc *comb* zinco-
zirconium *comb* zirconio-
zombie *base* zomb-
zoology *comb* zoo-
zygoma *comb* zygomatico-, zygomato-

PART III

Categories

ANIMALS

aardvark edent- (edentate)
adder colub- (colubrine)
agouti dasyproct- (dasyproctidae)
albatross diomed- (diomedeidae);
 procellar- (procellariid)
alligator eusuch- (eusuchian)
anchovy engraul- (engraulid)
angel fish pterophyll- (pterophyllous)
ant formic- (formicine); myrmec- (myr-
 mecine); myrmeco- (mymecology);
 myrmic- (mymicine)
anteater myrmecophag- (myrmecophagine)
antelope alcelaph- (alcelaphine);
 bubal- (bubaline)
ape pithec- (pithecoid); -pithecus (Australopithecus); sim- (simian)
armadillo dasypod- (dasypodid);
 tolypeut- (tolypeutine)
ass as- (assinine); ono- (onolatry)
auk alcid- (alcidine)
badger melin- (meline); mustel-
 (mustelid)
barracuda percesoc- (percesocine);
 sphyraen- (sphyraenoid)
bat desmodont- (desmodontid);
 megacheiropter- (megacheiropteran);
 microcheiropter- (microcheiropteran);
 noctilion- (noctilionid); pterop-
 (pteropine); vespertil- (vespertilian)
bear arcto- (cynarctomachy); urs- (ursine)
beaver castor- (castoreum)
bee api- (apiarian); bomb- (bombid);
 melisso- (melissean)
beetle coleopter- (coleopteral); lathro-
 (Lathrobium); scarab- (scaraboid)
bird avi- (avian); orneo- (orneoscopic);
 orni- (ornithology); ornitho- (ornitho-
 logical); volucr- (volucrine); *flycatching ~:* muscicap- (muscicapine);
 hanging nest building ~: pendulin-
 (penduline); *perching ~:* passer- (passerine); *singing ~:* oscin- (oscine);
 wading ~: grall- (gralline)
bittern botaur- (botaurus); ixobrych-
 (ixobrychus)

blackbird icter- (icterine);
 merul- (meruline)
black widow spider latrodect- (latrodectus)
bluebird sial- (Sialia); turd- (turdine)
boar apr- (apricide); suid- (suidian)
bobolink icter- (icterine)
buffalo bubal- (bubaline)
bug cimic- (cimicoid); entomo- (entomology); insecti- (insecticide);
 insecto- (insectology)
bull taur- (tauriform)
bullfinch pyrrhul- (pyrrhuline)
bunting emberiz- (emberizine);
 pyrrhul- (pyrrhuloxine)
butterfly lepidopter- (lepidopterous);
 papil- (papilionaceous)
buzzard buteo- (buteonine);
 cathart- (cathartine)
calf vitul- (vituline)
camel bact- (bactrian); camel- (cameline)
cardinal pyrrhul- (pyrrhuloxine)
carp cyprin- (cyprinoid)
cassowary casuar- (casuarina)
cat aeluro- (aelurophile); ailuro-
 (ailurophobe); feli- (feline); gale-
 (galeanthropy); gato- (gatophobia)
caterpillar bruch- (bruchus); -camp-
 (campodean); eruc- (eruciform)
catfish silur- (silurid)
cattle pecu- (pecudiculture)
centipede chilopod- (chilopodal);
 scolopendr- (scolopendriform)
chamois rupicap- (rupicaprine)
chickadee par- (parine)
chicken gallin- (gallinaceous); pull-
 (pullet)
chimpanzee sim- (simid)
chipmunk tam- (Tamias)
civet viverr- (viverrine)
cock alector- (alectoromancy);
 alectry- (alectryomachy)
cockroach blatt- (blatta)
coot fulic- (Fulicinae)
cormorant phalacrocorac-
 (phalacrocoracine)

cow bou- (boustrophedon); bov-
(bovine); bu- (bulimia); vacc- (vaccine)
crab cancri- (cancrine); gammar-
(gammarolite)
crane alector- (alectorine); grallator-
(grallatorial); grui- (gruiform)
cricket gryll- (gryllid); locust-
(locustarian)
crocodile crocodil- (crocodilian);
gavial- (gavialoid)
crow coraci- (coraciform); coraco- (coracoid); corvin- (corvine)
crustacean genus mysi- (mysid)
cuckoo cucul- (cuculine)
cuttlefish sepi- (sepiacean);
-teuth- (teuthologist)
deer cervi- (cervine); elaph- (elaphine)
docked tail colob- (colobus)
dodo did- (didine)
dog cani- (canine); cyn- (cynanthropy);
kyn- (kynanthropy); *bark:* gann-
(ganning)
dolphin delphin- (delphine)
donkey ono- (onocentaur)
dormouse glir- (gliriform); myox-
(myoxine)
dove columb- (columbine)
dragonfly libellul- (libellulid)
duck anat- (anatine); fuligul- (fuliguline)
eagle aet- (aetites); aquil- (aquiline)
earwig forficul- (forficulid)
eel anguill- (anguilliform); cyclostom-
(cyclostome); muraen- (muraenoid)
eland taurotrag- (Taurotragus oryx)
elephant elephant- (elephantine);
pachyderm- (pachydermic)
elk cerv- (cervine)
emu rat- (ratite)
ermine mustel- (musteline)
falcon accipit- (accipitrine); falcon- (falconry); raptor- (raptorial)
ferret mustel- (musteline);
viverr- (viverrine)
finch fringill- (fringilline)
firefly lampyr- (lampyrid)
fish icthyo- (icthyoid); pisci- (piscine);
bony ~: scopeli- (scopeliform). **Note:**
look for specific fish in this list
flamingo phoenicopter- (phoenicopte-
roid)

flea puli- (pulicine)
fly cyclorrhaph- (cyclorrhaphous); musc-
(muscid); myia- (myiasis)
fowl hunting aucup- (aucupation)
fox alopec- (alopecoid); vulp- (vulpine)
frog batracho- (batrachoid); bufo- (bufo-
tenine); phryno- (phrynoderma);
polyped- (polypedatid); rani- (ranine)
fruitfly drosophil- (Drosophilidae);
trypet- (Trypetidae)
gerbil cricet- (cricetine)
gibbon hylobat- (hylobatine)
giraffe artiodactyl- (artiodactylous)
gnat culici- (culiciform)
gnu connochaet- (Connochaetes)
goat caprin- (caprine); egagro-
(egagropile); hircin- (hircine);
trago- (tragopan)
goldfish cyprin- (cyprinid)
goose anser- (anserine); cheno-
(Chenopod)
gorilla gorill- (gorilloid); pong- (pongid)
grasshopper acrid- (acrid); forbi-
(forbivorous); gryll- (gryllotalpa);
locust- (locustid)
grebe podic- (Podicipedidae)
grouse gallinac- (gallinaceous);
tetrao- (tetraonid)
gull gavi- (Gaviae); lar- (larine)
hake merluc- (merlucine)
halibut hippogloss- (hippoglossoid)
hare cunic- (cuniculous); lago- (lagotic);
lepor- (leporine)
hawk accipit- (accipitrine); buteo-
(buteonine); falco- (falconine);
hieraco- (hieracosophic)
hedgehog echin- (echinate); erinac-
(erinaceous)
heifer damal- (damalic)
herd arment- (armentose)
heron arde- (ardeid); grallator-
(grallatorial)
herring clupeo- (clupeoid); halec- (hale-
comorphous); harengi- (harengiform)
hog hyos- (hyoscyamine)
hookworm ancylostom- (Ancylostoma)
hornbill bucerot- (Bucerotinae);
bucorac- (Bucoracinae)
hornet -sphec- (sphecoid); vespi-
(vespine)

horse caball- (caballine); caval- (cavalry); equ- (equine); hippo- (hippology); hippur- (hippuric); -hippus (eohippus)
horsefly taban- (tabanid)
hummingbird trochil- (trochiline)
hyrax chero- (cherogril)
insect wing angle torn-[2] (tornus)
jackass asin- (asinine)
jackdaw gracul- (graculine)
jay garrul- (garruline)
jellyfish discophor- (discophoran)
kangaroo macropod- (macropodine)
kestrel falco- (falconine)
kingfisher halcyon- (halcyonine)
kite milv- (milvine)
kudu tragelaph- (Tragelaphus)
lamb agn- (agnification)
lark calandr- (calandra)
leech bdell- (bdellatomy); discophor- (discophorous); hirud- (hirudine); sanguisug- (sanguisugous)
leopard pard- (pardine)
lion leo- (leonine)
lizard lacert- (lacertilian); saur- (saurian); sauro- (sauropod); -saurus (icthyosaurus); stellio- (stellion)
lobster astac- (astacian); gammar- (gammarolite); homar- (homarine)
locust locust- (locustarian)
louse pedicul- (pediculous); phthir- (phthiriasis); phthyr- (phthyriasis)
lynx lync- (lyncean)
macaw psittac- (psittacine)
mackerel scombr- (scombroid)
magpie corv- (corvoid); garrul- (garruline)
manatee trichec- (Trichechus)
marine flatworm nemert- (nemertion)
marlin istiophor- (istiophorid)
marmoset callithric- (callithricid)
marmot sciur- (sciurid)
marten mustel- (musteline)
martin hirund- (hirundine)
meadowlark icter- (icterine)
millipede arthropod- (arthropodal); diplopod- (diplopodal)
mink mustel- (musteline)
minnow cyprin- (cyprinid)
mite acar- (acaroid); miti- (miticide)

mockingbird mim- (mimine)
mole spalac- (spalacine); talp- (talpine)
mole-rat zemn- (zemnine)
mollusk malaco- (malacological); mollusc- (molluscous)
mongoose viverr- (viverrine)
monitor lizard varan- (varanian)
monkey cebo- (cebocephalic); pithec- (pithecoid)
moose cerv- (cervine)
mosquito aed- (aedine); anophel- (anopheline); culici- (culicid)
moth arct- (arctian); phalaen- (phalaenoid); tinea- (tineid)
mouse mur- (murine); mus- (musine); myo- (myomancy)
mullet mugil- (mugiloid)
muskrat cricet- (cricetid)
mussel mytil- (mytiloid)
muzzle capist- (capistrate)
neigh hinn- (hinnible)
nightingale philomel- (philomelian)
nuthatch sitt- (Sitta)
opossum didelph- (didelphine)
orangutan pong- (pongoid)
oriole icter- (icterine)
osprey ossifrag- (ossifrage)
ostrich rat- (ratite); struthi- (struthious)
otter latax- (Latax); lutr- (lutrine)
owl strigi- (strigine); tyto- (Tytonidae); ulul- (ululant)
ox bou- (boustrophedon); bov- (bovine); bu- (bulimia)
oyster ostrac- (ostracine); ostrei- (ostreiform); ostreo- (ostreophage)
parakeet psittac- (psittacine)
parrot psittac- (psittacine)
partridge gallinac- (gallinaceous); -perdic- (perdicine); perdri- (perdricide)
peacock pavon- (pavonine)
peck *bird:* becc- (beccafico)
pelican onocrot- (onocrotal); pelecan- (pelecanid)
penguin sphenisc- (spheniscan)
perch perc- (perciform)
pheasant alector- (alectorine); gallinac- (gallinaceous); phasian- (phasianine)
pig porcin- (porcine); sui- (suilline)
pigeon columb- (columbaceous);

palumb- (palumbine); perister-
(peristeronic); pullastr- (pullastrine)
platypus monotrem- (monotremal);
protother- (Prototheria)
plover charadr- (charadrine); pluvial-
(pluvialine)
polecat mustel- (musteline)
porcupine hystric- (hystricine)
porpoise delphin- (delphine);
phoecaen- (Phoecaenoides)
poultry gallin- (gallinaceous)
ptarmigan tetraon- (tetraonid)
quail coturn- (coturnine); gallinac-
(gallinaceous)
rabbit cunic- (cuniculous); lago- (lagotic); lepor- (leporine)
raccoon arctoid- (arctoidean); procyon-
(procyonine)
ram ariet- (arietine); crio- (criocephalous); krio- (krioboly)
rat mur- (murine)
rattlesnake crotal- (crotaline)
raven coraci- (coraciiform); coraco-
(coracomorphic); corvin- (corvine)
reptile batrach- (batrachian); her-
peto- (herpetology); -ophidia (Thanatophidia); ophio- (ophiolatry);
reptil- (reptilian); saur- (saurian); -sau-
rus (icthyosaurus); serp- (serpentine)
rhinoceros ceratorh- (ceratorhine)
roach blatt- (blattid)
roadrunner cucul- (cuculid)
robin turd- (turdine)
sable zibel- (zibeline)
sailfish istiophor- (istiophorid)
salmon salmoni- (salmoniform)
sandgrouse pterocl- (pteroclid)
sandpiper charadr- (charadrine);
tring- (tringoid)
scorpion pedipalp- (pedipalpous);
scorp- (scorpioid)
seagull lar- (laroid)
sea horse hippocamp- (hippocampine)
seal phoc- (phocine)
sea lion otar- (otarine)
sea urchin echin- (echinoid)
shark carchar- (carcharinid); gale-
(galeod); selach- (selachoid); *ham-
merhead* ~: sphyrn- (Sphyrna);
squal- (squaloid)

sheep ovi- (ovine); verv- (vervecine)
shrew soric- (soricine); tupai- (tupaiid)
shrimp macrur- (macruran)
silkworm bombyc- (bombycine)
skunk mephit- (mephitine); mustel-
(mustelid)
skylark alaud- (alaudine)
sloth xenarth- (xenarthral)
slug limac- (limacine)
smelt ather- (atherine)
snail cochlea- (cochleiform); gastropod-
(gastropodal); limac- (limacine)
snake angui- (anguiform); colubr- (colubrine); echidno- (echidnotoxin);
-glypha (episthoglypha); herpeto-
(herpetology); ophid- (ophidian);
ophio- (ophiolatry); reptil- (reptilian); serpen- (serpentine); viper-
(viperine)
snapper lutjan- (lutjanid)
snipe charadr- (charadrine); scolopac-
(scolopaceous)
sparrow passer- (passerine)
spider arachn- (arachnoid); arene- (areneiform); phalang- (phalangium)
squid cephalopod- (cephalopodal);
loligo- (loligopsid); teutho-
(teuthologist)
squirrel sciur- (sciurine)
stag cerv- (cervine); elaph (elaphine)
starfish asteroid- (asteroidean);
echinoderm- (echinodermatous)
starling psar- (psarolite);
sturn- (sturnoid)
stoat mustel- (musteline)
stork cicon- (ciconine); grallator- (grallatorial); pelarg- (pelargic)
sturgeon acipenser- (acipenserine);
sturion- (sturionic)
swallow chelid- (chelidonian); -hirund-
(hirundine); sturn- (sturnoid)
swan cycn- (cycnean); cygn- (cygnine)
swift cypsel- (cypseline)
swine porc- (porcine); su- (suoid)
swordfish xiphi- (xiphioid)
tapeworm cest- (cestoid); taeni- (taeni-
oid); teni- (teniacide)
tapir pachyderm- (pachydermoid)
tarantula theraphos- (theraphosid)
tarsier lemur- (lemuroid)

termite isoptero- (isopterous); termit-
(termitarium)
tern stern- (sternine)
thrush cathar- (Catharus); cichlo-
(cichlomorphous); muscicap- (muscicapine); turd- (turdiform)
tick acar- (acarine); ixod- (ixodid)
tiger tigr- (tigrine)
titmouse par- (parine)
toad batrach- (batrachian); bufo-
(bufonite); phryno- (phrynoderma)
tortoise chelon- (chelonian); emydo-
(emydosaurian); testud- (testudineous)
trout trocto- (troctolite); trutt-
(truttaceous)
turbot psett- (psettaceous); scophthalm-
(Scophthalmus)
turkey gallinac- (gallinaceous); meleagr-
(meleagrine)
turtle anaps- (anapsid); chelon- (chelonian); -chelys (Lepidochelys); testud-
(testudinal); turtura- (turturring)
viper viper- (viperine)
vulture vultur- (vulturine)
walrus oben- (obenid)

warbler vermivor- (Vermivora)
wasp sphec- (sphecid); vesp- (vespine)
weasel arctoid- (arctoidean); gale- (phascogale); mustel- (musteline)
weevil curculion- (curculionid)
whale balaen- (balaenoid); cet-
(cetaceous)
wolf lup- (lupine); lyc- (lycanthropy)
wolverine mustel- (musteline)
wombat phascolom- (phascolomian)
woodcock charadr- (charadrine); galli-
nag- (gallinaginous); scolopac-
(scolopacine)
woodlouse isopod- (isopodous);
onisc- (onisciform)
woodpecker pic- (picine)
worm ascari- (ascariasis); filari- (filariform); helminth- (helminthoid);
lumbric (lumbriciform); oxyur-
(oxyurifuge); scolec- (scolecoid);
scoleci- (scoleciform); scoleco (scolecobrotic); taeni- (taeniiphobia);
tered- (teredines); tinea- (tineid);
vermi- (vermiform)
wren troglodyt- (troglodytine)
zebra zebr- (zebrine)

THE BODY

abdomen abdomino- (abdominocentesis); alv- (alvine); celio- (celiomyositis); celo- (celoscope);
laparo- (laparotomy); ventri- (ventricumbent); ventro- (ventrodorsal);
abdominal sac: peritoneo- (peritoneoclysis); *distended ~:*
ventricoso- (ventricoso-globose)
adrenal gland adreno- (adrenotoxin)
amniotic sac amnio- (amniocentesis)
ankle bone astragalo- (astragalonavicular); tala- (talaria); tali- (taligrade);
talo- (talocalcaneal)
antibodies -valent (multivalent)
anticoagulant hepar- (heparin)
anus ano-² (anorectal); hedro- (hedrocele); podic- (podical)
arm acromio- (acromioclavicular);
brachio- (brachiocephalic)

armpit axill- (periaxillary)
artery arterio- (arteriosclerosis); -venous
(intravenous)
atlas *vertebra:* atlanto- (atlantoaxial);
atlo- (atloid)
atrophy tabe- (tabescent)
auricle atrio- (atrioventricular)
backbone rachi- (rachicentesis); rachio-
(rachiometer); rhach- (rhachitis);
-rrhachia (glycorrhachia)
bandy-legged valg- (valgous)
bile bili- (biligenic); chole- (cholecyst);
cholo- (chololith); gall- (gallbladder)
birthmark nevi- (nevoid); nevo-
(nevosity)
blind in one eye elusc- (eluscation)
blindness ableps- (ablepsy)
blister pemphig- (pemphigoid); phlyc-
(phlyctenous); pomph- (pompholyx);

pustul- (pustule); vesica- (vesicatory); vesico- (vesicoprostatic); vesiculo- (vesiculo-pustular)

blood cruent- (incruent); cruor- (cruorin); haema- (haemachrome); haemo- (haemogastric); hema- (hemachrome); hemato- (hematogenic); hemo- (hemophilia); sangui- (sanguicolous); sanguineo- (sanguineous); sanguino- (sanguino-purulent); *~ clot:* thrombo- (thrombo-phlebitis); *~ condition or disease:* -aemia (hyperaemia); -cythemia (leucocythemia); -emia (leukemia); *~ fluid:* lympho- (lymphocyte); *~ vessels:* hemangio- (hemangiosarcoma); vasculo- (vasculitis); vaso- (vasoconstrictor)

body corp- (corporeal); physico- (physicochemical); physi- (physiatrics); physio- (physiotherapy); somato- (somatology); -some (chromosome); *dead ~:* cadav- (cadaver); necro- (necrosis); *~ defect:* hamart- (hamartoma); *~ odor:* brom- (bromidrosis); *~ organ part:* -ite (somite)

bone ossi- (ossification); osseo- (osseomucin); osteo- (osteoplasty); *forearm ~:* ulno- (ulnoradial); *frontal ~:* fronto- (fronto-parietal); *~ joining hipbones:* sacro- (sacroiliac); *~ membrane:* periosteo- (periosteophyte); *bony process:* stylo- (stylohyoid)

brain cephal- (cephalitis); cerebri- (cerebritis); cerebro- (cerebrospinal); encephalo- (encephalocele)

breast mammi- (mammiferous); mammo- (mammogram); -mastia (macromastia); masto- (mastodynia); mazo- (mazoplazia); stetho- (stethoscope); *~ bone:* pect- (pectoral); sterno- (sternoclavicular)

breath afflat- (afflatus); anhel- (anhelation); -hale (exhale); halit- (halitosis); ozostom- (ozostomia); -pnea (apnea); pneo- (pneograph); pneumato- (pneumatometer); pneumo- (pneumobacillus); pneumono-(pneumonophorous); pneusio- (pneusiobiognosis); pulmo- (pulmnonary); spiro- (spirograph)

bruise sugill (sugillate)

buttocks nati- (natiform); -pygia (steatopygia); pygo- (pygopod)

cartilage chondr- (chondrify); chondrio- (chondriosome); chondro- (chondroblast); xiphi- (xiphioid); *eyelid ~:* tarso- (tarsoplasty)

cecum ceco- (cecostomy); typhlo- (typhlostomy)

cell alveolo- (alveolopalatal); celli- (celliferous); celluli- (celulliferous); cellulo- (cellulo-fibrous); -cyte (lymphocyte); -cythemia (leukocythemia); cyto- (cytology); -gonium (sporogonium); kyto- (kytometry); -plasm (neoplasm); plasmo- (plasmolysis)

cellulose cello- (cellophane)

celom celo- (celomate)

cervical cervico- (cervicodorsal)

cheek bucco- (buccolabial); -genia (microgenia); genio- (genioplasty); geny- (genyplasty); melo- (meloplasty); zygomatico- (zygomatico-auricular); zygomato- (zygomato-temporal)

chest pector- (pectoral); sterno- (sternocostal); stetho- (stethometric); thoracico- (thoracico-abdominal); thoraco- (thoracotomy)

childbirth loch- (lochia)

chin -genia (microgenia); genio- (genioplasty); geny- (genyplasty); mento- (mentoplasty)

chromosomes -ploid (diploid)

chyle chyl- (chylaqueous)

clavicle cleido- (cleidomastoid); clido- (clidomastoid)

clot grum- (grumous); thrombo- (thrombo-phlebitis)

coagulated pect-[2] (pectin)

coccyx coccy- (coccyalgia); coccygo- (coccygodynia)

collarbone clavi- (clavicle)

colon coli- (coliform); colo- (coloenteritis); colon- (colonic)

coma coma-[2] (comatose)

cornea corneo- (corneoiritis); kerato- (keratotomy)

corpse cadav- (cadaverous); necro- (necrophilia)

cough bech- (bechic); -tussis (pertussis)
cyst- sacc- (sacculation)
dandruff porrig- (porriginous)
defecation -chezia (hematochezia);
copro- (coprolagnia); fecu- (feculent); fim- (fimetic); fimi- (fimicolous); kopro- (koprophilia);
merd- (immerd); scato- (scatology); spatilo- (spatilomancy);
sterco- (stercoraceous)
diaphragm -phrenic (gastrophrenic);
phrenico- (phrenicotomy);
phreno- (phrenogastric)
ear auri- (auricular); auriculo- (auriculo-temporal); ot- (otitis);
oto- (otopyosis)
elbow ancon- (anconitis);
olecran- (olecranarthritis)
embryo- -blast (mesoblast); -blastic
(osteoblastic); blasto- (blastoderm);
-blasty; embry- (embryonic)
ethmoid bone ethmo- (ethmo-turbinal)
eustachian tube salpingo- (salpingitis)
eye eido- (eidoptometry); oculi- (oculiform); oculo- (oculomotor); op- (opalgia); ophthalmo- (ophthalmoscope);
-opia (diplopia); opsi- (opsiometer);
-opsis (coreopsis); ommat- (ommatophore); opsi- (opsiometer); opso-
(opsoclonus); -opsy (achromatopsy);
optico- (optico-papillary); opto-
(optometry); -scope (telescope);
-scopic (microscopic); -scopy (bioscopy); spec- (inspect); spic- (conspicuous); vid- (video); vis- (visual);
~ *ball:* glen-(glene); ~ *brow:* ophry-
(ophryosis); *cornea:* corneo- (corneoiritis); kerato- (keratotomy); *corner
of ~:* cantho- (canthoplasty); ~ *covering:* sclero- (sclerotomy); ~ *disease:*
albug- (albuginean); iris *of~:* irido-
(iridomotor); ~ *lash:* cili- (ciliary); ~
lid: blephar- (blepharotomy); *retina:*
retino- (retinoschisis). *See* **pupil**
face facio- (facioplegia); prosopo- (prosopagnosia); -visaged (round-visaged)
fallopian tube salpingo- (salpingotomy)
fibula peroneo- (peroneo-calcaneal)
finger -dactyl (dactyliology); dac-
tylo- (dactylology); -dactylous

(tridactylous); -dactyly (brachydactyly); digiti- (digitigrade)
fingernail -onychia (leukonychia);
onycho- (onychphagy)
foot ped- (pedal); pedi- (pedicure);
pedo- (pedopathy); pod- (podal-
gia); ~ *sole:* pelm- (antiopelmus);
plant- (plantigrade)
forearm ulno- (ulnoradial)
forehead metopo- (metoposcopy)
freckle ephel- (ephelis); lentig- (lentigo)
frontal bone fronto- (fronto-parietal)
gall bili- (biligenic); chole- (cholecyst);
gall- (gallbladder)
gargle gargar- (gargarism)
gastric chyli- (chyliferous); chylo- (chylocyst); chymo- (chymopoiesis)
genitals aede- (aedeagus); genito-
(genitourinary); *female ~:*
colpo- (colpospasm); *male ~:*
phallo- (phallocampsis)
gland adeni- (adeniform); adeno-
(adenomere); balani- (balanitis);
balano- (balanorrhagia)
goiter strumi- (strumiferous)
gonad gonado- (gonadopathy)
groin bubo- (bubonocele);
inguino- (inguinoscrotal)
gullet esophago- (esophagus);
oesophago- (oesophagalgia)
gums gingivo- (gingivoglossitis); oulo-
(oulorrhagy); ulo- (uloglossitis)
hair capilli- (capilliform); crini- (criniferous); pili- (piliform); pilo- (piloerection); piloso- (piloso-fimbriate);
hirsut- (hirsute); lanug- (lanugo);
thrix- (streptothrix)
hand cheiro- (macrocheiria); chiro-
(chiromancy); mani- (manipulate);
manu- (manual)
head capit- (decapitate); cephal- (cephalitis); -cephalic (dolichocephalic);
cephalo- (cephalocentesis); -cephalous
(brachycephaloius); -cephaly (dolichocephaly); cranio- (craniotomy);
kephalo- (kephalotomy)
heart cardi- (cardiagra); -cardia (tachycardia); cardio- (cardiology);
-cardium (myocardium); cordato-
(cordato-ovate); cordi- (cordiform);

pericardiaco- (pericardiaco-phrenic); pericardio- (pericardiostomy)

heel bone calcaneo- (calcaneo-fibular)

hernia -cele (perineocele); celo- (celotomy); hernio- (herniotomy)

hip cotyle- (cotyledonary); cotyli- (cotyliform); cotylo- (cotylosacral); coxo- (coxodynia); ischio- (ischiocapsular)

hyoid bone hyo- (hyoidal)

infectious disease diphther- (diphtheria)

inhale anhel- (anhelation)

insulin precursor nesid- (nesidioblast)

intestinal pouch caeci- (caeciform); ceco- (cecostomy); typhlo- (typhlostomy); ~ *rumbling:* borbor-[1] (borborygmus)

intestines entero- (enteropathy); ileo- (ileostomy); ilio- (iliosacral); intestino- (intestino-vesical); jejuno- (jejunocolostomy); viscer- (visceroptosis)

iris irido- (iridomotor)

jaw -genia (microgenia); genio- (genioplasty); geny- (genyplasty); gnatho- (gnathodynamics); -gnathous (prognathous); mandibulo- (mandibulo-maxillary); maxillo-(maxillo-palatine)

jejunum jejuno- (jejunoplasty)

joint arthro- (arthrodynia); articul- (multiarticular); ~ *socket:* gleno- (gleno-humeral)

kidney nephro-; pyelo-; reni-; reno-

knee genu- (genuflect)

labia minora nympho- (nymphoncus)

larynx guttur- (gutturo-labial); laryngo- (laryngoscope)

leg cnem- (gastrocnemius); crur- (crural); scel- (isosceles)

limb -mele (phocomele); -melia (macromelia); melo- (melorheostosis)

lips cheilo- (cheiloplasty); chilo- (chiloplasty); labio- (labiodental)

liver hepatico- (hepaticostomy); hepato- (hepatogastric); jecor- (jecorary)

loin muscle psoa- (psoadic)

loins laparo- (laparotomy); lumbo- (lumbodorsal); osphyo- (osphyocele)

lumbar lumbo- (lumbosacral)

lungs -pnea (apnea); pneo- (pneograph);

pneumato- (pneumatometer); pneumo- (pneumobacillus); pneumono- (pneumonophorous); pneusio- (pneusiobiognosis); pulmo- (pulmnonary); pulmoni- (pulmonigrade); pulmono- (pulmonobranchous); spiro- (spirometer)

lymph lymphato- (lymphatolysis); lympho- (lymphocyte)

marrow -myelia (micromyelia); myelo- (myelogenic)

mastoid mastoido- (mastoido-humeral)

membrane chorio- (choriocele); choroid- (choroideremia); hymeno- (hymenogeny); membrano- (membranocartilaginous); *eyeball* ~: sclero- (sclerotomy); *fetal* ~: allanto- (allanto-chorion); amnio (amniocentesis)-; *mucous* ~: muci- (muciparous); muco- (mucoprotein); mucoso- (mucoso-granular); ~ *sheath:* meningo- (meningocele)

mole nevo- (nevoid)

mouth -mouthed (open-mouthed); oro- (orolingual); stomato- (stomatalgia); -stome (cyclostome); -stomous (megastomous); *roof of* ~: palato- (palatonasal); uranisco- (uraniscoplasty); urano- (uranoschisis)

mucus blenno- (blennostasis); muci- (muciparous); muco- (mucoprotein); mucoso- (mucoso-granular); -myxia (hypomyxia); myxo- (myxomycete)

muscle musculo- (musculophrenic); myo- (myocardium); -tonic (myatonic); -tonia (isotonia)

nausea qualm- (qualminess)

navel omphalo- (omphalitis); umbilici- (umbiliciform)

neck atlo- (atloid); auchen- (maerauchenia); cervico- (cervicodorsal); coll- (decollate); jug- (jugulate); trachelo- (trachelodynia)

nipple mamilli- (mamilliform); papilli- (papilliform); papillo- (papillomatosis); papilloso- (papillosoasperate); thelo- (perithelium); umbo- (umbonulate)

nose nasi- (nasion); naso- (nasolabial); rhino- (rhinology)

nostrils nari- (narial)
occipital occipito- (occipito-axial)
ovary oario- (oariopathy); oophoro-
  (oophoritis); ovario- (ovariocentesis)
ovum oo- (oogamous); ovario-
  (ovariocele); ovi- (oviduct); ovo-
  (ovolecithin)
palate palato- (palatonasal); uranisco-
  (uraniscoplasty); urano- (uranoschisis); velar- (labiovelar)
palm palmati- (palmatifid);
  palmato- (pelmatopeltate)
pancreas pancreato- (pancreatotomy);
  pancreo- (pancreopathy)
pelvis pelvi- (pelvimeter); perineo- (perineocele); pyelo- (pyelocystitis)
penis med- (medorthophobia); men-
  tul- (mentulate); peo- (peotomy);
  phall- (phallic)
pericardial pericardiaco-
  (pericardiaco-phrenic);
  pericardio- (pericardiostomy)
perineum perineo- (perineocele)
periosteum periosteo- (periosteophyte)
peritoneum meso- (mesogastrium);
  peritoneo- (peritoneoclysis)
perspiration hidr- (anhidrosis); suda-
  (sudatory); sudori- (sudorific)
pharynx pharyngo- (pharyngology)
pimple pustulo- (pustulocrustaceous)
placenta mazo- (mazolysis);
  placenti- (placentiform)
pleura pleuro- (pleurotomy)
prostate prostato- (prostatectomy)
pubic area pubio- (pubiotomy);
  pubo- (pubofemoral)
pulse crot- (catacrotic); sphygmo-
  (sphygmograph)
pupil core- (corelysis); coreo- (coreoplasty); -coria (isocoria); coro-
  (coroplastic); -koria (leukocoria);
  pupillo- (pupillometer)
pus purulo- (purulo-gangrenous);
  pyo- (pyogenic)
pustular eruption mentig- (mentigo);
  psydrac- (psydracious)
pylorus pyloro- (pylorodiosis)
rash -anthema (enanthema)
rectum procto- (proctology); recto-
  (rectoscope)

retina retino- (retinoschisis)
rib costi- (costiform); costo- (costotome)
saliva ptyal- (ptyalogogue);
  sialo- (sialorrhea)
scapula scapulo- (scapuloclavicular)
scar cica- (cicatrix); epulat- (epulation);
  rhag-² (rhagades); ulo- (ulodermatitis)
scrotum didymo- (didymalgia); orchido-
  (orchidotomy); orchio- (orchiocele);
  oscheo- (oscheitis); scrot- (scotocele)
sebaceous secretion smegm- (smegma)
shingles herp- (herpes)
shoulder acromio- (acromioclavicular); humero- (humero-cubital);
  omo- (omodynia); scapuli- (scapulimancy); scapulo- (scapuloclavicular);
  spatul- (spatulamancy)
sinew chord- (chorditis); chorda- (chor-
  damesoderm); cord- (corotomy)
skeleton skeleto- (skeleto-trophic)
skin chorio- (choriocele); cuti- (cutisector); derm- (dermabrasion); -derm
  (endoderm); -derma (scleroderma);
  dermato- (dermatology); -dermatous
  (xerodermatous); -dermis (epidermis)
  ; dermo- (dermoneural); dora- (doramania); pell- (pellagra)
skull -cephalic (dolichocephalic);
  cephalo- (cephalometry); -cepha-
  lous (brachycephalous); -cephaly
  (dolichocephaly); cranio- (craniofacial); occipito- (occipito-axial);
  orbito- (orbitonasal)
smell deprivation anosm- (anosmia)
socket alveolo- (alveolopalatal);
  gomph- (gomphosis)
sphenoid bone spheno- (sphenoccipital)
spinal cord -myelia (micromyelia);
  myelo- (myelogenic)
spine rachi- (rachicentesis); rha-
  chi- (rhachitis); -rrhachia (glycorrhachia); spini- (spini-acute);
  spino- (spinobulbar); spinoso- (spinoso-dentate); spinuloso- (spinuloso-serrate); spondylo- (spondylitis);
  vertebro- (vertebroiliac)
spleen lieno- (lieno-gastric);
  splenico- (splenico-phrenic);
  spleno- (splenocele)
sternum sterno- (sternoclavicular)

stomach -gastria (microgastria); gastro- (gastroenteritis)

sweat hidr- (anhidrosis); suda- (sudaminal); sudori- (sudoriparous)

temple crotaph- (crotaphion); temporo- (temporomandibular)

tendon tendo- (tendolysis); teno- (tenotomy); tenonto- (tenontodynia)

testicle didymo- (didymalgia); orchido- (orchidotomy); orchio- (orchiocele); oscheo- (oscheitis); scrot- (scrotocele)

thalamus thalamo- (thalamocortical)

thigh mero- (merocele)

thorax thoracico- (thoracico-abdominal); thoraco- (thoracoplasty)

throat fauc- (faucal); gutturo- (gutturolabial); jugo- (jugo-maxillary); laryngo- (laryngoscope); pharyngo- (pharyngology); tracheo- (tracheotomy)

thumb pollic- (pollicate)

thymus thymo- (thymokinetic)

thyroid -thyrea (hypothyrea); thyreo- (thyreotomy); thyro- (thyromegaly)

tibia cnem- (cnemis); tibio- (tibiotarsal)

toe -dactyl (dactyliology); dactylo- (dactylology); -dactylous (tridactylous); -dactyly (brachydactyly); digiti- (digitigrade); halluc- (hallucar)

tongue -glossia (macroglossia); glosso- (glossoplegia); -glot (polyglot); lamino- (lamino-alveolar); ligul- (liguliform); linguo- (linguopalatal)

tonsil tonsillo- (tonsillotomy)

tooth cranter- (syncranterian); dentato- (dentato-serrate); denti- (dentifrice); dento- (dentosurgical); dont- (periodontal); laniar- (laniariform); odont- (odontalgia); -toothed (gap-toothed)

trachea tracheo- (tracheobronchitis)

tumor -cele (cystocele); -oma (sarcoma); onco- (oncologist); phym- (phymatosis); -phyma (osteophyma); struma- (strumectomy)

twitchy eye nystag- (nystagmic)

ulcer helco- (helcoplasty); ulcer- (ulcerate)

ulna cubito- (cubito-carpal); ulno- (ulnoradial)

umbilicus omphalo- (omphalitis)

ureter uretero- (ureterostomy); urethro- (urethroscopy)

urine mict- (micturient); ming- (bradymingent); ouro- (ouromancy); urea- (ureapoiesis); ureo- (ureometer); uretero- (ureterostomy); -uretic (diuretic); urini- (uriniparous); urino- (urinometer); uro- (urolith); -ury (strangury)

uterus hystero- (hysterodynia); metra- (metratonia); metro- (metrorrhagia); utero- (uterovaginal)

uvula staphylo- (staphylorrhaphy); uvulo- (uvulectomy)

vagina colpo- (colpocele); elytro- (elytroplasty); kolpo- (kolposcope); vagini- (vaginismus); vagino- (vaginomycosis)

vagus nerve vago- (vagotropic)

vein cirso- (cirsotomy); phlebo- (phlebotomy); varici- (variciform); varico- (varicocele); vene- (venesection); veni- (venipuncture); veno- (venostomy); venoso- (venoso-reticulated); -venous (intravenous)

ventral abdomino- (abdominoscrotal); celio- (celiopathy); laparo- (laparoscope); ventro- (ventrotomy)

ventricle ventriculo- (ventriculoatrial)

vertebra atlanto- (atlantoaxial); atlo- (atloaxoid); spondylo- (spondylopyosis); vertebro- (vertebrocostal)

vesicle vesiculi- (vesiculigerous); vesiculo- (vesiculo-pustular)

vocal cord cartilage aryteno- (arytenoid)

vomit -emesis (hematemesis); -emetic (antiemetic); emeto- (emetophobia)

vulva episio- (episiotomy); vulvi- (vulviform); vulvo- (vulvovaginal)

wart verruci- (verruciform)

windpipe bronchi- (bronchiectasis); bronchio- (bronchiogenic); broncho- (bronchoscope); laryngo- (laryngostenosis); tracheo- (tracheomalacia)

womb hystero- (hysteropexy); metra- (metralgia); metro- (metrophlebitis); utero- (uterolith)

wrist carpo- (carpoptosis)

xiphoid process xiphi- (xiphisternum); xipho- (xiphoiditis)

yawn oscit- (oscitation)
zombie zomb- (zombiesque)

zygoma zygomatico- (zygomatico-auricular); zygomato- (zygomato-temporal)

COLORS

Black

blue-black nigr- (nigrosine)
deep-black melan(o)- (melanous)
ebony-black eben- (ebeneous); ebon-
(ebonize)
inky-black atro- (atroceruleous)
reddish-black piceo- (piceo-
ferruginous)
sooty-black fulig- (fuliginated)

Blue

black-blue livid- (lividity)
dark-blue cyan(o)- (cyanean)
gray-blue caes- (caesious)
green-blue aerug- (aeruginous); glauco-
(glaucous)
milky-blue adular- (adularescent)
peacock blue pavon- (pavonine)
sea-blue cumat- (cumatic)
sky-blue azur- (azureous); -cerul- (cerulean); lazul- (lazuline)

Brown

acorn-brown gland- (glandaceous)
chestnut-brown castan- (castaneous);
-spad- (spadiceous)
dark-brown brun- (brunneous);
fusco- (fuscous)
dusky-brown phaeo- (phaeophyll)
reddish-brown testac- (testaceous)
yellow-brown fulv- (fulvous); gland-
(glandaceous); lur- (lurid); mustel-
(musteline)

Copper

brassy-yellow copper chalco- (chalcography)
gold-copper auricalc- (auricalceous)
red-brown copper cupr- (cupreous);

cupreo- (cupreo-violaceous); cuproso-
(cuproso-ferric)

Gold

copper-gold auricalc- (auricalceous)
yellow-gold aur- (aurulent); chryso-
(chrysography)

Gray

ash-gray tephr- (tephroite)
blue-gray caesi- (caesious)
dusky-gray phaeo- (phaeophyll); -phaein
(haemophaein); pheo- (pheochrome)
iron-gray feran- (ferant)
pale-gray polio- (poliomyelitis)
pearl-gray gris- (griseous)
silvery-gray glauco- (glaucodot)
white-gray can- (canescent);
canitud- (canitude)

Green

blue-green caes- (caesious); glauco-
(glaucous)
dusky-green oliv- (olivaceous);
olivaceo- (olivaceo-cinereous)
emerald-green smaragd- (smaragdine)
fresh-green thall- (thallium); -virid-
(viridescence)
grass-green verd- (verdurous)
leek-green porrac- (porraceous); pras-
(prasine)
light-green/blue beryl- (berylline)
pale-green celad- (celadon); festuc-
(festucine)
sea-green thalass- (thalassine)
slightly-green vir- (virescence)
turning green viresc- (virescence)
unripe-grape-green omphac-
(omphacitic)
yellow-green chloro- (chlorophyl-lose)

Orange

fruit-orange auranti- (aurantiaceous)
reddish-orange miniac- (miniaceous)

Purple

bright-purple blatt- (blattean)
dark-purple porphyr- (porphyrin)
metallic-purple indi- (indirubin);
    indo- (indophane)
red-purple amaranth- (amaranthine);
    phenic- (phenicine); -pun- (puniceous)
standard-purple purpureo-
    (purpurescent)

Red

blood-red cruent- (cruentous)
brick-red later- (lateritious); testaceo-
    (testaceo-fuscous)
bright-red -rub- (rubicund)
brownish-red -ruf- (rufescent)
cinnabar-red minia- (miniaceous)
copper-red pyhrro- (pyrrhotite)
crimson-red carmino- (carminophilous)
dark-red -rut- (rutilant)
deep-red grenat- (grenatite)
healthy-red -rud- (ruddy)
inflamed-red erysi- (erysipelatous)
orange-red miniac- (miniaceous); nacar-
    (nacarine); pyrrho- (pyrrho-arsenite)
poppy-red coquel- (coquelicot)
purple-red erythro- (erythrean); murex-
    (murexide); phoeni- (phoeniceous)
rose-red rhodo- (rhodophyllose); roseo
    (roseo-cobaltic)
rouge-red fuc- (fucate)
rusty-red ferrug- (ferruginous)
scarlet-red coccin- (coccineous)
vermillion-red minia- (miniaceous)

Silver

blue-silver glauco- (glaucescent)
white-silver argyro- (argyranthemous)
white-silver argent(i)- (argenteous)

Tan

light-brown fulv- (fulvous)

Violet

metallic-violet indi- (indirubin);
    indo- (indophane)
purple-blue ianth- (ianthine); io-
    (iopterous); -viol- (violaceous)

White

intense-white cand- (candescent)
ivory-white ebur- (eburnine)
lead-white ceruss- (cerussal)
leathery-white alut- (alutaceous)
milk-white lac- (lacteous)
pale-white leuco- (leucous)
snow-white niv- (niveous)
standard-white alb- (albicant)
yellowish-white ochroleuc- (ochroleu-
    cous)

Yellow

bright-yellow gambog- (gambogian)
brown-yellow fulv- (fulvous); lur-
    (lurid); ochreo- (ochreous)
canary-yellow melin- (meline)
gold-yellow chryso- (chrysocrous)
greenish-yellow icter- (icterus);
    jaun- (jaundice)
honey-yellow helv- (helvine)
lemon-yellow citr- (citreous)
light-yellow xantho- (xanthous)
metallic-yellow aen- (aeneous)
orange-yellow safran- (safranin)
pale-yellow flav- (flavescent); flavido-
    (flavido-cinerascent); gilv- (gilvous);
    helv- (helvenac); lurido- (lurido-ciner-
    ascent); ochro- (ochrocarpous)
red-yellow luteo- (luteous)
saffron-yellow croce- (croceous)
yolk-yellow lut- (lutein);
    vitell- (vitelline)

DIMENSIONS

deep batho- (bathometer); bathy- (bathysphere)

gigantic bronto- (brontosaurus); dino- (Dinotherium); giganto- (gigantology); mega- (megalith); megalo- (megalopolis); -megaly (hepatomegaly); super- (supernova)

high acro- (acrophobia); alti- (altimetry); alto- (altostratus); hypsi- (hypsicephalic); hypso- (hypsodont); super- (superstructure)

large ampl- (amplification); -fold (hundredfold); grand- (grandiflora); macro- (macrocosm); magni- (magnifying); maj- (majority); maxi- (maximum); plethys- (plethysmometry); super- (supertanker)

long dolicho- (dolichocephalic); -footer (ten-footer); longi- (longicaudate); macro- (macropterous); maxi- (maxicoat); procer- (procercoid)

low chamae- (chamaerops); hypo- (hypocaust); infero- (inferolateral); infra- (infrapatellar); sub- (subway); subter- (subteraqueous); under- (underground)

narrow/thin angusti- (angustifoliate); areo- (areolation); dolicho- (dolichocephalic); gracil- (gracile); isthm- (isthmian); lepto- (leptorrhine); phim- (phimosis); -stal- (staltic); stegno- (stegnotic); steno- (steno-sis); -strict- (stricture); tenu- (tenuity)

short brachisto- (brachistocephaly); brachy- (brachypterous); brevi- (abbreviation); chamae- (chamaerops); curt- (curtate); exig-[2] (exiguous); mini- (minidrama)

small -cle (particle); -cule (molecule); -culum (curriculum); -culuc (fasciculus); -een (colleen); -el (satchel); -ella (umbrella); -en (kitten); -et (rivulet); -ette (kitchenette); hekisto- (hekistotherm); -idion (enchiridion); -idium (peridium); -ie (laddie); -illa (cedilla); -illo (cigarillo); -isk (asterisk); -kin (lambkin); -le (icicle); -let (ringlet); -ling (duckling); micro- (microcassette); mini- (minibus); nano- (nanosecond); -ock (hillock); -ola (variola); -ole (variole); parvi- (parvipotent); parvo- (parvoline); -rel (wastrel); -ula (fibula); -ule (ampule); -ulum (speculum); -ulus (homunculus); -y (Billy)

thick cespitoso- (cespitoso-arborescent); -crass- (crassitude); dasy- (dasymeter); hadro- (hadrosaur); pachy- (pachyderm); pycno- (pycnometer); pykn(o)- (pyknic); spiss- (spissatus); visco- (viscosity)

wide ampl- (amplitude); eury- (eurygnathous); lati- (latisternal); platy- (platypellic)

DIRECTIONS

away from, apart a-[2] (avert); ab-[2] (abduct); abs-[2] (abstruse); apo- (apogeotropism); be- (bereave); de- (deplane); des- (descant); di-[2] (divest); dia- (diagnose); dif- (differ); dis-[1] (dismiss); e- (emigrate); ec- (ecdemic); ectro- (ectrotic); ef- (efferent); ex- (expatriate); for- (forgo); off-[1] (offload); se- (separate); with- (withdraw)

backward retro- (retroversion); opiso- (opisometer)

down a-[2] (abate); ab-[2] (abdicate); abs-[2] (abscond); cata- (catacomb); cath- (cathepsin); de- (decumbent); kata- (katabatic)

east euro- (euroboreal); orient-
(orienteering)
forward antero- (antero-frontal); fore-
(foredeck); pre- (preaxial); pro-¹ (pro-
jection); proso- (prosogaster)
into eis- (eisegesis); em-¹ (emigrate);
en-¹ (entomb); il- (illuminate); im-
(immerse); in- (instill); ir- (irradiate)
left laeo- (laeotropic); laevo- (laev-
ogyrate); levo- (levorotatory);
sinistro- (sinistrocular)
north borea- (boreal); septen-
(septentrion)
out of e- (eject); ec- (eccentric); ef-
(effluence); ex- (expulsion)
right dexio- (dexiotropic); dextro-
(dextrorotatory)

south austr- (Austronesia); noto-
(notothere)
toward a-¹ (ascribe); ac- (acclaim);
ad- (advance); -ad (dorsad); af-
(affirm); ag- (aggrade); al- (allege);
an- (announce); ap- (approve); ar-
(arrive); as- (assent); at- (attrition);
-bound (eastbound); il- (illuminate);
im- (impel); in- (inboard); ir- (irrigate); -ly (northerly); ob- (object);
-ward (outward)
up ana- (anabatic); ano- (anoopsia);
ex- (extol); super- (superscript);
sur- (surmount);
west hesper- (hesperian); occid- (occident); zephyr- (zephyrean)

DIVINATION

*To extract the root that shows the method being used,
simply drop the -mancy, which signifies telling the future.*

air ~ *blowing or moving:* aeromancy;
visions in the sky: chaomancy
angels angelomancy
animal(s) ~ *behavior:* zoomancy; ~
movement: theriomancy
appearance or form of a person
schematomancy
arrows with incised marks or words
belomancy
ashes cineromancy, spodomancy; ~ *of a
sacrifice:* tephromancy
ass head, boiled cephalonamancy
ax (balanced on a bar) axinomancy
barley meal alphitomancy
basin of water lecanomancy
belly noises gastromancy
Bible verses (randomly selected)
bibliomancy
birds ornithomancy; ornomancy
blood hematomancy; ~ *dripping in patterns:* dririmancy
bones osteomancy, osteomanty; ~
marked as dice: astragalomancy
bowl of water cylicomancy, kylixomancy
brass vessels (sound of) chalcomancy

breastbone sternomancy
bubbles rising in a fountain pegomancy
cake dough (sprinkled on sacrificial vic-
tim) crithomancy
candles (blowing them out) pneu-
mancy
cards cartomancy, chartomancy
cat (jumping and landing) ailuromancy,
felidomancy
cheese (patterns of coagulation)
tyromancy
cloud formations chaomancy
coals (burning) anthracomancy
contour of the land topomancy
counting mathemancy
crystal gazing crystallomancy;
spheromancy
cup scyphomancy
dead people (communication with)
egromancy, necromancy, necyomancy,
psychomancy, sciamancy, sciomancy,
thanatomancy
devil or demons demonomancy,
necyomancy
dice (or beans with points or marks on

them) astragalomancy, cleromancy, cubomancy

digging things up oryctomancy

dirt (thrown on the ground to produce patterns) geomancy

dots or points (drawn at random, originally on the ground) geomancy

dreams oneiromancy, songuary, sompnary

dust amathomancy

eggs oomancy, ovomancy

embryonic sac amniomancy

entrails of a human anthropomancy, splanchnomancy

evil spirits demonomancy, necyomancy

false divination pseudomancy

feces (examination of) scatomancy, spatilomancy, stercomancy

feet (soles of) paedomancy, pedomancy

figs or fig leaves botanomancy, sycomancy

fingernails onychomancy

fire empyromancy, pyromancy

fish (examining heads or entrails) icthyomancy

flour aleuromancy

flowers anthomancy

foolish divination moromantie

footsteps ichnomancy

forehead wrinkles metopomancy

fountain pegomancy

glass vessels (figures appearing in) gastromancy [one looks into the glass's "belly"]

gods (speaking through oracles) theomancy

handwriting chartomancy, graptomancy

hatchet axinomancy

head cephalomancy

heavens ouranomancy, uranomancy

horses (neighing) hippomancy

human features and form collimancy, frontimancy, metopomancy, physiognomancy, schematomancy

icons iconomancy

idols idolomancy

incense burning knissomancy, libanomancy

key cleidomancy, clidomancy

kidneys nephromancy

lamp or torch flame lampadomancy, lychnomancy

largest object nearby macromancy

laughter gelomancy

laurel tree or leaves daphnomancy

lead, molten (motions and figures in) molybdomancy

leaves phyllomancy; *tea ~:* foliomancy, theimancy

letters (of a person's name) nomancy, onomancy, onomatomancy, onomomancy

lines *~ on the forehead:* frontimancy, metopomancy; *~ on the ground:* geomancy; *~ on the neck:* collimancy; *~ on the palms:* cheiromancy, chiromancy; *~ on the soles:* paedomancy, pedomancy

lip reading labiomancy

logarithms logarithmomancy

lots cleromancy

Lucifer necyomancy

magic magastromancy

meteors meteoromancy

mice movements myomancy

mirrors catoptromancy, enoptromancy

molten lead (dropped on water) molybdomancy

moon selenomancy

names (including number of letters in) nomancy, onomancy, onomatomancy, onomomancy

neck wrinkles collimancy

numbers arithmancy, arithmomancy; *prophesy based on analysis of the measurements of the Temple of Solomon:* naometry

nursing baby (choice of breast) mazomancy

objects offered in sacrifice hieromancy

objects touched by another person psychometry

onions cromniomancy, cromnyomancy

oracle's rapturous statements chresmomancy, theomancy

palm reading cheiromancy, chiromancy

paper (written on) chartomancy

pearls margaritomancy

pebbles pessomancy, psephomancy

plants botanomancy, floromancy

playing cards cartomancy
pointed objects aichmomancy
posture ichnomancy
random lines or passages of books
   stichomancy
rings dactyliomancy, dactylomancy
rod rabdomancy, rhabdomancy
rooster (choosing grains of corn) alectoromancy, alectryomancy
sacred objects, sacrificial offerings
   hieromancy
sage botanomancy
salt alomancy, halomancy
secret means cryptomancy
serpents ophiomancy
sheep (shoulder blade) spatulamancy
shells conchomancy
shield aspidomancy
shoulder blades (charred or cracked)
   armomancy, omoplatoscopy, scapulimancy; ~ *of sheep:* spatulamancy
sieve (suspended on shears)
   coscinomancy
sleep meconomancy
smallest object nearby micromancy
smoke (ascent and motion) capnomancy
snakes ophiomancy
soles of feet (lines on) paedomancy,
   pedomancy
soul (emotional and ethical dispositions)
   psychomancy, thumomancy
spinning (in a marked circle until dropping) gyromancy
spots maculomancy
spring of water pegomancy
stars astromancy, sideromancy,
   uranomancy
sticks or wands rhabdomancy,
   xylomancy
stomach rumblings gastromancy
stones (or stone charms) lithomancy

stranger (studying the first one to
   appear) xenomancy
straws (burning) sideromancy
sword machaeromancy
teeth odontomancy
things seen over one's shoulder
   retromancy
thunder brontomancy, ceraunomancy
tide (motion and appearance)
   hydromancy
time chronomancy
tongue hyomancy
torch flame lampadomancy,
   lychnomancy
tree bark (writing on) stigonomancy
twitching limbs spasmatomancy,
   spasmodomancy
umbilical cord (number of knots in)
   omphalomancy
urine ouromancy, urimancy, urino-
   mancy, uromancy
verses or poems rhapsodomancy
walking ambulomancy
wand rhabdomancy
water hydromancy, ydromancy; ~ *in a*
   basin or shallow bowl: cylicomancy,
   kylixomancy, lecanomancy; ~ *fountain*
   or spring: pegomancy
wax (melted and dropped in water)
   ceromancy
weather aeromancy, meteoromancy
weights zygomancy
wheel tracks trochomancy
wild animals theriomancy
wind (observation of) aeromancy,
   austromancy
wine (its color, sound, etc. when poured)
   oenomancy, oinomancy
wood (pieces of) xylomancy
words logomancy
writing *on bark of a tree:* stigonomancy;
   on paper: chartomancy

EATING HABITS

air aerophagous
algae algophagous, algivorous

animals zoophagous; *specific animals:*
   see "Animals"

animal waste detrivorous
ants formicivorous, formivorous, myrmecophagous
anything omnivorous, pamphagous, pantophagous, pleophagous
aphids aphidivorous
apples pomivorous
bacteria bacteriophagous
bees apivorous
berries baccivorous
birds ornithivorous, ornivorous
blood hemophagous, hematophagous, sanguinivorous, sanguivorous
body's own tissues autophagous
bones ossivorous
books bibliophagous [metaphorical]
both vegetables & animal flesh herbicarnivorous
bread artophagous, panivorous
butterflies and moths lepidopterivorous
cats felivorous
cattle bovivorous
cells cytophagous
cereals graminivorous
children paedophagous [*see* Jonathan Swift]
coccids coccidophagous
coral coralivorous
corpse or carrion necrophagous
crab harpactophagous
crows corvivorous
crustaceans cancrivorous, carcinivorous
dead material necrophagous
decaying matter saprophagous
deer cervivorous, venisonivorous
detritus detriophagous, detritivorous
dirt chthonophagous, geadephagous, geophagous
divine beings divinivorous, theophagus
dogs canivorous
dolphins and whales cetivorous
dragons draconivorous
dry food xerophagous
dung coprophagous, merdivorous, scatophagous, stercovorous
eggs oophagous, ovivorous
everything omnivorous, pamphagous, pantophagous, pleophagous
feces coprophagous, merdivorous,

scatophagous, stercovorous; *one's own:* autocoprophagous
filth rhypophagy
fingernails onychoophagous
fish ichthyophagous, piscivorous; *all kinds of:* panichthyophagous
flesh carnivorous, creatophagous, creophagous, sarcophagous; *raw:* omophagous
flies muscivorous
flowers anthophagous, florivorous
fowl gallinivorous
fresh vegetable matter thalerophagous
frogs batrachivorous, batrachophagous, ranivorous
fruit carpophagous, fructivorous, frugivorous
full range of food omnivorous, pamphagous, pantophagous, pleophagous
fungi fungivorous, mycetophagous, mycophagous
gods divinivorous, theophagous
galls gallivorous
gold aurivorous
grain granivorous
grass or herbs graminivorous, poephagous
grasshoppers forbivorous
hair comeophagous, crinivorous
honey meliphagous, mellivorous
horns cornivorous
horses equivorous, hippophagous
humans androphagous, anthropophagous, feminivorous, homnivorous, paedophagous
ice pagophagous
insects entomophagous, insectivorous
insides of a structure endophagous, entophagous
iron ferrophagous, ferrivorous
knives cultrivorous (carnival act)
large creatures or plants macrophagous
larvae larvivorous
leaves foliophagous, frondivorous, phyllophagous
leeks prasophagous
legumes leguminivorous
lice phthirophagous
lichens lichenophagous, lichenivorous
light luminivorous

limestone calcivorous
living things biophagus
lizards saurophagous
lotuses lotophagous
many kinds of food euryphagous, pamphagous, pantophagous, pleophagous
mental energy psychophagous
metals metallophagous, metallivorous
milk galactophagous, lactivorous
mollusks molluscivorous
moths and butterflies lepidopterivorous
mud limivorous
narrow range of food oligophagous,
stenophagous
nectar nectarivorous
nematodes nematophagous
nutmegs myristicivorous
nuts caryophagous, nucivorous
oak leaves quercivorous
offal offivorous
onions cepivorous
only a few specific kinds of food oligophagous, stenophagous
only one type of food monophagous,
univorous
opium or heroin meconophagous
other species heterophagous
outsides of a structure ectophagous,
exophagous
oysters ostreophagous
palm trees palmivorous
parrots galliphagous
pepper piperivorous
pigs porcivorous
pine kernels pinivorous
placenta placentophagous
plankton planktivorous
plant juices mucivorous
plant lice aphidophagous
plants herbivorous, phytophagous, phy-
tivorous, plantivorous
plant sap phytosuccivorous, succivorous
plasma plasmophagous
poison toxicophagous, toxiphagous
pollen pollenophagous, pollinivorous
poultry gallinivorous

pupae pupivorous
rabbits leporinivorous
raw meat kreatophagous, omophagous
restricted range of food oligophagous,
stenophagous
rice oryzivorous
rock or stone lithophagous
rodents glirivorous
roots rhizophagous, radicivorous
same species homophagous
seaweed fucivorous
seeds clethrophagous, granivorous,
seminivorous
several hosts or sources of food plurivo-
rous, polyphagous
sheep ovivorous
shells conchivorous
skin cutaneophagous, cutisivorous
small creatures or plants microphagous
snakes ophiophagous, reptilivorous,
serpentivorous
society sociophagous [social predator]
spiders arachnophagous, arachnivorous
strange foods allotriophagous
termites termitophagous
thistles cardophagus
tissue histiophagous
too little hypophagous
too much hyperphagous
trays of ice pagophagous
trees dendrophagous
vegetables thalerophagous, vegetivorous
venison cervivorous, venisonivorous
water aqueophagus, aquivorous,
hydradephagous, hydrophagous
whales and dolphins cetivorous
wide variety of foods euryphagous, pamphagous, pantophagous,
pleophagous
women feminivorous; *See* **humans**
wood lignivorous, xylophagous,
ylophagous
wool or fleece mallophagous
words: large quantities of
omniverbivorous
worms scolecophagous, vermivorous

EMOTIONAL STATES

adversarial hostil- (hostile), inimic-
(inimical)

angry anim- (animosity), fur-¹ (furious),
invid- (invidious), ira- (irate)

annoyed vex- (vexed)

appeasing paca- (placation), placa-
(placation)

attracted to allect- (allectation), -phile
(Anglophile), -philia (logophilia),
-philiac (scopophiliac), -philic (bibliophilic), -philism (Francophilism),
philo- (philology), -philous (photophilous), -trope (heliotrope), -tropic
(glycotropic), -tropism (thermotropism), -tropous (plagiotropous),
-tropy (entropy), -urient (esurient)

belligerent anim- (animosity), fur-¹ (furious), invid- (invidious), ira- (irate)

bereaving dolor-, fleb- (flebile), flet-
(fletiferous), luct- (luctual), lype-
(lypemania), tapin- (tapinosis),
trist- (tristful)

bitterness acrim- (acrimonious)

blaming culp- (culpable), reprehen- (rep-
rehend), vituper- (vituperative)

braggart alaz- (alazon), jactan- (jactant)

brazen contum- (contumely), impud-
(impudent), procac- (procacity)

bullying procac- (procacious)

chastising castig- (castigation), peno-
penology, poine- (poinemania),
-pun- (punish)

cheerful beati- (beatific), chero- (cheromania), felic- (felicitous), hilar-, (hilarity), jubil- (jubilant)

coercive coerc- (coerce)

compassionate miserat- (commiserate)

craving appet- (appetite), conat- (conative), cup- (cupidity), eroto- (erotomania), -lagnia (kleptolagnia),
vell- (velleity), -urient (esurient),
-orexia (dysorexia)

cunning versut- (versuteness)

deceitful dolos- (dolose) ; perfid-
(perfidious)

dejected dolor (dolorous)-,

fleb- (flebile), flet- (fletiferous), luct-
(luctual), lype- (lypemania), tapin-
(tapinosis), trist- (tristful)

delighted beati- (beatific), chero- (cheromania), felic- (felicitous), hilar-,
(hilarity), jubil- (jubilant)

disgusted abom- (abominate), psoph-
(psophometer)

disparaging derog- (derogatory)

disrespectful derog- (derogation)

distressed miser- (miserable), perturb-
(perturbed)

doleful dolor (dolorous)-, fleb- (flebile), flet- (fletiferous), luct- (luctual),
lype- (lypemania), tapin- (tapinosis),
trist- (tristful)

downcast dolor (dolorous)-, fleb- (flebile), flet- (fletiferous), luct- (luctual),
lype- (lypemania), tapin- (tapinosis),
trist- (tristful)

dreading dirit- (dirity), pavid- (pavidity), tim- (timorous), trem- (tremble),
trep- (trepidation)

eager avis- (avidity), cupid- (cupidity)

envious invid- (invidity), zelotyp-
(zelotypia)

excited agit- (agitation), bathmo- (bathmotropic), -cit- (incite)

exulting beati- (beatific), chero- (cheromania), felic- (felicitous), hilar-, (hilarity), jubil- (jubilant)

fearful dirit- (dirity), pavid- (pavidity),
-phobe (technophobe), -phobia (claustrophobia), -phobic (ailurophobic),
phobo- (phobophobia), tim- (timorous),
trem- (tremble), trep- (trepidation)

frenzied corybant- (corybantic),
frenet- (frenetic)

glum dolor- (dolorous), fleb- (flebile),
flet- (fletiferous), luct- (luctual), lype-
(lypemania), -tapin- (tapinosis),
trist- (tristful)

greedy avar- (avarice), avid- (avidity),
cupid- (cupidity), edac (edacity)-,
gulos- (gulosity), pleonec- (pleonectic), pleonex- (pleonexia)

grieving dolor- (dolorous), fleb- (flebile), flet- (fletiferous), luct- (luctual), lype- (lypemania), penth- (nepenthe), tapin- (tapinosis), trist- (tristful)

guilt(y) culp- (culpability)

insecure ocno- (ocnophile)

insolent contum- (contumacious), impud- (impudence), procac- (procacity), proterv- (protervous)

intractable contum- (contumacious), obstin- (obstinate), pervic- (pervicacious), proterv- (protervity)

jocular beati- (beatific), chero- (cheromania), felic- (felicitous), hilar-, (hilarity), jubil- (jubilant), joc- (jocosity)

joyful beati- (beatific), chero- (cheromania), felic- (felicitous), hilar-, (hilarity), jubil- (jubilant)

lamenting myrio- (myriologue), thren- (threnetic)

loving agap- (agape), amor- (amorous), charit- (charitable), -phile (Anglophile), -philia (logophilia), -philiac (scopophiliac), -philic (bibliophilic), -philism (Francophilism), philo- (philology), -philous (photophilous),

meddling ardelio- (ardelion), tamp- (tamperproof)

miserable aerumn- (aerumnous), miser- (miseration)

obsessed –aholic (foodaholic), -lagnia (algolagnia), -philia (logophilia), -ridden (guilt-ridden)

panicky dirit- (dirity), pavid- (pavidity), -phobe (technophobe), -phobia (claustrophobia), -phobic (ailurophobic), phobo- (phobophobia), tim- (timorous), trem- (tremble), trep- (trepidation)

pleasant amen(t)- (amenity), ples- (pleasance)

pleased allubesc- (allubescency)

pleasure hedon- (hedonistic), volupt- (voluptuary)

revulsion invid- (invidious), ira(sc)- (irascible), miso- (misogamy), odi- (odium)

rude contum- (contumely), impud- (impudent), procac- (procacity)

sad dolor- (dolorous), fleb- (flebile),

flet- (fletiferous), luct- (luctual), lype- (lypemania), tapin- (tapinosis), trist- (tristful)

scared dirit- (dirity), pavid- (pavidity), -phobe (technophobe), -phobia (claustrophobia), -phobic (ailurophobic), phobo- (phobophobia), tim- (timorous), trem- (tremble), trep- (trepidation)

scornful deris- (derisive), sardon- (sardonic)

selfish avar- (avarice), avid- (avidity), cupid- (cupidity), edac- (edacity)-, gulos- (gulosity), pleonec- (pleonectic), pleonex- (pleonexia)

sincere prob- (probity), ver- (verity)

sorrowful dolor (dolorous)-, fleb- (flebile), flet- (fletiferous), luct- (luctual), lype- (lypemania), penth- (nepenthe), tapin- (tapinosis), trist- (tristful)

stubborn contum- (contumacious), obstin- (obstinate), pervic- (pervicacious), proterv- (protervity)

surly acerb- (acerbic), moros- (morose)

tender coupho- (couphomania), -storgy (philostorgy), tener- (teneritude)

thick-skinned callos- (callosify), pachy- (pachyhymenia)

timid dirit- (dirity), pavid- (pavidity), -phobe (technophobe), -phobia (claustrophobia), -phobic (ailurophobic), phobo- (phobophobia), tim- (timorous), trem- (tremble), trep- (trepidation)

trepidation dirit- (dirity), pavid- (pavidity), -phobe (technophobe), -phobia (claustrophobia), -phobic (ailurophobic), phobo- (phobophobia), tim- (timorous), trem- (tremble), trep- (trepidation)

trustworthy prob- (probity), ver- (verity)

uneasy agit- (agitated), anx- (anxious), trepid- (trepidation), -turb- (disturbed)

unhappy dolor-, fleb- (flebile), flet- (fletiferous), luct- (luctual), lype- (lypemania), tapin- (tapinosis), trist- (tristful)

untrustworthy apat- (apatitious),

decept- (deceptive), fallacy- (fallacious), insid- (insidious), ludif- (ludification), subdol- (subdolous), subrept- (subreptitious)
wrangling altercat- (altercation) ; obstrep- (obstreperous)

zany fatu (fatuity)-, inan- (inanity), moro- (moronic), stult- (stultiloquence)
zestful agito- (agitomania), alacr- (alacrify), ard- (ardently)

THE ENVIRONMENT

For mammals, birds, insects, and fish, see "Animals" in this section.

agate achat- (achate)
air aer- (aerate); aeri- (aeriferous); aero- (aerobic); anemo- (anemometer); atmo- (atmosphere); flat- (flatulent); physo- (physometra)
asbestos asbest- (asbestiform)
ash tree fraxin- (fraxinella); melia- (meliaceous)
atmosphere -bar (isobar); baro- (barometric)
beach littor- (littoral); thino- (thinolite)
beech faga- (fagaceous)
birch betul- (betulaceous)
blooming flor- (floriferous); thalero- (thalerophagous); vig- (vigorous)
bog telmat- (telmatology); turbar- (turbarian)
box-tree bux- (buxiferous)
bramble bat-³ (batologist); vepri- (vepricosis)
branch clado- (cladophyll); rami- (ramify)
buckthorn rhamn- (rhamneous)
bud gemm-¹ (gemmate); ~ *scaly cover:* perul- (perulate)
bug cimic- (cimicoid); entomo- (entomology); insecti- (insecticide); insecto- (insectology). *Also see* "Animals" *in Part III*
burr lapp- (lappaceous)
cactus cact- (cactaceous)
caraway plant car- (caraway seed)
carbon dioxide -capnia (acapnia); capno- (capnomancy)
cedar cedr- (cedrine)
celestial activity astro- (astronomy)
chaff acer-³ (acerate)

chasm vorag- (voraginous)
chloride muriat- (muriatic)
clay argillaceo- (arenaceo-argillaceous); argillo- (argillo-calcareous); limo- (limo-cretaceous); pelo- (pelophilous)
cloud fracto- (fracto-stratus); homichlo- (homichlophobia); mammato- (mammato-cumulus); nebul- (nebulous); nephelo- (nephelometer); nepho- (nephology); nubi- (nubiferous)
coal anthraco- (anthracomancy); carb- (carbonize)
coast littor- (littoral); maritim- (maritime)
cold alg- (algid); cheima- (cheimaphilic); crymo- (crymophilic); cryo- (cryogenics); frigo- (frigorific); gel- (regelation); kryo- (kryometer); pago- (pagophagia); psychro (psychrometer); rhigo- (rhigosis)
continent epeiro- (epeirogenic)
cone, pine strobil- (strobiliform)
copper auricalc- (auricalceous); chalco- (chalcocite); cupreo- (cupreo-violaceous); cupri- (cupriferous); cupro- (cupromagnesite); cuproso- (cuproso-ferric)
coral coralli- (corallidomous)
country *rural:* rur- (ruralize); rustic- (rusticity); *nation:* -ese (Japanese); -ia (India); -ian (Syrian); -land (Ireland)
crater crateri- (crateriform)
cress cardam- (cardamine)
cultivated land agra-¹ (agrarian)
cypress cupress- (cupressineous)
darkness achlu- (achluophobia); amaur- (amaurosis); ambly- (amblyopia);

crepus (crepuscular); fusc- (fuscous); lyg- (lygaeid); melan- (melatonin); nyct- (nyctitropic); obscur- (obscurity); tenebr- (tenebrous)

dawn auror- (auroral); eo- (eosophobia)

day diurn- (diurnal); ephem- (ephemeris); hemer- (monohemerous); hodiern- (hodiernal); journ- (journal); quotid- (quotidian)

decomposing enzyme -ase (amylase)

desert eremo- (eremophyte)

dewy roscid- (roscidating)

dry arid- (aridity); carpho- (carphology); celo- (celosia); sicc- (desiccate); xero- (xerophyte)

dust amath- (amathophobia); coni- (coniosis); -conia (fibroconia); conio- (coniofibrosis); conist- (conistery); konio- (koniosis); pulver- (pulverize)

earth agro- (agronomy); -gaea (Paleogaea); geo- (geocentric); hum- (inhumation); secul- (secular); tellur- (intratelluric); terr- (terrestrial); ~ *quake:* -seism (bradyseism); -seismal (isoseismal); seismo- (seismograph); tromo-(tromometry)

elder tree sambuc-[1] (sambucene)

elm ulm- (ulmaceous)

environment eco- (ecology); oeco- (oecology); oiko- (oikofugic)

evening crepus- (crepuscule); nocti- (noctilucent); nycto- (nyctophobia); vesper- (vespertine)

evergreen shrub ephed- (ephedroid)

fall autumn- (autumnal)

fern filic- (filiciform); pterido- (pteridology)

fir abiet- (abietic)

flax byssi- (byssinosis); lino- (linoleic)

flood antlo- (antlophobia); diluv- (diluvial); inund- (inundation)

flora -phyte (microphyte); phyto- (phytogenesis)

flower antho- (anthomania); -anthous (monanthous); flori- (floriferous); -florous (multiflorous)

fly tany- (tanystomate)

fog calig- (caliginous); homichlo- (homichlophobia); nebul- (nebulous);

nephelo- (nephelological); nepho- (nephology); nubi- (nubiform)

forest arbor- (arboreal); dendri- (dendritic); dendro- (dendrophilous); -dendron (rhododendron); hylaeo- (hylaeosaurus); nemor- (nemoricole); saltu- (saltuary); silvi- (silviculture); sylv- (sylvan); xylo- (xylophage)

fountain cren- (crenic); pego- (pegomancy)

foxglove digito- (digitalis)

frost cryo- (cryophyte); gel- (gelid); kryo- (kryometer); pachno- (pacnolite); pago- (pagophagia); pruin- (pruinose); rhigo- (rhigolene)

fungus fungi- (fungicide); -mycete (schizomycete); myceto- (mycetoma); -mycin (streptomycin); myco- (mycology); uredo- (uredospore)

garden horti- (horticultural)

glacier glacio- (glaciologist)

glassy feldspar sanid- (sanidine)

granite graniti- (granitiform)

grass gramin- (graminivorous)

hawthorn crataeg- (crataegin)

holly ilic- (ilicic)

hot aestu- (exaestuating); cale- (caleficient); calo- (caloreceptor); caum-; (caumesthesia) calori- (calorimetry); ferv- (effervesce); pyro- (pyromania); thermo- (thermonuclear); -thermy (diathermy)

hurricane lilaps- (lilapsophobia)

husk acer-[3] (acerate); glum- (glume); lepo- (lepocyte)

ice gel- (gelation); glacio- (glaciological); pago- (pagophagia); *icicle:* stiri- (stiriated)

island insul- (insular)

isthmus isthm- (isthmian)

ivy heder- (hederated)

jasper jasp- (jasperated)

lake lacus- (lacustrine); limno- (limnologist)

land agri- (agrichemical); agro- (agrology); choro- (chorography); geo- (geothermal); tellur- (telluric); terr- (subterranean)

landscaping *ornamental:* topiary- (topiary)

larch larix- (larixinic)
laurel daphn- (daphmomancy)
leaf bract- (bracteate); clad- (cladan-
thous); foliato- (foliation); -folious
(multifolious); frondi- (frondescence);
petalo- (petalody); -phyll (sporophyll); phyllo- (phyllomania); -phyl-
lous (diphyllous)
lettuce lactuc- (lactucarium)
lichen compound deps- (depside)
lightning astra- (astraphobia); fulgur-
(fulgurant); fulmin- (fulmination)
lily lili- (liliform); lirio- (liriodendron)
linden tilia- (tiliaceous)
maple acer- (aceric)
marble marm- (marmoreal)
marsh helo- (helobius); palud-
(paludicolous); palus- (palustrine);
ulig- (uliginous)
meadow prat- (pratal)
meteorological front fronto-
(frontogenesis)
meteor stone baetyl- (baetylic)
mineral -ite (anthracite); -lite (chrysolite)
mist calig- (caliginous); homichlo-
(homichlophobia); nebul- (nebulous);
nephelo- (nephelological); nepho-
(nephology); nubi- (nubiform)
mistletoe ixo- (ixolite)
moisture humect- (humectant); hydro-
(hydrobiology); hygro- (hygrophyte);
ulig- (uliginose)
moon luni- (lunisolar); lunu- (lunulate);
seleno- (selenodesy)
moss bryo- (bryophytic), musc- (emuscation); sphagn- (sphagnous);
splachn- (splachnoid)
mountain mont- (ultramontane); oro-
(orogeny); ~ ash: sorb- (sorbose)
mud lim- (limivorous); pelo- (peloid)
mulberry mor- (moriform); mur-
(muriform)
mushroom myco- (mycotoxin)
myrtle myrti- (myrtiform)
nard nard- (nardiferous)
nettle cnido- (cnidophore); urtic-
(urticaceous)
night -crepus- (crepuscule); nocti-
(noctiluca); nycta- (nyctalopia);

nycti- (nyctitropism); nycto- (nyctophobia); vesper- (vespertilionine); all
~: -pannychy (psychpannychy)
oak querc- (quercitron)
ocean enalio- (enaliosaur); halo- (halosaurian); mari- (mariculture); naut-
(nautical); nav- (navigation); pelag-
(archipelago); thalasso- (thalassocracy); thalatto- (thalattology)
orchard pomar- (pomarious)
orchid orchido- (orchidology)
oxygen oxa- (oxazine); oxy- (oxyacid)
ozone ozono- (ozonosphere)
peat bog turbar- (turbary)
pebble calcul- (calculous); pesso- (pessomancy); psepho- (psephology)
peninsula cherson- (chersonese)
petal petuli- (petuliform); -sepalous
(trisepalous)
pine -peuce (peucedaneous); pin- (pinaceous); ~ cone: strobil- (strobiliform)
pistil pistil- (pistillar)
plants -aceae (Rosaceae); -ad (cycad);
-ales (Liliales); botano- (botanomancy); -eae (Gramineae); herbi-
(herbicidal); -ia (zinnia); -phyte
(macrophyte); phyto- (phytography); vegeti- (vegetivorous);
vegeto- (vegeto-alkaline)
pollen pollini- (pollinosis)
pond lacus (lacuscular); limno- (limno-
philous); stagn- (stagnal)
poppy mecon- (meconidine); opio- (opiomania); papaver- (papaverous)
precipice cremno- (cremnophobia)
purslain portulac- (portulaceous)
pyrites pyrito- (pyritohedron)
quicksand syrt- (syrtic)
radiant emissions aurora- (aurora
australis)
rain hyeto- (hyetograph); imbri- (imbriferous); ombro- (ombrometer);
pluvio- (pluviograph)
reservoir lacco- (laccolite)
river amn- (amnicolist); flum- (fluminal); fluvio- (fluvio-terrestrial); potamo- (potamologist);
rip- (riparian)
rock -ite (anthracite); lapid- (lapidary);
-lithic (neolithic); litho- (lithotomy);

pesso- (pessomancy); petri- (petrification); petro- (petroglyph); rupes- (rupestrine); rupic- (rupicolous); saxi- (saxifrage)

rose rhodo- (rhodochrosite); roseo- (roseola)

rue rut- (rutaceous)

sand ammo- (ammocete); aren- (arenicolous); arenacio- (arenacio-argillaceous); psammo- (psammophilous); sabul- (sabulosity); saburr- (saburration)

sapphire sapphir- (sapphiric)

sea enalio- (enaliosaur); halo- (halosaurian); mari- (mariculture); naut- (nautical); nav- (navigation); pelag- (archipelago); thalasso- (thalassocracy); thalatto- (thalattology); ~ *shore:* thino- (thinolite)

seasons horo- (horology); *fall:* autumn- (autumnal); *spring:* vern- (vernal); *summer:* aestiv- (aestival); *winter:* hibern- (hibernal); hiem- (hiemal)

seaweed fuc- (fucivorous); phyceae- (Rhodophyceae); -phyceous (Rhodophyceous); phyco- (phycology); ~ *covered:* algos- (algose)

shell conchi- (conchiferous); lorica- (illoricated); -ostraca (Leptostraca); ostraco- (ostracoderm); testaceo- (testaceology)

shore littor- (littoral)

shrub fruticuloso- (fruticuloso-ramose)

sky coeli- (coelicolist)

snow chion- (chionodoxa); -chium (hedychium); ning- (ninguid); niv- (niveous)

soil agro- (agronomy); edaph- (edaphic); hum- (exhumation); paedo- (paedogenic); pedo- (pedology); terr- (terrarium)

spring of water cren-² (crenic);crouno- (crounotherapy); pego- (pegomancy)

stalk magyd- (magydare)

star aster- (asteraceous); astro- (astonomy); -sidere (hagiosidere); sidero- (siderostat); stelli- (stelliferous)

stone -ite (anthracite); lapid- (lapidary); -lithic (neolithic); litho- (lithotomy); pesso- (pessomancy);

petri- (petrification); petro- (petroglyph); rupes- (rupestrine); rupic- (rupicolous); saxi- (saxifrage); *stone-like deposit:* toph- (tophaceous)

straw carpho- (carphology); culmi- (culmicolous); festuc- (festucine); stramin- (stamineous)

stream fluvio- (fluviomarine); potam- (potamoplankton); rip- (riparian)

sun helio- (heliotropic); sol- (solarium)

swamp palud- (paludism); palus- (palustrine)

sweet plant fluid nectar- (nectared)

tendril cirri- (cirrigerous); cirro- (cirro-pinnate); pampin- (pampiniform)

thunder bronte- (bronteon); bronto- (brontology); cerauno- (ceraunoscope); fulmin- (fulminic); kerauno- (keraunograph); tonitr- (tonitrual)

tornado lilaps- (lilapsophobia)

tree arbor- (arboreal); dendri- (dendritic); dendro- (dendrophilous); -dendron (rhododendron); silvi- (silviculture); xylo- (xylophage)

twigs ramul- (ramulose); sarment- (sarmentaceous); scopi- (scopiform); surcul- (surculose); virgul- (virgulation)

twilight crepus- (crepuscular); lyg- (lygaeid)

universe -cosm (macrocosm); cosmo- (cosmology)

vegetation -aceae (Rosaceae); -ad (cycad); -ales (Liliales); botano- (botanomancy); -eae (Gramineae); herbi- (herbicidal); -ia (zinnia); -phyte (macrophyte); phyto- (phytography); vegeti- (vegetivorous); vegeto- (vegeto-alkaline)

vine ampel- (ampelopsis); pampin- (pampiniform); viti- (viticulture)

volcanic soil ando- (andosol)

water aqua- (aquatic); aque- (aqueduct); aqui- (aquiclude); hydro- (hydrophilous); hyeto- (hyetology); hygro- (hygrometry); rip- (riparian)

weed runc- (runcation); zizan- (zizany)

well phreato- (phreatic); putea- (puteal)

whirlpool vorag- (voraginous)

whirlwind prest- (prester)

wild vine labrusc- (labruscose)

willow itea- (iteatic); salic- (salicaceous)

wind anemo- (anemometer); vent- (ventilation); *north ~:* -borea (boreal); *south ~:* austro- (austromancy); *west ~:* zephyro- (zephyranth); favon- (favonian)

wood erio- (eriometer); hyle- (hylephobia); hylo- (hylophagous); ligni- (lignivorous); ligno- (lignoceric);

xylo- (xylophage); -xylous (epixylous); ylo- (ylomancy)

woods nemor- (nemoricole); saltu- (saltuary); silv- (silvics); sylv- (sylvan)

world -cosm (macrocosm); cosmo- (cosmography); -gaea (Paleogaea); mund- (mundane); secul- (secular); tellur- (telluric); terr- (terrain)

yew tax- (taxaceous)

EXPERTS AND THEIR TITLES

-ian (one skilled in or specializing in)
-ist (one who specializes in a specific art, science, skill or hobby)
-ologist (specialist)

abacus abacist

abnormalities *cellular ~:* cytotechnician; *diseases:* pathologist

abnormal states, physiology of pathophysiologist

abstract political theorizing metapolitician

acorns balanologist

acquired characteristics ctetologist

acupuncture acupuncturist

aerial photos *~ for accurate measurement:* photogrammetrist; *~ to identify geologic structures:* aerogeologist, photogeologist;

age of trees dendrochronologist

aging geriatrician, geriatrist; *~ and its problems:* gerontologist

agricultural geology agrogeologist

airborne microorganisms aerobiologist

airmail stamps aerophilatelist

algae algologist, desmidiologist

allergies allergist, allergologist

all religions pantheologist

almonds amygdalogist

alphabet formation acrologist

alphabetic systems of writing alphabetist, alphabetologist

ambiguity dilogist

amphibians amphibiologist

anarchy anarchiologist

anatomy of soft parts sarcologist

ancient *~ animals:* paleozoologist; *~*

diseases: paleopathologist; *~ geological features:* archaeogeologist, paleogeologist; *~ lake sediment:* paleolimnologist; *~ medicine:* thereologist; *~ plants, animals and environment:* paleoecologist; *~ soils:* paleopedologist; *~ topographic features:* paleogeomorphologist; *~ water use:* paleohydrologist

anesthesia anesthesiologist, anesthetist

angels angelologist

animal(s) zoologist; *~ and their environment:* zooecologist; *~ and human relationships:* anthrozoologist; *~ husbandry:* zootechnician; *~ lore:* ethnozoologist; *~ pathogens:* epizoologist, epizootiologist

anthologies anthologist

anthropomorphism anthropomorphologist

antibodies and antigens seroepidemiologist

anti-intellectualism misologist

ants formicologist, myrmecologist

anus, rectum, colon coloproctologist, proctologist

apes pithecologist; *~ diseases:* pithecopathologist

aphids aphidologist

applied biological science biotechnologist

Arab language and culture Arabist

archives archivist
arrangement of feathers at certain stages pterylologist
arteries arteriologist
artificial body part replacements prosthetist
artistic or philosophical tradition academician
Ascidiacea (sea organisms) ascidiologist
Assyria/Babylonia assyriologist
asthma asthmologist
astrophysics astrophysicist
atmosphere atmospherologist; ~ *dust and germs:* coniologist, koniologist; ~ *and weather:* meteorologist
atoms atomologist
automatic control systems cybernetician
bacteria bacteriologist; ~ *of the air:* aerobacteriologist
baldness phalacrologist
barley crithologist
baseball data sabermetrician
Basque language and culture Bascologist
baths balneo-
beards pogonologist
beauty kalologist; ~*in art:*aestheticist, esthetician
beauty treatments beautician
bees apiarist, melittologist; ~ *raising:* apiculturist
belief built around biological principles metabiologist
bells, bell-ringing campanist, campanologist
berries baccatologists
biblical literature, book lore bibliologist
biblical types typologist
bile choledologist
biological ~ *form and function:* morphophysiologist; ~ *rhythms:* chronobiologist; ~ *study of acquired characteristics:* ctetologist
biology biologist; ~*of bodies of water:* hydrobiologist
biotechnology ergonomist
biotypes biotypologist
birds aviarist, ornithologist; ~ *eggs:*

oologist; ~ *nests:* caliologist, nidologist; *raising ~:* aviculturist
blindness typhlologist
blood haematologist, hematologist; ~ *immunology:* immunohematologist; ~ *serum:* serologist; ~ **vessels:** angiologist
body forms somatologist
bones osteologist
book lore bibliologist; ~ *binding* bibliopegist; ~ *printed before 1501:* incunabulist
brain cerebrologist, encephalologist
brambles batologist
breasts mastologist, mazologist
breeding domesticated animals and plants thremmatologist
bridges gephyrologist
Buddha Buddhologist
butterflies lepidopterist
cabbages brassicologist
calculation logistician
calendar hemerologist
cancer cancerologist, chemotherapist, oncologist
cartilages chondrologist
cashews anacardologist
causes, origin aetiologist, aitiologist, etiologist
caves speleologist; *cave-dwelling organisms:* biospeleologist
celebrity cards (cigarette/gum packages) cartophilist
celestial ~ *bodies:* astrogeologist; ~ *mechanics applied to space vehicles:* astrodynamicist
cell(s) cytologist; ~ *abnormalities:* cytotechnician; ~ *disease:* cytopathologist; ~ *identification and abnormalities:* cytotechnologist; ~ *morphology:* cytomorphologist;~ *nuclei:* karyologist; ~ *physiology:* cytophysiologist; ~ *and tissues:* cytohistologist
ceramics ceramicist
chaos theory chaologist
character characterologist
cheese fromologist
chemical ~ *combinations:* stoichiologist; ~ *processes in immunology:* chemoimmunologist;~ *structure and its*

biological action: biochemorphologist

chemistry chemist; ~ *of interstellar space:* astrochemist

chemotherapy chemotherapist

chestnuts castanologist

childbirth obstetrician

children paedologist, pedologist, tecnologist; *diseases of~:* paedonosologist; *medical care of~:* pediatrician

China sinologist

Christ Christologist

chromosomes chromosomologist

church art, decoration, etc. ecclesiologist

cigar bands brandophilist

cinchona (large shrubs) cinchonologist

cities urbanologist

city contained in a single structure arcologist

climate(s) climatologist; ~ *and biological phenomena:* phenogenologist, phenologist; ~ *effect on organisms:* bioclimatician, bioclimatologist; ~ *past ages:* paleoclimatologist

clocks & watches horologophilist

clouds nephologist

Coccoidea (scale insects) coccidologist

code, secret language cryptologist

coins numismatist

Coleoptera (beetle) coleopterologist

colors chromatologist

comets cometologist

communist China pekingologist

comparative human body measurements anthropometrist

computer study cybernetician

concise writing brachylogist

continuity synechiologist

contradictions antilogist

controlled environment with few organisms gnotobiologist

cooking mageirologist, magirologist

cork phellologist

corkscrews helixophilist

corn spicologist

correct use of words orthologist

correspondences homologist

cosmetics cosmetologist

cosmos cosmologist

crayfish astacologist

crime victims victimologist

crime criminologist

criteria criteriologist

crop(s) ~ *cultivation:* agronomist; ~ *relationship with atmosphere:* agrometeorologist; ~ *relationship with climate:* agroclimatologist

crossword puzzles cruciverbalist

crustaceans carcinologist, crustaceologist

crystal(s) crystallologist; ~ *formations:* clinologist

crystallography leptologist, leptonologist

cucumbers cucumologist

cultivation of marine organisms mariculturist

culture culturologist

cultures ethnologist

customs of nonliterate peoples agriologist

cyclones cyclonologist

cysts cystologist

dance movements choreologist

dead people in the underworld nerterologist

death thanatologist

decadence; aging in nearly extinct groups geratologist

decay and mummification taphonomist

deformation or flow of matter rheologist

demons daemonologist, demonologist

dental occlusions gnathologist

derivation of words lexicologist

description and classification of phenomena phenomenologist

deserts, desert plants eremologist, desmidiologist

devil diabologist, diabolologist, satanologist

diabetes diabetologist

dialects dialectologist

dining aristologist

diplomats diplomatologist

Diptera (flies) dipterologist

disease(s) nosologist; ~ *affecting the extremities:* acropathologist; ~ *of the blood vessels:* angiopathologist; ~

caused by weakening: astheniologist; ~
of the ear: otologist; ~ *geographic factors:* geopathologist; ~ *of the joints:*
arthropathologist; ~ *of lower animals:*
zoopathologist; ~ *of the nervous systems:* neuropathologist; ~ *of nose and larynx:* rhinolaryngologist; ~ *in a population:* epidemiologist; ~ *symptoms:*
symptomatologist, symptomologist; ~
of trees: arborvirologist
divination mantologist
doctrines about faith pistiologist
dog(s) cynologist; ~ *diseases:*
cynopathologist
dolls planganologist
domestic economy oikologist
doses dosiologist
dragons draconologist
drama, esp. five-act plays pentalogist
dreams oneirologist
drugs pharmacologist; ~ *and the immune system:* immunopharmacologist; ~
and the nervous system: neuropharmacologist; ~ *and plant interaction:*
phytopharmacologist; ~ *prescription:*
pharmacist
earth ~ *relation to cosmic phenomena:* cosmecologist; ~ **surface:**
geomorphologist
earthquakes seismologist, tectonophysicist, tromologist
earthworms oligochaetologist
ecclesiastical ~ *buildings:* naologist; ~
calendars: menologist
echinoderms (marine animal)
echinologist
ecology aecologist, ecologist, oecologist;
~ *of cultivated plants:* agrioecologist,
agroecologist; *communities and environment:* synecologist; ~ *interaction with psychology:* ecopsychologist
educational methods educationalist
effect of light on chemical change
photochemist
effect(s) of ~ *drugs on mental states:*
psychopharmacologist; ~ *light on living beings:* photobiologist; ~ *low temperatures on organisms:* cryobiologist; ~ *sound on living beings:*
bioacoustician

eggs ovologist
Egyptian history Egyptologist
ethics of biological research bioethicist
elections psephologist
electrical ~ *currents:* galvanologist; ~
phenomena of living bodies: electrophysiologist; ~ *phenomena of living organisms:* electrobiologist
electricity electrician
elephants pachydermatologist
embryonic structures promorphologist
embryos cyemologist, embryologist
enigmas enigmatologist
enterobacteria enterobacteriologist
environment(al) environmentologist;
~ *effects on creatures:* hexicologist; ~
organisms en masse: synecologist; ~
pollutants: ecotoxicologist
enzymes enzymologist
erotic literature erotologist
ethnology of prehistoric humans
paleethnologist
Etruscan antiquities Etruscologist
events beyond natural law
parapsychologist
evil ponerologist
excrement; obscene literature scatologist, skatologist
excretion and secretion eccrinologist
experimental testing or inquiry
docimologist
exploitation of natural resources
geotechnologist
external secretions exocrinologist
extinct animals archaeozoologist
extraterrestrial life astrobiologist, exobiologist, xenobiologist
eyes ophthalmologist; *eye testing:*
optologist
eye, ear, nose, and throat specialist
otolaryngologist
faith pisteologist, pistologist
family descent genealogist
farming agriculturist
Fathers of the church patrologist
feathers pterylologist
feet podiatrist, podologist
female health gynecologist
fermentation fermentologist, zymologist
ferns filicologist, pteridologist

fetuses fetologist
fevers; heat pyretologist, pyrologist
figs sycologist
figurative language tropologist
films filmologist
filth or feces; obscene literature
  coprologist
fine dining aristologist, gastronomist
finger rings dactyliologist
fire science pyrotechnician
firearms ballistician
first principles archelogist
fish ichthyologist; ~ diseases: icthy-
  opathologist; ~ farming: aqua-
  culturist, pisciculturist; ~ fossils:
  icthyopaleontologist
fishing halieutician, piscatologist
flags and banners vexillologist
fleas pulicologist, siphonapterologist
flower raising floriculturist
flowers florist
flowers and their environment
  anthoecologist
folklore storiologist
folk psychology ethnopsychologist
fonts fontologist
food bromatologist, sitologist
foot care chiropodist
form and structure morphologist
fossil(s) fossilist, fossilologist, oryctologist; ~ birds: paleornithologist; ~ fish:
  paleicthyologist; ~ footprints: ichnol-
  ogist; ~ grasses: paleoagrostologist; ~
  insects: paleoentomologist; ~ plants:
  paleobotanist, paleophytologist; ~
  trees: paleodendrologist; ~ as organisms: paleobiologist
fractures agmatologist
fragrant essential oils aromatherapist
freshwater life limnobiologist
friction ~ as a medical treatment: ana-
  tripsologist; ~ in machines: tribologist
frost cryopedologist
fruit and seeds carpologist, pomologist
functions and activities of living matter
  physiologist
funeral dirges myriologist
funerals mortician
fungi mycologist
future trends futurologist

games ludologist
gem(s) gemmologist, gemologist; ~
  engraving: glyptologist
genealogy of the gods theogonist
general physiology biophysiologist
generative organs aedoeologist
geographical distribution of animals
  faunologist
germinal matter merologist
gestures pasimologist
ghosts phantasmatist
glaciers; ice glaciologist
glands adenologist
glass vitreologist
gnats; mosquitoes culicidologist
gnomes gnomologist
God theologian
gold or wealth chrysologist
goodness agathologist
governing politician
grammar grammarian, syntactician
grapes botryologist
grape vines viniculturist
grasses agrostologist, graminologist
grouped words or expressions
  onomasiologist
growth auxologist
growth & sexual development of children auxanologist
gum disease periodontist,
  periodontologist
gunnery artillerist
habits; behavior hexiologist
hair trichologist; ~ removal: electrologist
handwriting graphologist
head cephalologist
healing medicine physician
hearing audiologist
heart cardiologist
heat thermologist; ~ as a medical rem-
  edy: thermatologist
heavenly bodies uranologist
hell tartarologist
Hemiptera (insects) hemipterologist
Hepaticae (liverworts) hepaticologist
heredity or procreation genesiologist
heresies heresiologist
hernias herneologist
hickory nuts cichorologist
hieroglyphs hieroglyphologist

histology of the skin dermahistologist
history of the earth paleontologist
history annalist, historiologist; ~
  through historical data: cliometrician
Hittites Hittitologist, Hittologist
Homer Homerologist
honey bees apiologist
horse(s) hippologist; ~ *diseases:*
  hippopathologist
hotels and inns xenodocheionologist
human(s) anthropologist; ~ *activities:*
  demologist; ~ *biology:* anthropobiolo-
  gist; ~ *character:* ethologist; ~ *conduct
  and action:* praxeologist, praxiologist;
  ~ *fossils:* paleoanthropologist; ~ *ignorance:* agniologist; ~ *movement:* kine-
  siologist; ~ *settlements:*ekistician; ~
  types: typologist
humidity hygrologist
hurricanes; tornadoes lilapsologist
hygienic science hygiologist
hymns hymnologist
hypnosis hypnotist, neurypnologist
icons iconologist
ideas ideologist, sophiologist
identification and study of microfossils
  micropaleontologist
idioms idiomologist
immune reactions immunobiolo-
  gist; *immune responses to disease:*
  immunopathologist
immunity to disease immunologist
immunologic methods applied to histology immunohistologist
impaired word use aphasiologist
inanimate nature abiologist, azoologist
incorrect diction acyrologist, cacolo-
  gist
India indologist
indigenous diseases endemiologist
individual organisms and their environment autecologist
influence of emotion on disease
  psychoneuroimmunologist
influence of the stars astrologist
injurious effects of time on a living system catachronobiologist
inscriptions on monuments elogist
insect galls on plants cecidiologist,
  cecidologist

insects entomologist, insectologist
insects with 4 membranous wings
  hymenopterologist
interaction of radiation with living system radiobiologist
internal secretions of endocrine glands
  endocrinologist
intuition and reason noologist
Inuit culture Eskimologist
iris of the eye iridologist
Japan Japanologist
Jewish culture Hebrician
joints of the body arthrologist
jurisdiction dicaeologist
keys cagophilist
kidney beans phaseologist
kidneys nephrologist
kissing philematologist
knowledge epistemologist, gnoseologist,
  gnosiologist
lakes and ponds limnologist
language philologist; ~ *evolution:*
  glottochronologist
largest-scale aspects of the atmosphere
  macrometeorologist
larynx laryngologist
laughter gelotologist
laws *of the mind:* nomologist; ~ *of
  watery vapor:* atmologist
legendary animals cryptozoologist
legends; lying pseudologist
lepers leprologist
Lepidoptera (butterflies, moths)
  lepidopterologist
lichen lichenologist
ligaments or bandaging desmologist,
  syndesmologist
light photologist; *chemical effects of ~:*
  actinologist
lighthouses pharologist
light rays spectrologist
linguistic tones tonetician
linguistics glottologist, linguistician
literary work in three connected parts
  trilogist
literary work in four connected parts
  tetralogist
liturgies: formal worship liturgician, liturgist, liturgiologist
liver hepatologist

**living beings and atmospheric phe-
nomena** biometeorologist
living organisms biologist
locusts and grasshoppers acridologist
logic dialectition, logician
long-distance seismology
teleseismologist
lymphatic system lymphologist
machines mechanician
magic magician
magnetic measurements magnetician
makeup cosmetician
malaria malariologist
male impotence andrologist
mammalogy therologist
mammals mammologist
manuscripts codicologist
maps cartologist, chartologist
Mars areologist
martyrs martyrologist
match boxes cumyxaphilist
mathematics mathematician
Mayan culture Mayanist
measuring hearing audiometrist
mechanical insects entomechologist
medals & tokens exonumist
medical ~ *diagnoses:* diagnostician; ~
science or treatise: iatrologist
medicinal ~ *dosage:* posologist; ~ *herbs:*
herbologist
memory mnesiologist
menstruation emmenologist
mental diseases psychopathologist
mental life and biological processes
psychobiologist
mental processes psychologist
metamathematics metamathematician
metaphysics metaphysician
meteorites aerolithologist
meteoritic stones astrolithologist
meteorological ~ *phenomena of a small
site:* micrometeorologist; ~ *properties
of atmosphere:* aerologist
meter metrician
methods of success tactician
microfossils micropaleontologist
micro-linguistic analysis glossematician
microscopic life microbiologist
microscopic soil phenomena
micropedologist

midwifery tocologist, tokologist
**migrations and distributions of organ-
isms** chorologist
mills & milling molinologist
mineral drugs pharmaco-oryctologist
minerals oryctologist
minute details; microscopes
micrologist
miracles of gods and heroes aretalogist,
thaumatologist
missionary activity missiologist
mites and ticks acarinologist, acarologist
mollusks malacologist
monads monadologist
money boxes argyrothecologist
monsters; organic malformations
teratologist
moon selenologist
moral duty deontologist
moral values axiologist, ethician, ethicist
morphology of abnormal conditions
pathomorphologist
mosquitoes; gnats culicidologist
moss bryologist, muscologist
mountains orologist; ~ *and drainage:*
orohydrologist
mouth stomatologist
murder ctenologist, ktenologist
muscles myologist
museum collections museologist
mushrooms fungologist, mycologist
music musician, musicologist
music and the culture that produces it
ethnomusicologist
mystical meaning of numbers
numerologist
myths mythologist
narratives narratologist
natural communities biocenologist,
biocoenologist
nature ~ *of reality:* ontologist; ~ *of
truth:* alethiologist
nematodes nematologists
nerves neurologist; ~ *of the skin:*
dermatoneurologist
nervous system neurobiologist
nesting birds neossologist, nidologist
neural synapses synaptologist
neuropterous insects neuropterologist
neurosecretions neuroendocrinologist

neurotoxins neurotoxicogist
new expressions neologist
newborn infants neonatologist
nomenclature terminologist
nonsense morologist
nose nasologist, rhinologist
number computation arithmetician
nutrition alimentologist, dietician, trop-
hologist, threpsologist
obesity bariatrician
obituaries necrologist
obscenity; excrement scatologist
oceanography oceanologist
Odonata (dragonflies, damselflies)
odonatologist
oil exploration creekologist
one who speaks or writes in defense of
apologist
opium meconologist
optics optician
oracles chresmologist
orchids orchidologist
organic malformations; monsters
teratologist
organic tissue histiologist, histologist
organisms ~ as individuals: idiobi-
ologist; ~ pathogenic for plants:
phytobacteriologist
organization of words phraseologist
origin and causes aitiologist, aetiologist,
etiologist
origins; government archologist
orthopterous insects orthopterologist
otolaryngology otorhinolaryngologist
oyster farming ostreiculturist
palaeobotany phytolithologist
paleopsychic phenomena
paleopsychologist
paleozoology zoopaleontologist
papyrus manuscripts papyrologist
paradoxes paradoxologist
parapsychology metapsychologist
parasites entozoologist, parasitologist
parasitic worms helminthologist
past as indicated by geological data
geochronologist
past civilizations archaeologist,
archeologist
past events explained by laws of
causation palaetiologist, paletiologist

pathology pathobiologist, pathologist; ~
of the skin: dermatopathologist
pathological alteration of bodily function physiopathologist
peace irenologist
peaches persicologist
peanuts arachologist
pears piriologist
peat moss sphagnologist
pedometers pedometrician
penis phallologist
pharynx pharyngologist
phonemes phonemicist
phonograph records discophilist
photochemical effects actinologist
physics physicist
physiological psychology physiopsy-
chologist, psychophysiologist
physiology of organisms and environment ecophysiologist
physiology of the nervous system
neurophysiologist
picture-writing curiologist
plagues loimologist
planets; condensed matter of solar system planetologist
plankton planktologist, planktonologist
plant(s) botanist, phytologist; ~ and
animal organs: organologist; ~ bio-
climatology: phytoclimatologist; ~
communities: phytosociologist; ~ diseases: epiphytologist, phytopathol-
ogist; ~ ecology: phytobiologist: ~
nutrition: agriobiologist;~ physiology:
phytophysiologist; ~ viruses: phytose-
rology, phytovirologist; plant-like animals (coral): zootologist
playwright dramatist
pleasure hedonologist
poisons toxicologist
political and geographic factors
geopolitician
political parties stasiologist
pollen and spores palynologist; ~ in the
atmosphere: aeropalynologist
postage stamps timbrologist
postcards deltiologist
poverty & unemployment ptochologist
practical applications ~ of electricity:
electrotechnician, electrotechnologist;

~ *of medicine:* clinician; ~ *of psychology:* psychotechnician
practical details of an occupation technician
praise of God doxologist
prayers and rituals euchologist
preaching; sermons sermonologist
precipices cremnologist
precipitation hydrometeorologist, hyetologist
pregnancy cyemologist, cyesiologist, syllepsiologist
prehistoric antiquities paleologist
preparing mixed drinks mixologist
prevention of suicide suicidologist
primates primatologist
primitive societies and plants and animals ethnobiologist, ethnobotanist
prisons and criminal punishment penologist
problems of psychology and sociology psychosociologist
procedures methodologist
proper names or specialized field terms onomatologist, onomasiologist
prosthetic devices anaplastologist
Protista (non-animal or plant organisms) protistologist
Protozoa (single-celled animal-like organisms) protozoologist
proverbs paremiologist, paroemiologist
psychiatry psychiatrist
psychological and neurological correlations neuropsychologist
psychological ~ *methods for industry:* psychotechnologist; ~ *reactions:* reactologist; ~ *testing:* psychometrician, psychometrist
psychology as related to biology biopsychologist
public health sanitarian
pulse sphygmologist
purpose or end teleologist
purposelessness dysteleologist
pyramids pyramidologist
quicksand syrtologist
quinine quinologist
radiant energy radiologist
radiation ~ *applied to industrial problems:* radiotechnologist; ~ *effects on*

ecological communities: radioecologist
radioactivity's effect on geology radiogeologist
radiology of the nervous system neuroradiologist
radishes raphanologist
railroads ferroequinologist
rain ombrologist, pluviologist
rappings by spirits typtologist
recent organisms neontologist
record of nearby earthquake shocks engysseismologist
redundancies in speech or writing macrologist
refraction optometrist
relics lipsanologist
religion: final events eschatologist
religious ~ *calendars, festivals:* heortologist; ~ *literature:* hierologist
remedies accologist, iamatologist
repetition in writing or speech battologist, tautologist
residual magnetism in ancient rocks paleomagnetist
respiratory organs pneumologist
restricted climate microclimatologist
rhetoric rhetorician
rhetorical emphasis palilogist
rheumatic diseases rheumatologist
rhythm rhythmologist
river(s) fluvialist, fluviologist, potamologist; ~ *channel formation & characteristics:* fluviomorphologist
rocks geologician, geologist, petrologist; ~ *and minerals:* mineralogist; ~ *and stones:* lithologist
rubrics; established rules rubrician
runes runologist
rust uredinologist
saints' lives; sacred writings hagiologist
salvation soteriologist
science scientist
scientific approach to legal problems jurimetrician
sea thalattologist
seaweed or algae phycologist
secret language; code cryptologist
sedges caricologist
sediments sedimentologist

seeds spermologist
semantics semantician, semanti-
cist, semasiologist, sematologist,
semologist
semen spermatologist
senility nostologist
sensation and sense organs aesthiolo-
gist, esthesiophysiologist
senses and sense organs esthematologist
sermons; preaching sermonologist
serums serologist
sex sexologist
shells conchologist. conchyliologist
shiatsu acupressurist
shrouds, especially of Turin
sindonologist
sign language chirologist, dactylologist
signs or symptoms semeiologist,
semiologist
silkworm farming sericulturist
similarities homeologist
simple and complex reflexes
reflexologist
sin enissologist, hamartiologist
skin diseases dermatologist, pellagrolo-
gist; ~ nomenclature & classification:
dermonosologist; ~ and venereal diseases: dermatovenerologist
skull(s) craniologist; ~ shapes:
phrenologist
Slavic language and literature Slavicist
sleep; hypnosis hypnologist, hypnotist
slugs limacologist
small ~ community ecology: microecol-
ogist: ~ earthquakes: microseismol-
ogist; ~ systems of social behavior:
microsociologist
smells & olfactory process olfactologist,
osmologist
snake(s) herpetologist, ophidologist,
ophiologist; ~ diseases: herpeto-
pathologist
snow and ice cryologist
social interaction biosociologist
societal structure ethnomethodolo-gist
society ~ and biological science: sociobi-
ologist; human ~ groups: sociologist
sociological study of race
anthroposociologist
soils agrologist, edaphologist,

pedologist; ~ microstructure:
micromorphologist
soliloquies monologist
somatotypes somatotypologist
sound acoustician
Soviet government kremlinologist,
Sovietologist
species and genetic variations
genecologist
speech disorders: lalopathologist; ~ into-
nation: tonology; ~ sounds phoneti-
cian, phonologist
speech or writing to praise eulogist
spiders arachnidologist, arachnologist,
araneologist
spines acanthologist
spirits; Holy Ghost pneumatologist
spleen splenologist
sponges spongiologist
squid; cuttlefish teuthologist
star ages: cosmochronologist; ~ oscilla-
tions: astroseismologist
statistical study ~ of biological phenomena: biostatistician; ~ of economics:
econometrician, econometrist; ~ of
life forms: biometrician
statistics statistician
stomach gastrologist; ~ and intestines:
gastroenterologist
strawberries fragarologist
structural geology geotectologist
study of ancient human characteristics
ethnoarchaeologist
substances radioactively tagged
radioimmunologist
Sumerians Sumerologist
sun heliologist
surgical appliances acidologist
swamps; peat bogs telmatologist
symbols symbologist; ~ of language:
semiotician
synchronous events synchronologist
syphilis syphilologist
Syria syriologist
systematic view of all knowledge
pantologist
systematized belief dogmatician
taxonomy taxologist
tea tsiologist
technical terms orismologist

technological farming systems
agrotechnologist
technology technicologist, technologist
teddy bears arctophilist
teeth dentist, odontologist
tendons tenologist
terminology; language glossologist
termites isopterologist, termitologist
terms ending in -ology logyologist
terrestrial magnetism geomagnetician
theater arts theatrician
theology ~ *and evidence of purpose in*
nature: physico-theologian; ~ *based*
on observation of celestial bodies:
astrotheologian
theory of extended individuals
mereologist
therapeutic ~ *agents:* acologist; ~ *baths:*
balneologist; ~ *use of mineral springs:*
crenologist
therapeutics accologist, thereologist
three-dimensional properties
stereologist
thunder brontologist
tides tidologist
tightrope walking funambulist
time measurement chronologist
timepieces horologist
tissue ~ *changes in disease:* histopath-
ologist; ~ *organization:* histophysiolo-
gist
tooth ~ *irregularities and correc-*
tion: orthodontist; ~ *pulp diseases:*
endodontist
topographical study topologist
tornadoes; hurricanes lilapsologist
towers pyrgologist
trapeze artistry aerialist
trash garbologist
tree(s) arborist, dendrologist; ~ *farming:*
arboriculturist, silviculturist; ~ *growth*
& climate: dendroclimatologist
truffles hydnologist
tuberculosis phthisiologist
tumors oncologist
Turkic language and literature
Turcologist
turnips napologist
ulcers helcologist
underground water geohydrologist

unidentified flying objects ufologist
unintentional omissions haplology
universe macrocosmologist,
universologist
upper atmosphere physics and chemis-
try aeronomist
urinary organ surologist
use of x-rays roentgenologist
vaccines vaccinologist
values axiologist
vegetables lachanologist
veins phlebologist
venereal disease venereologist,
venerologist
vines viticulturist
Virgin Mary Mariologist
virginity parthenologist
virtue aretologist
viruses virologist
viscera enterologist, splanchnologist
vitamins vitaminologist
volcanoes vulcanologist
vomiting emetologist
walnuts juglandologist
warfare polemologist
water *its modifying power:* hydrogeolo-
gist; *subterranean ~:* hydrologist
wave motion kymatologist
wealth aphnologist, plutologist
weapons & fighting systems hoplolo-
gist
weather meteorologist; ~ *and celes-*
tial bodies: astrometeorologist; ~
and climate acting on living beings:
meteorobiologist
weight(s) ~ *and gravitation:* barologist;
~ *and measures:* metrologist
whales cetologist
whale diseases cetopathologist
wildfires using tree-ring data
dendropyrochronologist
winds anemologist
wine enologist, oenologist
wood xylologist
word history etymologist
work & its effect on humans ergologist
worms helminthologist, scolecologist,
vermeologist
worship; liturgies liturgician, liturgist,
liturgiologist

wounds traumatologist
writing systems grammatologist

zoology of present-day animals caeno-
zoologist, cenozoologist

FEAR OR DISLIKE OF

To extract the word part, simply drop "phobia" from each term.

abuse, sexual contreltophobia
accidents dystichiphobia
acid soils acidophobia
acorns balanophobia
aging gerascophobia
air aerophobia, anemophobia,
pneumatophobia
airplanes aeronautophobia, aerophobia, aviatophobia, avionophobia,
aviophobia
airsickness aeronausiphobia
alcohol methyphobia
alkaline soils basiphobia, basophobia
alligators eusuchophobia
amnesia amensiophobia, amnesiphobia
ancestors patroiophobia
anger cholerophobia
angina anginophobia
animals zoophobia; ~ *skins:* doraphobia;
wild ~: agrizoophobia, theriophobia
ants myrmecophobia
arts and crafts technophobia
ashes of cremation spodophobia
asymmetry asymmetriphobia
atomic explosions atomosophobia
automobiles amaxophobia, harmatophobia, ochophobia
bacteria bacteriophobia, microbiophobia
baldness peladophobia, phalacrophobia
banners/bumper stickers vexillophobia
base or low pursuits tapinophobia
baths ablutophobia
bats desmodontophobia, pteropophobia
beaches thinophobia
beards pogonophobia
bears arctophobia
beautiful women caligynephobia
beds clinophobia
bees apiophobia, apiphobia,
melissophobia
beggars/street people ptochophobia

being afraid phobophobia
being alone autophobia, monophobia,
eremophobia
being beaten rhabdophobia,
vapulophobia
being beautiful callophobia
being bound merinthophobia
being buried alive taphephobia,
taphophobia
being burned caustophobia
being clean balneophobia
being contagious tapinophobia
being dirty automysophobia
being pinched rrhexophobia
being ridiculed catagelophobia
being scolded enissophobia
being scratched amychophobia
being shot ballistophobia
being stared at ophthalmophobia, sco-
pophobia, scoptophobia
bicycles cyclophobia
birds ornithophobia
Blacks negrophobia
blindness scotomaphobia, typhlophobia
blood haemaphobia, hemaphobia, hema-
tophobia, hemophobia
blushing ereuthophobia, erythrophobia,
erytophobia
boasting kompophobia
boats scaphophobia
body odor autodysosmophobia,
bromidrosiphobia
bogs telmatophobia
books bibliophobia
boozing dipsophobia
breasts, developing mastophobia
bridges gephyrophobia
brothers adelphophobia
buffoons balatrophobia
bullets ballistophobia
bulls taurophobia

buttocks pygophobia
buzzards buteophobia
caffeine caffephobia
cancer carcinophobia, carcinoma-
   tophobia
cars harmatophobia, ochophobia; *riding*
   in ~: amaxophobia
cattle boustrophobia
cats aelurophobia, ailurophobia, eluro-
   phobia, felinophobia, galeophobia,
   gatophobia
caves speleophobia
Celts Celtophobia
cemeteries coimetrophobia
changes tropophobia, metathesiophobia
chatter, meaningless garrulophobia
chemicals chemophobia
chickens alektorophobia
childbirth lochiophobia, maieusiophobia, parturiphobia, tocophobia
children pediophobia, pedophobia
China/the Chinese Sinophobia
chins geniophobia
choice-making aboulophobia
choking pnigerophobia, pnigophobia
cholera cholerophobia
churches ecclesiaphobia
clergy hierophobia
clocks/watches chronometrophobia
closed spaces claustrophobia, cleisio-
   phobia, cleithrophobia, clithrophobia
clothes vestiphobia, vestiophobia
clouds nephophobia
cockroaches blattophobia
coitus coitophobia
cold cheimaphobia, cheimatophobia,
   cryophobia, frigophobia, psychrophobia, psychropophobia
colors chromatophobia, chromophobia;
   black: melanophobia; *blue:* caerulo-
   phobia; *brown:* fuscophobia; *cop-*
   per: chalcophobia; *gold:* aureophobia;
   gray: phaeophobia; *green:* verdopho-
   bia; *orange:* aurantiphobia; *purple:*
   porphyrophobia; *red:* erythrophobia;
   silver: argentophobia; *tan:* fulvopho-
   bia; *violet:* indophobia; *white:* leukophobia; *yellow:* xanthophobia
comets cometophobia
commitment zygophobia

computers cyberphobia, computer-
   phobia
constipation coprostasophobia
cooking mageiricophobia
corpse necrophobia
crevices chasmophobia
criticism enissophobia
critics criticophobia
cross or crucifix staurophobia
crossing a bridge gephyrophobia
crossing busy streets agylophobia, agy-
   rophobia, dromophobia
crowds demophobia, enochlophobia,
   ochlophobia
crystals crystallophobia
cyclones anemophobia
daggers pugioniphobia
dampness hygrophobia
dancing choreophobia, chorophobia,
   orchestrophobia
darkness achluophobia, lygophobia, nyctophobia, scotophobia
dawn eosophobia
daylight phengophobia
death necrophobia, thanatophobia
decaying matter pythophobia,
   septophobia
defecation, straining and painful
   defecalgesiophobia
deformity dysmorphophobia
demons and devils daemonophobia,
   demonophobia, necyophobia
dental work dentophobia, odontophobia
dependence soteriophobia
depth bathophobia
design or ultimate ends teleophobia
diabetes diabetophobia
dinner parties deipnophobia
dirt misophobia, molysmophobia, mysophobia, rhypophobia
disease loimophobia, nosophobia,
   pathophobia; *specific ~:* monopathophobia
disorder ataxiophobia, ataxophobia
dizziness dinophobia, illyngophobia,
   vertigophobia
doctors iatrophobia
dogs cynophobia, kynophobia
dolls paedophobia, pediophobia,
   pedophobia,

double vision diplopiaphobia, diplophobia
drafts aerophobia, anemophobia
dreams oneirophobia
drink alcoholophobia, dipsomanophobia, methyphobia, potophobia
drugs pharmacophobia
dryness xerophobia
ducks anatidaephobia
duration chronophobia
dust amathophobia, koniophobia; *dusty surfaces:* conistrophobia
dwarfs nanophobia
earthquakes seismophobia, tremophobia
eating phagophobia
eels anguillophobia
electricity electrophobia
emotions thymophobia
empty rooms cenophobia, kenophobia
England/the English Anglophobia
erection *maintaining:* ithyphallophobia; *loss of:* medomalacophobia
everything panophobia, panphobia, pantaphobia, pantophobia
excrement coprophobia, koprophobia, scatophobia
exhaustion kopophobia
experimenting peirophobia
eyes ommatophobia, ommetaphobia; ~ *opening:* optophobia
fabrics textophobia
faces prosopophobia
failure atychiphobia, kakorraphiaphobia, kakorraphiophobia, kakorrhaphiophobia
fainting asthenophobia
falling basophobia
falling downstairs climacophobia
falling in love philophobia
fat lipophobia, obesiophobia
father-in-law soceraphobia
Fathers of the early church paterophobia
fatigue kopophobia, ponophobia
fear phobophobia
feathers pteronophobia
feces coprophobia, koprophobia, scatophobia
fever febriphobia, pyrexeophobia, pyrexiophobia

fighting machophobia
filth rhypophobia, rypophobia, rupophobia
fire arsonophobia, pyrophobia
fish ichthyophobia
flashes selaphobia
flatulence physaphobia
flood antlophobia
flowers anthophobia
flute aulophobia
flying aeronautophobia, aerophobia, aviatophobia, avionophobia, aviophobia
fog homichlophobia, nebulaphobia, nephophobia
food cibophobia, sitiophobia, sitophobia,
foreigners xenophobia
foreplay malaxophobia, paizophobia, sarmassophobia
forests hylephobia, hylophobia, xylophobia, ylophobia
fountains pegophobia
France/the French Francophobia, Gallophobia
freedom eleutherophobia
French kissing cataglottophobia
friendship sociophobia
frogs batrachophobia
frost cryophobia, pagophobia, rhigophobia
fun cherophobia
funeral rites epicidiophobia, threnatophobia
fur doraphobia
gambling aleaphobia
garlic alliumphobia, scorophobia
gay people homophobia
genitals: genitophobia; *female ~:* colpophobia, eurotophobia, kolpophobia; *male ~:* phallophobia
Germany/the Germans Germanophobia, Teutophobia, Teutonophobia
germs bacillophobia, bacteriophobia, spermophobia, verminophobia
ghosts phantasmophobia, phasmophobia, spectrophobia
glass crystallophobia, hyalophobia, hyelophobia, vitreophobia
gloomy places lygophobia
God's wrath deiphobia, theophobia
going to bed clinophobia

gold aurophobia
good news euphobia
graves taphophobia
gravity barophobia
Greece/the Greeks Grecophobia,
  Hellenophobia
growing old gerascophobia,
  gerontophobia
hair chaetophobia, trichophobia; *curly ~:*
  ulophobia; *~ disease:* trichopathopho-
  bia; *excessive ~:* hypertrichophobia
Halloween Samhainophobia
happiness cherophobia
heart attack or disease anginophobia,
  cardiophobia
heat thermophobia
heaven ouranophobia, uranophobia
heights: *looking down:* acrophobia, alto-
  phobia, batophobia, hypsiphobia, hyp-
  sophobia; *looking up:* anablephobia,
  anablepophobia
hell Avernophobia, Hadephobia,
  stygiophobia
heredity patroiophobia
heresy heresiophobia
high places illyngophobia
holy things hagiophobia, hierophobia
home and environment domatophobia,
  ecophobia, oecophobia, oikophobia;
  returning ~: nostophobia
homosexuals homophobia
hornets vespiphobia
horses equinophobia, hippophobia
hospitals nosocomephobia
human beings anthropophobia
hurricanes lilapsophobia
hydrophobia hydrophobophobia
hypnotism hypnophobia,
  mesmerophobia
ice cryophobia, gelophobia
ideas gnotophobia, ideophobia
illness nosophobia, pathophobia; *specific ~:* monopathophobia; *wasting ~:*
  tabophobia
immobility of a joint ankylophobia
imperfection atelophobia
inability to stand basiphobia,
  basophobia
infection molysmophobia, mysophobia,
  septophobia

infinity apeirophobia
injections trypanophobia
injury traumatophobia
insanity dementophobia, lyssophobia,
  maniaphobia
insects acarophobia, entomophobia,
  insectophobia, isopterophobia; *stinging ~:* cnidophobia
Ireland/the Irish Celtophobia,
  Hibernophobia
irrational destruction atephobia
isolation eremophobia
Italy/Italians Italophobia
itching acarophobia, scabiophobia
Japan/the Japanese Japanophobia
jealousy zelophobia
Jews Judaeophobia, Judeophobia,
  Judophobia
jumping catapedaphobia
justice dikephobia
kidney disease albuminurophobia
killing dacnophobia
kissing philemaphobia, philematopho-
  bia; *tongue ~:* cataglottophobia
kleptomania kleptophobia
knees genuphobia
knowledge epistemophobia,
  gnosiophobia
lacerations sparassophobia
ladders scalaphobia
lakes limnophobia
large objects megalophobia
laughter gelophobia
law thesmophobia
lawsuits litigaphobia
learning sophophobia
left side levophobia, sinistrophobia
leprosy lepraphobia, leprophobia
lice pediculophobia, phthiriophobia
light phengophobia, photopho-
  bia; *glaring ~:* photoaugiaphobia,
  photoaugiophobia
lightning astraphobia, astrapophobia,
liquids aquaphobia, hygrophobia
lizards stelliophobia
lobsters homariphobia
lockjaw tetanophobia
loneliness eremiphobia, eremophobia
long waits macrophobia
loud noise ligyrophobia

love philophobia
lying mythophobia
machines mechanophobia
many things polyphobia
marriage gametophobia, gamophobia,
nuptophobia
materialism hylephobia
meat carnophobia, kreophobia
medicine pharmacophobia
meeting people anthropophobia
memories mnemophobia, nostophobia
men androphobia, arrhenophobia
meningitis meningitophobia
menstruation menophobia
metals metallophobia
meteors meteorophobia
mice muriphobia, murophobia,
myosophobia
microbes bacilliphobia, microbiophobia,
microphobia
milk galactophobia
mind psychophobia
mirrors catoptrophobia, eisoptrophobia,
spectrophobia
missiles ballistophobia
mistletoe ixophobia
mites acarophobia
moisture hygrophobia
money chrematophobia
monotony homophobia
monstrosities teratophobia
moon selenophobia
mornings matutinophobia
mortality thriptophobia
mother-in-law pentheraphobia
moths phalaenophobia
motion kinesophobia, kinetophobia
motor vehicles motorphobia
mountains orophobia
mummies mummiphobia
mushrooms mycophobia
music melophobia , musicophobia
myths mythophobia
names nomatophobia, onomatophobia
narcotics lethophobia, meconophobia
narrowness anginaphobia, stenophobia
navels omphalophobia
needles aichmophobia, belonophobia
neglect of duty paralipophobia
new things cainophobia, cainotophobia,

cenotophobia, kainophobia, kainotophobia, neophobia
night noctiphobia, nyctophobia
nipples, being seen through clothing
thelophobia
nocturnal emissions oneirogmophobia
noise acousticophobia, ligyrophobia,
phonophobia
Northern lights auroraphobia
nosebleeds epistaxiophobia
nuclear weapons nucleomitophobia
nudity gymnophobia, nudiphobia,
nudophobia
numbers arithmophobia, numeropho-
bia; *uneven ~:* perissophobia
nurses threpterophobia
nutritional food threptophobia
oceans thalassophobia
odors olfactophobia, ophresiophobia,
osmophobia, osphresiophobia; *foul ~:*
bromidrophobia, bromidrosiphobia,
old people gerontophobia
one thing monophobia
oneself autophobia
open spaces agoraphobia, cenophobia,
kenophobia; *high ~:* aeroacrophobia
opinions of others allodoxaphobia
opposite sex heterophobia
organic structure tectologist
otters lutraphobia
owls strigiphobia
pain algiaphobia, algophobia, odynepho-
bia, odynophobia, ponophobia; *from
light sensitivity:* photaugiaphobia,
photaugiophobia
pairs didymophobia
paper papyrophobia
parasites parasitophobia, pothiriopho-
bia, trypanophobia, verminophobia
parents-in-law soceraphobia
peace eirenophobia
peanut butter arachibutyrophobia
pellagra pellagrophobia
penis: peophobia; *erect ~:* ithyphallophobia, medorthophobia; *visible contour of ~:* medectophobia
people anthropophobia, demophobia
perfume myrophobia
philosophy philosophobia
physical love erotophobia

places topophobia
planning for the future teleophobia
plants botanophobia
pleasure hedonophobia
poetry metrophobia, musophobia
pointed objects aichmophobia, aichurophobia
poison iophobia, toxicophobia, toxiphobia, toxophobia
politicians politicophobia
pollen palynophobia
popes papaphobia
poverty peniaphobia
precipices cremnophobia
pregnancy maieusiophobia, tocophobia
prickly objects echinophobia
progress prosophobia
propriety orthophobia
prostitutes cyprianophobia, cypridophobia, cypriphobia, cyprinophobia, scortophobia
public places agoraphobia
public speaking glossophobia
pumpkins, especially jack-o'-lanterns pepophobia
punishment mastigophobia, poinephobia, rhabdophobia
puppets pupaphobia
purposive effort hormephobia
pus pyophobia
quarrels rixophobia
quicksand syrtophobia
rabies hydrophobophobia, lyssophobia
railways siderodromophobia
rain hyetophobia, ombrophobia, pluviophobia
rape stupraphobia, virgivitiphobia
rattlesnakes crotalophobia
razors xyrophobia
rectal disease proctophobia, rectophobia
referring to oneself autophoby
relatives syngenesophobia
religion sebastophobia, theophobia
religious ceremonies teletophobia
reproach enissophobia, enisiophobia
reptiles batrachophobia, herpetophobia
responsibility hypegiaphobia, hypengyophobia, paralipophobia
ridicule catagelophobia, katagelophobia
riding in a car amaxophobia

right side dextrophobia
rivers potamophobia
robbers harpaxophobia
room full of people koinoniphobia
ruin atephobia
Russia/the Russians Russophobia
rust iophobia, rubigophobia, uredinophobia
sacred things hagiophobia, hierophobia
sadness lypephobia
saints hagiophobia
salt halophobia
sand psammophobia
Satan Satanophobia
sausage allantophobia
scabies scabiophobia
scarring ulophobia
school didaskaleinophobia, scholionophobia
scissors forficophobia
scotomas scotomaphobia
scratches amychophobia
sea pelagophobia, thalassophobia
secretions crinophobia
secrets calyptophobia
semen spermatophobia, spermophobia
sermons homilophobia, keryophobia
severely deformed people teratophobia
sexual intercourse coitophobia, cypridophobia, erotophobia, genophobia
sexual perversion paraphobia
shadows sciaphobia, sciophobia
sharks carcharinophobia, selachophobia
sharp objects aichmophobia, belonophobia
shellfish ostraconophobia
shock hormephobia
sinning enissophobia, enosiophobia, hamartophobia, peccatiphobia, peccatophobia
sisters sororophobia
sitting cathisophobia, kathisophobia, thaasophobia
skin dermatophobia
skin diseases dermatopathophobia, dermatosiophobia
skin of animals doraphobia
skunks mephitophobia
sleep hypnophobia, somniphobia
slime blennophobia, myxophobia

small objects microphobia,
tapinophobia
smells olfactophobia, osmophobia,
osphresiophobia
smoke capnophobia
smothering pnigerophobia, pnigophobia
snakes herpetophobia, ophiciophobia,
ophidiophobia, ophiophobia
snoring rhonchophobia
snow chionophobia
society anthropophobia, sociophobia
solitude autophobia, eremiophobia, eremophobia, ermitophobia, isolophobia,
monophobia
sorcery veneficophobia
sound acousticophobia ~ of certain
words: onomatophobia
sourness acerbophobia, acerophobia
spasms choreophobia
speaking aloud phonophobia
speech defect laliophobia, lalophobia
speed tachophobia
spiders arachnephobia, arachnophobia
spiny creatures echinophobia
spirits demonophobia, phantasmapho-
bia, pneumatiphobia, spectrophobia
stage fright prosceniophobia,
topophobia
stairs climacophobia
standing or walking basiphobia, basophobia, basistasiphobia, basostaso-
phobia, stasibasiphobia, stasiphobia,
stasobasiphobia, stasophobia
stars astrophobia, siderophobia
statues agalmaphobia
staying single anuptaphobia
stealing cleptophobia, kleptophobia
stepfather vitricophobia
stepmother novercaphobia
stillness eremophobia, hesyphobia
stings cnidophobia
stooping kyphophobia, scoliophobia
strangers xenophobia
streets agyiophobia, agryophobia; crossing ~: dromophobia
string linonophobia
stuttering psellismophobia
sun/light heliophobia, phengophobia
surgical operations ergasiophobia,
tomophobia

swallowing phagophobia
swamps paludophobia
sweating sudoriophobia
symbolism semiophobia,
symbolophobia
symmetry [in Egyptian temples, mosque
decorations, etc.] symmetrophobia
syphilis luetiphobia, syphilidophobia,
syphiliphobia, syphilophobia
talking glossophobia, laliophobia,
lalophobia, phonophobia
tapeworms taeniiphobia, taeniophobia,
teniophobia
taste geumaphobia, geumatophobia, geu-
mophobia; sour ~: acerbophobia;
sweet ~: hedisophobia
technology technophobia
teeth odontophobia
teleology teleophobia
telephones telephonophobia
termites isopterophobia
terror enosiphobia
theaters theatrophobia
theology theologicophobia
thieves cleptophobia, kleptophobia,
harpaxophobia
thinking phronemophobia
thirst dipsophobia
thirteen tredecaphobia, tridecaphobia,
triakaidekaphobia, triskadekaphobia,
triskaidekaphobia
thunder brontophobia, ceraunophobia,
keraunophobia, tonitrophobia
tickling with feathers pteronophobia
ticks acarophobia
time chronophobia
toads batrachophobia, bufonophobia
tombs taphophobia; ~ stones:
placophobia
tooth decay cariophobia
tornadoes lilapsophobia
touching or being touched aphephobia,
chiroptophobia, haphephobia, hap-
nophobia, haptephobia, haptophobia,
thixophobia
train travel siderodromophobia
traitors proditophobia
travel dromophobia, hodophobia
trees dendrophobia
trembling tremophobia

trichinosis trichinophobia
tuberculosis phthisiophobia, phthiso-
   phobia, tuberculophobia
Turks Turcophobia
tyrants tyrannophobia
ugliness cacophobia
ulcers helcophobia
umbrella umbelliphobia
undressing deshabillophobia
urinating urophobia
vaccinations vaccinophobia
vampires vespertiliophobia
vegetables lachanophobia
vehicles amaxophobia, ochophobia
venereal disease cyprianophobia, cypridophobia, cyprinophobia, cypriphobia, venereophobia
vermin verminophobia
vertigo illyngophobia
virginity, losing esodophobia,
   primeisophobia
virgins parthenophobia
vomiting emetophobia
walking ambulophobia, basiphobia,
   basophobia, bathmophobia
warfare polemophobia
warts verruciophobia
washing oneself ablutophobia,
   balneophobia
wasps spheksophobia
wasting sickness tabophobia
water aquaphobia, hydrophobia
waves cymophobia, kymophobia
wax cerophobia
weakness asthenophobia
wealth chrematophobia, chrysophobia,
   plutophobia

weapons hoplophobia
weasels galeophobia
weight, gaining obesiophobia,
   procrescophobia
werewolves lycophobia
whirlpools dinophobia
whispering psithurophobia
white leukophobia
wickedness scelerophobia
wild animals agrizoophobia,
   theriophobia
wind ancraophobia, anemiaphobia,
   anemophobia
windows fenestrophobia
wine enophobia, oenophobia,
   oinophobia
winter cheimaphobia
witchcraft wiccaphobia
women feminophobia, gynephobia,
   gynophobia; *beautiful ~:* calligyne-
   phobia, venustaphobia
wood hylephobia, hylophobia, xylophobia, ylophobia
words logophobia, verbophobia; *long ~:*
   sesquipedalophobia
work ergasiophobia, ergophobia,
   ponophobia
worms helminthophobia, scoleciphobia,
   vermiphobia
wounds traumatophobia
wrinkles rhytiphobia
writing graphophobia, scriptophobia
x-rays radiophobia
yawning oscitophobia
young girls parthenophobia
zombies basinecrophobia

FOOD

Nonvegetarians should also see "Animals."

acorn balan- (balaniferous); gland-
   (glandiferous)
almond amygdalo- (amygdalaceous)
apple mali- (maliform);
   pom- (pomaceous)
avocado pers- (persea)
baking pistor- (pistorial)

banana musa- (musaceous)
barley alphito- (alphitomancy); crith-
   (crithology); horde- (hordeaceous);
   ptis-(ptisan)
bean cyam- (cyamoid); fab- (fabaceous);
   phaseol- (phaseolous)
beer cervis- (cervisial)

belch ruct- (eructation)
berry acin- (acinaceous); baccat-
  baccate; bacci- (bacciferous); cocci-
  (coccigerous)
blueberry vaccin- (vaccinium)
bran furfur- (furfuraceous);
  pityr- (pityroid)
bread arto- (artophagous);
  pan- (panivorous)
breakfast jent- (jentacular)
broth juss-[2] (jussulent)
butter butyro- (butyraceous)
cabbage brassic- (brassicacious)
caper cep- (cepaceous)
carbohydrate -ose (fructose)
cashew anacard- (anacardic)
cereal frument- (frumentaceous)
cheese case- (casefy); tyro- (tyromancy)
cherry ceras- (cerasin)
chestnut aescul- (aesculin); castan-
  (castaneous)
chew manduc- (manducation); mastic-
  (mastication)
citric citro- (citron)
cook -coct- (decoction); mageir- (mageiricophobia); magir- (magiric)
corn frument- (frumentation); spici-
  (spiciferous)
cucumber cucumi- (cucumiform)
cultivation -ponic (hydroponics)
digest chyli- (chyliferous); chymo- (chymotrypsin)-; peps- (pepsinogen);
  pept- (peptic); pepto- (peptogenic)
dill aneth- (anethated)
dine arist- (aristology)
dinner deipno- (deipnophobia); prand-
  (postprandial)
drink -ade (lemonade); bib- (bibulous);
  pino- (pinocytosis); pocul- (poculent); poto- (potomania)
eating alim- (alimentation); bromato-
  (bromatology); -brotic (scolecobrotic); cib- (cibarious); comest-
  (comestible); ed- (edible);
  escul- (esculent); gust- (gustatory);
  manduc- (manducation); mastic-
  (mastication); -phagous (creophagous); -phagy (anthropophagy);
  -sitia (asitia); sitio- (sitiophobia); -troph (heterotroph); -trophic

(heterotrophic); -trophy (hypertro-
  phy); -vora (Carnivora); -vore (herbivore); -vorous (omnivorous); ~
  disorder: bulim- (bulimia); ~ *-ori-
  ented:* edacit- (edacity); -phagia
  (dysphagia)
endive intubac- (intubaceous); intib-
  (intybe)
fig fici- (ficiform); syc- (sycoma)
fruit -carp (endocarp); -carpic (endocarpic); carpo- (carpophore);
  -carpous (monocarpous); frug- (frugivorous); pomi- (pomiform);
  pomo- (pomology)
garlic alli- (alliaceous); scoro- (scorodite)
gluttony adephag- (adephagia); helu-
  (heluation); lurc- (lurcation)
gooseberry grossul- (grossulaceous)
grain farr- (confarreate); farrag- (farraginous); frument- (frumentaceous);
  grani- (granivorous)
grape acini- (aciniform); botry-
  (botryose); racem- (racemiform);
  rhag- (rhagite); staphylo- (staphyline);
  uvi- (uviform); uvu- (uvula); vini-
  (viniculture); vino- (vinosity);
  viti- (viticulture); ~ *-gathering:*
  vindem- (vindemial)
hickory cichor- (cichoraceous)
honey melli- (melliferous); ~ *mixture:*
  muls- (mulse)
indigestion apeps- (apepsia)
kidney bean phaseol- (phaseolous)
leek porr- (porraceous); praso-
  (prasophagous)
lime tilia- (tiliaceous)
lunch prand- (prandial)
meal cen- (cenatory); coen- (coenaculous); deipno- (deipnophobia);
  prand- (anteprandial)
meat -burger (hamburger); carni- (carnivore); carnoso- (carnosity)
mint menth- (menthaceous)
mulberry mori- (moriform)
mustard sinap- (sinapistic)
nutmeg myrist- (myristic)
nutritious alibil- (alibility)
oats aveni- (avenaceous)
onion cep- (cepous); cromny-
  (cromnyomancy)

orange hesperid- (hesperidine)
parsley petrosel- (petroseline)
parsnip pastin- (pastinaceous)
pea pisi- (pisiform)
peach persic- (persicaria)
peanut arach- (arachidic)
pear apio- (apiocrinite); piri- (piriform); pyri- (pyriform)
pepper piper- (piperic)
pineapple bromel- (bromeliaceous)
pomegranate balaust- (balaustine)
provisions annon- (annonary)
pumpkin pepo- (pepon)
radish raphan- (raphania)
raspberry frambes- (frambesia)
rice oryzi- (oryzivorous); rizi- (riziform)
salad acetar- (acetarious)
salt halo- (halophile); sali- (desalination); salino- (salinometric); sals- (salsamentarious)
sandwich -burger (cheeseburger)
sauce embamm- (embamma)

sausage allanto- (allantoid); botul- (botuliform)
savory sapid- (sapidity)
seasoned stuffing farcin- (farcinate)
sesame sesam- (sesamoid)
sodium-containing natro- (natrocalcite)
strawberry fragar- (fragarol)
sugar gluco- (glucose); glycero- (glycerol); glyco- (glycosuria); levul- (levulose); saccharo- (saccharometer); sucr- (sucrose)
tea thei- (theiform)
truffle hydno- (hydnocarpous)
turmeric curcum- (curcumin)
turnip napi- (napiform)
unripe grape omphac- (omphacine)
vegetable lachan- (lachanopolist); oler- (oleraceous); olit- (olitory); vegeti- (vegetivorous); vegeto- (vegetarian)
walnut juglan- (juglandaceous)
wheat silig- (siliginous); tritic- (triticeous)
yam dioscorea- (dioscoreaceous)

LOCATION

above ano- (anocarpous); epi- (epidermis); ob- (obliterate); over- (overhang); super- (superscript); supra- (supraliminal); sur- (surbase)
across dia- (diameter); per- (peregrination); trans- (transmit); transverso- (transverso-cubital)
apex -apical (periapical); apico- (apicotomy)
behind after- (afterburner); back-(backdrop); meta- (metasternum); opistho- (opisthotic); post- (postscenium); postero- (posterolateral); retro- (retrocopulant)
between/among dia- (diagnosis); enter- (entergrave); entre- (entr'acte); epi- (epidemic); inter- (interval)
distant tele- (television)
front ante- (antependium); antero- (anteroparietal); fore- (forefront); pre- (preaortic); pro- (proscenium); proso- (prosogaster)

high(er) acro- (acrocephaly); alti- (altitude); alto- (alto-relievo); hypsi- (hypsistenocephalic); hypso- (hypsometry); super- (superstructure)
inside eis- (eisegesis); em- (embedded); en- (enclose); endo- (endoskeleton); ento- (entoparasite); eso- (esoenteritis); il- (illuminate); im- (implosion); in- (incarcerate); intero- (interoceptor); ir- (irradiate); intra- (intramural); intro- (introspection)
left laeo- (laeotropic) laevo- (laevorotatory) levo- (levogyrate) sinistro- (sinistrorse)
middle centri- (centripetal); centro- (centrolineal); -centric (heliocentric); medi- (medieval); medio- (mediodorsal); mes- (mesallantoid); mesati- (mesaticephalic); mesio- (mesio-sinistral); meso- (mesothorax); mezzo- (mezzotint); mid- (midsection)

near ad- (adjoining); by- (bystander); cis- (cismontane); epi- (epicenter); juxta- (juxtapose); para- (parametric); peri- (perigee); prox- (approximal) proximo- (proximocephalic)
outside ecto- (ectoparasite); epi- (epidermis); exo- (exoskeleton); extero- (exteroceptor); extra- (extraterritorial); extro- (extrovert); out- (outhouse); para- (paradox); preter- (preternatural)
right dexio- (dexiotropic); dextro- (dextrorse)
surrounding ambi- (ambiance); amphi- (amphithecium); be- (beset); circum- (circumference); peri- (periotic)
through dia- (diaphanous); per- (percolate); trans- (transparent); -wide (worldwide)

under hypo- (hypodermic); infero- (inferoposterior); infra- (infrastructure); sub- (subscript); subter- (subterfluent); under- (underpinning)
upon ana- (anaclisis); epi- (epilogue); ob- (obtrude); super- (superstructure); sur- (surcharge)
with co- (coterminous); col- (colleague); com- (commingle); con- (convulse); cor- (correlate); hama- (hamadryad); inter- (intermixed); para- (parataxis); syl- (syllable); sym- (symbiosis); symphyo- (symphyogenesis); symphysio- (symphysiorrhaphy); syn- (synagogue); sys- (system)

MEASUREMENT SCIENCE (-metry)

Item Measured/Name of Process
To extract the word part, simply drop "metry" from each word.

acid strength acidimetry
aerial photos for surveying and map-making photogrammetry
air or gas aerometry, pneumatometry, spirometry; ~ *purity:* eudiometry
alcohol proportion in liquor alcoholometry
alkali strength alkalimetry
alkaloids alkalometry
altitudes altimetry, hypsometry
ancient depths of the sea paleobathymetry
angles goniometry; ~ *of crystals:* crystallometry; ~ *of slope, elevation, or inclination:* clinometry
animal body dimensions zoometry
archeological materials archæometry
area dimensions (by using perspective) iconometry
area of plane surfaces planometry
astigmatism astigmometry
atmospheric pressure barometry
atomic weights stoicheiometry

axis axonometry
birds' eggs oometry
bladder pressure cystometry
blind spots caused by glaucoma scotometry
blood cells cytometry
blood-current velocity hemotachometry
blood force; blood corpuscles hematometry
blood pressure oscillometry, sphygmomanometry
blood quality hemometry
blueness of light cyanometry
bodily functions physiometry
body somatometry
boiling points of liquids ebulliometry
bones; skeletons osteometry
breadth of distant objects platometry
by using the foot podometry
carbon dioxide content micro-gasometry
celestial bodies—movements and positions astrometry

cell content (by measuring light
transmission after staining)
cytophotometry
cellular respiration respirometry
changes in intracellular activity:
micro-densitometry; ~ in the tympanic membrane: tympanometry; ~ in
weight as a function of inreasing temperatures: thermogravimetry
chemical proportions stoichiometry
chemicals: tiny quantities in electro-
lytic solutions voltammetry
chest curves; head curves cyrtometry
chlorine available in a liquid
chlorometry
circles cyclometry
cloudiness nephelometry
color blindness Tintometry
color for chemical analysis
spectrocolorimetry
coloring power of indigo indigometry
color intensity colorimetry,
chromometry
combustion comburimetry
conductivity conductometry
cornea of the eye: radius of curvature
ophthalmometry
correct versification orthometry
coulombs used in an electrolysis
coulometry
crossed eyes strabismometry,
strabometry
darkness of a substance densitome-try
degree of polarization polarimetry
density of a photographic negative
photodensitometry
depths in bodies of water bathometry,
bathymetry
diffraction diffractometry
dimensions of what was photographed
photogrammetry
direction radiogoniometry
disproportionate growth rates
allometry
distance(s) iconometry, longimetry; ~
between two stars: heliometry; ~ of
heavenly bodies: uranometry; ~ of
objects: apomecometry; ~ traveled:
odometry
distant ~ data: telemetry; ~ objects:

tacheometry, tachymetry, telemetry; ~
temperatures: telethermometry
doses medicine: dosimetry; radioactivity: dosimetry
duration & intensity of mental states
psychometry
ear sensitivity to various frequencies
audiometry
earthquakes seismometry; faint ~:
tromometry
eggs oometry
elasticity elastometry
electric currents rheometry
electricity in an eel electrometry
electromagnetic radiation
spectroradiometry
electromotive forces potentiometry
excess ametry
external form morphometry
expansion dilatometry
eye(s) crossed: strabismometry, strabometry; ~ muscles: phorometry; ~ pupil
diameter: pupillometry; ~ refraction: dioptometry; refractive power of
~: optometry; ~ sensitivity to colors:
chromatoptometry
faint earth-tremors tromometry
features of a literary style stylometry
ferrous salt titrimetry
figures that stand on the same base
epipedometry
flour quality aleurometry
flow of viscous substances rheometry
fluorescence fluorometry;
spectrofluorimetry
focal distance focimetry
foot stride pedimetry, pedometry
force of respiration pneumatometry
galvanic current galvanometry
gases gasometry; ~ emanating from the
sun: spectro-colorimetry
God theometry
group relationship patterns sociometry
handwriting constants graphometry
head cephalometry
hearing acoumetry, audiometry
heart size cardiometry
heat calorimetry; ~ of the sun's rays:
pyrheliometry; ~ quantities: calorimetry; ~ radiating from surfaces:

actinometry; *very small quantities of*
~: microcalorimetry
heavens uranometry
heights altimetry, hypsometry
hemoglobin hemoglobinometry
high temperatures pyrometry
human body at various stages of life
anthropometry
humidity hygrometry, psychrometry
hydrostatic pressure affecting ground-
water piezometry
inaccessible distances (by using staves)
baculometry
index of refraction spectrometry
infra-red radiation radiometry
intensity *of the blue of the sky:* cyanometry; ~ *of light in a particular part*
of the spectrum: spectrophotome-
try; ~ *of scattered light:* photogoni-
ometry; ~ *of the scintillation of stars:*
scintillometry
internal part endometry
interference phenomena interferometry
intraocular pressure
ophthalmotonometry
ion detection mass spectrometry
ionizing radiation radiation dosimetry
ions in solution voltammetry
isoperometrical figure isoperimetry
land embadometry
length and distance mecometry
lichen growth (to determine age of a
moraine) lichenometry
life expectation biometry
ligand binding micro-calorimetry
light *intensity:* photometry, spectropho-
tometry; ~ *polarization:* polarimetry;
~ *rays in a spectrum:* spectrometry; ~
wavelength, refraction, displacement:
interferometry
lines in ancient writers gnomometry
liquid volumes micro-fluorimetry
living cells micro-fluorometry
low temperatures cryometry
lung capacity bronchospirometry, pne-
ometry, pulmometry, spirometry
magnetic fields magnetometry
magnitudes in space geometry
malarial infection levels malariometry

manuscript text (by using lines of aver-
age length) stichometry
measurements pantometry
mental processes noometry
metric spaces metric geometry
microscopic objects micrometry
mountains orometry
movement of the walls of the chest
stethometry
movement range of joints arthrometry
muscular contraction dynamometry
number of soldiers depicted in a given
geometric figure stratarithmetry
odor(s) osmometry; ~ *intensity:*
odorimetry
one-to-one transformation of one met-
ric space into another isometry
optical density densitrometry
organism growth alloiometry, allometry
osmotic pressure osmometry
oxygen consumption rate respirometry
oxygenated hemoglobin in the blood
oximetry
ozone in the air ozonometry
pain pathometry; ~ *perception:* dolorim-
etry; *sensitivity to* ~: algometry
part related to height autometry
past time (by using radioactive ele-
ments) geochronometry
pelvis dimensions pelvimetry
perimeters perimetry
phosphorescence spectrophosphorime-
try
photometric measurements of very
small areas microphotometry
plane surfaces planimetry; *area of* ~:
planometry
plant responses phytometry
plasticity of a substance plastometry
plasticity or viscosity plastometry,
points, lines, angles, surfaces, solids
geometry
points on a survey tacheometry,
tachymetry
polygons polygonometry
polyhedra polyhedrometry
porosity; pore-size distribution
porosimetry
pressures tasimetry; *blood* ~:

oscillometry, sphygmomanometry; ~ *of gases and vapors:* manometry

projective properties projective geometry

proportion *of alkaloids in cinchona bark:* cinchonometry; ~ *of polarized light in a beam:* photopolarimetry

pulse sphygmomanometry, sphygmometry

quantity of sugar in a solution saccharimetry, saccharometry

quinine in cinchona bark quinimetry, quininometry

radiant energy radiation pyrometry, spectroradiometry

radiation radiometry; ~ *absorption:* absorptiometry

radii of curvature of the cornea keratometry

radioactivity doses dosimetry

radio wave direction radiogoniometry

rainfall pluviometry

rates of oxygen consumption respirometry

refraction refractometry

refractive indices reflectometry, refractometry

refractive power of the eyes dioptometry, optometry

remote measurement of human or animal activity biotelemetry

respiration stethometry; ~ *on a microscopic scale:* microrespirometry

retinal areas campimetry

rotation of the plane of polarized light as a function of wavelength spectropolarimetry

roughness of a surface profilometry

saline in a solution halimetry

salinity of water salinometry

senses relating to measurement metrical geometry

sensitiveness of photographic media sensitometry

sensitivity sensitometry; ~ *of smell:* olfactometry

shadows skiametry

shape and dimensions morphometry

shearing stresses rheogoniometry

shells conchometry

ship pitch and roll oscillometry

sides and angles of triangles trigonometry

size of pores (by means of mercury infusion) mercury porosimetry

size of the pupil of the eye pupillometry

skeletons; bones osteometry

skull craniometry

smell sensitivity olfactometry

soil moisture; tension; surface tension tensiometry

solid figures stereometry; *volume of ~:* volumenometry

solution *of an oxidizing agent:* iodometry; ~ *of a reducing agent:* iodimetry

sound phonometry

space-time geochronometry

specific gravity of fluids aræometry, hydrometry, volumenometry

speckled markings speckle interferometry

speech sounds phonometry

speed dromometry, tachometry, velocimetry ; ~ *of light:* phototachometry

spiral helicometry

squinting; strabismus strabismometry

stars: relative magnitude of astrometry

strata inclination clinometry

strength of a magnetic field magnetometry

structure of groups sociometry

sugar in a solution saccharimetry, saccharometry

sun's heat pyrheliometry

surface tension stalagmometry, tensiometry

surveying a country chorometry

suspended matter in a liquid turbidimetry

telescope magnifying power dynamometry

temperature(s) thermometry; ~ *of ancient climates and oceans:* paleothermometry **distant ~:** telethermometry; *very high ~:* pyrometry; ~ / *weight relationship:* thermogravimetry

tension *intraocular:* tonometry; *surface ~:* tensiometry

terrain features; plane surfaces planimetry

thermal expansion dilatometry
time chromometry, horometry
touch ethesiometry
topographical information (by means of aerial photos) photoclinometry
tremors of the earth tromometry
turbidity of a liquid or gas nephelometry, turbidimetry
tympanic membrane changes tympanometry
ultraviolet absorption micro-spectrophotometry
underlying substance or essence hypokeimenometry
universe cosmometry
urea ureometry
urine, specific gravity urinometry
velocity dromometry, tachometry, velocimetry
verses colometry
versification, correct orthometry

very high temperatures pyrometry
vinegar strength; acetic acid acetimetry
viscosity viscometry; ~ *of liquids:* viscosimetry
viscous substance flow rate rheometry
visual field limits perioptometry
visual powers optometry
volume volumetry; ~ *of respiratory air flow:* pneumometry; ~ *of a solid:* volumenometry
water hardness hydrotimetry
wavelengths of rays in a spectrum spectrometry
weak earth tremors microseismometry
weight or density gravimetry
weight/temperature relationship thermogravimetry
wind force, speed, direction, velocity anemometry
womb size hysterometry
X-rays roentgenometry

MENTAL PROCESSES

abstruse abdit- (abditory)
acknowledgment agnit- (agnition)
agreement pact- (paction)
ambiguity ambig, ancip-, dub- (dubious), pariso- (parisology)
amnesia amensi- (amensiphobia)
anticipation procata- (procatalepsis)
argument altercat- (altercation) ; obstrep- (obstreperous) ; vitilig- (vitiligation)
brain cephal- ; cerebri- (cerebritis), cerebro- (cerebrospinal) , encephal- (encephalalgia)
clever ingen- (ingenious)
competence quali- (qualified)
concept -cogit- (cogitation), -cogn- (cognition), epistem- (epistemology), –gnomy (physiognomy), -gnosia (dysgnosia), -gnosis (diagnosis), -gnostic (agnostic), gnoto- (gnotobiology), ideo- (ideology), -noe- (noetic), -noia (metanoia), -nomy (agronomy), phreno- (phrenology),

psycho- (psychosomatic), -sophy (philosophy); -put- (putative), ratio- (rational), -sci- (omniscient)
confusion atax- (ataxaphasia), ataxi- (ataxiamnesiac), -ataxia (psychataxia), ataxio- (ataxiophemia), ataxo- (ataxophobia); tarass- (tarassis), -turb- (perturbation)
consideration phrontis-
conversation –claim (exclaim), -clam- (exclamation), -dict- (contradict), -loc(u)- (elocution), logo- (logorrhea), -logue (dialogue), -lalia (echolalia), -lexia (dyslexia), lexico- (lexicographer), -lexis (catalexis), -lexy (kyriolexy), -logy (theology), -loqu- (loquacity), orat- (oratory), -phone (telephone), phono- (phonology), -phony (cacophony), - rhet- (rhetoric), verbi- (verbification), verbo- (verbotomy), voc- (vocalize), voci- (vociferous), -voke (revoke)

critical critico-, enisso-
decisive preempt- (preemptive)
determine -gnomy, (physiognomy),
  -gnosia (dysgnosia), -gnosis (diagnosis), -gnostic (agnostic), gnoto-
  (gnotobiology)
differentiate crimin-² (discriminate)
discerning *comb* -crit- (critical), -gnomy
  (physiognomy), -gnosia (agnosia),
  -gnosis (diagnosis), -gnostic (agnostic), -judic- (judicious), sagac- (sagacious), -soph- (philosophy)
dispute altercat- (altercation)
distinguish crimin-² (discriminate)
doubtful ambig- (ambiguous), ancip-
  (ancipitous), apor- (aporetic), dub-
  (dubiety), –skeps (omphaloskepsis),
  -skept (skeptic), vagu- (vagueness)
eloquent fecund- (fecundity)
estimate stoicheio- (stoicheiometry)
examine probat- (probative)
experiment peir- (peirastic)
faction factios- (factiose)
forecast prognos- (prognostication)
foreknowledge prognos- (prognos-
  tic)
idea -cogit- (cogitation), -cogn- (cognition), epistem- (epistemology),
  –gnomy (physiognomy), -gnosia (dysgnosia), -gnosis (diagnosis), -gnos-
  tic (agnostic), gnoto- (gnotobiology),
  ideo- (ideology), -noe- (noetic),
  -noia (metanoia), -nomy (agronomy),
  phreno- (phrenology), psycho- (psychosomatic); -put- (putative), ratio-
  (rational), -sci- (omniscient), -sophy
  (philosophy), -witted (quick-witted)
ignorance agnoi- (agnoiology) ;
  idiot- (idiotic), ignor- (ignorance),
  nesc- (nescience)
illiterate agramm- (agrammatic)
inference illat- (illative)
insanity ament-¹ (amentia), dement-
  (dementia), -mania (egomania)
instruct didasc- (didascalic),
  didact- (didactic)
interrogatory pysm- (pysmatic)
knowledge gnar- (gnarity)
learning -math- (polymath), mathet-
  (mathetic)

loss of knowledge –agnosia
  (prosopagnosia)
maxim gnom-² (gnomic)
meaning etym- (etymology)
memory -mem- (memorial), -mnem-
  (mnemonics) –mnesia (amnesia),
  -mnesis (anamnesis)
narrow outlook paroch- (parochial)
mull over rumin- (ruminate)
notion -cogit- (cogitation), -cogn- (cognition), epistem- (epistemology),
  –gnomy (physiognomy), -gnosia (dysgnosia), -gnosis (diagnosis), -gnos-
  tic (agnostic), gnoto- (gnotobiology),
  ideo- (ideology), -noe- (noetic),
  -noia (metanoia), -nomy (agronomy),
  phreno- (phrenology), psycho- (psychosomatic); -put- (putative), ratio-
  (rational), -sci- (omniscient), -sophy
  (philosophy), -witted (quick-witted)
opinion dox- (paradox)
perception esthes- (esthesiogenic),
  esthet- (esthete)
ponder rumin- (rumination)
pretended ignorance eiron- (eiron)
proficiency -apt- (aptitude), -bil-
  ity (capability), -ful (masterful),
  -habil- (rehabilitate), -poten-, (potential) -qual- (qualification), -ship
  (leadership)
proverb adag- (adage)
psychosis ament-¹ (amentia), dement-
  (dementia), -mania (egomania)
questioning pysm- (psymatic)
reasoning -cogit- (cogitation), -cogn-
  (cognition), epistem- (epistemology),
  –gnomy (physiognomy), -gnosia (dysgnosia), -gnosis (diagnosis), -gnos-
  tic (agnostic), gnoto- (gnotobiology),
  ideo- (ideology), -noe- (noetic),
  -noia (metanoia), -nomy (agronomy),
  phreno- (phrenology), psycho- (psychosomatic); -put- (putative), ratio-
  (rational), -sci- (omniscient), -sophy
  (philosophy), -witted (quick-witted)
reflective thought specul- (speculation)
refutation elench- (elenchus)
reject abdic- (abdicable), athet- (athetesis), relinq- (relinquish)
remembering memor- (memorize)

sagacious nasut- (nasuteness)
school-centered academ- (academics)
senseless –stup- (stupefied)
sound judgment phron- (phronesis)
study by candlelight
  elucub- (elucubration)
syllogism with unstated premise
  enthm- (enthymeme)
talented ingen- (ingenious)
teach didasc- (didascalic),
  didact- (didactic)
thought -cogit- (cogitation), -cogn- (cognition), epistem- (epistemology),
  –gnomy (physiognomy), -gnosia (dysgnosia), -gnosis (diagnosis), -gnos-
  tic (agnostic), gnoto- (gnotobiology),
  ideo- (ideology), -noe- (noetic),
  -noia (metanoia), -nomy (agronomy),
  phreno- (phrenology), psycho- (psychosomatic); -put- (putative), ratio-
  (rational), -sci- (omniscient), -sophy
  (philosophy), -witted (quick-witted)
truth verit- (verity)

understanding cogit- (cogitation),
  -cogn- (cognition), epistem- (epistemology), –gnomy (physiognomy),
  -gnosia (dysgnosia), -gnosis (diagnosis), -gnostic (agnostic), gnoto-
  (gnotobiology), ideo- (ideology),
  -noe- (noetic), -noia (metanoia),
  -nomy (agronomy), phreno- (phrenology), psycho- (psychosomatic);
  -put- (putative), ratio- (rational), -sci-
  (omniscient), -sophy (philosophy),
  -witted (quick-witted)
unreasonable alog- (alogism)
values axio-² (axiology)
vocabulary *comb* glosso- (glossology),
  -glot (polyglot), -lexia (dyslexia), lex-
  ico- (lexicography), -lexis (catalexis),
  -lexy (kyriolexy), lingu- (linguistics),
  -locu- (elocution), logo- (logorrhea),
  -logue (dialogue), -logy (eulogy),
  -loqu- (eloquent), rhema- (rhematic),
  -verbo- (verbosity)

NEGATIVES

a- *pre* not; without (atypical, atheist)
ab- *pre* away from (absorbent, absence)
an- *pre* not; without (analgesia, anorexia)
anti- *pre* opposite of; against (antidote,
  antistrophe)
apo- *pre* detached; apart (apogamy,
  apomixis)
-atresia *comb* absence of an opening
  (atresia, proctatresia)
atreto- *comb* absence of an opening (atretocyst, atretogastria)
cata- *pre* against (catachresis cataplasia)
contra- *pre* opposite; against (contradiction, contravene)
counter- *comb* opposite; against (count-
  er-clockwise, counter-culture)
de- *pre* deprived of; apart (detached,
  devaluation)
dis- *pre* apart; opposite (discrepant,
  disengage)
dys- *pre* badly; not correct (dysfunc-
  tional, dysphoria)

ectro- *comb* missing; absent (ectromelia,
  ectrosydactyly)
ex- *pre* former; deprived of (excaudate,
  ex-member)
il- *pre* not; opposite of (illegality, illicit)
im- *pre* not; opposite of (immature,
  impartial)
in- *pre* not; opposite of (inarticulate,
  insanity)
ir- *pre* not; opposite of (irreverent,
  irreligious)
-less *suf* without; unable to (defenseless,
  restless)
lipo- *comb* lacking; leaving (lipography,
  lipophrenia)
mal- *pre* poorly; not (maladapted,
  malnutrition)
mis- *pre* wrongly; not (misalignment,
  mismanagement)
miso- *comb* antipathy; hatred (miso-
  cainea, misogamy)
ne- *pre* not; opposite of (neglect, nescient)

nihil- *base* nothingness (annihilate, nihilistic)

no- *pre* not any (no-fault insurance, no-load fund)

non- *pre* not; absence of (nonallergenic, noncompetitive)

nulli- *pre* none (nullify, nulliparous)

ob- *pre* against; inverse (obliterate, obtund)

-priv- *base* lacking; taken away (deprivation, privation)

un- *pre* not; reversal (unbending, unimaginable)

with- *pre* apart; opposed (withhold, withstand)

NUMBERS

0 nulli- (nullipara)

1/10 decim- (decimate)

1/9 non- (nonan)

1/8 octan- (octant)

1/7 septim- (septimal)

1/6 sext- (sextant)

1/5 quint- (quintant)

1/4 tetarto- (tetartohedral)

1/3 trient- (triental)

1/2 demi- (demitint); dicho- (dichotomize); dimid- (dimidiation); hemi- (hemisphere); mezzo- (mezzo-relievo); semi- (semi-columnar)

3/4 triquadr- (triquadrantal)

1 eka- (ekaselenium); haplo- (haplopetalous); heno- (henotheism); mono- (monorail); uni- (unilateral)

1 & 1/2 sesqui- (sesquihoral)

2 ambi- (ambiversion); ambo- (amboceptor); amphi- (amphicarpous); ampho- (amphora); bi- (bicentennial); bin- (binaural); bis- (bissextile); deutero- (deuterogamy); deuto- (deutoplasm); di- (diplegia); dicho- (dichotomous); didym- (didymalgia); diphy-(diphyceral); diplo- (diplopia); disso- (dissogony); double- (doubleheader); du- (duplicate); duplicato- (duplicato-dentate); duplici- (duplicipennate); duo- (duograph); dyo- (Dyophysite); gemelli- (gemelliparous); gemin- (geminiflorous); twi- (twinight); zygo- (zygodont)

3 ter- (tercet); -tern- (ternary);

-tert- (tertiary); tri- (trifocal); triakis- (triakisoctahedron); triangulato- (triangulato-subovate); trigono- (trigonocephalic); triplo- (triploblastic); triplicato- (triplicato-pinnate); trito- (tritoencephalon)

4 quadra- (quadraphonic); quadrato- (quadrato-cubic); quadri- (quadrilateral); quadru- (quadruped); quart- (quarterly); quarti- (quartisect); quat- (quaternate); quater- (quater-centenary); quatre- (quatrefoil); tessara- (tesseraphthong); tetarto- (tetartohedral); tetra- (Tetragrammaton); tetrakis- (tetrakisdodecahedron)

5 cinque- (cinquefoil); penta- (pentacle); quin- (quinary); quinque- (quinquennium); quint- (quintuplets); quinti- (quintiped)

6 hexa- (hexahedron); hexakis- (hexakisoctahedron); seni- (senary); sex- (sexagenarian); sexi- (sexipolar); sexti- (sextisection); sise- (siseangle)

7 hebdo- (hebdomadral); hepta- (Heptateuch); septem- (September); septi- (septifolious)

8 octa- (octagon); octo- (octonary); ogdo- (ogdoastich)

9 ennea- (enneahedron); nona- (nonagon); -nov- (novena)

10 dec(a)- (decade); decem- (decempennate); deci- (decimeter); deka- (dekagram); -teen (sixteen); -ty (seventy)

11 endeca- (endecagon);

hendeca- (hendecasyllabic); undec- (undecagon); undecim- (undecimal)
12 dodeca- (dodecastyle); duodec- (duodecennial); duodecim- (duodecimfid); duoden- (duodenary)
13 tredecim- (tredecimal); triskaideka- (triskaidekaphobia)
14 quattuordec- (quattuordecillion); tessaradeca- (tessaradecasyllabon); tetradeca- (tetradecapod); tetrakaideca- (tetrakaidecahedron)
15 pentakaideca- (pentakaidecahedron); quindec- (quindecennial)
16 hexadeca- (hexadecachoron); hexakaideca- (hexakaidecahedron); sedecim- (sedecimal)
17 heptakaideca- (heptakaidecahedron); septendecim- (septendecimal)
18 duodeviginti- (duodevigintiangular); octakaideca- (octakaidecahedron)
19 enneakaideca- (enneakaidecahedron); undeviginti- (undevigintiangular)
20 eico- (eicosapentaenoic: 25); icosa- (icosandria); icosi- (icositetrahedron: 24); vicesim- (vicesimal); vigent- (vigentennial); viginti- (vigintiangular)
30 triaconta- (triacontahedral); triceni- (tricenary); triges- (trigesimal); trigint- (trigintal)
40 quadragen- (quadragenarian); quadrages- (quadragesimal)
50 pentacosta- (pentacostaglossal); penteconta- (pentecontaglossal); quinquagen- (quinquagenarian); quinquages- (quinquagesimal)
60 hexaconta- (hexacontahedron); sexagen- (sexagenarian); sexages- (sexagesimal)
70 septuagen- (septuagenarian);

septuages- (septuagesimal); septuagint- (Septuagint)
80 octogen- (octogenarian); octoges- (octogesimal)
90 enneaconta- (enneacontahedral); nonagen- (nonagenarian); nonages- (nonagesimal)
100 cent(i)- (centigrade); hecato- (hecatophyllous); hecatinicosa- (hecatinicosachoron: 120); hecto- (hectoliter); hekto (hektogram)
150 sesquicent- (sesquicentennial)
200 ducen- (ducenarious)
300 trecent- (trecentene)
400 quadricent- (quadricentennial)
500 quincent- (quincentennial)
600 hexacosi- (hexacosichoron); sexcent- (sexcentenary)
700 septingenti- (septingentenary)
800 octocent- (octocentenary)
900 enneacent- (enneacentenary)
1,000 -chili- (chiliarch); kilo- (kilogram); ~ *th:* milli- (millibar)
10,000 myria- (myriameter); myrio- (myriophyllous)
1,000,000 *one million* mega- (megavolt); ~ *th:* micro- (microgram)
1,000,000,000 *one billion* giga- (gigabyte); ~ *th:* nano- (nanosecond); nanno- (nannoplankton)
1,000,000,000,000 *one trillion* tera- (terahertz); trega- (tregadyne); ~ *th:* pico- (picofarad)
1,000,000,000,000,000 *one quadrillion* peta- (petameter); ~ *th:* femto- (femtometer);
1,000,000,000,000,000,000 *one quintillion* exa- (exameter); ~ *th:* atto- (attogram)

THE SENSES

Hearing

deafness -surd- (surdity)
ear auri- (auricle); auriculo- (auriculo-

temporal); ot- (othemorrhagia); oto- (otology)
hear acou- (acouasm); acoust- (acoustical); audi- (auditory);

audio- (audiology); auri- (auricle); ecoia (dysecoia)

sound echo- (echogenic); -phone (telephone); phono- (phonograph); -phony (euphony); -phthong (diphthong); son- (sonic); soni- (soniferous); sono- (sonometer); sonoro- (sonorous)

Related Perceptions

noisy crepit- (crepitation); frem- (fremitus); ligyr- (ligyrophobia); strid- (strident); stridul- (stridulous); strepi- (strepitus);
silent hesy- (hesychastic); tacit- (taciturnity)

Seeing

blindness caec- (caecilian); cec- (cecity); lusc- (eluscate); typhlo- (typhlosis)
eye blepharo- (blepharotomy); cantho- (canthoplasty); cili- (ciliary); corneo- (corneoiritis); irido- (iridomotor); kerato- (keratotomy); oculi- (oculiform); oculo- (oculomotor); ommat- (ommatophore); op- (opalgia); ophthalmo- (ophthalmoscope); -opia (diplopia); ophry- (ophryosis); opsi- (opsiometer); opso- (opsoclonus); optico- (optico-papillary); opto- (optometry); retino- (retinoschisis); sclero- (sclerotomy); tarso (tarsoplasty)
pupil core- (corelysis); coreo- (coreoplasty); -coria (isocoria); coro- (coroplastic); -koria (leukokoria); pupillo- (pupillometer)
see -blep- (ablepsia); eid- (eidetic); -opsia (hemianopsia); -opsis (synopsis); -opsy (biopsy); -scope (telescope); -scopic (microscopic); scopo- (scopophilia); -scopy (bioscopy); -scrut- (inscrutable); spec- (spectator); -spic- (conspicuous); -vid- (video); -vis- (vision); visuo- (visuosensory)

Related Perceptions

bright fulg- (fulgurant); helio- (helioscope); luc- (luciferous); lumin- (luminosity)
dark amaur- (amaurosus); ambly- (amblyopia); nyct- (nyctalopia); scoto- (scotophobia); tenebr- (tenebrous)

Smelling

nose nasi- (nasiform); naso- (nasology); rhino- (rhinology)
smell bromo- (bromidrosis); fet- (fetid); nidor- (nidorous); -odic (euodic); odori- (odoriferous); odoro- (odoroscope); -olent (redolent); -olfact- (olfactory); -osmia (anosmia); osmo- (osmodysphoria); osphresio (osphresiophobia); ozo- (ozostomia)

Related Perceptions

pleasant bene- (beneficial); eu- (euodic)
unpleasant cac- (cacosmia); mal- (malodorous)

Tasting

mouth -mouthed (dry-mouthed); oro- (orolingual); stomato- (stomatalgia); -stome (cytostome); -stomous (monostomous)
palate palato- (palatonasal); uranisco- (uranisconitis); urano- (uranoplasty); velar- (velarize)
saliva ptyal- (ptyalagogue); sialo- (sialorrhea)
taste geum- (geumaphobia); geumat- (geumatophobia); -geusia (parageusia); -gust- (gustatory); sapor- (saporific)
tongue -glossia (macroglossia); glosso- (glossodynia); hyo- (hyoglossal); lamino- (lamino-alveolar); ligur- (ligurition); ling- (lingible); lingui- (linguiform)

Related Perceptions

bitter alk- (alkaloid); picro- (picrotoxin)
salty alo- (alomancy); halo- (halophile); sal- (saline); sals- (salsamentarious)
sour acerb- (acerbity); acid- (acidulous); amar- (amarine)

sweet hedy- (hedyphane); melli- (mellifluous); dulc- (dulcify)

Touching

sensation -esthesia (myesthesia); esthesio- (esthesiometer)
skin cut(i)- (subcutaneous); derm- (dermabrasion); -derm (melanoderm); derma- (dermatherm); -derma (scleroderma); dermat- (dermatitis); dermato- (dermatology); -dermatous (xerodermatous); -dermis (epidermis); dermo- (dermoneural)
touch aphe- (aphephobia); -aphia (dysaphia); -apsia (parapsia); haph- (haphalgesia); hapto- (haptometer); -palp- (palpable); sens(i)- (sensiferous); sensori- (sensorineural); sent- (sentient); -tact- (contact); -tang- (tangible); thigmo- (thigmotaxis)

RELATED PERCEPTIONS

cold alg- (algid); cheima- (cheimaphilic); crymo- (crymophilic); cryo- (cryopathy); frigo- (frigorific); gelo- (gelosis); kryo- (kryometer); psychro- (psychroalgia); rhigo- (rhigolene)
dry -sicc- (desiccate); xero- (xerophyte)
hard dur- (duricrust); scler- (scleronychia)
rough salebr- (salebrous); trachy- (trachycarpous)
smooth glabr- (glabrous); leio- (leiotrichous); levig- (levigated); lisso- (lissotrichous); lubr- (lubricity); psilo- (psilodermatous)
soft malac- (malacissant); malax- (malaxation); -moll- (emollient)
warm calo- (caloreceptor); calori- (calorific); caum- (caumesthesia); pyr- (pyrogenic); therm- (thermal); thermo- (thermosensitive); -thermy (diathermy)
wet humect- (humectant); hydro- (hydrorrhea); hygro- (hygroscopic); madefac- (madefaction)

SHAPES

---

acorn-shaped balan- (balanoid); glandi- (glandiform)
agate-shaped agat- (agatiform)
almond-shaped amygdal- (amygdaliform)
anchor-shaped ancyr- (ancyroid)
angle -angle (quadrangle); angul- (rectangular); -gon (polygon); -gonal (polygonal); gonio- (goniometer)
antennae-shaped antenn- (antenniform)
anther-shaped anther- (antheriform)
apple-shaped pomi- (pomiform)
arc-shaped arcu- (arcuate)
arch-shaped arci- (arciform); cingul- (cingulate); fornici- (forniciform)
arrow-shaped bel- (beloid); *arrow head:* sagitt- (sagittate)
astragalus-shaped astragal- (astragaloid)
awl-shaped subul- (subulate)

ax-shaped dolabri- (dolabriform); pelec- (pelecoid); securi- (securiform)
axehead-shaped axini- (axiniform); pelec- (pelecoid)
bacterium-shaped bacteri- (bacterioid)
barrel-shaped dolio- (dolioform)
basilica-shaped basilic- (basilicate)
basin-shaped pelvi- (pelviform)
basket-shaped calathi- (calathiform)
bead-shaped monili- (moniliform); toruli- (toruliform)
beak-shaped aquil- (aquiline); corac- (coracoid); ornithorhynch- (ornithorhynchous); rhamph- (rhamphoid); rhyncho- (rhynchophorous); rostrato- (rostrato-nariform); rostri- (rostriform)
bean-shaped fabi- (fabiform)
bear-shaped urs- (ursiform)
beehive-shaped alve- (alveated)

beetle-shaped scarab- (scaraboid)
bell-shaped campan- (campaniform)
bent ancylo- (ancylostomiasis); ankylo-
(ankylosis); -campsis (phallocampsis);
campto- (camptocormia); campylo-
(campylodactyly); -clinal (anticlinal);
-clinate (proclinate); -cline (incline);
-clinic (matroclinic); clino- (clinom-
eter);-clinous (patroclinous); -clisis
(pathoclisis); clit- (heteroclital); cliv-
(declivity); curvi- (curvilinear); cyrto-
(cyrtometer); -flect- (genuflection);
flex- (flexural); lechrio- (lechriodont);
loxo- (loxotomy); repando- (repando-
dentate); scolio- (scoliokyphosis);
sinu- (sinuousity); -verge (diverge)
berry-shaped bacc- (bacciform)
bird-shaped orith- (orithoid)
bird's-head-shaped avicular- (aviculari-
form)
boat-shaped cymb- (cymbiform);
navi- (naviform); navicul- (naviculoid); scapho- (scaphoceph-
aly); scapulo- (scapulohumeral);
scyphi- (scyphiform)
bottle-shaped ampull- (ampullaceous); ascidi- (ascidiform); *leather
bottle-shaped:* utrei- (utreiform);
utric- (utricular)
bow-shaped arci- (arciform); arcu-
(arcuate)
bowl-shaped crater- (crateriform);
pateri- (pateriform); scyph- (scyphate)
bract-shaped bractei- (bracteiform)
branch-shaped rami- (ramiform)
breast-shaped mammi- (mammiferous,
mammiform)
brick-shaped plinthi- (plinthiform)
bristle-shaped chaeti- (chaetiform);
seti- (setiform)
broom-shaped scopi- (scopiform)
brush-shaped aspergilli- (aspergilli-
form); muscar- (muscariform)
bud-shaped gemm- (gemmiform)
bulb-shaped bulbi- (bulbiform)
bull-shaped taur- (tauriform)
buttock-shaped nati- (natiform)
canine tooth-shaped canini- (canini-
form); laniar- (laniariform)
cap-shaped pile- (pileiform)

caterpillar-shaped eruci- (eruciform)
catkin-shaped amenti[2] (amentiform);
juli- (juliform)
cell-shaped celli- (celliform)
cheek-shaped buccin- (buccinoid)
chisel-shaped celti- (celtiform);
scalpri- (scalpriform)
circle gyral- (gyrally)
clarion-shaped litui- (lituiform)
claw-shaped ungui- (unguiform)
cleaver-shaped dolabr- (dolabriform)
cloud-shaped cirri- (cirriform);
nubi- (nubiform)
club-shaped clav- (clavate, claviform)
cobweb-shaped arachn- (arachnoid)
coin-shaped nummi- (nummiform)
collar-shaped colli- (colliform)
column-shaped columelli- (columelliform); columni- (columniform)
comb-shaped pectin- (pectiniform)
cone-shaped coni- (coniform);
strobili- (strobiliform)
coral-shaped coralli- (coralliform)
corn-shaped grani- (graniform)
cowl-shaped cuculli- (cuculliform)
crab-shaped cancri- (cancriform)
crater-shaped crateri- (crateriform)
crescent-shaped crescenti- (crescentiform); lunul- (lunular);
menisc- (meniscate, meniscoid);
sigm- (sigmoid)
cross-shaped cruc- (cruciate, cruciform)
crown-shaped coron- (coroniform)
crystal-shaped crystalli- (crystalliform)
cube-shaped cubi- (cubiform)
cuckoo-shaped cuculi- (cuculiform)
cucumber-shaped cucumi- (cucumiform)
cup-shaped acetabuli- (acetabuliform); calath- (calathiform); calici-
(caliciform); cotyl- (cotyliform);
crin- (crinoid); cupuli- (cupuliform); cyath- (cyathiform); pocilli-
(pocilliform); pocul- (poculiform);
scyphi- (scyphiform)
curl-shaped calamist- (calamistration),
cirri- (cirriform)
curved gryp- (grypanian)
cushion-shaped pulvini- (pulviniform)
cusp-shaped cusp- (cuspate)

cylinder-shaped cylindri- (cylindriform)
dagger-shaped pugion- (pugioniform);
  sicula- (siculate)
dish-shaped patelli- (patelliform);
  scutel- (scutelliform)
disk-shaped disci- (disciform, discoid)
drop-shaped gutti- (guttiform); stilli-
  (stilliform)
ear-shaped aur⁻¹ (auriform); auricul-
  (auriculoid)
eel-shaped anguill- (anguilliform)
egg-shaped ov- (oviform); oval- (ovali-
  form, ovaloid); ovat- (ovate)
ellipse ellips- (ellipsoid)
embryo-shaped embry- (embryoniform)
eye-shaped ocul- (oculiform)
faced/faceted -hedral (hexahedral);-he-
  dron (polyhedron)
fan-shaped flabelli- (flabellate, flabelliform)
feather-shaped pinni- (pinniform);
  plumil- (plumiliform)
fern-shaped filici- (filiciform)
fiber-shaped fibri- (fibriform)
fibril-shaped fibrilli- (fibrilliform)
fiddle-shaped pandur- (panduriform)
fig-shaped fici- (ficiform)
finger-shaped dactyl- (dactyloid);
  digiti- (digitiform)
fish-shaped pisci- (pisciform)
fissure-shaped fissuri- (fissuriform)
flagon-shaped, flask-shaped ampulli-
  (ampulliform); lagen- (lageniform)
flat plani- (planimeter); plano- (plano-
  concave); platy- (platypus)
flower-shaped flor- (floriform)
foot-shaped ped⁻¹ (pediform)
forceps-shaped forcip- (forcipate)
forked -furc- (bifurcation)
fowl-shaped galli- (galliform)
frog-shaped rani- (raniform)
fruit-shaped fructi- (fructiform)
fungus-shaped fungill- (fungilliform)
funnel-shaped areten- (aretenoid); ary-
  ten- (arytenoid); choan- (choanoid);
  infundibuli- (infundibuliform)
gland-shaped aden- (adeniform)
globe-shaped glob- (globate)
gnat-shaped culici- (culiciform)
goat-shaped capri- (capriform)

globule-shaped globuli- (globuliform)
goblet-shaped pocul- (poculiform)
grape-shaped staphylo- (staphyloma);
  uvi- (uviform); uvu- (uvula); ~ cluster:
  acini- (aciniform); uvell- (uvelloid)
gregarine-shaped gregarini- (gregarini-
  form)
hair-shaped capilli- (capilliform); pili-
  (piliform)
hammer-shaped malle- (malleiform)
hand-shaped mani- (maniform)
handle-shaped ansat- (ansate)
hatchet-shaped dolabri- (dolabriform);
  pelec- (pelecoid)
heart-shaped card- (cardioid); cord-
  (cordate, cordiform); cordato-
  (cordato-ovate)
helmet-shaped cassid- (cassidiform);
  gale- (galeate)
herring-shaped harengi- (harengiform)
hinge-shaped gingly- (ginglyform)
honeycomb-shaped favi- (faviform)
honeycomb-shell-shaped alveolari-
  (alveolariform); alveoli- (alveoliform)
hood-shaped calyptri- (calyptriform);
  cuculli- (cucullate, cuculliform)
hook-shaped ancist- (ancistroid); hami-
  (hamiform); unci- (unciform)
horn-shaped corni- (corniculate, corniform); cornu- (cornuate)
horseshoe-shaped hippocrepi-
  (hippocrepiform)
horsetail-shaped equiset- (equisetiform)
hull-shaped naut- (nautiform)
human anthro- (anthropoid)
hydra-shaped hydr- (hydraform,
  hydriform)
icicle-shaped stir- (stirious)
irregular poikilo- (poikilocyte)
isopod-shaped isopodi- (isopodiform)
ivy-shaped hederi- (hederiform)
keel-shaped carin- (carinated)
kidney-shaped nephr- (nephroid);
  reni- (reniform)
knee-shaped genu- (genuform)
knife-shaped cultell- (cultellated);
  cultri- (cultriform)
ladder-shaped scalari- (scalariform)
lance-shaped lanceol- (lanceolate);
  lanci- (lanciform)

larva-shaped larvi- (larviform)
lattice-shaped cancell- (cancellate);
clathr- (clathrate)
layered -decker (double-decker); lamelli-
(lamelliform); lamin- (lamination);
-plex (cerviplex); strat- (stratified)
leaf-shaped clad- (cladode); foli- (foli-
ated, foliiform); phyll- (phylliform)
leather bottle-shaped utrei- (utreiform);
utric- (utricular)
lens-shaped, lentil-shaped lentic- (lenticular), phac- (phacoid)
lid-shaped operculi- (operculiform)
lily-shaped crin- (crinoid); lili- (liliform)
lip-shaped labell- (labellate, labelloid)
lizard-shaped lacerti- (lacertiform)
lotus-shaped loti- (lotiform)
lyre-shaped lyri- (lyrate, lyriform)
malformed -mutil- (Mutilla); pero-
(peropodous)
melon-shaped meloni- (meloniform)
miter-shaped mitri- (mitriform)
mole-shaped talpi- (talpiform)
moon-shaped luni- (luniform)
mulberry-shaped mur- (muriform)
mummy-shaped mummi- (mummiform)
mushroom-shaped fungi- (fungiform);
agar- (agariciform)
myrtle leaf-shaped myrti- (myrtiform)
neck-shaped colli- (colliform)
necklace-shaped monili- (moniliform)
needle-shaped aci- (aciform); acicul-
(acicular)
nipple-shaped mamilli- (mamilliform); mammula- (mammular);
papill- (papilliform)
nose-shaped nari- (nariform); nasi-
(nasiform)
nut-shaped caryo- (caryopsis); karyo-
(karyokinesis); nuci- (nuciform);
nucleo (nucleolus)
oar-shaped remi- (remiform)
oat-shaped aveni- (aveniform)
olive-shaped oliv- (oliviform)
ox-shaped bov- (boviform)
oyster-shaped ostrea- (ostreiform)
patella-shaped patelli- (patelliform)
pear-shaped piri- (piriform); pyri-
(pyriform)
pea-shaped pisi- (pisiform)

pebble-shaped calci- (calciform); cal-
culi- (calculiform); lapilli- (lapilliform)
pelvis-shaped pelvi- (pelviform)
penis-shaped pen- (peniform)
pen-shaped styl- (styliform)
petal-shaped petal- (petaloid); petuli-
(petuliform)
pillar-shaped columelli- (columelliform); columni- (columniform)
pinecone-shaped pin- (piniform);
strobil- (strobiliform)
pipe-shaped fistuli- (fistuliform)
placenta-shaped
placenti- (placentiform)
platter-shaped scutell- (scutellate)
pod-shaped siliqu- (siliquiform)
pointed aci- (acicular); acro- (acrocephaly); acu- (aculeate); acuti- (acutifoliate); -belon- (belonophobia);
cusp- (cuspid); mucroni- (mucroni-
form); muric- (muricate); oxy-
(oxyrhine); -punct- (punctured);
stylo- (stylograph)
pouch-shaped bursi- (bursiform); sacci-
(sacciform); scroti- (scrotiform)
purse-shaped bursi- (bursiform)
rattlesnake-shaped crotali- (crotaliform)
reed-shaped calam- (calamiform)
rhombus-shaped rhombi- (rhombiform)
rice grain-shaped rizi- (riziform)
ring-shaped annul- (annular); circin-
(circinate); cric- (cricoid)
rod-shaped -bacill- (bacilliform);
bacul- (baculiform); coryn- (coryne-
form); -rad- (radial); rhabdo- (rhab-
domyoma); vergi- (vergiform);
virgul- (virgulate)
roof-shaped tecti- (tectiform)
root-shaped radic- (radiciform)
rope-shaped funil- (funiliform);
resti- (restiform)
rotatory dinet- (dinetic)
round -annul- (annulate); -anu- (anulus);
-cing- (cingulum); cinct- (cincture);
circin- (circinately);-circul- (recir-
culate); -coron- (coronation); crico-
(cricoid); cyclo (cyclostomous);
disco- (discoid); globo- (globos-
ity); glomer- (glomerate); numm-
(nummular); -orb- (suborbital);

-rot- (rotund); -sphere (hemisphere);
sphero- (spheroid); stilli- (stilliform);
tereti- (tereticaudate); troch- (trochal); zon- (zonesthesia)
rush-shaped junci- (junciform)
sac-shaped bursi- (bursiform);
sacc- (sacciform)
saddle-shaped selli- (selliform)
salmon-shaped salmoni- (salmoniform)
sandal-shaped sandali- (sandaliform)
saucer-shaped acetabul- (acetabuliform)
sausage-shaped allanto- (allantoid);
botul- (botuliform)
saw-shaped serrati- (serratiform);
serri- (serriform)
scale-shaped lamelli- (lamelliform);
squami- (squamiform)
scimitar-shaped acinaci- (acinaciform)
scissors-shaped forfic- (forficate)
screw-shaped helic- (helicoid)
shell-shaped conchi- (conchiform);
strombi- (strombiform)
shield-shaped aspidi- (aspidiform);
clype- (clypeiform); pelti- (peltiform,
peltoid); scut- (scutiform)
shoe-shaped calcei- (calceiform)
sickle-shaped drepani- (drepaniform);
falci- (falciform)
sieve-shaped coli- (coliform); cribri-
(cribriform)
slanting loxo- (loxodromic); plagio-
(plagiodont)
slipper-shaped calceo- (calceolate)
slug-shaped limaci- (limaciform)
snake-shaped angui- (anguiform); colubri- (colubriform);
serpenti- (serpentiform)
spade-shaped pala- (palacrous)
spatula-shaped spatuli- (spatuliform)
spear-shaped hasti- (hastate, hastiform)
sphere-shaped spheri- (spheriform)
spider-shaped arene- (areneiform)
spike-shaped spic- (spiciform)
spindle-shaped fusi- (fusiform)
spine-shaped aculei- (aculeiform); spini-
(spiniform, spinoid)
spiral-shaped cirri- (cirriform); cochl-
(cochleate); gyro- (gyroidal); helici-
(heliciform); spiri- (spiriform);
voluti- (volutiform)

spoon-shaped cochleari- (cochleariform)
spur-shaped calcari- (calcariform)
square -quadr- (quadriform)
S-shaped sigm- (sigmoid)
stake-shaped pali- (paliform); sudi-
(sudiform)
stalactite-shaped stalacti- (stalactiform)
stalk-shaped podeti- (podetiiform);
stipiti- (stipitiform)
star-shaped aster- (asterisk); astr-
(astroid); stelli- (stelliform)
steeple-shaped campanili-
(campaniliform)
stem-shaped cauli- (cauliform)
straight ithy- (ithyphallic); ortho-
(orthogonal)
strap-shaped liguli- (ligulate, liguliform); lora- (lorate)
stirrup-shaped stapedi- (stapediform)
stylus-shaped styli- (styliform)
sword-shaped ensi- (ensiform);
glad- (gladiate); xiphi- (Xiphias);
xipho- (xiphoid)
tail-shaped caudi- (caudiform)
tea leaf-shaped thei- (theiform)
tear-shaped lachrymi- (lachrymiform)
tendril-shaped cirri- (cirriform);
pampin- (pampiniform)
tentacle-shaped tentaculi-
(tentaculiform)
thorn-shaped aculei- (aculeiform)
thread-shaped fili- (filiform); nemato-
(nematogen)
tongue-shaped lingui- (linguate,
linguiform)
tooth-shaped denti- (dentiform); laniari-
(laniariform); odont- (odontoid)
top-shaped strombuli- (strombuliform); trochi- (trochiform);
turbi- (turbiniform)
tower-shaped pyrgo- (pyrgoidal);
turri- (turriform)
trapezoid-shaped trapezi- (trapeziform)
tray-shaped hypocrater-
(hypocrateriform)
tree-shaped arbor- (arboriform);
dendri- (dendriform)
triangular delt- (deltoidal);

triangulato- (triangulato-subovate);
trigon- (trigonal)
trumpet-shaped buccin- (buccinoid);
litui- (lituiform)
tube-shaped fistuli- (fistuliform);
syringo- (syringotomy); tubi-
(tubiform); tubuli- (tubuliform);
vasi- (vasiform)
turnip-shaped napi- (napiform)
umbrella-shaped umbraculi-
(umbraculiform)
U-shaped hyoid- (hyoid); hypsi-
(hypsiloid)
valve-shaped valvi- (valviform)
vase-shaped urcei- (urceiform); vasi-
(vasiform)
vulva-shaped vulv- (vulviform)

wart-shaped verruci- (verruciform)
wedge-shaped cune- (cuneate, cuneiform); spheno- (sphenoid)
wheel-shaped roti- (rotiform); troch-
(trochal)
whip lash-shaped flagelli- (flagelli-
form)
window-shaped fenestri- (fenestri-
form)
wingcase-shaped elytri- (elytriform)
wing-shaped ali- (aliform); pteryg-
(pterygoid)
worm-shaped lumbric- (lumbriciform); scoleci- (scoleciform);
vermi- (vermiform)
x-shaped decuss- (decussate)
yoke-shaped zygo- (zygomorphic)

TIME

afternoon pomerid- (pomeridian)
ancient -antiq- (antiquity); arch(a)eo-
(archaeology); pal(a)eo- (Paleozoic);
proto- (protohuman)
day -diurn- (diurnal); ephem- (ephemeris); hemer- (hemerine); -journ-
(journal); quotid- (quotidian)
earlier ante- (antedate); fore- (forecast);
pre- (predawn); pro- (provision);
protero- (proterotype); proto- (pro-
tomartyr); retro- (retroactive);
yester- (yesteryear)
early period eo- (eolithic); paleo-
(paleolithic)
evening crepus- (crepuscular); noct-
(nocturnal); nocti- (noctilucent);
nycto- (nyctophobia); vesper-
(vespertine)
hour horo- (horology)
incomplete -esce (incandesce); -escence
(convalescence); -escent (incandescent)
lasting diuturn- (diuturnal); dur- (durable); perenn- (perennial); perm- (permanent); stabil- (stability)
later hystero- (hysterogenic); meta-
(metabiosis); post (postmeridian);
retro- (retrofit)

month -mens(i)- (mensal) *monthly:*
emmen- (emmeniopathy)
morning matut- (matutinal)
new caeno- (Caenozoic); caino- (Cainozoic); ceno- (cenogenesis);
neo- (neoplast); nov- (novelty);
thalero- (thalerophagous)
night crepus- (crepuscular); noct-
(nocturnal); nocti- (noctilucent);
nycto- (nyctophobia); vesper-
(vespertine)
old gerasco- (gerascophobia); gero-
(gerodontics); geronto- (gerontology); grand- (grandfather);
presbyo- (presbyacusis); -sen- (seniority); -vet- (veteran)
recent -cene (Miocene); ceno-
(Cenozoic)
same time co- (coexist); hama-
(hamarchy); simul- (simultaneous);
synchron- (synchronicity)
time chrono- (chronology); -temp-
(temporary)
today hodie- (hodiernal)
tomorrow crastin- (procrastinate)
twilight crepus- (crepusculine);
lyg- (lygophilia)

week -hebdom- (hebdomadal); septiman- (septimanal)

year -ann- (annual); -enn- (biennial)

yesterday hestern- (hesternal); prid- (pridian)

young juven- (juvenile)